SYNCHRONIZED SWIMMING

For Ross
for the many memories we shared
in our love for this sport
and for each other

# SYNCHRONIZED SWIMMING

## An American History

Dawn Pawson Bean

McFarland & Company, Inc., Publishers

*Jefferson, North Carolina, and London*

Library of Congress Cataloguing-in-Publication Data

Bean, Dawn Pawson, 1927–
Synchronized swimming : an American history /
Dawn Pawson Bean
p.     cm.
Includes bibliographical references and index.

ISBN 0-7864-1948-2 (softcover : 50# alkaline paper) ∞

1. Synchronized swimming — United States — History.
I. Title.
GV838.53.S95B43    2005          797.2'17 — dc22          2005000090

British Library cataloguing data are available

On the cover: Background ©2005 Creatas; U.S.A.'s duet of Tracie Ruiz (back)
and Candy Costie won the first Olympic synchro medals by
more than a point over Canada *(photograph by Ross Bean)*

Manufactured in the United States of America

*McFarland & Company, Inc., Publishers
Box 611, Jefferson, North Carolina 28640
www.mcfarlandpub.com*

# Acknowledgments

There are so many people to be thanked for the help they have given me in supplying information and photos for this book. These include the many, many friends from the world of synchronized swimming — Sue Ahlf, Rita Barr, Mary Black, Re Calcaterra, Jeannette Chase, Joyce Corner, Joy Cushman, Charlotte Davis, Jackie Douglass, Karen Eakin, Barbara Eaton, Pam Edwards, Emma Gene Edwards, Marion Kane Elston, Ike Eytchison, Lorraine Fasullo, Margaret Forbes, Rayne Gerhardt, Barbara Harrell, Jean Henning, Nancy Hines, Gertrude Hinrichs, Peg Hogan, Miwako Homma, Ginny Jasontek, Donald Kane, Marian Kretschmer, Barbara Longstaff, Sandra Valles Mahoney, Jackie McDaniel, Judy McGowan, Marna Moore, Ann Murphy, Pat Paterson, Mary Rose, Mary Jo Ruggieri, Helen Smith, Dorothy Sowers, Donn Squire, Carol Tackett, Mary Ellen Wiegand, Nancy Wightman, Louise Wing, Dawn Zajac, and Ruth Zink.

In addition, the following former members of U.S. Synchronized Swimming also sent items for my consideration and I thank them for their help and interest: Frances Jones, Margaret Mowrer, Bert Hubbard, Chelys Hester, Joanne Royer Meideros, Pearl Redding Huntley, Jeannette Chase, Mary Oppenheim, Millicent Heath, Joan Nelson, Lynn Hale, and Jan and Wilbur Luick.

I've had wonderful letters from and conversations with people from the past that I have gotten to know through this project — Lena Zimmerman Feinstein, Virginia Crabbe, Doris Dannenhirsch Beshunsky, Donna Glinka, Ruth Geduldig Winter, Nancy Hanna Rauworth, Phyllis Burrell, and Doris Dieskow Engerrand. Thank you so much for your contributions of memories and photographs.

I must also thank the leaders in the aquatic world with whom I've had discussions in past years. These include Clark Leach, Phil Patterson, Norma Olsen, Billie MacKellar, Mary Derosier, Theresa Anderson, Beth Kaufman, Harold Henning, Jan Armbrust, Robert Helmick, Lord Killanin and Javier Ostos. They have all been wonderful supporters who have helped the sport progress.

Thanks must also be given for the help I received from Rita and Preston Levi at the Henning Library at the International Swimming Hall of Fame in Fort Lauderdale, FL; Michael Salmon of the Ziffren Sports Resource Center, Amateur Athletic Foundation Library in Los Angeles; Woolsey Ackerman, Turner Classic Movies/Warner Brothers in Hollywood; Marigen Carpenter, mayor of Neenah, WI; Bobbie Burk, Stephens College archivist; Cathy Goodwin for research at the University of Illinois Library; and to the staff at the Chicago Historical Society.

Finally, my biggest thanks are for my family — my husband, Ross; our daughters, Kevis, Avilee and Lea; my sisters, Joan and Lynn; and my parents, Elna and Dick. They have all been involved with synchronized swimming in many different ways.

Thanks to Ross, who helped and supported me in all my synchro ventures and who was instrumental in the development of this book. Thanks for his critical analysis of the material, particularly the technical rules and figure changes. Thanks for the countless number of photos he took for my use in publishing *Synchro* magazine. And thanks for his editing and many rewrites of the chapters in this book. He helped with all but the last two which were finished after his death. The final chapter, "What's Next for Synchronized Swimming?" was his suggestion.

Thanks to our three daughters, who were champion synchronized swimmers and in adult life have all been involved with the sport and with this book. Thanks for their final help in editing, rewriting and proofreading. Special thanks to Lea for the recent help involving extensive Internet searching for athlete names that were incomplete in published results.

My final thanks are for the Pawsons, to my sisters who shared the early synchro years with me as teammates, and to my parents— Mom, a ballet dancer and teacher who was my inspiration for creating movements to music, and Dad, a speed and distance swimmer who clearly saw my interest in this new water ballet activity. He found San Francisco's Fairmont Water Follies team for me in 1941 and —*the rest is history*.

I apologize for any errors and omissions that may have occurred because I didn't have the information. However, I sincerely hope this book will bring to you the history of the sport as I have lived it and loved it.

*Dawn Pawson Bean*

# Contents

# Preface

"The sport that took 40 years to travel from Hollywood to Los Angeles."
*Quote from 1984 placemats of Olympic
sponsor McDonald's Restaurants.*

The McDonald's quotation above hinted at synchronized swimming's long struggle toward "making it" as an Olympic event but erred badly in perpetuating the myth that it was born in Hollywood and grew from Esther Williams' films. It also reinforced the impression that the sport version sprang full blown from the 1984 Los Angeles Olympic Games. The almost unrecognized truth is that, by 1984, U.S. national championships had been held for almost 40 years. Competitions had started as early as 1939 in locales far from Hollywood, and synchronized swimming had a background of multinational development going back to the early 20th century.

This is primarily the history of synchronized swimming (synchro) in the United States; however, the origins of synchro-like activities, possibly almost as old as swimming itself, can hardly be claimed by America. Related activities can be detected on ancient woodblock prints, vases and other items, which show water positions and actions that resemble synchro maneuvers. Well before the turn of the 20th century, Europe was working with floating patterns; England was experimenting with competitions in tricks and stunts (figures); and Canada had begun competitions designed to judge the form of the strokes and stunts. Descriptions of various stunts and tricks are found in turn-of-the-century books on water activities. These elements were not put to music until the 1920s. The United States can claim the origin of competition in the form that we today would recognize as synchronized swimming.

From novelty tricks in swim classes through the attraction of aquacades and movies, a sport grew and developed into the highly complex activity witnessed today. How that sport, synchronized swimming, grew and developed in the United States, the role the United States played in its worldwide acceptance and development, and the current status of synchronized swimming among world sporting events today will be what this book attempts to relate.

# 1

## *The Beginnings*

Although synchronized swimming is the youngest of the water sports, its precursors as "water ballet" or "water dancing" have a long history. In ancient Greece and Rome, there were group performances by girls and boys.[1] Public festivals were held in Roman times in *naumachias*, water-filled arenas or lake areas.[2] Larissa, Greece, contains the ruins of the principal structure of Greek theater. In the 4th century, the orchestra floor was converted to a water cistern with a blue and white marble floor and the nearby aqueduct brought in water. Programs featuring females as sea goddesses or nymphs were held.[3] The Roman poet Marcia, impressed by the beauty and elegance of motions in water, wrote, "Boys and girls were swimming like Tritons and Nimphas [nymphs], making beautiful figures in the water with their bodies."[4]

Water stunts were also practiced in the Orient. Bob Kiphuth, while the swimming coach at Yale University, brought from Japan some ancient wood-block prints showing male swimmers performing somersaults underwater and doing a figure much like modern synchro's Ballet Leg. In the Mid-East, a bas relief from the Assyrian palace of Nimrod, about 880 B.C., portrays swimmers in various underwater positions similar to those in certain of synchronized swimming's figures.[5]

Benjamin Franklin may have been America's first "stunt" swimmer. In a letter to Oliver Reeve, Franklin described his swim in the Thames from Chelsea to Blackfriars, performing, on the way, "many feats of activity, both upon and under the water, that surprised and pleased those to whom they were novelties."[6] He authored a book, *The Art of Swimming Rendered Easy*, with the following explanation on the cover, *With Directions to Learners. To which is prefixed Advice to Bathers*.[7] The booklet was published in Glasgow in 1781.

In the late 19th century, some German scientists, studying the behavior of the body in water, experimented with what they called picture swimming.[8] In this, they had large groups of ladies executing beautiful floating formations while background music played. As this type of activity migrated to Canada via England, Canadians added their own variations to create formation swimming. Formation swimming to music was also practiced in Japan.[9] Water ballet (still formations) became popular in Belgium and Holland.[10]

England struck off in a different direction in 1891 with ornamental and scientific swimming as part of the requirements for the Royal Life Saving Society.[11] The Society's *Handbook for Swimmers* gave one of their objectives as "the promoting of competition in Ornamental swimming, also known as *Scientific Swimming*." This consisted of what have been since called figures or stunts.[12] Only men competed in the events, executing various stunts individually, much as in a diving competition.

The first record of a competition in ornamental and scientific swimming appears to be one held in Yorkshire, England, in 1892. The competition was won by 14-year-old Bob Derbyshire, who later became a member of England's 1908 Olympic swimming relay team. In winning the competition, Derbyshire is reported to have performed front and back somersaults, torpedo, and other stunts.[13]

In 1898, professional displays in water were given by J.B. Johnson and his sisters at Blackpool Tower in London. The ladies wore black tights with sequined decorations and were called "the fast young things."[14] From 1912 to 1914, swimming star Eva Johnson was a sensation in England with her "Human Yacht" act. She swam around the pool balancing a model yacht which she had powered to light up when the house lights were dimmed. Not synchro, but a swimming performance nonetheless.

Between 1900 and 1902, displays in scientific swimming were given by Misses Ewart and Shafer, of the British Royal Life Saving Society, at St. George's Baths in London.[15] Misters Buller, Griffiths and Wilkenson of the Otter Swimming Club of London, originated the "Otter Wheel," a prototype of today's moving formations.[16]

The first recorded Canadian exhibition occurred in Winnipeg in 1898 with a competition in stunts and strokes for form.[17] The competitions there began as requirements for the Gold Medal of the Royal Life Saving Society which governed scientific swimming in both England and Canada at the time.[18]

Ornamental swimming became popular in Holland about 1900 with the Dutch Ladies Swimming Club H.D.Z., which was making what were called "propaganda tours" throughout the country. Herman Meyboom, director of the Cercle de Natation Bruxelles, trained floating patterns, first in Belgium and later in London. A Belgian document, around 1900, described the floats for other swimming teachers. Meyboom returned to Holland in 1914 and introduced trick swimming to his classes there. Descriptions of some of the "tricks," such as eating apples and drinking milk while submerged, suggest that his trick swimming may have been more of a detour than a milestone on the highway to synchro. While competitions

were said to have been held in trick swimming, no reliable evidence has been found to substantiate the claim.[19]

In Germany, the Isar-Nixon Club of Munich, under the direction of Frau Jacobi, specialized in floating formations and produced spectacular routines especially notable for their costuming effects.[20] One of the more striking effects seen in a photo was a float number costumed in stockings and black leotards with cloth "webbing" attached to the arms and sides of the suit to open to "wings" as the arms were raised in a pyramid float.

## Some Early Leaders

### ANNETTE KELLERMAN

Annette Kellerman played a very strong role in developing and popularizing water show activities in the United States in 1907 when she toured the country giving exhibitions in glass tanks.[21] Known as the first "underwater ballerina," Australian born Kellerman (1887–1975) had learned to swim to correct the results of what may have been a mild case of polio. "But for swimming," she said in 1918, "I might have been hobbling about on crutches instead of making my regular livelihood today as a moving picture mermaid."[22]

Kellerman won her first title, "Swim Champion of New South Wales," and set the women's world record for the mile. Her first diving display was from the 50-foot high board at Cavill's Bath in Sydney. She began her professional career, at age 15, giving two shows a day in a 60-foot glass tank, complete with eels and fish, at the Melbourne Exhibition Aquarium.

In 1904 her father took her to England in hopes of parlaying her swimming talents into money to support the family. At first, they got no attention, so Miss Kellerman swam 17 miles down the Thames River, from Putney Bridge to Blackwall, to call attention to her swimming feats. And it worked! The Thames swim brought her a contract from the *London Daily Mirror* to swim the English Channel. Though she failed in three tries at the crossing, feigning seasickness, these attempts brought her fame as the first important woman swimmer.[23]

Kellerman and her father traveled to the United States in 1907 and she toured the country giving exhibitions in a glass tank in theaters as part of a regular vaudeville circuit. After long runs in both Boston and Chicago, she was signed by the Keith Circuit for 14 shows a week for two years. Called the "Diving Venus," the "Perfect Woman," and "Daughter of the Gods,"[24] she demonstrated the approved styles of swimming and diving and performed "some fantastic stunts, porpoise swimming and the like."[25] Described as a "high diving and stunt swimming artiste," she performed stunts and dives that were forerunners of those found today in synchronized swimming and women's platform diving.[26]

Kellerman was strong willed and chose her own course of action, shocking to many at that time. In the Australian film on her life, Esther Williams said, "I have always had a warm feeling for any woman who stands her ground, 'I'm going to do this whether it's proper or not.'"[27] Williams was speaking of Kellerman's unconventional swimwear. She frowned on the wool swim suits fashioned with overskirts and sleeves that became very heavy when wet, not to mention the long stockings and shoes. She pointed out that "this attire wasn't only unattractive, but dangerous. A woman wearing such garments caught in a high wave or deep water, could find herself in serious trouble and might drown!"[28]

She was amazed seeing the bathing suits worn by American women. "What difference," she said, "is there [between] wearing 12 yards of linen in the water or lead chains?"[29] She was arrested on a Boston beach for wearing her famous "Annette Kellerman black one-piece suit." The suit, which might now be described as similar to a sleeveless leotard with tights, did much to liberate women's swimming as a sport.[30] In fact, Kellerman was inducted into the U.S. Swimming Hall of Fame for making swimming a sport for women through the use of this suit. But in 1975, she damned modern bikinis as too revealing, "shameful" and "much too brief."[31]

Annette Kellerman, called The Diving Venus, Daughter of the Gods and The Perfect Woman, was known as the first "underwater ballerina."

From vaudeville shows, she went to film. Her first film, *Neptune's Daughter*, made by the Universal Film Company of New York in 1914, cost $35,000 to make and grossed over a million dollars. Her other pictures, all made between 1915 and 1917, included *Diving Venus, Queen of the Mermaids,* and *Daughter of the Gods.*[32] The films attracted a great deal of attention and people began to try to imitate the water stunts. After five films, she returned to the New York Hippodrome in 1918 in what was billed as "the biggest mermaid spectacle ever seen live on stage." Forty years later, Kellerman was again seen on the screen when her life was portrayed by Esther Williams in a remake of *Neptune's Daughter.*[33]

Annette Kellerman's views on swimming for women were not what was generally accepted and why she created such a sensation. More normal for the times were the viewpoints expressed by George Corsans in his 1924 book, *The Swimming and Diving Book.* He explained his outlook, mirroring the common view of the time that women were all frail and delicate, that speed and distance swimming put too much of a strain on women's hearts. But, he also believed that a competition in stunts was possible. "Contests for women in fancy swimming should avoid heart strain while adding spectator appeal to a beneficial activity."[34]

Gertrude Titus incorporated water stunts into the professional course offered to future teachers at the Boston School of Physical Education Camp in 1915. "Teaching future teachers perfection of movement was always my aim," she said. She added music to help with the rhythm. In 1922, her students at Rochester University presented a water pageant for the Annual Physical Education Conference. Of this performance, it was reported, "Mass groups of costumed swimmers performed to a musical background. A story was recited. The music was used primarily for the rhythmic element to synchronize the swimmers with each other."[35] Titus had learned of the stunts as early as 1912 from Herbert Holm, coach of the Brookline Swimming Club. Holm was interested in a strong swimming team. To develop stronger swimmers, he experimented with tandem swimming using music to develop rhythm. To gain more body control, his swimmers retrieved things from the pool bottom and learned such stunts as surface dives, somersaults, log rolls and so forth. His aims were speed swimming and lifesaving ability, but stunts were also used to provide fun after a workout.

The YMCA and YWCA became interested in promoting water activities around 1915. In an article in *Physical Training*, they presented games and stunts to use with the increasing numbers of people learning to swim. Some of the ideas incorporated included marching in the water and adapting military formations to swimming formations.[36]

The Red Cross was interested in all types of water activity. Musical accompaniment of performances to this point was simply for background support. But during World War I the American Red Cross introduced a form of rhythmic swimming to music in their rehabilitation programs.[37] But, it was not until 1925 that music was used extensively in "water ballet" and even then it was mainly incidental or background.[38] It was only much later that water ballet used musical rhythms effectively.

Commodore Wilbert Longfellow, of the American Red Cross, in about 1920, conceived the idea that all swimming pools should have a formal dedication ceremony to promote the principles of health, fun, sport and safety. He wrote a pageant, *Showing Father Neptune* to dedicate the Washington University Pool in St. Louis, Missouri, in 1921.[39] When the Red Cross began to support water pageantry, it penetrated into almost every aquatic activity. In 1925, the pageant was used to dedicate the Hygiea Pool in Atlantic City. Music was supplied by the fire department band and the music and swimming were blended into the pageant. Longfellow stated there was need for this activity because racing reached so few people. The Red Cross promoted aquatic pageantry through their aquatic schools. The municipal beaches and pools throughout the country, which usually had Red Cross–trained personnel, began to use pageantry to show their yearly accomplishments.[40] The Red Cross continued this interest and in the late 1930s, Chauncy Hyatt, a staff member of the Chicago Chapter of the American Red Cross Life Saving Service, had a group presenting large water pageants. Through the Red Cross, he published a manual for wide circulation to aquatic instructors, the *American Red Cross Stunt Swimming and Water Pageantry* book.[41]

After World War I, making floating patterns became popular in Canada, Germany, Belgium, Holland and England and soon after, in France.[42] The Polytechnical Ladies and the Lewisham Ladies, both aquatic groups in London, were popular in the 1920s.[43] Floating patterns continued to develop in Europe and progressed to competitions in Germany in 1934. These performances were generally directed by whistle signals from the leader who stood on the deck. The swimmers formed a floating pattern and, on the whistle signal, sculled or swam into the next floating formation. Madame Morgen in France conceived the idea of introducing a theme with music for the floating routines during this time.[44]

## GERTRUDE GOSS

Gertrude Goss, a 1919 graduate of the Boston School of Physical Education, began combining strokes and stunts in her summer camp classes to make swimming more fun. At Winthrop College, Rock Hill, S.C., she taught all her classes to music and found it prompted greater endurance and easier breathing. In 1921, her students began performing in water shows.[45]

From Winthrop, Goss went to Smith College, where she was director of swimming for 27 years. She introduced rhythmic swimming at Smith College in 1924 and wrote the first significant publication dealing solely with the new activity, *Rhythmic Swimming Charts*, printed in 1930.[46] In this aid for swimming teachers, Goss, the women's swimming coach at Smith College, diagrammed a variety of water formations with stick figures. Detailed instructions were included for swimming using rhythms of the waltz and tango for "rhythmic" swimming and for moving from one large floating formation to another.

Her swimmers exhibited at the Yale Water Carnival in 1925. Under her tutelage, the lifeguards formed a club in 1926, the Smith College Lifeguards, which was the only formation swimming group in any of the New England colleges.[47] Nationally known for their precision swimming, they were an institution at Yale water shows, and much in demand in colleges with pools. They always did simple, well-synchronized routines wearing plain black or white suits with white pool caps. Their "glowworm" routine was much admired and imitated for its use of body lights.[48]

## KATHARINE CURTIS

Katharine "Kay" Whitney Curtis is credited with developing the athletic foundation for changing water ballet into a sport. As a student at the University of Wisconsin in 1915, she enjoyed creating and performing diving-like stunts in the water. She was encouraged in this interest by her coach, J.C. Steinauer, an old vaudeville acrobat. Curtis said, "I was a graceful, versatile swimmer, but had neither the speed nor the interest necessary for competitive swimming. Stunts, however, were a challenge to me. They stimulated my imagination."[49]

Alice Brownell Eyster organized the Dolphin Club for women at the University of Wisconsin in 1917. The club held its first water pageant in 1920 because, Eyster explained, "I got bored with swimming meets." She said she had never heard of water pageants, but while teaching a class on swimming techniques, she presented the idea to her students and asked them to write a play that would use as many swimming positions as possible. "The next thing I knew, there was a phonograph on the edge of the pool and the Dolphin Club members were swimming to music."[50] Eyster was inspired by some of the movements from Margaret H. Doubler's dance classes and adapted their movements to the aquatic medium using background music.[51]

As a teacher at the University of Chicago, Curtis formed the Tarpon Club, one of the first college women's swimming clubs, in 1923. The group executed "tricks" and floating formations for school programs. Curtis, in describing the activity, said, "Our programs were no longer composed of isolated tricks, such as the Monte Cristo sack trick, or swimming with one's hands and feet tied. [We] added music to group swimming." The early form of this type of swimming consisted chiefly of rhythmic swimming with added floating formations using transitional stroking and sculling maneuvers to move from one formation to the next.

Curtis originally used music merely as an accompaniment, but soon started coordinating the strokes and movements to the rhythms of the music, stating it was "just as in dancing. The movements of the individual swimmers are synchronized one with the other as well as with the accompaniment, be it vocal, percussive or instrumental." Since this involved the elements of musical accompaniment, composition, and the style in which the performers interpreted the music, she called it ballet swimming, or rhythmic swimming. She decried the use of water ballet for its non-rhythmic precursors, which she called stunt swimming.[52]

Whether it was the influence of the Kellerman displays and films, the Red Cross pool dedications showing water pageantry or the water displays in Europe, clubs and collegiate

Katharine Curtis is credited with developing the athletic foundation for changing water ballet into the sport of synchronized swimming.

programs began to spring up in many different areas of the country.

Lillian W. Reilly, swim coach of the Illinois Athletic Club, witnessed a demonstration of ornamental swimming by the Dolphinette Club while in Toronto for a dual swimming meet in the early '20s. She became very enthusiastic and started her own ballet team when she returned to Chicago. The Illinois Athletic Club developed the first water ballet club not connected with a university. This group and Curtis' Tarpon Club at the University of Chicago gave many exhibitions in the area.[53]

The Seals Club, formed at the University of Iowa in 1920, worked on water pageantry. In 1922, students at the University of Rochester, under Gertrude Gibson Meehan, presented a water pageant for the annual physical education conference.[54] A combination of dramatics and swimming, Water Plays was instituted as part of Commencement Day activities at Stephens College in Missouri, possibly as early as 1916.[55] These early plays were a combination of dramatics and swimming. The composition classes wrote the script and the swimming club presented the play. The earliest play for which a program is still in existence is the *Magic Pool*, presented in 1923.[56]

The Ducks Club was formed at the University of Oklahoma in 1922.[57] The Terrapin Club at the University of Illinois was organized in the fall of 1923 with 12 charter members. They held their first water pageant in 1928.[58] The Green Splash Club began at Michigan State in 1925.[59] The *Ohio State University Monthly* reported, in March 1928, "34 women students have been accepted as members of the Swan Club under Helen Saum, instructor." The Cygnets were composed of coeds who had "passed preliminary tryouts and were ready to take final exams in water ballet activities."[60] In 1929, the Fish Fans Club was founded at Washington State College by Lois Carrell.[61]

More and more college clubs developed. The University of California at Berkeley held its first water pageant in 1931.[62] Barnard College began formation swimming in 1934 and produced a water pageant, "Greek Games," that same year.[63] The Tarpons of Florida State, Tallahassee, began their club in 1937.[64] Kay Curtis developed a new team at Wright Junior College in 1937 and another in 1938 at the Chicago Teachers College.[65] The Terrapin Club of Mundelein College was pictured in *Discus* magazine in 1939.[66] Dorothy Maloney founded the Penguinettes of the University of Pennsylvania in 1940.[67] When Lois Carrell moved to Mills College in California, she began an effort, between 1939 and 1942, to develop movements to express a mood or theme and to put the emphasis on the actions of the swimmers rather than the staging of a performance.[68]

In San Francisco, Phil Patterson, primarily a diving coach who developed national diving champions Helen Crlenkovich, Vicky Manalo (Draves), Patty Elsinor and others, formed a private diving club in 1931 at the Fairmont Hotel. He added water ballet in 1933, as an added attraction to the water shows, featuring his champion divers. In an article in *The Amateur Athlete* in 1941, Patterson stressed the advantages that synchronized swimming could offer to the entire aquatic program. He said, "In the past, we have never had enough money to take all the kids we felt would have a chance in national competition. If we can raise good sized funds in this manner and our kids know they will get trips to distant points, they will work harder in training. Furthermore, they love the work they do in the ballet routines and this in no manner interferes with their training for competition. This synchronized swimming will be the greatest boon that competitive swimming has ever had."[69] The group of amateur swimmers and divers remained active as the Fairmont Water Follies, giving water shows throughout the state and in their home pool through most of 1942, when Patterson went into the armed forces.[70]

On the international scene, Canada was revising its early approach to competitive activity during these times. A provincial swimming championship was held at the Montreal Amateur Athletic Association pool in February 1924, listing competition in events titled tricks and water skills.[71] The competition was limited to ladies only.[72] Like the earlier Royal Life Saving Society competitions, proficiency was required in the performance of both strokes and tricks (figures). The tricks were taken from the scientific swimming section of the *Royal Life Saving Society Handbook*. Margaret "Peg" Shearer (Seller) of the Montreal YWCA won both events.

Another similar competition was held in 1925 which led to an official dominion (National) championship in "The Art of Graceful and Scientific Swimming" in 1926. Held in Montreal, it became known as the "Gale" since Mrs. Frances Gale had donated the trophy. Peg Shearer again won both events and she retained her titles until 1929, winning the dominion title for three consecutive years.[73] The Gale endured as a figure competition for many years. In 1950 it was changed to become the award for the aggregate winner of figures and solos.[74]

By 1928, Curtis began to wonder about competition as well. In the Amateur Athletic Union's "Official Aquatics Guide," she wrote, "Why must our competitive swimming be primarily speed with diving the only recognized form event? Why not center our interest on grace and ease of movement in the water, developing the aesthetic values of swimming? Why not a figures swimming contest? Canada

began the summer season in 1926 with such an event in Toronto. Let's not let the United States fall behind."[75]

While the Canadian competition was not synchronized swimming as we know it today, it was certainly the first recognized national event in a related form of swimming. Canada must get the credit for starting the technical or figures competition of synchronized swimming,[76] but the more characteristic combination of strokes, figures and floats, synchronized to the musical rhythms and tempos was evolving in the United States with Kay Curtis.[77]

## The Influence of Water Shows and Films

While the true precursors of the modern sport first appeared as swimming class activities, and then in water shows or water pageants, it was the Aquacade spectaculars that caught the public eye enough to stimulate interest in synchro development. Katharine Curtis produced many water pageants in the mid-'20s while teaching in the Chicago area. In 1927, the City of Chicago produced an aquatic show at the Navy Pier, called The Festival of the Lakes. There, the Illinois Womens' Athletic Club team exhibited its water ballet, introducing the disappearing ballet, in which "the team closed its performance by submerging behind a barricade."[78]

### BUSBY BERKELEY

Busby Berkeley was considered one of the top dance directors on Broadway in the late '20s. When sound came to films, Samuel Goldwyn brought Berkeley to Hollywood but movie musicals remained static until Berkeley began photographing dancers from every angle, including overhead. When first seen in 1930, it was said to cause audiences to gasp. In 1933, Daryl Zanuck, head of production at Warner Bros., gave Berkeley free rein for whatever grand and glorious ideas came to mind for the dance productions in *42nd Street*, a wildly successful

**Busby Berkeley created the first water ballet sequence for film in the scene "By a Waterfall" from *Footlight Parade*, produced in 1934 (Warner Bros. Studios).**

film. He followed this with *Gold Diggers of 1933*.

*Footlight Parade* was the third, and last, of the legendary Warner Bros. musicals of 1933. It included the first known water ballet sequence on film. An entire sound stage was turned into an Art Deco swimming pool, complete with glass sides so that Berkeley could film the swimmers underwater in their rhythmic actions. "By a Waterfall" is an aquatic dream sequence with 100 chorines splashing down a studio-built waterfall into a beautiful forest lake. There, the studio reported, he produced an "unparalleled water ballet sequence in the gigantic swimming pool, complete with golden springboards and some of Berkeley's best multifaceted kaleidoscopic top shots."[79]

The first extended-run water show was introduced in The Century of Progress World's Fair, 1933-34, on Chicago's lake-front.[80] Looking for something to accentuate the novelty of the underwater lighting in the lagoon, fair organizers asked Miss Curtis to provide a water ballet that would be effective over the lights.[81] She augmented her collegiate group, the Tar-

pons, with other swimmers in the area to make a 60-girl troupe, the largest group ever assembled for this type of demonstration. The Kay Curtis Modern Mermaids were born.[82]

The Modern Mermaids performed three shows a day during the entire summer fair season.[83] They entered from beneath a deck which had been built out over an area of Lake Michigan that had been partitioned off into a swimming pool arena.[84] Both the floating routines and rhythmic swimming routines were performed to a 12-piece band.[85] The audiences, seated on both sides of the pool area, were estimated at more than 10,000 people for each performance.[86] The Century of Progress Publicity Division's news release of August 24, 1934, said, "Performing ten complicated routines in perfect unison, thirty five modern mermaids are revealing to patrons of the Lagoon Theater at the Chicago World's Fair, the highly modern art of synchronized swimming."

The contracts for this new show reveal the tremendous response by the public. The swimmers were initially signed for one week of performances, the last week of June. This was extended another week, then two weeks, and finally, so popular was the show, the last contract was for the entire summer season. The publicity release stated, "They will be featured at the Lagoon Theater until ice forms in the Lagoon or the Fair closes on October 31st."[87]

Perhaps the first commercial sponsor for the sport, the U.S. Rubber Company supplied the rubber Krepe-Tex suits for the Aquacade. They were asked to partly underwrite the costs of continuing the Aquacade for the entire summer season ($750 per week for salaries for the swimmers and divers), but declined saying, "We appreciate very much the interest these suits have attracted ... but it will be out of the question for us to pay any money for their use."[88] Perhaps they still needed to work on those suits. Lena Zimmerman (Feinstein) recalls, "We were all given rubber bathing suits, (the newest thing at the time) for the shows. When we dove in, the suits split. It was fortunate that it happened at dress rehearsal," she said.[89]

The term "synchronized swimming" was officially born during the 1934 shows when announcer Norman Ross, himself a former swimmer, coined the term to describe the actions of the swimmers in the show.[90] Thus, a fairly sizable public segment came to enjoy and recognize synchronized swimming through the exhibitions of the Modern Mermaids, and thereafter the name was frequently applied to all kinds of water ballet.

The shows had proved so popular that on their final day at the Century of Progress, it was announced that the Mermaids would present their picturesque swimming act each Friday night during the coming winter in the pool of the Medinah Athletic Club in Chicago.[91]

These popular shows were the catalyst for the rapid rise in enthusiasm for and the developing popularity of water ballet activities. Swimming teachers all over the country soon wanted to incorporate it into their classes. In 1933, Olive McCormick in New York produced a book of *Water Pageants, Games and Stunts*. Published in 1933, it was intended as an aid to all those interested in producing aquatic programs from the standpoint of organization, costuming, music, scenery and lighting.[92] Notably, this publication preceded the Chicago World's Fair shows that brought wide attention and popularity to rhythmic swimming. Curtis was stimulated to publish, in 1936, *A Course Book of Water Pageantry*, detailing approaches to classwork and shows.[93] Then, also in 1936, she published *Rhythmic Swimming*, which gave more detailed descriptions of the stunts and a general outline of their use in water shows.[94] It was reprinted several times and served as the major source book for techniques and skills for many years.

During this same period of the mid–'30s a professional water show group came to life under the title Sam Snyder Productions of Boston. Initially giving shows mainly in Miami during the summer, the group eventually toured the U.S. and then many parts of the world as Sam Snyder's International Water Follies. Billed as the "world's longest traveling aqua show," the Water Follies shows continued to be well-received and they endured well into the '50s. The group included swimmers, divers, comedy divers and water ballet swimmers. At varying times, former Olympians such as Eleanor Holm, Buster Crabbe, Marshall Wayne and Dorothy Poynton Hill joined the show. Johnny Weissmuller appeared in the shows in London. Pete Desjardins, a 1928 Olympian diver who had been the USA's hope for extending Olympic diving dominance into 1932 and 1936, joined the shows and thus became labeled a "pro" and lost any further chance at Olympic competition.[95] Mary Dwight (Rose) and sister Fran (Gioe) began swimming with this show in 1953, right out of high school. "It gave an opportunity to continue doing what they really liked and earn their living at it," said Rose, who formed the St. Petersburg Aquabelles in the late '50s.[96]

A much smaller and shorter-lived group was part of a 1939–41 series of Sportsman's Shows appearing in Massachusetts, New York, Ohio, Rhode Island and Pennsylvania. Only five swimmers were involved in the shows, given for four weeks each summer. The swimmers performed in a portable tank whose water was supplied directly from a hydrant on the street. Each swimmer would dive in, swim a lap of her specialty stroke and then they joined together to present a short routine to the *Skater's Waltz*. Linda Brookman, a member of the group who later became coach at Villanova University, recalled one time that the water came in at 48°F. "All we could do was sprint the length of the pool," she said. A steamroller was brought in, its engine was fired up and used to pump live steam into the pool, raising the temperature, within 48 hours, to the contract-guaranteed 65°F.[97] Another member, Doris

Kelman (Dannenhirsch) recalled, "Even a hot shower for an hour afterward could not take the chill away, yet we never got sick."[98]

Florenz Ziegfeld, A.L. Erlanger, and Charles B. Dillingham, glamour merchants of the '20s, staged "girl-and-music" theater shows that were highly popular but with ticket prices that were generally out of range for the average working man. Movies and radio, emerging from their infancy, began to put the finest talents within the reach of millions, yet most theater owners didn't pay much attention to the changes taking place in the amusement business and continued to charge prices which the greater number of potential theatergoers could not afford.

Billy Rose was the showman who correctly read the signs of change. He recognized that if a show had "the sheen, the fun, the zest, and the romance of a Ziegfeld musical," and "was offered for the price of a movie admission, millions, not thousands, would throng to see it." He first put his new theories into practice at the Texas Centennial in Fort Worth in 1936 where he produced "a magnificent spectacle at prices the cowboys and farmhands could afford."[99] Later that year, Rose teamed with Floyd Zimmerman to develop a water show, the Cleveland Aquacade.[100] The program trumpeted that it had "the glamour of diving and swimming mermaids, in water ballets of breath-taking beauty and rhythm."

Rose's ideas really blossomed at the 1939-1940 New York World's Fair Aquacades where musical swimming was peddled as "an eye filling and stadium filling spectacle."[101] For the male lead, he latched onto Johnny Weissmuller, star of the 1924 and 1928 Olympics and the original "Tarzan" of the movies. In selecting the female lead and star, he shrewdly capitalized on the somewhat notorious fame laid onto Eleanor Holm from the 1932 Olympics. Holm, national backstroke champion and holder of a world record, was aboard the Olympic team ship on her way to expected easy victories in her events, but one evening sipped some champagne with officials. She was promptly expelled from the Olympic team for violation of the no-alcohol regulations. The hard-nosed official reaction made Holm an immediate sympathetic celebrity. Any leftover notoriety was quickly replaced by fame as multitudes admired her work in the World's Fair Aquacade.[102] The show, labeled "this marvel among girl extravaganzas," became the undisputed hit of the exposition.[103]

Rose's next endeavor was to be the Billy Rose Aquacade at San Francisco's 1940 Golden Gate International Exposition. Weissmuller went to San Francisco and Buster Crabbe, also famous as a movie Tarzan (the seventh) and the world record holder and 400 meter freestyle champion of the 1932 Olympics, replaced Weissmuller in the New York shows.[104]

With Eleanor Holm still performing in New York, Rose had to find a new female lead. Highly impressed with the photogenic good-looks of Esther Williams, then a three-time national swimming champion and a U.S. record holder, he talked her into trying out for the show. Weissmuller, who was to be the male star, seconded Rose's assessment of Williams by choosing her from a lineup of 75 hopefuls.

## ESTHER WILLIAMS

Williams' credentials to be Aquacade's "Number One Aquabelle," were very solid. Her U.S. 100 meter freestyle record would endure for six years and she was a part of the world record-holding relay team. Considered a lock for the 1940 Olympic team, her decision to go for the show world looked brilliant when the 1940 Olympic Games were canceled due to the war in Europe.[105]

With the famed New York show as precedent, and headlining the charismatic and beautiful Williams with renowned swimmer Weissmuller, the show leaped to popularity. Two to three performances were given each day for 7,000 spectators at each show and this was maintained the full year of the fair. The program touted the staging in a 250 by 50-foot wooden pool filled with 500,000 gallons of purified drinking water, continuously heated to a temperature of 72°.[106]

The Aquacade combined diving spectacles, on-deck comedy routines, comedy divers, song and dance numbers and a variety of water ballets. There were solos with Williams, duos with the Hopkins Twins, and giant water ballets with as many as 50 Aquabelles (including nearly every ballet-experienced swimmer from Patterson's Fairmont Hotel Water Follies) and their 24 Aquabeaux. The charisma of Williams and the beauty of the water ballets made this Aquacade a highlight of the fair and long lines snaked around the building awaiting tickets for each performance. MGM, sensing her potential, snapped up Williams after the Aquacade.

Her film debut, in 1942, was in *Andy Hardy's Double Life*. Oddly, no attempt was made to use her water show talents until her third movie when she starred in *Bathing Beauty* (1944). In this first attempt by *any* studio at making a swimming movie, they dove wholeheartedly into building a special back lot pool 20 feet deep and hiring chorus line swimmers galore. Williams said, "We just made it up as we went along" and "I ad-libbed all my underwater movements."[107]

Busby Berkeley, master showman of the time, now with MGM, choreographed the large group sequences, creating the elaborate water scenes with fountains, flame, smoke, mirrors and "lots of pretty girls swimming around with bows in their hair." Whatever it was in the combination of pretty girls, smoke, flame, mirrors and leading lady, the movie took off.[108] *Bathing Beauty* was the second most successful film of 1944, just after *Gone with the Wind*.[109] Several water spectacular movies later, Esther Williams was one of Hollywood's biggest stars. Her pictures appeared everywhere. She claimed she once saw her picture at a newsstand on the cover of 14 different magazines, all at the same time. As America's Swimming Sweetheart she made 26 movies in 18 years.[110]

Inspired by the success of the Rose New York Aquacade, Minneapolis producer Al Sheehan sold the city on his idea to emulate or surpass it with his own company.[111] The first of his popular Minneapolis Aquatennials was produced in the summer of 1940. By 1942, the show was staged in a specially built combination pool-stage, the Theodore Wirth Pool, on the shore of Wirth Lake.[112] During the four-week summer season, 6,000 spectators witnessed each show. The water ballet part of the show,

Esther Williams, star of the 1940 World's Fair Aquacade, is credited with popularizing water ballet through the MGM musicals that featured her.

the "Aqua Follies," remained one of the most popular acts throughout its long life. Helen Starr, who had been teaching water ballet to her University of Minnesota physical education classes, choreographed the Aqua Follies numbers.[113]

Coming back every summer, the Minneapolis Aquatennial was the largest extended-run water ballet in the nation and became the first to use champions from competitive synchronized swimming as its stars. The Aquatennials survived even beyond Sheehan's death in 1967. They inspired a number of copy-cat professional show groups during the '50s which provided an opportunity for employment for many later champions in synchronized swimming and diving. Fred Smith, stage manager for the Minneapolis Aquatennial, in comparing swimmers in other shows with the Aquatennial swimmers, said, "The poor girls couldn't swim in deep water. That was one of the secrets of our show. The old movie spectaculars

The Billy Rose Aquacades inspired Al Sheehan to produce the long-lived Minneapolis Aquatennial each summer.

ure, a fine sense of rhythm, a supple body and a fine impressionable mind. The fact that you have to be extra good to qualify gives those in the Aqua Dears the mark of distinction."[116]

Water shows continued to be a popular form of entertainment. In 1946, Elliot Murphy's Aqua Show was staged in Flushing Meadows, the site of the 1939 World's Fair in New York. These Aqua Shows brought audiences of up to 10,000 spectators. They featured exhibitions of fancy and comedy diving and 24 Aquadorables presented the water ballet.[117]

had swimming ballets that appear to be swimming, but really the girls stood in shallow water. Our girls were athletes, they really swam. It was an exhausting thing and they had to be well conditioned."[114]

Other cities also had the benefits of Al Sheehan's show productions. Seattle built an Aqua Theater on the shore of Green Lake and Sheehan's Minneapolis Aquatennial traveled there in 1950 to stage its popular aquacade, the first tour for the group outside Minneapolis. The local news media said, "the *Aqua Follies*, like the *Ice Follies*, play on speed and color and rhythm. The water ballet has the only women we've ever seen who look beautiful with their hair wet. They swim like metronomes, three beats, four beats, never missing a beat."[115] The shows in Seattle were staged under the title Seattle Sea Fair and the shows became a regular stop for the Aquatennial stars through the '50s.

In 1955, the Aqua Follies brought their show to Detroit. According to Detroit's Riverama Aqua Follies program, the Sheehan-produced annual water show was in its 16th year. Held on Belle Isle every summer, the Riverama aquacade numbers also had the Aquatennial's Dr. Helen Starr as choreographer and producer. The ballets involved 24 Aqua Dears whose "must have" qualifications were: "a shapely fig-

Buster Crabbe, the star of the 1940 World's Fair Aquacade, who had swum with Sam Snyder's professional group in Miami in the later '30s, joined the Sam Snyder Water Follies in 1946-47 and then, from 1948 through 1950, he produced his own water show, the Buster Crabbe Aqua Parade, which toured cities throughout the U.S., Canada and Europe. The 75-member troupe included divers, swimmers, dancers, and water ballet swimmers. The performances were given in two portable pools that had an attached stage. One pool was an 8-foot-deep diving pool with two 3-meter boards; the water ballet numbers were done in the big pool, 48 feet by 75 feet and 4-feet deep. In addition to large ballets and a fluorescent surfboard number, there were solo and duo numbers, including one that featured Crabbe swimming a duet with Madeline Rice.[118]

## *Acceptance by the Public*

After its start as a novelty activity for swimming classes in the '30s and '40s, it was the water ballet and aquacades of the late '40s and early '50s that were enthusiastically embraced by the public. Williams-inspired clubs for water ballet sprang up everywhere. Even though rules for competition in synchronized swimming national events had been adopted in 1940 (*cf.* Chapter 2) before Williams' immense popularity, her idolatry undoubtedly promoted popular acceptance and subsequent growth of competition as water ballet swimmers switched to synchronized swimming. Even though resemblance between the show-type water ballet and competitive synchronized swimming seemed meager at times, both were based on making a striking impression from actions in the water; each helped the other grow during this period.

In an interview with Kay Curtis in 1953, *Stars and Stripes* stated, "Her efforts led her to the 1934 World's Fair where she formed the 'Kay Curtis Modern Mermaids.' Thus was born the first 'water ballet' complete with musical synchronization. The ballet was elaborated on by Billy Rose at the New York World's Fair in 1939. Rhythmic or Synchronized Swimming was, of course, not entirely new. The Germans had experimented with *Picture Swimming* for years and Canadians had *Ornamental Swimming*. But both of these lacked what the Curtis method supplied, music."[119]

# 2

# *The Emerging Sport: 1937–45*

In the wake of widespread exposure to the charisma of the Modern Mermaid shows of the Century of Progress World's Fair, clubs began to spring up throughout the nation with eager young girls wanting to try to emulate the Mermaid's synchronized swimming, as water ballet had come to be known. Two 1938 photos from the *Chicago Tribune* show water ballet swimmers in paired stroking and in a float formation. The accompanying article quotes Stanley Brauninger, coach at Chicago's Medinah Athletic Club, saying, "One look at the lovely young women should convince you that [synchronized] swimming is a sure-fire beauty builder. Swimming exercises every muscle and does it rhythmically. The rhythmic exercise develops the streamlined well-proportioned figure."[1]

Swimmers were looking for programs and swimming teachers from all over the country were seeking information. A group that did much to further the knowledge of swimming activities was the Women's National Aquatic Forum that began meeting in Hollywood, Florida, in 1936.[2] The group, composed primarily of swimming teachers, met once a year to further their knowledge of all aquatic sports. A symposium on ballet swimming was held with the second annual meeting and has been part of the program ever since. Some of synchro's most famous swim coaches have taken part in the meetings.

Some forms of "synchronized swimming"

were being taught in Y summer camps and Red Cross Aquatic Schools as early as 1943.[3] There was widespread participation in synchronized swimming–related activities even before it had been well defined. To some, the term meant merely stroking to music or rhythmic swimming, while to others it meant creating movement expressive of mood or design.

Katharine Curtis, in her book *Rhythmic Swimming*, listed the following as rhythmic swimming's fundamental skills:

*Strokes:* Breaststroke, sidestroke, single overarm, trudgeon, crawl, reverse crawl [backstroke], waltz crawl, revolving crawl, shadow and tandem strokes.

*Sculling:* On the back: toward head, toward feet; hands at side, overhead; on the face, toward head, toward feet; on side making a single circle or figure eight.

*Stunts:* Surface dives, backward surface dives or kips, somersaults (forward and backward, tucked and piked); dolphins (head first, foot first, tandem and pinwheel), ballet leg, submarine, pendulum, mermaid's prayer, log rolling, tub, bicycle, plank and marching.[4]

Curtis stated, "This new form of rhythmic swimming requires endurance, not speed; versatility in the use of all strokes, not specialization in one; a keen sense of rhythm, the specific development of the ability to adapt one's strokes to the average strokes of the group. The degree of difficulty in any performance can be adjusted to the individual's ability; she can progress at her own rate of speed; her success depends not upon her strength, but upon her skill; her creative interest finds a wide field in the development of routines."[5] She wondered, "Why must our competitive swimming be primarily speed, with diving our only recognized 'form' event? Why not center our interest upon grace and ease of movement in the water, developing the aesthetic values of swimming: Why not a figure swimming contest?"[6]

Curtis became an instructor at Wright Junior College in Chicago in 1937 where she organized the nation's first Co-educational Synchronized Swimming Club. She took a new position at the Chicago Teacher's College in 1938 and organized a similar club there. The "natural rivalry" that sprang up between her former students at Wright and her new students at the teacher's college was soon directed toward arranging for a real (dual) competition. Curtis recalled, "Through their own interest and enthusiasm, the students, under the leadership of Frank Havlicek, student leader of the group, developed rules and events for a Dual Meet between the co-educational teams of the two institutions."[7]

## Early Competitions

### THE FIRST COMPETITION

The first competition in synchronized swimming was held at the Chicago Teacher's College on May 27, 1939, as part of the annual Teachers Day Program. Curtis was quoted in the program, "A synchronized swimming program should be designed to give the average swimmer a chance to perform in competition where speed is not the fundamental desire. The routines develop a sense of rhythm and improve the swimming ability of the participants. Creative skill is developed through this type of competition in as much as routines are created by the students."[8]

The competitive events were open to male and female swimmers, with no distinction, except in the fancy stunting, where one of each sex was required.

The events included:

1. Floating Routine: maximum of 14 persons, to music, maximum time 7 minutes.
2. Small Routine: 2 or 4 persons, to music, maximum time 4 minutes.
3. Large Routine: 8–12 persons, to music, minimum time 2 minutes, maximum time 4 minutes
4. Fancy Stunting: Teams of 2 persons, one of each sex, performing 4 required stunts and 4 optional stunts, one from each of four groups with points for difficulty.

Some of the interesting stunts that could be selected for the competition were:

*Sunfish:* Lie on side used for sidestroke. Extend arm overhead, the other straight behind. Swim, using scissors kick while splashing the surface of the water by fluttering movements of both hands. Smile sunnily.

*Muskrat:* Come up quietly to the surface from underneath and scull forward on the chest very quietly with legs extended and together. Suddenly, without a ripple, submerge and disappear.

*Mermaid's Prayer:* Assume position of prayer, hang in this position. Hollow the back and reach folded hands out in front.

*Double Flying Dolphin:* Executed by partners with one partner submerging and pushing or lifting the dolphin performer out of the water into the dolphin.

In regard to judging these and the other stunts that could be selected, the entry stated: "Each stunt is graded individually, as in diving, on ease, grace, form and rhythm. Routines are judged on timing, style, difficulty and composition."[9] There was no further clarification of how the scores would actually be determined.

Following the competition, the *Wright College News* reported, "Swim Club Wins Trick Aquatic Tilt. Wright Synchronized Swim Club came through for the alma mater Saturday May 27 by defeating the Chicago Teacher's College Tritons at their pool. The meet was the first of its kind ever held in the United States. Competition has been held in Canada, but for girls only. The program included a floating routine, a small and large routine and fancy stunting. Ellen Murphy and Dudley Field represented Wright in the stunts."[10]

David Clark Leach, Central Association chairman of the Amateur Athletic Union (AAU) Swimming Committee at the time of the dual meet, had been observing Curtis' work from as early as 1924. He had long believed that her rhythmic swimming might make an interesting competitive event to add to swimming and diving championships. The dual collegiate meet prompted him to discuss with Curtis the possibility of establishing rhythmic (or "synchronized") swimming as an AAU competitive event. Curtis initially reacted negatively on the basis that it might defeat her purpose of reaching the great masses of "mediocre" swimmers. But, after some thought, she reversed her stance. She rationalized that competitive rhythmic swimming might "offer an outlet for the [racing] swimmer who had passed the competitive age," and "still be a challenge for the mediocre swimmer."[11]

Leach enthusiastically set in motion the process of gaining approval for adding synchronized swimming to the AAU swimming program. He appointed Curtis to chair a rule preparation committee, composed of Bernice Lorber Hayes (coach at Wright Junior College), Eileen Scanlon (coach at Mundelein College), Isabelle Smith (teacher at Bowen High School), Victoria Vacha, Frank Havlicek and Leach. Scanlon and Smith had been part of the Century of Progress' Modern Mermaids while Havlicek had written the original collegiate rules.[12] They met at Curtis' apartment to discuss methods of marking and grading, divisions of competition to be included, requirements for the events and time limits.[13]

The group considered many options for methods of marking. One idea was to have a musician judge [Use of] Music, a dress designer to judge the Costuming, and a military officer to judge Precision. Leach suggested that the rules be patterned after those for fancy diving and figure skating with their scoring methods. Time was spent debating whether costuming should be given any points and it was finally decided that scoring the "appropriateness" of the costuming should remain part of the event.[14]

The name to be applied to the sport was also debated, noting that the activity had gone under many titles. An early name was ornamental swimming, then came the more popular water ballet, but picture swimming, water stunt swimming, stunt swimming, water pageantry, artistic swimming, rhythmic swimming and aquatic art had all been applied. Canada was then holding competitions in graceful and scientific swimming, later named fancy swimming. Synchronized swimming, which announcer Norman Ross had used to describe the actions at the 1934 Century of Progress World's Fair, finally won, "so as not to confuse the competitive form with Water Ballet as being done at the 1939 and 1940 World's Fairs."[15] Upon reaching initial agreement on a name and rules, two trial events, "a Ballet event and a Duet event," were scheduled in 1940 for the Central Association of the AAU.[16]

The first trial competition was an invitational meet at the Medinah Athletic Club of Chicago on February 13, 1940. Seven clubs competed in team and duet events. The winning team, composed of both men and women, was from Wright Junior College. Some adjustments to the rules were made following this meet.[17]

On March 1, 1940, a second competition was held at the Shawnee Country Club (now Michigan Shores) in Wilmette, Illinois, in conjunction with the Central Association Swimming and Diving championship meet.[18] Thus, it became the first synchronized swimming competition held under AAU auspices and was characterized as "The first synchronized swimming championship in the world."[19]

The entry sheets for this 1940 Central Association AAU Women's Swimming and Diving Championships included events for the Water Ballet and Synchronized Swimming Championships. The events were team ballet (8–12 members) and duet ballet.

The rules specified:

(1) Competitors may be men or women or both.
(2) The routine must include
   a. Any two of the following strokes: crawl, reverse crawl, breast stroke, side stroke, single overarm side stroke, elementary backstroke.

b. Any two of the following stunts: somersaults, porpoise, dolphins, kip.
(3) Length of Routine,
   a. Team ballet, 3–10 minutes.
   b. Duet ballet, 3–5 minutes.

Categories for the strokes and stunts were: (1) forward stunts, single and double, (2) backward stunts, single and double, (3) wheels, (4) stunt strokes, (5) twisting strokes and (6) twisting stunts. All strokes and stunts had to be selected from the approved list, which then included 59 actions each with a degree of difficulty.

The entry also stated "the Contest will be judged similar to a fancy diving contest."[20] Entrants were required to list everything they included in the routine on the master score sheet. Each judge was provided an assistant who read the list of stunts and strokes as they were to be performed. The judge announced a score for execution for each item listed. At the completion of each routine, the judge also awarded scores for style (included costumes and lighting effects), composition and accompaniment. Scorers added and averaged the awards to determine the placings.

The *Wright College News* reported, "Synchronizers cop AAU title. First Place in the first annual Central Association AAU Synchronized Swim Meet was awarded to Wright College Friday night after an evening of brilliant aquatic maneuvers at the Shawnee Country Club in Wilmette. Blazing away for the newsreel photographers, Bernice Lorber's crew outclassed the entire field composed of Chicago Teacher's College, Towers Athletic Club, Shawnee Country Club, Mundelein College, Blackhawk Park and the American College of P.E. Competitors placed in that order. Staged under Olympic conditions, judging was based on difficulty of the number, composition of routine, style, accompaniment and costuming."[21]

A meeting to evaluate the competition and rules was held afterward. Two major problems were dealt with. The scoring system was deemed too complex and difficult and judges felt that a better mechanism for evaluating and scoring the routine itself was needed. Subsequent revisions allowed judges to flash three scores at the end of each routine, for execution, originality and synchronization. Curtis said, "We had many discussion meetings, and a trial meet was held, before the rules were accepted, at least temporarily."[22]

The *Chicago Tempo* reported a second collegiate competition, listed as the second synchronized swimming contest of any type, on April 26, 1940. This competition was held in conjunction with the National Convention of the American Association for Health, Physical Education and Recreation (AAHPER). The article headlined, "Synchro Swimmers Beat Wright in Demonstration.... Four events test Tritons water ability." It reported, "Easily winning the Synchronized Swimming meet with Wright Junior College on April 26, the Tritons [Chicago Teacher's College] demonstrated results of careful practice, precision and concentration. Swimming before more than 100 spectators from throughout the country, the team splashed to victory in all four events. Frank Havlicek was first in Individual Stunts, Helen Cummings and Havlicek won in Duet, the Floating routine was taken by the Lake Shore Club, with the Tritons winning the Large routine." It further reported, "The competition gave visitors an excellent view of the possibilities in competitive water ballet or synchronized swimming."[23]

With the practical exposure of the tentative rules to these competitions, and the consequent revisions, it was feasible to develop a proposal for adoption of synchronized swimming into the AAU swimming program. The Central Association forwarded that proposal to the AAU for consideration at the 1940 convention in December of that year.[24]

## Acceptance by the AAU

Ironically, one of Katharine Curtis' most cherished concepts of synchro competition was dashed into oblivion soon after the adoption into the AAU. She had always presented rhythmic and synchronized swimming as a coed activity, in which men and women could benefit and contribute equally and together. But, when the Chicago Teacher's College Tarpons entered their usual coed team in an AAU event, they were informed that AAU swimming rules forbade men and women competing together (or even exhibiting together in a sanctioned event, as many later found to their dismay). The Tarpons had to reduce and revise their routine to compete without the men.[25] Thus, men involved in early synchro could be accommodated only where specific events for men were included. This prudish rule remained in force until the AAU was stripped of its overall control of sports and each sport formed its own national governing body under the Amateur Sports Act of 1978.

The Central Association of the AAU Board of Governors authorized Leach to present the new sport to the 52nd Annual AAU Convention, December 6–8, 1940, in Denver, Colorado.[26] The rules were referred separately to the Men's and Women's Swimming committees for study. The Men's Swimming Committee returned with approval for the sport, but the Women's committee rejected it, the main objection being, "It would require too much time to conduct competitions."[27] It gained acceptance for association competitions after a floor debate but joined softball and water polo as sports in which "There shall be no national championships."[28]

Ben York, president of the Florida AAU, said later, "Figure synchronized swimming may provide a formula for turning the U.S. into a nation of swimmers. For one thing, the galloping popularity of ballet type swimming will awaken Americans to the deplorable lack of swimming facilities." But Pete Desjardins, Florida coach, expressed some misgivings, "The very nature of synchronized swimming may provide its toughest hurdle. You see, when the AAU committee tried to fit synchronized swimming into its competitive bracket, they had to form some basis for judging.... In their passion for rewarding stunt execution, the AAU point-hoarders have lost sight of the whole ballet program. No matter how complicated the figures may be, or how dazzling the ballet routine, the AAU judges all judge on the basic stunt and stroke execution."[29]

Full acceptance finally was gained on the floor of the concluding general session of the 1941 AAU convention in Philadelphia.[30] However, it was not until 1945 when Yale's famous and influential swimming coach, Bob Kiphuth, championed synchro in recommending that synchronized swimming be added to the national championship events sanctioned by the AAU. The first official national championship would finally be held in 1946.

Synchronized swimming started operations as a subcommittee of the AAU Women's Swimming Committee.[31] Leach was appointed the first national chairman and he appointed Katharine Curtis to be his vice chairman. The balance of the National Synchronized Swimming Committee consisted of the local association chairmen. In most cases they also served as the men's or women's chair for swimming or diving. Even such famous swim coaches as Bob Kiphuth (Yale) and Ray Daughters (Washington) took on chairing the synchro committee for their associations. In the Pacific Association, renowned diving coach Phil Patterson chaired both the diving and synchro committees. Future Synchro National chairmen Mary Derosier (Michigan) and Norma Olsen (Iowa) chaired their local committees despite primary interests in swimming and diving, respectively. Lillian Whiting, who chaired the Women's Swimming Committee when synchro was accepted, subsequently served as synchro's registration chairman for many years.

Wright College cherishes the honor of winning the first Central Association meet, March 1940, with a team of six men and six women in "Dagger Dance."[32] Wright's trophy for the meet was presented to the Canadian Swimming Hall of Fame in Winnipeg, Canada.[33] They had wanted it because it was a *first* and because it was the only mixed competition. The next year the AAU ruled out mixed competition and, until recent years, the men had no chance to compete. Lake Shore won that next year and Wright placed second. Perhaps because men were ruled out or perhaps because of a very busy schedule and very large groups, interest in competition waned at Wright and the main event for them each year became "The Swim Show."[34]

Several clubs within the Central Association had already become experienced in competition in the trial synchronized swimming meets of 1940. They seized eagerly on synchro's new official status and both Indoor and Outdoor Central Association Championship competitions were staged in 1941.[35] Bernice Lorber Hayes, who became the coach at Wright Junior College when Kay Curtis left for Chicago Teacher's College, remembers the February [1940] Trial meet at the Medinah Athletic Club. She said, "Paramount and MGM sent photographers and it was fun to see it in the news reels at movie theaters."[36]

The Central Association Indoor Team Championship drew a capacity crowd and was held April 17, 1941, at the Shawnee Country Club in Wilmette, Illinois. Eight teams competed. Swimmers from the Lake Shore Athletic Club, won the title. *Discus* (the magazine of the Lake Shore Athletic Club), reported in May 1941, "This marks the first time in which water ballet [*sic*] has been recognized as an AAU championship event so the club's girls will go down in swimming history as the first champions in the sport. In winning, the girls had to beat five of the best teams in the Middle West. Team entries had included Shawnee Country Club, Wright Junior College, Niles Township High School, Blackhawk Park and the Midwest Athletic Club. Members of the winning team were Doris Dieskow, Rosemary Foster, Nancy Hanna, Marion Mittlacher, Jean Parks, Adeline Potter, Jeanne Roberts, Pauline Wesner, Jean Wilson, and Lillian Wilson."[37]

The CAAAU Indoor Duet Championships followed a month later on May 17, 1941, at the Madison Athletic Club. *Discus* (June 1941) reported that Polly Wesner and Lillian Wilson brought another gold trophy home to Lake Shore by defeating 18 pairs of swimmers from the Chicago Town Club, Wright Junior College, Shawnee Country Club, Midwest Athletic Club, Waukegan High School and the Chicago Teacher's College.[38]

In July 1941, CAAAU Outdoor Team Championships were held at Pekin, Illinois. The August *Discus* stated, "Never did 8 girls perform more beautifully in the water than the Lake Shore club water ballet in winning the CAAAU outdoor championship.... With easy grace and flawless execution, the girls annexed their 2nd title by an even wider margin than they held in winning the indoor championship at Shawnee Country club last April ... 2nd place went to Shawnee and 3rd to Naperville. More than 3,000 spectators attended."[39] Lake Shore continued winning and was triumphant over seven other entrants in the Outdoor Duet Championship, held August 1941 at the Glen Oaks Country Club, Glen Ellyn, Illinois. The September issue of *Discus* noted, "The win climaxed a brilliant season for the girls of the water ballet. They have been undefeated, both duet and team, through the entire season, both Indoor and Outdoor."[40]

The intense activity in the CAAAU immediately following AAU adoption of synchronized swimming was hardly representative of early activity in other areas of the country, as suggested by Leach's report to the AAU convention the following year. In his report, he said, "Due to the fact that the Swim Guide was not printed until very late this year, and due to the fact that Synchronized Swimming chairmen of various associations were not appointed early enough, it is impossible to report a great deal of progress nationally in this new sport.[41]

"Early this spring [1941], a Synchronized Swimming clinic was conducted at the Lake Shore Athletic Club of Chicago and 72 people attended. Five associations around Central sent representatives. Since that time, a great number of requests have been made and it is our intention to hold another such clinic in Central or elsewhere this winter.

"The Indoor Duet was held at Madison Athletic Club, Chicago, with 18 duets in the preliminary. The Outdoor Team was held at Pekin, Illinois, before a crowd of 3,000 spectators. The Outdoor Duet was held at Glen Oaks Country Club, Glen Ellyn, Illinois, with 8 teams. Both the Indoor and Outdoor championships were won by the Lake Shore Club of Chicago." He concluded his report with the statement, "Despite many requests, your chairman has been unable to secure responses from other associations concerning their activities."[42]

## *The War Years*

The entry of the U.S.A. into the war at the end of 1941 naturally had a severely inhibiting effect upon the emergence of synchronized swimming, but some development did continue. The Central Association of the AAU, the pioneer in competitive synchronized swimming, may be the only association with records showing competitions that continued through all the war years. The Lake Shore Athletic Club won the CAAAU titles from 1942 through 1944, but they lost their coach to war service.[43]

In the final Central Association AAU meet of the year, Sept. 5, 1943, *Discus* magazine published a photo of Jeanne and Lillian Wilson, winners of the Duet competition, captioned, "They swam to 'Taboo' in leopard skin costumes which were very effective in the unique jungle-like background of Idylwild Park." But while that description might make you wonder about the nature of the sport, *Discus* magazine in November 1943, wrote, "The old saying that swimming makes a woman beautiful might very well apply to Jeanne Wilson, star of the Lake Shore team. Her competitive ability and speed has been proved when she set a new American record for 100 meter breaststroke. At age 16, she is one of the top freestylers in the U.S. She is also the duet [synchro] champion with her sister Lillian."[44]

The next year, the core group from Lake Shore was swimming with Lorraine Thayer at the Edgewater Beach Apartments. They won the CAAAU title competing as Chicago Water Ballet.[45] *Discus* magazine reported, "Lake Shore water ballet — never defeated in competition, will perform with unbelievable accuracy, their ever changing formations in the water…. Lake Shore water ballet club defended their CAAAU title … the 5th title event in synchronized swimming since it was recognized by the AAU last year."[46] The *Chicago Herald American* reported, "Champions in the Central AAU Senior Synchronized Swimming event again…. Chicago Water Ballet girls add another trophy to their large collection. Lake Shore placed 2nd with Town Club third."[47]

But most synchro groups around the nation remember giving water shows during these years and little, if any, competition. Virginia Hunt Newman, a diver in such water shows in the '40s, remembers helping raise money for Uncle Sam through the sale of war bonds. The most lucrative of these shows, she said, was held at the Beverly Hilton Hotel in July 1945 and raised $25 million. Newman added, "You had to buy $25,000 worth of war bonds to attend. We had a lot of Hollywood's elite in attendance."[48]

Doris Dieskow, Lake Shore Club, remembers giving "lots of shows during the war. For the show at the Dayton Air Force Base, we had to collect gas coupons to get there. Since you couldn't get tires all during the war, we worried about that and had to get three flats fixed during that

The Central Association Championships of 1944 were won by the Lakeshore Club in 1944. From left to right are Marian Mittlacher, Irene Van Steen, Audrey Boessel, Jean Parks, Polly Wesner, Phyllis Burrell, Doris Dieskow, Nancy Hanna, and standing are Audrey Heuttenrauch and Lorraine "Larry" Thayer (coach).

trip. But, in spite of the war, it was an adventure, a fun time. We gave an exhibition in Davenport in the Mississippi River. We couldn't see a thing two inches under the water and had to dress and undress on a barge and start the routines from the barge."[49]

Leach managed to arrange for demonstrations of synchro routines and to hold a sample "national" team competition within the 1942 AAU Women's Outdoor National Swimming and Diving Championships, in Neenah, Wisconsin, August 14–16. Team and Duet exhibitions were given during each swimming and diving competitive session.[50] On the final day, a team championship competition was held.[51] The *Neenah Daily News* reported, "Special events tonight included synchronized swimming among three Chicago teams. Lake Shore Athletic Club won with 238 points. Skyline Athletic Club was 2nd with 143 points and Midwest Athletic Club was 3rd with 100 points."[52]

*Discus* magazine said of the Lake Shore team, "The nine girl water ballet team, swimming to Tchaikovsky's 'Piano Concerto,' gave a beautiful showing in Neenah. The ballet routine required more than nine months of training and the music was well adapted to the interpretation in the water."[53] Adeline Potter, a member of the winning team, said, "Our team made great preparations. We presented 'Piano Concerto' with a new idea in performing ballet legs and a 'first' in costuming — black leotards with only one long sleeve and hip length black capes with white satin piano keys appliquéd thereon. On the night of competition, the girls jauntily walked on deck with zip and enthusiasm, elbows high jutting out the black capes so the white piano keys could easily be seen and the same night, with the same zip and enthusiasm, walked off with the first national 'open' championship."[54]

A newspaper clipping noted that the swimmers were costumed as "black and white

The Lakeshore Club of Chicago won the 1942 Trial National Team Competition in Neenah, Wisconsin, held during the 1942 AAU National Women's Swimming and Diving Championship. Gold medalists included, top left to right: Adeline Potter, Jean Wilson, Polly Wesner, Lillian Wilson, Nancy Hanna, and bottom left to right: Doris Dieskow, Jean Parks, Phyllis Burrell, Marian Mittlacher.

piano keys." Another stated, "Although many persons got their first glimpse of this form of ballet at the New York World's Fair in the now famous Aquacade sponsored by Billy Rose, the Lake Shore Athletic Club has had a skilled team for many years. The girls who participate in this sport are all tireless swimmers, for water ballet routines, though beautiful to view, are tests of endurance. In spite of its difficulty, water ballet is especially effective entertainment because no effort is visible in the rhythmic strokes of the girls as they execute the various patterns."[55]

Marge Turner, the first Central Association duet winner [with Muriel Berndt] said of the Neenah meet, "The first national meet was awful. The best teams did not win. The rules were full of flaws and needed a grand overhaul. The meeting after the competition was a real battleground. What they needed then was a statistical specialist to help draw up the rules and computers to do the calculations."[56]

Even though this team event was the first

synchro competition held at a
national championship meet, it
has never been characterized as
the first synchronized swimming national championship
event because synchro was not
yet approved for national
championships. Wartime travel
restrictions obviously inhibited
participation and only three
clubs were entered where, the
year before, eight had been involved in the nearby CAAAU
events.

Chicago was the center of activity with clubs in colleges and athletic clubs. The first Central Association championships had eight teams entered. Swimmers pictured are, from left to right, Marian Mittlacher, Irene Van Steen, Jean Parks, Phyllis Burrell, Audrey Huettenrach, Doris Dieskow, Muriel Burns, Polly Wesner and Nancy Hanna of the Lake Shore Club.

In summing up her expe-
riences as a swimmer in that
meet and in her time with the
Lake Shore Club, Adeline Potter
stated in an article in *The Synchronized Swimmer*, "Interest accelerated the
progress of the sport. Ballet has come a long
way since that night [1942, Neenah] and our
team has come a long way, but in reflecting
back over the years, our team contributed a bit
to the progress of the sport, not only as active
contenders, but in the introduction of many
firsts. Lake Shore was the first to:

1. use leg make-up
2. wear leotards, turbans, painted caps
3. shed capes, sarongs
4. wear completely spangled bras
5. use wiltless ruffles
6. execute breast-side and inverted breaststroke hybrids.
7. perform somersub, split kip and cross-foot
   kips
8. create a contrast in rhythms in the same
   routine
9. perform a six person foot first pinwheel
10. enact a complete fairy tale with charac-
    ters."[57]

The high interest in this new activity
brought much favorable newspaper and magazine coverage. *Life* magazine had a feature titled, "Life Magazine visits Lake Shore Swim
Team." Photo captions read, "Pretty members
of a Chicago Club find a warm afternoon making ballet patterns in the cool water." Another,

"Girls form a 'flower' in Chicago's Medinah
Club pool where they give summer exhibitions.
Club has an indoor pool where they practice
all winter." Another read, "'Ballet legs' is one
of the formations that have made the ballet
team champions. This one is a lot harder than
it looks and requires hours and hours of practice on land."[58] The text stated, "The sportive
young girls demonstrating their water ballet
formations are all members of the Chicago
Town Club team, one of the best teams in the
U.S. Its impressive list of honors include 5 national and 3 local swimming and diving titles
as well as National Water Ballet champions.
Stars of the team are the Wilson sisters, Lillian
and Jeanne. Lillian is captain of the team and
was Central AAU freestyle champion and sister Jeanne holds 4 local titles and was runner
up in the National Breaststroke championship."

## *Seeds of Synchro Around the Country*

For the 1942 AAU Convention, Leach
asked association chairmen to report activity
in their districts.[59] The following reports from
his files are in the synchronized swimming
scrapbooks at the Henning Library, Interna-

tional Swimming Hall of Fame (ISHOF) Fort Lauderdale, Florida.

Connecticut Association: Bob Kiphuth reported, "Thanks to you and the girls for the demonstration. We have in times past had formation swimming by girls from Smith College, Wellesley and Vassar, but have never seen the type of work demonstrated by your stars. We regret we can't report any progress in our district, but we are very interested."[60]

Indiana Association: Bud Sawin reported, "No competitions were held, but three years ago, girls and boys teams from the Riviera Club used synchronized swimming to give exhibitions. This year, there is one girl scout troop, two University teams and a half dozen club organizations that gave exhibitions of synchronized swimming this past season. Will say that although the sport is in its infancy here, it has spread with great rapidity."[61]

Iowa Association: Norma J. Olsen reported, "In regard to my work as chairman of Iowa Synchronized Swimming, I took 5 girls to the state meet in Des Moines, last winter [1941]. We incorporated single and double synchronized swimming. My girls won first and 2nd place."[62]

New Jersey Association: Catherine D. Meyer, reported, "Only two active women's swim clubs, Newark Athletic Club and Watchung Lake Swim Club. Only one Duet competition was held, which was the first to be held in the east that I know of. Four duets (Newark and Watchung Lake) entered the competition held July 25, 1942, at Olympic Park in Irvington."[63]

Southeastern Association: John Foster with the U.S. Navy and traveling throughout the year, reported seeing synchro at a swim meet in Birmingham, Alabama; a Mid-South Open Swim meet in Chattanooga, Tennessee; and at a Middle Atlantic swim meet in Charlotte, North Carolina. "Exhibition Synchronized Swimming was held at all the above meets, but no actual synchronized competitions were held although events were promised for the next two years. I also observed professional exhibitions in Jacksonville, Miami, and Atlanta. I have seen the professional shows in New York and San Francisco, including the

Buster Crabbe shows with the Hopkins sisters, [but] Phil Patterson's Fairmont Hotel group in San Francisco was the finest that I have ever seen, although the Pacific Coast Association did not include any events for competition."[64]

Southern Pacific Association: Aileen Allen, coach of the Los Angeles Athletic Club, reported, "During the 1941-42 Indoor and Outdoor Swimming season, we used synchronized swimming to add showmanship to our swim meets. At each meet, we included tandem [duet] and teams up to 12 and found the public liked our programs. We did not hold Indoor competition in 1942 due to the tire shortage, but the La Jolla Tennis Club won the Outdoor meet held in their pool. We have four outstanding girls' teams in Southern Pacific Association and we have started two Junior boys teams here in the District. Numerous exhibitions have been given at army and navy camps."[65]

Newspaper clippings in the International Swimming Hall of Fame scrapbooks reveal the activity that had already started throughout the country during these years.

Bill Quinn, in a New Jersey newspaper's Sunday section, summarized the history of synchro there. In regard to the early development, he wrote, "Synchronized Swimming was introduced to the New Jersey area in the '30s. It has now reached a point where it is nudging speed swimming for the spotlight. Before 1940, Coach Kay Meyers, now tutoring Watchung Swim Club, started a Synchro group (Neptune's Daughters) within her Newark Womens' Athletic Club. Maplewood Country Club also staged synchronized swimming under the direction of Mickey Vogt, now freshman swim coach at Princeton University. Then came the NACettes of the Newark Athletic Club, really now the hub of synchronized swimming in the east."[66]

The Department of Parks and Recreation of the City of Detroit presented its first water pageant at the St. Clair pool in 1934. The water pageant was presented every spring until 1944. Mary Derosier and Frank Butler, swimming instructors who had worked on the St. Clair water pageants, formed the St. Clair Water Ballet Team in 1940 to fulfill requests for water shows at clubs and servicemen's organizations. After attending the Synchronized Swimming Conference at the Lake Shore Club in Chicago in 1941, the inspired Derosier attempted to "sell" synchronized swimming to Detroit, but most of the swimming coaches felt that "ornamental swimming" should be kept out of the competitive field.

A former member of Derosier's water ballet team, Rose Watson, inherited the team in 1945 and added a junior team with younger girls. After both senior and junior swimmers observed the first national team championships in Chicago in 1946 they started working on the skills they had seen. They entered a duet of Lorraine Stocking and Bernadette Timmins in the national duet competition at the Hinsdale Golf and Country club. With a sixth-place finish, these first girls from Detroit to enter a national competition stimulated the development of team capabilities that soon brought them to the national titles.[67]

During the 1936 AAU Women's National Swimming Championships, it was reported that the exhibition of synchronized swimming, given by the Lake Shore Athletic Club team, was the highlight of the program. Adeline Potter said, "Lake Shore had a ballet team prior to

that year but this was the first time I saw it done. Competition was unknown in 1938 when I joined the team."[68]

Jean Henning remembers in 1937, when she was a member of Chicago's Lake Shore Club, giving shows with routines full of "lots of stroking and sculling in various patterns. Unconsciously while practicing, I went into a Ballet Leg and from there into a Dolphin. Thus the new stunt, Ballet Leg Dolphin, was born."[69] Jean swam team and also performed exhibition duets with future husband Harold "Hal" Henning. In one, they taped lights all over their bodies and did tandem stroking. "The breaststroke was especially effective with the taped-on lights," she said.[70]

Marge Turner, a Kay Curtis water ballet swimmer at the Chicago Teacher's College from 1939 to 1942, wrote about a trip to Neenah, Wisconsin, to perform at the dedication of the new pool on the lake front. She wrote, "The first evening performance, the bright lights brought onto the pool surface a blanket of bugs. Every time we surfaced and tried to breathe, we got a mouth full of bugs, but we acted like they weren't there and did our thing, only to cough them out later."[71]

The Medinah Club of Chicago had an early start in water ballet as indicated by the photos of their swimmers in *The Chicago Tribune*. The captions read, "The Steed twins, Ruth & Minnie, putting rhythm into the crawl," and under the flower float, it read "Medinah Club swimmers in formation."[72] The following year they had "Medinah Girl Stars Sparkle in and out of the pool. Star formation is one of a series of water figures, executed by the Medinah girls' water ballet. Swimmers will give an exhibition during the swim meet with Milwaukee."[73]

Pat Paterson, Chicago, recalls, "Competitors from the early '40s felt that nose plugs were acceptable only for the weaker performers. The champions prided themselves on not

The Lake Shore Club continued as a dominant club in Chicago through most of the 1940s. Members of the team, above, who have continued with the sport through the years include Jean Henning and Nan Zack, second and third from left of seated swimmers.

using nose plugs which they said detracted from the appearance."[74] At that time, the only nose clips available were rather conspicuous, rubber coated half rings that came with a wide rubber strap to go around the head. She also remembered National Chairman Clark Leach saying that he was "almost another Avery Brundage." He was a stickler for rule interpretations and loved being the *major-domo* and head authority at early meets. He had his own flash cards made of metal so that water splashes wouldn't affect them.[75]

The Lake Shore Athletic Club began the first of its "Palm Beach Nights" water shows in February 1940. *Discus* magazine touted the coming Second Annual Aquacade: "Under the direction of coach Art Hejeland drilling 20 Aquabelles, the watershow will rival the famed New York Aquacade in perfection, if not in size."[76] In April of that year, John Hejeland became the new swimming director and Jacquelyn Nicholson became the new women's swimming coach. Nicholson had been a member of Chicago's first Athletic Club water ballet team at the Illinois Women's Athletic Club.[77]

In California, Millicent Heath, an engineer in Long Beach, began teaching swimming as an avocation at the YWCA in 1936. The Y officials didn't feel that racing was a suitable activity for girls and suggested she develop a water ballet team instead of a competitive swimming team. Using Kay Curtis' book, she developed a group which gave water shows in the area. Her example sparked the development of groups at the Pasadena Athletic Club, Los Angeles Athletic Club, San Bernardino's Arrowhead Springs Hotel and the Long Beach Pacific Coast Club.[78]

San Francisco's Fairmont Hotel Water Follies was the earliest club water show group in the San Francisco bay area. Producer Nick Kahler, while in San Francisco in 1942 with the Western Sportsman's Show, saw Marilyn Hanley and Jean Stanley swimming their duet in the 1942 Annual Water Follies production and invited them, on the spot, to become part of the Minneapolis Aquatennial. San Francisco's *Call-Bulletin* announcing the invitation said, "Jean and Marilyn have been Fairmont Phil Patterson's leading girls in his 'Swim to Swing' water

ballet which has revolutionized aquatic shows throughout the nation."[79]

Two women who later became well-known synchro names got involved with Fairmont's Water Follies in 1941. Kay Vilen, later the talented coach of the world champion Santa Clara Aquamaids, brought her daughter Sidney to join the Junior Water Follies team and Dawn Pawson (Bean) joined the team after seeing the Aquacades at the San Francisco World's Fair. But late in 1942, Coach Patterson was called to active duty. Soon after that, the hotel was turned into a temporary military hospital. The pool was boarded over and the Water Follies team, which had tried to continue its activities without its coach, was finally forced to disband.

The District of Columbia began synchro in the '40s as water ballet with D.C.'s American University water show group, the Aquianas. They were coached by Frank Martin, American Red Cross, who was instrumental in early clinic work at American University. Future national chairman Barbara Van Dusen (Eaton) swam with the Aquianas from 1950 to 1960.[80] The Baltimore downtown YWCA started a synchro program in 1950 with Dot Muhly as coach.[81]

Beulah and Henry Gundling, Cedar Rapids, recommended to the national committee in 1945 that an "Academy of Aquatic Arts" be formed which included solo swimming. Gundling demonstrated her solo for the 1949 AAU convention and solos were adopted in 1950.[82] In addition to winning the first AAU outdoor solo title in 1950, Gundling won Canada's first dominion solo title in 1949.[83] Gundling remembered seeing the University of Iowa Dolphin Club Water Show during her junior year in college. She was so inspired by the activity that she and several others who swam at the Cedar Rapids, Iowa, Ellis Park pool produced two "Aquacades." The highlight of this time was when they performed at a veterans' hospital in Clinton, Iowa. With such an appreciative audience, she was inspired to write in an autograph book, "I would like to do for swimming what Sonja Henie has done for figure skating."[84]

Synchro certainly had caught the attention of the public from the water shows and films. Norma Olsen, chair of the Iowa Association, received a letter from a local farm girl telling how she swam a "Milk Maid" routine in a prairie pond on her farm using a wind-up phonograph on the bank.[85] Teresa Andersen, at North High School of Des Moines, became Iowa chairman in 1946 when Olsen moved to California. Andersen became a synchro vice chairman in 1948 and coached teams that began entering national competitions in 1950 under KRNT radio station sponsorship.

The Synchro Club of Aquatic League at the University of Minnesota was putting on shows each spring in the 1940s under the direction of Dr. Helen Starr, physical education professor. Dr. Starr was the director of the water ballet performances at the Minneapolis Aquatennial and was synchro chair on the first AAU committee. Ruth Fife (Zink) took the synchro class from Dr. Starr in the winter quarter of 1945 and then swam in the 1946 Aquatennial water show. "Retirees" from the Aquatennial started a synchronized swimming group in 1950 which initially only indulged in show work, but later became involved in competition. The next step toward competitive synchro was in 1954 as Betty Forde (Swanson), Marion Anderson and Ruth Zink traveled to Chicago to watch the AAU National Championships. Inspired by the meet, the three returned to Minnesota and organized the state for competition.[86]

Synchronized swimming began as water ballet in the late 1940s at Kensington High School in Buffalo. Marie Felser started the first club after taking the American Red Cross synchro course from Billie MacKellar in 1950 at American University in Washington, D.C. Myron "Min" Hendrick and Mildred Moore were also instrumental in getting things going and the Niagara Association held its first competition in 1950.[87]

At the University of Oregon an aquatic art program in the late '40s was the precursor of synchro.[88] Pearl Redding (Huntley), a member of California's Pacific Coast Club's Aquabelles spent the summer of 1950 in Portland and started a group there. She invited the Multnomah Athletic Club and Cosmopolitan Club to participate with her group in a water show at the municipal stadium that summer. The three groups gave a combined exhibition for the water show held with the Portland Rose Festival on June 8–9, 1950. Huntley said, "They had band, drill team, trampoline acts, a paddleboard ballet by Santa Monica swimmers, diving, and two water ballet numbers."[89]

The Dolphins began at the Bangor YMCA in 1949 under Mrs. Richard "Binnie" Close. With 24 members, both boys and girls, they were the only water ballet troupe in Maine and one of the few in New England. In just three years, the Dolphins had given 25 performances at the YMCA pool and elsewhere in the state.[90]

# 3

# *Expansion and Structural Evolution: 1946–51*

As wartime travel restrictions ended in 1945, it was finally feasible to plan and stage the first official AAU National Championship in Synchronized Swimming for 1946. It was quite rightfully set in Chicago, long known as the "cradle of water ballet," and the home of the most active synchro proponents.[1] Water ballet was nursed through its infancy there in exhibitions, water shows and pageants and further matured in the World's Fair Aquacades. It was in Chicago that synchronized swimming evolved through dual competitions to the form in which it was adopted for AAU events, and it was the Central Association of the AAU that kept synchro alive through the war in its association championship competitions.

At the end of this incubating period, Town Club of Chicago emerged as the dominant club in Synchro. After winning the first junior national team event in 1946, it went on to win both team and duet events in the first true senior national championships. Town Club's swimming director, Walter J. Schlueter, was quoted in the *Chicago Herald American* saying, "Synchronized Swimming emerged from obscurity as merely an exhibition feature to a full fledged National AAU competitive aquatic event this summer."[2]

From synchro's adoption in 1940 through the inaugural national meets of 1946, its competition formats and rules remained totally sta-

tic. Only after the first national meets did dissatisfaction with its complexities arouse action toward simplification. Only a few minor changes were made for the 1947 season, but there was some growth as junior and novice competitions began to appear in association meets.

By 1948, the stifling complexities of judging and scoring procedures finally brought real reform for 1949 competitions. For the first time, judge awards would be publicly flashed immediately following each routine rather than waiting for scorers to carry out their complex calculations which had required each judge to give an individual execution score for every stunt and stroke along with routine scores for style, composition and accompaniment.

Then, for the 1950 season, another revolutionary change was made in expanding the competitive schedule to include a solo event. Perhaps even more revolutionary, though, was the adoption of a free routine concept for the solo event. No requirements, no restrictions would be applied, aside from fitting into a six-minute time limit. This was patterned on the solo event that Canada had added in 1948 to the national competitions in strokes and figures that had been held since 1924. The free routine solo event was a natural outgrowth of the individual competitions because the standard disciplines were adequately demonstrated in the stroke and figures events. Canada added the duet to the schedule in 1949 and the team in 1950.

Synchronized swimming was gestated, born and lived its infancy in the Midwest, but the basic elements for conversion to synchro had long existed in many areas. Water ballet, water show and aquacade activity was popular and provided the base for conversion in many places to competitive forms. Florida was a natural site for growth of such a water sport and proved it by producing a team, McFadden-Deauville, that won the second national team event in 1947. Parts of the West had been extremely active in water ballet, with Southern California actually involved in very early competition, but they were somewhat slower in appearing on the national scene. Once started, though, the West aggressively exerted its influence

The Midwest retained its national dominance through the 1946 to 1951 period with very few misses. Except for one escape to Florida, the senior national team titles remained in Chicago, Detroit, or Des Moines. Only Chicago's Town Club and Detroit's St. Clair Synchronettes were privy to the duet titles. The four solo titles were shared by June Taylor of Ontario, Canada, and Beulah Gundling, Cedar Rapids, Iowa. The Pacific Association, later to be totally dominant, first appeared in national competition at the 1951 Outdoor National Championships. Oakland's Athens Club Water Follies made a pretty big entry splash by taking silver medals in that first try but did not disturb the Synchronettes at the top.

Both the U.S. and Canada began looking toward international development and the possibilities for future inclusion on the Olympic program. Detroit's champions accepted an invitation to demonstrate at the 1948 Olympic Games but then were not able to raise sufficient funds for travel.[3] Both Canada and the U.S. did demonstrate at the First Pan American Games in Argentina in 1951, thereby paving the way for future international events.

Public and media acceptance was still a question: Was synchro a show or sport? While the public became fascinated with the sport from its first days, the publicity in the newspapers was quite different from what is found today. Sports editors were enamored with putting photos of girls in swim suits on their pages but feminists today would be up in arms with some of the photo captions of the '40s and '50s. They did attract attention so perhaps it wasn't too degrading to appear on the sports pages in swim suits with such captions as: "Bathing Beauties and Expert Swimmers Too"; "Can Can Cuties"; "Chorus Line? No, It's Synchronized Swimming"; "Bevy of Beauties"; "Not Only Are They Pretty, They're Champions"; "Six Visiting Eye-Tems"; "Synchro Swimmers Look Good In and Out of the Water"; "Yes, They're Pretty and So Is Their Show." Adjectives such as pretty, attractive, pulchritudinous, eye-catching, cute, shapely, or beautiful water nymphs hardly depicted a sport or athlete.[4]

## The National Championships, 1946–51

Although sporadic flare-ups of synchro competition occurred around the country during the war years, the Midwest, home of the pioneers in the sport, was still the hot spot as the 1946 to 1951 expansion period started. Not too surprisingly, during these first few years of regular national meets, clubs from Chicago and Detroit maintained a virtual stranglehold on team and duet national titles.

The Chicago Town Club emerged as the dominant club, taking first and second places in the first Official National Team Championships, held in Riis Pool, in Chicago, August 11, 1946.[5] They were followed, in the five-team final event, by Lake Shore Athletic Club, Forest Hills Country Club, and Garfield Park.[6] The members of the Town Club "C" team, the first national champions, were Polly Wesner, Nancy Hanna, Doris Dieskow, Marion Mittlacher, Shirley Brown, Audrey Huettenrauch, Phyllis Burrell, and Priscilla Hirsch.[7] Dieskow remembered the thrill in that first national competition of being on live television. "Most of us didn't own a TV so [we] had to go somewhere

Chicago Town Club wins gold in the First Official National Team Championships held in Chicago's Rees Pool in 1946. From left to right are Priscilla Hirsh, Shirley Brown, Audrey Huetterauch, Phyllis Burrell, Marian Mittlacher, Doris Dieskow, Nancy Hanna and Polly Wesner (photograph by Apex).

mer. Usually the younger girls are interested in competitive swimming and diving, but after their interest begins to wane in the more concentrated practice sessions necessary to excel in speed swimming, they turn to water ballet. While synchronized swimming requires practice for perfection, the periods are not quite as strenuous nor quite as many per week are necessary."[14]

In the 1947 Indoor Team Championship in Miami, an upstart winner surfaced. An eight-girl team from Miami Beach's McFadden-Deauville pool, the Dolphinettes, coached by famed diver Pete Desjardins, took the title from the Town Club. Town Club quickly regained its crown that summer in the Outdoor Championship but lost it again in the 1948 Indoor Championships to Detroit's St. Clair Synchronettes in a meet at Terre Haute, Indiana.

St. Clair won with a four-girl team of Alice Micus, Shirley Simpson, Marilyn Stanley, and Connie Todoroff. The Synchronettes, coached by Rose Watson, then went on to win five more consecutive championships, the 1948 outdoor meet in Des Moines, Iowa, and both indoor and outdoor meets in 1949 and 1950.[15] During this period the personnel of the four-girl team, five in one meet, remained almost constant. The success of their small teams was remarkable considering the difficulty and bonus points they gave away to larger teams, together with loss of the spectator appeal of large group action patterns.

The Synchronettes finally lost the 1951 indoor title to the KRNT radio station–sponsored team of Des Moines, coached by Teresa Andersen. Those new national champions from Iowa were Joanne Speer, Carla Courter, Barbara Springate, and Jean Grossman. Detroit regained the title that summer at the outdoor meet, for the seventh and final time.

Chicago Town Club's early strength was

to watch it."[8] But Hanna remembered the rubber suits they wore, saying "the suits held the water in and when we got out, a big gush of water would come out."[9] They at least seemed improved over the rubber suits given to the Modern Mermaids in 1934, which split upon diving in![10]

Four of the Town Club team, Dieskow, Hannah, Mittlacher and Wesner, were veterans of the Lake Shore team that had won the first trial team events in 1941[11] and two others had competed on the Lake Shore team in the CAAAU championships of 1944.[12] Now coached by Walter Schlueter, these swimmers had gravitated from the Lake Shore club to the Town Club, at the Hotel Continental, following the loss of their Lake Shore coach in 1944.[13] Coach Schlueter was quoted in a news clip after the 1946 team championships, "Ages of the 16 girls [the two Town Club Teams] who dominated the National Championship competition range from 16 to 26. This is an interesting point, for among most other types of competitive swimming, the ages of the girls would be, on the whole, much younger. Synchronized Swimming holds more interest for the older swim-

**Ruth and Gloria Geduldig, Chicago Town Club, won the First Official National Championship in duets, held in Hinsdale, Illinois, in 1946.**

also demonstrated in the duets, where sisters Gloria and Ruth Geduldig won the first national duet championship in Hinsdale, Illinois, Sept. 8, 1946.[16] Ruth Geduldig said she began synchro after a diving accident which resulted in a broken leg. "I turned to Synchronized Swimming and began swimming with my sister Gloria, who is three years younger than I am."[17] The pair went on to win the 1947 Indoor Championship at Chicago's Keymen's Club. By the outdoor nationals, a new duet power emerged, Alice Micus and Marilyn Stanley of Detroit's St. Claire Synchronettes. Micus and Stanley were surprised to hear their names called as the winners of the competition. They had gone hoping to be among the finalists, and then they were hoping for the bronze medal. A newspaper clipping quoted them saying they were so happy, they felt like tossing their coach into the pool, just as they had done in an earlier meet, "but she had her best clothes on," they said. "We just couldn't do that to her."[18] Micus and Stanley went on to win both championships in 1948.

The Town Club managed to retrieve the

title at the 1949 indoor meet with sisters Billie and Rosemarie Voelker, but not for long. The Synchronettes immediately reclaimed the top position at the outdoor meet, as Shirley Simpson and Connie Todoroff started a string of Synchronette victories that ultimately included 10 total titles (not all consecutive). In both 1950 meets, Stanley teamed with Simpson to win for St. Clair. In 1951, the Synchronettes won both championships with new partners and teammates, Ellen Richard and Connie Todoroff.

A solo championship was not added to the synchro program until near the end of this period, in 1950. In the first competition, the 1950 Indoor Championships, at the Illinois Athletic Club, June Taylor, from St. Catherine, Ontario, Canada, emerged as the champion. This was a turnabout from Des Moines' Beulah Gundling who had won the 1949 Canadian championship. Taylor was coached by Lillian "Billie"

**The St. Clair Synchonettes of Detroit won five consecutive national championships from 1948 to 1951. Above, from left to right, are Marilyn Stanley, Shirley Simpson, Connie Todoroff, and Ellen Richard.**

Connie Todoroff (left) and Ellen Richard, St. Clair Synchronettes,, won the national duet title four times from 1950 to 1954. They won gold in the First Official International Championships, the Pan American Games of 1955.

June Taylor, Kia Ora Swim Club, University of Western Ontario, won the first U.S. National Solo title. She won four times from 1950 to 1953 and completed her career swimming for the Hollywood Athletic Club.

MacKellar, who later emigrated to Hollywood, California, to spend many years helping to raise the quality of U.S. synchro.

At the 1950 outdoor meet, Beulah Gundling, Cedar Rapids, Iowa, won the chilly competition held in Lake Michigan. Judges were seated both on the shore and in boats. Bernice Lorber Hayes remembers trying to judge with waves rocking the boat. She said she had to keep one foot in the boat and the other on the dock to keep the boat from moving out while she was judging.[19] Teresa Andersen, later a national chairman, said she shudders when she thinks about judging that first outdoor solo event: "It was rainy and windy and the water was black. I could barely see a thing." Scorers were on a nearby pier. She told the story of Gundling rising from an underwater move with a lettuce leaf on top of her head.[20] This was the only national championship not held in a pool. In 1951, Taylor and Gundling split the titles once more to continue what was to become a four-year pattern with Taylor winning the indoor titles and Gundling the outdoor.

Junior national events began with team events in 1946. All titles went to Chicago or Detroit. Duets in junior nationals began in 1948 and the first three titles went to Peterborough (Canada), Detroit's St. Clair Synchronettes and to Chicago's Town Club. A men's duet event was added in 1949 with the title also going to Detroit. But the West was awakening. The Pacific Coast Club, of Long Beach, hosted and won the 1951 team event. Also in 1951, in the first junior national solo, Joan Fogarty, of San Bernardino, California, took the crown from the Midwestern favorites. Teammate Pearl Redding said of the win, "Fogerty won first place because she did three stunts in one [in succession] and then came up for air. We had never seen anything like that before."[21]

## Sport Administration

Synchro's first national chairman, Clark Leach, with his vice chairman, Katharine Curtis of Illinois, finally convinced the AAU in 1945 to remove the restrictions against holding

Beulah Gundling, winner of the 1949 Canadian Championship, did much to see that solos were added to the list of competitive events. She won four titles from 1950 to 1955 and was the first Pan American solo titlist (photograph by John Barry).

and Furney Jeffrey. Local (district association) chairmen still constituted the National Synchronized Swimming Governing Committee, which remained a subcommittee within AAU Women's Swimming.

As an AAU sport, the operation and competitive rules were determined by the national committee, but in practical terms, the local chairmen carried on all actual operation of the sport. A large proportion of synchro chairmen took on those duties in addition to a swimming or diving chairmanship they already occupied, so synchro promotion was often not their first concern. No AAU funds were provided to district associations aside from supplies for registration and sanctions and a small fraction of registration and sanction fees. Finances and help for everything else, organizing and conducting competitions, mailings, publicity releases, development clinics, etc., was on a do-it-however-you-can basis. Devoted volunteers ran everything, often volunteering substantial personal resources in the process. This, though, may not be considered much of a change from today. Richard Dodson, in explaining AAU synchro, wrote, "It is quite a miraculous organization! It is almost inconceivable that it would prove possible to develop such a far flung group of unpaid people who, in the aggregate, do such a tremendous amount of work for the benefit of the athletes, and in the long run, the public."[23]

The AAU's Code of Regulations imposed a very strict amateur athlete code, covering eligibility and participation in all sports. Athlete membership in the AAU was required. All competitions and exhibitions had to be approved and sanctioned by the AAU. Complete financial reports were required, even for exhibitions by club members in a club's home pool. A "travel permit" was needed for any athlete wishing to compete in any event outside her own district association. In any exhibition or competition that involved an appearance or demonstration by a "professional" athlete, a suitable time interval was required to separate the amateur and professional portions of the program. Lifeguards, "Learn-to-Swim" teachers and physical education teachers were "professionals" and ineligible for competition.

synchro national championships and then accomplished the staging of the sport's first true national championships in the 1946 Outdoor season.[22] The next year, synchro was able to conform to the normal AAU schedule of events and staged both indoor and outdoor national championships.

Detroit's Mary Derosier became the second national chairman in 1948 and served through 1952. She expanded the national committee to include four vice chairmen, Teresa Andersen, Richard Dodson, Katherine Meyer,

New books became available to help the new coaches. Gertrude Goss, the coach at Smith College, wrote *Swimming Analyzed* in 1949. It updated Curtis' earlier work. The demand was so great that this new book went through eight printings. Betty Spears, physical education professor and aquatic specialist at Wellesley College, published *Beginning Synchronized Swimming* in 1950. It was described as the best one in the field for practical use, covered beginning material and presupposed familiarity with basic strokes and techniques.[24] *Synchronized Swimming*, by Fern Yates and Teresa Andersen, was published in 1951. Synchro's Handbook Bibliography listed it as, "A well illustrated text showing the many stunts in synchronized swimming. Patterns, composition and staging and programs are covered most adequately."[25] A second edition was published in 1958. In 1951, Lillian MacKellar directed an educational 16mm film titled *Synchronized Swimming Stunts*. This was used in school classrooms throughout the country. The stunts were demonstrated by June Taylor.[26]

## Competitive Programs

The rules adopted in 1941 were added as a new section to existing swimming and diving rules. Thus, many of the more general swimming rules were automatically part of synchro rules. The competition classes, senior, junior and novice; the championship structure, association, invitational, and national, and the competition seasons, indoor and outdoor, were all applicable to synchro. The indoor season was before May and outdoor from May to September.

The first senior national competitions in duet and team events were held as separate events in different locations during the 1946 outdoor season. The team championship came first, August 11, at the Riis Pool in Chicago.[27] The duet championship was held a month later, September 8, at the nearby Hinsdale Golf and Country Club.[28] The next year, 1947, national indoor and outdoor meets were held, each meet including both duet and team events. This two-season approach was maintained until 1980.

As the new sport gained in popularity, J. Edwin Aspinall, chairman of the Women's AAU Swimming Committee, asked Mary Derosier in 1948, "How do you feel on mixed ballet swimming? I have several universities here in the state that have registered complaints with me that they are not able to have mixed duet teams. They feel that in their well-lighted pools that there is nothing wrong, and nothing the crowd can object to. They would like to see the rule modified so that duet swimming is permissible in clear water pools where there is sufficient underwater lighting."[29]

The first junior class national event was a team event that preceded the senior competition by one week in 1946.[30] No duet event was held until 1948. The junior class was not age-governed, as it is now. Instead, it was a developmental level in which eligibility was determined by placings in prior junior and senior competitions. Anyone having won any event in a given class of events at either junior or senior level was no longer eligible for junior competition in any event within that class. Thus, within synchro, as one of 10 classes of swimming events, winning a title in any of its three events disqualified the individual for junior competition in the other events.

When solos were adopted in 1950, the junior class eligibility was changed to make winners of a junior solo not eligible for junior duet or team, but members of a winning junior duet or team still remained eligible for other two events in junior.[31] Then, in 1954, synchro established its own rules to allow synchronized swimmers to win junior titles in each event. Similarly, the AAU novice class competitions were closed to anyone who had ever taken any medal place in *any* synchro competition. Novice class competitions were normally held only at association levels.

With the idea that spreading junior national events widely around the country would stimulate further interest and participation, each junior national event, solo, duet or team, could be awarded to a different sponsor and site. Actually, most bids came from sponsors hoping to facilitate a title for a local competitor.

Zone competitions in synchro were still

35 years in the future, but in the west, the Far Western Swimming and Diving Championships had long been a popular event. At the instigation of the Pacific Association (San Francisco Bay area), a Far Western Synchronized Swimming Championship was organized in 1951. That first Far Western, held in Oakland's Temescal Pool, attracted 10 clubs, all from California.[32] The Far Westerns were continued annually until synchro adopted the zone concept in 1981. The title of the long-existing meet was then changed to Western Zone Championship.

## Technical Rules

The synchro portion of the 1946 *Official AAU Swimming Handbook*[33] constituted a grand total of 12 pages for rules, stunt descriptions, stunt and stroke difficulty tables, and sample master routine and judging sheets. The only events were team (eight to 12 members) and duet. Preliminary events were to be held when more than five teams or seven duets entered. The five highest-scoring teams and seven highest-scoring duets qualified for finals. Scores from the preliminaries were totaled with those of the finals to determine the places. By 1948, minimum team size had been reduced to four members to improve participation from clubs with fewer members. The maximum remained at 12 members. In 1949, a bonus point rule was instituted, adding 0.5 points to the team score for each member exceeding four. Thus a team of 12 would earn a total of eight bonus points in a competition involving both preliminary and final events because the bonus was applied in each event and both scores were added for the final placing score. The rationale for this gift was that as numbers increased, it became more difficult to maintain uniform synchronization and higher levels of performance for the more difficult stunts.

The duet and team rules of this period left very little room for creative choreography. On routine entry forms (five judging and one master scoring) every stunt and every stroke sequence had to be listed, each with its difficulty multiple. Initially, two low difficulty stunts from a list of four (somersault, porpoise, dolphin and kip) and at least two of eight listed strokes (done in sequences of at least three stroke cycles each) had to be included. The routine could then be filled out with any number of additional strokes or stunts that would fit into the time limits of five minutes for duet or *10 minutes* for teams.

Through 1946, though, any such fill-in stunts or strokes had to be taken from those listed in the difficulty multiple lists in the rules. Luckily, repetitions were not counted for difficulty or judging, nor used in the averaging calculation, so low-difficulty fillers could be used. The probable reason for this dispensation was to avoid having routines crammed with repetitions of high difficulty stunts to raise routine difficulty averages. The rules stated, "No stunt may be repeated more than three times...." However, no punishment was suggested for overuse infractions. Indeed, referee penalties were remarkably absent. Another multiple stunt rule was, "Not more than two stunts may be done at the same time." Nothing specified how to arrive at a difficulty for two different stunts done simultaneously that each had different difficulties.

For 1947, in a great victory for choreography, use of any "unlisted" movement and stunt was to be allowed. Unlisted actions had to be fully described and listed as a "position change."[34] These "PCs" were not graded, nor included as part of the total number for averaging. They were not overused in those days because they impacted on the time needed to maximize the number of high difficulty stunts that could be included.

Every movement had to be performed in the exact order specified on the routine sheets, or deductions would be made (by the judges) on every stunt thereafter from the point of an error. Consequently, routine sheet preparation, listing every stroke and stunt in proper order together with its assigned difficulty multiple, and describing (in order) every position change, every transition and all float movements, was a vital and major undertaking.

In 1948, Dick Dodson and Ellen Murphy Wales were given the task of revising the rules (changes to be effective for the 1949–50 handbooks and seasons). Simplifying the complex judging and scoring procedures and providing more freedom in choreography were particular concerns. They were eminently successful with judging and scoring but only produced moderate reforms in choreographic freedom. The new requirements list substituted five compulsory stunts, not to exceed 1.5 in difficulty, for the former two of four specific stunts and two of eight listed strokes. Since the five could be selected from the entire difficulty table, this did improve choreographic flexibility.

In addition, a new and bigger change came into being with the statement, "All strokes, standard or hybrid, executed within a routine shall be listed and described, but shall receive no grade and shall not be included in the total number of stunts for purposes of computation of results. They shall be considered in the award for style."[35] This eliminated strokes from individual judgment and from affecting difficulty and opened the way for stroke creativity. Hybrid stunts (as "position changes") were already allowed. The entrance and exit were also dropped from items to be individually graded but had to be considered in the award for style. Routine sheet composition was eased with the notation, "Position Changes and simple body movements, or incomplete stunts, need not be listed on routine sheets."[36] In exchange for being liberated from having every stunt evaluated and judge penalties being assessed on every stunt following an error in listing, though, one would now be subject to the first referee penalty, five points off the final score, for not performing the routine as listed.

Themes, which had always been a central part of choreography, became more important in 1949 as a title was added to required listings on the master scoring sheets. Even though theme, as such, was never recognized as a specific judging factor in the rules, it had probably always been the primary influence on choreography, musical interpretation and costuming. For new routines, first thoughts were usually, "What can I be and what will I wear?" Choice of music and choreographic ideas were usually secondary.

Routine time limits were also changed to a uniform maximum of six minutes (no minimum), replacing the three to 10 for teams and three to five minutes for duet. Deck time was completely open, governed only by an ambiguous, "All movements on the deck, if they are included as part of the routine, must be performed to the music."[37] Since many routines of that period would *finish* with deck action in addition to their entry action, significant time might be involved.

The six-minute routine limit was a rather curious choice in view of the running times of the old 78 rpm recordings that were the only source of accompaniment then. The only two disk sizes then widely available, 10" or 12", held a maximum of three or five minutes of music, respectively. Since competitors often wished to use the maximum time in order to pack in as many high-difficulty stunts as possible, at least part of the accompaniment recording would have to be repeated. If the complete 10" recording was played completely through twice, the music interruption while the tone arm was moved back to the beginning of the record would occur in the middle of the water action. If the transfer was not expertly performed, unexpected delays could occur. A 1951 home movie shows the improvised fluttering, splashy hand and foot movements made by one soloist during one such unexpectedly long break.

The 12" disk allowed either a swim through at the five minutes or a couple of options for placing the interruption more strategically. An introductory section might be used for deck action and then an entry made to water positions during the music break for restarting the record. Alternatively, the record could be played to the end, then return to the beginning to repeat an introductory section. The 1951 Athens Water Follies "Can-Can" used the latter to advantage. Finishing the water action at the end of the recording, they used a *long* music pause to climb out and regroup on deck, then repeated the introductory music and the can-can kick line that had started them off.

Oddly, the duet and team time limit disappeared from the rules in 1950 as the rules format was extensively changed to incorporate solo competition. A six-minute limit still appeared, but only within the newly inserted solo routine rule section, in which all rules were obviously intended to apply only to solos. Duet and team time limits did not reappear until 1954, after a second total rules revision, making the same limit apply to all events. In the meantime, a tacit accord must have existed for the solo limit to apply to all.

The solo event was introduced in 1950 with revolutionary changes in competition philosophies. Solos were given *carte blanche* choreographically with no requirements or restraints on routine content. This constraint-free format was based on the Canadian solo event introduced into the dominion championships just two years before, but influential protagonists of this form Beulah and Henry Gundling had, as early as 1945, tried promoting restriction-free routines to the AAU under an "Academy of Aquatic Arts."[38]

The AAU solo routine, as adopted, would "consist of any listed or new figures, stunts, or strokes or parts thereof," but total freedom of regulations had not yet arrived. A single copy of the solo routine still had to be submitted (not five judging plus a master score sheet, as for duet or team) with the title of the routine and the stunts and strokes listed in order. Further, "Original [*sic*] figures [Canadian terminology used], stunts or strokes must be described." The soloist was, though not explicitly stated, bound to perform the routine exactly as listed. Further, there seemed to be a hint of some suspicion that the soloists might not be above carrying out some skullduggery, in the form of instant plagiarism of attractive novelties seen in other competitors' routines in practices. Thus, "Changes in the listed routines necessary to adapt the routines to the competitive pool have to be made in conference with the referee. Changes must not include figures, stunts or strokes which are the same or similar to original [*sic*] stunts named and described in other competitors' routines submitted for the same competition."[39] Once again, however, despite the forceful warnings, no hint of penalties for violations appeared in the rules.

It might be noted, the practice of making routine listings public following the competition (by rule), together with the nature of accompaniment of the day, made appropriating entire routines feasible. Commercial, single-piece recordings were normally used without editing. So the same music was available for anyone wishing to try out the listed routine. With the complete routine posted on the wall, along with descriptions of all the stunts and hybrid stunts, it was fairly easy to copy either hybrid stunts or the entire routine.

Duet and team regulations were also slightly altered for 1950. Of the five required stunts, three would now have to have a difficulty of 1.3 or less, and the other two 1.5 or less. So, to offset these low difficulties, as many other stunts (as time permitted) of the highest possible difficulty would be incorporated. However, the use restriction "no more than two stunts from each number group" had now been inserted. This still allowed, for example, both 10a, flamingo half twist, and 10b, flamingo full twist, difficulties 1.9 and 2.0, to be used in the same routine.

There were also many changes made in the stunts. Stunt difficulty tables in 1946 still followed the original 1941 classification into forward stunts, single and double; backward stunts, single and double; group stunts; and twisting stunts. As previously noted in Chapter 2, some stunts from this first list have endured, at least in name, into today's listings. There are still ballet legs, ballet leg submarine, dolphins (head first and foot first), dolphin twists, somersaults (front and back, tuck and pike), log roll, porpoise, kip, tub and corkscrew, but one might not recognize them today. Desirable performances were distinctly different. For the ballet leg, some swimmers might demonstrate great flexibility by bending the knee as close to the chest and chin as possible, shin at the surface, then extend to a sharp angle before straightening the leg to the normal perpendicular ballet leg.

The dolphin was described and performed, insofar as possible, as a layout somersault. Swimmers were supposed to make as deep an arch as possible before flipping around, as in a somersault, never submerging deeply. For any front pike action, it was considered in very bad form to have the buttocks showing at the surface. Tempo? The basic precept was to move into the stunt vigorously. Indeed, in one case, a two butterfly stroke momentum gathering action was listed as desirable. Remember though, these were stunts being done in routines, not by themselves. Only Canada had separate figure competitions at this point.

By 1949, the difficulty multiple tables appeared in an alphabetical listing, each stunt given a number for the position in which it appeared. A stunt with an added twist had a different number from the base stunt. That was changed the next year so that a stunt modified from its base by adding a twist or by doubling would have the same number as the base with a letter, *a*, *b*, etc., appended.

Four stunts, in which action was repeated consecutively (doubling) for a higher degree of difficulty, were parenthetically designated Canadian, probably in relation to some requirements for similar repetitions in Canadian figure and stroke competitions. A log roll was 1.1 but log rolling (log rolling, Canadian) was worth 1.5. A seal was 1.5, but repeating the seal three times in a row made it a seal, Canadian, with difficulty 1.7. A crane done once was 1.8, but a repetition made the difficulty 1.9 (crane, Canadian). The dolphin, foot first, ballet leg, worth 1.8, repeated, as a Canadian walkover, increased the value to 2.0. Although not specified by the rules, swimmers performed a right ballet leg first and then the left for the latter two stunts.

For someone who has never seen the stunts as they were performed then, some of the 1951 relative difficulties for several stunts might make a puzzling comparison with our present order of difficulties. For example, in the table below, the low difficulties of the porpoise and walkovers relative to ballet leg and somersub might seem strange.

|  | *1951* | *2003* |
|---|---|---|
| Dolphin | 1.2 | 1.4 |
| Ballet Leg | 1.4 | 1.6 |
| Kip | 1.5 | 1.8 |
| Porpoise | 1.2 | 1.9 |
| Somersub | 1.3 | 2.0 |
| Front Walkover | 1.2 | 2.1 |
| Back Walkover | 1.2 | 2.0 |

In fact, these inversions from present relations were a realistic reflection of differences in

manner of performance. Porpoises and walkovers used abrupt leg lifts, with little or no support at any point. Split position? There was hardly any time to see a split in the walkover ("runover" might have been a better name).

New stunts were being added almost as quickly as the competitors could dream them up. Twins Jeanette and Minnette Levinson, silver medalists in the first duet competition, swimming to a popular song of the day, "Flamingo," created the flamingo figure for the routine and appliquéd flamingos on their suits. Their coach, Ellen Murphy Wales, created the marlin turn and the catalina stunt for their team routine the same year.[40] Some help was given to those who had not seen the new stunts performed when stick figure illustrations (by Roy Weber, Richard Dodson and Ellen Murphy Wales) were added to the rulebook descriptions in 1948.

Driven by the urge to add more difficulty to duets and teams, the stunt list proliferated. Some of the least useful stunts (e.g., walking on hands, in deep water) were dropped. Twists were added to many stunts. Some advantage was taken of creative actions that were introduced by soloists. Interestingly, where 50 stunts were included in the 1946 table, there were only 39 numbered stunts in 1951. However, the added twists, doubling or other variations of those numbered base stunts added up to a grand total of 95 stunts. Several other now-familiar figures, catalina, crane, spiral, swordfish, tailspin and walkovers, had been introduced. The highest difficulty was now 2.0, for a flamingo with a full twist and for several dolphin derivatives.

Much higher overall routine difficulties could be derived from use of dolphin chains and dolphin pinwheels or moving floats with a large team. For each member over the base of two or three, 0.1 was added to the base difficulty. Consequently, a 12-girl team doing a mixed dolphin chain got a neat 2.6. Even better would be a dolphin, foot first pinwheel, escalating to 2.9. And there was nothing against using both of these stunts in the same routine.

## Judging and Scoring

From 1940 through 1946, judging and scoring procedures remained completely static. Judge assistants read the stroke sequences and stunts from the judging sheets as they were being performed. For each one the judge announced a score for the assistant to record. At the completion of the routine the judging sheets were delivered to the scorers who transferred the awards of all five judges to a master sheet. High and low judge scores for each stunt and stroke were struck out. The remaining scores were added for each stunt and stroke and each sum multiplied by the listed difficulty multiple average. All the results were added and that sum was divided by the total number of stunts and strokes being judged. That quotient was divided by the number of judge scores summed, three or five. Then that quotient was finally multiplied by a weighting factor to produce the final score for the performance. This may be considered an execution score, but no name for it was ever given in the rules. It became execution, officially, only after a drastic revision of judging and scoring processes in 1949.

Judges also announced, at the conclusion of the routine, separate scores for style, composition, and accompaniment. The only instructions on what was to be judged under these award categories were that costume and lighting effects were considered part of style. Each of these awards was also multiplied by an individual weighting factor (three, three and two, respectively) before being added for the final score. Since 15 to 30 stunts and strokes might be listed in the 10-minute team routines then allowed, scoring was obviously a monumental task.

With all the calculations required for the execution score (personal computers were still more than 30 years in the future), it is obvious that scores were not announced until some time after each performance. Nevertheless, according to Bud Harvey, Florida news reporter, in a review of the 1947 national meet, it really did get done. "Results are tabulated and averaged, and strangely enough, final results are usually announced the same day."[41]

A slight improvement was made for 1947 by combining the three choreographic scores into a single style award. An augmented definition of the award was also offered now. "Style shall include: Costuming, Showmanship, Manner of Performance, Combination of Units to Compose a Harmonious Routine, Timing, Music, Effectiveness. It shall be judged on a comparative basis as of the given competition."[42] The final phrase suggests that judges were expected to adjust their standards to fit the level of each competition.

A landmark change was finally made for 1949. Judges would now announce a single 0 to 10 award for execution along with the 0 to 10 style score.[43] Recording an award for each stunt was no longer required, but it was clear that the judge was still expected to judge each stunt mentally and to integrate those awards into the final single score. Some expert mental gymnastics were certainly needed to satisfy such demands as, "Any stunt omitted ... shall be considered '0' and all stunts from this point on ... marked down one third. (This deduction shall be made by the individual judges....)"[44] But at least spectators no longer had to remain in the dark about what judges thought of each routine until scorers finished their massive calculations. Execution and style scores would now be flashed immediately following each routine.

Scoring operations were also benefited by this change. Now it was only necessary to use an average degree of difficulty for the routine. This could be calculated before the competition, adding the multiples for all listed stunts and dividing by the number of stunts. Strokes no longer muddied judging or calculations. For the final execution score, high and low judge scores were stricken and the average of the remaining scores multiplied by the average degree of difficulty and then that product multiplied by five. The style score was calculated similarly as an average of the judges but finally multiplied by six, rather than five. The six to five weighting may have been an adjustment for incorporating three original scores into the single style score. The difficulty multiple, which could rise to two or more, still made the execution weigh more than style. The sum of these scores, along with any bonus points, determined the final routine scores.

All of the above judging and scoring antics applied to duet and team only. When solos were introduced in 1950, judge's awards for solo were as different as the soloist requirements had been. Four awards, for execution (0–40 points), synchronization (0–20 points), composition (0–20 points), and showmanship (0–20 points), were recorded and flashed after each routine. Composition and showmanship were to be graded on a comparative basis "as of the given competition," helped by keeping a "Comparative Form" for all these scores through the competition. Final scores were obtained by averaging remaining judge awards in each award after striking high and low and summing the four averages.

## International Development

Canada, first to have "trick" and stroke competitions, added a type of solo routine to their Gale competition in 1948. Music was optional that first year. Jane Houghton, coach in 1948 of Detroit's junior national duet and team champions, responding to an invitation, entered swimmers in Canada's meet in Peterborough. One of her swimmers performed a solo, "à la Canadienne," to become the first U.S. swimmer in Canada's Gale Trophy representing a non–Canadian club.[45] The next year, music was required for the solo event.

When Canada held its first dominion (national) championship in 1949, it was also the first in the world to offer a solo synchronized swimming championship. That meet also included duet but no team competition. Winners in that championship were: figures, Jean Mowat, Montreal; solo, Beulah Gundling, Cedar Rapids, Iowa; duet, June and Gale Taylor, University of Western Ontario; and stroking, Marjorie Cochland, Montreal.[46] Canada's Ornamental Swimming Association changed its name to Figure Swimming briefly. In a move to promote international participation, its rules were revised to allow nonresidents to enter any competition.[47]

Mary Derosier was the prime instigator of a clinic held in Detroit in 1948 to which the Canadians were invited.[48] Peg Seller, Canadian chair, said of that meeting, "That was our first get-together. From the very first, Mrs. Derosier was interested in our Canadian rules and was trying to devise means whereby we could have a common basis for competition for our two countries and maybe someday for world competition."[49] An informational flyer for a 1949 clinic in Peterborough stated that two types of synchronized swimming competition, Canadian, with solo, figures and stroking, and the U.S.A.'s AAU competition, with duet and team, would be demonstrated. Their hope was toward "developing acceptable rules for international competition." The clinic did accomplish the acceptance of the name "synchronized swimming" for Canadian competitions.[50]

In 1947, Let van Feggelen and Nel van Vliet, Holland, toured the U.S. and became acquainted with modern synchronized swimming techniques. The next year, van Feggelen attempted to recall the stunts from memory and train the girls from his club. France was also experimenting with interpretive stunts between floats in musical routines.[51] Jan Armbrust of the Netherlands, using stunts from the American AAU rulebook, wrote a series of articles in 1948 about synchronized swimming for the Dutch *Swimming Chronicle*. Demonstrations with music were held in Holland and Belgium that year and in 1950 the first synchronized routines were performed in a water show given by the L.Z.C. club from Leiden and the Z.A.R. club from Amsterdam.[52]

In 1949, basketball promoter Lou Bittner and Norma Olsen, manager of the Athens Water Follies, arranged for an exhibition tour of AAU swimmers, divers and water ballet to the Philippines, Hong Kong and Japan. Associated Press sports editor Russ Newland traveled with the group. Olympic swimmers and divers were the featured stars but the group included Oakland's Athens Club Water Follies team. The group introduced synchro as a sport to the areas they traveled.[53] Unfortunately the troupe ran into trouble almost immediately with the AAU. Bittner, sponsor of the tour, had failed to finalize the required AAU travel permits before the group flew off and performed in Manila and

Hong Kong. AAU officials demanded cancellation of the planned Japan finish of the tour and demanded an immediate return home. Reporters and photographers from all the Bay Area newspapers accompanied Frank Geis, Pacific Association registration chairman, in meeting their flight. As they deplaned, Geis instantly suspended everyone for participating in "unauthorized exhibitions." Under two-inch banner headlines about the suspension, Olsen was quoted saying, "As far as I can see, it is all a technical misunderstanding. Mr. Bittner said he would get the sanction and apparently never did."[54] The suspension lasted nine months, but the *Tribune*'s front page headlines and photos for this escapade are probably still without equal for synchronized swimmers.

Synchro enthusiasts in both the United States and Canada worked diligently to spread the gospel of synchro to the world, always hoping, given worldwide interest and participation, synchro could eventually be part of the Olympic Games. Town Club's swim director Walter Schlueter was quoted after the 1946 national championships saying, "Synchronized swimming is here to stay and may well be found in the next Olympic program, if only as an exhibition feature of the 1948 Games in England. However, in the future, the pioneers of the new sport feel sure it will develop into a recognized international event."[55]

Both Canada and the United States were invited to exhibit at the 1948 Olympic Games in London. Detroit's champion St. Clair Synchronettes initially accepted the invitation, then found it impossible to finance the trip. R. Max Ritter, secretary-treasurer of the Federation Internationale de Natacion Amateur (FINA), reported that Canada, through its representative, Mr. Daly, did propose that ornamental swimming be added to the Olympic program at that time. The FINA Congress referred the proposal to the FINA Bureau for further study.[56]

The Amateur Swim Union of the Americas (ASUA) was organized at those 1948 Olympics. FINA chairman, Javier Ostos, Mexico, said, "The Pan American arena succeeded with the help of the American Amateur Swimming Association, in inducing the Pan American Sport Federation to include synchronized swimming in the program of the Pan American Games in Mexico in 1955."[57] In his report announcing that ASUA would conduct its first Pan American Games in 1951, Lawrence Johnson, chairman of the AAU's Men's Swimming and Diving Committee, and chair of the Olympic Men's Swimming Committee, expressed the hope that synchronized swimming would be included on the Olympic program, "providing mutual agreement could be reached on the size of the teams." Dan Ferris, secretary-treasurer of the AAU, said he believed that FINA and ASUA would "be making a step in the right direction if they adopted the AAU Synchronized Swimming Rules."[58]

No agreement could be reached within the short time before the first Pan American Games, in Buenos Aires. But, synchronized swimming was demonstrated there by both Canadian and United States groups who performed every day of the Games and at a special performance for President Peron.[59] The U.S. delegation included Marilyn Stanley and Connie Todoroff, the duet from the St. Clair Synchronettes, and Beulah Gundling, soloist from Cedar Rapids, Iowa. Henry Gundling represented the AAU. Teresa Andersen, of Des Moines, Iowa, with her swimmer, Joanne Speer, participated in an unofficial capacity. Billie MacKellar led the Canadian delegation that included the duet of Gail and June Taylor and soloist Marjorie Cochland.[60] These demonstrations and ASUA meetings at those games resulted in agreement on rules that should be used in the first official multinational championship for synchronized swimming, the II Pan American Games, scheduled for Mexico City in 1955. The rules were to involve a stunt competition plus free routine competition using the U.S. solo routine awards.[61]

## Spreading Throughout the Country

Bob Ballard, diving coach from Chicago's Lake Shore Club, was hired by the Athens Club of Oakland, California, in 1945 to coach the diving team. He showed the 1945 *AAU Handbook*, with its synchro rules, to backstrokers Ruth Helm and Dawn Pawson, who began to incorporate some of the stunts they found there into their exhibition duet ballets. Asked to perform their duet at the AAU Men's Junior National Swimming Championships being held in their Athens Club home pool in 1946, Pacific Association officials were so horrified by a "vulgar and immoral" action they had performed that registration chairman Frank Geis advised "suspension or reprimand" immediately. The disgraceful action? Alternate ballet legs, the first ever seen in the Pacific Association! In the hearing, learning that it was really *condoned* by the AAU, dumbfounded officials dropped the charges.

Upon returning to the San Francisco Bay area from war duty in 1946, Phil Patterson took up where he left off with the Fairmont Hotel Water Follies by starting a new Water Follies diving and water ballet group at the Athens Athletic Club in Oakland. Following his sudden death one year later, Pawson became the volunteer swimmer-coach for the Athens water ballet. Norma Olsen, who had moved to Oakland so Patterson could coach her future national and Olympic medalist diver daughter, Zoe Ann, took over managing the Water Follies. Olsen had been synchro chairman in Iowa and was appointed Pacific Association synchro chairman in 1948. Like Patterson, she arranged for exhibitions for the Water Follies throughout California and then began to look beyond its borders, first for shows and then for competition. She entered a Water Follies team in its first competitions in 1951.[62] At the outdoor nationals that same year, a four-girl Water Follies team took a surprising second place. Across the Bay, the Crystal Plunge Swimming Club also started getting involved in synchro, sending a duet to the 1951 Outdoor Nationals and a solo in 1952.

In Southern California, Bill Engle, city recreation director, was instrumental in helping the Pacific Coast Club in Long Beach establish its water ballet team, the Aquabelles, in 1948. They swam their first local competition that year.[63] With several active clubs in the area, interest was great enough for the Pacific Coast

Club to host a junior national team championship in 1951, which they won. That same year, the San Bernardino Ripples entered a team in the outdoor nationals in Detroit.

Louise Wing became swimming director at the Boston YWCA in 1946. "I knew synchro was starting in the Midwest, so I offered it," she said. Wing had belonged to the synchro club at Wellesley and had taught synchro at the Pittsburgh YWCA before the war where she was able to put on many shows to promote Y programs, open country club pools, and show Red Cross programs. "At the time AAU registration was fifty cents, but Frank Ryuel lowered the fee to twenty five cents for our first AAU meet in 1950," she said. "Competing with my three groups, the Aquateens, Swimphonics, and Mermatrons, was a large group from Pittsfield, Massachusetts, coached by Phyllis Rhiel, daughter of one of my Mermatrons." Wing wrote, "I enjoyed cranking up the old Victrola to teach basic strokes. To this day, Skaters Waltz means 'breathe, two, three; blow, two three; kick, two three.'"[64]

The NACettes, of the Newark Athletic Club, had developed a synchro group sometime before 1946. The Newark Park and Recreation Department sponsored a group to give water shows each summer from 1946 to 1950. It was converted to a Synchro team in 1950 under the coaching of Emma Biase.[65] During this period some dual competitions were held. A NACettes duet took fourth in the outdoor nationals in 1950. At that same meet, Alicia Elliot competed as a soloist for the Montclair YMCA, winning fifth place in the first national solo competition.

Synchro was popular in Florida very early with Miami's professional water shows so it was natural that amateur clubs would spring up. The second national championship, in 1947, was won by the McFadden-Deauville Swim Club of Miami Beach. Pete Desjardins, coach of the MacFadden-Deauville Dolphinettes, said, "Water Ballet is attracting girls who never thought of swimming competitively."[66]

Michigan State College showed a strong and lasting interest in synchro. Their Spartanettes had entries in early national championships and continued regular national participation into the '70s. Rose Watson, who became the coach of Detroit's St. Clair Synchronettes in 1945, led the group to win their first national duet and team titles in 1947 and 1948.[67] The group eventually won a total of 16 national titles and included exhibitions at the 1951 Pan American Games in Buenos Aires and the 1952 Olympic Games in Helsinki.

The Penguinettes of Penn State University were organized in the fall of 1947 in response to a request for a High School Day performance. A news clip read, "It has grown by leaps and bounds with credit now being given for the P.E. class. Tryouts are held to select 15. The big event is the All College Synchronized Swimming Program." Participants in the 1952 All College program included Swarthmore, Bryn Mawr, Temple University, Beaver College, Baldwin School, and Penn State University. Prudence Fleming, Temple's coach, said, "[It] gives a fascinating outlet for college swimmers in this area."[68]

Betty Baldwin, of Sharon, Pennsylvania, divided her Allegheny Mountain Association into a number of sections with a divisional chairman for each section in 1948 and was conducting workshops for coaches and officials. She requested the national committee to divide the United States into eight divisions to facilitate the work of answering requests for information on synchronized swimming.[69]

In 1948, Joy Cushman and Jeanette Chase were involved in a water ballet class at the Houston Downtown YWCA.[70] Learning of national synchro competitions, they entered their duet that year. When the group gave a show at the Shamrock Hilton Hotel in 1949, the hotel management was so impressed they made it a regular feature and provided use of their giant pool for practices. Swimmer-coach Cushman got the team to the 1950 national meet as the Cork Club, using the same name as the Shamrock Hilton's swimming club which had been founded by Col. Ben Jolly. A 1951 article in *Shell Employee News* quoted Cushman: "Synchronized Swimming is fun, but it's work too…. [She was] a YWCA recreation instructor when the team was formed two years ago. The Corkettes, now with more than 50 in the group, draw crowds whenever they appear. Her duet took first in Texas. The Corkettes team took first and second in other Southwestern competitions. The Corkettes are the [Cork] Club's best known representatives."[71]

Nanette Taylor, a PE teacher at the University of Utah who had performed in the water shows of Esther Williams movies, developed the first synchronized swimming in the Salt Lake City area in 1948. The entry of a group in the 1949 nationals resulted in arrangements for a clinic with Mary Derosier and Beulah Gundling which drew participants from as far as Tooele, 50 miles away.[72] Soon after that, Florence Anderson began a synchro group at the Deseret Gym. Both junior and senior competitions were held in 1952. The team entered senior national competition in 1954.

Peggy Krame, Ginny Myers, and Shirley Theodore started a club for formation swimming at the St. Louis Jewish Community Center in 1948. With divers, they gave water shows and later competed in local Synchro meets. The same year, Re Calcaterra started a water show group at the St. Louis Downtown YMCA/ YWCA with 45 "mostly men" members. With the men's power, they could do lift pyramids three to four bodies high. Calcaterra then organized the Clayton Shaw Park Synchronized Swimming Team, with 32 young swimmers, to enter into competitions, a team she continued coaching for more than 50 years.[73]

The Milwaukee Athletic Club became active in synchro early, as evidenced by the second place their team entry gained in the 1950 Outdoor National meet. Their soloist also took silver at the indoor meet that year.

Water ballet began in the Inland Empire Association at Spokane's North Central High School in the early '50s with competition starting in the late '50s. Ann Murphy reported, "Bess Milton [Carlson] did it all; she coached and she ran the Association. At a 1954 show at the park, the girls wore silver suits and silver caps (said to be 'super-heavy' and full of glitter), and thus were dubbed the Silver Mermaids."[74] Their first competitions didn't start until 1957.

In 1951 a Twin City team, from South Bend and Mishiwaka, entered the outdoor nationals. During this period, synchro faced a very antagonistic, pro-swimming Indiana AAU hierarchy that made growth difficult even after an enthusiastic audience reception for the exhibition the Athens team swimmers gave there on their way to the national championships.

Synchronized swimming began in Colorado in 1951. Gertrude Hinrichs was developing a synchronized program at the Denver YWCA when she met Ninetta Davis who had also started a program in the area. They joined forces and the Synchronettes became an outgrowth of the Y program at the Denver Athletic Club. Hinrichs, Davis, and Louise Bower along with Harry Shade, Red Cross water safety director, decided to change from water ballet and move toward competitive synchronized swimming. "Competition wasn't great in those days," Hinrichs said. "Swimmers prepared for the August competition by swimming every day all summer. Year round swimming came later."[75]

# 4

# *Reshaping and Growing— The West Emerges: 1952–56*

Remodeling with growth may be the best characterization of synchro during this period of some turbulence. While gaining widespread recognition and enthusiasm, it was its adoption in the West, already the stronghold of women's speed swimming, that began to put a new face on synchro. Western swimmers and coaches, long accustomed to more rigorous competition training, started applying those concepts to synchro and looked askance at the existing fixations on deckwork, costuming and props for thematic interpretation, especially in solos. Even in the early '50s, Western clinics stressed fluid movement, stating that a good routine should cover "a length a minute" and never remain statically in place for a collection of stunts, hybrids, and arm waving.

Growth was sweeping. In contrast with some of the early AAU national competitions in which entries rarely surpassed the five-team limit for finals, three to four hours were needed to conduct some preliminary events. International interest and growth surpassed even that in the United States. Much of the international attention could be attributed to promotional tours made by swimmers and officials from the U.S. and Canada. Those exhibitions and promotions paid off in 1952 with the adoption by FINA (Federation Internationale de Natation Amateur) of rules to govern international synchro competitions. Global activity was

certainly piqued with seeing synchronized swimming in its first major international role, as an event in the Pan American Games of 1955.

With national meet participation spreading over the continent, synchro began generating more media attention. A particularly favorable early report came from George Lineer, sports editor of the *San Francisco Chronicle*, in a *Beach and Pool* article titled, "Synchronized Swimming and the Olympics."[1] It was, he stated, "an argument for the admission of Synchronized Swimming to the Olympics, based upon the facts that the sport calls for skill, physical condition, and imagination plus the beauty and the music." Note that this article appeared before the demonstrations at the 1952 Olympics. Still lobbying in 1954, he wrote, "There may be considerable opposition to admitting Synchronized Swimming because those who oppose it will, for the most part, be those who know little or nothing about it. Speed and straight muscle events now dominate the Olympics."[2]

Another favorable review came from sports editor Bernard Kahn, of the *Daytona Beach Evening News*. Reporting on the 1953 national championships in Elinor Village, he wrote, "When the AAU Women's Synchronized Swimming Championships loomed before me, I was thrown for a loop ... synchronized swimming was shrouded in intriguing mystery. Now, after almost a week of watching, listening and tagging after swimmers, coaches and officials, I think I've gained a perspective that puts synchronized swimming in a spotlight as one of the most exciting and spectacular competitive sports recognized by the AAU."[3]

However, a negative note was sounded about the 1954 Outdoor National meet. *Sports Illustrated* wrote, "It is difficult for one not a 'synchronized swimmer' to describe synchronized swimming ("Ever hear of it, Mac?") as a sport, without, shall we say, a certain unsynchronized crassness of tone. Synchro swimmers engaged, singly and also in teams of two and four, in exactly the same kind of contortions which are employed by the chorus mermaids in aquatic shows. Synchro-swimmers costume themselves, if possible, even more gaudily. Of course, if the drive to keep American youth out of the soda parlors is to succeed, a good deal of this sort of thing must and will go on."[4] But, for the same national event, Carl White, *Santa Monica Outlook* sports editor, was a bit kinder. "A stranger to the newest and fast growing sport of Synchronized Swimming, one can hardly realize the scope or how rapidly it has increased in popularity until he talks with Mrs. Olsen. To one who has never seen a meet such as this, it is amazing to see the gyrations the girls go through in the water."[5]

Luckily, seeing the sport as part of the Pan American Games seemed to make a more favorable impression on all sports periodicals and writers. A spate of local and national publicity broke out, mostly favorable. *Sports Illustrated*, with six color pages, had Athens team member Lynn Pawson featured with a full-page head shot, a centerfold spread of the team's open spin action, and a good explanation of the sport, quite a change in outlook.[6] Lee Griggs wrote, "Norma Olsen scored a notable triumph at the Pan American Games when she cornered Kenneth (Tug) Wilson, President of the USOC, and badgered him into watching the Synchronized Swimming competition. Wilson was unexpectedly impressed. "You know, I've changed my mind," he said, "the control, the physical conditioning, and coordination [of] these girls convinced me that this is as much a sport as

speed swimming and diving." Said Olsen, "Let's face it, the swimming meets of the past didn't draw anyone, but with the showmanship and pretty girls in brilliant costumes, you've got a talking point."[7]

Following the Pan Ams, the *Saturday Evening Post*[8] presented five color pages and the Sunday newspaper magazine *Parade* had four color pages with the Athens team on its cover.[9] Color features were still not common in any print media in that day, so synchro was getting very special notice. In the article, John W. Noble wrote, "California's aquatic chorus girls have drawn wolf whistles around the world. They show people how to do lots of things in the water besides swim. The young ladies are waging a calculated battle. They want Synchronized Swimming to be included as the newest competitive event in the ancient Olympic Games. They are campaigning now to demonstrate the sport at Melborne next year, and in 1960, they hope to be regular Olympic participants. Critics objected, 'It isn't a sport!' Norma Olsen only smiled. She is convinced that all critics of 'bottoms up swimming' as the speed swimmers call it, will be won over when they know the facts."[10]

Early in 1956, Lineer wrote, "though rhythmic swimming is not part of the impending Olympic Games in Australia, girls at the Athens Club have developed the new art in aquatics which someday will rightfully find its place on the list of competitive events in the Olympics."[11] But sounding the negative view, the *Oakland Tribune*'s Alan Ward asked, "Can Synchronized Swimming be classed as a sport? Mrs. Norma J. Olsen thinks so, but A. Ward is dubious. If a decision had to be made, it probably would be against aquatic ballet being part of bona fide athletics. Synchronized Swimming, in my opinion, can be ranked with the rodeo, figure skating and a dog show as on the borderline between sports and theater."[12]

The more synchronized swimming was presented to the public as a sport, though, the more it was debated whether it was that or entertainment. The sport-oriented contingent within the AAU made a bold move toward improving its athletic image character in 1954 with a complete rules overhaul that applied the same rigorous performance standards to all events, solo, duet and team, equally. No longer was the solo an artistic refuge with no athletic requirements. The artistic advocates fought the changes savagely, then having lost the battle, they split off from the AAU, founding the International Academy of Aquatic Art. Even with their loss, synchro continued to thrive, looking forward, at the end of this period, to even greater change.

## National Championships 1952–56

Until 1952, nearly all the senior national champions had come from the Midwest but this changed after the Athens Water Follies team entered the national picture in 1951. After placing second in their first meet, the 1951 Outdoor in Detroit, they vowed to take the gold the next year. They came to the 1952 Outdoor meet in Florida, and did just that. Following that win, the senior national team title never strayed away from the Pacific Association. Duet and solo titles also went west one and two years later, respectively, but have not been quite so

consistently retained there, occasionally wandering to other areas.

The Des Moines KRNT champions of 1951 successfully defended their indoor team title and won the 1952 Indoor meet in Des Moines. At the 1952 Outdoor National Championships in Ormond Beach, Florida, the Athens Club under coach Ross Bean, defeated the seven-time national champions from Detroit and took the synchronized swimming title west for the first time, an act which was described some years later in the February 1972 *Synchro-Info* as "the beginning of the total domination of the sport by swimmers from the Pacific Association."[13]

The Athens team extended its triumph to beat the indoor champions from KRNT Des Moines the next spring in Des Moines' home pool. In 1953, though, they lost the outdoor title to a 12-girl team from Peterborough, Canada. That defeat, despite higher judge awards to Athens than those given to the Canadian team, was the result of a combination of overwhelming bonus points and the very high difficulty multiples for large group pinwheels, chains and floats. This led to further rules revisions. The Athens team regained its title the next year and continued to take top honors through 1960.

"From Aquabelles to Aquachamps" was the title of Norma Olsen's article in the *Amateur Athlete* that recounted the Athens Club's trek to its first national competition. "The six girls, a chaperone and coach drove the 7200 miles in two cars to compete in Senior Nationals. They literally 'swam for their suppers' across the country and back, giving clinics and shows along the way in exchange for housing and gasoline money to make the trip ... before they embarked, the actual practicing began and the swimmers decided that if they were to win a championship, they must work together every day, six days a week and sometimes twice a day."[14]

The Athens Club Team of 1952, the first team from the West to win the national title. Swimmer are, from left to right, Lynn Pawson, Dawn Pawson Bean, Sally Phillips and Joan Pawson. Athens Club won 17 national championships from 1952 to 1960 (photograph by Bob Kirwan).

So quickly had the sport advanced in the west that in the indoor meet in 1955, all team finalist positions were filled with California swimmers. Actually, all were from the city of Oakland with the Athens Water Follies placing first through fourth and the Oakland Moose Club Naiads fifth. Oakland teams took the next two places with the Oakland Naiads sixth and Oakland Park and Recreation Department Sea Sirens team seventh. This disproportionate share of local finalists was probably instrumental in advancing a movement that was finally successful, at the next convention, in raising the number of teams in finals from five to seven.

The site of the indoor meet, in Oakland, was somewhat responsible for the unusual distribution in finals. In Houston that summer for the outdoor nationals, the participation was a little closer to normal. The Shamrock Hilton Corkettes pleased the home crowd by garner-

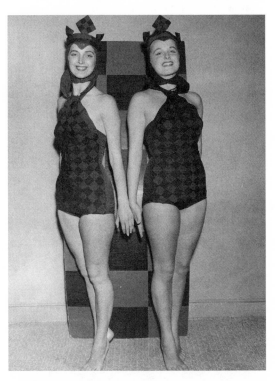

Joan and Lynn Pawson brought the senior national duet title west for the first time and won three titles in 1953 until 1955. Their "Checkmate" duet led to the adoption of the Castle and Knight figures into the competitive rules (photograph by Leonard Stallcup).

ing the bronze, Mexico's Centro DePortivo Chapultepec team took home fourth, and Athens teams could take only the first, second and fifth spots. The Lansing Sea Sprites were sixth with the Chicago Swim Club next. Meet manager Joy Cushman encouraged foreign entries and was instrumental in helping the Chapultepec team from Mexico and soloists from the University of Mexico and from Guatemala take part.

In 1956, full coaching responsibilities for the Athens Water Follies fell onto Joan Pawson Nelson as previous coach Bean moved from the area. Nelson brought in other Oakland swimmers and produced an eight-girl unit that made the team championship their private domain through 1960. Their example soon ended the era of the small teams of only four or five members that had started with the St. Clair Synchronettes.

In contrast to the team event, duet titles were widely shared during this period. Carla Courter and JoAnn Speer, KRNT Des Moines, won the 1952 and 1953 indoor season titles. Ellen Richard and Connie Todoroff, St. Clair Synchronettes, won the 1952 outdoor and 1954 indoor competitions. The Athens Club's Joan and Lynn Pawson won the 1953 outdoor, 1954 outdoor, and 1955 indoor while teammates Joanne Berthelson and Jackie Brown took first in the 1955 outdoor and 1956 indoor. In 1956, the outdoor title went to Judy Haga and Sandy Giltner, of the Lansing Sea Sprites, coached by Frances Jones.

June Taylor and Beulah Gundling, the alternating winners of the solo titles from 1950 and 1951, continued their reigns the next two years. Taylor, who had moved from Canada to Hollywood with her coach, Billie MacKellar, won both the 1952 and 1953 indoor titles while Gundling won the outdoor titles the same years. However, with the change in solo rules for 1954, many of the "elite" soloists of the first years took leave. In the first meet under the new rules, Beulah Gundling still competed but had to share the indoor title with KRNT's JoAnn Speer, actually losing to Speer in the prelim.

None of the Midwest or East elite designed to make the trek to the outdoor meet which

**Judy Haga and Sandy Giltner of the Lansing Sea Sprites took the duet title back to the Midwest, winning three duet titles in 1956 and 1957.**

was held on the West Coast, in Santa Monica, for the first time. The father of 1953's silver medalist, Alicia Elliot (New Jersey), belittled that competition in the October 1954 *Synchronized Swimmer.* "I have reluctantly reached the conclusion that competitive synchronized swimming is deteriorating to a marked degree. Of the 32 soloists, 23 were from California or Texas, all but 3 of the duets were from California and Texas, and all but 1 of the 12 teams came from California or Texas. It seems rather farcical to call this a national meet. It is my opinion that many contestants deferred from undergoing the effort and expense involved by not knowing whether they are supposed to be artists or athletes."[15]

In a scathing response in the December issue, Athens coach Bean asked, "With whom does the fault lie that they did not participate? Must they pick the time and site for their defense of the positions? The East and Midwest have had a monopoly on sites for the championships. Does anyone think it is any easier for California participants to go to Florida than it

is for other parts of the nation to come to California? Far from being a deteriorating sport, it proved that in Texas and California, it is a vigorously growing and surging sport. The East and Midwest had better look to their laurels now. Our California teams, many isolated by inordinate distances to travel, have had their first taste of national competition and they like it."[16]

The solo title at that controversial meet went to a westerner for the first time, to Joanne Royer, of Riverside. She had previously trailed June Taylor and Jo Ann Speer for a third place in the 1953 indoor meet, then followed Beulah Gundling and Alicia Elliot for the bronze in the 1953 outdoor, and took another bronze in the 1954 indoor, behind Gundling and Speer. Royer went on to prove that her title was not a fluke by winning both indoor and outdoor titles in 1955 and then the 1956 indoor title. Beginning with the 1956 outdoor competition, won by Linda Ridings of Fort Lauderdale, the solo title would change with each competition.

*Sports Illustrated*, in writing of the 1954

**Joanne Royer, Riverside Aquettes, brought the solo title west for the first time, winning the national title from 1954 to 1956. She placed second in the 1955 Pan American Games.**

competition, was not kind. "The [Solo] championship went to 19 year old Joanne Royer who shot an arrow weakly into the pool before diving and demonstrated in the course of something called "The Huntress" that her toenails were painted bright green. Another young lady wore plaid kilts, plaid stockings and a plaid hat with a feather and posed with two fencing foils before taking her initial dive. Her act was entitled, "Scotch and Water...."[17] Obviously, synchro still had a long way to go.

Competition for the men had been eliminated when synchronized swimming became part of the AAU, but it was still a widely discussed issue as the colleges, among other groups, still had a number of men participating. A junior national competition for men was held in Detroit in 1949, then there was a five-year hiatus. In November 1953, Bert Hubbard pleaded for mixed competition in *The Synchronized Swimmer*, writing, "Mixed Synchronized Swimming needs you now!" Several associations had already approved the event but the general AAU rule prohibiting competition between women and men prevented its introduction.[18] However, approval was given to hold another men's junior national championship in 1954. There were only four entries. Hubbard won the solo and paired with Lee Embrey to win the duet. In 1955, a senior national men's solo was held in Rockford, Illinois, again with only four entries. Donn Squire, now from San Francisco, became the first (and only) senior men's solo champion.

Now there was something else to debate at the national convention, how to select the representatives for the first official international championship conducted under FINA rules. Synchro's first trials were held to determine the U.S.A.'s entries for the 1955 Pan American Games. The trials were held in Tooele, Utah, using the recently adopted FINA rules that were to be applied at the Games in Mexico City. Eleven swimmers were selected for the two solos, two duets, and team event. Beulah Gundling, who had left the sport to form the IAAA, and retired champions Ellen Richard and Connie Todoroff, returned to the sport and were selected along with the Athens team (Joan and Lynn Pawson, Dawn Pawson Bean, Sally Phillips and Loretta Barrious). Joanne Royer, Riverside, placed second in trials to win the second solo spot and Joanne Berthelsen and Jackie Brown, Athens Club, were second in duet to win that spot. These were the first competitors to represent the U.S. in the sport's inaugural international competition under the newly adopted FINA rules. The II Pan American Games in Mexico City marked the beginning of a new era in international competition for the sport.

## Sport Administration

Mary Derosier, Detroit, Michigan, remained chairman in 1952. One finalizing highlight of her administration was the demonstration of synchronized swimming at the 1952 Olympic Games in Helsinki by U.S. and Canadian swimmers.[19] Derosier's term ended soon after that and she soon dropped from prominence in synchro activities.

Donn Squire, Pacific Association, as the "Golden Buddha," won the only men's national solo title in 1955.

Norma Olsen, even though she had been the Iowa Association synchro chairman before moving to California and had been named Pacific Association synchro chairman in 1948, was still considered a relative newcomer in the synchro world when she accompanied the Athens Club team to the national championships in 1951. She soon showed she was hardly naive as a promoter and savvy politician. She replaced Derosier as national chairman in 1953. Not only did she push major rule reorientations through the 1953 convention, she promoted many international eye-opening exhibition tours during this period. The latter included a 1956 round-the-world tour with exhibitions in 12 countries, ending with eight days of crowd-pleasing demonstrations at the Olympic Games of Melbourne.

Some fairly rapid changes were made in how synchronized swimming was administered. The synchro committee itself was initially merely a subcommittee of the Women's Swimming Committee but was soon split off as an independent national committee, composed of a chairman, as many as eight vice chairmen and local association chairmen. Legislative matters were conducted by committee meetings at the annual convention and at each national championship, but increasing loads of day-to-day business put increasing responsibilities on the chairman and vice chairmen. Olsen realized more could be accomplished faster by smaller, specialized working groups and started developing subcommittees. One of the first, intended to establish independent control of the increasing international activity which up to this time was managed through the AAU's Foreign Relations Committee, was the Olympic Synchronized Swimming Committee (OSSC). This was organized with Olsen as chairman and four other members appointed by Olsen. This committee, in its various forms, became very instrumental in the development of synchro activities internationally and domestically.

The other committee that Olsen established almost immediately upon taking office was the All America Committee, chaired by William Groeniger. Following guidelines set by AAU Swimming, Olsen saw that synchro's first

All American swimmers were named at the 1954 convention. The mechanism established then was for a committee to select a solo, duet and team from those having won one or both of the senior national titles within the year.

By 1956, six more subcommittees had been born. These, with their chairs, were: stunts, Teresa Andersen; rules, William Royer; judges rating, Florence Anderson and Betty Brandelein; public relations, William Royer; bibliography, Eleanor Wright; and age group, Beth Kaufman. Kaufman, known to U.S. Swimming as the "Mother of Age Group Swimming," chaired both synchro's and swimming's age group program. Her daughters participated in both sports.

Along with persuading passage of drastic rule changes in her first year, Olsen managed to pry the synchro rules out of the AAU's Swimming and Diving handbook and into a separate handbook. This first *Official Synchronized Swimming Handbook* was published for 1954.[20] A 48-page pamphlet, the new handbook included a directory listing AAU and Synchronized Swimming Committee members and addresses, excerpts from the swimming rules as they applied to synchro followed by general and technical synchro rules, officials and duties and methods of marking the competitions. It also listed all the stunts with their degrees of difficulty and descriptive movement sequences which were diagrammed with stick-figure drawings. There were master scoring forms and judging forms for the judges to record their scores for execution and for the comparative judgment of style. Finally, results from the 1953 national competitions were included, both senior and junior (for the first time.) This first synchro book also had photos of the previous year's winners and a history section listing all prior champions.

A big change in the look of the rulebook took place in 1956 when the stick-figure illustrations of the stunt sequences were replaced with somewhat more realistic figure drawings by Phyllis Williams. Unfortunately, some of these drawings, most of which survived for about three decades, showed beginner-like execution faults (bent knees, open pikes, arched necks and backs in verticals) or strange anatomical behaviors (legs themselves arching to conform to dolphin circles).

One new teaching book appeared. Colleen and Gordon Bennett produced a *Handbook of Synchronized Swimming* in 1955.[21] That same year, Lillian MacKellar supervised the production of a 16mm film, *Synchronized Swimming Stunts*, produced by Helen Cardan. The film illustrated all the standard synchro stunts with surface and underwater shots of performances by national champion June Taylor.[22]

The movie and television industries began to take notice of the new sport. In 1953, 20th Century Fox made a short subject film, *Dancers of the Deep*, to accompany the major studio release *King of the Khyber Rifles* in theaters around the country. The 20-minute film, made in Silver Springs, Florida, included eight Athens Club team members, U.S. solo champion-to-be Joanne Royer and the Canadian Peterborough team of 12 women.[23]

For a short period, television networks, with interest in synchro aroused by publicity from the 1956 world tour, featured the champions on national shows, including Art Linkletter's *You Asked for It* and the *Ed Sullivan Show*. Local television suddenly had short filler pieces on the "new sport," featuring swimmers in their areas.[24]

Advances were made in technology. Even a common thing like a microphone was a great technical advance for coaches. "When coaches could hold a mike on pool deck, they no longer returned from practice with a hoarse voice."[25] But the big advance technically came with the use of underwater speakers, first begun in 1952. Before these became available, swimmers would signal each other underwater by grunting or screaming. By 1954, their use became official and the rule book specified that among other personnel needed to run a championship, there should be "a listener for underwater speakers." Under the general rules, it read, "If an underwater speaker is used, it must be checked by a listener underwater before each routine."[26] It might seem this would cause some delay in competition, but it already was policy (not a rule) to allow each contestant a music check for loudness and speed. Initially the rule was obeyed fairly strictly. A young girl

would pop into the water, duck underneath as a short section of the next routine's music played, and pop up again to nod or shake her head to indicate whether it was audible or not. Soon, though, checks were made only at the competitor's request.

While not really a technology advance, a big help to the appearance of the swimmers in the water arrived with the relatively inconspicuous, rubber-coated wire noseclip, the Laxto, from England. It was seen in the AAU competitions for the first time in the early '50s. Until its arrival, the only ways to prevent entry of water into the nose during upside-down maneuvers were controlled exhaling, adhesive tape, a curled upper lip, or an ugly, broad rubber half ring "nose plug." The latter can still be found in drug stores, sporting its conspicuous rubber band head strap. For water show action, without much obligatory upside-down action, swimmers usually went unprotected. In competition and synchro practice, one or another of the nose clips was used. For the 1955 Pan American Games competition, where the U.S. team wanted to make a particularly good impression on the international audience, they devised a water barrier of adhesive tape that could be hidden by makeup for a nearly natural look.

## Competitive Programs

One of the first results of the AAU's adoption of synchro was the loss of its prior coed character, due to the AAU's rule prohibiting men and women competing in the same event. There was no discrimination, though, as synchro was listed equally in the swimming rules among the men's events, as well as women's. However, few sponsors appeared eager to take advantage of the opportunity to hold championships in the men's events. With only minor competitor activity and absent any sponsor interest or bids for future men's competitions, the men's events simply disappeared.

The first synchro handbook of 1954 made no mention of the sport being either for men or women. Neither the U.S. nor FINA excluded male events or participation, except at world and Olympic levels where FINA listed synchro as an event for women. Indeed, in recent years, there are instances of males rising to national championship prominence, in both the U.S. and Europe.

The only competitive classes existing in swimming when synchro started were novice, junior and senior. An athlete having won a medal in novice then found that level totally closed. After winning any junior event, only the senior level remained open, no matter what the swimmer's age or capability. That class transition was liberalized for synchro, with other major changes of 1954, to allow an athlete to compete in each class until winning in all three events.

In the early '50s, several associations started conducting competitions in age classes, or "age group" events. The Pacific Association held a trial Junior Olympic competition (age groups 14 and under, and 15–16 in duet and team) with its first Far Western competition in 1951. An invitational national 12 and under solo event was held with the 1954 Outdoor National Championships in Santa Monica. In 1956, a national age group program was approved for association-level competition only. The age categories, for synchro as well as swimming, were: 10 and under, 11–12, 13–14, and 15–16. Swimmers participated only in their own age events. This greatly expanded opportunities for competition. There were no exclusions except by age. Each swimmer might win as many titles in a given age level as capabilities permitted, then look toward the next age level for further fields to conquer. It allowed competition among those below the AAU minimum junior and senior age of 12. The age group program took off, increasing the number of athlete registrations like no other program had.

Collegiate competition programs continued strong growth. Doris Bullock, coach at the University of Illinois, hosted the First Intercollegiate Synchronized Swimming meet under AAU rules on March 1, 1952. The response was so great that each of the 12 schools had to be limited to three routines.[27] A Midwest intercollegiate meet was held at Bowling Green State University on April 18, 1953, with four schools participating.[28] The National Section on Girls

and Women's Sports (NSGWS) decided to use the AAU rules and published them in its 1953–55 *Sports Guide*.[29]

The Third Annual Intercollegiate Synchronized Swimming Conference, held at Michigan State on December 5, 1953, included competitive events that brought participants from nine schools.[30] Another such meet was held at Michigan State in 1954, this time with 150 participants.[31] The University of Illinois held a competition in February 1955, with eight schools participating.[32]

Wheaton College in Norton, Massachusetts, hosted the First Annual Conference of Synchronized Swimming for College Women in 1955. Swimmers from college clubs were invited to demonstrate routines at the conference. Margaret Lloyd, dance critic of *The Christian Science Monitor*, wrote, "It wasn't a dance event, it wasn't an athletic competition, but it had the beauty of dance design, the skill of athletics and the motor impulse of both.... The girls gave a wonderful show, all the more refreshing for being an experience in physical education rather than a professional production, though glimmers of Hollywood influence could be seen here and there."[33]

A second annual conference was held at Mount Holyoke College, South Hadley, Massachusetts, in 1956. The *Penn State News* reported that 300 swimmers from 50 colleges participated.[34] A third conference was held at Vassar College in 1957.[35]

## Technical Rules

In April 1953, Olsen appointed Ross Bean to chair an ad hoc committee to study all the existing rules—American, Canadian, Pan American, and the proposed FINA rules—to try to develop more useful concepts for unified rules. Bert Hubbard commented on the formation and aims of this committee in *The Synchronized Swimmer*: "Before we can seriously consider this problem, we [AAU synchro] should unify our own present Duet, Team and Solo rules."[36]

The Ad Hoc Rules Revision Committee report, published in October 1953, began, "It has been recognized for some time that extensive changes are needed…. The first decision that must be made is whether we wish to have synchronized swimming evolve into a pure art form or a pure sport, or a compromise between the two extremes. The rules as they stand, incorporate a little of both in a most unbalanced manner. The solo has been allowed to become largely an interpretive art while duets and teams have been made to be largely an exhibition of physical skill and ingenuity in overcoming the restrictions." Bean added, "an attempt must be made to make the rules compatible with those of other countries, insofar as possible. This does not mean lowering our standards but alterations should be made so that our competitors will not find themselves at a disadvantage when competing under international rules."[37]

Following favorable action by the committee, Olsen and Bean undertook a rewrite of the AAU synchro rules to incorporate the main suggestions of the report. The primary goals were to design rules that were equally applicable to all events, solo, duet and team, and to open paths for nearly unrestricted compositional creativity while still retaining some athletic skill requirements that might help cast a better public image of synchro as a sport. After the product of their efforts was reviewed, amended, and approved by members of the Pacific Association and Southern Pacific Association, Olsen took the rule proposal to the 1953 AAU convention. Despite hot debates, Olsen's political skills got the rule proposal passed essentially intact.

The convention floor debates were mild compared with the public storm that followed. R.J. Dodson, editor of *The Synchronized Swimmer*, deplored the changes, saying "the artistic element is of prime importance and the athletic element is secondary."[38] He claimed the new rules would stifle creativity and cause a loss of interest in the sport. Bean countered, "We should consider our public image if we want to be accepted as a sport. It is easier to get a swimming suit picture on the sports page of a girl advertising a horse race or a boat show than a synchronized swimmer, who is often referred to the entertainment editor."[39]

Henry Gundling and Peg Seller (president, Canadian Amateur SSA) protested that the rule changes would injure solos, which, they said, were the most popular event. Further, they felt the U.S.A. should have adopted the FINA rules with free routines for all events in order to facilitate international participation.[40] Bean pointed out that in the most recent outdoor championships, under the far more inhibiting old rules, the number of swimmers in the team event exceeded those in solos, and had for a while. He noted that AAU competitors had been doing very well in other countries or international competitions, indicating that adapting from stringent to more liberal rules doesn't appear to be a problem, and is certainly easier to do than the opposite.[41]

The protests about hurting entries were also rebutted at the 1954 Indoor Championships in Chicago, the first under the new rules. There were more entries in each event than in any previous championship. The top two soloists of the 1953 outdoor championships boycotted the 1954 outdoor meet, held on the West Coast (Santa Monica) for the first time. Their supporters vehemently labeled that meet a "farce."[42] The answer was that the "farcical" meet still attracted more competitors than any prior outdoor championship.

The chasm between the artistic freedom advocates and supporters of the new rules could not be closed. After proposals for regaining their position failed to make headway at the 1954 convention, the "artists," led by the Gundlings, left the AAU. With Seller of Canada, they formed the International Academy of Aquatic Art (IAAA) in 1955.[43] The first festival was held at the University of Michigan in 1955.

The IAAA, still operating today, made their activity everything that could not be impressed onto the AAU. No restrictions or requirements are imposed on routine composition. Men and women compete together. At their "festivals" the routines are judged, but only to place them into various merit levels and it is possible for all contestants to gain the same highest level award if seen that way. The IAAA outlook has remained attractive to certain swimmers and swimming groups. Summer recreation programs, school programs and individuals with little time to prepare and perfect athletic skills have often gravitated toward its minimum requirement view. Its membership exceeded AAU synchro memberships for many years.

The new AAU rules still required a complete listing of everything done in the routines for all events, solo, duet and team. But no longer did duets and teams have to pack in as many standard, high-difficulty stunts as possible to optimize the routine average difficulty. In place now was an "athletic" specification that each routine must include five standard stunts, upon which the average routine difficulty multiple would be calculated. These could be any stunts from "different number groups" of any difficulty, but the maximum difficulty multiple that would be used for calculations would be 1.8. This top difficulty multiple limitation was a critical factor in final acceptance of the five-stunt approach. The five-stunt concept was welcomed, but had been resisted initially for fear that the same five highest difficulty stunts would automatically be used in every high-skill routine. The 1.8 limitation opened the way for general approval because a large number of stunts could be selected to balance out to that value.

Duet and team choreography was joyfully liberated by this change. Not so happy were soloists, on whom the same requirements were now imposed. No longer could a soloist depend upon showmanship to offset the obvious lack of anything more difficult than a front pike somersault, kip and ballet leg in a routine.

A routine time limit of six minutes now applied to *all* events. Finally, a limit of 30 seconds for deck work was specified. Patience at last had worn thin with abuses such as: a soloist's mother reciting, at the microphone, a long poem about Pele, the Hawaiian fire goddess, "to set the stage"; a swimmer, wearing pink satin toe shoes, performing about 30 seconds of ballet, then devoting another 30 seconds to unlacing the shoes; or the 12-girl team doing "jumping jack" pop-ups from large prop boxes on deck through an entire three-minute recording before climbing out of the boxes to repeat that record for the water portion of their routine.

The half-point bonus for team members

over four dropped out for 1954, but was restored for 1955. The team size remained four to 12 until 1956, when the present eight-swimmer maximum was imposed.

The list of stunts remained basically unchanged in the great revision of 1954. But soon the list began to expand with new, high-difficulty stunts that filled the need to allow even the five stunts for difficulty to contribute to creative sequences. Interestingly, in the face of the view that soloists were the inventive artists, the sources of most of the new figures (e.g., spins, barracuda, heron, knight, castle) entering the stunt lists in the next few years were from duets and teams. The Athens team introduced the heron and split (open) spin in Mexico City.

Some figure descriptions were changed in 1954. The dolphins were, for the first time, described as a circle, rather than a somersault. A number of simpler, rarely used stunts, along with surface propulsion actions (canoe, lobster, torpedo, muskrat, marching on water) were gradually dropped from the list. "Canadian" repetitions disappeared. Shadow stunting, with one swimmer performing a stunt at the surface and the partner performing the same action below the surface, was eliminated because of the difficulty in judging it. The dolphin ballet leg twists were also deleted due to judging problems.

## Judging and Scoring

The main change in judging with the new (1954) rules was that the judges would now apply the same awards, execution and style, to all events. They were still expected to consider the perfection of all parts of the routine in execution. Unfortunately, the instruction for the judge assistant, "shall read the routine as each stunt is performed and *record the judges scores on the routine sheet*" [italics added] was ambiguous and led to a somewhat heated debate over the next few years. Chairman Olsen wanted an award assigned to each of the five stunts for difficulty with an execution award based upon the average of those scores. Bean argued the intent of the instruction was for recording the final execution and style awards and the execution award should be based on consideration of all parts of the routine. The new definition for the execution award certainly supported the latter view: "Execution covers the performance of stunts, strokes and parts thereof and the synchronization of the swimmers, one with the other and also with the music."

The style award also had a new definition, varying somewhat from the old one: "Style shall include the construction of the routine, and the interpretation of the music by utilization of figures, stunts and strokes to form a flowing pattern, and the appropriateness and interpretiveness of costuming, manner of presentation and spectator appeal."

The convergence of solo with team and duet procedures simplified the scoring procedures and precompetition work was reduced in having only to verify the average of the five stunts listed for difficulty. No longer was the averaging of a dozen or more stunts necessary.

In 1956, a new section, penalties, appeared in the handbook. The only assessable penalty in prior times had been the five points for failing to perform a routine as listed. Now there could also be a five-point penalty for failure to do a required stunt, failure to start or finish with the music, failure to perform a required stunt simultaneously (duet or team), or for exceeding the deck time limit. A two-point penalty for interruption and restart of deck movements was also added. An interruption after entering the water, though, resulted in disqualification. Also, officials had to approve the costume as *appropriate* or the contestant would not be allowed to swim.

## International Development

In 1951, during the Amateur Swimming Union of the Americas [ASUA] meetings at the First Pan American games, an agreement had been reached for rules expected to govern synchro's first competitions to be included in the Second Pan American Games.[44] The result was a novel twofold competition. First a set of five stunts would be done individually, then a free

In the first official international competition, Beulah Gundling of Iowa wins the Pan American Games solo (photograph by Ross Bean).

routine for all events. Individual stunt scores would be averaged for members of duets and teams. The routines were to be scored with the same four awards as were then current for the AAU solos, with the same 40, 20, 20, 20 base for execution, synchronization, composition and showmanship. Nothing in the rules specified *how* the *stunts* were to be judged or scored. Those rules were never used.

Peg Seller (president for Canadian synchro) and Mary Derosier (chairman for AAU synchro) collaborated in drawing up a set of rules to be submitted to FINA at their congress at the Helsinki Olympic Games. It is not surprising that the hodge-podge of AAU rules of that period did not form the model for the international rules. Instead, the rules adopted were patterned after the Canadian rules which featured free routines for all events, but with awards that followed the AAU four-award solo scoring of that time. The point distributions and descriptions of factors covered by each award were identical with those of the AAU solo rules. In addition, a *five*-minute total time limit was specified, but only a maximum of 20 seconds was allowed for deck movements within that limit. The entire set of rules covered two typewritten pages since no standardized stunt descriptions were needed in the free routines and no stunt competition was included in this proposal.

Min Hendrick, Niagara Association chairman, invited Canadians to participate in an annual open competition in his association in 1952. With the title changed to the Canadian-American Championships the next year, this meet was the first to be designed for competition between representatives of different countries. It was helpful as a means of communication and fostering mutual understanding between the two nations while each was busy developing and building its programs. Peg Seller said, "It was self-evident that very little separates us. We have come a very long way towards merging into one type of competition. I feel that before too long, we will basically have the same rules. The FINA rules, loose as they are, bind us together."[45]

The international exposure of synchro continued at the 1952 Olympic Games in Helsinki, Finland. Mary Derosier, U.S.A., and Peg Seller, Canada, each accompanied a group of their swimmers who gave daily exhibitions and at the following Olympic Gala. They also exhibited at the subsequent Danish National Championships. Swimmers for the Olympic demonstration were soloists Beulah Gundling (U.S.A.) and Joan Orser (Canada); Connie Todoroff and Ellen Richard (U.S.A.) and Evelyn Orrice and Beverly Sutcliffe (Canada), duet; and the U.S.A. team from the St. Clair Synchronettes, Todoroff, Richard, Shirley Simpson, and Laurine Stocking.[46]

Beulah Gundling said, of her 1952 Olympic experiences in Helsinki, "We never failed to attract considerable attention, no matter what time of day we practiced. People would crowd to the edge of the pool, watching every move with interest, even though we used no music and merely worked on stunts." Cameramen, newsmen and coaches were always on hand for pictures or to ask questions. The photographers invariably wanted us to do a 'ballet leg' which seemed to have a peculiar fascination for everyone. The Finnish people were a most appreciative and responsive group. They were particularly intrigued with twists and each time a twist was performed they broke into delighted laughter and then applauded enthusiastically. In fact every stunt we did in our routines, no matter how simple, brought forth loud applause.... The water in the pools at the swim stadium was heated to about 75° which made swimming pleasant even though the temperature of the air hovered in the low 60s most of the time we were there."[47] Those appearances in Helsinki were instrumental in stimulating formation of an international committee within the framework of FINA which considered and adopted rules for governing the sport.

Personal friendships did much to pave the way in Latin America. Joy Cushman had a personal friend in Mexico, Rosa Pardo, coach of the Mexican team, but Pardo was also private secretary to Javier Ostos. Ostos, who would later head FINA, was very instrumental in synchro's

St. Clair Synchronettes, from left to right: Connie Todoroff, Shirley Simpson, Laurine Stocking and Ellen Richard, demonstrate at the 1952 Olympic Games in Helsinki. The popularity of the sport there helped it onto the Pan American Games program.

gaining acceptance into world competitive events. Cushman was warmly accepted for her knowledge and enthusiasm for the sport in clinics and the help she freely volunteered. She encouraged competition between the two countries and established exchange programs and clinics with Cuba, Puerto Rico, Aruba, Guatemala and Santo Domingo.[48]

The demonstrations of competitive-type synchro in Argentina and then in Helsinki had been enough to convince the FINA Congress that synchro was a worthy sport for international competition. FINA approved the submitted rules in 1954.[49] These rules superseded those of the ASUA and were used in the II Pan American Games in 1955.

For the 1956 FINA Congress, in Melbourne, a proposal was submitted to adopt the new version AAU rules, intact except for imposing an absolute limit on the sum of the difficulties for the five routine stunts rather than limiting the sum only for calculations. This proposal was competing with concepts in another proposal, coming from a meeting of representatives of six countries in Rotterdam at the Second International Conference of Synchronized Swimming. The latter simply suggested a stunt competition be added to the existing free routine competition. This was much more warmly greeted than the AAU proposal. A six-stunt competition was recommended and finally adopted by FINA, but only to be initiated in the quadrennium starting in 1960.[50]

Another demonstration was arranged by Olsen for the Olympic Games of 1956 in Melbourne. Culminating an around-the-world tour of exhibitions and clinics, the 11 swimmers (Appendix D) exhibited twice daily during the nine days of the swimming and diving events. The Athens Water Follies team's first experience with the large Australian Olympic crowd was something of a shock. As they stepped out in front of the audience in their "Dance of the Eagles"

theme costumes—feathered and beaked headpieces, bells decorating the suit at the neckline and waist—they were greeted, not with applause, but with a chant of "Cock-a-doodle-doo."[51] Much chagrined and sensing the feelings of the sports-minded audiences, thereafter they performed, for the entire nine days of the swimming and diving events, in plain white suits and caps, to tremendous ovations.[52] Demonstrations continued to be offered at the Olympic galas in Rome (1960), Tokyo (1964) and in Mexico City (1968). These exhibitions gave a wide variety of sports audiences all over the world a taste of synchronized swimming.

## The First International Competition

The international evangelism paid off when synchronized swimming was seen for the first time in multi-international competition in the 1955 Pan American Games. Despite poor participation with only three nations—the U.S., Canada and Mexico—the competitions

The Athens Club demonstrates during the 1956 Olympics Games in Melbourne. "Dance of the Eagle" swimmers are, in back, left to right, Joanne Berthelsen, Jackie Vargas, Joanne Brobst, Loretta Barrious. In front, left to right, Jackie Brown, June Young, team manager and tour director Norma Olsen, Lynn Pawson and Evelyn Oremus (photograph by Bob Kirwan).

were immensely popular even though held in Chapultepec Park instead of the main swimming stadium. Exhibitions and medal presentations were performed in the main stadium between swimming and diving events.

Two entries were allowed in solo and duet and one in team. The competition was in routine only, using free routines. But the AAU-style routines needed little adaptation (except to ensure maintaining consciousness in the thin Mexico City air) to make winning performances. The U.S. won everything: Beulah Gundling the solo; Ellen Richard and Connie Todoroff, duet; and the Athens Water Follies, now a team of five, beat the same 12-girl Canadian team that had upset them in the U.S. Nationals two years before.

The Athens team at the Pan American Games had an experience not likely to be duplicated. Practices and competitions were held in Chapultepec Park. One afternoon, Rosa Pardo, the Mexican coach who was running the practice sessions, came to the Athens team saying, "I have someone who wants to meet you." The team got out of the pool and a very distinguished gentleman stood before them. Pardo introduced him, telling the team that he lived in the Chapultepec apartments which directly overlooked the pool. When she gave his name, Luis Sandi, they immediately realized he was

the composer of the team music they had chosen, the *Ballet Bonampak*, an original work based on ancient Aztec themes. Dawn Bean remembered saying something to the effect that we loved all of the *Ballet Bonampak* but our rules only let us use five minutes. He said he was honored we had chosen it and enjoyed how we had put it together.

Of this competition, *Sports Illustrated* commented, "Synchronized Swimming, long considered nothing more than an exhibition, has found new popularity as a full-grown sport. Pretty girls have been making meaningful movements to music in pools for years, but until 1946, when it was given official AAU status, Synchronized Swimming has reached the public eye largely through gaudy, sequin-studded aquacade productions which bore little resemblance to sport in any form. There are still those who refuse to admit its validity, but thousands of women (and some men too), have taken up Synchronized Swimming as a demanding, but not exhausting sport, which puts a premium on grace and coordination rather than muscle power. This year, for the first time, Synchronized Swimming was admitted to the Pan-American Games, and adherents of the sport are looking toward the day when it will be sanctioned for Olympic competition."[53]

Rosa Pardo coached the large Chapultepec Club swimmers of Mexico City in grand aquacades. After acquiring a set of U.S. rules and organizing a synchronized swimming group, she arranged for a 1953 dual competition in Mexico City with Joy Cushman's Shamrock Hilton Corkettes. In 1954, the Chapultepec team turned up as a surprise entry in the U.S. outdoor nationals. Displaying amazingly sophisticated and entertaining routines, they went home with third-place medals in both team and duet. Their next appearance was the Pan American Games of 1955, in their home city, winning silvers in solo and duet and bronze in the team event.[54]

That year Mexico also sent competitors to the AAU outdoor

The Athens Club won the Pan American Games Team title. From left to right are Sally Phillips, Loretta Barrious, Dawn Pawson Bean, Lynn Pawson and Joan Pawson.

meet, in which their team again took third. With the strong support of Mexican synchro by President Ostos and Coach Pardo, Mexico has continued to maintain a vigorous international presence to this day. They, along with Canada and the U.S., have entered every Pan American Games where synchro was included.

Claudia Noonan, a competitor from Chicago's Lake Shore Club, moved to Brazil in 1952. In a letter home in January 1952, she told of the first synchro competition in Sao Paulo. "It was tough," she said. "We had to teach all the contestants everything, translate all the stunts and rules into Portuguese, and teach the judges too.... The kids were beginners in [water] ballet and the music was mostly waltzes. In fact my record of 'Beautiful Ohio' has become a hit song in Sao Paulo, I guess they'd never heard it before."[55]

Even though Canada had started having competitions related to synchro long before any other nation (1924), national involvement had been largely restricted to the central provinces of Quebec and Ontario until the '50s. The dawning of that decade, though, saw rapid expansion across Canada. The start of the spreading interest was nearly coincident with Canada's somewhat delayed adoption of a full program of true synchro, as teams were finally put into their program in 1950.

A review in *Synchronized Swimming, 60 Years to Celebrate* (Canadian Synchro) attributed much of the expansion to help from the Women's Intercollegiate Athletic Union, which offered financial support for a program of competition in figures, strokes, solos, duets and *trios*. The University of British Columbia soon sponsored the B.C. Open Championships. Nationwide participation was not attained until the '60s when Newfoundland finally became involved.[56]

But Canadian competitors were highly active and successful in international activities during this period. Canadian champions continued international demonstrations with an exhibition in Helsinki in 1952. Toronto's June Taylor won four successive AAU indoor solo championships, (three while still living in Canada). Peterborough's team numbers smothered the AAU's 1953 outdoor team event. Their

swimmers won a second (team) and two third (duet and solo) places in the 1955 Pan American Games.

With Peg Seller, Canadian synchro's president, also serving as secretary to FINA in the early '50s, they were also quite influential on the developing international scene. The result of her collaboration with Mary Derosier in rules for international events was adopted by FINA in 1952.[57] It was largely Canadian pressure, with their long experience in "trick" or "figure" competition, that brought stunt competition into international meets.

Japan's early exposure in the sport came through the U.S. State Department's sponsorship of Far Eastern tours. For the first, in 1954, an Athens team accompanied by Norma Olsen and other leaders, gave exhibitions and several clinics in Japan and Korea. The *Oakland Tribune* reported, "An exhibition of synchronized swimming was given in the beautiful Meiji Pool (Tokyo), and 15,500 people turned out. Everything the swimmers did drew tremendous applause from the people."[58] The instant enthusiasm aroused in Japan inspired rapid development and the desire to learn more. In 1956, the first U.S.A.–Japan dual competition was held in Osaka. Athens Water Follies members, not too surprisingly, won all events. Thereafter, Joy Cushman began a regular exchange program between the two countries where one year, Japan came to the U.S., and the following year the U.S. went to Japan.

Numerous synchronized swimming groups sprang up across Europe in this period. The Koninklijke Nederlandse Zwembond (Dutch Swimming Federation) added a synchronized swimming committee to its structure in 1952 to coordinate and stimulate synchronized swimming. Jan Armbrust was made chairman and he organized a series of clinics to promote the sport.[59]

Beulah Gundling gave demonstrations in Paris at the International Congress of Physical Education for Girls and Women, a special exhibition for the French minister of education and for the Racing Club of France.[60] The swimmers of the Racing Club were making great progress under Mlle. Monique Berlioux, French backstroke champion and a 1948 Olympian.[61]

Gundling then toured England, giving demonstrations in 16 cities while husband Henry, a national committee member, led clinic sessions for British swimmers.[62]

Dawn Zajac, then a London trapeze artist and theater performer, was fascinated by the exhibitions. She went to California in 1954 to learn more under Lillian MacKellar, who had moved to Hollywood with star competitor June Taylor.[63] Zajac returned to London to become the leading coach of British swimmers.

By 1954, French participation had advanced to staging its first synchronized swimming competition. A small group of synchro champions from the Racing Club of France went to give England its first taste of competition duet and team routines. That year, demonstrations of synchronized swimming were included in the British Empire Games and both the German and the European swimming and diving championships.[64] "However, it was in 1956," said George Rackham, president of the British Swimming Teachers Association, "that we saw for the first time how polished and technically perfect the U.S. teams were. The Athens Water Follies, AAU Team champions, were on their way to demonstrate at the Olympic Games in Melbourne. The demonstrations they gave were fantastic, such precision and perfect synchronization had never been seen here before."

London's *Daily Mirror* underwrote the costs for the Gundlings' tour of 16 cities in England in 1953 (they paid their own airfare). Canada's Peg Seller, credited by the *Mirror* as "the world's leading authority on Synchronized Swimming," was along to help. Seller was quoted saying, "Beulah was superb and the U.S. can be justly proud that one of their swimmers had the honor of introducing Synchronized Swimming to Britain."[65]

The first of the promotional tours arranged by Olsen, to further the development of the sport came in 1953. This was arranged through the Special Services Department in Washington, D.C. For one month following the 1953 national championships, performances were given in military bases throughout the East and Southeast, ending in Michigan at the Great Lakes Naval Training Center.[66]

From 1954 to 1958, the U.S. State Department sponsored tours with U.S. synchro swimmers and divers through the Far East, Europe, and even around the world. Largely budgeted under entertainment for U.S. troops abroad, they also enabled exhibitions and clinics for sport enthusiasts wherever they went. State Department tours went to Japan and Korea in 1954, 1955 and 1956. Walter Bouillet, director of entertainment for the Far East Command, reported they had never received so many letters of commendation all stressing the need for this type of sports entertainment for the morale of the troops. The *Saturday Evening Post* reported, "...there were the 4000 soldiers in Seoul murmuring, 'You're like the kids back home' ... but one swimmer complained, 'I get sort of embarrassed if they whistle too much.'"[67]

Then came the globe-circling tour that had a major influence on the sport's world acceptance and worldwide growth. This 90-day tour was cosponsored by the AAU with the U.S. State Department under the International Educational Exchange Services, so exhibitions and clinics could be given in various cities in Denmark, England, Italy, Sweden, Switzerland, the Netherlands, Egypt, Pakistan, India, Malay Peninsula, and New Zealand. The pinnacle of the tour was a 10-day stint at the Olympics in Melbourne, with twice-daily demonstrations during the competitions, finishing with participation in the final gala.

The synchro swimmers in the group included the Athens Club team from Oakland, the duet from the Shamrock Hilton Corkettes of Houston, and soloist from the Riverside (California) Aquettes. The divers were Fletcher Gilders of Detroit and Roland Smith of Kansas. Norma Olsen and Teresa Andersen were synchro leaders. The group was headed by Lawrence J. Johnson, representing the AAU. Olsen praised Johnson's leadership: "As the official representative of the AAU, Lawrence Johnson was superb in his relationship with the leaders of amateur sport and with the consulates."[68]

After exhibitions and clinics in Scandinavia and Europe, the group arrived in Egypt for a planned week of appearances there. The plans abruptly changed as the Suez crisis erupted. As the hostilities between Israel and Egypt escalated, headlines in San Francisco Bay Area papers reported the tour's plight. Contra Costa County's *Independent* read, "Bay Girl Swimmers in War Zone"; the *Oakland Tribune*, "Athens Club Girls Team is Missing"; the *San Francisco Examiner*, "Bay Mermaids Trapped in Cairo"; and finally, the *San Francisco Chronicle* reported, "Swimmers Escape War Zone." The latter went on to report, "The Oakland Athens Club swimming group, caught in Cairo by the hostilities, is safe and being evacuated, the Associated Press reported today, See story page 1."

For a period of three days, no one at home knew where the girls were. They were evacuated onto the U.S. Navy destroyer *Chilton*, bound for Naples, Italy. The *San Francisco Chronicle* in reporting, "Local Mermaids Saw Part of War," quoted Joanne Brobst "This first morning we saw a British plane crash into the harbor at Alexandria after being shot down," and "before the *Chilton* left Alexandria, Egyptian ships were firing over it at the British planes." From Naples, the group resumed their tour itinerary, first to Rome, through India and then on to Melbourne.[69]

The group arrived in Bombay where crowds greeted them. *The (Bombay) Times of India* reported on Nov. 15, 1956, "A brilliant exhibition of synchronized swimming was given by 11 U.S. women, now on their way to Melbourne to give demonstrations at the Olympic Games. At the Mahatma Gandhi Memorial Pool, this marked the first time the sport has been seen here."[70] The *Times* reported 5,000 interested persons in the audience.

To coincide with the tour's travels in Europe, Netherlands synchro chairman Jan Armbrust scheduled the Second International Conference of Synchronized Swimming in Rotterdam. It was here, as noted previously, that the six nations represented agreed to recommend to FINA the addition of a six-stunt competition (in black suits and white caps) and a free routine competition. The FINA Congress in Melbourne adopted those recommendations and established a Technical Synchronized Swimming Committee (TSSC). Armbrust was appointed the TSSC chairman and Norma Olsen was named honorable secretary.[71]

## Development Around the Country

In many areas of the country, local water show activity flourished as preludes to subsequent development of competitive synchro interests. And the number of synchro clubs was increasing and expanding as shown in the pages of competition results in the handbooks. Colorado added the Lakewood Synchronettes, Loretta Heights Swim Club and Colorado A & M University. Illinois had teams at Waukegan High School, Lorelei Club of Northwestern, Chicago Independence Park, Illinois Wesleyan University, Sovereign Hotel Club, and Chicago's Community Builders. Results from national meets reveal Tucson YWCA, Minneapolis YWCA, Fargo (North Dakota) Swim Club, Nebraska's Doan College, Erie YWCA, Pennsylvania, and the Milwaukee Fin Club had all entered national meets during this time. Florida continued to grow, adding the Nauti Nymphs of Fort Lauderdale, Sunlando Springs Swim Club, and new clubs in Glen Springs and Winter Park. In Iowa, competitions were reported with four new clubs in Des Moines, Build Lincoln High, East High School, Waterloo High School, and the Des Moines Golf Club. Fort Dodge also began a program.

In Connecticut, Hope Smith started the Dolphin Club at Windham High School in Willimantic. It was the only high school in the state with a full-fledged water show. Synchro competitions began between clubs at the Stamford YWCA, Bridgeport Women's Athletic Club, Bristol Synchronettes and the Willimantic Dolphins.[72] And synchronized swimming began in the Adirondack area when Mary Oppenheim taught water ballet classes in 1956 and then organized the first competition that year.[73]

Organized competitive synchronized swimming in the Pacific Association was an outgrowth from several water show groups with the Athens Athletic Club (Water Follies) leading the way. Within this period, several strong clubs developed, including the Oakland Moose Club Naiads, the Oakland Park and Recreation Department Sea Sirens, Crystal Plunge in San Francisco, and the San Francisco Merionettes, the club that would dominate the 60s in national events. Others that entered national competitions included the San Francisco Women's Club, Livermore Swim Club and Vallejo College.

The 1952 Far Western meet again included a Junior Olympic competition for the age groups 14 and under and 15–16. In 1953 the meet included a "midget" division for solos 12 and under. Joanne Royer won the senior solo and the 12 and under was won by 7-year-old Papsie Georgian.[74] A West Coast indoor synchro meet was held at Mission Beach in San Diego in May 1953. A newspaper headlined, "Southern California's crack teams entered in Synchronized Swimming Meet. Entries include Los Angeles Athletic Club, Huntington Beach, Monterey Park Club, Pacific Coast Club of Long Beach, Santa Monica Synchronized Swimming Club, and possibly USC and UCLA."[75]

Wesleyan College in Macon, Georgia, staged an aquacade in 1952 as, "something new … [using] swimming more as a creative art with interpretation wound around the music and some creative poetry."[76] Joyce Hillard, coach of the Minden Water Sprites (New Orleans area), entered a team in competition in 1952 and they went on to win the Louisiana state title.[77] Jean Maeys, director of aquatics for women at Northwestern State College at Natchitoches, held an open meet followed by a clinic with Beulah Gundling.[78] Thereafter, competitions were held with the New Orleans Royettes, Minden's Tidettes and Auburn Park of New Orleans.

In the Potomac Valley Association, the Aqua Gems began water ballet in the 1950s, but did not begin competition until 1961. Vernon "Ike" Eytchison, Barbara Van Dusen (Eaton), Mae McEwan, Jean Ackerman, Sonja Lazarowitz and Barbara Browne were all involved.[79] Peg Hogan, now the University of Richmond coach, joined the Aqualites under coach Dot Muhly at the Baltimore YWCA in 1956. The group had started a few years earlier and was

the only competitive synchro team in the area at that time.[80]

Activity was just beginning in Montana where a water show was given at Montana State College at Bozeman, in the fall of 1952, according to Dorothy Kennemer, who wanted "to put Montana on the map."[81] The Ducks club at the University of Oklahoma, coached by Carole Hass, reported feeder clubs in the local high schools. "We've had open competitive meets in Bartlesville and Blackwell," reported Hass in December 1952.[82]

Furney Jeffrey, coach of the Summit YMCA, now had more than 50 girls registered in New Jersey in 1952, the local newspaper reported. It noted the leading teams in the state were the Westfield Dolphins, Newark Mermettes, and Newark Park and Recreation Aquabelles. Colleges with synchronized swimming included St. Elizabeth Junior Centenary, New Jersey College for Women and Trenton Teachers College. Alicia Elliott was a three-time state senior champion and runner up for the national solo title and Lorraine Muzenski (Fasullo) won the 1954 junior national solo title.[83]

Strong growth continued in pioneering Michigan. Lansing reported a new club, the Sea Sprites, for girls 15 to 17, with Frances Jones as coach. They placed third in the nationals in Des Moines in 1952.[84] By 1953, the Sea Sprites had replaced the St. Clair Synchronettes, Michigan's early champions from Detroit, as the top group in Michigan. The Sea Sprites grew to more than 60 members during this time.[85] The Lansing Y Ripples, Detroit City Club, Detroit Patton Madcaps, Monticello College, Ferndale's Lincoln High School, Dearborn YMCA, Ann Arbor Swim Club and Chandler Club of Detroit were also active.

The Berea Aquateens grew from a backyard pool activity of Dr. Robert Lechner who started synchro in about 1954 with six to eight neighborhood girls. The club grew to 30 members when Dean Kraus, who had coached synchro at Kent State University, took over coaching the club. Kathy Brooks and Gretchen Lechner won the junior national duet in 1956 swimming "The Hobos" in which they blackened their faces with cork. Kraus left in 1958 and Jo Birt, also from Kent State, became the head coach.[86] Other clubs that entered Ohio competitions in this period were the Kent State Sharks and the Columbus Kipettes. In the Lake Erie Association there were the Cleveland Penguins, Toledo Synchronettes and an adult group, the Monaquas. One of U.S.A. synchro's few male swimmers, Donn Squire, started with the latter.[87]

The Neighborhood House of Portland offered a water ballet team and several of the Y's had synchronized swimming classes by the mid-'50s. The Neighborhood House team, later renamed the Chinook MerMiss, was coached by Florence Godfrey, who taught children the basics of all four aquatic sports. Marna Moore, Oregon Association, remembers that to be on the Neighborhood House team you also had to be on the racing team. In fact, she said, "Only after you proved your worth in swimming were you invited to join synchro. Godfrey taught every child she instructed the basics of all four aquatic sports since she felt that the more you knew of all aquatic skills, the more it enhanced the one you wanted to focus on." Other early pioneers in Oregon were Gloria Hicks, who started the Tualatin Hills Club; Betsy Austin, who began the MerMacs of Multnomah Athletic Club; and Mike Popoviche, Portland's aquatic director. Popoviche, an early advocate of all four aquatic sports, oversaw the building of pools in Portland and he insisted that all Portland's pools must be able to accommodate all four aquatic sports.[88]

The early starting Shamrock Hilton Corkettes continued to bring attention to synchro in Houston. Margaret Swan (Forbes), visiting in Houston in 1955, saw a duet swimming and had never seen anything like it. She joined an adult group in San Antonio and soon began helping coach its younger swimmers. When the coach left the area, she became head coach. She brought this team, the Silver Fins, to their first national competition in Hartford in 1957.[89] During this period, competitions were reported with the Crystal Pool in Houston, Dallas Athletic Club, Catalina Club of Dallas, Fort Worth Athletic Club and the Southern Methodist University Dolphins.

Bowling Green University, under coach Iris Andrews, had a longstanding program. Dorothy "Dottie" Dahms got started under that program and then founded the Dayton Synchronettes in 1956 as a show troupe, which changed to the Dayton Aquanymphs as they became a competitive team. Soon after, Edna Hines started synchro at the Coralina Club in Columbus. While Bowling Green University continued its activity, it added a new program, an adult club which also offered synchronized swimming.

# 5

## *Growing Pains Here, Promotion Overseas: 1957–62*

AAU Synchronized Swimming made another dramatic change in its competitive structure during this period, feeling that it might improve its sport image by following FINA's example of adding a stunt (figure) competition for 1958. Here every athlete would be judged individually on the performance of a series of selected stunts. The gratification in having a more objectively and relatively easily judged event very quickly became eclipsed by the frustrations of attempting to fit the event into schedules already overburdened by burgeoning numbers of competitors.

The synchro national committee took on new dimensions as additional subcommittees were added for more efficiency and to utilize the growing numbers of volunteers eager to take part in organizing and developing the programs. A long-overdue judges' training program was initiated and regulations for maintenance of national ratings were instituted. Outstanding athletes and contributors to synchro began getting recognition for the first time, through nominations to the Helms Athletic Sports Hall of Fame.

Synchro took another step toward more independence within the AAU as it established its own committee for international affairs rather than continuing to depend on the AAU's international committee for all its relations as closer attention to the international fields was becoming essential. More multinational events were developing, but it was really the U.S. tour programs that were doing the most to accelerate overseas development. The Far East tours continued through most of this period and European megatours were undertaken in 1958 and 1960.

And always, the question lingered, show or sport? A live, half-hour broadcast on KGO-TV was seen nationwide on July 4, 1957. The Richfield Oil Company's program, *Success Story*, was advertised to viewers as "The story of the Athens Water Follies of Oakland, California, an organization that has developed from a small group in 1944 to an internationally famous aquacade that has competed or exhibited around the world."[1] Glen King wrote in the *Berkeley Gazette*, "We will be watching with great interest. It will be a visit to the Athens Club to see the Water Follies in action. While we rejoice that synchronized swimming is getting more, long-overdue, recognition, we will be holding our fingers crossed to see who gets credit for what. Too often the pompous speechmakers proved they knew nothing about the years of daily practice, thousands of dollars of out of pocket expense ... and the humiliating cold shoulders from sports authorities who refuse to consider such swimming a 'sport.'"[2]

Norma Olsen continued her optimistic

views. Following the Olympic demonstrations in Melbourne, she had arranged for an interview with Mr. Brundage. She was upset that he had called synchronized swimming "aquatic vaudeville." Saying, "I was so nervous when I first met Mr. Brundage that I could hardly state my case to best advantage. I was surprised and delighted to find him a very amiable man willing to listen, watch and eventually change his mind," said Olsen. "We induced him to watch competition in this sport and could see that he had never fully realized what skill, training and physical condition was needed for the sport." But she added, "This doesn't mean that Mr. Brundage is ready to advocate the event for the 1960 Games."[3]

## The National Championships, 1957–62

This was a transitional period in club domination on the national scene. The Athens Club of Oakland seemed to be maintaining its firm grip on national titles at its start, but the power had shifted, before it was over, to the San Francisco Merionettes. Their rapid rise was certainly due largely to the innovative choreography of their coach, Marion Kane, coupled with even more rigorous training than Athens had instituted.[4]

A major change in the program of the national championships took place when stunt competition became a requirement, a score added to the routine score to determine placements. While already a requirement in FINA, it was first tried in 1957 at the national championships, then added in 1958 as a requirement for all the national competitors. Some results of these early stunt competitions brought a few surprises. For the first time, judges had a chance to analyze critically every swimmer's individual performance. It was always assumed that soloists were the most skillful competitors, but the first stunt competition placed doubt on that orthodox wisdom. Solo winner Toni Stewart did win that first stunt competition, but other soloists were pushed for places as members of Athens Water Follies team, notoriously

nonchalant about solo competition, took five of the top 10 spots. Ross Bean, coach of the Athens team said, "This suggested that it was only their indifference to solos, and not a lack of individual capabilities, that had kept them from dominating all events rather than just the team and, usually, duet."[5]

As Eastern and Midwestern clubs struggled to catch up again by adopting the more rigorous Western training, the Athens Club of Oakland continued to hold a lock on the team event through 1960. It was from a neighbor just across the San Francisco Bay, though, that the real threat to Athens' dominance was developing. That threat was the team that grew up under the wing of the San Francisco Park and Recreation Department. The S.F.P.R.D. Merionettes first appeared in national team competition in 1957 and took sixth place in finals. By 1959, now as the San Francisco Merionettes, they had risen to third. Teams from other parts of the country were coming up also. The Columbus Coralinas, Lansing Sea Sprites, Houston's Shamrock Hilton Corkettes, Berea Aquateens, and Detroit Park and Recreation Department's Penguinettes all broke into the recently exclusive California territory of finals.

Despite the competitive rebuilding elsewhere, at the close of the '50s Oakland's Athens Club seemed resurgent as it won every 1960 title — solo, duet and team — in both the indoor and outdoor meets. However, that outdoor team title, their 17th, turned out to be their last. The Merionettes, relentlessly surging up the placement ladder, were right behind Athens in second place at the 1960 Outdoors. Then, decimated by the retirements of their veterans after the world tour of 1960, Athens didn't even enter a team in the 1961 nationals, the first time in 10 years. The Merionettes took over to start a new era as an *Oakland Tribune* sports headline lamented, "Golden Age of Athens Ends."

The Merionettes' succession to the throne took place in the 1961 indoor championships before a home crowd in their Balboa Park Pool. With a sharp Spanish routine, "La Fiesta Brava," the Merionette team of Margaret Durbrow, Claire Vida, Phyllis Firman, Louella Sommers and Sharon Hood forged the first of

The San Francisco Merionettes win the first of 17 national team titles in 1961. With coach Marion Kane, swimmers are, from left to right, Louella Sommers, Margaret Durbrow, Claire Vida, Sharon Hood and Phyllis Firman.

played any kind of lock grip on duet titles when this period began, the best record having been four titles in a row. In fact, the results of the 1957 and 1958 duet events seemed to suggest that the West might never master duets as it had teams. Judy Haga and Sandy Giltner of the Lansing Sea Sprites won both the indoor and outdoor titles in 1957. Then, Roz Calcaterra and Mary Jane Gury of St. Louis Shaw Park won both the indoor and outdoor competitions in 1958.

It was not for the West's lack of effort as three Western clubs, University Athletic Club of Hollywood, Athens, and the Oakland Naiads, took on Shaw Park, KRNT Des Moines, the Columbus Coralina Club, Ohio State University, the Lansing Sea Sprites, the Shamrock Hilton Corkettes, and Cuba in vying for top places in the finals of the two 1958 meets. The University Athletic Club, with 1957 solo champion Betty Vickers and Mary Ellerman, was runner-up behind Shaw Park both times with an Athens duet following in third.

many victories. It was a convincing win, by more than nine points, but Oakland's Moose Club Naiads, coached by Betty Brandelein, put on a performance that had an influence on the style of synchronized swimming for years to come with their attractive, flowing "Return of the Swallows." The Merionettes, however, began a fabulous reign that would endure for the next 10 years.

At that year's outdoor championships in New Jersey, the Merionettes confirmed their hold on top but Shaw Park of St. Louis (coach Re Calcaterra) accomplished the feat of occupying the runner-up spot, previously taken by California teams for the past six years. But, a new group of Athens swimmers was already nipping at their heels. At the 1962 Indoor, the Merionettes continued to consolidate their position and Shaw Park repeated for second place, but by summer, the new Athens team replaced Shaw Park in second position.

California swimmers had not yet dis-

The next year, though, California and Athens resurged with both 1959 duet titles going to Athens' Sue Laurence and Jackie Vargas. They repeated in 1960 where it appeared that Shaw Park could be on its way back to duet ascendancy as the Calcaterra and Gury duet rose to follow them in both meets. The Merionettes, however, dashed those hopes in the 1961 Indoor as Phyllis Firman and Louella Sommers culminated their rapid rise to the top. But, in the 1961 summer meet, Joanne Schaak and Barbara Burke of the University Athletic Club, Hollywood, won. Beyond that point, though, the Merionettes started a six-year domination of duet competition as Sommers, with new partner Claire Vida, succeeded in winning both indoor and outdoor titles in 1962.

The closely fought solo title never stayed

**Betty Vickers, Hollywood Athletic Club, with coach Lillian MacKellar, after winning the 1959 solo title (photograph by Hanson Williams).**

**Papsie Georgian, Athens Club, winner of the national 12 and under solo title in 1958, became the youngest senior national solo champion, winning in 1960 at age 14 (photograph by Bob Kirwan).**

long in any one place during these years. Tony Stewart (Essick), unattached from Chicago, won the 1957 Indoor at Lansing and Betty Vickers, of Hollywood, won the 1957 Outdoor meet in Oakland. Stewart, now representing the Chicago Town Club, reclaimed her Indoor title in 1958, but the Outdoor title went to Sandy Giltner of the Sea Sprites, who also won the 1959 Indoor championships. Then, Vickers, who had last won in 1957, took home the Outdoor title in 1959.

Athens' diminutive Papsie Georgian, only 14 years old but already a veteran who won the 1958 12 and under national title, became the youngest swimmer to win a senior solo championship when she took the title at the 1960 Indoor.[6] She made it a double when she added the Outdoor title and then kept it, winning both indoor and outdoor meets in 1961. Papsie didn't defend her titles in 1962 and the title passed to Barbara Burke of the University Club, Hollywood, who also doubled in winning both 1962 titles. In second place was Paso Robles' Roberta Armstrong, who had made a quick rise to the challenging position.

Qualifying trials to determine AAU synchro's representatives to the 1963 Pan American Games were held in City of Commerce, California, in December 1962. As in 1955, the Pan American Games competitions would be governed by FINA rules, which now included a stunt competition. Those rules were applied at the trials to ensure qualifying the competitors most likely to do well at the Games. Some rather unexpected results ensued. The placing varied dramatically from the results the AAU scoring procedures would have produced. The AAU scoring summed two awards for routines,

Mary Jane Gury (left) and Roz Calcaterra, Shaw Park, St. Louis, won the national duet titles in 1958 (photograph by Leonard Stallcup).

Louella Sommers (left) and Clair Vida of the Merionettes, won the senior duet title in 1962. Sommers won with Phyllis Firman in 1961 and Vida won with Judy Wejak in 1963.

one of those awards being nearly doubled by the difficulty multiple, to give rise to a maximum routine score nearly 50 percent greater than the maximum stunt score where the stunt score comprised only about 38 percent of the total score. Under FINA rules, though, routine and stunt scores were weighted nearly equally, making the stunt score worth about 50 percent of the total score.

In the trials, Papsie Georgian, the 1961 solo champion who had returned to competition to try for a spot on the Pan Am Team, won the solo routine event. Barbara Burke, the 1962 solo champion, had the highest stunt score. But, it was Roberta Armstrong who placed second in both routine and stunts that turned up with the highest total score in an unbelievably close event. Armstrong scored 138.80 to Burke's 138.59, and Georgian had 138.53. Favorite Georgian missed being one of the two solo qualifiers for the Pan American Games by just 0.07 points.

The duet contest was also an upset. The Merionette duet with Claire Vida had rather easily won both 1962 national duet championships. But with Vida swimming with new partner Judy Wejak, their weaker stunts dropped them to third place. Barbara Burke and Joanne Schaak, University Club, took first on the strength of their stunt scores, with Athens' Marcia Blixt and Marian Whitner second. Scores were 132.08 for Burke and Schaak, 130.83 for Blixt and Whitner, and 128.35 for Vida and Wejak.

The most unexpected upset occurred in

Duet titles had been held by Midwestern swimmers since 1956 when Sue Lawrence (left) and Jackie Vargas, Athens Club, brought the duet crown back to the West Coast in 1959. They won four duet titles (photograph by Bob Kirwan).

the team contest. Athens Club, which had last won the national team title in 1960, managed to outscore the four-time national team champions from San Francisco by four points in stunts, a lead impossible for the Merionettes to overcome, even with their convincing win in the routine. The final score totals, Athens 131.76 to Merionettes 128.87, gave Athens the coveted trip.[7]

## International Development

While synchronized swimming was becoming increasingly popular in Europe, Scandinavia and the Far East, it seemed to be lagging in the Western hemisphere. U.S., Canadian and Mexican synchronized swimmers had looked expectantly to another competition in the 1959 Pan American Games in Chicago. It was a major disappointment when the synchronized

swimming events were canceled for failing to attract the then-required entries from four nations. Nonetheless, demonstrations and clinics were given throughout the duration of the Games by both the United States and Canada, hoping that such efforts would bring synchro back as a full medal sport in 1963.

After the initial success of the Pan American Games, the Central American and Caribbean Associations fought for the inclusion of synchronized swimming in their regional games, but that didn't happen immediately.[8] In fact, it was quite a number of years before South American and Central American competitions came into being.

While Germany had competitions in floating patterns since 1934, their first synchronized swimming competitions began in 1957.[9] Thereafter Europe began to develop many more national competitions and then the Netherlands hosted the first known multinational competition in Europe, the Festival of Europe. Nine countries competed in the meet held in Amsterdam in 1958 with the Netherlands winning all events.[10] Czechoslovakia reported starting synchronized swimming in 1957 with the club ZKL Brno. Founder Stanislav Krajicek reported more than 100 girls practicing in groups according to their ages, from six to 20 years.[11]

England was visited by two Canadian teams in 1959, the Sea Sprites from Quebec and the Peterborough Ornamental Swimming Club from Ontario. Pansy Forbes, coach, was instrumental in getting synchro water skills introduced into the British school aquatic program.[12] South Africa reported holding a beginner program in 1961.[13] But, obviously still more were needed to make synchronized swimming a worldwide sport.

Norma Olsen cornered Avery Brundage in 1952, urging the president of the International Olympic Committee (IOC) to accept synchronized swimming into the Olympics. He turned her down flat. "He was tough to talk to," Olsen said, "he didn't want any new sports in the Olympics that needed judges." Actually, Brundage, in rebuffing Olsen, had energized her. "I figured the best approach then was to educate people about the sport in other parts of the world."[14] And that is just what she set out to do.

The annual tours that Olsen had started in 1953 were continued throughout this period. The 1957 tour to the Far East included swimmers from Oakland's Moose Club Naiads, Fort Lauderdale Swim Club, Shaw Park St. Louis, and divers Sam Hall and Frank Fraunfelter from Ohio State. Joy Cushman, national chairman, led the group, giving clinics and serving as coach and manager as well.[15] U.S. swimmers easily won the competitions held in Tokyo, Osaka, and Nagoya.

The tours escalated to an even bigger scale in 1958, as three tours were offered. The first two were six weeks each, one to Europe, ending in Spain, and the other to the Far East sponsored by the Armed Forces Professional Entertainment Branch, Special Services Division. That fall, a third tour exhibited at the Spring Games in Rio de Janeiro.

Dorothy Donnelly of Connecticut was the manager of the 45-day tour of Europe. The itinerary, arranged by the AAU's Daniel Ferris, provided for a series of exhibitions beginning at the Brussels World's Fair, then to Paris for more exhibitions with the tour ending in Spain.

The tour started in Belgium. Clinics and shows were given in La Louviere, Serang, and Brussels. There, a news clipping reported, "This is the first time the swimming pool has seen such a large audience, and those present were enchanted by the show. The gracefulness, suppleness, and surety of technique of the American swimmers won the audience. The perfect demonstration of the most difficult figures was warmly applauded." The announcer enthusiastically introduced the swimmers, at one point saying, "Make way for the champions. There now is a graceful, pretty little golden butterfly. It is Linda Ridings, who flies and glides and the spectators, not being able to catch this beautiful lepidopteron, must content themselves with applauding."[16]

Mr. Gill Van den Broeck, chief of guides at the Brussels Fair, wrote, "Water ballet is show; Synchronized Swimming is sport." One week of the Americans' visit was enough to persuade the public and the swimming officials to change their minds to "It really *is* a sport!" He continued, "There is no competition possible with the perfect technique of the U.S.A. girls. The entire tour was a triumph of technique assisted by the girls' good figures, their spontaneous smiles and expert showmanship."[17]

After two weeks in Belgium, the tour moved to France where 12 days were spent giving clinics and shows in and around Paris, at Evreoux, LeHavre, and Fertes Allais. Everywhere they went they received royal treatment. Dorothy Donnelly said in a report in *The Amateur Athlete*, "I feel the tour helped to promote synchronized swimming in Europe where the sport lags behind our amazing development in recent times. We were impressed to learn that many spectators had traveled great distances to view the exhibitions, [and] had remained to question and observe. At one of our exhibitions in France, the audience sat in a cold and driving rain for two hours time to watch the performances. The interest is tremendous."[18] Competitions were held in Paris, Brussels and Barcelona. The U.S. won all competitions. *Synchro News* reported the swimmers had their first taste of competition under French rules where "they were required to perform dives from the deck, strokes and stunts."[19]

Spain was the last country on the tour, with stops in Madrid and Barcelona. For nine evenings the group took part in the Seventh Annual International Swimming Festival where the Sociedad de Athletic Barcelona had gathered swimmers from Holland, Sweden, Denmark, Belgium, France, United States, Germany, Italy and Spain for the competition. Sandy Giltner (solo), Linda Ridings and Roz Calcaterra (duet), and the Athens team were the class of the competition, winning every event by a wide margin.[20]

The second tour in 1958 was to the Far East, taking the team through Japan, Korea, Okinawa, the Philippines, Guam and Hawaii, as they presented 23 water shows and many clinics. Manager Marge Dineen said, "I am really impressed with the quality of Japanese synchronized swimming. Betty Vickers knows most of the girls from the tour into this area last year and she commented several times on the tremendous improvement these girls have shown in a year's time. The Japanese routines show imagination in their creation and execution."[21] This was an early insight into the creativity of the Japanese synchro routines that, even today, remains their outstanding trademark.

The swimmers also competed in a Japan-America meet while on this tour and won all the events. But, Manager Dineen said, "I caution any reader not to underestimate the Japanese synchronized swimmers. The margin of superiority for the U.S. was small indeed and they will undoubtedly press the United States for top honors when international competition becomes more widespread."[22] Dineen managed yet another tour to the Far East in 1959.

The third tour, led by Helene Harms of New Jersey took the swimmers for a week of exhibitions in Brazil during the 10th Annual Spring Games in Rio de Janeiro.[23]

Olsen made really big plans for 1960. Not one, not two, but three tours were arranged for Europe and a fourth tour was again going to the Far East. Each European tour had approximately 20 swimmers, plus divers. Each tour was of seven weeks duration. Tour number one took the group to Sweden, the Netherlands, and Finland; tour number two went to Brussels, West Germany, and Czechoslovakia; and tour number three went to London, France and Spain. These three tours all ended in Rome with the combined group demonstrating at the Olympic Gala following the 1960 Games.[24]

The total personnel of the delegations of the three tours in Europe numbered 85! To fill the numbers needed, applications to participate were taken from swimmers from all over the U.S. Even though swimmers had to pay their own transportation costs of approximately $1,100, there was no scarcity of applicants. Titled the American Water Follies Syn-

The 1958 tour group to the Far East included, left to right, swimmers Papsie Georgian, Sharon Gray, Janet Anthony, Jackie Vargas, Loretta Barrious, Rosalind Calcaterra, Mary Jane Gury and Sue Lawrence, and kneeling, left to right, divers Lou Vitucci and Tom Gompf.

chronized Swimming Tour, they were listed as a "good will" activity by the AAU Foreign Relations committee, with the caveat, "The members [of these tours] are not official representatives of the AAU."[25]

The fourth tour, to the Far East, was again under the auspices of the Armed Forces Professional Entertainment Branch, Special Services Division, and this group did officially represent AAU synchronized swimming.[26] Dineen once again managed the group of swimmers from the Athens Club and Shaw Park and divers Lou Vitucci and Tom Gompf. The group toured the Pacific area for five weeks giving exhibitions and clinics in Hawaii, Japan, Korea, Taiwan, Iwo Jima, Okinawa and Guam.[27]

The 1961 Pacific and Far East tour was the last State Department–sponsored tour. Re Calcaterra managed the six-week tour to Hawaii, Japan, Guam, Korea, the Philippines, Okinawa, and Sri Lanka. Exhibitions and clinics were given by swimmers from the San Francisco Merionettes, Athens Club and the Hollywood Athletic Club with divers Darlene Georgian, Ron Jaco and Bob Webster.[28]

## Sport Administration

Norma Olsen still chaired the national committee as this period began. The final year of her term saw her still busily pursuing media interest for the sport, and pushing growth both domestically and worldwide. The U.S.'s Olympic Synchronized Swimming Committee became increasingly busy with growing international activity and requests for help in overseas development, for which Norma Olsen's State Department tours of the world and Far East were largely responsible. Olsen continued to represent the U.S. on the FINA Technical Committee as honorable secretary.[29]

Joy Cushman, a former swimmer and coach of the Shamrock Hilton Corkettes, became, in 1958, the first ex-competitor to be elected chairman. In her first year, at the national championships held in her hometown, Houston, she succeeded in getting the team event televised live. She said the television was truly a marvelous experience, made possible largely because of an underwater mirror technique developed by the television station.[30] Synchro was indeed rising in the eyes of the networks.

As synchro grew, there were more members with stakes to protect and interests in having a hand in giving it direction. The attendance at the AAU annual conventions began to multiply. *Synchro-News* reported that more than 50 people had attended the national convention meetings in Chicago in December 1957, with 29 members of the national committee present.[31]

The sport was growing and changing rapidly and the number of rules also grew. The initial four pages of general rules in the swimming handbook expanded, by 1962, to 10 pages. The original six pages of stunts had multiplied to 29. New committees were established for judge training, judge rating, Junior Olympic, visual aids and publications and hall of fame, to address a variety of growing pains. Technical advances also were made. In Maryland, Dot Muhly reported using tapes for the music reproduction at their 1958 competition. She wrote, "Before the meet, three inch reels were taped and tagged with the contestant's name

and title of routine. In my opinion, this method can be more successful than using records."[32]

There had been no specific newsletter or magazine for synchronized swimming after *The Synchronized Swimmer*[33] changed to *The Aquatic Artist*[34] in 1955. Wilbur Luick of Santa Clara, in 1957, began publishing *Synchro-News*.[35] He published throughout 1958 and then publication was suspended indefinitely in 1959 after only one issue. It resumed again in 1960. Chairman Joy Cushman said, "The Committee was advised that Will Luick, Editor of Synchro-News, has made a diligent effort to save the publication.... The (national) committee voted enthusiastically to support Mr. Luick and expressed the hope that this magazine, which has been of such tremendous value to the sport, would continue to thrive."[36] Three issues were published in 1960, one in 1961, and then it was again suspended. Billie MacKellar and Jean Maeys attempted a rescue operation in 1962 but found the time commitments were too great and income minimal so they suspended operations after only two issues. However, there was still a great demand for printed information.

Gertrude Goss, Smith College, produced another book in 1957, *Stunts and Synchronized Swimming*,[37] with suggestions for using the various items with different levels of skill. Yates and Anderson's *Synchronized Swimming*[38] came out with a second edition in 1958 that added the newer stunts and illustrated a total of 87 with underwater and surface photography sequences. A revised edition of Spears' *Beginning Synchronized Swimming*[39] was also published in 1958. It was promoted as an aquatic guide for the instructor who wanted to start a synchronized swimming program in universities and colleges, Y's and civic organizations.

Two films were produced with the purpose of aiding instructors and coaches. In 1957, Don Canham in Ann Arbor, Michigan, produced *Champions on Film, Synchronized Swimming*,[40] with the assistance of Frances Jones, coach of the Lansing Sea Sprites. Beulah Gundling demonstrated 32 stunts from the simple tub through the more complex crane.

In 1958, Helen Cardan in Hollywood, assisted by Billie MacKellar, produced an educational classroom film on three reels titled *This Is Synchronized Swimming.*[41] Beginning, intermediate and advanced skills were demonstrated by Betty Vickers.

## Competitive Programs

Immediately after age group competition was initiated in 1956 as an association-level-only program, thoughts turned toward enabling competitions to be held with other associations. One step toward this was made in 1958 with the introduction of a national 12 and under solo event to be held with the Outdoor Senior National Championships.

The AAU had established a Junior Olympic age group program with a regional structure, dividing the nation into four wide-area competition regions. In 1959, synchro adopted the AAU's Junior Olympics as a separate age-based program. If the program had been fully implemented, it would have permitted three placewinners from each event at the association championships to compete at the higher-level Regional Junior Olympic Championships. Despite the enabling rule specifying that the competition "may be held in conjunction with the AAU Junior Olympic program," no enthusiasm was generated and participation lagged until the late '60s.

## Technical Rules

Simplification of entry preparation was made for 1959. In place of the tedious descriptions of all the stunts, standard or hybrid, and strokes in order of performance, competitors now were only required to show a "skeleton" routine, listing their compulsory stunts with number and difficulty, but with all other action between simply listed as "strokes" or "hybrids." In 1960, the burden was decreased still further as the requirement to submit five judging sheets was dropped.

In a very late pragmatic move, recognizing the limitations of recording systems then available, routine time limits were finally changed to five minutes in 1958, from the extant six minutes. At that time, there was no way to use the full six minutes without replaying part of a five-minute (12-inch) disc, or using very expensive 16-inch transcription discs (requiring special turntables). Perhaps the preemptive pressure of FINA's adopting the five-minute limit some six years earlier might have had some influence as well. The FINA limit of 20 seconds for deck work was also adopted.

And in a move to lower the weight of the execution award relative to the style award, the useful average difficulty of the five stunts used to calculate the routine difficulty was lowered from a maximum of 1.8 to 1.7. This lowered the maximum execution score correspondingly. This limit remained throughout this period.

A trial stunt competition was held with the 1957 Outdoor National Championships in Oakland. Three required stunts of 1.7 or less were drawn from a list of 20 possible and the competitors would choose three additional, higher difficulty stunts as optionals. The competition took two and one half hours for the 42 contestants. The consensus of judges and contestants was that they liked this very much. Norma Olsen said, "It brought about the most objective type of judging that had been found to date in synchronized swimming."[42] Rules chairman W.C. Royer began working on plans to present this plan for future competition at the coming national convention.

The competitive program then made its biggest change since the addition of the solo event when stunt competition was introduced in 1958. At all levels, competitors would be required individually to perform six standard stunts, one at a time, before a panel of five to seven judges. It became evident at its introduction to national competition, at the indoor national championships at Des Moines, that it was a much greater change than anticipated. That first AAU national stunt competition took more than seven hours to complete. Even worse than the child outgrowing its clothes before they are worn a second time, stunt competition had become an unmanageable teenager immediately upon birth.

For the competitive procedure, after random draw, the competitors were divided into "flights" of six. The first swimmer of the flight would perform all three of the compulsory stunts before the panel, one right after the other, waiting only for judge awards to be called between each stunt, and then move to the end of the flight. After each member of the flight had performed the compulsories in turn, they each returned to do all three optionals in the same manner. Then it was the turn for the next flight of six competitors. Only a single panel was used for the entire competition. The early draw competitors could be finished six to eight hours ahead of those drawing late positions. No matter what position was drawn, the three and three in a row made for a very grueling experience. Even more arduous was the task for the judges, attempting to maintain concentration over that period of time.

These problems became more crushing as the numbers of competitors increased making it almost impossible to get through the event in a single day. The 1961 nationals in San Francisco saw a marathon 11-hour stunt competition. This pushed the next convention into adopting a suggestion that national stunt competition be limited to competitors qualifying through preliminary routine competition. Thus, final stunt competition was limited in 1962 to the top 10 solos and duets and the top eight teams. That meant that preliminary routines would always precede stunt competition. AAU synchro was alone in adopting this approach. Other nations and FINA continued allowing all competitors into stunts (figures) so it always preceded all routines.

At the senior level, each competitor performed three "compulsory" and three "optional" stunts before a single panel of judges. Compulsories were drawn only half an hour before the competition from 17 different groups of three stunts each. No compulsory stunt exceeded 1.7 difficulty. Swimmers submitted with their entries a list of three optional stunts, chosen from three different stunt categories, of any difficulty of 1.8 or more. The initial set of 17 senior draw groups included just about every stunt in the book of 1.4 to 1.7 difficulty. In 1962, the number of draw groups was reduced to 10. Representative stunts were assigned to include

most basic actions. Different stunts were to be rotated onto the list every four years.

Accompanying the introduction of stunt competition was a total revision of the stunt groupings. Stunts had been listed alphabetically, with numbers assigned according to their position in alphabetical order. A "number group" was simply a group made up of a single base stunt and its derivatives with added twists or spins. Now, all stunts were placed into five "categories of stunts," based upon some common action of the stunts in each category. The categories were: I, ballet leg; II, dolphin, head first; III, dolphin, foot first; IV, somersault, front and back; and, V, diverse. This reclassification affected not only the selection of stunt competition optional stunts since it required choice from different categories, but also significantly changed the selection of required stunts for routines. A competitor who might have previously chosen several somersault or ballet leg action stunts could no longer do so.

A variety of additions and deletions to the stunt list took place in this period. In 1959, the 360-degree spin was added to those stunts that had previously been adorned by 180-degree spins. At the same time, though, the head first dolphin listings were greatly reduced by dropping those with twists while they were left attached to foot first dolphins. Subsequent growth added modifications or extensions of existing stunts (straight leg swordfish, elevator, sub-crane, dolpholina, swordalina, ballet leg roll), as well as novel actions, as in the subalina, subilarc, and gaviata, which used a rising rotation for the first time, and in the hightower, knight, and pirouette.

Actions that were not useful in either stunt competition or routines were gradually deleted. Gone by 1962 were: foot first surface dive, pendulum and reverse, periscope, flying porpoises, seal, shark figure 8, all the flying dolphins, including those with flips and twists; and all the tandem (partner) actions.

For lower classes of competition, Novice, Junior Association, Junior Olympic and Age Group, a single group of compulsories—kip, somersub and dolphin—was used, with just two optionals. In 1959, junior national competitors were added to the lower requirement group.

## Judging and Scoring

The first National Judges Training Program began in 1958 under Florence Anderson of Salt Lake City. *Synchro News* said, "Mrs. Anderson holds that the problems associated with the judging of AAU Synchronized Swimming present a never ending challenge." She said, "A judge should accept the responsibility of training and qualification as a contestant accepts the requirement that many hours of arduous practice and application will be necessary before championship skills can be achieved."[43]

Anderson corresponded and conferred with leaders throughout the country to derive workable judging standards. A new judges board, composed of Chairman Anderson and five regional chairs, implemented a training and rating program in 1960 with the requirement imposed that "judges for national competition shall be chosen only from an accredited list submitted yearly by the National Rating Board." Originally, judges had been simply appointed by the national chairman and later were chosen by vote of the national committee.

In 1960, routine judging sheets, listing the compulsory stunts were eliminated. Now judges could concentrate on everything seen in the routine and not be concerned about whether or not the five required stunts were performed. This put total responsibility on the referee and assistant to check for possible infractions.

The entire routine penalty structure was altered. Most of the prior five-point penalties, for failing to do the routine as listed, omitting a required stunt, (duet or team) failing to do a required stunt simultaneously, or failing to start or finish with the music, became one-point penalties. Exceeding the deck time joined exceeding the routine limit as a two-point penalty. The omission of one of the listed five stunts drew a more serious additional penalty, though. The routine degree of difficulty would be recomputed by totaling the difficul-

ties for the four remaining stunts and dividing by five.

A new section appeared for stunt competition penalties, dealing with balks or false starts (reducing judge awards by one-third), authorizing a second attempt for a failed stunt if circumstances warranted it, or deducting a point if the swimmer "moves out of the designated area" during performance.

Certain routine judging elements started an oscillating migration in 1958 as they moved from one award category to the other and back again. Synchronization moved from execution to style. Thus, execution became solely "the performance of stunts and strokes and parts thereof from the standpoint of perfection." Style was defined as "the synchronization of the swimmers, one with the other and also with the accompaniment; the construction of the routine; the interpretation of the accompaniment by the utilization of stunts and strokes to form a flowing pattern; the appropriateness and interpretiveness of the costuming; the manner of presentation, spectator appeal and originality."[44]

Second thoughts, after only a year, moved synchronization back under execution in 1959, where it remained for the next two years. Then in 1961, it was moved back to style where it stayed until many years later, when the need for compatibility with FINA forced yet another move.

Theme was specified as a judging factor, for the first time, in 1959. Even though a routine title had been required on all routine sheets since 1949, there were no admonishments to judges that it should be a specific consideration. Now, the style award was defined to include, "construction of the routine, interpretation of the accompaniment and *theme* [italics added] of the routine by the utilization of stunts and strokes to form a flowing pattern...."[45] Actually, this change was probably simply bowing to the long-standing *de facto* influence of theme. There was no doubt that the interpretation of a theme, suggested by the title, had been a major factor not only for the competitors, but for the judges as well.

Attempts to define standards of performance for the stunts began in 1959. A new part of the description of stunts section described tuck, forward pike and backward pike positions as they should appear during the execution of a stunt using them. Proper starting positions, front and back layouts, were described for the first time. Basic principles of design and control were listed. Traveling was dealt with too, specifying that stunts were to be done in a relatively stationary position unless otherwise called for.

Finally, at the convention of 1962, the wording, "On forward moving stunts it is optional whether or not one stroke is used in assuming the layout position," was deleted. But, in spite of having specific descriptions of the "starting positions" as layouts, a number of stunts, catalina, flamingo and crane, were described as starting from an extended ballet leg position, leaving it optional on the action used to gain that position.

## Development Around the Country

During this period, many areas of the country failed to report activity other than water ballet classes or water shows. In others, the only evidence of involvement found was in meet results, such as the Montgomery (Alabama) Montrose Loreleis and the University of Tennessee.

The Missouri Valley Association held its first indoor meet in Topeka in 1957 with competitors from the Kansas City Sea Sprites, Topeka Synchronettes, Leawood Country Club, Leavenworth Aquadettes, Kansas City YWCA Aquabelles, and Springfield Swim Club. Millicent Heath, who had started programs in Southern California and then Oregon, moved to Kansas. In 1958 she held a series of clinics and workshops in Wichita, Salina, Kansas City and Springfield. The clinic in Wichita was the first of its kind for the area.

In Ohio, the Berea Aquateens succeeded in winning the junior national team title. Karen Luedke (Eakin) "remembers that all the team members were cheerleaders in high school, so it was natural to do a routine titled 'The Cheerleaders,' with red and blue beanies on our heads.[46] Five clubs, the Dayton Aquanymphs, Lima Aquabelles, Lima Cygnets, Glass City Aquatic Club of Toledo, and the Coralina Club of Columbus, competed in the 1958 Ohio championships. By the next year, additions to the club list included the Jewish Center Nereides of Columbus, the Coshocton and Scioto Country Club teams and Youngstown's Spray Club.[47]

The Michigan and Iowa associations combined to host the 1958 Indoor Senior National Championships in Des Moines' new $3 million North High School.[48] Papsie Georgian of Oakland's Athens Club won the special 12 and under competition held in conjunction with the outdoor championships in Houston.[49]

Connecticut was busy with competitions, hosting the 1958 Junior National Indoor Solo Championships in New Britain,[50] a senior solo and duet competition in May and then the first outdoor meet in Hartford in July. The *Hartford Times* reported stiff competition between the 24 competitors in solo and duet. Storr's Club and Newington Recreation Department also began competing in this period.[51] The Bristol Synchronettes participated in Yale's Annual Water Carnival for the fourth consecutive year in 1958.[52] In New York, the Coquins of Glens Falls were doing workshops and giving demonstrations in 1958 and competing whenever possible. They reported helping new groups get underway at New Hartford, Utica and Albany. The Coquins won both duet and team in the first state championships.[53]

The Adirondack Association hosted the Outdoor Junior National Team Championships in 1958. The same year, the New York State Indoor Championships brought entries from Rochester, Glens Falls, Niagara Falls, Delmar Aquatic Club, Albany Optimettes and the Buffalo Swimkins.[54] Other New York clubs appearing in meet results were the Rome Aqua-Galas, Mount Hope Aquamaids, and Lockport, Rochester and Orchard Park clubs. Niagara Falls Recreation Department, Kenmore-Tonawanda Recreation Department, Franklin Aquatic Club of Rochester, the Aquarora Club, and the Buffalo Swimkins. The Swimkins competed in the 1958 Niagara Association Championships. Team winners included Mary Ellen Witt (Wiegand), who later became the club's coach.

Libby Felton, Mechanicsburg, Pennsylvania, reported in 1959 that her club, the Catalinas, had just secured the sponsorship of the Harrisburg YMCA. She noted that because there were few indoor pools in the area and the demand for pool time was so great, they found it difficult to further their skills. "In spite of the handicaps, we push on," she said.[55]

Out West, the Naiads at Arizona State University at Tempe staged a water carnival in 1958 soon after they formed.[56] That year, junior and senior competitions were held in Arizona with competitors from Perry Pool, Dick Smith Swim Gym, and Nelson's Pool.[57] Nearby, New Mexico synchro began as water ballet in 1960 at the Albuquerque City Pool and at the YMCA. The first competitive event was held in 1964 with Barbara Harrell and Charlotte Piper, University of New Mexico, instrumental in its development there.[58]

In California, the Athens Club team, on its way to nationals in Houston, stopped in Long Beach to defend its Far Western title, then went inland to present a water show in Riverside where former teammate Dawn Bean was planning to start a synchro team. The *Riverside Daily Press* publicized the free show with a large picture and article, "Championship Team Will Exhibit Talents."[59] Subsequent tryouts for the new team brought more than 50 swimmers from which the Riverside Aquette team was formed. Bill Royer, chairman for the Southern Pacific Association, reported holding the first age group competition. He said, "Fifty-six entrants indicate the potential for this type of meet ... the success of the event has prompted the scheduling of two more age group meets for 1959."[60]

In 1958, Revajean Porter coached the Tacoma Trim Trouts, Floreine Harrington organized the Bremerton Blue Fins and Frances McLean reported on the University of Washington's Silver Fish Club and four new synchro programs at the Seattle YWCA. Cora Mae Kintz, from the University of Washington's Silver Fish Club, started a new club at the Washington Athletic Club in 1960 where the first national coach for the U.S., Charlotte Jennings (Davis), began her synchro career.[61] Helen Smith said of Kintz, "except for her, synchro would not have happened in Seattle."[62]

Chelys Hester, chairman of the Nebraska Association, said, "I became involved in the sport in 1960 when a pool was put in at our university. I told the President that I would like to see Synchronized Swimming added to the Physical Education program, beginning with water shows. And we did that."[63] And it was masters synchronized swimming that made the news in Colorado in 1959. The Lakewood Synchronettes were featured in the *Rocky Mountain Sportsman*. Stan Zamonski wrote, "Swimming is more than just wading in a pool for a group of pretty housewives in Lakewood.... The Synchronettes are unique in the area, their club is composed entirely of housewives with children ranging between the ages of two and sixteen. They were first organized in 1956 as an activity of the YWCA.... Unlike most sporting activities, the Synchronettes make swimming an all year affair."[64]

In the South, the Florida Association held a state championship in 1958 with clubs from Ft. Lauderdale, Orlando, St. Petersburg, Redington Beach, and Clearwater participating. St. Petersburg hosted the 1958 Junior National Outdoor Solo. The Florida Gold Coast Association began with recreational programs but by 1960 had started a competitive program. Diving coach Bill Parks passed information on to Si Forman of North Miami. There were three clubs in the association that year, Pompano, North Miami and Margate. The Dade County Blue Sharkette team was started by Madge Fiddy Noble in 1961. Madge had taken a crash course from Billie MacKellar, but she soon moved to Cuba and started a team there.[65]

Only two clubs participated in the 1958 Oklahoma Junior Championships, Tulsa's Aqua-Y-ettes and Bartlesville, but there was progress through the school systems. An Oklahoma high school and collegiate state championship was reported in 1962. More than 100 swimmers competed from high schools in Capital City, Oklahoma City, and Tulsa. College competitors were Northwestern State at Natchitoches, Oklahoma State University at

Stillwater, Northeastern State College at Tahle-quah and the University of Oklahoma at Nor-man.[66]

The existing Texas clubs continued to grow. Dallas' Catalina Club competed in the 1957 Junior Nationals and was encouraged to seek more honors. The Shamrock Hilton Cor-kettes won the 1958 Southwestern champi-onships. The Catalina Club of Dallas and the Crystal Athletic Club of Houston also com-peted. Margaret Swan (Forbes) formed her own club in 1962, the Cygnets of San Antonio.[67] The club rose to finalist positions in all events in national competitions in the late '60s and '70s.

## Awards and Honors

The Helms Athletic Foundation,[68] which had given awards to outstanding athletes in many amateur sports since the mid–'30s offered, in 1958, to establish two awards for synchronized swimming.[69] An ad hoc commit-tee was appointed to set guidelines and select nominees for the athlete and contributor awards. Synchro's recommendations were sub-mitted to the Helms Athlete Sports Board for approval.

The standard established for athlete in-clusion was four solo titles or a combination of 10 duet and team titles. Also considered were the efforts made toward helping the sport grow and develop. In 1961, the first athlete award winners were June Taylor (Gregory) and Joan Pawson (Nelson). Taylor, the first national solo champion, won the title four times and she had given countless demonstrations throughout the country with her coach, Billie MacKellar (Hall of Fame contributor in 1962), as they worked to promote the sport. Pawson won 11 duet and

team titles. She took over the coaching of the Athens team in 1956, which led them to four more years of national titles including the demonstrations at the 1960 Olympic Games and the team representing the U.S. at the Pan American Games in Brazil. In 1962, the Athens Athletic Club Team of 1958 that had demon-strated at the Melbourne Olympics was hon-ored into the Hall of Fame.

The first Hall of Fame awards, in 1959, went to synchro's two pioneer contributors, Katharine Curtis and Annette Kellerman. Kellerman's role in performing in turn-of-the-century swimming exhibitions and in films in swimming suits that allowed women to truly swim instead of bathe, opened the door for women in all aquatic activities. Curtis is cred-ited with the development of the sport of syn-chronized swimming. Curtis was working for Uncle Sam in Europe in 1958 when notified of her selection. She wrote, "I am director of Travel during leave time for the U.S. Army in Europe. It will be 1962 before I return to the U.S.A., but I am looking forward to the time when I can once more see the AAU Synchro Competitions. The action of 'sainting me' be-fore I am really dead is touching and flattering. Thanks to you all."[70]

In 1958, Roz Calcaterra, national duet champion from Shaw Park, St. Louis, was the first synchronized swimmer nominated for the Sullivan Award. Gillian Hall, of the Bristol, Connecticut, Synchronettes, was named na-tional Deaf Athlete of 1959 for her achieve-ments in synchronized swimming. She won the junior outdoor solo title in 1957 and went on to win the junior outdoor duet in 1959 with partner Dale Benson. She said she was able to participate in the sport by sensing the vibra-tions of the music underwater.

# 6

## *Change, Change and Still More Change: 1963–68*

A 21-year-old person is usually welcomed to maturity, at least in official terms. In its 21st year of official existence, synchro seemed much more like a gawky preteen, still looking for ways to be accepted and loved while trying to come to terms with the world around it.

All the growth and adaptation of the last decade seemed only a prelude to more of the same in this new period, sometimes seeming, unfortunately, to be changing only for the sake of change. The legislative process was opened wide with committee meetings available to everyone interested. Everyone, it seemed, had an idea and everyone else was willing to try it. So it would be 'tried, then adjusted' in some manner the next year or so— then possibly returning to the original after another year of trial. The age group age determinant mechanism jumped back and forth; maximum difficulty allowed for routines fluctuated; synchronization oscillated between execution and style.

For judging, standards for a national judge rating were established; different methods for selecting judges for national events were tested and a code of ethics entered the picture. The good news was that more people were involving themselves, bringing more thought and work to improving synchro. Some of the international competition picture was murky, at least for the Pan American Games. After being omitted from the Pan American Games in 1959 for too few entries, synchro was restored for 1963 but deleted again for 1967. All this was due to the requirement that five nations enter in order to include it on the program. It would be restored as more ASUA (Amateur Swim Union of the Americas) federations developed programs. Then only the same few would turn up when staging time arrived. It was an unsettled period for ASUA synchro.

But, throughout the world, synchro was growing at an accelerated pace. U.S.–led international tours and Olympic demonstrations brought much attention and not only were programs being developed, but multinational competitions also came into being. Nine countries participated in the first Criterium de Europe held in 1967. This competition was the forerunner to the now familiar European Championships.

In an attempt to promote interest in women's sports, the AAU, in 1964, supported a beauty contest of sorts. Registered competitive athletes submitted photos from which an AAU panel would select the winners. Clubs around the country had been urged to send nominees with photos and athletic bios to the AAU for the contest. Synchro's Patty Willard was named Miss AAU Synchronized Swimming for 1964.[1]

But to the age-old argument whether synchronized swimming was show or sport, the

81

myth that synchronized swimmers just float around looking beautiful, the San Francisco Merionettes took on the challenge of swimming the Golden Gate in 1963. The strait, nearly two miles wide, is known for treacherous currents and cold water, usually about 50 degrees to 54 degrees Fahrenheit. The *San Francisco Chronicle* reported after the event, "All 23 girls who took part completed the event with Margo McGrath, a skinny 13 year old finishing in a time of 34 minutes, 35 seconds." Later that same year, the Official Golden Gate Swim was won by Joe Taylor in a time of 44 minutes and 50 seconds.[2] The same McGrath went on to win all four senior national titles in 1966.

## *The National Championships 1963–68*

The atmosphere was charged at the indoor championships of 1963. It was just one month before the Pan American Games in Sao Paulo, Brazil, and only a few months after the December trials for the Games where upset representatives had qualified due to the influence of FINA stunt scoring.[3] Would the defending national champions retain their titles in the face of those trial reversals? Could sentiment for showing the Games' representatives as unequivocally the U.S.A.'s strongest affect the contest?

In the solo, Roberta Armstrong, the prime Pan American Games solo qualifier, did surpass the 1962 champion, Barbara Burke, who was the second qualifier. In team and duet, though, the Merionettes retained their national titles, putting the Pan American representatives into the runners-up positions.[4] The Merionettes trampled the Athens team by four points under U.S. rules, but it made no difference for the Games.

The San Francisco Merionettes almost totally ruled the decade of the '60s. Not only did they continue the team and duet monopoly started in 1961, they added solo crowns from 1965 to 1968 as well. Oddly, it would turn out that their reign would end and their invincibility disintegrate just as they equaled the

Athens Club record of 17 national championship titles. Their accumulation of duet and solo championships ultimately far exceeded those of any before as they amassed an amazing total of 47 senior national titles.

In the team event, following their easy win in the 1963 Indoor meet, the San Francisco Merionettes repeated with an overwhelming 13-point victory at the 1963 Outdoor Championships. With an even greater margin, 15 points, they again successfully defended their indoor title at the 1964 championships, also moving their "B" team into the third-place spot. That summer, Merionette teams took both first and second places. Marion Kane had become renowned for routines with innovative choreography, superb showmanship and a masterful blending of music and movement.

Not only did the Merionettes maintain their powerful grip on the team crown in the 1965 Indoor Championships in winning their ninth straight crown, they won in such a manner that the USOC's *Amateur Athlete* (May 1965) would report, "For the second time in the history of the sport, one club won all the titles. The San Francisco Merionettes won with their 'March of Triumph' [routine]." The article continued, "but one of the most memorable team entries was the bright and bouncy second place 'Keystone Kops' entry of the Riverside Aquettes coached by ex–Athens genius Dawn Bean. Sister Joan Nelson, whose name is also legendary synchro-wise, wrote another medal winner, the third place 'Gypsy Violins' from the Athens Club."[5] Not mentioned in this article was the team that had rapidly risen to take fourth in that event, the Howell Swim Club, coached by Jay Howell, the first team from the Walnut Creek area to enter the national competitions.

The 1965 Outdoor meet at Lorraine, Ohio, was the biggest to date, with 68 solos, 47 duets, 24 teams and 192 competitors. The Merionette exploits were repeated there, all three titles won for a second time. At this meet, though, the Howell Swim Club replaced Athens in third. The Merionette story was repeated twice more in 1966 as they easily won in both the indoor and outdoor meets. The Howell team, though, had moved into second at both meets and the

The San Francisco Merionettes dominated the sport in the '60s, winning 17 total team titles. This is the 1967 All American team: back, left to right, Andrea Welles, Margo McGrath, Carol Redmond, Sharon Lawson, Norma Fish, and front, left to right, Barbara Trantina, Kathy McBride and Kathy Bryant.

Santa Clara Aquamaids, only two years old, made themselves known by displacing the Riverside Aquettes for third in the summer meet.

The Merionettes dominated the team event again in both 1967 championships. Reporting on their Russian routine, *Synchro-Info* marveled, "They dance, they kick, they cartwheel into the water and they introduced some new skills — a hybrid open spin that *stopped* at the ankles and *pressed up again* for another open spin; a Heron was *stopped at the height, held*, and then *arched over* for a foot first return."[6] Support scull had come into being. Innovative moves of this kind paved the way for a whole new look in the sport.

The upstart Santa Clara team was threatening, though. Now in second place positions, they were achieving scores that might have assured victories in the past. By 1966, just two years after their founding, the Santa Clara Aquamaids had already gained strength by acquiring skilled transfers from other established clubs. It was further fortified for 1968 with three strong swimmers from the Howell Swim Club. Aquamaids' coach Kay Vilen, taking full advantage of the new strength, was not to be denied! At the 1968 Indoor Championships, their strong, one-point advantage in stunt average helped them to gain a lead in the routine final, as well. Santa Clara had arrived at the top. Pam Albin, Kathy Craig, Nancy Hines, Diane Howell, Carol Reynolds, Melinda Sellers, and Kim and Kris Welshons were the swimmers savoring that first triumph.[7]

At the outdoor meet the routine scores were tied, but Santa Clara's 0.57-point stunt edge pushed them into a 128.82 to 128.25 overall victory again over their San Francisco rivals. Down in a distant third place was another Merionette team with 107.14. Then came another Santa Clara team. This would be the beginning of six years of fierce, vacillating competition for the top spot between the two clubs. However, the circumstances of Santa Clara's winning unmistakably changed the direction of club growth. This first victorious Santa Clara team was unusual in that it did not include a single swimmer who had started synchronized swimming at Santa Clara; all eight were transfers. Three had just moved from the Howell Swim Club, two were former Athens Club swimmers, one was from the Riverside Aquettes, one came from the Columbus Coralinas and one was from the University Club of Hollywood.

A Midwestern coach, in *Synchro-Info*'s "Athlete's Corner" questioned, "Is it fair for a team to recruit all the top swimmers, from all over, and put them on a team to win a championship? What will the sport come to? Is there a Code of Ethics that can be drawn up to stop this recruiting?"[8] But soon, "recruiting" was hardly the word; there were young swimmers from all over tripping over each other in their

Santa Clara wins its first national team title. At left, from the top down, are Kathy Craig, Kris Welshons, Nancy Hines, Pam Albin. At right, from the top down, are Diane Howell, Melinda Sellers, Kim Welshons, Carol Reynolds (photograph by Lee Pillsbury).

mad scrambles to work with the entourage of the top coaches in California's Bay area.

The duet championships, for a while, became even more a Merionette private domain than the teams. In 1963, Judy Wejak and Claire Vida won both indoor and outdoor titles with other Merionettes winning both second places. Margaret Durbrow and Patty Willard took over the top spot in 1964 with their San Francisco teammates also earning a second at the indoor meet and both second and third at the outdoor competition. Pam Morris paired with Willard to win in 1965 with seconds to the Merionettes. Teammates Margo McGrath and Carol Redmond moved to the top in 1966 and 1967, but the other place medals began going regularly to other clubs. In 1968, the duet title changed at the same time as the team. Santa Clara Aquamaids Kim Welshons and Nancy Hines won both the indoor and outdoor titles, beating McGrath who was now swimming with Kathy Bryant. The battlegrounds were cleared for years of fierce contention for this title in the years to come.

In the solo championships, following her Pan American trials victory in late 1962, Roberta Armstrong, Paso Robles, won every solo in sight — both indoor and outdoor U.S. solo titles in 1963 and the 1963 Pan American Games solo crown as well. Armstrong was the first to perfect the rapid spinning action. Before her techniques were analyzed and taught, spins tended to be "hit or miss" gambles for any athlete attempting them. Armstrong won her titles again in 1964.

In 1965, the Merionettes, winners of all the duet and team titles since 1961, took over the solo crown as well. Pam Morris not only won both indoor and outdoor titles, but she was the first swimmer to win all three routine titles (solo, duet and team) in the same year. She made spectacular use of the rocket action in her routine. Then Margo McGrath, swimming appropriately to "I Left My Heart in San Francisco," did the same in 1966 but added the stunts title as well. Her routine included the first-seen use of the eggbeater kick with arm stroking. *Synchro-Info* praised her performance: "The amazing performance of Margo McGrath, was not just in capturing all the ti-

Pam Morris (left) and Patty Willard, San Francisco Merionettes, won duet titles in 1965–66. Morris became the first swimmer to win all three events in one year and Willard became Miss AAU Synchronized Swimming in a special contest the AAU held to increase interest in women's athletics.

tles (the first time anyone has won all four), but in the manner in which she accomplished this. Though we have all read 'seemingly effortless' in the rules, her solo performance brought real meaning to those words."[9]

McGrath repeated her titles in 1967, but not as easily. She had to rely on the lead she carried from the stunt competition into the routine competition. Teammate and duet partner Carol Redmond, using a spectacular un-

derwater rocket, was on top in the routine portion of the score with her stirring "Joan of Arc." *Synchro-Info* noted how effective her interpretation of the theme had been (theme was dropped from rules the following year), and also pointed out, "The rocket hybrid actually rose above waist level on the thrust."[10]

McGrath successfully defended her indoor title in 1968, but at the outdoor meet Kim Welshons, of Santa Clara, captured the solo title as well as winning the stunt competition to complete the Aquamaids' takeover of all the events.

## International Developments

This period started in 1963 on an invigorating high point with the return of synchro to the Pan American Games program in Sao Paulo, Brazil. But the disappointing four-country participation there led to another rejection by ASUA for synchro as a medal sport for the 1967 Pan Am Games.

The competition for places on the podium at the 1963 Pan Am Games in Sao Paulo was almost anticlimactic after the excitement of the upsets at the Trials and the reversals of those results at the indoor national championships that had immediately preceded the Games. Not only did the U.S.A. win all the gold medals, they also took second places in solo and duet. Two entries from each country were still allowed. Roberta Armstrong won the solo and Barbara Burke and Joanne Schaak won the duet. The U.S.A. team won by more than 10 points over Mexico's team, which led Brazil by more than 15 points. Canada had sent only two swimmers, making up a single duet and two solo competitors. Synchro was popular on television, too. National chairman Joy Cushman, who had accompanied the group in Brazil, reported how satisfied the ABC producer had been with the synchro television coverage, mentioning that he had told her they had more than 100 letters complimenting them on the presentation.[11]

Although synchro had been popular in Brazil in 1963, it was deleted from the 1967 competitive program in Winnipeg due to the

Carol Redmond (left) and Margo McGrath won four duet titles in 1966 and 1967. They spent almost a year teaching and touring in Europe in 1967–68.

Santa Clara's first solo title went to Kim Welshons at the outdoor championship of 1968. She successfully won both solo titles in 1969 (photograph by Lee Pillsbury).

poor participation in the previous Pan Ams. Jae Howell, Danville, California, suggested in *Synchro-Info*, "It is evident that Synchro will have to be sold first to the officials in authority in the AAU and in other areas of the U.S. before we can expect other countries to buy it. I feel everyone in this sport should do something constructive to further this purpose."[12] She set the machinery to work by arranging for an exhibition at the next AAU convention with swimmers Kathy Craig, Gail Gardner (Emery), Kathy Knibbe and Debbie Howell.

Great efforts were exerted by Olympic International chairman Joy Cushman, AAU officials, and Canadian synchro committees to obtain a change in the decision to exclude synchro from the Games in Winnipeg, but to no avail. An exhibition was allowed in the Games-ending gala. Both Canadian and U.S.A. (San Francisco Merionettes and Hollywood Athletic Club) swimmers participated. Four thousand spectators saw the show with 2,000 more turned away at the gate. In 1969, Harry Hainsworth, AAU aquatics administrator, advised, "As you are probably aware, the Pan American top brass has approved synchro for the 1971 Pan-Am Games in Cali and it is now the responsibility of all of us to stimulate national participation by countries other than the U.S. and Canada. We believe Mexico is a prospect as well as Brazil, but it is important that we pressure them into taking part."[13]

In 1965, U.S.A. competitors began crossing the northern border again for competitions and succeeded in winning open titles in the 1965, 1966, and 1967 Canadian nationals. Marion Kane reported in 1966, "The Canadians have adopted the U.S. performances on the kip, dolpholina, swordfish, knight, flamingo, porpoise and catalina. However, they

These are the winners of the gold medals in the team event in the Pan American Games of 1963. From the Athens Club swimmers are, from left to right, Marcia Blixt, Judy McFadden, Marian Whitner, Linda McFadden, Kim Welshons, Margie Lawrence and Papsie Georgian (photograph by Leonard Stallcup).

are proud of our national champions, I don't want to take away from the progress synchronized swimming has made around the world. The ability is there and I am sure that seeing the American swimmers perform, it will not take these countries the time it has taken us to obtain the perfection of skills and swimming."[17]

Once again, synchronized swimming was demonstrated at the Olympic Games, in 1964 in Tokyo and 1968 in Mexico City. In 1964, the group included swimmers from the Lansing Sea Sprites, Shaw Park and New York's Bronx Community College. In 1968, Eva Govezensky (Mexico) and Kim Welshons (U.S.A.) demonstrated their solos during breaks in the speed swimming events and the Santa Clara Aquamaids demonstrated a team number at the Olympic Gala. Synchro backers were still looking for an admission into the Olympic program, but Dr. Harold Henning, FINA president, offered a discouraging report in 1965, saying, "Members in the FINA were against the proposal for [including synchro in] the World Championships as well as for the Olympic Games and added that such championships were frowned upon by the IOC and that it would affect FINA's income from TV money."[18]

The U.S. touring program continued, but with no U.S. government funding for tours after 1961, Norma Olsen took matters in hand and arranged for a self-funded international tour in 1964. This time it included a mix of swimmers from Michigan, Missouri and New York. Fran Jones, of the Lansing Sea Sprites, and Joyce Lindeman, of the University of Michigan, led the group. Clinics and demonstrations were given in 15 countries in Europe and Asia before the final stop at the Olympic Games in Tokyo, Japan. Of this tour, George Rackham, president of Great Britain's Swim Association,

prefer to thrust from the compact pike in the back pike barracuda without sculling toward the surface."[14] Of the competition, Don Kane said, "I was impressed with the ability of their soloists to cover the pool. I also noticed that they did not put as much emphasis on control as we do. However, the conduct of the meet impressed me; every judge dressed in white ... [and] absolutely no one was allowed on pool deck while the competition was in progress."[15]

Two multinational events in 1967 brought focus to the international scene. The United States held its first truly multinational meet in 1967 when the San Francisco Merionettes hosted the Golden Gate Invitational Solo Championship. U.S.A. solo champion Margo McGrath was the winner, followed by Cinde Stevens of Canada and Carrie Berenson of the Netherlands. Seven nations participated.[16] And the Criterium de Europe, was held in 1967 in Amsterdam. The San Francisco Merionettes won all the titles. Carol Redmond's solo, given two awards of 10, left the audience crying, "More, more, more." She also scored a synchro first, a 10 in stunts! Joy Cushman, accompanying the group said, "Synchronized swimming on the international level is strong. While we

wrote, "In 1964, the USA team on their way to Tokyo demonstrated to a capacity crowd at the Crystal Palace pool.... In 1965 the Amateur Swim Association of Britain was formed.... In 1967, the tour of the fabulous San Francisco Merionettes showed such ease and a degree of execution hitherto thought impossible."[19]

In a turnabout tour, the Japanese national champions from the Hamadera Club in Tokyo came to the United States in 1966 for a month of visiting U.S. synchro clubs. Accompanied by doctors Saburo Kitamura and Kiyohiko Takahashi, they competed and won seventh-place finalist positions in the outdoor national championships and then toured the country, training with clubs in San Francisco, Danville, Riverside, Corpus Christi, San Antonio, St. Louis, Chicago, Lansing, Buffalo-Tonawanda, New York City and Washington D.C. Of their trip, Dr. Kitamura wrote, "It makes me happy to inform you that the number of applicants for a district championship in Japan has tripled due to the stimulation and zeal crystallized from the Japanese-American Good Will competition and tour held bi-annually."[20] The Japanese-American exchange was resumed in 1968 with Santa Clara traveling to Japan for exhibitions and clinics. They competed in and won the All-Japan Championship that year.

## Sport Administration

In 1963, Joy Cushman remained chairman of the national committee. She also headed its Olympic international committee. During this final year of her term, she presided over fundraising efforts to send synchro swimmers to the Pan American Games in Sao Paulo, Brazil, and, for the first time, ABC televised synchro's national championships on national network television — *live*! Cushman accomplished this television miracle in time for the national championships held in her home town of Houston.[21] ABC, for the next three years, covered both the indoor and outdoor national championships on its *Wide World of Sports* program. Unfortunately, the broadcasts were discontinued after three years. ABC cited lack of national interest and noted that our outdoor

championship was really just a "live re-run" of the indoor competition.

In a blistering critique of those who wrote to ABC about dropping synchro, Patsy Bauch, a coach in Texas, wrote, "I have had my fill of hearing criticism of ABC's failure to film our wonderful sport of synchronized swimming. Until the world of synchronized swimming realizes that it is a sport and conducts itself as such, it will not be recognized as such, regardless of how much work and training is involved. I find nothing athletic about having a theme, and worse, having to interpret that theme with sometimes outlandish makeup and costumes. Return the feathers to Mr. Ziegfeld and let the Barrymores take bows for 'dramatic interpretation.' As it now stands, I simply cannot see synchro in the Olympics when we insist on rehashing *Carmen*, *Cinderella*, and *World War II*."[22]

Teresa Andersen was elected in the 1963 convention to replace Cushman and served through 1966. She had long been active in synchro administration and was the coach of the KRNT team in Des Moines, Iowa. During her administration important changes were made in the conduct of the national committee and its subcommittee meetings. Synchro had been tightly controlled by a small group of chairman-appointed committee leaders whose meetings were open only to their appointed committee members. Even though progress had been made with this benign dictatorship approach, more and more synchro enthusiasts resented lacking a voice in the decision-making process. Their exasperation reached a climax at the 1963 convention when many coaches sat outside a closed hotel room for more than five hours before the rules committee emerged with word of changes that had been made. The ensuing pressure they put on the AAU resulted in opening all meetings in 1964 to anyone interested.

Anderson was replaced by Donald T. Kane, San Francisco, who served from 1967 through 1968. He made a striking move when he created an athletes' representative position on the national committee and appointed Pam Morris to that position. Morris was the first active athlete to sit on any AAU governing committee. In 1968, Gene Ahlf suggested that the athletes should elect their own representative rather than having one appointed. Rather critical of the status quo, Ahlf said, "Although I feel Pam Morris got little or no encouragement at the National Committee meetings, I feel it is high time these girls had a voice in what should be their sport, run with their interests in mind."[23]

To this point, synchro still had no national budget. Only its shares of AAU registration fees and meet sanction fees provided funds for any essential equipment, supplies, and mailing. Volunteers continued to perform all functions with whatever resources their local AAU might grant and anything they could dig up themselves. When it became necessary to find a way to send athletes to the Pan American Games in Brazil, synchro's Olympic international committee (OIC) attempted to help through selling pins and decals. This effort raised $1,700. In addition, the "hat" was passed for donations at all junior and senior national meets to help send athletes to participate in the Pan American Games and the growing number of European competitions.

Increasing numbers of entries impacted meet schedules more and more and mechanisms for speeding up the meets were sought. Music checks for turntable speed still occupied an undesirable amount of time between routines. An attempt had been made to limit the music test time to 30 seconds, but there were too many objections. Most speed checks were not very long, but a few competitors insisted on listening to the full record for timing, and even a repeat if the overall time was off from what they wanted. Sound manager Will Luick cut some of that time waste by conducting those checks on a monitor as scores for the just-finished competitor were flashed and announced. Then, Ross Bean tried using a dual sound system, one turntable to play the active competitor's music over the public address while the next competitor would check her music through earphones to the other turntable. When one routine ended, a simple switch exchanged the turntable roles and the speed-checked recording became immediately ready to play over the PA with no delay at all.[24]

Dot Muhly, Maryland, had touted the advantages of magnetic tapes over cut discs as early as 1958.[25] In 1965, Barbara Harrell of New Mexico brought tapes to that year's national championships and asked for official provisions for using audio tape recordings. Roberta Swartz of Mentor, Ohio, in a note to *Synchro-Info*, suggested that tapes should be allowed for accompaniments. She pointed out, "The cost of making a record is enough to discourage many swimmers. Tapes do not get scratched or broken and can be used for practice and performance. I hope the rules will be changed to allow this as an option."[26] Her request was not implemented, though, because the only tape decks of that time were bulky, awkward-to-load, reel-to-reel decks, impractical for general use. Simple, fast-loading cassette decks were still in the future.

In a sport as young and complex as synchro, technical and interpretive change and advance came at such a furious pace that it was difficult for most participants to keep abreast of the latest ideas and trends. To help disseminate the knowledge of the few to the many, a national clinic program to be held at the annual national convention was proposed. It became a reality in 1965 with the first clinic conducted for coaches and judges, held in Washington, D.C.[27] These educational seminars were the forerunners of a biennial feature of the convention schedule.

Written material was still in demand and more books were published. In 1963, Beulah Gundling produced *Exploring Aquatic Art*,[28] which *Synchro-Info* characterized as "an encyclopedic reference book with useful information despite much excess material."[29] Dorothy Donnelly's *Synchronized Swimming Instruction Book*,[30] printed by the Girls Clubs of America, was aimed at helping the beginning teacher. In 1965, Betty Vickers produced *Teaching Synchronized Swimming*,[31] also aimed at basic teaching. Its wealth of illustrations made it the best available for current techniques of that time. Betty Spears added another book in 1965, *Fundamentals of Synchronized Swimming*.[32] It too was listed as "Primarily for the beginning teacher, but current coaches found a number of conflicts with present techniques and ideas."

Overseas, George Rackham, president of the Great Britain Swimming Association, produced in 1968 *Synchronized Swimming*.[33] Its review cited it as having the best analysis of applying physical principles (hydrostatics, buoyancy, balance, force) to synchro, and the best analyses of propulsion and sculling techniques.

During this period, synchronized swimming began to publish its own series of manuals and guides to aid those in the sport. Marion Kane authored the first *Judges Training Guide* in 1964.[34] It was the first printed material defining steps for training and testing new judges. The same year, Kane wrote the first *Meet Managers Guide* to instruct meet managers on what should be done in hosting an AAU meet.[35] Don Kane produced the *Press Relations Guide* in 1966 to guide local clubs in the kind of information needed and manner of submission to the press,[36] and in 1968, Kane produced the *Guide to the Administration of Synchronized Swimming*.[37] This was the first outline showing the structure of organization of the national committee and a guide as to what was expected of national chairs and members.

*Synchro-Info*, edited by Dawn Bean, began filling the gap left by the demise of *Synchro-News*. It published its first issue in February 1963. The rulebook bibliography assessment was, "an excellent source to keep one well informed of everything that is of importance to all synchro people. The byline is most apt, 'News and Views for Everyone interested in synchronized swimming.'"[38] In contrast with its short-lived predecessors, *Synchro-Info* (later *Synchro*) maintained its bimonthly publication schedule for a full 30 years.

## Competitive Programs

In 1964, the age group program was said to be "BOOMING."[39] Four national regions (East, West, Central and South) were established to initiate a higher level of regional championships. The top three in each age division from each association could advance to the regional championships. The four-region division, however, ran into trouble from excessive size and complaints about long distances to travel. In 1966, nine regions were approved. Heated discussions took place on whether the 10 and under division should become 8 and under with a 9 to 10 division as well. The fear that starting too young might cause dropouts at the older age levels led to adoption of the 10 and under group. Internationally, the youngest age division has always been 12 and under.

In the meantime, the AAU's Junior Olympic program, adopted by synchro in 1957, languished with minimal participation despite advantages such as medals provided by a national sponsor. As a "developmental" program, some of the better athletes in the upper age divisions who participated in senior events were excluded from the Junior Olympic eligibility rules. Consequently, it suffered somewhat from the image of not having "true champions." The Junior Olympic chairman's report in 1967 complained of having only seven association Junior Olympic meets that year, and pointed to some of the attractions of the program. This stimulated a campaign to improve participation.

Legislation was adopted in the 1968 convention to make the age group and Junior Olympic programs more complementary, the main step being to adopt 13 age group regions to match the number in the AAU's Junior Olympic program. The AAU sponsored association awards (through a national sponsor) for all age divisions, but provided for only the 13–14 age group in regional championships. Regions were encouraged to include the other age divisions in their meets by buying the medals themselves.

From the start of the age group program, a swimmer's age had always been established as the age as of the first day of the meet. Recognizing that this would frequently force changes in members of a duet or team routine during the year, a "universal birthday" of June 1 was adopted in 1965. This was changed to May 1 for 1966 and 1967. Then, in 1968, two birthdays were put in place, January 1 for the indoor season and May 1 for the outdoor season.

Athletes in senior class programs were also feeling restricted by the lack of any kind of competitive program between local association and national meets. This was not a great problem in the West, which had conducted a Far Western Championship each year since 1951. That program was finally emulated elsewhere when an East zone invitational championship was initiated in 1968 as the Far Western Championship held its 18th annual meet. The stage was set for the start of a national zone championship program.

The colleges were beginning to think of synchro in more than aquacade terms. In 1968, the (Synchro) College Coaches Association was formed which established governing rules and instituted an All American system. While training and competitions in synchro-like events had been taking place for some time, the steps taken by the coaches association made progress toward more uniformity.[40]

## *Technical Rules*

During this period, changes in rules were nothing revolutionary, but were important nonetheless. Cost and time containment pressures finally caused the reduction of mandatory precompetition practice time at nationals from eight to four days in 1963. Junior national compulsory stunts moved up from the same list of four stunts that served all classes other than senior to being drawn from the senior stunt groups. Alternate swimmers for (qualifying) teams and duets were finally allowed to participate in stunt competition for the first time in 1964. The same year the number of teams that would qualify for final stunt competition at national championships was increased from eight to 10.

Because of the ever-increasing numbers entering the competitions, some sort of seeding procedure was needed. The order of performance (order of draw) for final events had always been by random draw, for all seven positions. But a seeding approach was adopted for 1964 that had the top three qualifiers draw for start positions numbers five to seven. Fourth to seventh qualifiers drew for start positions one to four. This was changed, in 1968, to make the fourth qualifier automatically take the fourth starting position.

By 1968, seeding began even for preliminary events at the national championships. A "block" of the late-starting positions was set aside in each preliminary with the number of positions corresponding to competitors present from the previous year's top 20 solos, 15 duets, or 10 teams along with the most recent senior association champions. Those competitors were allowed to draw from this "last block of numbers." Foreseeing changes in personnel from one year to another, for maintaining seeding qualification a "50 percent rule" was invoked. This meant that at least 50 percent of the members of a team or duet must remain from those who were members at the time of qualification.

There were also changes in the routine rules. A small move toward more choreographic freedom was made in 1964 in allowing direction changes to be made during the ballet leg or flamingo positions of any routine stunt listed for difficulty. On the negative side, soloists had their routine time cut down to four minutes in 1965; routine sheets were further simplified in 1967, changing from a "skeletal" form to requiring only a list of the five required stunts; and the maximum allowable degree of difficulty for routines, set at 1.7 in 1963, jumped back to 1.8 for 1967–68.

Referee responsibilities increased in 1968 as a one-point penalty was imposed for improper spin or twist performance in either stunts within a routine or in stunt competition. It would be assessed for failing to perform a 180-degree spin or full twist within limits of 90 degrees more or less than specified; or failing to perform a 360-degree spin within a limit of 90 degrees less than specified. In this first go at controlling spins and twists, no mention was made of half twists, assuming, presumably, *no one* could be so awkward as to be off that little rotation. Both the 180 degree spin and half twist were expected to be exact (too much rotation on the 180-degree spin would change it to 360 degrees), but the only object of the penalty on the 360-degree spin was to ensure competitors could accomplish *at least* the full rotation.

Many changes were also made during this period to the stunt competition. Sporadic pressure arose to add the rocket, a rapid, high vertical thrust from a nearly submerged level, to the list of stunts. The basis was the desirability of the spectacular high thrust. It never made it to the lists, possibly because it resembled too closely the actual performance of the barracuda. This stunt, despite a description very specifically demanding a rise to the knees before thrusting, was almost always thrust from ankle level, very much like the rocket. Since judges appeared to condone that performance, another name for the action didn't seem warranted. Rocket never appeared in the rules until, with the adoption of FINA's technical routines in 1994, a split rocket was made one of the required movements in the routines.

Good support sculling for vertical positions began to appear in the early '60s. It was still sufficiently novel in 1964 for *Synchro-Info* to report, of the Merionette team routine, "Probably the most remarkable feat [at the national competition] was the Heron 180 degree spin which upon completion of the spin was held at thigh level for a *full 4 counts* before submerging slowly in precise unison."[41] Twists, which had generally been performed at float level, started moving higher as vertical scull techniques improved, so the twist description was changed in 1964 to allow twists to be executed with the water level between the ankle and the hip instead of between the ankle and knee.

Forty-six "new" stunts were proposed during this period, driven by pressure for greater versatility in filling the five-stunt requirement in routines. Most were variations or take-offs of existing stunts (sub-tower, kip-tail, Eiffel reverse, gavalina, elevator-rocket, somer-pirouette, subalette and knightalina). The stunts committee was not receptive to most of them, explaining, "While we are in favor of increasing the number of high difficulty options, too many of the new proposals are simply 'freight trains,' hitching one stunt on to another. New stunts should embody some new principle of movement or design."[42]

Actually, the only alterations allowed until 1968 were "add-ons," twists and spins on some stunts that previously had none (Eiffel Tower, subalina); spins on stunts previously having only twists (flamingo, bent knee flamingo, kip, porpoise); and adding opposite somersaults to those already in use (front pike barracuda, back pike heron). Even the three new figures introduced in 1968, the castle, contra-crane and Eiffel walk, had little novelty.

One variation of open spins, actions that had been used in routines since the mid–'50s was finally introduced into the figure lists for 1968. This was the addition of the gaviata. As performed, though, it could not meet the "rapid rotation" definition of spins, so the word "spin" was simply dropped, making the figure simply gaviata, open 180 degrees. This opened the way for many future variations on opening and closing split rotations.

## *Judging and Scoring*

The new judges training chairman, Marion Kane, developed the first judges training manual in 1964 and incorporated the requirements and standardized test procedures that had been established for earning and maintaining a national judge rating. To reach that level, national judge candidates were required to pass a stunt identification test, a written test on rules, practice judging at competitions, and take an oral examination. Maintaining the national rating required passing a written examination every other year, attending specified national competitions, and participating in a national or regional judges' clinic each year.

Judge selection for national events was originally a simple designation by the national chairman and later by the national committee. In 1968, a blind draw system was proposed by Gene Ahlf.[43] That proposal couldn't muster enough votes at the time, but a proposal that judges be elected by the *coaches* did pass. Unforeseen at that time was the strange politicking that would soon come about as coach cliques worked to elect judges considered most beneficial to their causes.

In 1966, George Sellers asked that a code of performance for judging be established and proposed an evaluation mechanism similar to that actually in use now in computerized evaluations.[44] Those involved in synchro were not ready for that yet, but another suggestion he made, that judges not discuss a competition while it was in progress, was adopted into the rules in 1967.

Judges who had long complained of being cramped in ranking competitors with only half-point intervals for their scores finally had their wishes granted in legislation passed at the convention in Las Vegas in December 1968. One-tenth point intervals were established for grading routines, but the judges would have to wait until 1970 to use the new grades, to allow time for scoring charts to be prepared. It wasn't easy getting the one-tenth point division passed. There were many advocates of changing to one-quarter-point and there were some for one-fifth-point intervals. The former finally lost because it would require space for a second decimal place on flash cards (for x.25 and x.75), and the latter because if five divisions were to be used, it might just as well be 10.

A victory for the "synchro is a sport" advocates was registered in 1966 with legislation that removed most of the theatrical display factors from judging guidelines. All reference to theme, costuming and spectator appeal were deleted from the style score. Manner of presentation and originality were also taken out, the latter replaced with creativity. The boiling up of sentiment for this move had been encouraged by comments in *Synchro-Info* in 1964 and earlier, castigating excessive make-up and elaborate costumes. Further fuel was added in 1965: "Why should dance ability [deck work] be regarded as a judging point in a swimming sport, and why should the athletes be rewarded for the sewing skills of their mothers [costuming still being judged], or why should we reward the originality of a hybrid that may have been copied? Judging should only be on those factors that have a direct bearing on performance."[45]

Screams of protest flooded *Synchro-Info*'s "Mailbox." "How will we attract audiences?" asked one. Ross Bean replied, "I haven't seen our overdress and excessive makeup has done much to attract them now; besides we are not outlawing theme and costuming, just asking the judges to disregard them in the scoring." Judy McGowan added, "I definitely agree that simple costumes are best. A judge need not judge the costume. However, if a hat falls off, some small penalty should be given. A swimmer's hat shouldn't be that heavy or put on with such haste."[46] The sport advocacy victory was not complete. For another eight years a line remained on entry blanks to list theme or title and deck work remained part of judge responsibilities.

Synchronization continued to be batted back and forth between being part of the execution score or part of the style awards during this period. After a reasonable resting period in execution, it was sent back to style again in 1968 where it was to be considered along with judging the variety, construction, difficulty and originality of the routine.

Where the judges were placed was finally discussed and determined in 1967. The rules specified, for the first time, that judges were to be placed in elevated positions on more than one side of the pool. In 1968, the number of routine judges was increased from five to seven. U.S. judges studied the observations Don Kane had made of the Canadian judging system when he reported, "Scores were written before being flashed and the judges were also required to write down the breakdown of their scores according to the formula of 50 points for execution, 25 for composition, 20 for synchronization, and 5 for showmanship."[47]

The competition structure was still having a hard time dealing with the numbers of athletes in stunt competition. In 1965, the use of two judging panels for stunts was officially condoned. That is, two panels of seven judges each were permissible if 14 judges could be found. In 1964, to obtain enough judges, seven "non-coaches" judged the compulsories, while seven coaches were used to judge the optionals. With a record 205 entries at the Eastern Regional Age Group Championships in 1965, the committee decided to run four stunt panels simultaneously and to limit soloists competing in stunts to only those 10 with the highest routine scores in each age group. That way, they said, they had time to process all the duet and team routine entries.

## *Around the Country*

This period was marked with numerous clinics throughout the country as leaders in the sport attempted to further its development throughout the country. Lee Skidmore reported that South Carolina was organizing the first synchro programs there in 1963 and a competition was held that summer in Greenville, South Carolina. Jill Harms (Griesse) reported giving an exhibition in Kaneohe where she was coaching a speed team in 1964. There was plenty of interest she reported; 60 girls wanted to start, but no one would give her a pool to use. In 1966, Dottie Alverson, Hawaiian synchro chairman, reported holding their first competition in 1966. They also held a water show with all Hawaiian clubs invited to participate. Evelyn Sims reported holding the first Virginia Association clinic in 1963 with just one club attending. However, at the clinic held in 1964, eight clubs participated. Pamela Wainscott was teaching synchro at the Louisville YWCA and Charlotte Howard reported in 1968, "We are trying to help her build a good strong group in this area." Springfield, Massachusetts, held the Senior New England Association Championships in 1965 with clubs coming from New York, Connecticut, New Jersey, and New Hampshire. In Tennessee, Chattanooga reported an age group competition in 1966. All swimmers who entered the meet were from the Chattanooga Synchro Nymphs.

## *Awards and Honors*

The Lawrence J. Johnson Memorial Award is a United States Aquatic Sports (USAS) award given on a rotating basis to a female swimmer, male swimmer, female diver, male diver, synchronized swimmer, water polo player, and long distance swimmer. In 1968, Margo McGrath became the first synchronized swimmer so honored.[48] Johnson was interested in all aquatic sports and was instrumental, along with Max Ritter, for adding synchronized swimming to the program of the Pan American Games in Mexico City.

In 1965, Pam Morris became the first syn-

Margo McGrath, San Francisco Merionettes, won the first of her five solo titles in 1966 and in 1968 she was the winner of the Lawrence J. Johnson Memorial Award.

chronized swimmer inducted into the International Swimming Hall of Fame in Fort Lauderdale, Florida. She participated in the dedication of the pool and presentation of the first slate of honorees in December 1965. At her induction, the announcer said, "Pam has won 10 national championships and is the only swimmer to hold simultaneously the solo, duet and team crowns."[49] Beulah Gundling was inducted into the aquatic art division of the International Swimming Hall of Fame in 1965.

Joy Cushman, at the 1963 AAU convention in San Diego, was presented a special award by AAU president Jesse Pardue for distinguished service in promoting the sport of synchronized swimming. The plaque read: "with the admiration of the National AAU Vice Chairmen." Peg Seller, early Canadian champion, first president of the Canadian Amateur Swimming Association, and who was instrumental in the development of the FINA rules (with the U.S.'s Mary Derosier), was honored to be named to Canada's Sports Hall of Fame in 1966.[50]

The Helms Hall of Fame continued to honor synchronized swimming's Hall of Fame athletes and contributors. Duplicate awards were displayed at its Sports Hall of Fame in Los Angeles (see Appendix A).

# 7

# *New Programs, New Ideas, Here and Abroad: 1969–75*

Growth of existing programs with development and adoption of new categories for competitive programs may have been the most significant progress of this period. Collegiate and masters programs were begun. The Junior Olympic program finally gained popularity partly as the result of synchro's inclusion in the AAU's multisport National Junior Olympic Championships. Both the junior Olympic and the age group programs were expanded from nine to 13 regions.

The international image looked suddenly brighter as synchro passed a recognition landmark when it became part of the program in the first World Aquatic Championships. This had to mean that at least part of the sports world considered synchronized swimming a real sport. Many in the other three aquatic disciplines would really see synchro for the first time in Belgrade.

To cope with the burgeoning size of both junior and senior nationals domestically, many hopeful "solutions" were floated and some were tried. More panels of judges for figures helped shorten the time there. Qualifying scores from specified competitions were required for entries in some national events. Semifinal events were added. Even a divided flight or heat system for preliminary events was tried. Still, more relief was needed.

Synchro sought to define a more respectable image via better word impressions. In 1974, the style award for routines was abandoned in favor of the term content as being better expressive of the meaning of the award; stunt would become figure, the term already used for some time internationally. To avoid confusion, the newer terms will be used throughout this transition chapter.

Routines were developing different looks. Where maximum sustained height had been thought of as applying only to figure execution, swimmers were perfecting techniques for holding height both right side up and upside down. They learned to keep both arms above the surface by "sculling with the legs." The first such "eggbeater" kick was noted in national competition in 1969. The "crane scull," first used in attempting to maintain high levels in the twists of the crane figure, had metamorphosized into a "vertical support" scull used increasingly for higher and higher levels in all upside-down positions, bent knee, crane and double vertical. For most of this period, quick-paced, "supersharp" action was the dominant team style. Santa Clara's 1975 team introduced a slow-down tempo midway through the routine that was impressive for its stark contrast. Competitors applauded the "slow part," but hedged, "We're glad *they* did it because they're the only ones who could try something so different without worrying about their place."[1] And finally, joining the rest of the world, the name "stunt" was officially changed to "figure" at the convention of 1973.[2]

In the world of officials, training and testing of judges was standardized and a judge evaluation mechanism was adopted. Judges selection would be from an election by coaches at national events. Written scores had to be turned in prior to flashing scores. The new one-tenth-point intervals for judging routines started putting lots of scores into the nines. Even a judge uniform was adopted, all white. Things certainly *looked* better.

Synchro was also getting noticed by film again. Marion Kane directed 32 former synchro swimmers from the Bay Area clubs to recreate the Billy Rose Aquacade swimming sequences for the film *Funny Lady*, starring Barbra Streisand. Merionette Heidi O'Rourke did the swimming part of Aquacade star Eleanor Holm.[3] Kane was congratulated by a former swimmer who said, "It is another of your innumerable contributions to synchronized swimming by exposing our beautiful sport to the thousands of movie goers who never have seen synchro before."[4]

But a somewhat confused picture of what synchro was all about surfaced in an article in the April 1971 issue of *Sports Illustrated*.[5] Miriam Courtney, Oregon synchro chairman, wrote *Synchro-Info* about the piece, stating, "Author Blount has written about everything that has ever been said to explain the sport from Esther Williams and Water Ballet bug-a-boos to a resume of the real training and athletic ability it requires ... through it all he has woven a personality study of the [San Antonio] Cygnets and their mentor-owner Margaret Swan ... and over it all, has showered a list of Routine titles and Club names, just because they sound so colorful. For synchronized swimming, at this stage of development, we imagine almost any publicity on a national level must be considered good publicity, but one is not sure just what sort of an image this article will leave in the minds of readers since even one thoroughly familiar with the sport emerges from the experience somewhat confused as to what has been said."[6]

The *Toledo Blade*, reporting the 1969 na-

tional championships, wrote, "What's the one sport that requires its participants to be experts in gymnastics, ballet and swimming and have a good ear for music? In high pressure competition, it's known as synchronized swimming; in recreational activities as water ballet. Either way, for both audience and swimmers alike, the sport has a beauty and grace all its own."[7] An article in the September 1975 issue of *Women-Sports*, by Pat Tashima, said, "Synchronized Swimming ... you know, Esther Williams.... From water ballet to full fledged sport, synchronized swimming has made quite a splash."[8]

Always though, the question, is it show or sport? Teresa Andersen, coach of KRNT Des Moines, wrote of the 1969 nationals, "Are we moving in the direction of an aquatic sport or aquatic vaudeville, as Avery Brundage called it? Some of the numbers could have fit well into Billy Rose's Aquacade with overly fancy suits. Shall we set ourselves back 15 years by incorporating such aquatic vaudeville? If so, we can forget about acceptance to the Olympics."[9]

## The National Championships 1969–75

The years from 1968 to 1974 were the most closely contested period the sport has known. Where most of the '60s belonged to the San Francisco Merionettes, in the early '70s, the Merionettes and the Santa Clara Aquamaids fought fiercely back and forth for the top spots. Titles switched from one to the other into the summer of 1974 when Santa Clara finally took over and reigned until the '80s. It sounds as if it were relatively easy to do this, but a swimmer on Canada's Hollyburn Club, after competing in the 1969 AAU nationals, marveled, "For those who have never been to the AAU nationals, the sheer number of competitors is staggering.... We expected a high caliber meet, but you have to see it to believe how difficult it is to be in the top 20!"[10] But something of a balance was provided as a foreign visitor at a junior association competition that same year said, "It was rather pleasant to see that all U.S.

swimmers aren't just born great; that you too have developing swimmers."[11]

Television was also taking notice. CBS came to the 1973 Indoor National Championships in Hershey, Pennsylvania, to televise parts of the competition for its June 3 *Sunday Sports Spectacular*. Kim Welshons, as commentator, said that cards of appreciation to CBS following the event, with comments, would be of great value.[12] The next year, Donalda Smith, FINA Technical Committee secretary, wrote, "The TV Broadcast of the International Solo [Ottawa 1974] proved so popular that it was repeated two days later. I doubt you'll be able to see it [in the U.S.] but it is the best showcase for synchro to date…. They have excerpts from all the solos with the top three shown complete."[13] Even nonnational meets were getting attention. *Newsweek* magazine videotaped portions of the Far Western Championships at Huntington Beach for later release to major television stations across the country. In the Bay Area it was shown on the morning *Today* show but Marian Kretschmer reported seeing it in Ohio on their *Women's World* news program.[14]

Doug Smith, in the *Lorain* (Ohio) *News*, wrote of the 1972 nationals, "Last night's crowd seemed to favor the team competition, and with good reason, this event is the very essence of synchronized swimming, each swimmer trying to duplicate her teammates' movements at exactly the same time. The entire competition was an impressive thing to watch, an exercise in discipline and devotion by girls that, for the most part, are in their teens. Their composure in the water and on the performing deck was magnificent, and their little girl squeals of joy as the results were announced somehow seemed to fit right in, too."[15]

Teams were always closely contested, no matter who won. After the Aquamaids took over the title from the Merionettes in 1968, they successfully defended it at the both the indoor and outdoor championships in 1969, but then lost the indoor title to San Francisco in 1970. Santa Clara prevailed again for the 1970 outdoor title but lost both meets in 1971 to San Francisco. Santa Clara finally displayed its dominance as it came back to win again in the spring of 1972 and remained undefeated in the team event until 1980.[16] The margins of victory in these powerhouse battles were often less than a single point.

While Santa Clara and San Francisco exchanged the two top spots, there was turmoil and pitched contention for the lower places. It was now difficult for other clubs to push past the Santa Clara and San Francisco "B" teams, sometimes even their "C" teams, but invaders did move up from obscurity. The San Antonio Cygnets (coach Margaret Swan Forbes) were seen in finals for the first time in 1966 and moved steadily upward with innovative team routines. In 1969 and twice in 1970, they became the only non–California team finalists (top 7) for this period. They were the first winner of the national Edwin Olsen Trophy, given to the high-point "non–California" club.[17]

The Walnut Creek Aquanuts,

Santa Clara successfully defended its 1968 team title through 1969, winning with, in back, left to right, Pam Albin, Kathy Bryant, Gail Johnson, Carol Reynolds, Nancy Hines, and in front, left to right, Teresa Andersen, Kim Welshons and Kris Welshons (photograph by Lee Pillsbury).

San Francisco overtook Santa Clara and won the 1970 team title. Swimmers are, in back, left to right, Chris Jeffers, Amy Miner and Lona Albano, and in front, left to right, Joan Lang, Heidi O'Rourke, Barbara Cooney, Bede Trantina and Sue Morris.

archaic remnant from water ballet days, five more clubs entered without titles at the outdoor meet.[20]

The 1973 outdoor meet in 1973 in Paso Robles had a different novelty. One of the most interesting developments this year was the entry of the Women's Army Corps team into senior nationals. The team was started when the Pentagon Sports Office wanted full-time sports programs for women comparable to the modern pentathlon for men.[21] Margaret Swan was hired to coach and, in less than six months, she taught the army team the sport and took them to nationals. They placed 29th of 36 in national team prelims.[22]

The duet also migrated back and forth between Santa Clara and San Francisco. Merionettes Heidi O'Rourke and Barbara "Bede" Trantina,

partly an offshoot of the dissolved Concord Mermaids, rose into the finals in 1971 and finally displaced San Francisco from its second-place spot in 1974. *Synchro-Info* noted, "The rapid rise of Walnut Creek (coach Sue Ahlf) suggests that the domain of the top two teams can be invaded by a thoroughly dedicated group."[18] The California Coralettes (coach Judy Graun), a split-off club from the Aquamaids that even used the same pool for practices, made the finals in 1973 and moved past Walnut Creek into second place in 1975. Others teams moving into the finals were the Riverside Aquettes, Dayton Aquanymphs, Tustin Meraquas, Berea Aquateens, and the Tonawanda Aquettes.

A novelty of the 1973 indoor meet was the independent decision by four clubs to experiment with entering their routines without titles.[19] It was rather apparent from the results that the omission had no adverse effects. With demonstration that requiring a "title" was an

overtook Santa Clara's defending champions Kim Welshons and Nancy Hines at the 1969 indoor competition, but Welshons and Hines bounced right back to win the outdoor championship. Then the duet title returned to San Francisco for the next two years, O'Rourke winning in 1970 with Bede Trantina and in 1971 with Joan Lang. O'Rourke and Trantina received five awards of "10" in 1970, the first time straight "perfect" scores had ever been awarded in the U.S.[23]

Santa Clara rose again in 1972 when Gail Johnson and Teresa "Terry" Andersen won both titles. They kept winning through 1973, but Kathy Kretschmer and Amy Miner won back the 1974 indoor crown for the Merionettes. Johnson came back with Sue Baross to win the 1974 outdoor and then Santa Clara's Robin Curren and Amanda Norrish won both meets in 1975.

In solos, the 1968 champion, Kim Welshons of Santa Clara, continued winning

Kim Welshons (right) and Nancy Hines won the first duet title for Santa Clara in 1968 but lost in 1969. They won three titles in 1968 and 1969 (photograph by Lee Pillsbury).

through 1969. Upon her retirement, teammate Carol Reynolds rose to win the 1970 indoor title, but San Francisco moved in again with Bede Trantina winning the outdoor. Trantina then lost to teammates Joan Lang in the 1970 outdoor and Heidi O'Rourke, who won the titles in 1971.

The 1972 solo title returned to Santa Clara with Gail Johnson winning both meets. She lost the 1973 indoor championship to her duet partner, Terry Andersen. That win qualified Andersen as the U.S. soloist for the first World Aquatic Championships, and she went on to win the gold in Belgrade late that summer. In the meantime, though, Johnson had beaten her to reclaim the outdoor solo title. Kathy Kretschmer restored the title to San Francisco by winning the 1974 indoor meet, but the title ricocheted back to Santa Clara as Johnson won the 1974 outdoor meet. Johnson continued by winning both titles in 1975, and so became the champion of all solo titlists with six solo championships.

## International Developments

The premier international event for synchronized swimming had been the Pan Amer-

Gail Johnson (left) and Terry Andersen won the first world duet title in 1973 in Belgrade (photograph by Lee Pillsbury).

Heidi O'Rourke (left) and Bede Trantina won three national titles in 1969 and 1970. O'Rourke won two more in 1971 with Joan Lang.

Lang, took the duet as well. The Merionettes were outstanding in their team victory over their neighbor and rival at Santa Clara which was competing in its home pool.

The most remarkable thing about these trials, however, was the number of 10s given. O'Rourke got five for her solo, but so did second-place Lang. Johnson, in third, had three 10s. The winning duet, O'Rourke and Lang, scored *all* 10s while second-place Johnson and Andersen got three. In the battle for the team title, San Francisco received six 10s against Santa Clara's four. One official remarked that it almost seemed with such tremendous competition between the two top clubs, that it was more a contest for the judges to see who could give the highest scores.[25]

Once more, all the pre–Games enthusiasm seemed to peter out before entry time, and only four countries, Canada, Colombia, Mexico and the U.S., participated in the sixth Pan American Games. The U.S. won all the events easily. Heidi O'Rourke was effortless and captivated the audience with her solo. After O'Rourke and Joan Lang swam their duet, the tremendously enthusiastic audience chanted, "*Once! Once!*" (Eleven! Eleven!) as if mere 10s could not be enough for what they had just witnessed. After the team swam, the audience stayed in their seats applauding and applauding, refusing to accept the athletes' departure. This time they conveyed what they really wanted, "*Otra vez, otra vez!*" (another time, another time).[26]

The U.S. official in Cali, Dawn Bean, said that one of the more interesting sidelights was watching the Canadians deal with a national team, their first for nearly a decade. The five swimmers from Quebec (coach Suzanne Eon) twisted and spun the opposite direction from the three from Calgary (coach Mary Ann

ican Games. While the "Pan-Ams" did not have the participant attendance of some of the European meets, they were essential for U.S. synchro as part of the USOC's commitment to the Games. ASUA secretary Dr. Harold Henning and ASUA president Lic. Javier Ostos, announcing the return of synchro to the Pan American Games, said, "It now becomes our responsibility to demonstrate to the Pan American Sports Organization that the growth of synchronized swimming has achieved justifiable international recognition."[24]

Synchro had waited eight years for the sport to return to the Pan American Games. Trials were held in Santa Clara to determine the U.S. representatives for the Games to be held in Cali, Colombia, in 1971. This time, San Francisco would not be defeated. Heidi O'Rourke won the solo and, with partner Joan

Reeves.) Neither coach would allow a change in direction for her swimmers, so the routine was performed with each swimmer spinning and twisting her own way.

Qualifying for the seventh Pan American Games in 1975 was based upon performances in the national events. Santa Clara's domination was continuing so all the U.S. entries were from the Aquamaids again. In the Games in Mexico City, Gail Johnson won the solo, just 0.67 points over Sylvie Fortier of Canada. Teammates Robin Curren and Amanda Norrish won the duet. U.S. official Billie MacKellar described the Aquamaids' gold-winning team routine as "throwing every audience-pleaser from the past decade into the routine — 'down-the-drain,' lift-assist figures, fans and reverse fans, ballet leg lines, a crown lift, and a fake ending. They flashed from one formation to another in perfect unison," she said.[27]

## The First World Championships

As important as the Pan American Games had been to synchro, a real milestone was passed when synchro was included with swimming, diving, and water polo in the First World Aquatic Championships to be held in Belgrade, Yugoslavia, in 1973. Dr. Harold Henning, then FINA president, said, "Some FINA member countries did not really feel that all four of the FINA sports could be conducted at one time because of the expense involved. However, the FINA Bureau determined with past President Javier Ostos urging that that all four sports must be held at the same locale or not at all."[28]

No qualifying trials were held to choose the U.S. representatives for the first world championships. By this time, the mechanisms had been established for selecting international competitors on the basis of placement in the national competitions (hoping to avoid the previous embarrassments of having a representative who was defeated in a national championship between the trials and the international event). For this competition, the winners of the senior indoor meet were listed for the corresponding events in the world competition. Santa Clara had won everything, hence its swimmers would represent the United States in this first world championship.

Synchro's first test in the FINA World Championships in Belgrade was a real success with 15 participating countries. The U.S. won all three gold medals, Teresa Andersen, solo; Andersen and Gail Johnson, duet; and the Santa Clara Aquamaids winning team. Almost the best of all, synchro was instrumental in the U.S.'s winning the overall medal count for all four sports because it was only as Andersen won the solo, the final gold medal awarded at the Games, that the U.S. passed the others to win the overall championship. Joy Cushman, U.S. official, reported, "The overwhelming response and acceptance from top sports people was a great step forward for our sport."[29]

The meet also marked the first contact with Soviet coaches. The Russians felt Sue Randell's performance in figures was so outstanding that they spent two days filming her after the competition. It was widely believed that when the Soviet Union began entering synchro competitions, the door to the Olympic Games might be opened.

FINA wanted the world aquatic championships to be held on a four-year schedule, midway between the Olympics. Since the first championship was held only one year after the Olympic year, rather than waiting five years,

Terry Andersen won the solo at the first world championships and earned enough points to secure the overall team win for the United States (photograph by Lee Pillsbury).

until 1978, to get to that midway schedule, they chose to have an intermediate championship. The second World Aquatic Championships were scheduled for only two years after the first, then the next interval would be three years. The expense of travel to Cali, Colombia, site of the second championships, resulted in a great reduction of European participation. Just 10 countries participated in synchro this time, with only seven entering the team event. Nevertheless, it was considered a highly successful event, with enthusiastic crowds and much media interest.

Billie MacKellar, U.S. official at the Games, said that many teams went to great lengths to try to upset the U.S. The Canadians arrived early and undertook a great publicity campaign. The Japanese and Dutch had their top swimmers training in the U.S. for a year and several teams had American coaches or sent their coaches to visit and study U.S. training methods.[30] All the intensive training was beginning to show in improved and attractive performances. The Canadian team was filled with eye-grabbing and attention-getting lifts.

The Santa Clara swimmers, though, had little difficulty in retaining all titles. Gail Johnson Buzonas had waited two years for another chance at the world solo title after losing the chance to be the U.S.'s first solo representative to the world event to her duet partner, Terry Andersen, in 1973. She prevailed over Canada's Sylvie Fortier by nearly 1.7 points. With some relief, she remarked, "I am glad I'm retiring because I wouldn't like to meet Sylvie in a few years."[31] The duet of Robin Curren and Amanda Norrish won by a similar margin. The Aquamaids went into the team routine with a figure average of 80.31, comfortably leading

The Santa Clara Aquamaids won the first world team title in 1973. Swimmer are, in back, left to right, Jackie Douglass, Robin Curren, Dana Mills, Amanda Norrish, and in front, left to right, Gail Johnson, Suzanne Randell, Sue Baross and Terry Andersen (photograph by Lee Pillsbury).

Gail Johnson had been edged out for the solo title at the World Championships in 1973, but came back to win both the World and the Pan Am Games titles in 1975 and a total of six national solo titles (photograph by Lee Pillsbury).

Japan with 78.19 and Canada with 76.82. Thus, it hardly mattered that Canada's flashy routine managed to gain awards that tied the U.S.'s routine score, except in reflection upon possible future events.

Around the world, synchro was making great strides. In 1971, FINA reported that 26 nations were conducting competitive synchronized swimming programs. To this time, there had been relatively few international competitions open to U.S. swimmers except for the Pan American Games. When an invitation to a foreign country was received, it had traditionally been extended to the national champions who would attend, if they could, since all such participation was at their own or their club's expense. With an ever-increasing number of competitions developing, it became necessary for the OSSC to establish a priority order of who would be approved to go where. Thus, the "club option" policy was developed in 1973. This established an order of choice based on order of placement in the previous national competition for the top seven solos, duets, and teams.

There were many new "open" competitions. More and more international events began to appear on the world calendar. U.S. swimmers participated in Expo '70 in Osaka, Japan; the Denmark International in 1970; the West German International Age Group in 1972 and in the Canadian Open championships in 1969 and 1972 (see Appendix D). In 1974, in an attempt to gain more international competition for countries that were not included in the developing competitions among the LEN (League of European Nations) countries, the U.S. hosted the first Pan Pacific Games in Honolulu. Five countries participated. The meet was such a success that those attending decided to organize Pan Pacific competitions every two years. The next meet was scheduled for Osaka, Japan, in 1976.

Tours and exchanges of swimmers between countries continued, but as many or more swimmers were now coming to the U.S. as U.S. swimmers were traveling abroad. In this period, swimmers from South Africa, Japan, Czechoslovakia, Panama, Canada, Holland, Australia, Switzerland and France came to train with clubs mainly in California but also in New Jersey, Michigan and Texas.

And as eager as the U.S. had been for education and clinics to help start programs in the U.S. in the '60s, now it was the rest of the world seeking information. The first world conference for coaches and judges was held in Ottawa, Canada, in 1974.[32] Forty-two delegates from 15 countries participated. The conference was held in conjunction with an international solo competition. The U.S.'s Kathy Kretschmer was the winner of the solo event.

## Sport Administration

Frances "Fran" Jones, coach of the Lansing Sea Sprites, Orchard Lake, Michigan, was elected chairman for 1969 and 1970, but served only until early 1970 when health problems forced her to resign. Her energies had been focused on using educational resources to develop the sport. To this end, she instituted a series of national seminars to be held the day after the national championships, beginning with a judging seminar in Toledo in 1969.[33] This was followed by a coaching seminar in Dallas in 1970.[34] Though health problems caused her resignation, the national seminars were continued. In 1974, a separate coaches camp was held at Millersville State College.[35] Another was held in 1975, at Wright Junior College.

Joy Cushman was asked to return to fill the balance of Jones' unexpired term. She accepted, saying, "I consider it an honor to again serve in this capacity. I will do my best to pick up the loose ends and complete the business of the year on this short notice."[36] *Synchro-Info* reported, "We feel this is an admirable choice." Her evenhanded firmness at meetings and in many preliminary actions leading into the meetings minimized irritability and led to a feeling of confidence in the sport and the people in it.[37] As chair of Synchro's OSSC, she had been representing synchronized swimming at U.S. Olympic Committee (USOC) meetings and in 1971 was appointed to the USOC's Board of Directors.[38] In 1973, the AAU instituted a new policy requiring that members of all the sport Olympic and International committees be elected. A nine-member OSSC was elected at the first opportunity, the 1973 Indoor National Championships. The members of the OSSC, in turn, chose Cushman as their chairman. She continued as the USOC representative into 1976.

The Olympic Synchronized Swimming Committee, with funding only from the USOC participation in the Pan American Games, sought financial support for sending a team to the first world championships in Belgrade, Yugoslavia, in 1973. The OSSC began selling pins and patches to help support competitors in international events. Local associations were asked to donate $1.00 for every registered athlete in every club for which the proceeds would be donated to the International Travel Fund.[39]

Until 1972, all national subcommittee chairmen were appointed by the national chairman, who also chose the subcommittee members. This had resulted in many of the same people being asked to serve on multiple committees. Somewhat following the lead of the OSSC, where the AAU required, in 1973, that members be elected to the committee, synchro put signup sheets for any in attendance to indicate their desires to serve and in which areas they would prefer working. This resulted in a much wider geographical representation and more diversity on the committee makeup.

Only a single, appointed athlete representative position on the national committee had been set up for 1968. The representation was expanded to two members for 1969, then to three for 1970. In 1970, it was decided to make the positions elective, with athletes voting for one representative from each of three zones, East, Central and West, plus one at-large representative. For 1971, Kim Welshons, Santa Clara; Angie Taylor, San Antonio; and Duffy Bopp, Tonawanda; became the first elected athlete representatives from their zones; Pam Morris was elected the at-large representative. Welshons managed to establish a travel fund, which still exists today, to help send athlete representatives to convention.

Lillian "Billie" MacKellar, Hollywood, California, was elected to serve as chairman at the 1971 convention and served through 1975.

She maintained a sense of order and peace even during the period of fierce competition between the top two clubs. The Lillian MacKellar Distinguished Service Award was established in her honor and she was named its first recipient.

A crisis of sorts broke out when the AAU mandated in 1972 and 1973 that rules for all aquatic sports be combined in a single AAU Aquatics Handbook. This book would not include any of the subcommittees, directory, or historical information that synchro had been publishing in its own handbook. Synchro was forced to publish a supplementary directory in 1973 to provide information on committee chairmen, judges, and important addresses and phone numbers. The combined rulebook was so bulky and unmanageable that all the aquatic sports revolted against it and separate sport rulebooks were allowed again for 1974, but with an AAU-mandated common cover.[40]

Hosts for national championships were becoming increasingly difficult to find since the costs of staging a senior national generally exceeded income by a large margin. The national committee tried to make hosting more attractive by approving a sponsor fee in 1972, allowing hosts to charge and keep a set entry fee for each swimmer for each event entered.[41]

The swimmers named "All American" had followed AAU guidelines since the All American program was started in 1954. They were designated by event, solo, duet and team All Americans, according to who won the three events of the senior national championships during the year. The committee would make a choice if there had been a split in winners of the indoor and outdoor meets. The total number named would also depend on the number of members on the winning teams.

In an attempt to give "more realistic, individual recognition to many outstanding synchronized swimming competitors," *Synchro-Info* published its own list of "1969 All-Stars" in the February 1970 issue. This was to be "an annual presentation of those competitors, who, in our opinion, have achieved the highest level of performance during the previous calendar year."[42] The *Synchro-Info* selections were based upon individual point accumulation from a set of performance criteria in national events, including the figure competition, which was not involved in the usual All American selections. Eleven swimmers, to encompass members for solo, duet and team, would be selected, but listed without relation to any particular event qualification. The *Synchro-Info* All-Star Team was published for 1970 and 1971. The national committee finally recognized the advantages of the *Synchro-Info* approach and adopted a similar point system to select a more representative All American team.[43] With some modifications, that point system is still used today.

Early in this period, all competition music was still on grooved discs. A method of speed adjustment using stroboscopic calibration had been devised to accurately reproduce the desired playback speeds. In 1971, a mandatory marking of competition recordings for a stroboscopic speed setting became effective. However, by that year, the days of the disc were numbered. Unofficial use of cassette decks was already widespread in lower-level AAU meets. The official ushering in of the tape era might have been the First World Aquatic Championships in 1973, where a reel-to-reel tape deck was provided in addition to the three-speed turntable. Some cassette recordings were used at national meets in 1972 and 1973 with the adventurous coaches having to supply the tape decks that could be plugged into the existing system.

The cassette became officially acceptable under 1974 rules which specified "No tape shall contain more than one accompaniment per side…," thus making note of problems that had already been discovered in their unofficial use.[44] By 1976, two inexpensive models of portable cassette decks were available with speed (pitch) controls that allowed the same kind of speed adjustments as were used with disc recordings and cassette decks became part of the normal equipment for major meets.

Other advances in technology allowed the first use of computers for scoring in 1972. Robert Mueller, in Pennsylvania, brought a portable computer to an association competition. Mueller, who wrote the program, offered a print-out or cassette of the program, with directions for its use, to anyone desiring it.[45] He

was not overwhelmed with requests for it. Computers were still expensive, awkward and needed some significant skill to use.

Two books appeared during this period. In 1971, Bernard Hasbrouck, coach at Creighton University, produced *Synchronized Swimming Self Taught*, a manual for beginning teachers.[46] In 1975, Fran Jones and Joyce Lindeman's *Components of Synchronized Swimming* was published. The jacket cover read, "The most up-to-date and complete manual available, featuring a scientific new approach to learning each skill, guidelines for competitive coaching and directions for producing water shows."[47]

The Jole Company, with the help of the U.S. Olympic Committee, produced a series of 8mm loop teaching films in 1971. Gail Johnson and other Santa Clara swimmers demonstrated for the 32 films, each devoted to a single figure or skill. The loop cartridge structure allowed continuous repetitions with simple loading but the need for the special loop film projectors reduced the potential distribution of the films.[48]

*Synchro-Info* added photo pages to its mimeographed text newsletter format in 1968, inspiring Lillian DeSha, of Cincinnati, to write, "The pictures have served to convince anxious mothers that the sport does not develop masculine type girls."[49] *Synchro-Info* finally became a true magazine in 1970 as it shifted to full photo-offset printing and commercial binding and trimming. But it lost its status as the sole magazine in the world devoted entirely to synchronized swimming in 1971, when Canadian Synchro began *Synchro Canada* as its official publication with Joyce Coffin as editor.[50] *Synchro Japan* appeared in 1975, with Nakako Saito as editor.[51]

## Competitive Programs

The nine sections of the age group program (AG) were replaced in 1969 by applying the AAU's 13 Junior Olympic regions to the AG program, as well. A single birthday, January 1, allowed competitors to remain their age of that date for the entire year. This was established for all age group and Junior Olympic competitions in 1972.[52] In order to bring the Junior Olympic (JO) program back into the development, grass-roots, area restrictions were placed on entry into the JO competitions. First, senior national place winners became ineligible for their events. The next year, all national finalists were excluded in their events.

The first national Junior Olympic competition was conducted by synchro's national JO chairman, Barbara Eaton, and committee in Norfolk, Virginia, in August 1971. Synchro's separate JO national continued through 1973, then the AAU included synchro in its multisport national in 1974, but only for the 13–14 age events. Quaker Oats had started the regional and national competition and had provided medals and some funding, but it was replaced by Chevrolet automobiles.[53]

An Eastern Intercollegiate Synchronized Swimming Conference was formed in 1969 and a figure competition was held at Stonybrook College. A routine competition event was held the next year at State University of New York at Albany. A tentative set of rules for intercollegiate competition was drawn up in 1971 and tested in a Midwest regional competition at Ohio State University in 1972. Ohio State hosted the first College Association meet in 1973.[54]

Rules were finalized at the Intercollegiate Synchronized Swimming Coaches Association meeting at Penn State in September 1974.[55] Under guidelines established by the National Association of Girls & Women in Sport (NAGWS), a coaches academy was established in 1975. The AIAW [Association for Intercollegiate Athletics for Women] became the governing body for all women's collegiate sports in 1975.[56] It encouraged the coaches academy to set up a committee to promote and develop regional and national collegiate competition.[57] Michigan State staged the Big Ten championships and Eastern regional championships took place at the University of Pittsburgh in 1975. National championships would not begin until 1977.

A letter to *Synchro-Info*'s Mailbox in April 1975 from Louise Wing pleaded with masters to set up a program, saying that the "[rules] committee is already far too busy providing synchro for the younger age groups. Obviously, it is up to those of us who enjoy synchro and would like a little friendly competition among our peers to come forward and volunteer to do whatever is necessary to set up a Masters Program for ourselves."[58] In response to Ms. Wing, the national committee went on record as not being in favor of conducting a masters program since it did not recognize masters. They did approve, however, an experimental masters meet to be held that fall under the auspices of the U.S. Swimming Federation.[59]

That fall, a first national Masters competition was held in 1975 in Reading, Pennsylvania. Marjorie Murphy, aquatic director of the Summit YMCA and host of the meet, said, "Although the meet was small in numbers, it was a huge success. It gave us [masters] an opportunity to do many satisfying things—compete with others in our own age group (the first time in many years we owned up to our real ages), and meet old and new friends, all enthusiastic about the same thing, Synchronized Swimming!"[60]

## Technical Rules

In another attempt to reduce the length of overstuffed routine events, semifinals were introduced in 1969. Some of the top competitors from the previous year's events would be seeded directly to those semifinals and others would qualify from the preliminary events. The preliminaries had become so large that there was some worry that the best competitors could get lost in the crowds. Now, the best from the previous year — 20 solos, 15 duets and 10 teams — would be vying in the semifinals with the 10 high scores from the now smaller preliminaries. Athletes were pleased. Both those who were seeded directly and those who advanced from prelims said they gained a real sense of accomplishment in the new events. They also felt the comparisons among competitors would be better and more meaningful with the smaller semifinals consisting of a more uniform level of capabilities.

The change failed, however, to make much of a dent on the preliminary event problems. The solo preliminary in 1969, with 106 entries, had to start at 6:00 A.M. and lasted more than 10 hours. Judge Judy McGowan asked, "Are you as exhausted as I am after judging for 10 straight hours? The time has come for scheduling some kind of qualifying meet."[61] The next year, with an atmosphere within the pool enclosure of Southern Methodist University at around 100 degrees F, 134 solos, 102 duets, and 47 teams competed in the 1970 outdoor meet. There was universal agreement that something, anything, had to be done to control the flood of entries.[62] That fall, a qualifying routine score was imposed upon solo and duet entries.[63] Entries were required to achieve a qualifying score at a prior national, regional or senior association competition. After seeing the entries in the 1971 meets, the Senior Association was dropped as a qualifying meet. It was evident that local scores were simply rising enough to qualify the local favorites. Qualifying score requirements were also applied to entrants for 1974 junior national events.

Nothing arrested the flood. Faced with more than 120 solos and 90 duets at a three-day junior national in Walnut Creek in 1973, more creative solutions were invoked. With a rather liberal rule interpretation, preliminaries were divided into two flights, or heats. Each heat would be judged by a separate panel, halving the number of competitors each set of judges would have to compare. Each heat qualified 10 for the semifinal.[64] This, of course, increased the size of the semifinal undesirably.

This strategy was suggested for use at the 1973 Outdoor Senior Championship where more than 90 solos were entered in prelims. The athletes voted against using it. After they watched the upward-drifting, late-afternoon scores with judges trying to survive nine hours of the central California sun, with temperatures as high as 110 degrees F, the athletes reconsidered. For subsequent meets, heats would be used whenever entries exceeded 60. But this meant that the size of the semifinal events was raised from an easily managed 20 to 30 contestants to the more difficult comparison of 30 to 40 competitors.

The proverbial straw that really broke the camel's back was the schedule of the 1974 junior national meet in Baltimore.[65] Dealing with the 153 solos and 117 duets in the allotted two days verged on the impossible. Saturday's preliminary competition began at 6:00 A.M. and concluded at 1:40 A.M. Sunday. Through the luck of the draw, the Meraqua duet of Teri Pickett and Avilee Bean swam last in the Saturday night event and started their swim at 1:35 A.M. Then it was back in the pool for Bean a little more than four hours later, swimming her solo at 6:05 A.M. that same Sunday morning as the number two solo draw. Officials subjected to the same schedules were probably no less tired and frustrated.

There was no shortage of proposals at the following convention of 1974. Despite the sense of urgency, the fear of losing opportunities for national meet participation prevented an acceptable plan from developing. The only recommendations agreed upon were for trying to decrease the amount of time between routines and events and continue discussing various options. The problems lingered on.[66]

As interest in international competitions increased, the question of how to handle those participating in the U.S. national championships was again visited. Foreign competitors had taken part, without restriction, in U.S. championships for many years, even winning national championships in the early years. But the adoption of seeding procedures made coaches worry that the foreign swimmers could displace their swimmers from a seeded position. So, starting in 1972, foreign countries were restricted to one federation-certified entry each in solo, duet, and team event. Simply restricting the numbers obviously didn't take care of the coach's worries. One or more single entries could still cause a critical displacement. So, for 1973, a duplicate place and award arrangement was instituted. No U.S. athlete could be displaced by a foreign entry. Any U.S. competitor would be awarded the same place as the immediately preceding foreign competitor. Both would have the same places, the same seeding privileges, the same medals. Everyone was happy except, perhaps, the host facing the prospect of purchasing duplicate awards.

Another major change of the rules was more in interpretation. "Themes" were dropped as a judging criterion in 1968, but the master scoring entry sheets still retained a line for theme through 1969.[67] In 1970, with the master sheets now having to be purchased from the scoring committee, that line was replaced with one labeled "title." The announcer continued to use the title for introductions. Many coaches simply used the music title or something related: *Song of Norway, Scheherazade, Finlandia,* etc. There was some real descriptive imagination shown: "O'er Icy Steppes the Russian Wind Doth Blow," "Mortality, Behold and Fear," "Loudly Sings the Druid Hymn." Perhaps, though, the revolt against titles could have been with "Corn-Cob Cuties and Barn Yard Beauties," or "Last of the Red Hot Mommas!" These were actual titles sent with the results of the competition to the sports media.

Patsy Baugh, in San Antonio wrote *Synchro-Info*'s *Mailbox*, saying, "I find nothing athletic about having a 'theme,' and worse, having to interpret that theme with sometimes outlandish makeup and costumes. To add more ridicule to such a beautiful sport is the 18th Century mimetics attempted by untrained and inexperienced would-be actresses…. For theatrics we go to the theater, not a swimming pool…. This theme business has gotten completely out of hand. If the swimmers could be freed of this burdensome trivia, and the judges could be spared the knife of *Madame Butterfly* and the *Bomb at Hiroshima*, perhaps the fathers of the Olympics would cast a kinder eye in our direction."[68]

College student Kevis Bean wrote to *Synchro-Info*'s Athlete's Page, "I hope our swimmers will seriously think of reconsidering their desire to keep titles. The title is a relic from our watershow past and may actually harm our position in striving for Olympic recognition. Can you imagine Janet Lynn (skating) or Olga Korbut (gymnastics) being announced as *Scheherazade, Anastasia, Scarlett O'Hara, Desdemona, Saint Bernadette, Lorelei* [all titles taken from the top 20 placing soloists in the results in the 1972 rulebook]?"[69]

Still, many coaches thought that titles were needed for music interpretation. Several clubs in 1973 set out to prove otherwise. The Tustin Meraquas, Walnut Creek Aquanuts and Berea Aquateens all submitted entries with blank "title" lines in 1973. When announcers asked for their titles, Walnut Creek used "untitled," and the Meraquas listed theirs as "Routine Number ___."[70] Judges seemed to have little problem with evaluating their routines on execution and content. At the national convention that fall, the title line was officially dropped from the master scoring sheets.

In another effort to move away from the theatrical aspect of the sport, deck work was removed as a judging responsibility in 1974 with a rule specifying that judging "begins upon entry into the water." The stimulus for this was not a belated reaction to the 1960s criticisms for irrelevance and excessive theatricality, but to the dangers involved in the complex, multilevel team antics that had become commonplace. Potentially serious slips and falls had already occurred several times so it was believed best to remove the incentive for excessive display by making it irrelevant to the judging process. A penalty for deliberate standing or walking on the bottom was introduced in 1971 after one club performed head and waving arm motions while walking for half the length of a shallow pool, effectively continuing its deck work for another half minute in the water.

Rule changes in figures for 1969, changed the penalty for omission of a required figure in a routine. The five standard figure requirement was still retained, but omission of a required figure would be penalized by a standard one-point deduction in place of the cumbersome recalculation of the difficulty. A major change came for 1970 with standardizing the starting position for all figures to either a front or back layout. No longer could a figure start from a ballet leg (e.g., flamingo, Eiffel tower) or a vertical (spiral). And a five-point penalty for swimming out of the draw order was approved in 1974. This rule allowed a duet or team to swim instead of having to be disqualified because of the tardiness of one member.

In 1971, the five figure categories were compressed to four by combining the head first and foot first dolphins into a single dolphin group. At the same time, the practice of creating a totally new number for each figure to which a twist or spin was added was abandoned in favor of adding a letter to the number of the base figure. Each twist and spin was given a specific letter designation so that the figure and its appended action could be recognized by the number-letter combination. This ended the inconvenience of having to renumber all figures that were listed following a new spin or twist addition to an existing figure. It also altered the credit a swimmer would maintain if, for example, a figure with a half twist was listed or called for and a full twist was performed. Under the prior system, a full twisting figure would be a different number and therefore a totally different figure. The wrong amount of rotation, then, would be a failure to do the proper figure or a zero score. Now it would only be subject to the penalty for exceeding the limit of the twist.

The addition of a 180-degree spin to the hightower for 1971 made it the figure with the highest difficulty multiple, 2.2. To ensure better selection of high-difficulty actions, the difficulties for two other figures, castle and tailspin, were moved up to 2.2, along with introducing the provision that only one 2.2-level figure could be used as an optional. During this period, the swordasub, albatross, and catalarc were added, each involving at least one new transitional action. The aurora, added in 1972, included several novel transitions.

The three compulsory plus three optional senior figure competition gave way in 1972 to six required figures in five draw groups.[71] In its first national test, the performances revealed a number of weaknesses in some top competitors that had not been at all obvious when athletes had been able to perform their favorite optionals. For junior nationals, figures were still drawn from the senior groups. Junior Association figures were changed from the kip, dolphin, and somer-sub to a draw from two groups of four figures as compulsories while retaining two optionals.

A complete reevaluation of figure difficulties had started in 1974.[72] Historically, an initial difficulty was set based upon the ease with which a swimmer could perform the figure in a recognizable manner. Thus, low-difficulty figures were those which a novice could get through; more difficult figures were those with

more complex sequences that needed more training to obtain a recognizable performance. As skills and techniques improved, it became apparent some of the listed difficulties bore little resemblance to the skills needed for superior performances of the figures. Occasional individual changes aggravated rather than cured the problems. Jan Paulus chaired the ad hoc committee studying the relative difficulties of all figures. Parts of the long-awaited report on the "major-minor" figure judging analysis, led by Paulus, were presented at national seminars in 1973 and 1974. The main drive of the study had been to define what constituted the "major" and "minor" performance deficiencies in judging each and every figure. This was obviously an overwhelming task, complicated by many conflicts of definition. Nonetheless, a printed report was presented in 1975. The results of this 500-sample survey of coaches, "top 10" swimmers and officials, revealed many perceived problems in existing difficulty multiples. The committee studied the relative difficulties of all the transitional actions, essentially from one stable position to another position included in the figure, and set the stage for better figure difficulty analysis. The subsequent study group established new difficulty listings, passed at the convention of 1975, with more realism for top-level performances.[73] Major changes in difficulty multiples for many figures were made in 1975.

## Judging and Scoring

Ellen Murphy Wales, winner of the women's stunt competition in representing Wright College in the first competition held in the U.S., was guest speaker at the 1972 national championships banquet. Asked to describe what competition was like in 1946, she said, "How did [the swimmers] work? They got in there and swam! How did they coach? They got in there and howled! How was it judged? They got in there and fought! Hasn't changed a bit!"[74] While this achieved the expected laugh, the U.S. judges and officials felt they had come a long way from those days.

Swimmers were supposed to become

anonymous in figure competition in 1969 when it was ruled that they must all wear dark, one-piece suits, and be announced only by order number. This came about after *Synchro-Info* had editorialized in 1968, "A long overdue restriction should be applied to costumes for figure competition. A standard one-piece black suit would aid greatly in maintaining a uniform discrimination based upon body position. White and vari-colored suits frequently make comparisons of body position difficult. Judges have been asked to wear white clothing for judging; it is time to ask the competitors to wear black suits for figure judging."[75]

The restriction to only two judging panels for figures was finally relaxed in 1974 as mechanisms for using up to six panels were defined. This included dividing the competitors to allow simultaneous starts at all panels and progression through each panel in turn. This greatly reduced the total time involved and, for the swimmers, it lessened the "penalty" of an early draw.

Following a longstanding Canadian practice, judges were required to submit written scores for routines prior to their flashing of scores. The written score was the official award, no matter what was flashed. This was to ensure that no onlooker could possibly think a judge might be tempted to alter the content award after hearing the other judges' execution awards read.[76] The collection of these scores did not delay progress as much as expected because swimmers could be making their exits and the announcer could fill the time with the name introductions of the exiting swimmers. When the style award was retitled content in 1974, nothing was changed as far as the factors being judged were concerned. Execution remained everything done from a standpoint of perfection. Style or content was everything else: synchronization, creative action, fluidity, difficulty and diversity (substituted for "variety").

Use of one-tenth point intervals for routine awards was legislated in 1968 but initiation was delayed until January 1970 to allow time for the technical details to be worked out, such as new scoring tables and flashcards. Associations were urged to use it earlier if they wished. While many trying it liked it, others thought

it too unwieldy for scorers and enablement was rescinded in 1969. Tenth-point intervals were finally adopted for use in routines for 1972, but half-point intervals still prevailed for figures.

Judges were happy with their new freedom in using tenths of a point. Ranking of the top competitors was simpler, without so much need for juggling content and execution scores irrationally to obtain the desired ranking. But an overlooked "penalty" of the closer packing of routine scores with one-tenth-point separations was that the figure scores gained a heavier influence. This had been predicted, but disregarded in the enthusiastic rush for more flexibility in ranking routines.

In the continued effort to improve the judging process, the officials committee itself was further divided into three subcommittees in 1971, for training, testing and evaluation. In addition, field representatives were appointed to standardize training around the country. Fees for training and testing were established. And to ease the burden on the scorers, standardized figure and routine forms were made obligatory in 1970 to facilitate scoring. The competitor-generated forms, which had been allowed to this time, tended to show a rather cavalier disregard for uniformity and little resemblance to the form sample published in the rulebook.

Judge evaluation procedures were set up in 1969. Initially, only bias detected with either of the top two clubs was reported. Later the report was broadened to include the entire competition. The officials committee suggested that two unsatisfactory evaluation reports should require taking another oral exam to retain the rating. Discussions over which evaluation method was the best caused a lot of controversy, but, in 1970 a method that plotted each judge's deviations from the averaged scores of the other judges was adopted. After evaluations by that mechanism had been used for a year, Gene Ahlf worried, "Many judges want to know their record. Coaches and competitors want the judges evaluated ... however, the system has a tendency to pressure a judge to attempt to stay in the middle to protect their evaluation. Unless we have a balanced panel of judges, the results of the evaluations are not completely valid."[77]

In 1972, coaches and relatives of an athlete were barred from judging panels. Panels of seven judges were to include two from each of the three zones with a random draw for the zone of the seventh judge. These rules were intended to assure an equitable distribution and utilization of judges without biases, but they failed to recognize the very unequal distribution of rated judges throughout the country. All the restrictions made choosing judges a very lengthy process.

Requirements for becoming national judges were revised in 1969. A judge would have to be at least 18 years old and not an active competitor. A recommendation from the association would be needed to begin work to move toward a national rating. A three-year period between retesting was established, oral exams were started, and newly accredited national judges would be allowed to judge only preliminary events in the national competitions in their first year of national championship judging.

## Around the Country

Most development now occurred more like cities growing beyond their boundaries. As the sport became popular in one area, more clubs would be developed in surrounding areas as they too sought to join the nearby competition. Most new development was dependent upon finding coaches to lead the programs. The far-flung Alaska Association reported a club of 40 to 50 swimmers, the Petersburg Porpoises, who were busy preparing a water show, appropriately titled *Winter Wonderland*.[78] Bette McInnis reported starting a program at the municipal pool in Santa Fe, New Mexico. She wrote, "The sport of Synchronized Swimming has become so popular that every organized swim program wants to offer such a class to its members. And when you are the one chosen to teach it, believe me, you need all the help you can get."[79]

## Awards and Honors

The Helms Athletic Foundation had sponsored a Sports Hall of Fame for many AAU sports since the mid–'30s, since 1959 for synchronized swimming, where awards were displayed in the Helms Hall of Fame Museum in Los Angeles. But in 1971 the Helms Bakery that had supported the awards was sold. In 1972, United Savings Bank became a one-year sponsor of the Helms Athletic Foundation. In 1973, Citizen Savings Bank took over the Helms Athletic Foundation and continued to sponsor the Hall of Fame awards.[80] Duplicate certificates were now sent to the International Hall of Fame in Florida where it was hoped they would be displayed since the Helms Hall of Fame Aquatic Museum was no more. The awards continued under Citizen Savings (see Appendix A).

To honor the work that pioneer synchro coach and teacher Lillian "Billie" MacKellar had had done in developing the sport, a new award was established in her name, the Lillian MacKellar Distinguished Service Award. To reflect how MacKellar and those following her had impacted and influenced the sport, the criteria included the words, "to one who has given unselfishly of oneself for synchronized swimming without thought of personal gain and with a particular emphasis on working for the benefit of the athlete." The committee felt it only appropriate to make the first honoree Billie herself in 1971.[81]

In 1974, Gail Johnson became the second synchronized swimmer to be awarded the Lawrence J. Johnson Memorial Award.[82] This award is presented at the annual convention on a rotating basis to an outstanding athlete from one of the aquatic disciplines. The first synchro recipient, in 1968, was Margo McGrath.[83]

# 8

# *National Teams and Autonomy: 1976–82*

A truly pivotal event for all amateur sports in the United States took place during this period as the Congressional Amateur Sports Act of 1978 was put into effect. As a result, synchronized swimming and many other amateur sports became self-governing and independent of the AAU. Synchro set up its own governing body, code of operations and sport rules, without any oversight from the AAU. Independence, though, also added responsibilities, so, synchro passed a major milestone when a U.S. Synchronized Swimming National Office was established and an executive director hired to conduct the business of the new United States Synchronized Swimming, Incorporated (USSSI).

The progress of the sport paid little heed to the maneuvering involved in gaining independence, and that new status did little to solve any of the competition problems. National meets were still bloated with entries to the point of being nearly unmanageable. New techniques and new fashions in choreography evolved. Introductory sequences of long series of complex actions without coming up for air for a full pool length became the standard for solos. A "long" figure also became *de rigueur* in duets and teams. Spins were longer and more numerous. Duet and team "spectaculars," throw somersaults and dives or complex assisted lifts and platforms, all became frequent,

almost to the point of becoming commonplace.

A major factor in this transformation toward complexity was undoubtedly the decision, at the 1979 convention, that the U.S. should finally join the rest of the world in allowing unrestricted, free routines in all events. No longer would space be needed for five mundane and unimaginative required figures in the routines. The evolution had certainly started before that, but now U.S. swimmers were totally free to show the world what they could do with their creativity.

The rest of the synchro world was progressing too. Meeting the challenges of international competitions with other rapidly improving federations brought on another major accommodation, the formation of the first U.S. National Team in 1979. Long resisted as impractical due to the difficulties of bringing members together from all corners of the nation for long training camps, the concept triumphed in 1978 at the first Olympic Sports Festival. There, it was proved that it was feasible to bring together the talented swimmers from everywhere and integrate them into smoothly functional and beautifully performing teams, even with only a single week of practicing together as was allowed at the sports festival.

The U.S. Olympic Committee had wanted to establish a major all-sports event within the country to bring attention to its outstanding athletes in more than just the Olympic years so the USOC established the National Sports Festival in 1978.[1] This was to be a "National Olympic Games" in which top athletes from each of the four zones (East, West, North, South) would compete against the others, much as nation against nation in the Olympic Games.[2] It was a great opportunity for some of the money-starved "minor" sports because the USOC provided all the funding for athletes' and officials' travel, housing, and training. For synchro, ten athletes, enough for a team, two solos and two duets, were invited from each of the four zones. Each sport was responsible for establishing its own criteria for qualifiers to represent the zones and synchro initially used the figure rankings from the previous year's national championship. The 10 highest-scoring athletes from each zone would go to the festival. Coaches and managers were selected by their respective zones.

Upon arrival in Pueblo, Colorado, in 1978, coaches and athletes had one week to prepare to compete in solo, duet and team events. This would be little problem for soloists and most duets, where a little refreshment on their own routines would get them ready to start. But each of the zone teams included members who had never worked together before, or had any acquaintance with the team routine to be done. Here was the opportunity to determine whether swimmers from different clubs and different areas of the country could be brought together for a relatively short training time and refine a team routine to the point that it would be competitive in international events.

The result of the festival experiment and experience was a resounding success, far beyond synchro's expectations. The winners of those first events were of little consequence in comparison with the triumph of a concept. When it was over, there was no doubt in anyone's mind that high-level synchro swimmers could be brought together from all over the nation to work with their archrivals to develop a highly integrated team effort. Coaches and swimmers worked with a spirit of give and take, teaching, listening, absorbing, and practicing. In the end, four highly competent teams battled for the honors. Few spectators would

have believed the swimmers had not worked together all season. *Synchro-Info* reported, "Who won what seemed less important than what U.S. Synchro won in this new competition, a sense of accomplishment and camaraderie never before seen, and new approaches and vistas for the future."[3]

The obvious lesson from the first national sports festival was that a national team was feasible for the U.S. and that paved the way for the decision, at convention later that same year, to approve selecting a national team for the 1979 Pan American Games.[4] This move was an inspiration to talented members of smaller or weaker clubs with its implications for having a chance to grab the gold ring of participation in world-class competition. Any girl, from any club, could make the team! In the small print, though, was the need first to measure up to qualifying for entry into the team trials competition.

The first team trials consisted of three days of figure competitions in Walnut Creek, California.[5] Two teams were selected, one for the Pan American Games and the other to represent the U.S. in the Swiss Open. The national coach was designated as the club coach having the most athletes on each team. The first national coach was Gail Johnson (Pucci), Santa Clara, who became the coach for the 1979 Pan American Games Team. Gail Emery, Walnut Creek, became the national coach in 1980 with Johnson heading the national coaching staff again in 1981. The honor went back to Gail Emery in 1982.

Much progress had been made with the question of show or sport, particularly after the publicity at the first world championships in 1973. However, there was still work to be done. Lyle Makowsky, executive director of Synchro Canada, said during a visit to a U.S. competition in 1976, "If we ever intend to develop the sport throughout the world and have it accepted as a sport, we will have to appreciate the realities that describe the normal 'sports fan.' To get the public excited, you have to emphasize its competitive aspect.... We must accept the fact that people are more excited about watching something which pits one human being against another, or a human being against the limits of space or time, and even greater excitement is engendered by events which involve contact.... We must change the presentation, give names, histories, points ... identify parts of the routines and figures that are extremely difficult and say why."[6]

Soon after synchro was announced as the newest sport on the Olympic program in 1980, magazines began exploring and explaining it. *Women's Sports, The Olympian, Sportswoman, Young Athlete, American Girl, Small World, Swimming World*, airline magazines and Sunday sections of the many newspapers all had synchro articles. The *Los Angeles Times* in a special Olympic sports issue commented that "Perfect body control and split second coordination" are needed in synchro.[7] Miwako Motoyoshi, Japan's technical committee member, wrote in the *International Swimming and Water Polo* magazine in 1982, "Not so long ago the rules always had to be explained. Now it's a full house. It was marvelous to see the packed stands around the pool in Ecuador."[8]

*Life* magazine, in July 1982, did a feature on Tracie Ruiz and Candy Costie, U.S. champions, and explained how to become a success in the sport, "Start with a great body, strengthen with weightlifting, slantboard sit-ups and dozens of underwater laps. Master 'eggbeating' and sculling with hands and arms. Practice 'grunts' while submerged to signal partner...." *Sports Illustrated*, August 2, 1982, also covered Ruiz and Costie, and spoke almost admiringly of synchro for a change, "Synchronized Swimmers may look like cupcakes, but they're tough cookies.... Half the routine is performed upside down in a pool."[9]

Chris Georges of *Swimming World* wrote in 1979, after participating in a synchro workout, "I supposed I could handle the eggbeater and swan kicking. As expected, the eggbeater went well, I even beat a few girls to the wall, but the swan kicking was harder than I imagined.... But, after a few pathetic attempts at an upside-down split, I got out, forced to admit the defeat I had half anticipated ... and we hadn't even done the hard stuff yet! I learned my lesson that night, and I for one, will never scoff again at a synchronized swimming workout!"[10]

## International Developments

In 1976, FINA changed to the use of tenth-point intervals for routine awards. It deleted all references to themes, routine titles, or music titles; required submission of a written score for routines and added rules for age group competitions. Technical Synchronized Swimming Committee chairman Jan Armbrust, wanting synchro to maintain an appearance of maturity and stability to promote its campaign for Olympic status, resisted making any other changes.

Many forces were then working toward the Olympic goal. Lic. Javier Ostos, past president of FINA said, "The success scored at the Regional and Continental contests, coupled with the endeavors of Japan and the European League, considerably strengthened the arguments FINA was to put forth in its debate with the Olympic Program Committee and with the International Olympic Committee (IOC).... The future of synchronized swimming as an Olympic discipline stands on firm foundations even though there are still some international officials who look askance and do not consider it a technical sport."[11]

The prospect of at least being a part of the 1984 Olympics brightened in December 1977. Dr. Harold Henning, past president of FINA, put a question to the Los Angeles delegation at the meeting at which Los Angeles was selected as the U.S. city to bid for the 1984 Games. He said, "One of our disciplines is not on the Olympic program now, and if it is not [on the program] by 1984, would you accept it as a demonstration sport and provide a venue for it? I'm speaking of synchronized swimming."[12] The Los Angeles delegation agreed that they would. Henning said that the IOC agreed that "Swimming is one sport and thereby the disciplines of swimming, diving, water polo and synchronized swimming are considered events for the purpose of these rules. This meant that the IOC would then consider synchronized swimming as an event of the Olympic [swimming] program."[13] At the IOC meeting in 1980, the duet event was accepted for the 1984 Olympic Games.[14] Early in 1984, partially in response to the Soviet Union's boycott of the

Olympics, the solo event was abruptly added since it was observed that no additional athletes would be involved.

Synchro enthusiasts were totally puzzled over the failure to include the event that, to them, *was* synchronized swimming: the team. One reason given for team event rejection was that IOC members could not understand how an event with the number of team members varying between four and eight could be a fair contest. In 1980, FINA changed its rules to require eight-member teams, no more, no less, in Olympic, world, continental and regional championships. Four- to eight-member teams would still be allowed in other international events, but a penalty of 0.5 points would be deducted for each member fewer than eight.

The FINA World Aquatic Championships held in Berlin in 1978 marked the first time in international event history that the U.S. failed to dominate every event. Starting with the figure competition, Canada's strength leaped to attention. Helen Vanderberg gained an insurmountable lead of 3.55 points in the figure competition over U.S. solo champion Pam Tryon and she went on to easily win the solo title. The Japanese duet earned the highest routine score but Vanderberg and Michelle Calkins' high figure average won them that title. The U.S.A.'s Tryon and Michele Barone took second. The U.S.A's team depth, however, still proved too great for the others. Despite their number one starting position, they presented such a thrilling performance that they could not be denied the gold medal.

Lord Killanin, president of the IOC, with three members of the Olympic Program Commission, attended the duet event at the world championships in Berlin in 1978. Killanin said, "All the time, I thought it was like a show, an amusement, not a sport. Now I saw it was a sport." He added, "I am very impressed. I saw syn-

chronized swimming for the first time today. It is a very elegant sport."[15]

The U.S. felt the interest shown by the Russians at the world championships was a sign they already thought that it would eventually become part of the Olympics. A meeting was arranged with Valentina Sharova, the Russian synchro coach, and the U.S. delegation. In inquiring about the progress of USSR synchronized swimming, she was asked when they would enter an international competition. Sharova's answer was, "When we can beat you." After the figure competition, she was asked to compare her swimmers with those just seen. Her answer, "Not as good as your best," suggested they might not be far below either.[16]

The fourth World Aquatic Championships were held in Guayaquil, Ecuador, in 1982.[17] Wildly enthusiastic crowds saw the 50-meter synchro venue totally sold out and tickets being scalped for double and triple face value. Sponsors finally sold tickets for seats in the adjacent 50-meter speed pool bleachers.

Canada won the solo and duet events at the third World Championships in Berlin, but Santa Clara's team of (from left to right) Michele Barone, Linda Shelley, Erin Barr, Pam Tryon, Tami Allen, Gerry Brandley, Jane Goeppinger and Michelle Beaulieu, succeeded in keeping the team title with the U.S. (photograph by Lee Pillsbury).

Some spectators would sit more than 150 feet away from the action.

U.S.A.'s Tracie Ruiz was mobbed for autographs every time she walked from the hotel. Gaining a three-point lead in figures, she easily won the solo. But problems with partner Costie's figure performance allowed the Canadian duet to develop a 2.5 figure average lead, so they won easily. Even in the team event, U.S.A.'s usually strong aggregate figures fell behind Canada by 1.3 points. With that figure deficit showing clearly on the electronic scoreboard during routines, there was little that could be done to overcome a talented Canadian team performance. Candy Costie, in the post-competition interview, clearly stated the problem: "You can knock them dead with your routine, but if you've blown the figure competition, you can kiss winning goodbye."[18]

After the 1982 world championships, *Swimming World* wrote, "How should U.S. synchro team spell 'relief?' F–I–G–U–R–E–S, that's how! The lack of unquestionable figures superiority spelled the difference between a clean sweep of all three events and one gold and two silvers that the U.S. eventually earned."[19] U.S. official Dawn Bean said, "I left with mixed emotions; happy to see the remarkable progress of so many countries, but sad to find many countries with well established programs unable to participate because synchronized swimming is not on the Olympic program and therefore their Federation would not allot any funding. Yet, without world wide acceptance as a sport, we may never become part of the Olympics."[20]

CBS was diligently taping all the synchro final events at the world championships in Guayaquil while its directors and technicians were commenting on what a great event it was. U.S. synchro enthusiasts were encouraged to hope that the U.S. public would see a good part of the competition. As it turned out, to everyone's great dismay, CBS never had any plans at all to show any of the synchro events on the U.S. network. "No demand for it," they said.[21] The tapes were only made to sell to television broadcasters in other nations.

International competition had become more and more of a challenge for U.S. synchronized swimming. Going into 1978, the U.S. had dominated the world events, but with Canada's solo and duet wins at the 1978 World Aquatic Championships, tight battles between these two synchro "superpowers" would be the rule for many years.

The effort to overcome Canada's building strength in world competition had spurred the U.S. to develop and field its first national team for the 1979 Pan American Games in San Juan, Puerto Rico. That national team gained an 0.8-point advantage in figures which enabled them to secure the team title, but world champion Helen Vanderberg overcame the 0.4-point lead the U.S.A. soloist, Michelle Beaulieu, had earned in figures to win the solo title. Vanderberg, with partner Kelly Kryczka, had a figure average lead of almost a full point, and had little trouble topping Michele Barone and Linda Shelley.[22] The first experiment with a national team was successful and the U.S. continued choosing a national team to represent it at the major events each year thereafter

National Team I also participated at the first FINA World Cup that same year and a National Team II was selected to represent the U.S. at the Swiss Open in 1979. Other international competitions of the period were still open to the club option policy and the Santa Clara Aquamaids, Walnut Creek Aquanuts and Ohio State Synchro all competed well in foreign competitions. (See Appendix D.)

The Soviet Union, having first observed the sport at the 1978 world championships, initiated its own international event in 1982, the Soviet Women's Day International Solo and Duet Invitational. Held in Moscow the first week in March, Ruiz and Costie greatly outdistanced the European and Canadian competition. Of that meet, in Moscow's Olympic pool, U.S.A. official Don Kane said, "The Soviets do not hide the fact that the emphasis of their national program is aimed toward a good showing in Los Angeles in 1984. They apparently do not plan to emphasize the team event until after 1984."[23]

Taking note of the large number of international meets developing in Europe, synchro's Olympic international committee decided that the U.S. should try hosting a major international event. Concord, California, became the 1980 site for the first American Cup.[24] CBS was there to televise the events. The producers were so enthusiastic after the filming that they broadcast 28 minutes on the national network rather than the planned 13 minutes.

For an international competition, the American Cup was novel in allowing two entries per federation in the solo and duet events. From the preliminary event, the higher-placing contestant from each country would advance to the final event; the lower one would go to a consolation event. A surprise, possibly shock is a better word, developed when four champions of their country found themselves relegated to the consolation solo event after losing to teammates in the preliminary event. Only the national champions from the U.S.A. and the Netherlands qualified to swim in the solo final. This might be taken as a measure of how close the competition was, or it could possibly reflect on how judges assess the relative merits of two contestants that they have not watched developing over a long period of time.

We hardly seemed gracious hosts. The U.S. won all three final events and topped all consolation events as well. Linda Shelley led the parade to the victory stand in solo. She triumphed again in duet with Suzanne Cameron and U.S. National Team I was outstanding in their victory. Future Olympians Tracie Ruiz and Candy Costie won the solo and duet consolation events.

Once more, the importance of a conglomerate national team was demonstrated. The large advantage gained in figures allowed a very confident, nerve-free routine performance. Judges noted the uniform strength of all eight competitors and the sharp, clear action through difficult maneuvers. The U.S. earned an edge in routines in the face of the Canadians' striking showmanship which featured the first "platform" ever seen in competition.

The second Pan Pacific Cham-

With increasing challenges from other nations, the U.S. selected a national team in 1979. Members are, in back from left to right, Tracie Ruiz, Michele Barone, Linda Shelley, Laura Florio, and Tara Cameron, and in front from left to right, Marie White, Pam Tryon, Michelle Beaulieu, Gerri Brandley, Karen Callaghan and Suzanne Cameron (photograph by Ross Bean).

Kurt Gowdy, ABC-TV, interviewed the U.S. National Team following its gold medal performance at the first American Cup. From left to right are Linda Shelley, Tracie Ruiz, Suzanne Cameron, Candy Costie, Robin Waller, Julie Olsen, and Gowdy (photograph by Ross Bean).

*Left:* Linda Shelley and Suzanne Cameron (back) won both the national and American Cup duet titles in 1980. Shelley was also the reigning national solo champion since 1978 (photograph by W. Salvatore). *Right:* Sue Baross, 1976 U.S. solo champion, won again in 1977 and paired with Linda Shelley to also win the duet title. Baross was the gold medalist in solo at the third Pan Pacific Games in Mexico City in 1977 (photograph by Lee Pillsbury).

pionships were staged in Nagoya, Japan, in 1976, with Santa Clara representing the U.S. Although their team and duet of Robin Curren and Amanda Norrish had no problem winning against entries from Canada, Japan, Mexico, Australia and New Zealand, Curren lost the solo to Canada's Sylvie Fortier.[25] One year later, at the third Pan Pacifics in Mexico City, Santa Clara's Sue Baross had little problem defeating Helen Vanderberg in solo, and the U.S. team overwhelmed the Canadians again, but the duet fell to Canada's Vanderberg and Michelle Calkins.[26]

Going to a biennial schedule, the fourth Pan Pacifics were held in Christchurch, New Zealand, in 1979. This time, Santa Clara's Shelley and Barone took back the duet title, but their team lost to Quebec and Vanderberg overwhelmed Shelley for the solo title.[27] Tracie Ruiz won the solo in the fifth Pan Pacific Championships in Calgary, Canada, in 1981, then paired with Candy Costie to win the duet.

The U.S. National Team suffered a surprising loss to Canada. The accelerated drift toward very flashy and theatric routines, so evident in this meet, led FINA technical chairman Jan Armbrust to express some concern: "Pantomime playing has nothing to do with sport. The public may like it, but we must really think about the difference between show and sport … some things are not illegal, but they may be headed in the wrong direction. We may have to push a bit to get them going the right way," he declared.[28]

FINA added World Cups to the list of events and scheduled the first for Tokyo in 1979.[29] The first Central American championships were held in 1977.[30] Robert H. Helmick, secretary of FINA, sent word that Sri Lanka had reported holding its first synchronized swimming meet in February 1977. He said, "It's important to our efforts to include synchronized swimming in the Olympic program to have as many nations as possible conducting competitions and holding champi-onships. Therefore, it seemed like especially good news."[31]

The U.S. hosted the first ASUA age group competition in Florida in 1982[32] and "club op-tion" competitions offered a new world of op-portunity to many U.S. swimmers. Clubs who took the chance to compete internationally par-ticipated in the Swiss Open, Mallorca Open, Soviet Women's Day Invitational, Mazda Invi-tational-England, Scandinavian Open, Egyp-tian Open, Netherlands Invitational, and International Age Group in Mexico. (See Ap-pendix D.)

FINA appointed an International Judges Study Group to develop a judge training man-ual. The group met at the U.S. Olympic Train-ing Center in Squaw Valley in 1978 to write its first FINA manual. This was presented the next year at the International Conference for Judges in Washington, D.C. The first World Confer-ence for Coaches was held in Calgary, Canada, following the 1981 Pan Pacific Championships. In 1982, FINA established its first list of rated international judges in 1982 and selected Dawn Bean, Judy McGowan and Betty Wenz as the first FINA judges from the U.S.A. More judges would be added in following years until an al-lotment of 10 international judges per federa-tion, three "A," three "B," and four "G" (gen-eral), was fulfilled.

## The National Championships 1976–82

By 1976, Santa Clara had firmly estab-lished itself as the top club in the nation. The 1975 world team had mostly retired, but the new group succeeded in keeping the title at home even while dealing with the death of their brilliant coach, Kay Vilen. Just retired Gail Johnson (Buzonas) took on the challenge of stepping into Vilen's shoes.

Whatever else happened at the 1976 In-door Nationals in The Woodlands, Texas, it will last in memory as the "Night of the Flood." As participants headed for the airport after finals, they found it was totally inaccessible with all roads and underpasses leading to it flooded by the torrential rains that had fallen continuously during the final competition. A few abandoned their cars to wade a half mile through water as high as their knees to reach the airport. Others simply returned to the ho-tels they had just left to try again the next day.

Earlier in the day, the television crew tap-ing the events, looking at the dark indoor com-petition pool, had tried to get the finals moved to the outdoor diving well. Commenting on how lucky it was the move hadn't been made, with the tremendous volume of rain water falling during finals, one observer said, "It would have been very difficult to determine whether the swimmers were on the surface or under it because the rain was coming down so hard, the water seemed continuous from the bottom of the pool to any height above it."[33]

Santa Clara won easily in 1976, but com-petition was heating up with their San Jose neighbors, the California Coralettes, coached by Judy Graun. By the outdoor nationals of 1977 in Hilo, Santa Clara led by only 1.5 points. A notable aspect of this competition was that, for the first time in many years, no "B" teams from any club appeared in finals. Talent had risen throughout the country, allowing their entrance into the final field.

At the 1978 indoor championships in Commerce, California, obeying recent policy decisions, figure averages were kept secret until after the last routine. As the routine scores were flashed, the Coralettes appeared to lead by 0.8 points and it seemed they might finally be victorious. It was not to be. As the withheld figure averages were added, Santa Clara won by just 0.2 point. That was too much for some of the Coralette swimmers. By that summer, the Aquamaids had little trouble winning as the Walnut Creek Aquanuts moved into second place over a depleted, four-girl Coralette team.

In the 1979 indoors, for the first time in more than 30 years, college teams were in finals. Not only in, but threatening the cham-pion. Both the University of Arizona (coach Kathy Kretschmer) and Ohio State University (coach Mary Jo Ruggieri) were loaded with strength recently skimmed from the top seven clubs, while Santa Clara, with only three returning members of their 1978 team, had been forced into prelims for the first time in memory. "Against the odds, the failure to turn everything upside down must be attributed largely to the miracles wrought on the Aquamaids by their young coach Gail Johnson, who must now be considered one of the truly great coaches," reported *Synchro* [*-Info*] magazine.[34] Arizona took second and Ohio State third. Collegiate recruiting had depleted many teams, but the Hamden Heronettes, Seattle Aqua Club, Walnut Creek Aquanuts, and Tustin Meraquas managed to stay in the finals.

Santa Clara coasted to victory again at the 1979 outdoor nationals in Long Beach, California, over the usual clubs. No university team had yet converted to club status that would allow competition outside the collegiate season. Hamden and Seattle moved into the second and third places the colleges had vacated. But there were to be no more easy wins for Santa Clara.

At convention that year, it was decided to change to a single senior national championship in place of the two each year that had been held under the AAU. With no indoor senior meet that spring, it was a long period of anticipation and preparation for the summer event.[35] The anticipation was heightened by awareness that contention for the titles had never been tighter since the Merionettes and Aquamaids exchanged titles back and forth in the early '70s. This meet, in the new facilities at Irvine, California, became the largest senior national ever held to that date, with 439 total entries and 272 competitors in preliminary figures. Even with four panels, eight hours were needed for those figures. Prelim figure competition might have been shorter than alternative mechanisms for weeding out the preliminary solo and duet contenders but something more effective was still obviously needed.

As the two-per-year senior national schedule ended in 1979, so did the reign of the Aquamaids. Their overturn by the Walnut Creek Aquanuts at the single 1980 senior national in Irvine was the closest contest ever. Just 0.04 point separated Walnut Creek from Santa Clara in that contest. Monica Mendenhall, Julie Olsen, Jill Van Dalen, Becky Roy, Mary Vis-

niski, Marie White and Sara White celebrated their capture of the pinnacle. They did not realize, at that time, that it would be the start of an unbroken string of team titles lasting until 1990. Walnut Creek went on to win both the 1981 and 1982 championships.

Some relief developed in 1981 when all entries, including teams, were required to qualify through zone championships.[36] This greatly reduced the number of entries in the preliminary events, and allowed discarding the preliminary figure competition. A much-improved schedule followed.

From 1975 through 1980, Santa Clara had a continuous series of duet winners. First it was Robin Curren and Amanda Norrish, then Sue

Walnut Creek won the first single year championship and then added 12 more team titles before Santa Clara began its string of victories. Swimmers include, in back, from left to right, Becky Roy, Sara White and Jill Van Dalen, and in front, from left to right, Julie Olsen, Mary Visniski, Marie White and Monica Mendenhall.

Baross and Linda Shelley, followed by Michele Barone and Pam Tryon. Then Barone paired with Shelley and the next year Shelley paired with Suzanne Cameron to keep the title in Santa Clara.

It was not always easy though. In 1978 Barone and Tryon twice lost the routine competition to the Coralettes' Sara and Marie White but prevailed due to higher figure averages. Then in 1979, Barone, with new partner Shelley, had to face off against Barone's 1978 partner Tryon and former teammate Michelle Beaulieu, both now swimming for the University of Arizona. In 1980, Shelley and Cameron were the victims of the Seattle Aqua Club's Candy Costie and Tracie Ruiz in the routine competition, but the figure average gave Shelley and Cameron the title once more, but by only 0.06 of a point. Costie and Ruiz showed an exciting new dynamism that would inject new energy in the sport for many years to come.

The long Santa Clara and even longer California domination of the duet event finally gave way at the 1981 senior nationals in Fort Lauderdale. Seattle's Ruiz and Costie broke the grip that California had held on the title for 24 years, ever since the victory of Shaw Park's Roz

Tracie Ruiz, Seattle Aqua Club, had been a close second in the nationals of 1980. By 1981 she achieved the gold and remained undefeated in national and world competition through 1984. Ruiz won five national and world championship titles and was the first Olympic Games solo gold medalist.

Calcaterra and Mary Jane Gury in 1958. Costie and Ruiz were solid victors in 1982 as two sets of twins flanked them on the victory stand in Hilo, Hawaii. The Coralettes' twins, Marie and Sara White, were second, and Hamden's twins, Karen and Sarah Josephson, were third.

The solo title was distributed between several Santa Clara swimmers from 1976 to 1980. Robin Curren won the indoor 1976 title, then was upset by teammate Sue Baross in the outdoor meet. Baross won both indoor and outdoor titles in 1977, then Pam Tryon took the 1978 indoor and Linda Shelley rose to win the 1978 outdoor. Shelley won both competitions in 1979 and comfortably defended in the single event of 1980. At that meet though, the rapidly rising challenger Tracie Ruiz of the Seattle Aqua Club, rose to second.

The solo title had resided in California since 1960, but it migrated with the duet, to Washington in 1981 when Tracie Ruiz also took the solo gold home. Defending for the first time in Hilo in 1982, Hawai-

Amanda Norrish (left) and Robin Curren, U.S. national duet champions in 1975, also earned the World and the Pan Am Games duet titles that same year. They successfully defended their national crown in 1976 (photograph by Lee Pillsbury).

ian-born Ruiz (middle name Lehuanani) was a big hit with the spectators as she easily won the title again.

The first Collegiate (AIAW) National Championship, held at Michigan State University in 1977, brought entries from 15 schools.[37] Ohio State won all the titles with Sue Flanders winning the first solo; Cory Lamb and Cindy Ott became the first duet winners and joined with Jill Vincent to win the trio. Joanmarie Barris, Jill Vincent, Terry Edwards, Heather Bruce, Jane McGorrum, Donna Burian, Cory Lamb and Cindy Ott made up the first winning team for the Ohio State Buckeyes.

During the next years, many top swimmers took advantage of the scholarship programs offered by several colleges and the collegiate winners were generally well-known names from the AAU and USSSI championships. Solo champions included Linda Shelley and Pam Tryon from the Aquamaids swimming for San Jose State and the University of Arizona; Tara Cameron of the Coralettes went to Ohio State; and Tracie Ruiz of the Seattle Aqua Club went to the University of Arizona.

Collegiate duet champions were often combinations of swimmers from different established clubs. Duet winners of the first championship were Ohio State, Cory Lamb from the Meraquas with Cindy Ott of the Coralinas. Next it was Karen Callaghan from the Aquanuts with Tara Cameron of the Coralettes. They were followed by Karen and Sarah Josephson from the Heronettes. The University of Arizona won titles with some intact pairs, Sara and Marie White from the Coralettes, Becky Roy and Julie Olsen from the Aquanuts and Candy Costie and Tracie Ruiz from the Seattle Aqua Club. From 1977-1982, Ohio State and the University of Arizona each won three duet titles. Trio titles were also divided between Ohio State and the University of Arizona with Ohio State winning four and Arizona two. Ohio State forged a string of six consecutive team victories from 1977 through 1982.

## Sport Administration

Barbara Eaton, Virginia Beach, was synchro's chairman from 1975 to 1977. During debates over the Amateur Sports Act in Congress, she followed the examples of other aquatic sports and organized a restructuring committee to develop the articles of incorporation and code of regulations under which synchronized swimming would operate upon the sports act's execution. Her efficient organization and conduct of the sport during the restructuring made her widely respected in the AAU and she was appointed to the AAU's parliamentarian's committee at the end of her term.

Judy McGowan, York, Pennsylvania, was elected in fall of 1977, and served as both the last AAU synchro chairman and the first president of United States Synchronized Swimming, Incorporated (USSSI). Following her 1977 to 1980 AAU term, she was eligible, under the new organization rules, to run for president of USSSI. She was elected to two consecutive two-year terms, designed to make the synchro term of office for its head officer coincident with the Olympic Quadrennial. This 1981–84 USSSI term made her the only leader of U.S. Synchro, in any of its incarnations, to serve a seven year stint in office.

Synchro began to prepare for autonomy when Eaton named McGowan to chair an ad hoc restructuring committee to develop plans for the conversion. The progress in defining the organization that would ensue was presented at the 1977 convention and passed.[38] Before the Amateur Sports Act was passed in 1978, there had been a pitched lobbying battle during the two prior years to influence Congress on the final nature of the act. The AAU, which included all the aquatic sports, fought hard to maintain its position as the official representative for amateur sports in the U.S., while the National Collegiate Athletic Association (NCAA) attempted to maintain its position as the international representative for some sports. The United States Olympic Committee (USOC) finally won the designation as the coordinating agency and international representative for all amateur sports in the Olympic and Pan American Games programs.

The USOC specified that each sport set up its own autonomous incorporation and hold its own international franchise. In the case of the aquatic sports, the structure of sports representation to the International Olympic Committee required that an intermediate corporate structure, United States Aquatic Sports, Inc. (USAS), be formed as the primary coordinating agency for the international aquatics franchise, FINA.

The four aquatic corporations, including synchro, would each have a seat on the USAS Board of Directors as well as on USOC's Executive Board. Judy McGowan became the first representative to USAS and Dawn Bean, Olympic International chairman, became USSSI's first representative to the executive board to have a vote at USOC meetings. Another part of the act specified that athletes should be given more influence in the operations of the new autonomous sports. An Athletes Advisory Council (AAC) was set up within USOC and Kathy Kretschmer served as synchro's first representative to that committee.

The legal papers for incorporating USSSI were filed in December 1977, to become effective January 1, 1979. Until USAS was fully operative, synchro continued working with the AAU for administrative purposes. The first convention of the four aquatic sports under USAS took place in fall of 1980. Judy McGowan, then USSSI president and synchro's representative to the USAS board, was appointed "chef de mission" for the 1982 World Aquatic Championships.

USSSI found an initial home in 1981 for its new national office in the National Governing Body (NGB) Building at the Olympic Training Center in Colorado Springs. For the executive director to head that office, an excellent choice was made with Paula Oyer. Brenda Scandaliato was added to the staff in 1982 as a general assistant.

National chairman Judy McGowan initiated changes in the way the national committee operated in 1978. The 25 formerly independent subcommittees, reporting only to the chairman and board of governors, were all reorganized under five vice chairmen, each in charge of specific functional areas: development, finance, international, officials, and technical. All the subcommittees were allocated responsibility under an appropriate vice chairman. Their titles changed to vice president in 1980 and four zone representatives were added. With incorporation, a board of directors was established to provide a more efficient operation. The makeup of the board of directors included the officers, the vice presidents, zone representatives, the athletes representatives, ASUA and FINA representatives and past presidents and chairmen.

Athlete representative terms of office were increased from one to two years in 1977, and a collegiate representative was added to USSSI's Athletes' Board. The number of athlete representatives was increased to six in 1978 to meet the Amateur Sports Act's requirement that athletes comprise 20 percent of the membership on all committees.

Funding for international competitions continued to be a grievous issue. It was immediately apparent that the money raised from sales of pins and patches, meet sanctions, and donations would never be enough to cover the costs of multiple overseas expeditions. At the 1976 convention, the finance committee reported, "The growth and development of international competitions within FINA dictate that the National Committee face up to the fact that national funding has become a prime need.... We must all join forces to develop ways and means to finance U.S. participation, both internationally and nationally."[39] Such resolutions were not much of a solution. The problem might have been even more acute for USSSI and the OIC after establishing a national team in 1979. The real bite was delayed for a year as USOC funding provided for the Pan American Team travel while Japan funded all participants to the first FINA World Cup competition. The OIC was able to use the balance of its pin and patch money to help National Team II compete in the Swiss Open.

In 1980, all USSSI clubs were asked to donate to the National Team Travel Fund. The suggested donations were $50 from clubs participating at the national level and $25 from all other clubs. Again, Team I received funding under USOC's allocation to USSSI, so the collected funds could again be used for Team II.[40] Despite intensive efforts by USSSI to attract commercial sponsors, the OIC sales of pins and patches remained the only non–USOC source of funding in 1981.

With new technological advances, the comparative ease of making home-edited cassette tape recordings for synchro accompaniment had almost crowded out the more expensive edited discs as the decade of the '70s came to a close. Cassettes made their final triumph when they were made mandatory for USSSI national competitions in 1982.[41] But, in recognition of the vast reservoir of existing discs that might be repetitively used for developing swimmers, the provision, "disc recordings will still be allowed at local and regional championships during the transition," was approved for all but national meets. The change to tapes was a great relief to sound managers tired of having winds blow records off the turntable and bumps to the sound table that often resulted in delayed re-swims, generally in more favorable later positions. The advantage the tapes provided was somewhat offset by the prevalence of poor quality, home-edited tapes that assaulted the ears with distortions and terribly mismatched bits of different pieces of music.

The USOC opened its first Olympic training center at Squaw Valley, California, in 1977. The first sport to make use of the new facility was synchronized swimming.[42] Santa Clara trained there before the August Pan Pacific Games in Mexico City and a workshop for swimmers and coaches was scheduled for fall. Synchro was back again in November holding the first "top 10" camp.[43] This camp brought one athlete and one coach from each club that had placed in the top ten of any event in the 1977 senior nationals to a specially designed program at Squaw Valley. Funding from the USOC's Development Program provided for sports medicine testing of athletes' physical traits for the first time. Experts were brought in to offer sessions on techniques, strength development, conditioning, nutrition and psychology. OIC chairman Dawn Bean said, "All participants of this first camp felt that the sharing of techniques, ideas, and concerns was the most

beneficial thing that had happened and they enthusiastically await the next camp. Not only did they learn many things that will help their own development but they were able to work with and get to know the other competitors in a friendly, non-competitive atmosphere."[44] Mary Tope, coach of the Riverside Aquettes, said, "I am always saying I am alone at the pool, but I'm not. Every night there is an entire army of people helping me with all the things they have shared with me through the years since I began [in 1962 in Indio, California]. It is this sharing of knowledge that had made this sport grow and the continued sharing will take it to where we all want to see it, in the Olympics."[45]

The next year, 1978, a second "top 10" camp was held in Squaw Valley but it had been preceded by an "intermediate" camp, for those just below the "top 10" cut-off.[46] Its theme was "How to Become an Elite Swimmer." The sports medicine testing from that intermediate camp showed one astonishing result. A young swimmer from Seattle, Tracie Ruiz, had tested with the same strength and physical agility as Linda Shelley, the current national solo and duet champion. Some wondered at the time whether that offered some portent for the future.[47]

Two camps were offered in 1979, the elite camp in Squaw Valley[48] and a coaches' camp at the new Olympic Center in Colorado Springs.[49] USSSI squeezed in one more intermediate camp at Squaw Valley before that facility closed forever in 1980. That fall the elite camp was held in Colorado Springs. With pressure mounting for developmental camps that would respond to regional and zone athlete needs, the Olympic International Committee offered a plan for alternating intermediate (athletes not qualified for national semifinals) camps in odd years with beginner camps in the even years. However, this was scrapped before its inauguration in favor of a zone camp plan for 1981, that would minimize travel distances and costs. The zone camps would serve the functions of both intermediate and beginner camps. These camps laid the foundations for the National Clinic Network (NCN) that would begin in 1988.

National Coaches Camp had been held in

1975[50] and again in 1976,[51] but coaches lost interest in those specialized camps when the camps at the Olympic Training Centers offered the opportunity to attend with their athletes. The last USSSI Coaches Camp, open to all who wanted to attend, was held in Colorado Springs in 1979.[52] There were alternatives. Mary Jo Ruggieri, coach of the Ohio State University team, began the R & R Sports Academy programs for athletes at all levels in 1979, providing as many as six camps each summer in various locations around the country. This program has continued to the present, but on a reduced scale.

Obviously, coaches and swimmers were seeking information to help them achieve the highest levels. To meet the expected upsurge in demands for written materials after synchro's first Olympic Games in 1984, the development committee was writing a teaching manual, *Coaching Synchronized Swimming Effectively*, that would include six levels of achievement and a "patch" reward program for new and recreational swimmer awards. More new books were added to the list of synchro texts. Mary Jo Ruggieri and Jean Lundholm authored *Introduction to Synchronized Swimming* in 1976. The book included concepts of stability and motion, body positions and movement progressions for rotation, unrolls and transitional movements as well as dry-land exercises, pool conditioning and unit plans for coaching and teaching.[53] Betty Wenz, chairman of the sports medicine committee, with the cooperation of American Alliance for Health, Physical Education and Recreation (AAHPER) produced *Sports Medicine Meets Synchronized Swimming* in 1980. The book held information relating to work physiology, warm-up and flexibility, injury classification, common orthopedic problems, body composition and weight control, nutrition, and psychological aspects of elite women's athletics.[54] Nancy Wightman and Nancy Chiefari authored *Better Synchronized Swimming for Girls* in 1981. The book was written for young readers, 8 to 14 years old, as part of a sports series published by Dodd, Mead and Company. The cover jacket read, "This book shows you how to perform the basic body positions, sculling movements, and figures

used in beginning level synchronized swimming. The synchronized swimmer is a skilled, trained athlete. Yet any girl who can swim can learn the skills necessary to enjoy the sport."[55]

USSSI published its first and only *Yearbook* in 1982.[56] The yearbook included the results and photos of the year's national and international events which had been dropped from their usual residence in the rulebook. The yearbook was, of course, planned as an annual publication but this first one was delayed until so late in the year that most remained unsold. Consequently, no others were published. *Synchro Canada*, *Synchro Japan* and *Synchro Magazine* continued publication and a new magazine, *Synchro News*, appeared in the United Kingdom in 1981, under Chris Harrison.[57] *Synchro-Info* dropped the *-Info* to become simply *Synchro* in 1979. A major motivation for the change was that "Info" seemed to suggest to many people that the magazine's publisher was the repository for all information, past and present and future, about synchro.

## Competitive Programs

The longstanding AAU tradition of holding two senior national championships, indoor and outdoor, was finally abandoned as competitors as well as officials became increasingly concerned about the costs of attending two senior meets each year as well as the many other national events that had sprung up. The change to a one-a-year summer senior national was voted in at the 1978 convention, to take effect in 1980. The single senior national concept had been simmering for more than 10 years, after ABC discontinued its television coverage giving, as one reason, the outdoor nationals was a live rerun of the indoor competition.

The division of the nation into competition zones was stimulated by the start of the USOC's Sports Festival competitions. The USOC had designated four zones from which teams of athletes would be drawn for competing with each other at the festival.[58] Synchro used those zone divisions in 1980 to push through a plan that was hoped would finally put a cap on the numbers in national competitions. Qualification for nationals would take place through zone competitions. Often proposed and always rejected previously, the new proposal sweetened the package by allowing additional qualifiers for each zone based on the number of contestants the zone had in finals of the most recent championship. This maintained eligibility for all the top athletes from each zone and ended the main objections. North, South, East and West zones were established and qualifying allocations were enacted. By 1980, selection of sports festival athletes was based upon performances in meets within the zones as well as the national championships. This event had become a bonus for athletes, who wanted more competitions to be considered for qualifications. For two years a cumbersome system was used, involving various national and zone meets; then, in 1983, qualification became based solely on the zone meets.

Each junior national event traditionally had been awarded separately to sponsors in different locations but there was considerable sentiment generated for changing to an integrated meet. Beginning in 1977, the policy was adopted to award the solo and duet events to a single sponsor-site, and the team events to a different site and sponsor. Another compromise action was taken in 1978, to take effect in 1980, to hold a three-event indoor junior national championship during the period that would be vacated by the demise of the senior indoor in 1980. The outdoor juniors would continue on the same basis of solo with duet and a separate team event. That combination actually was never used. Instead, two full-event junior nationals were awarded and held in 1980. The first three-event meet took place in Hamden, Connecticut, at the Easter holiday period. The outdoor juniors were held in July at Mission, Kansas.

As age group competition continued advancing in popularity, some reorganization was done. The 15–17 age group was split and expanded in 1977 into 15–16 and 17–18 for solo and duet and 15–18 for team. The new divisions were added to the national Junior Olympic program in 1978. International age group events started to be offered, so an international age group trials event was initiated in 1982 to determine the representatives to such meets. The next year, a national age group championship was combined with the international age group trials in Denver, Colorado.[59] This national event differed from the Junior Olympic national in allowing a younger age group, 11–12, but more importantly, by not excluding the age groupers who might also be active in senior national events and would be the likely international competitors in age group events.

For 10 years, the "regional" groupings for age group and junior Olympic programs were identical, corresponding to those of the AAU's Junior Olympic regions. Partially in the hope of promoting synchro development in some of the weaker areas by bringing them together a with stronger associations for competitions, the association groupings for the age group program were reorganized for 1982.[60] The associations within each of the four zones were distributed into four, A, B, C and D Age Group "sections." Besides bringing different associations together, this also generally prevented the age group and Junior Olympic regional events from mirroring each other.

The USOC encouraged the development of State Games. Both the Empire State Games in New York, beginning in 1978, and the Sunshine State Games in Florida, starting in 1980, included synchro. Although more states would be added through the years, the state games program never developed whole-hearted backing. But, in the enthusiastic early starting states, like New York and Florida, the state games remain strong promoters for the sports they include.

Although collegiate competitions were the original source of competitive synchro, and the Association for Synchronized Swimming for College Women was formed in 1955, formal rules under a national body governing intercollegiate competitions were not formulated until 1975. The first National Intercollegiate Championships were scheduled for Michigan State College in 1977.[61] Some colleges and universities in the East and Midwest had been conducting competitive synchro programs (club) for some time. The "official" status allowed several to have thriving programs going very quickly, offering the opportunity to synchro-

devoted swimmers to go to college while continuing competition in their sport. Some could even offer scholarships to the swimmers for their "varsity" program. These attracted some of the AAU clubs' top swimmers who might otherwise have devoted several more years to the support of their club while attending a close-by, synchro-less college.

Club coaches did not always look kindly upon the collegiate opportunities. One said, "I have put my life and soul into developing these swimmers. I will quit [coaching] before I become a farm club for some University!" From another, "Since it is a well known fact that it takes eight to ten years to develop a national competitor, will the coaches continue to develop swimmers if, at the moment they become good, the colleges offer scholarships that cannot be turned down?"[62] But for parents, the lure of scholarships was real and understandable, as exemplified by the comment from the parent of a swimmer whose brother had a basketball scholarship, "Now all that swimming may finally pay off."[63] Pat Gorman, editor of the *College Coaches Academy News*, said, "Recruiting

puts pressure on an athlete. Coaches, collegiate and otherwise, must consider what each can offer the athlete in the way of contributing to her total life and help her think through without pressure. The final choice must be her own. Nobody owns an amateur athlete."[64]

Further aggravation arose because the swimmers were not simply lost to the limbo of intercollegiate events but they were returning to face their former teammates in the AAU nationals as well. The AAU code had long had a rule against recruiting athletes into "super clubs." But the collegiate recruiting of star swimmers into what the club coaches saw as super clubs was a normal feature of collegiate sports. The super club designation seemed appropriate for a University of Arizona team that had not even existed two years before it won second places in all three of the 1979 indoor national events with swimmers who, only the year before, had been members of other finalist clubs. Even before that happened, alarmed reactions had resulted in forming an ad hoc committee in 1978 to study the problem. The only outcome was a reminder to collegiate coaches and representatives to adhere strictly to the NCAA recruiting rules. In particular, it was believed that some flagrant violations of proscriptions against coach and athlete recruiting contacts at meets had occurred.

In 1977, AAU synchro followed U.S. Swimming's lead into the world of masters competition, officially adopting rules to govern this new group of athletes.[65] An initial masters national championship was held in 1975 and a second in 1976 in Washington, D.C.[66] However, the 1977 championship at the University of Richmond was listed officially as the first National Masters Championship. This competition brought 39 competitors, distributed into 22 solos, 11 duets and 5 teams.[67] By 1982, there were 148 participants in 76 solos, 40 duets, 5 trios, and 23 teams.[68] Several U.S. clubs participated in Canada's senior age games in Toronto in 1978 and won medals.[69]

Winners of the first collegiate national championship from Ohio State University include, in front, from left to right, Cindy Ott, Joan Marie Barris, Terry Edwards, and in back, Heather Bruce, Jane McGorrum, Donna Burian, Cory Lamb and Jill Vincent (Department of Photography, Ohio State University).

## Technical Rules

After initially requiring athletes to compete in their own age group, as done worldwide, U.S. synchro liberalized its rules to allow a single athlete to advance upward to the next higher age group "to complete a duet or team." The swimmers moving up an age group were still required to perform figures within their own age group. In 1977, the rules were relaxed to allow competing in figures for any age group entered for routines. By 1979, any number of swimmers could now move up to higher age group routines, with no restrictions on the extent of the upward movement.[70] And a sixth required figure was added to the age group figure competitions in 1978 to make better scoring more relative to senior competitions where the athletes competed with six figures. Then in 1980, the figures for all developmental programs were revised with new groups based on a progression of skills.

There were still more changes to the rules. A new order of draw procedure for finals was adopted for 1977 with the top four qualifiers drawing for the last four performance positions; the three lowest places would draw for the earliest positions. But, for 1978, another draw system was instituted which is in place today. In this, the highest-scoring qualifier draws from among the last three swimming positions and the draw continues adding the next earlier swimming position after each draw, each qualifier drawing in order of placing in qualification, until all swimming positions have been drawn.

With the expanding numbers of nationally rated judges available for the figures competition, an allowance was made for using as many as six panels for figures for 1978.[71] Contestants were divided into six equal groups for starting, and flowed through all panels continuously. This would make, in essence, six swimmers suffer the stigma of performing as number one, but sharing assuaged the pain a little and any score drift became less obvious with shorter judging times. The decision was made, in 1976, to publish only individual figure scores, listed under the figure competition draw numbers of the competitors, until after

the last final event started. Only then would composite figure averages be known except through tedious matching and calculating. This anonymity was supposed to minimize any possible influence figure results might have upon judging of routines.

When the international rules were first developed in 1954, a "free routine" was adopted for simplicity in understanding rules throughout the world. The U.S., however, had continued with its five-figure requirement since it felt this imposed some measure of athleticism. After stunt (figure) competition began in 1958, many felt the figure competition was an adequate test of athletic skill and that the free routine should be adopted. Five standard figures were still required in routines in 1976 but the penalty for omission of a required routine figure was changed in 1977 to a three-point deduction for solo, two for a duet member and one for a team member. Use of a "substituted" figure, by all members of a duet or team, was made a two-point penalty rather than penalizing as an omission.

It took 25 years, until 1979, for the U.S. to accomplish joining the rest of the world with free routines.[72] 1980 was the first year that routines didn't have compulsory figures. Immediately they became more innovative and creative, particularly at the senior level. However, the next few years saw many abuses of the new freedom, particularly with age group swimmers who rarely completed a vertical and seemed to "back-tuck" out of everything. It was a good move for USSS but the U.S. coaches needed time to learn to use some judgment on what should be put into age group routines.

Although the U.S. had adopted the free routine, it still felt its two-award scoring system was superior to FINA's single award and continued to use two scores. The U.S. system also had been using a difficulty multiplication factor of 1.8 on the execution score, making that score's weight nearly twice that of the content score. This factor continued in use but was changed, in 1982, to 2.0 to make it easier for the audience and parents to figure out the scoring.

National championships still had far too many entries for judges to work through. To try to whittle the national preliminary solo and duet lists down to something more manageable for judges and meet hosts, a preliminary figures competition began in 1976. It was believed that a tremendous number of swimmers could be judged in a relatively short time with four figures judged by four panels. A preliminary figure competition was required whenever there were more than 60 routines entered in junior or 45 in senior events. The preliminary figure competition did cut the time needed for solos and duets at the 1977 national championships, but national chairman Frances Jones noted a disturbing element. "With almost 200 swimmers in Preliminary Figures, all scores seemed to be in the 5 to 6½ mode," she said, "We must do something to liberate the 7 to 8½ point scores."[73]

Figure changes were made as well, again generally to conform with the international requirements. In the early '60s, AAU synchro had deleted twists from head first dolphins, considering them, as then performed, incompatible with the circle definition of the dolphin. FINA had always retained the dolphin twists. Twists were finally restored to the AAU dolphins for 1976. Not only had the pathway for added twists changed to allow better conformation to a circle but it had become obvious that U.S. swimmers would have to be doing them in international events. The introduction of the nova brought a totally new transitional action. Open and closing split rotations multiplied with kip split, closing 180 degrees, open 360 degrees, and the gaviata open 360 degrees. Spins and twists were added where needed to make U.S. figures match those of FINA. The Catalina was reworded to prevent sideways (lateral) movement of the torso during rotations. The timing of the opening on the gaviata was more closely defined. The acceleration in the aurora open spins was revised in 1978 to align better with FINA's description, bringing about a change in manner of performance for U.S. swimmers. At convention, an athlete representative objected saying, but this is a U.S. figure! It was pointed out that the rest of the world had interpreted it differently and unless we could make FINA change, we had better learn to do it the way of the rest of the world.

## Judging and Scoring

The first code of ethics for swimmers and officials was adopted in 1977. Originally meant to deal only with international participants, it was made to cover all athletes and officials, at home or abroad.

A radical change was made in 1980 to select judges for an event by random draw from all available (and qualified) judges in place of the previous election by coaches. It was further specified that all rated judges must be used ahead of unrated judges who might otherwise be brought into service to maintain geographical balance. This meant that an appropriately rated judge would have priority over all non-rated judges, regardless of affiliation or geographical distributions.[74]

And a major factor in judging at all levels was changed based on the improving skills. For 1978, a clause was introduced into the figure performance standards calling for maintenance of "maximum height … in all parts of a figure in which the legs, or part of a leg, extend above the water."[75] Along with the prior year's change in definition of twist level from between ankle and knee to between ankle and hip, this ended the debate on preference for a low-level stable twist versus the bouncier but higher twist level. Twists were pushed upward to new levels, as only three of 102 swimmers in the 1978 indoor meet showed a midcalf water line on the dolphin, full twist. All others were near knee level to above the knee.

## Awards and Honors

The sponsor of the Helms Hall of Fame was changed once again in 1980 when First Interstate Bank became the new sponsor. Awards were still presented with duplicate certificates sent to the International Swimming Hall of Fame for display. In a first for synchronized swimming, the United States Aquatic Sports Award, formerly known as the AAU Swimming Award, was presented to Lillian MacKellar for her contributions in pioneering the development of the sport at the 1982 USAS Annual Convention.[76]

# 9

# *The Olympic Era Begins: 1983–88*

At last, the long-awaited synchro debut in the Olympic Games was approaching. From the first demonstrations in Argentina (1951) and Helsinki (1952), every synchro devotee had felt the sport was more than ready to fit into the Olympics. In retrospect it was easy to see that the progress and changes that had been made during the long delay before acceptance had been beneficial. The shaking out of problems and improvements in concepts and actions had brought synchro to a maturity and stability that would fit much better into the Olympic program. Despite that evolution, the International Olympic Committee (IOC) still had reservations. It finally adopted only the duet event for the program. Then, at the last minute before the Games, the solo was added. Although thankful for what they could get, synchro enthusiasts were still crushed. Only the inclusion of the showpiece event, the team, could give a sense of mission completed. As the time grew closer, though, the excitement in anticipation of synchro's first competition in the Olympics grew to overwhelm and quench that disappointment.

The Olympics certainly had not solved all of United States Synchronized Swimming's domestic problems. Rules, protocol, and even national meet size all seemed reasonably under control, but synchro still had troubles with financial resources, media exposure and image,

and now stagnant growth. The slow pace of growth motivated the development of programs aimed at grassroots development, with the first steps accomplished by the publication of coaching development books. The status as an Olympic sport began helping synchro out of its financial morass as it became more attractive for corporate sponsorships. Many factors combined to drive USSS to rely less on volunteerism and more on the paid office staff to maintain the organization on a solid operational basis.

National teams saw some changes in this period. Where in 1979, the U.S. had selected its first national team, by 1984, it chose an Olympic team of three athletes plus two national teams to compete in the other international events. This paved the way for choosing three national teams in 1987, one of which was the first U.S. junior team which would compete in the French Open and Vienna Open age group competitions. In 1988 the U.S. again selected an Olympic team plus two national teams. However, with the addition of a world junior championships scheduled for 1989, the U.S. began selecting a junior national team each year.

In the international arena, USSS competitors seemed back on the right track with national teams gaining more gold than silver, and this was capped by the brilliant gold coming

Olympic trials were held in Indianapolis in 1983. Team U.S.A. includes, bottom, left to right, Candy Costie and Tracie Ruiz; center, Sarah Josephson, alternate; and back, left to right, Charlotte Davis, coach, and Gail Emery, manager (photograph by Nancy Hines).

many were undoubtedly attracted to the broadcast because of her involvement, the result did not please many in the synchro audiences. Following the broadcasts, Barbara Koch wrote *Synchro* magazine, "After years of trying to convince people of how athletic the sport really is, Esther's 'expert' commentary on ABC ruined all the strides made. I was very embarrassed by this woman's description of the high points, 'Knox gelatin is a must!' The topper was her comment on how much she liked the 'sequins and glitter' on one country's costume. What a shame! The audience knows little more than they did before seeing it on television."[3]

The question of show or sport was increasingly asked by the American media. Responding to a *San Francisco Chronicle* inquiry about the sport being in the Olympics, Gail Emery said, "People think of Esther Williams. She's the reason we are here, she popularized the sport, but it's not Esther Williams any more."[4] Jennifer O'Connor wrote *Synchro* magazine, "I'm amazed and shocked, and heart sickened at the appalling lack of seriousness the media has shown at what we've waited for so long. I very naively believed that finally we'd be taken for the sport and art we are. This just proves that the struggle for recognition must continue."[5]

David Gritten, *Los Angeles Examiner*, wrote, "For millions of viewers, a star is born. I'm not talking about any individual athlete, but a whole sport — synchronized swimming — a bizarre meld of figure skating, gymnastics and Busby Berkeley musicals which takes place in the water. As anyone who watched the duets yesterday, it truly resists comparison with any other sporting event."[6] But Capt. Mark Phillips criticized the International Olympic Committee in an article to the *London Times* where he said he had read, "with some regret of the changes to the Olympic Games ... saying that when [professional] tennis players were admitted to the Seoul Olympics, the world realized that the Games were taking on a new

from the first Olympic experience. But, this period ended on a somewhat depressed note for the U.S. as the Canadians recovered and jumped to the front in the second Olympic battle.

Although synchro was now an Olympic sport, many still questioned its status and predicted it would soon be dropped. Getting acquainted with the newest Olympic sport was still a continuing process for periodicals. *MS* magazine put synchro into the perspective of the Modern Mermaids in the Chicago World's Fair of 1934, to "set the record straight on this 'NEW' sport."[1] The demonstration at the IOC meeting in Los Angeles (January 18, 1983) by the top U.S. and Canadian teams, found many delegates who were seeing the sport for the first time, surprised that it had not been included in the Olympics earlier. The Los Angeles Olympic Organizing Committee had arranged for both new sports, rhythmic gymnastics and synchronized swimming, to give a demonstration at these meetings.[2]

Plans for the Olympic Games were well underway as this period began. ABC felt it needed to have Esther Williams do the commentary in order to draw audiences. While

image." When it was pointed out that it was not only tennis players, but also professional football players, he said, "Snooker could well be next. We already have Synchronized Swimming, so why not ballroom dancing and bowls as well?"[7] Tracie Ruiz summed up her thoughts on the subject: "The public has become more aware of synchronized swimming as a sport since the 1984 Games. It has usually been associated with Esther Williams, but now is really coming into its own."[8]

But the entertainment world was also looking again at synchronized swimming. "America Swims," a spectacular revival of the 1940s style aquacade, was the smash hit of the 1984 Worlds Fair Aquacade in New Orleans. Director Marion Kane Elston trained a group of 35 U.S. and international swimmers for the performances that were seen by more than 3.5 million people. Sara and Marie White headed the cast of former synchronized swimmers. Linda Shelley joined the cast of an Aquacade titled "Splash" at the Riviera Hotel in Las Vegas. The cast relied heavily on other synchronized swimmers to provide the rest of the cast. Then Elston directed another large-scale aquacade for Expo '88, held in Brisbane, Australia, with the cast primarily U.S. synchronized swimmers.

With only a few routines shown during the 1984 Olympic Games, synchro was certain that television coverage would be good with the 1987 Pan American Games in Indianapolis. With Olympian Tracie Ruiz-Conforto swimming in the solo, they felt certain the cameras would be there preparing for Seoul. Not to be! CBS packed up its equipment as the swimming events finished, deserting the venue the day synchro started. Synchro's events were totally sold out but CBS said it thought the public was not interested in watching synchronized swimming. Haven't we heard that before?[9]

By 1988, the media was taking aim at synchro once more. *Time* magazine wrote after the Games in Seoul, "The Ax Is Out: It sure is pretty, but is it sport? Devotees of rhythmic gymnastics and synchronized swimming will defend the events to the last ribbon-reeling pirouette and surface-breaking toe point, and both clearly require dedication and skill. But the IOC is planning to trim the Games' current profusion. Does anyone have worthier sacrificial lambs to offer?"[10]

## International Developments

Everyone and everything was building toward that grand Olympic moment, synchronized swimming in the Olympic Games. The 1983 American Cup, staged in the pool built to be used for the 1984 Olympics, was a meet designed to test staff and procedures for the next year's Games. Even though only the duet was scheduled on the 1984 Olympic program at that time, synchro's OIC chairman asked the LAOOC sponsors to hold the solo and team events at the American Cup as well. Sixteen nations came with 25 solos, 17 duets and seven teams. During the middle of a 90 degree heat wave in Los Angeles, synchro drew more than 7,000 paid spectators to the events where Tracie Ruiz and Candy Costie won the solo and duet and USSS National Team I succeeded in winning the team event.[11] A month later, speed swimming drew only 2,300 for its pre–Olympic competition in the same pool. The staff, under LAOOC competition director Dawn Bean, and synchro proved their readiness for hosting the first synchro Olympic Games competition. Everyone was eagerly awaiting 1984.

In one of the best television presentations of synchro to that time, ESPN televised the American Cup in Los Angeles, 1983. Two one-hour broadcasts were prepared, one for solo and duet, the other for team competition. These shows were then repeated around the country at various times prior to the Olympics. Chelys Hester in Nebraska wrote, "The ESPN coverage has been great. It has been a real eye-opener to see how unique the routines are now."[12]

The next step for American athletes was to qualify for the Olympics through synchro's first Olympic trials, to be held in Indianapolis in April 1984. To no one's surprise, since they had dominated duet competition for four years, Tracie Ruiz and Candy Costie won the trials and the right to represent the sport in its first appearance in the Olympic Games. The audience gave them a standing ovation as their winning score was announced, the highest ever recorded in a U.S. competition. "That standing ovation meant more than anything to us," Ruiz said, "We love to swim for the audience. It was inspiring." The *Los Angeles Times* wrote, "It was what went on in the water, not what went up on the scoreboard that brought the crowd to its feet. Ruiz and Costie's innovative choreography and unusual hand and arm work is making them the 'Torvill and Dean' of Synchronized Swimming." Their coach, Charlotte Davis, said, "Sure it would take a disaster for them to lose, but we want to do more than just win. We want people to go away thinking, 'Hey, they are awesome.'"[13]

Finally, the goal of the past 30 years, since the first FINA rules were written in 1954, was to be reached in Los Angeles in 1984. Within only a few weeks of the start of sales for seats at the Olympic events in July 1983, all tickets for the synchro duet events, 15,500 each for prelims and finals, had been sold out.[14] Synchro was one of the first sports to completely sell out. The venue seating was expanded by 1,000 seats the following January and those tickets all sold immediately.

Then, a synchro miracle happened. With the help of the LAOOC and USOC vice president Robert Helmick, the solo event was added to the program just two months before the Games began.[15] Helmick, FINA secretary, said, "The [Soviet] boycott has served to benefit Synchronized Swimming. Synchronized Swimming has been virtually untouched by countries choosing to remain at home for the Olympics. [Adding the solo] is a logical choice because the competition at the Olympics will be stronger with the addition of the solo. The proposal [for its inclusion] had been narrowly voted down in 1983, mainly by the Soviet and Eastern Bloc, whose programs are underdeveloped compared to the U.S., Canada and Japan."[16] Again, tickets for the solo prelim and final events were sold as fast as they could be printed.

## Synchro's First Olympic Games

The Olympic Games were synchro's dream finally come true. For once, it even seemed eagerly welcomed by the media. The *Los Angeles Examiner* enthused, "For millions of viewers, a star is born. I'm not talking about any individual athlete, but a whole sport, synchronized swimming, a bizarre meld of figure skating, gymnastics, and Busby Berkeley musicals, which takes place in the water. It truly resists comparison with any other sporting event."[17] But synchro's image was still a problem to some of the media. "Now take the phrase *Solo* synchronized swimming. It just doesn't make sense. If you are swimming all by yourself, who are you gonna synchronize with?" asked a television standup comedian. But the *Los Angeles Times* had it figured, "There's always the music." They still wondered about the judging, "It doesn't take a judge with years of experience to notice when partners fall out of sync, which doesn't happen often, but the solo event requires an even more esoteric level of understanding."[18]

Twenty-two countries were represented in the 18 duets and 17 solos entered in synchro's first Olympic Games. In a departure from the normal international order of events, duet routine preliminaries preceded the figures competition. Costie and Ruiz carried their slim lead from prelims into the figure competition. Of the latter event, the *Los Angeles Times* reported, "There were no sequined suits and hats, no bright make-up, no Michael Jackson hits, just plain black suits, goggles, swim caps and concentration!"[19] Synchronized swimming shed its Hollywood image during the figures competition."[20] Ruiz led Carolyn Waldo, Canadian soloist, by 2.76. Costie placed fifth, much better than her 18th at the 1982 world championships where, ironically, the same group of figures had been drawn. Their combined average was only 0.55 points better than the Canadians.

In duet prelims, the first event staged, Candy Costie and Tracie Ruiz revealed a startling new maneuver which they called "threading the needle" and which the *Los Angeles*

U.S. National, Pan Am Games and World Champions Tracie Ruiz and Candy Costie, Seattle Aqua Club (photograph by Nancy Hines).

U.S.A.'s duet of Tracie Ruiz (back) and Candy Costie won the first Olympic synchro medals by more than a point over Canada. The *Los Angeles Times* said their show-stopping "Yankee Doodle" music at the end of the routine sent the flag-waving Americans overboard in their enthusiasm (photograph by Ross Bean).

*Times* attempted to describe: "The two girls spin underwater with their feet out of the water touching and then perform a move that makes it appear as if their legs are going under and then up and through the opening created by their other legs."[21] Got that? They were slim winners in that prelim over the Canadian pair. There really was no doubt, however, as to the outcome of the duet finals. *Synchro* cheered, "USA had an outstanding swim, ending with the show-stopping *Yankee Doodle Dandy* that set flag waving Americans overboard in their enthusiasm." The U.S. outdistanced its Canadian rivals by more than a point and had its first Olympic synchro gold. Canadian silver medalists Kelly Kryczka and Sharon Hambrook were not happy with the results. They felt the American hype for U.S. gold medal winners had stacked the deck against them. "All I can say," said Kryczka darkly, "was that I wish it had been in a different country. I think we would have been up against very different odds."[22] But Ruiz and Costie were speechless. "I don't know whether I'm happy or sad," Ruiz said, "I mean, I do know, I'm both. [It's] all the years we've spent together." Costie wasn't so introspective. "How do I feel? It feels absolutely incredible."[23]

The solo event had been a surprise to everyone. Ruiz' reaction when informed of the May 29 announcement was, "Oh thank you for calling. I can't believe it. It's a miracle, a dream come true."[24] Coach Charlotte Davis said, "Oh my God," three times in a row, and then, "This is so neat!"[25] The short notice meant the USSS Board of Directors had to take a quick vote to confirm Ruiz as their soloist, but there was no question. Even the *Los Angeles Times* reported the obvious: "For Tracie, the reigning world champion, it was almost as if the IOC was mailing her the medal. She had not been beaten in international competition in the past four years."[26]

The late addition meant the solo literally had to be squeezed into the program. Prelims were scheduled for 8:30 A.M. the morning after the duet finals. Six soloists, who had competed in the duet the afternoon before, had scant time to prepare. Even Ruiz said she felt "sub-par" in

*Above:* Tracie Ruiz was undefeated in solo for four years leading up to her victory in the first Olympic Games to include synchronized swimming, in 1984 in Los Angeles. Her strength, style and charisma made her the undisputed champion of the world (photograph by Ross Bean). *Left:* Tracie Ruiz posed to begin her Olympic solo. She has been called the "greatest soloist ever" and the International Swimming Hall of Fame named her Synchro Athlete of the Century (photograph by Nancy Hines).

her swim that morning, but it motivated her to make amends in the afternoon finals. She told the *Los Angeles Times*, "Even if I had won, I would have been disappointed if I didn't swim well. I put on a new suit and hat [for finals] and started to get excited."[27] The *Times* added, "Ruiz's routines are difficult, innovative, and charismatic. Waldo would have to outscore her by 2.8 to capture the gold medal."[28] For Ruiz, her dream did come true. She won by 3.1 points. *Synchro* wrote, "The charisma, strength and grace that has made her the world's premier solo and figure swimmer these past four years was evident. She stood alone atop the synchronized swimming world."[29]

Javier Ostos, Mexico, past president of FINA, wrote in the *International Swimming and Water Polo* magazine after the events, "There was strong opposition by the IOC who looked upon it as a frivolous attraction that had nothing to do with sport.... After the success in Los Angeles, the IOC will seriously have to reconsider the inclusion of all three events into future Olympics to safeguard the prestige and fame of the Olympic Games. I do wish this dream could come true in Seoul."[30] But FINA's request for the inclusion of the team event in the Seoul Games was rejected. This response

was due "on the one hand to gigantism and on the other to the fact that synchro is regarded more as a spectacle than as a sport."[31] There was still work to be done, but *Synchro* magazine summed up the experiences, saying, "The anticipation, the Games themselves, and now the memories of those wonderful weeks, are something that can never be forgotten, nor ever duplicated in our lifetime."[32]

As Judy McGowan was leaving her long residence as USSS president following the 1984 Olympics, she was selected to chair the FINA Technical Synchronized Swimming Committee (TSSC).[33] She continued in that position through 1992. The conservative, "don't rock the boat" policies of the previous chairman were replaced with driving motivation for beneficial progress. She led the international synchro governing group through significant changes in competitive structure, including the use of two routine awards, introduction of a technical routine, and the development of a "biomechanical" base for evaluations of difficulty multiples for figures.

USSS teams and clubs were increasingly involved in a growing number and variety of international competitions where they usually earned medal places. In just five years, U.S.

swimmers competed in two Pan American Games, three Pan Pacific Championships, two American Cups, two FINA World Cups, and the Rome Open, Swiss Open, French Open, Mallorca Open, Scandinavian Open, Soviet Women's Day, Hans Christian Andersen Cup, Lotte Cup — Japan, Petro Cup — Canada, French Grand Prix, Swedish Invitational, Australia's Inaugural Games, Scotch Centenary, and Loano Invitational. Age group swimmers competed at the Swiss Open Juniors, Mexico Age Group, Japan Age Group and Vienna Age Group. (See Appendix D.)

World tensions dampened some U.S. athletes' overseas activities in 1986. Terrorist groups had seized an airplane and killed hostages, airports were bombed, and the U.S. State Department advised against travel to certain areas. USSS considered the risks, then cancelled Team II and club option participations in competitions in Italy, and took extra precautions for Team I at the World Aquatic Championships. With the isolating precautions and safeguards, the environment of that event seemed almost like isolation in a fantasy world, an aquatic Disneyland. Synchro participants were never aware of any security problems.

The exhilaration of the USA's 1984 Olympic performance was completely deflated at the world championships of 1986 in Madrid. The meet attracted the largest number of synchro participants ever to compete in the world championships, but few in the audience. Hosts explained that all of Europe is on vacation in August, so there were, for the first time in a major synchro event, many empty seats. But the athletes were there and ready, with 24 solos, 20 duets and 15 teams. And, for the first time, China and Russia were entered. Canada took every gold medal. Carolyn Waldo easily beat Sarah Josephson in solo; Waldo and Michelle Cameron won the duet over the Josephson twins, Karen and Sarah. U.S.A. Team I kept the score gap narrow by winning the routine competition, but still lost to Canada's superior figures.[34]

The last international event for synchro in 1987 was a source of major ego restoration for USSS. The FINA World Cup in Cairo saw the newly returned Tracie Ruiz-Conforto overcome Carolyn Waldo's 1.5-point lead in figures to win the solo. The Josephsons tied Waldo and Cameron in the routine competition but had to settle for silver with a 0.5-point lower figure average. In contrast, U.S.A. Team I topped the Canadians by 1.5 points in their figure averages, thus paving the way for the first Team I victory over their Canadian counterparts in seven years.[35]

In Madrid in 1986, the U.S.A. team earned the top score in the routine, but lost the title to Canada in the combined score in the world championships. At the top, from left to right, are **Kristen Babb, Mary Visniski, Lisa Riddell;** at center are **Michele Svitenko** and **Tracy Long;** and at bottom are **Karen Josephson, Susan Reed,** and **Sarah Josephson** (photograph by Nancy Hines).

In early 1988 the glow continued, but with some puzzling overtones. In Moscow, Kristen Babb (Walnut Creek) defeated Canada's Sylvie Frechette, but unexpectedly also led her own teammate, 1984 Olympic champion Tracie Ruiz-Conforto. Karen and Sarah Josephson won the duet easily over Canada's Frechette and Natalie Guay, who actually took third, behind USSS' second pair, Babb and Michele Svitenko.[36] At the Seoul Pre-Olympic warm-up meet in June, Ruiz-Conforto easily vanquished Carolyn Waldo. The Josephsons won the routine competition but lost again by a narrow margin on figures to Waldo and Cameron.[37] Still, USSS entered into the Olympic contest full of optimism for the coming games in Seoul.

Seoul hosted 18 solos and 15 duets for the second synchro competition in the Olympic Games. Synchro had returned to popularity in spectator sales, the only sport other than gymnastics to sell out before the Games began.

Tracie Ruiz-Conforto was back in the solo to face off with Carolyn Waldo once more; Karen and Sarah Josephson, USSS' four-time national and three-time collegiate champions, would battle again with Canadians Waldo and Cameron. Once again the heavy weight given to figures in the last major international meet to use a single award for routines made predictions of the probable final outcomes too easy. Going into finals with a 2.5-point figure lead, a relaxed and confident Waldo could easily swim with nearly flawless execution. The charismatic Ruiz, even with superb presentation, strength and power, only tied Waldo in the routine, failing to overcome any of the figure deficit.[38] Prophetically, Ruiz-Conforto had said in a *Sports Illustrated* article prior to the Games, "Whoever wins figures at Seoul will win the gold medals."[39] In a later issue, *Sports Illustrated* in reporting the event said, "In Seoul, Waldo built a huge lead over Ruiz-Conforto in the compulsory figures which count for 55% of the final score and thereby all but clinched the solo title before the freestyle competition even started." After the events, *Sports Illustrated* also noted, "If synchro weren't such a show biz sport, complete with gelatin-molded hairdos and plastered-on smiles, and if its judging were not so political, it might be worth questioning the curious scoring system. The heavy emphasis on figures robs the event of any drama!"[40]

Karen and Sarah Josephson brought their score up from preliminaries by more than a point, winning the routine competition in a

Team U.S.A. overtakes Canada in the World Cup in Cairo in 1987, the first team gold medals in almost a decade. At the top, left to right, are Kristen Babb, Lori Hatch, Lisa Riddell, Tracy Long; at center are Michele Svitenko, Karen Madsen, Susan Reed; and at bottom are Sarah Josephson, Tracie Ruiz-Conforto, Karen Josephson (photograph by Ross Bean).

In 1988 in Moscow, Karen and Sarah Josephson (left) won the duet event with teammates (from right) Michele Svitenko and Kristen Babb placing second. The solo had unexpected results with Babb beating Tracie Ruiz (center) for the title.

Heading for the Seoul Olympic Games in 1988 are, from left to right, Sarah Josephson, Tracie Ruiz-Conforto, and Karen Josephson. U.S.A. took silver in both solo and duet events (photograph by Nancy Hines).

Canada. Over and over, spectators seeing the television presentations (without figures) asked how it could have happened that way — what was wrong with the rules? *The Olympian*, a daily newspaper distributed in the Seoul Olympic Village, did not equivocate. "A coronation for the Canadians, but a popular triumph for the Americans. The result of the duet performance is identical to what was established in the figures and doesn't reflect the valor of the Americans' presence…. The American twin sisters did what others couldn't do in four minutes and four seconds, they attained perfection! The Canadians are the Olympic Champions, but the Americans got the ovation of the public!"[41]

U.S. officials, coaches and teams were still helping, with missionary-like zeal, in a variety of overseas clinics and camps, still on the path that Norma Olsen had set out more than 30 years before. Education was still a key. More than 80 coaches and judges stayed for an International Coaches and Judges Seminar held at the University of California–Los Angeles [UCLA] following the pre–Olympic American Cup competition in 1983. Another international seminar was held in Madrid following the 1986 world championships and yet another, specifically for coaches, was held following the 1987 Pan American Games in Indianapolis. Former swimmers were in demand for coaching in foreign countries. At the 1984 Olympics, four U.S. coaches attended as the primary coaches for Switzerland, Mexico, Venezuela and Australia. Many others were coaching overseas. (See Appendix D.)

There still were mixed messages from the media to synchro's inclusion in the Olympic program. Few nations, however, have shown the lack of interest the U.S. has had from

spectacular display of perfect spins, more spins and a shattering split rocket at the end. Their superior difficulty alone seemed enough to capture the day, but their 1.3-point deficit in figures did not go away. Carolyn Waldo and Michelle Cameron took the gold home to

sportswriters and media. It is a different situation in other countries around the world. In Japan, synchronized swimming on television was immensely popular. Mikako Kotani (1988 Olympic bronze medalist) became a superstar in her country. The press there wrote, "Young girls dream of becoming synchronized swimmers as they watch Mikako's graceful performance. Her fame has spread throughout the world and her performances have captured the hearts of all those who love the sport."[42]

In France, where television had also found synchro a good audience-getter, Muriel Hermine, the 1988 Olympic fourth-place soloist, had the same kind of impact. Largely due to her presence on television, French synchro swimmer registrations in 1994 were more than double those in the United States. Switzerland, though, never had any television coverage of any of its competitions until Mikako Kotani took part in a Swiss Open Championship. Arriving with her was a Japanese television crew, sent along, as usual, to tape her performances. The local Swiss television station, upon receiving a courtesy call from the Japanese crew to apprise them of their intent to tape the competition, was so impressed that Japan would send the crew to Switzerland that they decided there must be more to synchro than they thought. Swiss television then sent its own crews out to televise a synchro meet for the first time.

One piece of good news for all synchro enthusiasts came from the FINA Bureau's meeting at the 1988 Olympic Congress. They stated that their first priority in supporting additional Olympic events would be for the addition of the team event in synchronized swimming. They reasoned that it would provide greater opportunities for a greater number of athletes as well as increased opportunities for the participation of women in the Olympic movement. Synchro's hopes were riding high again with this support.

Walnut Creek's 1984 team received the first scores of 10 for technical merit. From the top, left to right, are Holly Spencer, Julie Olsen, (center) Lisa Babb, Ginnylee McGilton, Kristen Babb, Mary Visniski, (bottom) Michele Svitenko and Kim Stanley (photograph by Nancy Hines).

## The National Championships 1983–88

Although not so momentous as the first Olympic trials, the 1984 U.S. National Championships, held in conjunction with those trials, were very exciting. NBC was there to televise the event. A sell-out crowd of spectators for all events at the Indianapolis Natatorium gave exhilarating support. Esther Williams came to present the awards. She remarked, "This is not show business. These girls work so hard. They're true athletes. I can't believe that after so many, many years, I'll be in my hometown when these girls prove to the world that this is a great sport."[43]

Walnut Creek won its fourth straight team title in 1983 at the competition held in the famous Yale Bowl. And they won again convincingly at the 1984 Nationals and Olympic trials. Walnut Creek remained invincible through

1989 with as many as 25 different swimmers cycling through those winning teams during this period. (See Appendix B.)

From 1983 through 1988, only two pairs of duet competitors won gold. Candy Costie and Tracie Ruiz from the Seattle Aqua Club defended their title in 1983 and 1984. Then from 1985 through 1988, Karen and Sarah Josephson, initially at Ohio State and then Walnut Creek after their college graduation, took over the duet championships. Their twin matching produced synchronization unequaled by any previous competitors, complemented by difficulty such as never seen before. The colleges had always made trios part of their program. In 1983, USSS added trios to all levels except for senior national but that exception was waived in 1984 and Kristen Babb, Michelle Svitenko and Kim Stanley, of Walnut Creek, became the first winners. Walnut Creek continued to dominate this event, taking all senior national titles through 1988.

Tracie Ruiz repeated her solo victories in 1983 and 1984 for a total of four consecutive titles and retired after the Los Angeles Olympics. Sarah Josephson, swimming for Ohio State, won the solo in 1985 and successfully defended her title in 1986. In 1987, with her amateur status restored, Tracie Ruiz-Conforto came back to win the USSS title again and in her 1988 victory, she was awarded straight 10s, the first such award since Heidi O'Rourke in 1971.

As might be expected with the continuously changing personnel of collegiate competitors, collegiate nationals did not show the same repetition of gold medalists as USSS nationals. The collegiate solo title moved from one campus to another every year during this period. Julie Olsen won for the University of Arizona in 1983, then Sarah Josephson won for Ohio State in 1984. Sister Karen followed in 1985. Lori Donn won for the University of Arizona in 1986, but Ana Amicarella reclaimed the title for OSU's Buckeyes in 1987. Then Stanford got into the act when Ginny Cohn won in 1988.

The duet title was stable for a while as Karen and Sarah Josephson kept it at Ohio State for the three years from 1983 through 1985. Then Karen Brinkman and Lori Donn

from the University of Arizona won in 1986. Stanford's Deidre Cohen and Ruth Weinberg won in 1987. Ohio State brought the title back in 1988 with Cathy Cramer and Jessica Hudacek. The trio went to Ohio State in 1983, switched to the University of Arizona in 1984, then returned to stay at Ohio State from 1985 through 1988. And in the team event, the University of Arizona took top honors from 1983 through 1985. Then Ohio State University rose up again to win the team event from 1986 through 1988.

## Sport Administration

Judy McGowan remained president when the USSS National Office moved from Colorado Springs to Indianapolis in 1983. Synchro activities and staff had outgrown the space that USOC could allocate in the NGB Building in Colorado Springs when the Lilly Foundation and Indiana Sports Corporation made an attractive offer for grants and assistance that would help offset office rental costs in Indianapolis. It could not be refused.

The USSS moved to a biennial legislative and rule book cycle in 1983. Looking at the attendance at the first "off" year convention, President McGowan chortled, "They said it couldn't be done, that no one would come to convention in the "off" year. I suggested if we made it appealing enough, attendance would be good."[44] The educational seminar, scheduled for the non-legislative years, had drawn 120 registrants, the most ever to attend the national convention!

This period was marked with setbacks and solutions. The status as an Olympic sport had brought increased financial support from USOC and stimulated some sponsorship activity, so USSS seemed to be sailing relatively smoothly onward through early 1983. However, in late summer an athlete filed a lawsuit against both USSS and USOC which required the expenditure of a great deal of time and funds for the next several years. A major part of the suit hinged upon errors in the original code of regulations as it was drawn up for incorporation in 1978. The eventual result of the suit, aside from nearly bankrupting USSS, was to change the code on athlete hearings and appeals to bring USSS code into compliance with that of the U.S. Olympic Committee.

In the Olympic year, McDonald's Corporation became a major synchro sponsor.[45] Fuji Films and the Mary Kay and Elizabeth Arden cosmetics firms also made donations in that year. These sponsorships enabled USSS to double the office staff, adding an educational director and a secretary-bookkeeper. A half-time public relations director was added early in the Olympic year. And following the Olympic Games, the staff was expanded by adding Charlotte Davis, the 1984 Olympic coach, to become USSS' first full-time national coach.[46] Kim Van Buskirk was also added after 1984 as synchro's first educational director. Margo Erickson was hired in 1987 to become synchro's first technical director.

Following the 1984 Olympics, USSS developed a series of special aquacades, titled "Classical Splash" to showcase their athletes. The first used the Indianapolis Symphony Orchestra to accompany the show, directed by Santa Clara coach Chris Carver. The shows were artistically and financially successful. The next year, retitled "Splash," the shows were accompanied by the Air Force Academy Jazz Band. Those performances were also very successful, but a winter "Splash," held just before Christmas in Indianapolis, was poorly attended and the program was put on hold. "Classical Splash" programs have been offered occasionally as club options in subsequent years.

Dawn Bean, competition director for synchro's first Olympics Games, was elected USSS president in 1984. Bean, the first national champion to head the sport, looked optimistically toward the future, hoping to build upon the Olympic excitement to further growth throughout the country. Ad hoc committees were set up to meet some special needs of USSS. The outreach committee was to encourage national organizations with swim programs to add synchronized swimming; the athlete eligibility committee was formed to keep records for eligibility to national competitions; the video committee developed policies for videotaping and for distribution of videos; and ath-

lete concerns on the subjects of ethics, recruitment, and retirement were debated by another committee.

The sports medicine committee developed a plan for research into the physiological and biomechanical demands of the sport and into an investigation of injuries and their relationship to training practices. The research projects and the testing of national team athletes were started with Dr. Fred Roby and Dr. Betty Atwater at the University of Arizona. In 1988 they reported, "Synchro swimmers are about the same physiologically as they were in 1984, but now they are a lot more fit, less fat, and more competitive in laboratory testing. They require the same aerobic and anaerobic capacity as speed swimmers, but are less sensitive to high levels of blood carbon dioxide. In comparing elite with junior elite athletes, the elite athletes were more flexible, had lower bone mineral content and greater shoulder strength."[47] The coaches certification program became a reality with two levels established by the fall of 1984. Levels III and IV were added soon after. The history committee created and produced "president plaques," which now hang in the Indianapolis office. In 1988, the sound and equipment committee suggested that a decibel meter to monitor sound levels should be required for all national championships. Its use would assure equivalent music volume for all competitors and spare spectators potential ear-damaging sound levels often demanded by coaches.

The rulebook took on a whole new look with a complete revision in 1987. It adopted a loose-leaf binder format that would accommodate page and addendum alterations in nonlegislative years. The new format included a complete new set of figure illustrations. The previous figure drawings had lasted since 1955 with only minor changes made by as many as seven different illustrators in the intervening years. The insertions didn't always match and more and more changes were needed to keep the drawings relevant to the changed methods of performance through the years. The new illustrations were drawn by Avilee Goodwin, a former junior national champion, who had been selected by Human Kinetics to illustrate the intermediate teaching book. The drawings were later computerized (in 1995) and loaned to FINA for their rulebook use. All this was done in conjunction with a decision to go with desktop (computer layout) publication in place of the usual commercial preparation.

But while solutions were being found to handle old problems, new problems started appearing early in 1985. USSS' first executive director, Paula Oyer, who had been responsible for bringing in sponsors and running a highly effective office, resigned to become U.S. Rowing's executive director. In August, Betty Watanabe, the marketing director for Logo 7, an Indianapolis firm, was hired to replace her.[48]

The end of that year brought another surprise when McDonald's rescinded its expected sponsorship for 1986.[49] At the time McDonald's first signed as a sponsor, Judy McGowan had commented, "It has been said that getting a sponsor is easy, keeping a sponsor is hard."[50] McDonald's had given a bright report for the future at the 1985 convention but kept dragging its feet on signing the 1986 contract, waiting until two days after Christmas to announce dropping their sponsorship. "Poor TV exposure" was cited as the main reason. They soon dropped diving and swimming as well. Half the planned 1986 budget disappeared with McDonald's. An emergency meeting of the board of directors in January tackled the problems with a 50-percent reduction of both staff and programs. Two full-time and one part-time office positions were eliminated. Most activity budgets were drastically cut, but the national team program was spared by a grant from the USOC.

Some fiscal relief finally arrived out of the large pool of Olympic Games profits that the Los Angeles Olympic Organizing Committee had distributed to the USOC. Those funds could be used to augment USOC's annual allocations to individual sports. The USOC initiated the distribution plan in 1985 by requiring each sport's NGB to develop an extensive four-year sport plan before receiving any allocations. With only a few months allowed for preparation, a special meeting of the USSS' vice presidents was called for June. The resulting plan the vice presidents came up with was regarded warmly by USOC and brought substantial increases in USOC's annual support for synchro. The success of the January board meeting and the June vice presidents' meetings in problem solving turned them into regular annual events.

Of its Games surplus funds, LAOOC distributed 40 percent to the USOC, with an additional 20 percent to the USOC to distribute in lump sums to the sports on the Olympic program. The remaining 40 percent went to fund programs established under the newly organized Amateur Athletic Foundation (AAF) in Los Angeles, for Olympic sport development throughout the greater Los Angeles area. Upon receiving its allocation in 1985, USSS set up the United States Synchronized Swimming Foundation (USSSF) under chairman Judy McGowan. A policy was established that 50 percent of the annual interest and dividend earnings of the fund would be distributed in grants to Synchro activities, with the remaining 50 percent reinvested for maintaining growth. Its subsequent influence has been substantial; more than $600,000 was distributed in its first 12 years to various synchronized swimming programs and projects.

Meanwhile, creative approaches to increasing income were being tested. Booster memberships were added in 1985. The life member program was made more attractive in 1987 with added benefits, the most visible being a breakfast or luncheon gathering for life members at convention. Speedo, the Gap Stores, and Lady Hathaway began providing equipment and supplies for the national teams. Tambrands became a one-year sponsor, discontinuing their sponsorship citing a lack of television news coverage. Synchro developed a set of products that would be marketed from the office and USSS meets: towels, patches, pins, sports bags, sunglasses, T-shirts, swim caps, posters, rulebooks, directories, coaching books and instructional videotapes. In 1988, Ultra Swim took on the sponsorship of the national camp program. Coca-Cola became a partial sponsor under the USOC's joint sponsorship plan and the USSS staff could finally be expanded. A public relations firm was engaged in a part-time program to increase attention, improve image and boost membership.

Not until 1987, though, did USSS come

out from under the hanging sword of the law-suit.[51] An arbitration judge finally dismissed USSS from any liability in the suit although several individuals were still left dangling for potential personal liability if the plaintiffs wanted to continue action. Time eventually ran out on all such possibilities in 1989.[52]

USSS sponsored its own summer camp program in 1984, authorizing The Sports Group to direct the camps for two years using the national achievement program in *Coaching Synchronized Swimming Effectively* as the curriculum. Then, in 1986, R. & R. Academies was authorized to direct the camps the next year and they held seven camps in various parts of the country. The first elite (coaches of national semi-finalists) coaches seminar was held in the summer of 1985 at the USOC's Colorado Springs Training Center. Three intermediate camps were held in 1986. Then, the National Clinic Network (NCN) plan was developed for zone camps to start in 1988. Technical director Margo Erickson said the clinics marked the beginning of an organized effort to share techniques developed at the elite level with athletes and coaches throughout the competitive system, presenting them in a manner appropriate to the level of the participants.

Plans to issue a 1983 *Yearbook* were abandoned after the poor sales of the 1982 *Yearbook*. An *Athlete's Newsletter,* then a *Masters Newsletter* were started in 1985. USSS newsletters for the membership continued through this period. But, USSS' planned series of coaching texts was finally off the drawing board and into print. Margaret Forbes edited *Coaching Synchronized Swimming Effectively,* published in 1984.[53] Kim Van Buskirk, USSS educational director, edited and published *Coaching Intermediate Synchronized Swimming Effectively* in 1987.[54] Human Kinetics produced a video to accompany *Coaching Synchronized Swimming Effectively,* which was previewed by international participants at the FINA World Cup in Egypt in 1987.[55] In 1988 Charlotte Davis and Dawn Bean collaborated on the *Three Month Curriculum,* which included "Lesson Plans for Recreation Departments and School Programs" based on the *Coaching Synchronized Swimming Effectively* book's unit plans.[56]

The USSS printed several new utility manuals in 1985. The *Publicity Manual,* by Mary Rose, instructed clubs on developing effective media interaction and coverage; Norma Longmire revised the *Scoring Manual;* Jean Struck updated the *Meet Managers Manual.* In 1986, Peg Hogan compiled a *Directory of Colleges* with synchro programs, and in 1988, the *Officials Training Manual* was developed by Barbara McNamee in conjunction with the zone officials chairs.

*Synchro* Magazine remained something of an anomaly, still increasing in size and coverage, but still dependent on volunteer effort and the publisher's personal subsidies to keep it going. In 1985, Australia joined a growing group of countries publishing newsletters with *Synchro News Australia. Synchro Switzerland* added photos to its newsletter format, but *Synchro Canada* did not survive the post–Olympic retirement of its editor of 14 years, Joyce Coffin. Two years later, Synchro Canada's attempted restart of the magazine ended after only two issues were published. *Synchro World,* which began in England in 1984 under editor Jennifer Gray, ceased publication after 1989 when its publisher discontinued underwriting it. It had become apparent that survival of magazines for synchro depended on either heavy subsidies or extremely bare-bones, economical newsletter formats.

## Competitive Programs

National championships remain the most important event for the majority of those involved in synchronized swimming in the United States. But as the number of international events has grown, so has the U.S. representation to those events. From the first national team of 1979, three national teams of 10 became the norm except for the Olympic years when two teams plus three athletes were selected. In 1986, three full teams were chosen. However, because of State Department travel advisories against travel in 1986, only Team I competed overseas that year. In 1987, three teams were again selected for international competition and these did compete. In 1988, two teams, plus the Olympic team of three, were selected.

With more athletes going on to the national teams, an alteration was made to the date of the senior national championships, which changed in 1984 from the traditional summer to spring, to be held before May 1. The object of the change was to give national teams more time to prepare for summer competitions. It also gave clubs more flexibility for participating in the summer international events. And the only change to the junior national program was a tightening of eligibility rules in 1984 which made members of Olympic, Pan American, U.S. national teams, and winners of open international events ineligible in their events.

Participating in the Olympic Sports Festival became a major goal for swimmers just below those of the national team although solos and duets from the national teams continued to be part of the festival in order to provide some of the top names the USOC wanted. This was done whenever it would not conflict with an international event that one of the national teams was training for. The 1985 Olympic Sports Festival benefited from the Olympic association and synchro was one of 12 sports chosen for television coverage. However, this involvement brought on a major snafu when the starting time for the events was advanced by one hour to accommodate television. The changed time was not transmitted to the people of Baton Rouge. Many arrived late and missed half the competition. Realizing the distress of the audience, the swimmers put on a demonstration for them following the award ceremonies. ESPN did a much better job at the 1987 Olympic Festival, broadcasting the entire solo and duet finals. Unfortunately, the team broadcast lost out to preemption by a lengthy Davis Cup tennis final.

Changes were happening in the junior programs as well. Facing realities, the competition that had been called "international age group trials" was officially changed in 1985 to the "National Age Group Championships." Swimmers qualified for the competition through their sectional championships. By 1986, more than 600 competitors and 500 routines were entered. Age group chairman

Kaaren Babb complained, "Seven days was not enough. It is imperative that we streamline the direction of the whole age group program.... Logically, we should start at the Association, go to Section, to Zone, and then to National."[57] For 1987, the competition stretched to 10 days; in 1988, there were 900 competitors with no peak in sight. The national Junior Olympic program, which reached more grassroots levels, expanded in 1986 to include three qualifiers from each region, instead of only the winner. However, holding the competition in August kept the numbers at manageable levels; in 1988, there were 287 participants.

Collegiate programs had begun to flourish under the Association for Intercollegiate Athletics for Women (AIAW). Then, when the NCAA made an offer to "take over" and "support" women's intercollegiate sports, it was an offer that most colleges could not afford to refuse. Unfortunately, less than half the sports operating under the wing of the AIAW would be accepted in the transfer, making the support of the rejected, "minor" sports in college programs financially difficult. Colleges and universities very quickly started discontinuing most remaining AIAW sports. Synchro lost its varsity status at the University of Michigan in 1984 and at the University of Arizona in 1985 despite Arizona coach Kathy Kretschmer's pleas: "What more can be said than the 1984 Olympic gold medal winners in synchronized swimming were U. of A. girls?"[58]

Most varsity programs were reduced to club status, but Mary Jo Ruggieri won her battle to keep varsity status at Ohio State. USOC allocated some funds to support collegiate developmental clinics in 1988, but growth was still stagnant. Barbara Bernard, Northwest Missouri State University, wrote to *Synchro* magazine in 1988, "After a long association with the sport, our club folded due to a lack of interest after the 1984 Olympics. I thought with the Olympic coverage, there would be more interest but the reverse seemed to occur. The only conclusion I have been able to draw is that the swimmers saw the high caliber of skill and felt it was too difficult for them as beginners."[59] Despite the problems, collegiate national championships continued and many colleges still participated under their college club sport banners.

The masters program also flourished as entries in the masters national championships grew from 200 in 1984 to 276 from 42 teams and 21 states in 1988. About the program, Carol Mitchell wrote to *Synchro*'s Mailbox, "I have just experienced the most enjoyable meet of my lifetime, the 1987 Masters National Championships. Never before have I been so inspired by a meet. I just wish a greater number of our younger swimmers could have seen the enthusiasm and sheer enjoyment shared by these competitors, not to mention their level of skill … we should be proud of the fact that many of our masters swimmers could compete with the top swimmers of today."[60]

International competitions for most masters began with the World Masters Games in Toronto, Canada in 1985. Swimmers came mostly from the U.S. and Canada. U.S. swimmers won seven of the events at that first competition. Calgary hosted an international masters meet in 1987 and Ontario scheduled an invitational international meet in Ottawa in 1988 since the Second FINA World Masters championships in Australia did not include synchro.

## Technical Rules

Longstanding definitions of amateur status began to loosen during this period. FINA started, in 1983, by allowing teachers of elementary swimming to retain amateur status. However, transgressions such as, "Capitalizing on their athletic fame, by advertising teaching elementary skills in swimming, and/or by directly preparing an athlete for competition," remained certain grounds for loss of amateur status.[61]

Then, in 1984, another accommodation made even those transgressions acceptable under specified conditions. FINA rules would allow an athlete's trust fund to be set up into which an athlete's earnings from "professional" activities could be deposited and held in trust for distribution when amateur status was no longer desired. It was even feasible for a "pro-

fessional" to return to "amateur" competition, as in the case of Tracie Ruiz-Conforto. Having become professional after the 1984 Olympics, she sought a return to amateur status for the 1988 Games. Under terms of a National Board of Review, she was able to deposit into a trust an amount that covered her professional earnings and she regained her amateur status in 1986. The review board stated, "The recent FINA rules concerning trusts, and the requirement that USSS's rules not be more restrictive than those of FINA, were important to the final decision."[62]

The U.S. adopted the FINA figure competition groupings in 1983 so that USSS competitors would be trained in the figures they would draw in international events. A few problems still arose from differences in figure description language and action interpretations. In adopting the swordasub from USSS, FINA required that a totally different underwater action from that used in USSS be adopted. Their inclination toward loose descriptions allowed rotations in either direction for figures such as kip, split closing 180 degrees and open 360 degrees, in conflict with the closely defined directions imposed by USSS rules. For several years, national team members practiced discrepant figures both ways before, in 1988, USSS gave up hoping to change FINA and revised its descriptions to conform to the international demands.

New figure additions also followed FINA additions with the 1986 adoptions of the ibis, alba and dalecarlia and the additions of ascending, descending, continuous and combined spins to various figures. And the balk penalty was changed, in 1988, to a simple two-point deduction.

Attempting to adapt to new FINA regulations was becoming an ever-greater factor in USSS rules modifications. An exception to this normally one-sided action was FINA's switch to two-routine awards after longtime use of a single score. However, even in appearing to be changing toward the USSS system, the system adopted by the 1986 FINA Congress for initiation in 1989 digressed in many details. USSS was again forced into substantial accommodation measures for compatibility with FINA's new award system. The two FINA awards, for technical merit and artistic impression, were quickly adopted by USSS for use in 1987, even while decrying the "artistry" image invoked by the name of the second award. More than a name adjustment was involved. The distributions of the basic six judging elements within the two FINA awards were different from those used by the USSS for more than 20 years. USSS judges had to be retrained to include synchronization and difficulty along with execution under technical merit rather than within artistic impression, the content equivalent. Conversely, manner of presentation had to be moved to artistic impression, no longer coupled with execution. Whether real or imagined, the consensus was that the changes seemed to make an immediate difference in choreography. *Synchro* reported in 1987, "Creativity is back."[63]

Another "follow FINA" change was made in 1987 to allow the competing members of a duet or team to be altered up to two hours before the start of the event. This meant the lineup of swimmers could be changed between preliminaries and finals, inserting an alternate, if desired, to take advantage of higher figure scores. Another change, in deference to spectators for once, was to allow announcement of competitor names and club affiliations in the introductions before the performances.

The U.S., however, acted alone in 1988 introducing a penalty for the deliberate return to or hanging onto the pool deck after entering the water. This was in reaction to several routines that had used poses involving hanging from or sitting on the deck in the middle of a routine.

## Judging and Scoring

The major change in routine scoring occurred when FINA decided at the congress, in 1986, to adopt a two-score system, but the elements considered under the new categories of technical merit and artistic impression, were different than those the U.S. had been using for some years. The U.S. had based its categories on *how* they did whatever they did and *what* they

did which had included difficulty as part of the content score. Now, difficulty was in the technical score while manner of presentation was in the artistic merit score along with choreography and interpretation of the music. The change resulted in massive retraining of all U.S. judges, from national down to local level. Every U.S. judge was required to attend a retraining seminar before being eligible to judge any event in the new year.

At the world championships in Madrid in 1986, an electronic scoreboard was used to keep track of the figures competition which lent some interest, actually even excitement, for spectators following individuals through the contests. They could not only identify who was performing but knew, as quickly as anyone there, the award from each judge, the contestant's figure total and her rank in relation to those preceding her.[64] However, this was never used in the U.S., nor was it used internationally again. Figure competition was increasingly looked upon in world circles as something that needed to be changed.

The U.S. continued its usual competitions, but with computers becoming more available, Bill Reed, of New Jersey, developed a new scoring program which was successfully tested at the 1983 national championships. Another change was the rescinding of the longstanding practice of using the same judges for the final event as had been used for the semifinal event. The change was aimed at minimizing the practice of simply maintaining identical rankings from one level of competition to the next through the use of more judges. It also allowed making use of judges in finals whose "affiliation" disappeared as their swimmers were eliminated in the semifinals. A minimum age of 16 years for association and 18 years for regional judges was adopted in 1984. Practice judging was added as a requirement for achieving regional and zone ratings. Statistically based judge performance evaluations were made a routine part of all meets where entry numbers were large enough to provide statistical reliability. The regular feedback to judges on their performances would, it was hoped, lead to improved effectiveness.

A standard set of uniforms was mandated

for officials in 1985. Red, white, or navy shirts would be worn in specified combinations with white or navy trousers or skirts and a navy blazer. This abandonment of wearing all white for all occasions was instigated by the effectiveness of seeing officials in color on television at the 1984 Olympic trials where NBC had provided red shirts for the judges. However, all white remained the requirement for figure competition and continues to this day in international events, except where a separate uniform is provided.

## Awards and Honors

The original Helms Hall of Fame suffered another major change when Citizens Savings Bank reported in May 1986 they were donating the museum and library to the new Amateur Athletic Foundation (AAF) in Los Angeles. The AAF changed the nature of the museum and exhibits to feature Southern California athletes only. After a period of indecision, USSS decided, in 1987, to sponsor its own USSS Hall of Fame with awards that fall. No display hall was provided, but duplicate certificates of award continued to be sent to the International Swimming Hall of Fame in Florida.

The USSS awards committee studied ways to honor more deserving individuals for their work in many different areas with the results that in 1983, an annual Coach of the Year honor was given to the coach whose swimmers earned the highest number of points at the senior national championships. The first recipient was Charlotte Davis of the Seattle Aqua Club. In 1984, USSS began the Athlete of the Year award, for the overall highest points at the senior national championships. Tracie Ruiz was the first to be named to this award. In 1986, a Developmental Coaches Service Award was begun for coaches who work primarily on the local level and bring age group athletes to the national Junior Olympic level. The first recipient was Mary Tope of the Riverside Aquettes. Then, in 1987, the New Coach of the Year award was started to honor coaches whose athletes make national age group finals for the first time and the recipient was Cindy Coe of the Ken-Ton Kipettes. The USOC began the USOC Sportswoman of the Year award in 1987 to honor each sport's most outstanding athlete, asking for the one who had the most impact on the sport during the year. Tracie Ruiz-Conforto was named the first recipient of this award.

The Southland Corporations' Olympia Award, in 1983, was given to Tracie Ruiz,[65] and to Louise Wing, masters synchro competitor.[66] Candy Costie was honored in 1985[67] and Sarah Josephson in 1986.[68]

USSS nominated McDonald's, then a sponsor for U.S. synchro, for the Women's Sports Foundation's Corporate Contribution Award in 1985.[69] Awarded at WSF's annual banquet in early December, McDonald's accepted the award just a month before announcing it would drop its sponsorship of synchro.

# 10

## *Growth and Popularity Worldwide: 1989–94*

Even while anticipation of the 1992 Olympics in Barcelona was just beginning to build, the announcement came that changed the focus almost immediately to four years in the future. In April 1991, the IOC announced that the 1996 Olympic Games would include the team event. That was the good news. The bad news was that the solo and duet events had been dropped from the Olympic program and the Olympic team event would include only eight teams.

The years leading to the 1992 Olympics were exciting for both USSS and international synchro. Titles of all kinds were to be strongly contested and as they approached, it was hard to predict the outcomes. The announcement of the new Olympic program though, seemed to pull attention immediately to the more distant future. Swimmer goals changed instantly. No chance as an Olympic duet or solo? Keep swimming and look for that team spot now! The air was charged with anticipation. We would finally show the world the real synchro! The Olympics of 1992 did turn out well for U.S.A. synchro, but the real goal was four years down the road. Work, plan, work and plan to reach out and grab that bright shining star.

Growth and popularity of the sport continued to accelerate throughout much of the world. A 1990 FINA report revealed that 65 nations were now conducting synchronized

swimming programs. In May 1992, 104 participants from 57 countries attended the first World Synchronized Swimming Coaches Seminar, sponsored by FINA, in Olympia, Greece.[1] Other sports and FINA were finally taking a good hard look at synchro. In 1989, FINA put a limit on the distance that backstrokers could dolphin kick underwater, citing health concerns as one factor. *Sports Illustrated* chuckled, "Regarding FINA outlawing the underwater backstroke kicking, Berkhoff, whose world record of 54.51 seconds will still stand, calls the ruling a personal slap in the face. He points out that he stays underwater only 16 seconds compared to more than 55 seconds for synchronized swimmers."[2]

Recognition was finally coming that synchro was truly a strenuous athletic event. In 1990, *Health* magazine commented, "Synchronized swimming looks almost easy. But, like a glimpse at an elegant tapestry's underside, a look below the water's surface reveals the enormous effort behind the perfection. Because the swimmers hold their breath during many moves, a four minute routine makes aerobic demands similar to running for the same amount of time."[3] Writing about the 1991 Olympic Festival, the *San Francisco Chronicle* wrote, "Synchronized Swimmers, long viewed as jokes by many sports fans, are due to receive the credit they deserve for the long hours of training they endure on their way to aquatic perfection. Synchronized swimming is hard work. It's water polo without the ball; it's dancing without the dance floor. The pasted-on smiles hide an extraordinary effort. The trick, as in practically every sport this side of professional wrestling, is to make the difficult appear easy."[4]

But synchro was still having difficulty attracting an audience in the U.S. except for the earlier Olympic Games. The problem extended to the lack of television coverage, even of its important events. On the 1991 Olympic Festival in Los Angeles, Lea Bean, local synchro media coordinator, wrote, "If only we had been able to hold our events at a time not dictated by ESPN, who didn't cover us anyway. Trying to entice spectators to come out when, as the saying goes, 'Only mad dogs and Englishmen go out in the noon-day sun,' was hard on everyone."[5] The lack of coverage may have been influenced by the *Los Angeles Times*' Mike Downey who, in thumbnail sketches of the sports, wrote, "Every gelatin-head from Maine to New Mexico will be here to watch the team of Candy and Cookie Cutter, who will swim with lit sparklers in their teeth to the soundtrack music from 'Backdraft.'"[6]

Obviously, synchro was still not regarded as a sport with much of the media. At the Olympic trials of 1992, the *Pasadena Weekly* wrote, "Does synchronized swimming, with its languid turns and out of sight underwater gamboling, belong in the Olympic Games where speed, strength, endurance and courage have always been the test? Do performers who mainly embody the spirit of Esther Williams' musicals belong on the same winners' platform as a Carl Lewis, Flo Jo, or Sergei Bubka? Not in my time!"[7] But the *Los Angeles Times* said, "Part of the problem synchronized swimming has in earning respect as a sport is that spectators can only see the ballet-like movements that are demonstrated above the water. Beneath the surface, these athletes put their bodies through a rigorous workout."[8]

The NBC network television presentation of the 1992 Olympics in Barcelona was fairly standard, one solo and two duets shown late at night, well after prime hours. But for those willing to pay $125 for cable coverage through NBC's Triplecast, a fantastic treasure of sports coverage could be gained. On three cable channels, complete preliminary and final events in many of the Olympic contests, including synchro, could be followed. Every preliminary and final solo and duet was shown. Unfortunately, so few people bought into the Triplecast that NBC dropped any plans for subsequent cablecasts.

For some countries, complete or near-complete presentation of synchro is the expected norm. The German network, for example, surveyed viewers to determine which two sports should be presented in their entirety in 1992. Synchro was one of the top two sports. Some U.S. enthusiasts of synchro, living near major Canadian border cities, have been able to tap into CBC's more complete network reviews of synchro events. France and Japan generally have extensive coverage of synchro. Dick Ebersol, president of NBC Sports, reported in *USA Today* that there was a 15-percent slump in viewers in the second week of broadcasts (1992). "We ran out of female-appeal swimming and gymnastics, and men turned attention to the baseball pennant races [going on at the same time], [viewers] were gone. The Olympics ought to add more female-appeal sports." Rudy Martzke, columnist for *USA Today*, said [about NBC's programming], "Worst moves, under use of female-appeal, diving and synchronized swimming in week two."[9]

In 1994, with the assistance of the USOC Broadcast Properties division, synchronized swimming not only aired on Prime Network, a national cable station, but also on CBS' *Eye on Sports* as part of the USOC Olympic Television package. A CBS executive informed [USSS] the viewing audience doubled from the previous week. "This is a reflection of how well everyone in synchro spread the word," said marketing vice president Ed Wodka.[10]

## International Developments

In 1990, FINA once more redefined and liberalized the definition of "amateur athlete." Athletes would be eligible to compete unless their sport was their sole occupation or business on which they were financially dependent for their living. Athletes could deposit any earnings from USSS-approved commercials and ads into the previously established USSS trust fund to become available at the end of their competitive careers.

Previous rule changes had been made during the congress sessions held at the Olympic Games. These took effect the first of the year following the Olympics. But, starting in 1991, changes in the governing rules for all of the aquatic sports were now to be decided at the FINA Congress held each fourth year at the world aquatic championships. Many synchro changes were made in Australia in January 1991 which, because of the unusual time of holding the championships, went into effect only 60 days later. The date forced some rapid adaptations to all national programs for the coming season. The next congress was scheduled for Rome in conjunction with the world aquatic championships in the summer of 1994. Changes made then would go into effect on January 1 of the following year.

Two new events were added to the world calendar. Internationally, various age group competitions had been held since 1976, but in 1989, FINA added a Junior World Championship to its international schedule. It was the first world meet solely for swimmers ages 14 to 17. Another major world stage for synchro came about with addition of synchro's duet and solo events to the 1990 Goodwill Games. Seattle was the site for the first Goodwill Games held in the United States. This was an excellent promotional opportunity for synchro. Not only were costs of participation totally covered by Turner Enterprises, but the Games-covering television network, Turner Broadcast Systems, recognized that synchro *was* an appropriate sport for television.

The idea for a short program came during discussions at the world seminar being held in conjunction with the 1985 FINA World Cup in Indianapolis. The Japanese delegation outlined a concept for a short program event as a possible substitute for figure competition. They suggested routines of about two minutes in duration with the required performance of a number of specified actions within all the rou-

tines. After a few years of deliberation and discussion, the FINA Technical Synchronized Swimming Committee submitted a formal proposal for technical routines to the FINA Congress in Perth in January 1991. Although the proposal was rejected by the congress, the TSSC was sufficiently influenced to decide to put the concept to a test at a meet over which they had total control of content, the FINA World Cup that was to be held late that summer. The fifth World Cup in Bonn, in September 1991, became the first testing ground for the new technical routines. Results would be determined by the totals of scores in three events rather than two. Technical routine and figures would each be 25 percent of the final score and the free routine would comprise the other 50 percent.

In the solo championships, with or without the new event, Sylvie Frechette would have triumphed over Kristen Babb, but only by the slimmest of margins. Frechette's final lead was 0.17 point after winning both routine events with Babb winning the figures, but her lead in the free event would have been enough. Fumiko Okuno of Japan won the bronze and Olga Sedakova of the Soviet Union followed. Karen and Sarah Josephsen had no difficulty in any of the three events, leading by a wide margin after figures. Okuno and Aki Takayama, 1.61 points back, upset the usual order, leading Canada's Christine Larsen and Kathy Glen by 0.33 points. Again, the Soviet Union followed in fourth. China's duet drew two very damaging penalties and they dropped to seventh behind France and Italy.

The U.S.A. National Team I prevailed in the team event as well, winning by nearly a point over Canada. But there were some glitches. Differences in interpretation of the meaning of specifications for required elements caused some severe penalties. The new event brought disaster to Japan's team. For their entry, they surfaced in two sequential sets of four, violating the requirement that everything be done by all eight, simultaneously. The resulting penalty dropped them behind the Soviet team, which took home a bronze medal for the first time in a senior international event.

After the competition in Bonn, the consensus of the officials was outlined: "While the

After the loss of the gold medals at the Olympics in 1988, the 1989 World Cup in Paris brought some surprises. Michele Svitenko and Tracy Long were duet winners. Long won the solo and the U.S. team edged by Canada 188.9 to 188.8 (photograph by Charles Long).

long programs of top athletes are all performed almost perfectly, the short programs did show differences, particularly in Duets and Teams, where not all verticals were exact, and spins varied in the number of revolutions, and timing errors were seen on the more difficult actions ... judges found it an excellent way to compare athletes on the identical skills. The requirement that everything in the routines be performed simultaneously by members of teams and duets was considered a major aid in evaluating performances. Judges said they were surprised to see how creative the short programs were."[11]

Despite unhappiness in some quarters about penalties, the consensus was that the time had come for technical routines. The TSSC decided to work out the problems and try the technical routine another time, at the 1993 World Cup in Lausanne. Judy McGowan, USSS FINA representative, commented, "Adding a Short Program is a big step, and it has many benefits besides a technical evaluation of routine skills with a common denominator. It is a way to educate the public about the technical aspects of synchronized swimming. It will also generate greater media attention because of a variety in events, thus greater exposure. The Short Program for synchronized swimming is an idea whose time has come!"[12] After its test at the World Cup in Lausanne in

1993, the TSSC decided that it should be recommended for integration into future world cups and other FINA events. Action was soon put in motion to develop the proposal for the technical routine to be part of the competitive structure for the next congress in 1994.

After the loss of the gold medals at the Olympics in 1988, the U.S. took a large step toward recovery of its international status in the final international event of 1989. That world cup event in Paris brought some surprises.[13] With Kristen Babb, the U.S.A.'s top soloist, injured, all speculation was on whether Sylvie Frechette of Canada or Mikako Kotani of Japan, would move to the solo pinnacle. Instead, U.S.A.'s Tracy Long put on a surprising display of vivacity and skill and triumphed over both, edging Frechette by 0.24 points with Kotani only another 0.64 points farther back in third. Michelle Svitenko had stepped into Babb's place as Long's duet partner and the new pair had demonstrated its strength in winning the duet at the Japan Open, French Open, and Swiss Open before arriving at the world cup. Thus, winning the duet over Japan's Kotani and Takayama was not as surprising as their winning margin, 191.03 to 190.03. The team event was very close. U.S.A. Team I squeaked by Canada 188.94 to 188.85. Almost a decade had passed since the U.S. had earned a sweep of all events in a major international meet.

The first Junior World Synchronized Swimming Championships were held in Cali, Colombia, in July 1989. The swimmers were all between the ages of 14 and 17 so no clear favorites had been established through prior competitions and the outcome was sure to be unpredictable. The Cali newspaper headlines, soon told the story: "U.S.A. Gano en Figuras" (U.S.A. wins in figures), "Becky se Bano en Oro" (Becky bathes in gold), "Dyroen-Sudduth, el Dueto de Oro" (Dyroen-Sudduth, duet of gold), and finally, "E.E.U.U. Gran Champeon" (U.S.A. a great champion). "In a great demonstration of strength, speed and synchronization, the United States won all events and overcame, in great style, their rivals from Canada and Japan."[14] Despite the freshness of the entries, results still seemed to reflect the usual pattern of major international events with the U.S.A., Canada, and Japan taking the medals in all events. In solo, Becky Dyroen was followed by Canada's Karen Clark and Fumiko Okuno of Japan. Duet and teams followed the same order. But a message for the future could be seen in the Soviets stepping up to fourth place in teams.

In an unprecedented turnaround, all the second Junior World Championship gold medals went to Japan. Held in Salerno, Italy, in 1991, Laila Vakil of Great Britain turned up with a win in the figures competition. Miya Tachibana won the solo and duet, with partner Rei Jimbo. The Salerno competition saw U.S.A.'s Heather Pease drop to fifth in solo, but Laurie McClelland and Jenny

The U.S. won all three events at the first Junior World Championships in Cali. Team winners, from left to right, are Lori McCoy, Jill Savery, Suzannah Dyroen, Margot Thien, Tina Vorheis, Kristy Donn, Becky Dyroen, Jill Sudduth.

Ohanesian won bronze medals in duet for the U.S.A. and the U.S. Junior National Team took silver. Also noted was the rise of the Soviet Union delegation moving upward in all events, taking fourth in solo, second in duet and third in team.[15]

By 1993, the rising skill level of the rest of the world became apparent at the Junior World Championships in Leeds, Great Britain. Russia had achieved a major goal, taking gold medals in a major competition. Olga Brousnikina won the solo and duet events but the Russian team still had work to do and placed third behind Canada and Japan. It was apparent that the U.S. would also have more work to do in the future as they saw soloist Kristina Lum place fifth and both the duet and team were in fourth.

Ted Turner's second off-year Olympics, the Goodwill Games, added the Olympic program events of synchro duet and solo to its program in 1990. Synchro found that the Turner Broadcast Network that was covering the Games for television was much more enthusiastic about synchro's audience impact than others had been. In the competition, Kristen Babb won the solo with Japan's Mikako Kotani second. Canada had not sent its leading soloist, still harboring feelings that it had lost in 1984 only because of the U.S. audience en-

vironment. In the duet, Karen and Sarah Josephson, who had come back to competition wanting to fulfill their Olympic dream of gold, had little difficulty prevailing over Canada's Alexander and Clark.[16]

With the sixth World Championships being held in southern hemisphere Perth, the normal 1990 schedule for the competition was deferred to January 1991 to fit into Australia's summer climate. Synchro had an outing in beautiful weather, bathed in glorious popular attention. Neither the press nor the organizing committee believed synchro would draw much interest. But synchro was the first final event to sell all its seats in presales, so organizers hastily constructed additional bleachers and added deck chair seating. Even with those last-minute measures, seating failed to approach demand. When competition finally arrived, resourceful spectators resorted to buying tickets for water polo or diving. Paying $5 more than the synchro tickets, they gained entrance to the Aquatic Complex where they lined the bridge between the swimming and synchro pools and filled the balconies of the building overlooking the pool, just to stand and watch the synchro action.

A letter appeared in the *Weekend Australian* on January 6, 1991, complaining, "The decision to allow a synchronized swimmer to carry the Australian flag at the World Swimming Championships is an affront to all serious athletes." Australia's *Synchro-News* replied that, "Karen and Sarah Josephson carried the American flag into the Entertainment Center [Opening Ceremony]; Mikako Kotani of Japan carried her country's flag in the Opening Ceremonies and so did Canada's Sylvie Frechette. Carolyn Waldo carried her nation's flag into Opening Ceremonies in Seoul."[17] And Gail Emery told of marching in the Opening Ceremonies in Barcelona. "Everyone wanted to be next to the *Dream Team* [U.S.A. basketball]. I spent Opening Ceremonies standing (truthfully being squished) next to Magic Johnson, Scotty Pippin and Coach Daly. I gave Magic a synchro pin and asked if he knew about our sport. He said, 'Sure I do! That's like dancing in the water. See, I got you covered, babe.'"[18]

Karen and Sarah Josephson were eagerly anticipating a real battle after the easy Goodwill Games victory. Their routine, filled with spins, split rockets, and intricate paired movements, earned two 10s in technical merit and five 10s in artistic impression. Karen said, "Because of our comeback, we knew our performance had to be better than in the [1988] Olympics." Sarah added, "Everyone remem-

The Josephson twins, Sarah (left) and Karen, were undefeated in the U.S. from 1985 until 1988 and came back to win again in 1991 and 1992. They were the Olympic favorites in the duet for 1992 and didn't disappoint (photograph by Ross Bean).

bered our performance there, and it was important to perform as well or better here." There was little doubt who was best that day, but the usual ranking was upset with Japan's Mikako Kotani and Aki Takayama besting the Canadian duet for second place.

Sylvie Frechette, Canada, felt comfortably safe going into solo finals with a 4.1-point figure lead over rival Kristen Babb of the U.S. With strong Commonwealth audience support, she gained another 0.2-point advantage on her routine to win going away. Babb philosophized, "I did my best. My best will get better! This is one time. We are even now in wins and losses. We are going head-to-head the next two years."[19]

Never before had there been such quality from all the teams. Canada, swimming fifth, earned what looked like an insurmountable score, garnering six out of seven awards of 10 for artistic impression; the U.S. had finally learned some of its lessons on figures, though. Its 2.5-point lead there allowed it to reclaim the world championship, last won in 1978. After receiving straight 10s for artistic impression, Michelle Svitenko, U.S.A. team captain, said, "It was a very satisfying experience."[20] FINA chairman Judy McGowan said, "The Canadians took the art of the theater and made it into sport. The Americans took the sport of synchronized swimming and made it into an art."[21]

Following the events, *Sports Illustrated* castigated ESPN for its failure to include synchro coverage in its telecasts from the world championships, "Judgment Calls—thumbs down to ESPN which pulled out of its planned coverage of synchronized swimming at the World Championships because it didn't want to pay rights fees for music such as that used in the swimmers' programs."[22]

Now the course was set for Barcelona. The news was encouraging in 1991 with major victories at the Pan American Games, the Pan Pacifics and the FINA World Cup. At the German Open in March 1992, the Josephson twins, Karen and Sarah, beat Canada's Vilagos twins, Penny and Vicky. Frechette's lead over newly married Babb-Sprague had been narrowed greatly. Then, in the Mallorca Pre-Olympic competition, Babb-Sprague defeated Frechette for the first time since her back injury in 1989. Things looked golden for the 1992 Olympic Games in Barcelona.

Bolstered by nine consecutive international victories, there was little doubt who was favored in the Olympic duet as Karen and Sarah Josephson came onto pool deck. FINA TSSC chairman Judy McGowan said, "The level of difficulty in their routine was truly in a class by itself, as was their flawless execution of that difficulty. They demonstrated variety and creativity within the difficulty of the routine."[23] Their awards, four 10s in both technical and artistic scores, reflected that perfection. Canada's Vilagos twins were second and Japan's Fumiko Okuno and Aki Takayama were third.

The solo event was a different situation. Beginning as early as the 1986 Moscow event, the rivalry had raged between the U.S.A.'s Kristen Babb-Sprague and Canada's Sylvie Frechette as first one and then the other would take the lead. The contest took a forced hiatus early in 1989 as Babb mended a near career-ending back injury. Frechette was far in front as the rivalry resumed but Babb-Sprague kept narrowing the margin through meetings at Rome, Bonn and the Barcelona Pre-Olympic. Finally, in Mallorca, Babb-Sprague had more than closed the gap in her first triumph since her back injury. The stage was set for an Olympic showdown.

Routine scores were as close as they could be, Frechette leading by 0.12 points. But the final figure scores had Babb 0.25 points in front of Frechette for an apparent victory by only 0.13 points. It should have ended there but with the figure scores came a major controversy that threw synchro, FINA and the IOC into bitter recriminations and turmoil. The controversy arose when the Brazilian judge, after the panel's awards were read and displayed on the electronic scoreboard, announced she had entered the wrong score and wanted to correct it. On the normally accepted basis that the time to correct a hand pad score was before sending (entering) it, the referee refused to allow the change. Unfortunately, that score had been for Frechette's figure. Canadian protests went to the technical committee and then to the FINA

Bureau, both upholding the referee's decision that a judge may not change a score "after the fact."

When someone asked Babb-Sprague if she felt her gold was tarnished because of the scoring mistake, she replied, "Absolutely not, I came here and had the greatest performance of my life."[24] Following the contest, McGowan reflected, "The solo was a question of the technician versus the artist. Kristen was better technically. Her ability to master the difficult spins and her height above the water during the other figure movements made a difference. Sylvie was the winner of the artistic impression part of the score. Her manner of presentation was exceptional, demonstrating the ability to swim with great passion."

The Games ended with Babb-Sprague winning the solo. McGowan said, "The friendly

After recovering from major back surgery, Kristen Babb-Sprague went on to victory in Barcelona. Some months later, Sylvie Frechette of Canada was awarded a duplicate gold medal because of a scoring error.

rivalry of Kristen and Sylvie has been good for synchronized swimming and will be missed by all. Perhaps it is indeed fitting that for one special moment in time, each of these fine athletes was crowned the best soloist in the world, Sylvie at the World Championships at Perth and Kristen at the Olympic Games in Barcelona."[25]

The rivalry was not, however, so friendly in other quarters. Canada carried the appeals to the IOC with the aid of IOC vice president Richard Pound (Canada) and the Canadian Olympic Association. Finally the IOC decided to award a second gold medal to Frechette and list the two as co-champions. When informed of the decision, Babb-Sprague said, "At the Opening Ceremonies in Barcelona, we all took an oath to be the best we could be as competitors, without regard for the outcome. As the Olympic Oath states, the true honor is to participate. The issuing of a tandem gold medal to Sylvie in no way changes the pride and satisfaction I felt then or now."[26]

The 1992 Olympic Games were over. Now the U.S. began to travel down the road to At-

Becky Dyroen-Lancer became the most decorated swimmer at the 1994 World Championships in Rome where she scored the first grand slam (gold in all events) in the World Championships since 1973. Dyroen-Lancer is the only U.S. synchronized swimmer to have been awarded the FINA Prize Eminence (photograph by Nancy Hines).

lanta. Team U.S.A. made its new position atop the synchro world clearer still in its sweep of all events at the 1993 FINA World Cup in Lausanne, Switzerland.[27] Becky Dyroen-Lancer was the big winner with her second grand slam performance and became the third athlete in the history of the world cup to win figures, solo, duet and team. She and long-time duet partner Jill Sudduth had faced a real challenge for the first time in Russia's Olga Sedakova and Anna Kozlova. That duet took second, Russia's highest place in world competition. The U.S.A.'s superiority extended into the team event where Canada came in second and Japan third once more.

This was also the first world event in which former states of the Soviet Union were competing as separate federations. This factor raised the number of contending nations, but hurt the Russian team which had lost crucial swimmers to Ukraine and Belarus. The growth in numbers was also evident at the third Junior World Championships, in Leeds, Great Britain, in 1993.[28] There, 33 nations participated, but the U.S. Junior National Team had little to boast about in the results. Canada won the team event with the U.S. falling to fourth. Russian juniors offered warnings for the future in winning both the solo and duet, as the U.S.A.'s Kristina Lum earned fifth in solo and, with Kim Wurzel, finished fourth in the duet.

The first major international event of 1994 was the Goodwill Games in St. Petersburg, Russia. Becky Dyroen-Lancer and Jill Sudduth won the duet but Dyroen-Lancer suffered her first defeat in solo since 1993, coming in behind Russia's Olga Sedakova, 197.20 to 197.02.[29]

Then came the 1994 World Championships. "It took more than a day, but the U.S. National Team conquered Rome and the World with their grand slam sweep at the World Aquatic Championships," said U.S. media director Laura LaMarca. Synchro's Becky Dyroen-Lancer was the most-decorated American athlete at the championship with three gold medals. She said, "I am very happy about this win. As a soloist, it will be my biggest win ever, because solo and duet are not included in the Olympics. You can't get any bigger than this."[30]

The figure competition was grueling. With almost 200 competitors and two panels of judges, the event took more than 15 hours over two days' time to complete. The judges toiling in the heat could take small comfort in the realization that this would be the last such event within the world aquatic championships, as technical routines would now replace figure competition. Heading into the solo finals, Dyroen-Lancer had a 2.73-point lead in figures and went on to augment that lead with five awards of 10 for technical merit and four 10s for artistic impression. She was the first American to win a World Championship solo title since Tracie Ruiz-Conforto in 1982. Fumiko Okuno, Japan, earned straight 10 awards for artistic impression, placing her into a strong second over Canada's Lisa Alexander.

The duet was much closer with the Japanese duet trailing Dyroen-Lancer and Jill Sudduth by 0.01 points after figures. The judges recognized the U.S. pair's flawless swimming with five 10s in technical merit and three more in artistic impression to give them the gold. Japan's Okuno and Miya Tachibana and Canada's Alexander and Woodley had identical final scores, 186.259. For the first time in any major international competition, FINA's tiebreaker rules were invoked to award Japan the silver medals by virtue of having the higher artistic scores.[31] The U.S. team, with a 1.1-point figure lead over Japan and 1.6 points over Canada, headed confidently into the final swim and won the largest (20 teams) world championship team event by 2.6 points. Canada pulled up to second and Japan was third, only 0.05 points out of second place. Of that team win, Nathalie Schneyder, team captain, said, "We feel within ourselves that we had the best swim and are satisfied we have achieved our goal. Four years ago I was on the award stand in Perth and didn't know if I would ever achieve another World Championship medal. I'm terribly lucky to be swimming with such a good group."[32]

## The National Championships 1989–94

After two years of application of the new routine awards for technical merit and artistic impression in USSS competition, their influence in boosting the importance of the artistic side of synchronized swimming was beginning to be realized in 1989. *Synchro* Magazine mused, "A new style of routine was developing…. The thing that made [Heather Simmons and Patti Lynn's] routine really stand out was the change in style and emphasis that Santa Clara brought by using only Ravel's 'Bolero.' While the trend has been to use bits and pieces of this and that, this duet used only Bolero and was reminiscent of Torvill and Dean's [ice dancing] Olympic program. The synchro version was masterfully choreographed and scored the highest number of 10s at the meet."[33] The next year, swimming to *Scheherazade*, the same pair received six 10s for artistic impression and tied the Josephsons in routine score.

The Walnut Creek Aquanuts continued their long string of team victories into 1989, but their position was much more precarious in that meet. For the first time in many years, there was no insurmountable figure average apparent as team finals started. Walnut Creek led Santa Clara only by 0.55 points. Walnut Creek's routine swim execution was nearly per-

Santa Clara's Jill Sudduth and Becky Dyroen dominated all duet competitions, winning U.S.A. Nationals for three years and almost every international event, World Championships, World Cup, Goodwill Games, Pan American Games, American Cup, Junior Worlds and numerous open meets (photograph by Nancy Hines).

fect, but Santa Clara outdid them on the artistic scores. Walnut Creek still won, but by only 0.72 points.

In 1990, Santa Clara's routine finally earned the margin needed to overcome a small figure deficit and stop Walnut Creek's consecutive victory streak at 10. The team accomplishing this feat consisted of Becky Dyroen, Suzannah Dyroen, Jill Sudduth, Heather Simmons, Natasha Haynes, Patti Lynn, Laurie Martin and Anna Miller. It had been a long road. Becky Dyroen, Sudduth, Simmons and Lynn had all been part of the impressive 12 and

under demonstration team at the Los Angeles 1983 Pre-Olympic competition. Also to be noted, the two teams each were competing with four future Olympians on each team.

With the return of the Josephson twins to their team in 1991, Walnut Creek was competing with seven past and future Olympians—Kristen Babb-Sprague, Karen and Sarah Josephson, Jill Savery, Nathalie Schneyder, Margot Thien, and Laurie McClelland—and easily regained the team title. They held it in 1992 as only one team member changed, Jenny Ohanesian replacing Michelle Svitenko. Then the 1992 Olympic champions, Babb-Sprague and the Josephsons retired and Santa Clara came out strong in the 1993 figures competition, earning a 1.4-point edge. The Aquamaids performed with flawless execution and outstanding artistry in their routine to receive four 10s for technical merit and all 10s for artistic impression. They successfully defended their title in 1994.

Karen and Sarah Josephson had retired after their 1988 Olympic silver medal performance and Kristen Babb and Tracy Long were crowned the new duet champions in 1989. In 1990, Karen and Sarah Josephson returned to the competition, saying, "We both feel we can't live the rest of our lives saying 'what if….'"[34] They reclaimed the title in 1990 and went on to win twice more in 1991 and 1992, before finishing their competitive career with the Olympic gold they so richly deserved.

In 1993, Santa Clara's Becky Dyroen and Jill Sudduth moved to the top to start what would be a new and fabulous reign. They would never be beaten in any subsequent national or international competition they entered and fairly easily defended the duet title through 1994.

The Aquanuts' Kristen Babb quickly stepped up to the 1989 solo championship as Tracie Ruiz-Conforto retired for good. She continued

After losses to Walnut Creek in the '80s and in '91 and '92, this team of Aquamaids succeeded in bringing the title back to Santa Clara. In back, from left to right, are Jenny Mayer, Laurie Martin, Anna Kozlova, Becky Dyroen; at center are Heather Simmons and Kari Kreitzer; and at bottom are Mary Wodka, Jill Sudduth, and Suzannah Dyroen (photograph by Nancy Hines).

winning USSS top honors until she retired after the 1992 Olympics. Then, Becky Dyroen's strength in figures put her in position to take over the number one spot in 1993. A substantial obstacle arose in teammate Heather Simmons' routine performance, which received six awards of 10 for artistic impression, but Dyroen's 1.5-point lead in figures was enough to give her the solo crown. Dyroen commented, "It is really hard when your toughest competition is on your own team. You support your teammates 100 percent, but you want to do well also."[35] Dyroen became the most decorated swimmer of this period, succeeding in grand slam performances in every competition she entered. Before her solo final event in 1994, she said, "I've got to keep myself into reality here. I can't let my head get too big. But, if I win this competition, it increases my confidence because I feel Heather [Simmons] is the second-best competitor in the world."[36]

In 1994, synchronized swimming was dubbed an emerging sport by the NCAA and athletes were cautioned to follow full NCAA eligibility requirements. NCAA's definition of amateur is more strict than either USSS or FINA, so athletes were carefully instructed on the differences in rules.[37] Such things as performing in a paid exhibition or receiving compensation for teaching synchro or even getting pay for judging at a synchro meet can all professionalize an athlete and make her ineligible for college competition.

Under coach Mary Jo Ruggieri, Ohio State was the dominant team through most of these years of collegiate competition. In the team event, Ohio State won every team title during this period. The trio title went west to Stanford in 1989, but Ohio State had it again from 1990 to 1994. The University of California at Berkeley won the trio in 1994. In the duet competition, Dee Cohen and Karen Madsen won for Stanford in 1989. Then Ohio State won the title for the next four consecutive years: with Maria Guisti and Cheryl Schemenauer in 1990; Guisti and Carrie DeGuerre in 1991; and DeGuerre and Kim Ochsner in 1992 and 1993. With future Olympians Jill Savery and Margot Thien, U.C. Berkeley won the duet in 1994. The solo title wandered about a little more. Maria Guisti, Ohio State, won in 1989 but Stanford's Karen Madsen claimed the title in 1990. Guisti won it back in 1991, then it went West again to Emily Porter of Arizona State University in 1992 and in 1993. Finally, in 1994, U.C. Berkeley won with Savery.

## Sport Administration

Barbara McNamee, of Des Moines, Iowa, was elected president of USSS in the fall of 1988. She served for four years and oversaw the development of a new look for USSS with a new logo and redesigned products, aided by a new public relations agency, The Design Group. Extensive revisions were made to the code of regulations and the competition rules were totally reorganized.

Nancy Wightman, from Troy, New York, took over from McNamee in 1992 and served through 1996. One of her first tasks was getting *Synchro Swimming USA* magazine started as it became part of the national office operation with Laura LaMarca as editor.[38] It filled the vacancy left by the cessation of *Synchro* magazine's publication at the end of 1992. The new magazine was seen as a potential marketing and public relations tool as well as for communication and education. It turned toward a colorful, glossy format to fulfill those purposes. In its first issue, Wightman said, "Greetings and welcome to the first edition of *Synchro Swimming USA* magazine. We are very excited about the opportunity of carrying on the *Synchro* magazine tradition and USSS having its very own official magazine."[39]

Financially, USSSI was finally making strides. The "Classical Splash" aquacade was revived in a new form in 1990. A National Team III was selected to provide an all-star cast that would perform daily at Sea World in San Diego. While U.S. teams had performed previously at special commercial shows in Cypress Gardens and Sea World, this was the first time USSS swimmers would be involved in a show on a long-term basis, the full summer season.[40] The sponsor base began to improve somewhat. Colorado Timing Systems supplied a portable electronic scoreboard unit for national meets.

Coca-Cola and Max Factor were added as new sponsors in 1991. Speedo was the supplier of national team equipment through 1993. The major source of USSS funding, however, remained the U.S. Olympic Committee, with some augmentation from membership fees and the U.S. Synchronized Swimming Foundation. The excitement over the team event in the Olympics encouraged Jantzen, in 1994, to become a national sponsor and synchro's supplier for national team outfitting. Roger Yost, Jantzen's vice president of advertising and sales promotion, was very excited about the mutual opportunities that a Jantzen–synchro swimming U.S.A. partnership would create.[41]

With FINA further loosening the amateurism rules by 1993, some federations began to provide subsistence-level incomes to athletes in training for Olympic sports. The USOC now offered, to its member sports, annual grants to help defray training costs for Olympic and Pan American athletes. For the USSS athletes, the first grants from the USOC were $2,500 per year to each of the top 10 athletes (Level I grants). By 1993, the grants had risen to $5,000 a year and an Olympic job opportunities program was also in place for the Level I athletes. Additional grants up to $2,500 for Level II athletes were available based on need. Some tuition assistance was available for collegiate athletes also.

The biggest change came in the Operation Gold program which rewarded the NGB competition programs for the level of performance reached in international events, thereby encouraging and assisting athletes to continue training for future international events including the Olympic Games. In non–Olympic years, each sport would select a qualifying world-class event and athletes were awarded Operation Gold funds based on their achievements in the selected competition. For synchro, the 1993 Operation Gold competition was the FINA World Cup. A first-place finisher would receive $5,000, second place $4,000, third place $3,500, fourth place $3,000 and fifth through eighth places $2,500. As Sarah Josephson reported, these awards were intended to help offset training expenses for the top athletes. Then, in the summer of 1993, the USOC announced that cash awards would be given for performance in the Olympic Games — gold medalists to receive $15,000, silver $10,000, bronze $7,500 and fourth $5,000.[42] The definition of the amateur obviously was no longer related to any of the old proscriptions against competing for prizes of monetary value.

Sound became even more manageable in U.S. competitions with the allowance for "pretiming" of senior national routines. This began in 1989. Under this regulation, the sound manager would time and verify the playing times for tapes in practice and use a frequency calibration procedure to ensure playing it back at exactly the same speed and timing in the competition. Actually having been used by sound managers since 1984, the practical effect at this point was only to eliminate the need for timing competition to determine whether over or under time penalties should be assessed.

Spreading knowledge throughout the country has been an continuing effort since the sport began. In 1988, a new plan which became known as NCN (National Clinic Network) was formed. An NCN pre-elite camp was held in the fall and the curriculum for the camps was designed for that level of skill. Then, four zone clinics, NCN "A" camps, would be held in four sections of the country on the same January weekend beginning in 1989. The top 30 athletes in each zone were eligible to participate. Instruction was under the direction of a national coach with the assistance of a national team athlete and designated zone clinicians.

Following participation in the "A" camps, zone clinicians would offer two NCN "B" camps within each of their zones to reach the next 30 ranking swimmers in each of their areas. Finally, as the final part of the zonal plan, a total of 16 "C" camps, four in each zone, were to be held. Unfortunately, those "C" camps were rarely offered, primarily due to the difficulty of determining participant eligibility since many swimmers for whom the camp was aimed were not able to participate in a zone championships figure competition where assessments could be made. With a shift to association level organization, "C" camps became more successful. Technical director Margo Erickson said, after the first camps had been held,

"We gave premature birth to a new baby," but the consensus of all participants was that the new baby was alive and doing well.[43]

The camp program USSS had previously authorized under the direction of R & R Sports Academies continued through 1992. Demand declined and fewer camps were held each year as the NCN program, with access to Olympic coaches and help from national team athletes, satisfied more of the demand. USSS finally dropped sponsorship of the summer camp program completely but R & R Academies has continued as an independent summer camp program.

In 1989, USSS published a separate figures handbook, to make that section of the full rulebook available to athletes and coaches in handy form, undiluted and more readable by young readers with simplified rules and without the code in which they had little interest.[44] Photos of prior years' champions were added in 1991. Two USSS Manuals came out in 1990. The *Adapted Manual*, by Vera Hammel, was to help adapt programs involving swimmers with special needs to include forms of synchronized swimming.[45] The *Safety Manual*, by Margaret Forbes, dealt with water safety from pool safety to electrical safety and also some legal issues that might involve the coach.[46] In 1992, the sports medicine committee published a *Sport Training Manual*, edited by Rebecca Skidmore and Marti Tucker.[47] It covered training, conditioning, mental preparation, injury prevention, and other topics. A nutrition section was added to the manual in 1994. Betty Hazle edited the latest revision of USSS' *Meet Management Guide*, giving step-by-step instructions for hosting a U.S. championship.[48]

The most venerable of synchronized swimming magazines finally asked *Synchro* readers if the magazine was obsolete now that we had the USSS office newsletter. The resulting letters of support had no effect upon stagnant circulation numbers. Its publishers decided that personal subsidy of *Synchro* had reached its limits. They pulled the plug at the end of 1992, fulfilling a full 30 years of independent publication. U.S. Synchronized Swimming took on its subscriptions to start publication of *Synchro Swimming USA* in 1993.

Other magazines had suffered the same fate. *Synchro Canada* had been discontinued in 1986. Jenny Gray, *Synchro World* editor, complained in 1989, "Subscriptions are well down from last year and we will be hard pressed to continue, perhaps this is what people want." She started up again in late 1990 but after several issues explained, "Unfortunately, the economic situation has gotten the better of us and the magazine will close. Subscriptions have been insufficient to cover the printing costs and without a sponsorship we are unable to continue."[49]

## Competitive Programs

For 1991, the USSS Senior National Championships underwent a name change to the U.S. National Championships and this name held until Jantzen's sponsorship in 1994 when it became the Jantzen U.S. National Synchronized Swimming Championships. The competition was governed by international (FINA) rules. Stricter qualifying requirements were imposed to make an elite entry slate of about 20 solos, 20 duets and 12 teams who would qualify through prior national, junior, zone and collegiate competition. Complying with international rules meant dropping trios from the U.S. Nationals, but they were retained at all other levels. A new minimum age of 13 years for senior level competition was also adopted.

The tight qualifying requirements were designed to eliminate the need for a preliminary event, maintaining only the semifinal and final events. Subsequent erosion of restrictions on the entry eligibility, allowing more entries from various sources, found the goal of only 20 entrants soon inflated to 35 to 40 in duets and solos. Minor changes in eligibility had developed in the subsequent years, opening it to a few more entrants from zone, collegiate and junior programs.

With entry to the U.S. National Championships becoming tightly restricted, another senior event, the U.S. Open Championships, was added as a summer event. Qualifications were similar to those of the previous senior nationals except to exclude all members of the

U.S. National Team I from entry. Not only did this event provide a high-profile competition opportunity for the athletes no longer eligible for the U.S. Nationals, with the top athletes excluded and out of the club line-ups, chances for mixing up the normal power structures were greatly enhanced. The first Open Championship was held in July 1991.

The international definition of junior, or as near an approximation as USSS coaches would agree to, was finally adopted for USSS events in 1991. The junior class became age restricted for 13- to 18-year-old athletes, rather than being based upon level of accomplishment. The age limitations differed from the international 14 to 17, but it was a step in the right direction. At the same time, the biannual junior nationals were reduced to a single meet, named the U.S. Junior Championships. For 1993, the junior championship was made subject to FINA rules, but with some exceptions, as using the U.S. 13–18 age range and retaining the trio event.

The Junior Olympic program, always touted as being developmental, moved closer to that base in 1991 as the classes of athletes to be excluded were expanded to include all U.S. national qualifiers, all U.S. open finalists, U.S. junior medalists and all national age group winners. The changes had some rapid and striking effects. The elite club denizens of U.S. national semifinals continued to dominate the still-unrestricted 1992 National Age Group Championships but the National Junior Olympics found other clubs battling for unaccustomed medal opportunities. In 1993, the top age for U.S. age group competition was extended upward to include 19 years, providing a spot for a previously neglected age.

Collegiate synchro competition managed to survive the NCAA takeover of women's sports from the AIAW, but not without some casualties, and with a much-reduced rate of growth. The Gender Equity Act of 1972, better known as Title IX legislation, may still provide the basis for some future growth. This act prohibits discrimination based upon sex in funding of sports activities in colleges receiving federal assistance or grants. Only in 1993 did the NCAA take up a serious study of the issues raised by that act and it recommended that synchronized swimming be added to the NCAA Gender Equity Task Force list of "emerging sports," a designation suggesting a sport with potential for balancing support of women's and men's activities. Under favorable circumstances, the USSS Collegiate Championships could become an NCAA event, but only after attaining 40 institutional member participation.

The masters rules were stripped of all references to gender in 1991. The earlier rules included specific men's and mixed events, with all the age divisions as well, producing a tremendous and complex list of potential program events. Although men had sometimes constituted a significant presence, with as many as 10 males at national championships, their events were very underpopulated. Most of the men dropped out when their special events were removed. From 10 men competing in 1990, male entries dropped to just one in 1994. The change to genderless age divisions still left a large number of divisions for medals because the masters and grand masters divisions effectively doubled the age groupings.

International competitions for masters also became more numerous. Indianapolis hosted the Pan Pacific Masters in 1989. The third FINA World Masters Championships was held in Rio de Janeiro in 1990, and this time it included synchro. Indianapolis held a Masters World Games in 1992 and the fifth World Masters Swimming Championships, held in Montreal, also had synchro. The World Masters Championships remain unique in allowing unlimited entries from each nation, hence many U.S. clubs have participated.

## Technical Rules

The trial introductions of a technical routine made dramatic changes in the competition structure of some international meets during this period. Impressed by the concept of a short program which included required actions and movements, Dawn Bean snapped up the idea to make a legislative proposal to USSS for use in developmental progressions for age group and qualifying progressions for higher levels. Although the shorter routines should have been very useful in age group programs, the proposal was rejected resoundingly. Later proposals were also rejected while FINA continued to test the concept in competitions at the World Cup meets in Bonn and Lausanne. With favorable reactions and most problems solved, machinery was set in motion to make the technical routine a normal part of some FINA events by 1995. The U.S. continued with its program of figures and free routines, rejecting the technical routine as impractical because of the scarcity of pool time faced by most clubs.

When the difficulty multiples for all figures were revised by FINA in 1991, USSS considered some of the new FINA values wildly unrealistic, despite the much-touted "scientific biomechanical" base, and stuck with the old values while looking at ways to produce better results. FINA had also altered some action descriptions for 1991, intending to reintroduce some element of risk. One of the main changes, requiring a rapid, high thrust action in the barracuda and heron was returning to the rocket-style thrust USSS had temporarily adopted for those figures more than a decade previously. Another was calling for a uniform but *rapid* rotation of at least 720 degrees on continuous spins. USSS adopted these changes as well. Finally, in one of the most radical changes, FINA's new figure competition groups for senior and junior events were adopted. This meant going from groups of six figures to groups of only four figures. Juniors in nationals would have their figures drawn from five junior groups rather than from the senior groups, as previously. Age group figures were also changed to four required figures, eliminating the long-honored optionals. USSS was greatly indebted to FINA for finally bringing about long-overdue simplifications of the competitive structure.

## Judging and Scoring

In the most drastic change in scoring since the initial rules were accepted was the change in FINA from a single-score routine award to the new categories of technical merit and artistic impression. Although the approval had come in 1986, implementation was delayed to start January 1, 1989, because it had meant such drastic changes to most sport rules. While the U.S. had never left its own two-score system, it too had to revise to the newly designed categories. Everywhere else, the change to two scores was universally hailed as a major advance for the sport. Judges could now really distinguish between the two different scores.

Desperate for more flexibility in figure awards, tenth-point intervals for judging figures was finally put into effect in 1989, replacing the traditional half-point scale. In 1991, with international as well as USSS judges finally fed up with competitors' interpretation of "executed slowly, high and controlled" to mean infinitesimal motion, "slowly" was dropped from figure execution instructions. Uniform tempo, maximum height and other factors of movement control took precedence over attempts to demonstrate how slowly a motion could be accomplished.

## Awards and Honors

Becky Dyroen-Lancer and Jill Sudduth were selected as *Swimming World* magazine's World Synchronized Swimmers of the Year in 1993. For the second consecutive year, Dyroen-Lancer was selected World Synchronized Swimmer of the Year by *Swimming World* in 1994.[50] She won more gold medals than any other U.S. athlete at the world championships in Rome and was the first American to sweep all the gold medals in synchro since 1973.

# 11

## *Olympic Teams, at Last!: 1995–99*

At the XXVI Olympic Games in Atlanta, almost as if celebrating the 50th anniversary of the first U.S. National Synchronized Swimming Championship, the team event finally appeared on the Olympic program. Not only was the dream fulfilled of having synchro's premier event finally on stage in the Games, but the U.S.A. National Team seized the opportunity to put a glorious climax to a spectacular competition in winning the first Olympic team title before a wildly enthusiastic home audience. A more consummate celebration could hardly be imagined.

It had been a long wait, with difficult battles along the way. Unfortunate victims of the skirmishes were the solo and duet events which had been undeservedly banished from the Olympic program to make room for teams. Continued misunderstanding of the sport was mainly responsible. There were still those who opposed having synchro in the Olympics at all, and enlisted the "bus is full" refrain, i.e. efforts to minimize growth of the Olympic population, to try to keep synchro out altogether. Thus, it was considered a synchro victory when their advocates bowed to the limitation pressures and agreed to drop solos and duets and allow only an eight-federation entry into the team event. Hence, an Olympic qualifying meet became necessary for selecting the lucky eight.

Fortunately, there had been no problem in gaining approval for including the new technical routine as a replacement for figure competition. In fact, teams might not have been accepted into the Olympics at all if the figure competition had continued, so the new technical routine provided an interesting, venue-filling preliminary event, separate from the free routine.

The years before this finale had been filled with vigorous international activity with sometimes dramatic alterations of the player positions. Russia had started to show real strength again as it recovered from the disintegration of the Soviet Union and its support of the synchro effort. Both China and Korea were making their presence felt. The introduction of technical routines was making a difference in meet structure and synchro training.

The wailing that the Olympic "bus was full" had been replaced with, even more urgent, "the bus is overloaded," as the time approached to decide the program for the 2000 Olympics. There were proposals to banish several sports to reduce overcrowding, even while new sports were being crammed into the program. Synchro was a prime candidate for ejection on some lists and the U.S. media definitely saw it as gone.

With the program decisions to be made in late 1994 for the Olympic program of 2000, a delegate to the January 1994 International Judges Seminar in Toronto suggested that a worldwide effort be made to petition the IOC on synchro's behalf. Such a flood of letters ensued that President Samaranch finally had to ask them to stop. There was a collective sigh of relief in the synchro community when the announcement came that the team event would remain on the program, contrary to the media predictions.

No synchro enthusiast, though, had been happy with only the single event in 1996 and the effort to restore the other two events was immediately increased. Luckily, some of the IOC hierarchy looked favorably upon the sport, perhaps in part because it had proved itself as a prime ticket-selling sport in four Olympics. The reward came in 1997 as the IOC announced that the duet would also be on the Olympic program in 2000. The very good news was that the duet would not only return but it would include a preliminary event to qualify 24 duets with the stipulation that eight of the duets must be derived from among the members of the teams qualifying in the team event. The bad news, though not as bad as it might have been, was the loss of the second alternate for teams. Now just one reserve, instead of two, would be permitted, reducing team delegations to a total of nine members.

This was a period of relative stability for the USSS, organizationally and financially, with adequate support from the USOC and other sources for its important programs. Competitive program structure changes were made for better skill progressions. At the top of the competitive ladder, the U.S. national titles were now totally under Santa Clara's control. The outlook for international competition was brightening as the national teams kept winning.

However, for the USSS, the Olympic excitement and glow fell behind too soon. There

Finally, synchro's premier event, team competition, was on the Olympic program. U.S.A. won the gold medals before madly cheering thousands. From left to right are Suzannah Bianco, Tammy Cleland, Becky Dyroen-Lancer, Emily Porter-LeSueur, Heather Pease, Jill Savery, Nathalie Schneyder, Heather Simmons-Carrasco, Jill Sudduth and Margot Thien (photograph by Dan Helms).

would be no resting upon 1996 laurels. The entire Olympic team was retired and gone. New national team members would be chosen and would have to prove their mettle. It would be a new era, with new goals and new players. A new administration with a new, young president was in charge. Where would they and the new athletes lead us?

## International Developments

The technical program was adopted at the 1994 World Congress in Rome. Since upper-level IOC officials had already been sending strong rumblings against further use of figure competitions in the Olympic Games, technical routines were immediately installed in the Olympic Games and world aquatic championship programs, replacing figure competition. However, figure competition would be retained for the junior world championships. There the competition would be free routine and figure competition and the FINA World Cup would include all three events, free and technical routines and figure competition. Hosts of other international events were encouraged to include all three events but only required to have two. While no words actually specified that the free routine must be part of all international events, its inclusion was guaranteed by not providing a scoring procedure for a program omitting it.[1] With the option of having just technical and free routines, figure competition for senior-level events was soon history.

With the advent of the technical routine, the retreat from the original excessive weighting given to figure scores was carried still further. Earlier changes had changed the figures value from almost 60 percent of the total score to about 50 percent. With the introduction of the technical routine, scoring procedures were altered so that in competitions with three events, the free routine would constitute 50 percent and figures and technical routine would count for 25 percent each of the final total. In two-event competitions, either free routine plus figures or free routine plus technical, the free routine would provide 65 percent of the total score.

The FINA World Cup had always been restricted to eight qualifiers for each event, with qualifying based on placement in the prior world aquatic championships. Now, qualifying for the world cup was expanded to include a member from each continent if not otherwise qualified. An exception to all qualifying requirements was made for the team event for the 1995 World Cup in Atlanta because it would be used as the first step of the qualifications for the Olympic team event. That event was opened to all federations so all those interested could try to be among the 12 teams admitted to the final Olympic qualifying trials that would immediately follow the world cup events.

The number of finalists in international meets was changed from the traditional eight to 12. At least part of the motivation for this change was the hope that it might be used to justify increasing the number of entries in the Olympics to 12 to fill a normal final event. It didn't work for that purpose but it did force some changes in meet schedules.

Another major change involved judging. Two separate panels of judges for judging technical merit and for artistic impression were used officially for the first time in the 1995 Pan American Games in Argentina. Unanimously acclaimed by judges as a great improvement, almost every subsequent international competition in 1995 used two panels. Judy McGowan said, "I seriously doubt we will ever go back to one panel of judges. The judges like it better because they can be more precise when only judging Technical Merit or Artistic Impression. The coaches and athletes feel the judging is better and it allows more people to be part of the decision making process."[2]

However, approval from upper levels was not unanimous. Strong opposition arose from FINA Bureau to using 10 judges instead of the traditional seven in the 1996 Olympics. The main argument was the necessity of asking the IOC to allow more officials. Another factor was probably the desire to avoid adding more view-blocking judges, often poorly placed on deck in high, lifeguard station chairs. After demonstrating at the 1995 FINA World Cup that a more acceptable 10-judge seating arrangement was feasible, permission was granted for the use of two panels of five judges each for the Olympic Games.

The XII Pan American Games, held in Mar del Plata, Argentina, was the first international competition for the U.S. in 1995 and the first to use separate panels of judges for each of the two routine scores. Becky Dyroen-Lancer again led the U.S. team to victory and scored her seventh grand slam victory. She said, "Ever since I won the 1993 FINA World Cup where I established myself, the pressure has been different. No one realizes what it is like to have to defend a title."[3] Dyroen-Lancer won the solo by 1.5 points and the duet with Jill Sudduth by a point. The team also won by more than a point. Canada took all silver. Maria Elena Guisti, U.S. collegiate champion, won the bronze medal for Venezuela in solo. Mexico was third in duet and team.

The fourth Junior World Championships were held in Bonn in 1995. The U.S. Junior Team's goal was to improve over its 1993 placing in Germany. The team succeeded in duet by earning bronze medals, but remained trapped in the same fifth place in solo and fourth place in team that it had achieved in the prior meet.

The large entry included 18 teams, 28 solos and 26 duets. The team medals went to Canada, Japan and Russia.[4]

The USSS staged a separate Olympic trials to determine the 10-member "Dream Team" that would compete in the first Olympic team event in Atlanta. The October 1995 trials were held in Indianapolis. The athletes swam technical and free routines singly, in small groups, and larger groups, accumulating individual judging points in each swim until the 10 athletes were selected. The televised event revealed the agonies of a special swim-off competition between best friends for selection of the 10th member. U.S.A.'s first Olympic team members included Tammy Cleland, Heather Pease, Jill Savery, Nathalie Schneyder and Margot Thien from Walnut Creek; Suzannah Bianco, Becky Dyroen-Lancer, Heather Simmons-Carrasco, and Jill Sudduth from Santa Clara; and Emily Porter-LaSueur from Arizona State University.[5]

With the addition of eight teams for the Olympic Games, it became necessary to have a world competition to determine the qualifiers. Rather than the normal prequalified number of contestants for previous world cups, an unlimited entry into the team event of the 1995 World Cup in Atlanta was allowed, so it could be used as part of the qualifying program for the 1996 Olympics. Sixteen nations entered the world cup team events from which 12 would advance to the Olympic team qualifying event. That competition, one day after the world cup finals, would select the eight teams to be allowed the honor of competing in the Olympic Games.

As in the previous two world cups, the competition involved the new technical routine as well as the free routine and figure competition. The U.S.A. swimmers handily won everything in sight: figures, technical, and free routines in solo, duet, and team. Dyroen-Lancer scored her ninth consecutive grand slam. Canada was also consistent in earning all the second places while Russia took all the

The U.S.A. junior Team captured gold at the 1998 American Cup in Cerritos. With their "Circle of Light" formation above, team members included Alison Bartosik, Erin Dobratz, Julie Drexler, Alysia Jones, Stephanie Joukoff, Christina McClelland, Katie Norris, Andrea Nott, Kim Probst and Kendra Zanotto (photograph by Nancy Hines).

thirds and Japan sank to fourth in all events, followed by France.

The following day, the U.S.A. team won the Olympic qualifying technical contest in the morning. That evening, as its free routine performance was awarded an unprecedented set of straight 10s, five for technical merit and five for artistic impression, they clinched the top qualifying spot. "I really didn't expect a perfect score," exclaimed Coach Chris Carver. "I told the team to look at the scoreboard and cherish it."[6]

The Olympic year finally arrived for this team that called themselves the "Team with a Dream."[7] These 10 girls of the U.S.A. Olympic Team had first been assembled for the Swiss Open of 1992. Every subsequent year, the same 10 won the top spots on the national team while sharing the dream of being the first to win gold medals in the team event of the Olympic Games.

During the training time before the events began, synchro again issued a "media challenge" to sports writers to get in with the team and try it themselves. A syndicated columnist from the *Miami Herald*, Dave Barry, gave synchro great coverage in Atlanta after he and fellow journalist Dan Le Batard took synchro's *challenge* and gamely tried the sport. Some excerpts from his column: "Dan and I started learning our synchronized maneuvers, The first one was called Eggbeatering…. When Dan and I gracefully raised our arms, our entire bodies, arms and all, immediately sank like anvils. When we all tried the maneuver together, there was a circle of a dozen young women, smiling and raising their arms, and in the middle of the circle, there was this bubbling, violently turbulent patch of water, underneath which were Dan and me, trying desperately to eggbeater our way back to the surface before our lungs exploded…. We gave up on eggbeatering, and tried the ballet leg…. When Dan and I attempted it, we hit the bottom so hard we left dents. My favorite maneuver was the vertical split…. We attempted this as a group, with Dan and me again in the middle, and I will never forget the sight from the bottom of the pool, where I, of course, immediately found myself…. After 45 minutes of alternately eggbeatering and sinking, I came to the surface and using what little air I had left in my lungs, shouted, 'This is the hardest sport in the world.' Then, and only then, did they let us out of the pool."[8]

Synchro was the hardest ticket to get in Atlanta. Offers in excess of $500 came from people begging for tickets to free routine finals. Even after the event had started, wishful folks still milled outside wanting to find a latecomer's ticket or a crack through which a glimpse of the action might be caught. Arriving judges reported their slow-moving bus had been stopped by a woman frantically waving her arms in front of the bus. Climbing aboard, she asked pleadingly "Does anyone have any tickets for the synchronized swimming finals, I'm desperate."

Synchro in these Olympic Games had little resemblance to its previous appearances in the Games. Gone were the solo and duet events, replaced by team. Gone was the figures competition, replaced by a technical routine. But staying were more than 15,000 wildly cheering spectators who couldn't get enough of the sport; arriving early to be certain that not a second of competition would be missed; loudly voicing their support in the competition; and finally, staying long after the victory

ceremony to wave at, or, if lucky, talk with the swimmers.

Synchro gained new respect from other sources at the Games. After setting a world record in the 200-meter running event, America's Michael Johnson responded unexpectedly to a press conference question on what he was going to do next. Instead of the expected champion's cliché, "I'm going to Disney World," he said "I'm going to be a spectator now and take in some of the other sports, like synchronized swimming. I respect those athletes." When some of the reporters started to snicker, he quickly jumped to synchro's defense saying, "Come on, you don't think that's not [sic] a sport? Those athletes train harder than I do!"[9]

High expectations rested on U.S.A.'s team, undefeated for the last five years and ranked number one in the world. They came through the technical routine with a 0.442-point lead over Canada and 0.537 over Japan. That event counted for only 35 percent of the final score and the team members knew they had to perform flawlessly if they were to win. Some observers at their last practice runs had their doubts as they watched the team flub a final raft action twice in a row. False alarm! Their final performance was as flawless as anyone could hope for. They were rewarded with a score of 100. For the first time in synchro's Olympic history a perfect score had been achieved. Emily LeSueur probably expressed the team's thoughts best: "I think, for us tonight, it was a perfect swim and we'll always remember this moment as being a perfect moment."[10]

The other team performances were hardly less spectacular. Canada's second-place performance was outstanding but was handicapped by a ponderous section of music that temporarily reduced the excitement of the action. Japan's expression of the seasons was beautiful and superbly creative. Russia fell back to fourth despite an exciting and difficult routine with spectacular multilevel rafts and connected actions. France, Italy, China and Mexico, finishing in that order, all displayed routines and performances that left the audience wanting more. No one at the stadium that day failed to realize that the greatest competitive synchro spectacle ever seen in the Olympics had just gone by.

But the excitement was all in Atlanta. The home audiences got to see very little of what went on. By the time NBC started putting the 1996 Olympic Games on the air, its own conclusions on the 1992 Olympic coverage seemed forgotten. The president of the NBC Sports Division had suggested then that more attention should have been given to female-appeal sports in the second week to avoid audience losses that occurred. The outlook for synchro did seem more positive initially as five of the technical routines aired in sporadic bursts across the broadcast day. Then it was back to normal as only two of the free routine finalists, the U.S.A. and Canada, were shown.

In 1996, the U.S. had named three full teams, an Olympic team, a junior team and National Team I. This team actually was a second team behind the Olympic team, so it was something of a surprise that it had squeaked through to a win over Canada, Japan and Russia in the 1996 Swiss Open. All members of that team returned to form the 1997 USSS National Team I and see what they could do in the 1997 FINA World Cup in Guangzhou, China. But now, they faced an entirely different set of competitors. All the leading teams at this event included some returning Olympians. The U.S. team was the only contender with no Olympic swimmers. For the first time in a major competition, Team U.S.A. dropped out of all the medal places, taking fifth in the team, sixth in duet, and seventh in solo. Russia finally fulfilled the promise it had been showing for years and won all three events.[11] One of their officials consoled a U.S. official, saying the team was young; much can happen in the next four years.

With five years together as the U.S.A.'s National Team I, the swimmers achieved a level of performance unmatched by any in Atlanta. Swimming together to win gold at the Swiss Open in 1992, they reached their goal in Atlanta, the first Olympic team gold medals (photograph by Dan Helms).

For the first time in the Olympic history of the sport, a perfect score (100 points) was achieved in the tree routine. Swimmers are overwhelmed with emotion as they see the scoreboard (photograph by Dan Helms).

Members of the new Team II took gold in solo and duet at the 1997 Swiss Open in St. Moritz and silver in team. The unique aspect of these victories was that the solo champion was a male who also was part of the winning duet. The international rules that limit synchro events to women are the Olympics, World Aquatic Championships and the FINA World Cup. In Europe, where there are no gender restrictions in many of the international events, male synchro swimmers have been infrequent, but not unheard of. The French National/Open Duet title was won in 1990 by a male-female pair, Stephane Miermont and Anne Capron. Santa Clara's Bill May first won the Swiss Open solo title in 1997 and paired with Stacey Scott to also win the duet.[12] May continues competing and winning gold medals at the Swiss Open competition through 2003.

The U.S.A. Junior National Team rose to its highest finish in several years by taking a bronze medal in team, fourth in duet and fifth in solo at the Junior World Championships in Moscow in 1997. "Seeing such a high level of competition was great for the team," said Lauren McFall (solo, duet and team competitor). "Having to pull together as a duet and with the team was a great learning experience for all of us. We swam well and really showed our strengths in the free routines."[13]

For the first time in the 25-year history of the world aquatic championships, the U.S.A. would find itself fighting for a medal, any medal, in any event, in Perth at the eighth World Championships in 1998. The U.S. team did come from behind in the final to win the bronze, passing by the other perennial power, Canada. Russia topped the field with Japan taking second. Russia won both the solo and duet. Olga Sedakova won the solo, Virginie Dedieu of France was second with Miya Tachibana of Japan third. Kristina Lum, the U.S. soloist, was fourth. In duet, Sedakova paired with Olga Brousnikina to win the gold with Japan second, France third and the U.S.' Carrie Barton and Elicia Marshall placing fourth.[14]

Again, some consolation may be found in the fact that the U.S. team was the only one in the "new order" with no returning Olympians. In addition, Canada, as instrumental in the worldwide development as the U.S.A. and also as accustomed to silver and gold, had also fallen, to fourth in team, fifth in duet and sixth in solo. Thus, taken optimistically, the change may not be so much an ebbing of U.S. and Canadian excellence as a rise in the rest of the world. U.S.A. synchro could take some sort of maternal pride in seeing the rise of those it has helped so much in the past.

Synchro's previous two appearances in the Goodwill Games, 1990 and 1994, had included only the solo and duet events, the events of the Olympic program. For 1998, however, the team event was contested for the first time, and because the IOC had recently reinstated the duet event for the 2000 Olympics, it was also included. Reigning world champion Russia swept the gold medals in both events, but the U.S.A.'s young team continued its climb to the top of the medal stand with a second-place finish in both events. This marked a definite improvement over the 1997 World Cup and 1998 World Championship placements. However, the inclusion of a male, Bill May, on the U.S. team turned into the story of the Games. The novelty and skill of May and Lum caught the attention of international and national media. The pair was featured on all the major networks' national morning shows and evening news along with stories and photos in all the major national newspapers, international wire services and even Russian and Italian television stations.

May caused the media to sit up and take notice at the 1998 Games. The Olympic Games are seemingly reverse discrimination, a man prohibited from competing in a sport because it is listed as a sport for females. His partner at the Goodwill Games, Kristina Lum, has said about swimming in the Olympics that if she couldn't compete with Bill, she is lucky because she can still compete on the team and that she intends to stay with Bill as long as he lets her. May said, "We did this because we wanted to give people a new perspective on synchronized swimming by utilizing the different skills and inferred passion of a man and woman. We want to help the sport evolve and expand, kind of like figure skating has during the last quarter century."[15]

Bill May was the talk of the town at the Goodwill Games held on New York's Long Island in the summer of 1998. Swimming with partner Kristina Lum, the pair had won the national duet title, and his participation in the Games brought much attention and publicity to the event (photograph by Nancy Hines).

While her Santa Clara teammates went off to international competitions, Anna Kozlova kept training and waiting for the day when she would be eligible to represent her new country. First winning the U.S. solo crown in 1996, she achieved citizenship in 1999 and led the qualifiers for the 2000 Olympic Games in Sydney (photograph by Nancy Hines).

Junior swimmers were also working toward putting the U.S. team atop the medal stands again. The 1998 American Cup, an open international junior competition since 1980, was held in Cerritos, California. Team U.S.A. succeeded in taking the gold in the team event by a point and rose to silver in solo and duet. With the addition of ASUA age group events, the meet brought competitors from 17 nations and was termed the premiere international junior meet of the season.

Led by Bill May, Team II won all gold medals at the Swiss Open in Zurich in 1999. The most interesting aspect to this competition was that it marked the first major international competition that included the free routine combination event, a seven-minute routine unique to the Swiss Open. "Team USA amazed the crowd with an Elvis medley featuring none other than Bill May as the King. The routine earned not only a pair of 10s for Artistic Impression, but burning love displayed by the audience prompted the announcer to call for an encore," wrote Brian Eaton, U.S.A. media director.[16]

The U.S.A. continued its push toward the medal stand in Sydney with an overall third-place finish at the FINA World Cup held in Seoul in 1999. The overall points title went to Russia with 498, Japan was second with 467, and the U.S.A. third with 437. Canada placed fourth with 435. "This has been a long, difficult summer for our athletes with Olympic Trials, Pan American Games and the World Cup," said USSS President Laurette Longmire.[17]

Olympic trials were again staged as a separate event in 1999. Held in Federal Way, Washington, a 13-member Olympic training squad was selected to begin training for the 2000 Games. Qualifying at the top of the list was Anna Kozlova, finally able to represent her new country. "You don't know how long I have waited for this day," Kozlova said. "These past five years have been very difficult and often times lonely for me, staying behind as my teammates traveled abroad to represent the United States."[18] Kozlova and Tuesday Middaugh won the competition to select the duet entry. Final team selections were made early the next year. The 2000 Olympic team included

Carrie Barton, Tammy Cleland-McGregor, Bridget Finn,, Kristina Lum, Elicia Marshall, Tuesday Middaugh, Heather Olson, Kim Wurzel and Kozlova.

## *The National Championships 1995–99*

Becky Dyroen-Lancer and Team U.S.A. continued their winning ways through 1996, but substantial change became the norm following the Olympic Games in Atlanta. Those waiting in the wings finally had their chance to step up to the plate. Anna Kozlova began her reign as solo champion and the top-ranking swimmer on an entirely new team from the Santa Clara Aquamaids. It was the dawning of a new era.

Santa Clara successfully defended its championship in 1995. That 1995 event was especially significant to many of the veterans on the teams because the members of the Olympic team in training would not be participating at the 1996 national championships. Dyroen-Lancer expressed their thoughts: "This is a special win for me. It is the last Jantzen Nationals of my career and this is a really special team. We have worked incredibly hard together and have a special bond. This is our three-peat on the wins of the past two years." Coach Chris Carver said, "I can't even imagine what it will be like to coach without these girls. I've tried not to think about it. They're like my daughters."[19]

The 1996 Jantzen National Championships marked the beginning of a new era in the United States. With the absence of the nation's top 10 swimmers, the U.S. Olympic Team, the competition was wide open for new stars to be crowned. But Santa Clara met Walnut Creek's challenge in a successful defense of the crown. Ohio State, maintaining full strength and high hopes from the 1995 team, was still unable to capitalize on its opponents' member losses and remained in third place.[20] Santa Clara continued to win through 1999 with Walnut Creek continuing in the silver medal spot and Ohio State generally remaining in third place, al-

though in 1998, Santa Clara's B team moved into the bronze medal position and repeated in 1999.

Santa Clara's Becky Dyroen and Jill Sudduth fairly easily continued to defend the duet title they had first won in 1993 and continued to win through 1995. During this period, they also won two world cups and the world aquatic championship titles. They did not defend in 1996 while they were training with the Olympic team. Following the Olympics, they finished their synchro careers by winning the FINA qualifying events for solos and duets that was held in Scotland. These wins qualified the U.S.A. for entry into solo and duet events for the 1997 FINA World Cup.

With all the medalist duets of 1995 absenting the 1996 event to continue training for the coming Olympics, the U.S. national title was open for new stars at the top. Santa Clara's Anna Kozlova and Annemarie Alm quickly filled the vacancy for the duet gold. Kozlova returned with another partner, Charlotte Massardier, a French champion training in the U.S. for one year, to win the title in 1997. In 1998, she was paired with Tuesday Middaugh but the mixed duet of Kristina Lum and Bill May moved ahead to win the event by just 0.23 points. May described the routine as synchro's twist on ice-dancing: face-to-face interaction, intertwined dance moves and a series of lifts swum to the driving rhythms of Ravel's Latin romance "Bolero."[21] Was this the start of a new era or a return to synchro's collegiate mixed-gender start? May and Lum were still strong in 1999, but Middaugh and Kozlova took the gold back by a very narrow margin, 95.86 to 95.42.

Becky Dyroen-Lancer also strongly defended her solo title through 1995 to remain undefeated for four years. As she vacated the title for Olympic team training, former Soviet swimmer Anna Kozlova took it over, winning in 1996 through 1999. In 1998, she earned a perfect score of 100 in the free routine with her interpretation of Stravinsky's "Firebird." Ironically, the crown stayed in the same household. Kozlova, who had emigrated from Russia, was living with Dyroen-Lancer's parents while training with Santa Clara. Kozlova said, "Honestly, [putting in a second grand slam performance in 1997] was a lot harder than the first time. I had more fears and I didn't want to disappoint anyone. I never assume that I will win. I look at the others and think they are very good."[22]

Ohio State continued its dominance in national collegiate championships through 1997, winning 18 meet championship trophy titles since the collegiate program's inception in 1977.[23] However, 1998 saw Stanford rise to take the overall trophy by winning solo, duet, trio and figures and taking second in team. Olympian and Stanford student Heather Pease said, "I was so proud to be swimming with Stanford at Collegiates. Our team was so motivated all year and it was exciting to watch it pay off in the swims we had." Coach Vicky Weir said, "It took the hard work of the entire team to achieve this goal. It's an unbelievable accomplishment for our team and Stanford athletics."[24] Ohio State had been victorious in the team event since 1986 but, in 1999, Stanford won its first team event title and successfully defended the overall title it had won the previous year. "This is a great victory for Stanford athletics," said first-year team coach Gail Emery. "Our consistency and all-around strong effort is a real credit to the quality of athletes on this team."[25]

The duet title returned to Ohio State in 1995 with Emily Marsh and Becky Jasontek who successfully defended in 1996. Then Heather Pease and Vanessa Shaw won it for Stanford in 1998. In 1999, Brazil's Olympic hopefuls, Carolina and Isabella Moraes, took the duet title back to Ohio State. The trio returned to Ohio State for 1995 and 1996. Stanford won in 1997 and was able to successfully defend in 1998 but the title then returned to Ohio State in 1999. The solo story was different: it was Western all the way. Every title from 1992 to 1999 went to one of the California schools. Jenny Mayer of San Jose State won the title in 1995. Stanford won the next four solo titles with Bridget Finn in 1996, Heather Pease in 1997 and 1998 and Vanessa Shaw in 1999.

## Sport Administration

Nancy Wightman was president in 1995 and served through 1996. In a move aimed at increasing participation in the sport by bringing synchronized swimming to organizations that already had established aquatic programs, the USSS entered into a relationship with the national YMCAs late in 1994. The YMCA bulletin stated, "The objective of the project is to help 150 YMCAs develop the leadership and resources necessary to add synchronized swimming to their programs." The USSS trained the instructors who were to return to their YMCAs, implement the program, and then conduct similar training programs for the YMCA instructors in their geographical areas. The USSS would serve as the resource center for the program.[26]

The USSS joined a partnership with the Susan G. Komen Foundation in 1995 in the "Fight Against Breast Cancer." Wightman commented, "With a membership base that is 99 percent female, there is no better organization for us to support."[27] Synchro swimming members were encouraged to work with their local chapters in fund raising and awareness efforts. National team members served as spokespersons in national and international events. A National Team III was selected in 1995 that might well have been called the "National Exhibition Team." It was to take part in a new form of the "Classical Splash," the "Jazz Splash." The team performed, along with Olympic team members, at the U.S. Military Academy in West Point. Proceeds from the show went to benefit the Susan G. Komen Breast Cancer Foundation.[28] This same group participated in a "Classical Splash" aquacade to dedicate the new Atlanta Olympic swimming venue in early 1996.

Laurette Longmire, of Tujunga, California, a former competitor from Riverside and Ohio State, was elected president in 1996 and served the quadrennium. "If you truly believe this sport is one that can rival figure skating and gymnastics," she said, "then talk up the sport. If we all promote the positive image we know the sport contains, then the media and public awareness will expand. This expansion can and will lead us to where we want to be, unrivaled in the public eye as an athletic sport that develops talented and articulate athletes." With her professional career in computers, she was of great assistance as USSS joined the world on the Internet. The Web site (www.usasynchro.org) was activated in July 1997. In the first month of operation, 25,000 hits were listed.[29] Synchro is alive!

Betty Watanabe, USSS's executive director since 1985, resigned her position in 1994. Debbie Hesse, from Arlington, Texas, who had previous marketing director experience with a nonprofit organization in Dallas, was selected the new executive director. She said, "With this opportunity and inspiring group of people, we must rise to the challenge that lies before us. We must constantly promote the positive aspects of our sport so that our organization will grow and prosper during the next few years."[30]

A 20-percent increase in USSS membership after the 1996 Olympic Games was the stimulus for expanding the office staff with addition of an education coordinator, a publications coordinator and a media relations director. Also contributing to support of and the need for new staff were the United States Olympic Committee and synchro's recent sponsors. And it did happen. There was a big upsurge in registrations following the 1996 Olympic Games and its television showing. Media director Brian Eaton said, "Swimmers are taking to Synchronized Swimming like ducks to white bread."[31]

The excitement over the potential public relations value of the team event in the Olympics began drawing in new sponsors. Before the Olympics arrived, Eastman Kodak, Baquacil, Avon Products, United Airlines, Coca-Cola, National Pool and Spa Institute and NationsBank had joined in offering products and support for the USSS.[32] In 1999, Chicken of the Sea became the newest addition to the sponsor list. In the summer of 1999, Kodak and the USSS jointly debuted a new membership poster that became highly sought. Titled "Waiting to Inhale," Kodak offered to customize the posters for individual clubs, and for special events and watershows.[33]

The major partner in synchro's funding, however, was still the United States Olympic Committee. Its grants supported USSS programs for grassroots development, coaching education, elite athlete clinics and education, and additionally helped fund synchro's Olympic and national team activities. A joint marketing agreement with USOC further enhanced the programs.[34] Under the USOC's new plan for determining funding levels for its member sports, performance goals would be determined and established by each sport and funding would be based on the sport's success in meeting those goals. The USSS had already developed a set of long-range goals and only needed to establish mile-post markers for gauging progress on the road to their goals. New markers would be set for each quadrennium that would relate to the present established goals of the USSS, which were: 1) maintain the excellence of the national team program; 2) athlete development through coaching education; 3) increased member development through gender equity advocacy; 4) enhance public image; 5) financial diversification; and 6) improved international relations.[35]

A new music playback technology was introduced at the 1995 Olympic Festival. All music for competition and practice sessions played flawlessly at CD quality and at the proper speed from the hard drive of a personal computer. The "tapeless" playback system was introduced by Denver's Jack Pelon, a Denver radio station operator who was the announcer and sound coordinator for the event. He transferred all the original tapes brought to the competition to the computer and then played them back with an access program he set up. The system eliminated all starting glitches and long tape leader waits.[36] Then, a different system, digital audio tape, was introduced at the 1996 Olympics. These systems offered absolutely reproducible timing and automatic cueing to the start of the music.

The NCN camp program continued with the pre-elite camp, four zone "A" camps, regional "B" camps for junior swimmers and association "C" camps for age group athletes. For 1996, the pre-elite clinic was divided into junior and senior camps. Performance standards and technical routine elements were presented and by year's end, all competitive programs within Synchro U.S.A. would be presented with the appropriate training. Zone clinicians were replaced by national coaches and coaching staff for all national clinics.[37]

Although the USOC's San Diego Olympic Training Center was opened in 1997, there still was no pool. USSS top athletes continued to prepare for major competitions using pools in Santa Clara and Walnut Creek with occasional training time at the Olympic Training Center in Colorado Springs. To this day, the USSS is hoping for pool access that will allow synchro to join other sports at the Olympic Training Center in San Diego.

A revised coaching certification program was adopted in 1995 with programs for both recreational and professional teachers and coaches. More than 200 coaches responded to the initial questionnaire surveying their educational background, coaching tenure and achievements. The new program was officially implemented in 1997.

## Competitive Programs

The present-day "amateur" had come a long way from the original English gentry characterization of competing only for the joy of it! But this was a far more conservative action than it appeared in view of other sports, such as basketball, having allowed long-time professional athletes to form "Dream Teams" for the 1992 Olympic competitions. Also, prize money for Olympic medalists would be awarded by the USOC. Now, U.S. Synchro was looking at its own Dream Team for 1996. The athletes selected had been the top 10 in the U.S. ever since winning the Swiss Open as National Team I members in 1992.[38]

The National Sports Festival, retitled the Olympic Festival, had been staged in all non–Olympic years through 1995. The USOC discontinued the festivals at that point, citing ever-increasing costs and failure to attract the media and public interest the originators had been seeking. Most sports, rather than displaying their top athletes in intensely competitive contests, as originally envisioned, had used the festival as a training field for lower-level athletes. For the USSS, though, the festivals had a special meaning as they provided a testing ground for the national team concept. It was bringing swimmers from all over the country to work together for one week at the festival that proved a national team could be successfully molded, even in a nation as large as the United States. Kristina Lum, solo winner said, "I think the festival is special because the teams are mixed up together. Everyone is always friendly with each other. The crowds that come are always excited to watch."[39]

At the 1996 convention, as part of an ongoing restructuring effort to try to establish better tracking through several choices of developmental and upper-level competitions, the USSS decided to drop the old age group program in favor of a new intermediate class. This would resemble age group except for changing the 18 to 19 group to 18 and over, and abandoning the national championship. Reverting back to the days of five required figures in routines, U.S. synchro embarked on a path toward better development of age group competitors in 1997 by requiring technical routines in certain developmental levels, for the 13 and under age group program, the new intermediate class and as "prescribed" routines for novices. Led by Karen Paulk, Florida, the process came about after two years of work by the competitive restructuring committee.

Initially, the Junior Olympic program was to be continued as before, but making the U.S. [National] Junior Olympic Championship independent from the Amateur Athletic Union. This would follow the example of other sports that appeared to have set up independent JO nationals. Those new rules were actually in the printing process when the word was received that some of their premises were misbegotten and the Junior Olympic title could *not* be used without fees and other concessions. Instant revisions were made to the printing and the program was renamed age group, but with all the dressings of Junior Olympic. It would take over the developmental aspects of the JO program, assuming the same exclusions of all upper level competitors from the new AG competition.

In the colleges, it had taken until 1993 for the NCAA to undertake a real study of the meaning and consequences of the Gender Equity Act of 1972. The report of that study was published in 1994. Soon thereafter, synchronized swimming was prominent on the list of "emerging team sports for women" to be considered as useful for colleges attempting to bring their gender equity program up to par by adding women's programs. Synchronized swimming was recognized as one of the safest sports, relatively inexpensive, and offering optimal physiological benefits. USSS president Wightman stated, "I am pleased to report that conferences and colleges are beginning to look seriously at synchronized swimming as an opportunity for growth in women's sports."[40]

In 1996, synchronized swimming was a varsity sport at Canisius College, Keuka College, Ohio State University, Stanford University, University of Richmond, Walsh University, Wheaton and York Colleges and a club sport at 17 other colleges and universities. The Eastern Collegiate Athletic Conference (ECAC) became the first collegiate association to incorporate synchronized swimming into the conference competitive structure. This step was aided by a grant from the USOC that will facilitate the expansion of synchro programs within the member schools of the ECAC. It is expected to be a model for conferences elsewhere in the country. The first ECAC Synchronized Swimming Championships were conducted at Wheaton College in Norton, Massachusetts, in 1998. Joanne Wright, coach of Canisius College, winners of this first conference championship said, "A sanctioned conference championship like this is important to the development of synchronized swimming and gives a wide variety of athletes and schools a chance to excel in this NCAA 'emerging' and Olympic sport."[41]

The masters program continued to grow with the only changes in U.S. competition being in the list of figures in the figure groups. With more and more international competitions being held, many former USSS swimmers were returning to swim again. One competitor said, "This is my family and they are what keeps me coming back." The masters group describes its program as "Athletes for Life."[42] U.S. masters' swimmers competed in the FINA World Masters in Sheffield, England, in 1996 and in Casablanca, Morocco, in 1998, and brought home numerous gold medals.

While professional water shows had nothing to do with U.S. synchro, the opening of Cirque du Soleil's *O* show in the Bellagio's 1.5 million-gallon aquatic stage on October 19, 1998, provided a new outlet for retired synchronized swimmers. The show has been highly successful and some of U.S. synchro's stars are performing there. Said Joe Delaney, theater critic for the *Las Vegas Sun*, said, "Just as Bellagio sets the new standards for elegance in hotels, *O* sets the new standard for production shows. Despite a very complicated physical setup, the show is seamless, perfectly-paced production and performance.... *O* tops any production show I have seen in 66 years."[43] The old-time aqua spectacular was revived in the summer of 1999 in the Pacific Northwest when athletes from all aquatic disciplines came together for the 50th Seattle Sea Fair. This was the first time in 35 years that synchro had been included in the event and planners were so impressed they were trying to figure out a way to involve synchro in future sea fairs.

## Technical Rules

Technical routines had been adopted at the 1994 FINA World Congress in Rome and inserted into Olympic Games, World Aquatic Championships and World Cup programs. Federations were urged to add the technical program to their events. Some USSS officials, having seen the handwriting on the wall after the Bonn experiment in 1991, attempted soon after to get the USSS to integrate some form of technical routines into its programs. The proposals were curtly rebuffed. Even knowing FINA had just made the technical routines part and parcel of international events, further technical program proposals at the 1994 convention were thrown out by the rules subcommittee. Opposition was based largely on fears of overloading coaches and athletes with the need to develop more routines.

Only after national teams and some USSS clubs had been faced with technical routine competition everywhere they traveled in 1995 and 1996, including the Olympic Games, did the USSS face up to realities. Technical routines had started appearing in most international events beginning in 1995. The U.S. kept dragging its feet but finally bowed to reality after the Olympic Team survived technical routines in Olympic qualifying competition in 1995 and in the 1996 Olympic Games. The program adopted at the 1996 convention differed only in details from 10-year-old proposals for short routines with technical requirements, but when the U.S. added technical routines for the senior level in 1997, it was only in teams. Team technicals were introduced into the U.S. national and U.S. senior open competitions. Solo and duet technicals were not approved for U.S. use until 2000.

FINA once again recalculated the figure difficulty multiples on a new biomechanical base in the summer of 1994. With the USSS Figures Committee chairman taking part this time, a number of errors in base data were corrected before they affected the calculations. The new values seemed more valid and the USSS adopted the new difficulties immediately for 1995.

The size of the senior competition had grown through relaxation of some qualifying standards, but remained small in comparison with other national meets. One small change was in the age for senior level. In 1995, the minimum age for senior-level competition was moved up to 14 years. In 1994, FINA changed its rules to allow 12 qualifiers into final events in place of the traditional eight. The USSS, which was operating its U.S. national and junior national under FINA rules, was then forced into having 12-competitor finals in those meets but retained eight for all other competitions. However, because it had added so much time to the final events, the USSS reverted to eight finalists for all competitions in 1996.

Qualification for entry into the U.S. Open events remained dependent upon achieving minimum standard scores in other USSS competitions. Events for two age group categories,

14 to 15 and 16 to 17, were added to the U.S. open program for 1998.

The age for junior competition seemed to change year by year. Not satisfied with the 18-year-old age limit previously set for USSS juniors because it excluded some high school seniors, the USSS upped the age to 19 in 1994. Then, finally beginning to realize the problems of trying to define teams for international meets from events involving the variant ages, the USSS took the inevitable step of adopting the international 14- to 17-year standard for 1995. Of course, FINA soon took action to restore its divergence by adopting a new set of determining ages, 15 to 18, effective in 1998. In the fall of 1998, the USSS adopted the new FINA ages of 15 to 18 for juniors. But something still needed to be done with the junior national program. Harkening back to the days of the overloaded entry lists of the '70s, the 1998 Junior Nationals brought 72 solos, 66 duets, 44 trios and 42 teams. Since the U.S. had decided to have FINA rules apply to the U.S. junior national competition, all 370 competitors took part in the figure competition that, even with four panels, lasted more than nine hours and was followed by another four to five hours of team competition. Obviously, changes still needed to be made in the qualifying procedures.

In an effort to reach every age group, an intermediate class was started which opened the 18–19 events to all 18 and older competitors. This also provided an overlap into the masters level of competition, allowing post–high school competitors to continue club affiliations indefinitely. The new intermediate class would not include a national championship event. President Longmire said, "Overall, I believe [the changes] will foster improved athlete development and allow us to focus on completing proper skill development."[44]

## Judging and Scoring

Proposals for U.S. synchro to use different panels of judges for the two-routine award categories had been made as early as 1977. The concept had even been tested with unofficial panels at the 1978 Senior National Outdoor Championships.[45] However, it was not until it became another "follow FINA" reflex that the USSS actually used two panels for judging routines in a major event. The first use of two panels took place early in 1995 at the Pan American Games in Argentina.[46] Shortly thereafter, the idea was finally tested at the U.S. junior national. Surprise! It was instantly popular because it cut the judging overload by a factor of two and largely eliminated the usually apparent dependence of one award upon the other when both were given by a single judge. Two panels are now used whenever the number of judges available allows.

## *Awards and Honors*

Becky Dyroen-Lancer was awarded the 1995 FINA Prize Eminence, the highest distinction worldwide that can be made to an individual or organization in recognition of their outstanding positive action in the aquatics community. Dyroen-Lancer is the first American athlete to receive the award since diving's Greg Louganis won in 1983.[47] The International Swimming Hall of Fame, in 1996, established a new award, the Paragon Award. It is given "to an individual who has shown hard work, dedication, motivation and discipline in competitive swimming, synchronized swimming, diving, water polo, aquatic safety or recreational swimming."[48] Dorothy Sowers was synchro's first Paragon honoree.

For outstanding coaching accomplishments and contributions to synchronized swimming, Gail Emery was inducted into the International Women's Sports Hall of Fame in the contemporary coaches category at ceremonies held in New York in October 1997. In her acceptance speech, Emery said that the values she learned as a synchro competitor inspired her to coach.[49] Emery is credited with helping dispel the old-school notion of synchronized swimming as water ballet. In the 1980s, the Aquanuts introduced a precise, fast-paced technical style that led to the acceptance of the sport as a physically demanding athletic event. So that her athletes could meet the rigors of this new style, Emery implemented scientifically designed training methods and cross-training regimens.

Emery was honored in 1998 by the California State Legislature as a California Woman of the Year for her efforts to introduce synchronized swimming to the Olympic Games. In 1999, Mervyn's established a new set of awards in conjunction with the Women's Sports Foundation, the Spirit of Sports Awards. Synchronized swimming was honored to win two of the five national awards. Emery was honored as the Professional Coach of the Year for her development of the Walnut Creek Aquanuts and Dawn Bean was honored as the Community Coach for her work with the Unsyncables masters team.[50] At the USOC's 3rd Annual Coaches Recognition Weekend in 1999, Sue Nesbitt of Riverside was named Developmental Coach of the Year for Synchronized Swimming and Chris Carver, Santa Clara head coach, was named Coach of the Year for Synchronized Swimming.[51]

# 12

## Rising to the Challenge: 2000–03

Norma Olsen, in 1952, had urged Avery Brundage, president of the International Olympic Committee (IOC) to accept synchronized swimming into the Olympics. He turned her down flat. In rebuffing Olsen, Brundage actually inspired her and pointed a direction for her to follow. "I figured the best approach then was to educate people about the sport in other parts of the world," she said and that is what she set out to do.[1] Both the U.S. and Canada embarked on numerous international tours, giving clinics and seminars, teaching local swimmers and coaches, holding international exchanges and hosting foreign competitors in their homes for training. The U.S. and Canada shared their knowledge to help develop the sport throughout the world. But now their once-dominant leadership and athletic superiority were being challenged from every side by worldwide development.

In the 64 years from that first competition between the Chicago Teachers College and Wright Junior College in 1939, U.S.A. synchro's fondest hopes of developing into an Olympic sport had really come true. But where once the U.S. had stood atop the podium wreathed in gold and laurels, now it is Russia firmly entrenched in the top spots they first reached in 1997. Now it is Russia setting the standard for excellence. The 2000 Olympic Games marked the first time that U.S.A. Synchro did not earn a medal at the Olympics. Japan stood alone as the only nation to have won a medal in every Olympic Games since synchronized swimming was included in the program. Japan and France were winning some gold medals; Italy, China and Spain were challenging to move up. The U.S. and Canada were contending with each other for a spot on the award stand.

Olsen's vision, her dream of teaching the world, had certainly been achieved. In an interview for the Canadian Broadcast film, *The Mermaids Club*, the announcer is saying, "Today the Russians and the Japanese often dominate the sport. But what's important to Dawn Bean is not who wins the medals—it's the fact that the whole world is competing for them." Bean said, "I always felt we would have 50 to 100 countries competing, once they knew about it. It just surprised me how long it took. I expected this to happen in the first 10 years. Instead, it had taken my entire lifetime to see it develop to this extent. But I knew it would happen."[2]

Prior to the first Olympic inclusion, many people did not know what synchronized swimming was all about. Now, apparently, it has become so familiar that images of synchro come to mind from many different areas. In an article about the work of traffic police to relieve rush-hour madness, Danny Perez of the *Houston Chronicle* wrote, "This intricate system resembles synchronized swimming in that all the officers have to move and react at the same time."[3]

Sprinter Jon Drummond, at a USOC Athletes' Summit in 2002, learned a bit about synchro and was impressed. "I have to eat crow," said Drummond, who won gold in Sydney as a member of the 400-meter relay team. "I was one of those guys who thought synchronized swimming is not a sport. After trying their workout, I have new respect for them. When I go to the Olympics in 2004, I'm going to have a lot of people to root for. These athletes are inspiring."[4]

*Sports Illustrated*, in a 2002 article on "Underrated and Overrated Sports" put synchro in the "underrated" category saying, "Synchronized Swimming is an all-too-easy target. It's showy, with Chucky-doll smiles and Crystal Barbie getups. But the physical prowess required in this sport takes a distance runner's endurance and a speed swimmer's strength. Throw in the control needed to suspend breathing for up to a minute and synchro is one of the toughest sports around.... Sure, some of synchro's superficial elements need to move beyond the *Million Dollar Mermaid* era, but this is a sport with substance — even grit — beneath the surface."[5]

Truly, the Olympic motto, "Swifter, Higher, Stronger" can now be applied to synchro. At a seminar at the U.S. convention in the fall of 2001, Gail Pucci stated, "I think the Olympic statement really applies to synchro more than ever. Music is faster, movements are swifter and height is at its all-time most important. One thing that stands out most is theme versus no theme. Some go to great lengths to have a theme, others, including the winners, have little to none." Pam Edwards (officials vice president) said, "Routines seem to be less 'theme-y' and more designed to show the swimmers' strengths. The top place finishers look more athletic and toned while remaining lithe and flexible." Lorraine Fasullo (past officials vice president) said, "Routines are non-stop, even in slow sections, swimmers leave the water physically drained." FINA honorable secretary Ginny Jasontek said, "The choice of music [was] characterized by a force-

ful beat. What was valued highly included very fast movement and an emphasis on height and strength and unusual arm movements."[6]

## International Developments

The year 2000 was important for the United States. Unlike most other nations in the 1996 Games, Team U.S.A. experienced a 100 percent retirement of its Olympic team. This had forced the U.S. into a rebuilding phase in 1997. Since then, Team U.S.A. had steadily improved, but had not returned to its former favorite status. From fifth at the 1997 World Cup, Team U.S.A. moved up to bronze in the 1998 World Championships and up to silver at the 1998 Goodwill Games. A third-place overall finish at the 1999 World Cup definitely placed the U.S. within Olympic medal contention.

When teams were added to the Olympic program for 1996, it was with the stipulation that only the top eight could participate. The pre–Olympic competition in Atlanta had determined the qualifiers for 1996. For 2000, the Olympic qualifying competition was different because now it included duet qualifying. The duet event had been put back onto the Olympic program. It was open to the top 24 duets from the qualifying competition, provided that eight of the duets would come from those also qualifying for team. In the qualifying event held six months prior to the start of the Games, Russia was first, Japan second, Canada third and the U.S. fourth. Team member Carrie Barton said, "I think we really made a strong showing for the future; there's still six months to go before the Games and a lot can happen during that time. We came here to make a great impression and leave people talking about how bright the future is for the Americans."

Anna Kozlova and Tuesday Middaugh were the duet expected to swim for the U.S. in the Qualifying, but Middaugh's back injury forced them to withdraw. Former Olympians Heather Pease-Olson and Tammy Cleland-Mc-Gregor had come out of retirement to try to qualify for the Olympic team again and were asked to replace Kozlova and Middaugh. They had a scant four weeks to prepare. Olson said,

"I felt we had a great swim and did the best we could possibly do." Three judges placed them third in the technical routine because of their mirror-like precision on every spin. Russia won the event, with Japan, France, and Canada ahead of the U.S. in fifth.[7]

Part of the preparation for the Games in Sydney was a series of international competitions for the duet of Kozlova and Middaugh. They faced their first major test in 1999 at the Swiss Open, followed by the Rome Open. In Switzerland, they led the event after the technical routine but Canada moved ahead in the free routine. "The technical routine was pretty darn good, but you could see the free routine was new and that they were new," said coach Chris Carver. "A few minor synchronization errors are all that needs fixing in their free program. The difficulty of their program and superior base skills should make this end up in a good place."[8] Kozlova and Middaugh took second in duet behind Canadians Claire Carver-Diaz and Fanny Letourneau. Bill May won the solo for the third consecutive year.

U.S.A.'s Olympic duet of Tuesday Middaugh and Anna Kozlova rose to the top of the medal stand for the first time in more than a year when they captured the gold medal at the Rome Open in 2000. Said Kozlova, "Rome was a big success for us, not only in our placement, but how we have progressed as a duet. We have the technical skills, now we will put our training emphasis on the artistic skills and performance aspects."[9] The U.S. took all the gold medals in Rome. Team II won team; Middaugh and Kozlova took gold in duet and Bill May won solo. Based on May's two wins in Switzerland and Italy, the U.S. proposed adding a men's solo along with the mixed duet to the FINA Congress.

The Olympic Games in Sydney, Australia, were Anna Kozlova's return to Olympic competition, this time swimming for the U.S.A. Kozlova had finished fourth in the duet at the 1992 Olympics while swimming for Russia. She sat out the 1996 Games while awaiting U.S. citizenship and finally had a chance to represent her new country at the 2000 Games in Sydney. Paired with Tuesday Middaugh, their marks were just shy of the medal stand in fourth

Anna Kozlova (left) and Tuesday Middaugh began their efforts toward the medal stand in Sydney by winning gold at the Rome Open in 2000. They placed fourth in Sydney (photograph by Nancy Hines).

place. Olga Brousnikina and Maria Kisseleva of Russia were first, Japan second, and France third. For Russia and France, the duet brought their first Olympic medals. The U.S. was also pleased, "We had a good feeling about this swim," Kozlova said. "It's our first big international meet. We came in with no ranking, no comparison to the others, I think we needed that exposure." Partner Middaugh said, "I waited so long for this moment, I'm finally here, and now it's already over.... I wanted to stay out there forever."

The team event was exciting, but an error in the technical program dropped the U.S.A.'s team to fifth place. Although they swam well in the free routine, the deficit from the previous day was too great and the final score showed the team still in fifth place. Carrie Barton remarked, "The team felt 10 times better than the tech routine. Every time I was up, everyone looked so strong and so precise, I could feel the energy."[10] But on this day, it wasn't enough. Defending world champion Russia snared the gold, Japan earned the silver, Canada finished third with France fourth.[11] This was the first time in Olympic history that Team U.S.A. had been shut out of medals. It just wasn't meant to be. That's all that can be said about Team U.S.A.'s final outcome. Former Olympian Heather Pease-Olson had an opinion too. "Our long program was an extremely strong routine. It really focused on our strengths. We per-

The 2000 Olympic Team looked strong but had one minor error. They placed fourth in Sydney. Swimmers included, from left to right, Anna Kozlova, Tuesday Middaugh, Heather Pease-Olson, Carrie Barton, Kim Wurzel, Kristina Lum, Tammy Cleland-McGregor, Becky Jasontek and Elicia Marshall (not pictured: Bridget Finn) (photograph by Nancy Hines).

formed some very unique new lifts that I think demonstrated our creativity as well."[12]

With years to prepare for the 2004 Olympics in Athens, it was back to work again for the U.S. athletes with the next big challenge to come in 2001 at the ninth World Championships in Fukuoka, Japan. Thirty-one nations came to compete and the U.S. came close to the medal places, taking fourth in all three events. Russia and Canada repeated their 2000 Olympic routines while others swam new routines. Becky Jasontek said, "I think swimming new routines makes it more exciting because the judges have never seen our routine. We had the opportunity to really go out there and impress them, to show them something they've never seen before." Many positive remarks were made about the progress of the U.S. team, which was encouraging for the new squad. Lindsey Wiggington said, "I think we showed that we're back and we can compete with the top three teams in the world. We received some very positive comments from other countries on how strong we looked and how intricate our routine was. It's a sign that people are starting to sit up and take notice of the USA again."

Miya Tachibana and Miho Takeda of Japan took the duet title away from Anastasia Davydova and Anastasia Ermakova of Russia. Canada placed third and the U.S.A.'s Becky Martin and Lauren McFall were fourth. In solo, Anna Kozlova was fourth behind Russia's Olga Brusnikina, Virginie Dedieu of France and Miya Tachibana of Japan. Kozlova was the fourth different soloist to represent the U.S. since 1997 when Becky Dyroen-Lancer won in Scotland. Kozlova said, "This was the most exciting solo competition of my life."[13]

Juniors were also busy in 2001. Russia, exhibiting unmatched energy and fitness, secured its second consecutive sweep of the Junior World Championships at the competition held in Federal Way, Washington. "There wasn't as much pressure on us this year as in 1999," said Anastasia Ermakova, who, with her solo victory, had earned three gold medals. "After our success in Fukuoka [Senior World Championships] we felt very confident against the competition at the junior level," she said.[14] Alison Bartosik (U.S.A.) was fourth in solo behind Canada and Japan. The U.S.A. duet of Bartosik with Sara Lowe placed sixth.

Russia won the junior team with Japan second, China third, Canada fourth, and the U.S.A. fifth. But it was China that proved to be the fan favorite, moving ahead of Canada. Head coach Gail Pucci said, "We were surprised by the level of some of the nations here, some have improved dramatically since we last saw them. This has been an eye-opening experience for our coaches and athletes, that there are some things we need to work on and some areas in which we need to expand and improve if we want to continue to be a leader in this sport."[15]

Now there were just two years to be ready for Athens. The U.S. got back on the award stand at the 2002 FINA World Cup in Zurich by taking the bronze in team. Russia was the winner in the team event, a victory without surprise for the young squad which, with almost the same team, had won this event last year in Fukuoka. The Japanese maintained their placing in the world hierarchy and took second. But the most interesting duel was between the U.S.A. and Canada. The fight was intense for the remaining place on the podium. The U.S.A. held a slim lead after team technicals. Alison Bartosik said, "Our team tech swim felt incredible. We entered the water from the deck with half of our team flipping and when we did, the audience went crazy with cheering and clapping. We were energized and ready to show our stuff." Separated by just 0.01 point after the technical program, after the U.S. presented its free program it was evident that the third position was almost a certainty for the U.S. The U.S.A. outscored its long-time rival by 0.334 point in the final free routine. Coach Chris Carver said, "In the career of any coach, there are certain unforgettable moments that do not necessarily have to do with gold medals. The bronze medal swim in Zurich was one of those moments for me. It was exciting to see the work of this great team come to fruition and it was a thrill beyond words to see the Stars and Stripes raised once again."[16]

In the duet finals, the *FINA News* reported, "The two Anastasias gave absolutely no chance to their opponents in a spectacular free program. Davydova and Ermakova (RUS) set the standard in duet showing superb synchronization and elegance, beating Tachibana and Miho Takeda who had won the 2001 World Championships."[17] Canada was third and Alison Bartosik and Anna Kozlova of the U.S.A. were fourth.[18] France rose to win its first gold medal in a major championship when soloist Virginie Dedieu surpassed Miya Tachibana of Japan and Anastasia Davydova of Russia. Dedieu impressed the judges, who rewarded her with five 10s for artistic impression and one 10 and four 9.9s in technical merit. Anna Kozlova (U.S.A.) placed fifth.

Wins in Switzerland boosted U.S.A. spirits that summer. Gold for the U.S.A. came in solo, duet and the new combo team at the 27th Annual Swiss Open Championship in Geneva. Bill May captured his fifth consecutive solo title and his efforts with National Team II won the gold in the combo team event. Silver and bronze in solo went to Japan and Canada. The U.S.A.'s Victoria Bowen placed fifth. In the team final, the U.S. placed third behind Japan and Canada.[19] Anna Kozlova and Alison Bartosik started a winning streak in 2002 with gold, first at the German Open, followed by the U.S. National Championships and then at the Swiss Open, where Canada was second and Switzerland third.

Russia ended the 2002 Junior Synchronized Swimming World Championships in Montreal with a sweep of all the gold medals in the regular events and did not participate in the new combo team event. Thirty-three countries came to the competition, with 204 swimmers participating. "In the Team Final," *FINA News* reported, "There was no doubt [about the outcome of the team event] once the Russians performed. Their routine had the best synchronization and greatest height and was amply rewarded with the highest marks." Japan was second and Canada third. The new synchronized event, the free routine combination, made its FINA debut with nine countries. "Because the competition was among juniors, it was obvious that the teams were enjoying their performance hugely. Japan emerged on top, Canada was second and Spain third."[20] The U.S.A. juniors placed fourth.

More than a year earlier, Stephanie Nes-

**Anna Kozlova and Allison Bartosik, shown above with coach Chris Carver, won the Olympic trials in duet and won the bronze in Greece in 2004 (photograph by Nancy Hines).**

bitt, Riverside Aquettes, and Sara Lowe, Santa Clara Aquamaids, had the idea that they should swim a duet together. When Lowe and Nesbitt qualified one and two in figure competition, they knew that it was time to give it a try. Together these two took third for the U.S.A. in the duet event. Winners were Natalia Zlobina and Olga Larkina. Canada was second with Nicole Cargill and Courtney Stewart. In solo, Lowe placed fourth behind Natalia Ichtchenko of Russia, Nicole Cargill of Canada and Tina Fuentes from Spain.[21]

Finally, the goal is coming into sight. There is just one more year to Athens. In the first major event of 2003, the U.S. swept all the gold medals at the Rome Open. Anna Kozlova held a three-point margin over Italy's Lorena Zaffalon to place first in solo; Kozlova, with Alison Bartosik, won the duet by 2.2 points and the team dominated the field, winning the event by five points over second-place Brazil.[22] It was a good beginning to the year.

Ever since the FINA World Swimming Championships began in Belgrade in 1973, it has been just behind the Olympics in importance to the U.S. and to the world. It had been held every four years, midway through the Olympic quadrennial, but was changed in 2001 to twice in the Olympic quadrennial, the year after and the year before the Olympic Games. Barcelona was the site in 2003 and Sue Edwards, FINA technical committee member, said, "If we look to statistics and following a survey made by the FINA Technical Synchronized Swimming Committee, there are more than 90 countries worldwide where their respective aquatic federations have an active section of synchro. But looking at the world medal tally including Olympic Games, World Championships and World Cups, only five countries appear, U.S.A., Canada, Russian, Japan and France. This reality is surely about to alter; a new wave of change is reaching this discipline and new nations will emerge."

Barcelona was the first competition in the world championships to include the new free routine combination. "The acceptance and enthusiasm from the athletes, officials, media representatives and spectators was evident," reported Pedro Adrega, FINA communications department.[23] But not only was this the first time it had been held, the occasion marked the first medal for Spain at a world level in synchronized swimming and this brought huge crowds to the stadium. Japan had a spectacular program and the six 9.9s they received attested to this quality. The U.S. was impressive and moved into second place, but Spain, swimming to "Barcelona," got the crowd on its side and when scores appeared Spain was tied with the U.S. for second place. It was a historic moment, both for the new event and for Spain.

Synchronized swimming is by definition a team event, but the popularity and success of the sport has managed to create a few stars. Virginie Dedieu of France is one who did not disappoint. Previously the winner of the World Cup and the European championships, Dedieu clearly outclassed all her rivals and won the first gold medal for France in synchro at a world championships. Her scores included three 10s in technical and all five 10s in artistic impression. "In the past, I had all the qualities to win, but some mental strength was missing when I entered the water. I managed to improve on that and now I just had to concentrate on the interpretation of my program," said Dedieu. With such a performance, the only suspense was for the two remaining places on the podium. Anastassia Ermakova of Russia was second, but it was Gemma Mengual of Spain who provided the upset, taking third and assuring herself a place on the medal stand. Veterans Miya Tachibana of Japan and Anna Kozlova, U.S.A., placed fourth and fifth.

Pedro Adrega reported the duet event, saying, "It was Russia on one side and the rest of the world on the other." Anastasia Davydova and Anastassia Ermakova of Russia, already first after the technical routine, finished with a score of 99.084, leaving scant room for anyone to surpass them. No one could. Tachibana and Miho Takeda, the previous world duet champions, earned 98.084 to put them in second with another "Spanish Surprise." Mengual, who partnered with Paola Tirados, was in third with 96.667. The U.S.A.'s Anna Kozlova and Alison Bartosik were close behind with 96.334.

To date, only four countries had won a

medal in any world team event. At this competition, the fight remained between these four countries. Russia once more proved its supremacy. Describing the competition among the "rest of the world," Adrega said, "The Japanese team presented a program which made the spectators cheer the swimmers and this joyful atmosphere was also rewarded by the judges." The Japanese secured the silver medal leaving three countries battling for the bronze. Adrega continued, "The American swimmers did not risk too much and the final result reflected the correctness of their routine. More original were the Canadians and the Spanish, but with more creativity came the inevitable mistakes of too many risks." The U.S.A. won the bronze with Spain in fourth and Canada fifth.

For the U.S., claiming the bronze medals at the world championships in Barcelona was a major step on their way to Athens. "Obviously, I'm very happy we were on the medal stand," said head coach Chris Carver. "They had lots of competition and they held up to it very well, which is all part of the education that will put them in a better position for the main round in a year at the Olympics." People in the crowd had booed when the United States team walked out before its performance. Carver was impressed with the way the team handled the distraction. "It was a good day," she said. "We were put to the test. People decided to express their political viewpoints towards the United States, but that made [the team] more tenacious."[24]

The final event of the last year before the Olympics was the Pan American Games, held in August in Santo Domingo, Dominican Republic. The duet of Alison Bartosik and Anna Kozlova held onto the slim lead they earned in the technical routine and, swimming last in the free routine, earned a total of 95.917 to defeat Canadians Fanny Letourneau and Courtney Stewart with 95.584. The Moraes twins, Carolina and Isabela, U.S. collegiate champions from Ohio State, placed third for their home country of Brazil with 91.833.

"Too close for comfort" read the headlines after the first day of team competition as the U.S. and Canada stood 0.167 point apart going into the free swim. Of the technical swim, Kendra Zanotto was pleased. "It felt good. We had a lot of energy walking out there. It was great to do a Latin-inspired routine in a Latin American country. The crowd really cheered for us, which was inspiring. It was great to have them behind us." Final scores were U.S. 97.000 with Canada scoring 96.416. Coach Chris Carver was pleased with the free swim, "This is a turning point for this team. To get 9.8s means we are on the verge of excellence. We continue to improve and are definitely better than last year." But Becky Jasontek summed up the team's feelings perfectly, saying, "I was very happy with the two silver medals last time around, but the one gold means the world."

With the Olympics in Greece next year, the sense is definitely that the U.S. is emerging from its fall from grace. Jasontek said it all, "This win just brings us a step closer to the podium at the Olympics. I enjoyed ending the season on a golden note."[25]

## U.S. National Championships 2000–03

The Santa Clara Aquamaids remained the dominant club in U.S. national championships, winning every solo, duet and team title in the four-year period. Bill May, though ineligible for major international events, has become the top synchro swimmer of the period.

Santa Clara surpassed Walnut Creek's record of 10 consecutive team titles (1980–89) by winning the title all four years, totaling 11 consecutive overall team titles. Remarkably, the win in 2002 was with their "B" team since the majority of their "A" team members were training for the summer's world championships in Barcelona.[26] They won again in 2003. Of the victory, head coach Chris Carver said, "The Aquamaids are very proud of the tradition established by their first head coach, Kay Vilen ... it is a tradition of excellence and our recent victory at the Senior National competition in Long Island, New York, validated our efforts to keep Kay's bequest on-going."

In 2000, May, with Kristina Lum, recap-

Santa Clara, in its second period of dominance in U.S. national championships, surpassed Walnut Creek's 10 consecutive wins by winning its 12th consecutive title in 2004. Added to the 1968–79 years, the team has been victorious for 23 years (photograph by Nancy Hines).

tured the duet title they first won in 1998. Said Lum, "Our duets are so unique, so different, that I believe we have to be judged in a different view than the normal duet. I'm not saying mixed duets are necessarily better, they're just different."[27] Though barred by international federation rules from competing in most elite international events, including the Olympics, May made his case for serious consideration for equal status for men in synchro. However,

Bill May, ineligible for Olympic or World Championships, has continued to excel in competitions which allow males. He has won the U.S. title three of four years and has won five consecutive Swiss Open solo titles (photograph by Nancy Hines).

the proposal for mixed duets was rejected by FINA and thus there was no event for May in the 2001 World Championships. May paired with Kozlova to win the 2001 U.S. title. Then, May and Lum won again in 2002 and 2003.

Bill May wrote another chapter in his already famous legacy by sweeping all four events at the 2000 Jantzen National Championships in Landover, Maryland.[28] But not only did he win, he became the first male to win the U.S. solo championship since the men's solo championship was discontinued in 1956. In 2001, Kozlova, who placed second in solo, said, "Bill and I are such perfectionists. Being paired with him this season has not made us rivals in solo. It has only made us better as we push each other on a daily basis through training."[29] Technically, May can be higher, swifter and stronger, but he also is the cream of the crop in the artistic score as well. He won both the Kay Vilen High Point trophy and the Esther Williams Creative Achievement award at the nationals of 2001.[30] May lost the title only once, to Kozlova in 2002, but regained it in 2003.

Olympian Kozlova, for the U.S. in 2000 and Russia in 1992, said that life in Russia didn't offer many options so children were very goal oriented. "I remember working very hard and thinking, 'One day I will be able to go and visit a foreign country and I'll become a completely different person.'" She said that the hardest thing since she came to America was the inability to compete internationally. "I was a person without a country in terms of competing, but I never doubted my decision to come to, or to stay in, America."[31] Kozlova earned her citizenship in 1999 and thus became eligible to compete for the United States in 2000 and she is working toward competing in 2004.

In the colleges, in the four-year period, Ohio State and Stanford have each won two solo crowns with Shannon Montague and Katie Norris winning for Stanford and Carolina Moraes winning for Ohio State. The duet, however, has been all Ohio State. The Moraes twins, Carolina and Isabela, have won all four titles. Three wins were accomplished by the trio of Isabela and Carolina Moraes and Mary Hofer, but Stanford's Stephanie Joukoff, Jennifer Kibler, Ashley McHugh won the crown in 2003. Ohio State captured all four team titles. The 2003 championships marked their 22nd overall collegiate title.

## Sport Administration

Betty Hazle, who had swum with the San Antonio Cygnets, was elected president of U.S. Synchronized Swimming in 2000. She stated her overall organizational goal was to increase participation in synchronized swimming and also to get back the fun in the sport. She asked everyone to ask themselves these questions as they prepare for the season, "Why do I swim/coach/judge? Is it for friendships developed over years, a feeling of accomplishment or achievement, the thrill of good clean fun in the water? Is it traveling to different places, the excitement of competition, working with others to reach a goal, the freedom to express your creative side, creating something new each year?" She concluded by saying, "Love what you do and feel that it matters; how could anything be more fun?"[32]

In the second year of her presidency, she was severely challenged with the 9/11 attack coming on the eve of the 2001 national convention. Meetings had been scheduled to begin on September 11 in Dearborn, Michigan. Instead, everyone who had already arrived spent their time by television screens, watching and worrying. Everything stopped for more than a day while those already there tried to figure out what to do next. It was hard being away from home and a difficult decision was made to proceed with the convention. With no flights arriving or departing, convention delegates continued with the work at hand, many volunteering to lead committee meetings in the absence of the chairmen. Only necessary changes were made and passage of emergency legislation was kept to a minimum. President Hazle said, "I have never been prouder to know

and be associated with the members of US synchro as I was during that week in Dearborn ... meetings and seminars were held with the help of members and staff filling in whenever and wherever needed. Meetings were adjourned for the candlelight vigil on Friday night arranged by the Hyatt staff. Moments of silence were observed, verses of 'God Bless America' were sung, tears were shed and words of comfort were extended to each other ... the tragic events of 9/11 were felt by all of us."[33]

The office staff saw many changes during this period. Charlotte Davis announced her retirement after the Olympics of 2000. As national team director, she concluded a career of more than 30 years as a leader in the world of synchronized swimming, a career that included seven Olympic gold and silver medals, including the sport's first gold medalists in 1984.[34] Heather Pease-Olson resigned her briefly held position of national team director to take over the coaching of the Stanford University team after the resignation of Gail Emery.[35] Linai Vaz de Negri was named national team director. She said, "I hope to bring leadership and vision to the relentless pursuit of excellence in the national team program."[36]

Debbie Hesse, who had been executive director since 1994, overseeing all facets of the organization, primarily marketing, revenue development, personnel and USOC relations, resigned in 2001 and Terry Harper, who had been the executive director of U.S. Sailing, became the new executive director. Margo Erickson, a 14-year employee and long-time member of the USSS, moved into the newly created role of education director and former president Nancy Wightman accepted the newly created position of emerging programs director.[37] Brian Eaton, media director, who had started with synchro as an intern during his college years in 1995, left to become the new director of communications for U.S.A. Gymnastics.[38]

Synchro joined the cyberspace world in 1997 and became almost completely Web based by the start of 2000. Entries, forms, registration and other necessities could all be downloaded directly from the USSS site. The new system streamlined the entry process, saved mailing costs, provided the option for direct ordering, and became an instant source of news and information.

Sponsorships began to flourish. Synchro was very much in the public eye, beginning in January 2000 when, during Super Bowl XXXIV, VISA aired its new commercial which featured the U.S. Olympic Team athletes. There were both 30-second and one-minute versions which graced the television screens for almost half a year. Chicken of the Sea became a sponsor during the Olympic year and incorporated synchro logos and athletes in advertising and other promotions. To help promote sponsor relations, the USSS hosted a sponsor summit in February 2002 at the Cheyenne Mountain Conference Resort in Colorado Springs. The meeting provided an opportunity to share up-to-date information as well as brainstorm cross-promotional ideas with fellow sponsors. Highlights of the trip included a visit to the USOC Training Center as well as a brief synchro exhibition by Carrie Barton and Heather Pease-Olson.[39] National Pool and Spa Institute signed on for another year as did United Airlines, Colorado Time Systems, Ocean Engineering, Kodak, and Bacquacil. E-Synchro enlisted to provide educational assistance with workbooks and videos.

The USSS Foundation, which had been founded by investing synchro's share of the profits from the 1984 Olympics, established a planned giving program to ensure the financial stability of the organization. Synchro's members and friends were invited to invest in synchro's future with membership in the Founders Society. The goal is to raise $1 million through gifts or as part of estate plans.[40]

## Competitive Programs

The impetus for starting the U.S. Open in 1991 was to provide a quality senior-level meet in the summer for athletes who were not participating in national team events. In fact, national team athletes were specifically made ineligible. By 2003, the focus had changed totally. Not only were national team members now allowed to participate, they were encouraged to swim when it did not conflict with their international schedule. Where international competitors were once excluded, then allowed to compete if they were not the national champions of their country, by 2003, all foreign entries were encouraged to enter. The U.S. had reached the point of realizing that to improve its overall world status, more of the U.S. athletes and coaches needed to be exposed to what was going on in the world. The new format made the U.S. Open a true international competition.[41]

The collegiate programs still continue and add member schools fairly slowly, much too slowly to assure that enough varsity programs could be achieved by 2006 in order to qualify as an NCAA sport. When the NCAA listed synchronized swimming as an emerging sport, synchro was given until 2006 to establish 40 varsity programs around the country in order to host a NCAA championship. A Collegiate Development Task Force was formed to act upon a long-term strategy to reach that goal.[42] With 90 percent of synchro athletes going on to college, they and their parents were encouraged to ask when applying for admission whether or not synchronized swimming was offered. Universities offering synchronized swimming under the club program were requested to actively seek varsity status.

The National Clinic Network (NCN) got a new look and developed a four-year plan. In 2000 there would be clinics with Olympians. For 2001, the first National Coaches College was scheduled. Zone clinics were to be held in 2002 and sectional clinics in 2003.[43] After first being proposed in the late '80s, by Linda Loehendorf and Carol Tackett, the coaches' college finally came into being. Held at the Olympic Training Center in Colorado Springs in December 2002, 104 participants, including national team staff, judges and coaches throughout the country, came together to focus on the development of 13 and under athletes. "Being able to interact with the entire National Team staff was very helpful as they contribute in so many ways," said Tammy Crow. The sharing of knowledge and experiences throughout the weekend was reminiscent of the old "top 10" and intermediate training camps held in Squaw Valley and Colorado Springs in the '70s and

'80s. Dr. Peter Haberi, USOC coaching and sports science staff, presented "Effective Coaching from a Sports Psychology Perspective." Synchro staff included Sandra Mahoney, who explained Esynchro's "1-2-3 Method"; Sue Nesbitt addressed flexibility; Pam Edwards shared her judging experiences; and national team director Linai Vaz De Negri explained, "Efforts such as the Coaches College are part of a larger plan to extend and improve our overall communication, sharing of knowledge and the commitment to invest in coaches in all areas."[44]

Masters programs continue to grow and the ever-increasing numbers make it difficult to include all the age-based events in the normal three-day competition. U.S. masters rules have remained much the same as when the program began in 1977 with the only changes being in eligibility and figure lists. Following FINA's change to individual technical routines, the U.S. included their use at the 2000 national championships. However, a complicated compromise had been crafted so that athletes could meet their technical requirement by choosing to compete either with an individual technical routine or in figure competition. This caused great difficulty for the judges and scorers in trying to equate scores in the vastly different events and as 2003 ended, both events remained, but were scored as separate events.

Worldwide, masters programs have grown as well. FINA replaced figure competition with individual technical routines in 1998 with the first widespread use of the new rules at the 2000 World Championships in Munich and these rules were still in use in masters worlds in New Zealand in 2002 but this competition was the last to require that event since, at the FINA Congress there, individual technical routines were replaced with technical routines for each event. Technical routines and free routines each count for 50 percent of the final score in every event.

## Technical Rules

A change that was expected in the winter of 2000 was the announcement that mixed pairs would join the FINA program in 2002. The U.S. had brought the proposal to FINA on behalf of Bill May, U.S. national champion and the world's foremost male synchronized swimmer. May had became a symbol of discrimination in the sports world. Where most sports were dealing with issues of women breaking new barriers, synchro had the reverse, men wanting to compete in the predominantly female sport. FINA rules offer competition only for women while men have been allowed to compete in many countries. In the U.S., starting with the Sports Act of 1978, men and boys have been allowed. However, few men have competed in the last 12 years, although there are some boys in recreational programs. Only Bill May has reached the national level.

The FINA General Congress did approve, in concept, the addition of a mixed pairs event to all FINA-sanctioned competitions beginning with the FINA World Cup in Zurich in 2002.[45] The congress asked the technical committee to adapt rules for the event following the 2001 World Championships in Fukuoka, Japan, where a demonstration was scheduled to be held. However, the demonstration was not held and FINA continued with the program of events for Olympic Games and world championships with synchronized swimming listed as only for women. It was even suggested that synchro would jeopardize its position on the Olympic program if it was open to male and female competitors.

But while mixed pairs was not approved, a new event was added to the world program, for use in any international competitions. Led by the Swiss Federation, the major change that began at the turn of this century was the addition of the free routine combination event to FINA programs beginning in 2001. The free routine combination is a five-minute program for 10 swimmers which includes one to two solos, one to two duets, and a team of four to eight swimmers that swims one or two times for a total of at least two minutes of the five. It is difficult to explain and difficult for judges to determine weighting of the various parts, but it is definitely a crowd pleaser. Although it has made favorable impressions, it has not been approved for Olympic inclusion.

Concerned with the increasing amount of glitter and flash on swimsuits and headpieces, FINA set a policy for 1998 that said, "Swimwear … must reflect the sporting nature of Synchronized Swimming. *Our public image is very important*"[46] (italics added). What is worn in the future may influence composition to minimize interpretive drama and theme, instead enhancing the power and inherent beauty of human motion.

## *Judging and Scoring*

In looking at the international scene, Vaz De Negri stated in the convention seminar of 2001, "Sheer speed was used as a showcase of talent and difficulty. Our over emphasis on smoothness and flow in figures to the detriment of height and power was definitely not awarded, or simply viewed as a weakness."[47] Everywhere now, two panels of judges are the norm. This has resulted in a better evaluation of the elements that must be considered under both categories, technical merit and artistic impression.

## *Awards and Honors*

Chris Carver and Tracie Ruiz-Conforto were inducted into the Women's Sports Foundation's International Women's Sports Hall of Fame in 2000.[48] Carver was recognized in the coaching category and Ruiz-Conforto as a contemporary athlete. Carver has a 39-year coaching record, 17 years as a national team coach and has many years as head coach of the Santa Clara Aquamaids where, at the time of her induction, seven of her athletes represented the U.S. in the 2000 Olympics.

Ruiz-Conforto at the induction was called the greatest soloist in the history of synchronized swimming. From her gold medal debut at the 1979 World Cup to her gold medal sweep in the inaugural 1984 Olympic competition and her remarkable resurgence at the 1988 Olympic Games, she was named one of Xerox's Top 100 Olympic athletes of All Time.[49] In 2001, she was named Synchro Swimmer of the Century by the International Swimming Hall of Fame.[50]

# Epilogue: The Future of Synchronized Swimming in the 21st Century

Unless one experienced a national championships of the first decade as well as the team events in the 1996 and 2000 Olympic Games, it is difficult to realize just how much synchro has changed—from show to sport to Olympic spectacular! As the era of U.S.A. synchronized swimming was dawning in 1946, the Chicago *Herald Tribune* had it nearly right in its prediction: "Synchronized swimming is here to stay, and may well be found in the next Olympic program, if only as an exhibition feature of the 1948 Games in England. The pioneers of the new sport feel sure it will develop into a recognized international event."[1] Unfortunately, synchro was not seen in the 1948 Games, but only because the invited groups could not raise the funds to appear there. However, synchro now seems here to stay as a respected international event.

The road has been tortuous, and not always certain. The future looked brighter in 1955 when synchro's national chairman, Norma Olsen, got Kenneth "Tug" Wilson, president of USOC, to admit "the control, the physical conditioning, and coordination of these girls convinced me that this is as much a sport as speed swimming and diving."[2] Larry Johnson, honorable secretary of ASUA, summed up synchro's growth in 1958: "No other new sport has had such a phenomenal rise in amateur circles on good solid ground with such a crowded background of experience worldwide." Olsen said, "It isn't just the United States where the sport is booming; it's countries all over the world."[3] But the Olympics seemed farther and farther away with each passing year, particularly while Avery Brundage, long-lasting head of the IOC, refused to even consider it. "It's show biz," he said.[4]

When synchro finally became part of the World Aquatic Championships in 1973, it was drastically different from those early days and it had evolved still further before it joined the Olympic family of sports in 1984. Even the solo and duet made it a major attraction at each Olympic Games, but only as the team events flashed before the 1996 Olympic audiences in Atlanta did the world finally see and admire what synchronized swimming really is. As we now look forward to the future, the question is, "Is synchro all that it could be?"

The answer is obvious. Synchro can be and will be better yet. Even as this chapter is being written, changes in international rules are being made that may improve the sport. We can hope for early granting of some items on the wish list of progress, bringing back the solo to the Olympics, for example; others may take a great deal of stubborn persistence to achieve. "One thing I have learned over the years while involved in this sport is that 'change does not come easy to us,'" USSS president Betty Hazle said. "We tend to be resistant to change, whether it is because we are afraid, it is too much work, or for whatever reason, NOW is the time for everyone in the organization to grasp hold of these goals and work together in accomplishing our plans."[5] As we look forward to the next Olympic Games in Athens in 2004, it indeed is the time for the United States to reach for the stars once more.

## *Changes Over Time*

Changes for the better have taken place through the years. The USSS competition structure offers competitive programs for nearly every level of skill and age, with the chance to win visible evidence of prowess in contests. USSS competitions include association-level novice, age group, intermediate, junior, senior and masters championships. Regional, zone and national championships are held for age group, junior, senior, collegiate and masters levels. National trials competitions designate competitors for Olympic Games, World Championships, World Cups, Pan American Games and other international contests.

Training programs have produced enough officials so there is seldom a problem filling the judge seats at major national events, but judges and scorers may still be scarce at some association and even regional competitions. Synchro's progressive program for training, rating and evaluating judges has been a model for other judged sports. Dissemination of information is better handled now than it was in the past. The U.S. Synchro office distributes teaching and training books and videos. *Synchro Swimming USA* magazine fills some of the information gaps and offers a newsletter on the internet as well as access to a wide variety of materials.

A coaching certification program has been established. Clinics and seminars are held to educate coaches. Athletes at all levels have clin-

ics for training so that information is spread widely throughout the country. The most elite athletes are selected to train together to represent the United States in world events.

And the sport's visibility may be improving as evidenced by this note in *Sports Illustrated* in an article on college basketball. Marc Salyers, of Samford College in Birmingham said, in describing his team's offense, "When we play, well, it's like synchronized swimming, everyone knows where everyone else is."[6]

## *Problems to Overcome*

Problems that have continued through the years and still need better resolution include the following:[7]

1) Poor Sport Image — The problem of synchronized swimming's image, particularly in the U.S., has been at the top of every list of synchro's problems since the beginning. Lack of acceptance as a sport has generally been attributed to the theatrical origins and theater-associated factors in synchro performances and awards. Improving synchro's image must deal both with overcoming its arty and theatrical impressions and with making its competitive character much more clear to the spectator in order to gain true synchro sports fans.

2) Dealing with Aquacade Origins — Synchronized swimming remains haunted by its show business background. "Theme" has made a strong comeback in choreography, even in the face of clear disapproval. FINA technical committee chairman Jan Armbrust in 1982 stated, "Pantomime playing has nothing to do with sport ... we must really think about the difference between show and sport...."[8] Still, many of the free routines in the 1996 and 2000 Olympics attempted to relate a story, portray a subject or send a message. In describing the action of Team U.S.A. in its 1996 Olympic free routine, *Synchro Swimming USA* described the action as portraying "a progression through the string, woodwind, percussion and horn sections of the orchestra."[9] We have passed the time that this symbolism would have been read to the judge during the performance so the in-

terpretation could be evaluated. Now, the judges, if following the letter of the rules, only grade how well the action interprets the *music*, and not how it portrays theme or story. The insistence of many teams in relying on a theme appears to be a 30-year step backward.

FINA took a positive step toward costume control in a guideline adopted in 1998 which has now become part of the FINA Judging Manual. "In Synchronized Swimming's ongoing endeavour to be accepted without question as a 'real sport,' public image is important. Appropriate swimwear enhances this image — inappropriate 'costumes' detract. Swimwear should reflect the athletic nature of synchronized swimming and not be a costume more suited to a stage production." "For Technical Routines, swimsuits should be one piece and with minimal adornment. Headpieces may be worn, but should be minimal and unobtrusive." "For Free Routines, swimsuits should be one piece and not have excessive decoration, additional adornment, or added features who are not part of the actual suit. Headpieces should be neat, not excessive in size or style, and in harmony with the suit and music. They should not cover any part of the face or neck." It further states, "Excessive or unnatural make-up is often highlighted by close-up television shots and detracts from any attempt to project an athletic performance."[10] This appears to state the case for simpler apparel very clearly and forcefully and has made the appearance of the swimmers much less theatrical and more in the tone of sport, although some work still needs to be done.

Category names probably should be changed to neutral terms in relation to factors that can be graded objectively. The category of "artistic impression" does not seem to describe a sports contest. Synonyms for "artistic" include aesthetic, cultured, elegant, refined and exquisite. "Impression" is defined as an effect, feeling, sensation. This simply confirms that this award is based on personal *feelings* about the aesthetic *sensations*. Rhythmic gymnastics more astutely uses "composition" for essentially the same award. Similarly, subfactors of the artistic impression score, such as choreography, music interpretation and creativity, may

need to be renamed and reworked to become more objective standards of performance.

3) Complexity for Judges and Audience — Limiting the number of elements might assist judges in making real performance comparisons. No other sport has a judge training manual with a set of award-defining tables listing nearly 50 factors that judges should be considering and evaluating in a routine. The critical elements at the heart of the quality of the performance should be the core of evaluations. Gymnastics and figure skating programs also appear complex but judge evaluations are made upon a much more limited set of criteria, most of which become apparent to even untrained but devoted observers. Triple jumps are better than doubles. Any jump completion is better than a pratfall. Falling off the beam or bars is an instant half-point deduction. By contrast, decisions in upper-level synchro competitions depend upon tiny discrepancies in the vertical lines, a small difference in height, tiny errors in synchronization, all subject to dispute from a different chair or angle. Audiences, as well as judges, may be baffled seeking to compare one routine to another on these obscure observations.

The introduction of the technical routine is a positive step toward clearer relations between performance and awards. Both judge and spectator have a better chance of discerning performance differences between identical required elements than within the many variations seen in a completely free routine. Media and audiences may learn the language of the identifiable key actions and, with practice, even learn to distinguish the good from the excellent. The television commentator, program order in hand, can guide the audience into the critical actions and comment on the differences in performance between competitors or even replay and compare two competitors on split screens.

4) Synchro Access and Visibility — To compete successfully with other activities for attention and potential athletes, synchro must become familiar to a wide population with convenient opportunities to test its characteristics for themselves. In places where a public familiarity and good image has been promoted by

Technical perfection of positions with height, strength and control has always been part of the execution score, but the levels go higher and higher, requiring even more strength and control. Above, 1984 Olympian Tracie Ruiz in her Olympic routine (photograph by Ross Bean).

Timing is everything in achieving simultaneous jumps and throws. Not only are the swimmers above performing a risky movement, it takes perfect timing beneath the water to lift and throw the swimmers. Above is the 1996 Olympic team action (photograph by Dan Helms).

television and press coverage, as in Canada, Japan and France, synchro growth has been relatively much greater than in the U.S.A. But, even where interest may be aroused by media support, opportunities for participation are sometimes hard to find. Access to competitive synchro programs remains extremely limited in most areas of the country. Municipal recreational offerings are offered in only a small minority of towns; school programs are found only in a few areas; collegiate programs are growing, but are still scant and dependent upon club programs to feed them. Club programs exist in clusters in limited numbers of regions across the country. The USSS has tried to expand the YMCA-YWCA participation in a nationwide program, but with slow progress. Gender equity requirements may improve college support. This, in turn, would increase visibility and credibility for introduction into high school physical education and interscholastic programs.

5) Facility and Teaching Deficiencies— Swim facilities are costly and municipal and school facilities are usually driven to prioritize activities to obtain optimal cost efficiency in their use. Although some school districts and municipalities offer their facilities to community groups at minimal or no cost, synchro may not compete well with other activities on the comparative cost effectiveness of facility use. Many more lap swimmers may be accommodated than synchro swimmers. Costs of rent-

Platforms are an audience-pleasing action that have found their way into the technical rules. Now swimmers must include an acrobatic move, a platform (above), stack or jump (throw). These actions add difficulty because of the risk involved. Above, Kristina Lum with her Santa Clara teammates (photograph by Nancy Hines).

ing facilities are usually prohibitive for the small numbers in most synchro groups.

Paradoxically, synchro programs proposed for some recreational facilities may founder for lack of experienced teachers or coaches. Few collegiate synchro teacher training programs exist. As in all amateur sports, competent coaches coming from the coaching certification program that the USSS has offered since 1984 find there are few places that offer well-trained coaches or teachers a living salary. With few exceptions, synchro coaches continue to be selfless devotees to the promotion and advancement of synchro, rewarded almost entirely by seeing the product of their efforts in action. The clubs that do find themselves with both facilities and coaches usually devise all sorts of approaches to making the most efficient use of both to keep operations within funding limitations.

6) Single Area Domination — At the time of the advent of national teams, with members selected on the basis of individual performance, one firm hope was that they would spread the sport to all areas of the country. That has not proved to be the case. The San Francisco Bay area was dominant before national teams and remains the destination of ambitious synchro swimmers from all parts of the country still. In the collegiate ranks, the fully funded scholarship program at Ohio State University continues to draw top athletes although Stanford has increased its scholarship program and is challenging the long-reigning Buckeyes.

7) Scarcity of Officials— Synchro not only asks its judges to work hard in the process of judging, it asks them to spend personal funds and many long hours while doing so. Even so, the national judge roster is well filled with synchro devotees who have embarked upon the time- and money-consuming training programs to gain national judge ratings. U.S. national championships seldom lack for officials. A limited number now receive housing reimbursement for their participation. But in local competitions, finding enough officials is more difficult. Only in the most active synchro areas is there any certainty of having enough fully qualified officials at every competition. Almost all officials, judges, scorers and others come from the ranks of the personally interested, former swimmers or parents of active swimmers, but even this pool may be largely untapped due to lack of recruiting and training programs. Until synchro gathers enough participants to support defraying expenses of officials, their availability will probably remain cloudy.

8) Participant Costs— Synchro may not be as costly for the athlete as figure skating or gymnastics, but it remains an expensive activity. Athletes and their parents are responsible for costs of coaching, facilities, equipment, music, apparel and travel. Club sponsorships by cities, schools or businesses are rare. This still limits participation by all income levels. Only when the athlete reaches elite levels is there some support in the form of Olympic funding. The USOC assists in helping fund training camps and programs for all levels. For the elite swimmers, there are education grants to assist those in college, some funding for training expenses and for those in the work force, USOC's corporate sponsors help with a job opportunity program where athletes work for companies who allow time in the work day for training and who cooperate with the competitive schedule of the athlete. In addition, the USOC has a financial reward system in which funds are given for Olympic medal winners. But these benefit only the most elite athletes and are based on their placement in the Olympic Games.

## What Does the Future Hold?

There are now more than 90 federations that include synchronized swimming in their aquatic programs, well more than the required minimum for acceptance into the games. The world swimming championships, the FINA Junior World Synchronized Swimming events and the Olympic qualifying competition all regularly have 30 or more federations participating in synchronized swimming.

Since its debut in the 1984 Olympic Games, synchro has been one of the Olympic spectators' favorite events. It was the second event, right after women's gymnastics, to sell out all its tickets in 1984. Again, it sold out very quickly in Seoul, Barcelona and Atlanta. All three routine events have been very popular within the world aquatic championships and now, with the addition of the free routine combination, spectators have an even more engrossing event.

But not all is rosy. Synchro support was dealt a severe blow in many countries when restrictions were placed on the number of entrants into the Olympic competition. With only eight teams, many nations saw little chance for participation in the prestigious Olympic event and reduced their funding for synchro. The addition of 24 duets to the 2000 Olympics helped restore some of the troubled programs since more countries can take part in the Olympic Games.[11] Thus, the qualifying competitions with their unrestricted entry in both duet and team events have helped keep interest alive. Perhaps the Olympic ticket sales for the sport may spur the return of the solo event to the Olympic program by 2008.

Figure competition was criticized as the "hidden" competition that too often determined the victors, before a routine was ever swum. In large meets, figure competition took a great deal of time and the figures performed in this competition became almost totally unrelated to actions in routines. Figure skating dispensed with its compulsory figure competition after 1990. Synchro has partially followed suit by requiring technical routines instead of figure competition at the senior level. But figure competition is retained at the junior and age-group levels where it is considered a useful development tool.

We are still dealing with theme, drama, pantomime and flashy costuming. While these have been eliminated from being part of the judgments, they still play an important part in the minds of coaches and athletes although Olympic coach Chris Carver recently said, "Creativity is less important than doing the routine well. To be competitive today, routines must have several highlights and points of interest. Tessellated patterns moving into one another add interest, excitement and motion to routines. Themes are not necessary. Music interpretation and the use of music are much more important than themes. Routines should showcase the swimmers' strengths."[12] To that point, national team director Linai Vaz de Negri, stated "[Routines] have a high number of lifts that accentuate height and power, more intricate single leg movements and sheer speed as a showcase of talent and difficulty. Our overemphasis on smoothness and flow in figures to the detriment of height and power was definitely not rewarded, or it was simply viewed as a weakness."[13] Hopefully the speed and intricacy of routines will also prevent the athletes from the overdramatization, pantomime and play-acting that have become so prevalent in recent years.

The word is out that apparel for the routines should be more conservative. Unadorned suits are advised for technical routines. Sequins and beading are not specifically proscribed, but the strong message that gaudiness is not desirable has somewhat inhibited their use. As Jan Armbrust, the first FINA technical committee chairman said more than 20 years ago, the accelerated drift toward very flashy and theatric routines is a cause for concern: "Pantomime playing has nothing to do with sport," he said. "The public may like it, but we must really think about the difference between show and sport.... Some things are not illegal, but they may be headed in the wrong direction."[14]

The question of events for men is still there. While synchro is commonly thought of as an activity for women, at the turn of the last century competitions in the equivalent of figures or stunts were for males only. Then, Annette Kellerman and the aquacades and film spectaculars, particularly those with Esther Williams, turned the focus toward women. Still, early synchro precursors in collegiate events did not discriminate between men and women. Only as AAU rules prevailed were men and women segregated. Men's championships were allowed in any of the events but those separate men's events were finally dropped for lack of competitor interest. Present USSS rules do not limit male participation in synchro. Synchro is restricted to women only in FINA world cups, the world aquatic championships and in the Olympic Games.

A few men taking part in synchronized

swimming in Europe and in the United States have managed to rise to high levels of achievement. The 1990 French Open champion duet was a mixed pair, Anne Capron and Stephane Miermont. In USSS competition, Bill May rose to win all the senior level events and is the current national solo, duet and team champion. Although qualifying high enough in national team trials to be a member of the world championship and Olympic teams, he has had to be satisfied with swimming on Team II and winning gold medals in competitions where male participation is allowed. He opened the eyes of many top FINA and Olympic officials at the 1998 Goodwill Games with his silver medals there. However, at the moment, it appears unlikely that the rules will soon be changed to allow male participation since no demand has been established and there are few males actually competing. There has been little sympathy or interest for such a move in the IOC hierarchy. May clings to hope and has said, "I know the addition of the mixed pairs event, much like figure skating, will only improve the popularity of our sport and promote the development of our sport worldwide."[15]

The question of life after years of involvement with synchronized swimming is taking a return to the past. Prior to the start of this century, the only outlets for someone who wanted to keep involved with the sport were through coaching. Now, the first major professional aquacade since the Worlds Fair spectaculars of the '40s opened in Las Vegas in September of 1998. Cirque du Soleil, a Montreal company that had been highly successful in its shows that combine circus, dance, and old time vaudeville acts, decided to open a water show spectacular, called *O*, that would be based in Las Vegas. They auditioned for synchronized swimmers throughout Canada, the U.S. and Europe. The synchro portion of the show is directed by Canada's Olympian Sylvie Frechette and has included many top U.S. swimmers such as Olympians Becky Dyroen-Lancer, Jill Sudduth, and Suzannah Bianco. Stephane Miermont, French national duet champion, was also among those in the early casts. The show is still a strong favorite five years later and continues indefinitely.

Esther Williams is planning a spectacular water show for Las Vegas scheduled to open in the spring of 2005. With the return to water show spectaculars, there is now a professional athletic opportunity for swimmers when they leave the competitive ranks.

## *Show or Sport?*

Show or sport, the question lingers still. The media, never willing to grant sport status to anything that can't qualify winners under "swifter, higher, stronger" standards, always answers, "theater!" But even *Sports Illustrated*, despite habituation to less than flattering reviews of synchro, admitted in its 1984 Olympics report, "Synchronized Swimmers may look like cupcakes, but they're tough cookies, half the routine is performed upside down in a pool."[16]

If Avery Brundage, the crusty old czar of the IOC, had remained in charge, synchro probably never would have been admitted to the Olympics. He remained firm in his convictions: "It's not sport, it's show biz."[17] Joy Cushman reported, "I do know Avery Brundage said it would be over his dead body, and it was!"[18] Acceptance came only after Lord Killanin, then-chairman of the International Olympic Committee, saw it for himself in 1978. "I am very impressed," he said, "I saw synchronized swimming for the first time today. It is a very elegant sport."[19]

The question remains, is synchronized swimming show or sport? Perhaps there will never be an answer, for in truth, it is both show and sport and, in its best incarnations, transcends both categories to become truly unique, an art form unto itself.

# Appendix A:
# Awards and Honors

---

## U.S. Synchronized Swimming Hall of Fame*

Established 1958

*To honor those who have made significant achievements
in the sport, as an athlete or contributor*

### Athletes

1961   June Taylor, Hollywood Athletic Club
      Joan Pawson, Athens Athletic Club, Oakland
1962   Athens Athletic Club, Team of 1958: Janet Anthony, Loretta Barrious, Sue Lawrence, Lynn Pawson, Jackie Vargas
1963   St. Clair Synchronettes, Team of 1952: Ellen Richard, Marilyn Stanley, Shirley Simpson, Connie Todoroff
1964   Papsie Georgian, Athens Athletic Club
1968   Roberta Armstrong, Paso Robles Roblettes
      Pam Morris, San Francisco Merionettes
      Patty Willard, San Francisco Merionettes
1969   Margo McGrath, San Francisco Merionettes
      Claire Vida, San Francisco Merionettes
1970   Carol Redmond, San Francisco Merionettes
1971   Nancy Hines, Santa Clara Aquamaids
      Kim Welshons, Santa Clara Aquamaids
1972   Heidi O'Rourke, San Francisco Merionettes
      Margaret Durbrow, San Francisco Merionettes
1973   Barbara Trantina, San Francisco Merionettes
1974   Teresa Andersen, Santa Clara Aquamaids
1975   Gail Johnson, Santa Clara Aquamaids
1976   Kathy Kretschmer, San Francisco Merionettes

1977   Amanda Norrish, Santa Clara Aquamaids
      Robin Curren, Santa Clara Aquamaids
1978   Sue Baross, Santa Clara Aquamaids
1979   Santa Clara Aquamaids, Team of 1973: Jackie Douglass, Dana Moore, Teresa Andersen, Gail Johnson, Sue Baross, Suzanne Randell, Robin Curren, Amanda Norrish
1981   Michele Barone, Santa Clara Aquamaids
1983   Pam Tryon, Santa Clara Aquamaids
1984   Linda Shelley, Santa Clara Aquamaids
1986   Michelle Beaulieu, Santa Clara Aquamaids
1988   Candy Costie, Seattle Aqua Club
1989   Amy Miner, San Francisco Merionettes
1990   Mary Visniski, Walnut Creek Aquanuts
1992   Tracie Ruiz Conforto, Seattle Aqua Club
1993   Tracy Long, Walnut Creek Aquanuts
1995   Michelle Svitenko, Walnut Creek Aquanuts
1996   Karen Josephson, Walnut Creek Aquanuts
      Sarah Josephson, Walnut Creek Aquanuts
1997   Kristen Babb-Sprague, Walnut Creek Aquanuts
1998   Joan Lang, San Francisco Merionettes
2001   Becky Dyroen-Lancer, Santa Clara Aquamaids
2002   Jill Sudduth, Santa Clara Aquamaids
2003   Jill Savery, Walnut Creek Aquanuts

*The U.S. Synchronized Swimming has been known as the Helms Hall of Fame 1959–71, the United Savings, Citizen Savings, First Interstate Bank Hall of Fame 1972–85, and the United States Synchronized Swimming Hall of Fame 1986–present.

2004  Nathalie Schneyder, Walnut Creek Aqua-
      nuts

### Contributors

1959   Katharine Curtis, Chicago, IL
       Annette Kellerman, New York, NY
1962   Lillian MacKellar, Hollywood, CA
1963   Teresa Andersen, Des Moines, IA
1964   Joy Cushman, Houston, TX
1966   Clark Leach, Wilmette, IL
       Lawrence Johnson, Boston, MA
1967   Marion Kane, San Francisco, CA
1968   Dawn Bean, Santa Ana, CA
1969   Norma Olsen, Oakland, CA
1970   Re Calcaterra, St. Louis, MO
       Irene Pierce, St. Petersburg, FL
       Kay Vilen, Santa Clara, CA
1971   Ross Bean, Santa Ana, CA
       Edna Hines, Columbus, MO
1972   Margaret Swan, San Antonio, TX
       Wilbur Luick, San Jose, CA
1973   Frances Jones, Orchard Lake, MI
1975   Lillian Whiting, Des Moines, IA
1976   Ninetta Davis, Denver, CO
1977   Harold Henning, Napier, IL
1978   Barbara Eaton, Virginia Beach, VA
       Don Kane, San Francisco, CA
1979   Marian Kretschmer, Dayton, OH
       Judy McGowan, Lancaster, PA

1981   Jan Paulus, San Jose, CA
       Dottie Sowers, Tonawanda, NY
1982   Louise Karkut, North Olmsted, OH
1983   Sue Ahlf, Walnut Creek, CA
       Ella Peckham, Oakland, CA
       Betty Wenz, Hayward, CA
1984   Gail Emery, Walnut Creek, CA
1986   Norma Cocklin, Dallas, TX
       Lorraine Fasullo, Clark, NJ
1987   Ruth Zink, Edina, MN
       Vernon Eytchison, Silver Springs, MD
1988   Peg Hogan, Richmond, VA
1989   Ed Kaminski, Santa Clara, CA
1990   Sue Albrecht, Solon, OH
1991   Virginia Jasontek, Cincinnati, OH
       Carol Tackett, Littleton, CO
1992   Charlotte Davis, Seattle, WA
       Barbara McNamee, Des Moines, IA
1993   Pam Edwards, Santa Clara, CA
1994   Margo Erickson, Indianapolis, IN
1995   Rita Barr, Santa Clara, CA
1996   Chris Carver, Santa Clara, CA
1997   Joyce Lindeman, Ypsilanti, MI
1998   Mary Rose, Altamonte Springs, FL
1999   Fred Day, Richmond, VA
2000   Nancy Wightman, Hammondsport, NY
2001   Del Neel, Carmel Valley, CA
2002   Norm Donofrio, Southport, CT
2003   Kaaren Babb, Clayton, CA
2004   Laura LaCursia, Walnut Creek, CA

---

## MACKELLAR DISTINGUISHED SERVICE AWARD

Established 1970

*For unselfishly giving of oneself for synchronized swimming, without
thought of personal gain and with particular emphasis
on working for the benefit of the athlete*

1971   Lillian MacKellar, Glendale, CA
1972   Joy Cushman, Houston, TX
1973   Dawn Bean, Santa Ana, CA
1975   Kay Vilen, Santa Clara, CA
1977   Teresa Andersen, Des Moines, IA
1978   Don Kane, San Francisco, CA
1979   Re Calcaterra, St. Louis, MO
1980   Dottie Sowers, Tonawanda, NY
1981   Ross Bean, Santa Ana, CA
1982   Judy McGowan, Lancaster, PA
1983   Marian Kretschmer, Dayton, OH
1984   Ginny Jasontek, Cincinnati, OH
1985   Mary Jo Ruggieri, Columbus, OH
1986   Barbara McNamee, Williamsburg, VA
1987   Norma Cocklin, Dallas, TX
1988   Pam Edwards, Santa Clara, CA

1989   Marna Moore, Milwaukie, OR
1990   Joyce Lindeman, Ypsilanti, MI
1991   Mary Rose, Altamonte Springs, FL
1992   Rita Barr, Santa Clara, CA
1993   Vernon Eytchison, Silver Springs, MD
1994   Lorraine Fasullo, Clark, NJ
1995   Nancy Wightman, Hammondsport, NY
1996   Ed Kaminski, Santa Clara, CA
1997   Gail Emery, Lafayette, CA
1998   Peg Hogan, Richmond, VA
1999   Jeanne Struck, Tucson, AZ
2000   Margo Erickson, Indianapolis, IN
2001   Ruth Zink, Anna, IL
2002   Mary Ellen Wiegand, West Seneca, NY
2003   Betty Hess, Pennsbury, PA
2004   Barbara Eaton, Virginia Beach, VA

## Lawrence J. Johnson Memorial Award

*United States Aquatic Sports Outstanding Athlete*

1968  Margo McGrath, San Francisco Merionettes
1974  Gail Johnson, Santa Clara Aquamaids
1980  Linda Shelley, Santa Clara Aquamaids
1985  Tracie Ruiz, Seattle Aqua Club

1990  Karen & Sarah Josephson, Walnut Creek
Aquanuts
*Award has been discontinued.*

## United States Aquatic Sports Award

*For Outstanding Contributions to Aquatic Sports*

1982  Lillian MacKellar, Pioneer Contributor
in Synchronized Swimming

## F.I.N.A. Prize Eminence

*To an individual or organization in recognition of
their outstanding positive action in the world aquatic community*

1995  Becky Dyroen-Lancer, Athlete

## International Swimming Hall of Fame

*Fort Lauderdale, FL*

1965  Pam Morris, Athlete: San Francisco Merionettes
1965  Beulah Gundling, Aquatic Art Pioneer: Des Moines, IA
1974  Annette Kellerman, Pioneer Swimmer: Australia
1978  Kay Vilen, Coach: Santa Clara Aquamaids
1979  Katharine Curtis, Coach: Chicago Teachers College
1980  Heidi O'Rourke, Athlete: San Francisco Merionettes
1981  Marion Kane, Coach: San Francisco Merionettes
1983  Gail Johnson, Athlete: Santa Clara Aquamaids
1985  Helen Vanderberg, Athlete: Canada
1986  Teresa Andersen, Athlete: Santa Clara Aquamaids
1988  Kim Welshons, Athlete: Santa Clara Aquamaids
      Peg Seller, Pioneer: Canada
1989  Margo McGrath, Athlete: San Francisco Merionettes
1989  Carol Redmond, Athlete: San Francisco Merionettes

1991  June Taylor, Pioneer Athlete: Hollywood Athletic Club
1993  Billie MacKellar, Pioneer Coach: Canada/ Hollywood Athletic Club
1993  Tracie Ruiz-Conforto, Athlete: Seattle Aqua Club
1994  Carolyn Waldo, Athlete: Canada
1995  Candy Costie, Athlete: Seattle Aqua Club
1996  Dawn Bean, Contributor: Santa Ana, CA
1997  Karen Josephson, Athlete: Walnut Creek Aquanuts
      Sarah Josephson, Athlete: Walnut Creek Aquanuts
1998  Norma Olsen, Pioneer Contributor: Oakland
1999  Kristen Babb-Sprague. Athlete: Walnut Creek Aquanuts
2000  Michelle Cameron, Athlete: Canada
2001  Michelle Calkins, Athlete: Canada
      Gail Emery, Coach: Walnut Creek Aquanuts
2002  Margaret (Peg) Hogan, Masters Athlete: Octopi of Richmond
2003  Sylvie Frechette, Athlete: Canada
2004  Becky Dyroen-Lancer, Athlete: Santa Clara Aquamaids

## International Swimming Hall of Fame Paragon Award

Fort Lauderdale, FL
*For Outstanding Contributions to the Sport of Synchronized Swimming*

| | | | |
|---|---|---|---|
| 1996 | Dorothy Sowers, Tonawanda, NY | 2001 | Charlotte Davis, Seattle, WA |
| 1997 | Judy McGowan, Lancaster, PA | 2002 | Virginia Jasontek, Cincinnati, OH |
| 1998 | Ross Bean, Santa Ana, CA | 2003 | Sue Ahlf, Walnut Creek, CA |
| 1999 | Barbara McNamee, Williamsburg, VA | 2004 | Nanette Zack, Mount Prospect, IL |
| 2000 | Ed Kaminski, Santa Clara, CA | | |

## Women's Sports Foundation International Sports Hall of Fame

East Meadow, NY
*Recognizing Outstanding Women in Sports*

| | | | |
|---|---|---|---|
| 1985 | McDonald's Corporation, Contributor, nominated by U.S.S.S. | 1999 | Tracie Ruiz-Conforto, Athlete |
| | | 1999 | Chris Carver, Contemporary Coach |
| 1997 | Gail Emery, Contemporary Coach | | |

## U.S.S.S. Athlete of the Year
## U.S.O.C. Sportswoman of the Year
## and Sullivan Award Nominee

*The athlete who has made the greatest impact in the sport during the past year*

| | | | |
|---|---|---|---|
| 1987 | Tracie Ruiz-Conforto, Seattle Aqua Club | | Heather Simmons-Carrasco, Jill Sudduth, Margot Thien |
| 1988 | Tracie Ruiz-Conforto, Seattle Aqua Club | | |
| 1989 | Tracy Long, Walnut Creek Aquanuts | 1997 | Carrie Barton, Santa Clara Aquamaids |
| 1990 | Karen Josephson, Walnut Creek Aquanuts | | Anna Kozlova,* Santa Clara Aquamaids |
| 1991 | Sarah Josephson, Walnut Creek Aquanuts | 1998 | Kristina Lum, Santa Clara Aquamaids |
| 1992 | Karen Josephson, Walnut Creek Aquanuts | 1999 | Kristina Lum, Santa Clara Aquamaids |
| | Sarah Josephson, Walnut Creek Aquanuts | | Bill May,* Santa Clara Aquamaids |
| 1993 | Becky Dyroen-Lancer, Santa Clara Aquamaids | 2000 | Anna Kozlova, Santa Clara Aquamaids |
| | | | Bill May,* Santa Clara Aquamaids |
| 1994 | Becky Dyroen-Lancer, Santa Clara Aquamaids | 2001 | Anna Kozlova, Santa Clara Aquamaids |
| | | | Bill May,* Santa Clara Aquamaids |
| 1995 | Becky Dyroen-Lancer, Santa Clara Aquamaids | 2002 | Anna Kozlova, Santa Clara Aquamaids |
| | | 2003 | Anna Kozlova, Santa Clara Aquamaids |
| 1996 | U.S. 1996 Olympic Team: Suzannah Dyroen-Bianco, Tammy Cleland, Becky Dyroen-Lancer, Heather Pease, Emily Porter LeSueur, Jill Savery, Nathalie Schneyder, | 2004 | U.S. 2004 Olympic Team: Alison Bartosik, Tammy Crow, Erin Dobratz, Becky Jasontek, Anna Kozlova, Sara Lowe, Lauren McFall, Stephanie Nesbitt, Kendra Zanotto |

*Sullivan Award Nominee only

## U.S.O.C.–U.S.S.S. Coach of the Year

*The coach who has made the greatest impact in the sport during the past year*

| | | | |
|---|---|---|---|
| 1983 | Charlotte Davis, Seattle Aqua Club | 1986 | Gail Emery, Walnut Creek Aquanuts |
| 1984 | Gail Emery, Walnut Creek Aquanuts | 1987 | Gail Emery, Walnut Creek Aquanuts |
| 1985 | Gail Emery, Walnut Creek Aquanuts | 1988 | Gail Emery, Walnut Creek Aquanuts |

| | | | |
|---|---|---|---|
| 1989 | Gail Emery, Walnut Creek Aquanuts | 1997 | Chris Carver, Santa Clara Aquamaids |
| 1990 | Gail Emery, Walnut Creek Aquanuts | 1998 | Chris Carver, Santa Clara Aquamaids |
| 1991 | Gail Emery, Walnut Creek Aquanuts | 1999 | Chris Carver, Santa Clara Aquamaids |
| 1992 | Gail Emery, Walnut Creek Aquanuts | 2000 | Chris Carver, Santa Clara Aquamaids |
| 1993 | Gail Emery, Walnut Creek Aquanuts | 2001 | Chris Carver, Santa Clara Aquamaids |
| 1994 | Gail Emery, Walnut Creek Aquanuts | 2002 | Chris Carver, Santa Clara Aquamaids |
| 1995 | Gail Emery, Walnut Creek Aquanuts | 2003 | Chris Carver, Santa Clara Aquamaids |
| 1996 | Gail Emery, Walnut Creek Aquanuts | 2004 | Chris Carver, Santa Clara Aquamaids |
| 1996 | Chris Carver, Santa Clara Aquamaids | | |

## COLLEGIATE ATHLETE OF THE YEAR

| | | | |
|---|---|---|---|
| 1984 | Sarah Josephson, Ohio State University | 1995 | Emily Marsh, Ohio State University |
| 1985 | Karen Josephson, Ohio State University | 1996 | Sadie Pietras, Ohio State University |
| 1986 | Adrienne Lehman, Ohio State University | 1997 | Gina Pietras, Ohio State University |
| 1987 | Anna Amicarella, Ohio State University | 1998 | Ana Cukic, Ohio State University |
| 1988 | Cathy Cramer, Ohio State University | 1999 | Gina Lighthall, Wheaton College |
| 1989 | Karen Madsen, Stanford University | 2000 | Julie Enos, Stanford University |
| 1990 | Maria Guisti, Ohio State University | 2001 | Shannon Montague, Stanford University |
| 1991 | Maria Guisti, Ohio State University | 2002 | Lindsay Kaufman, University of Iowa |
| 1992 | Carrie DeGuerre, Ohio State University | 2003 | Suzanna Hyatt, Ohio State University |
| 1993 | Carrie DeGuerre, Ohio State University | 2004 | Asha Bandal, University of Richmond |
| 1994 | Jill Savery, University of California, Berkeley | | |

## MASTERS ATHLETE OF THE YEAR
## (MAE MCEWAN MEMORIAL AWARD)

| | | | |
|---|---|---|---|
| 1979 | Nancy Weiman, D.C. Synchro Masters | 1993 | Elizabeth Knowles, Fredrick Swans |
| 1980 | Peg Hogan, Octopi of Richmond | 1994 | Sherry Weinberg, Seattle Kaleidoscopes |
| 1981 | Louise Wing, New England Synchro | 1995 | Jeanne Ulrich, D.C. Synchromasters |
| 1982 | Barbara Eaton, Tidewater Aqua Aerials | 1996 | Scotti Nichols, Michigan Synchro Masters |
| 1983 | Barbara McNamee, D.C. Synchromasters | 1997 | Fred Wing, New England Synchro |
| 1984 | Marian Kretschmer, Dayton Synchronettes | 1998 | Mary Kay Adams, Dayton Synchronettes |
| 1985 | Eleanor East, Dade County Blue Sharkettes | 1999 | Barbara Browne, Redwood Empire Synchro |
| 1986 | Linda Lash, Columbus Sync-or-Swim | 2000 | Laura Soles, Octopi of Richmond |
| 1987 | Jane Katz, Manhattan Plaza Masters | 2001 | Holly Kyle, Redwood Empire Synchro |
| 1988 | Margaret Forbes, San Antonio Cygnets | 2002 | Penny DeMeules, Southern California Unsyncables |
| 1989 | Sue Dmytryszyn, St. Louis Masters | | |
| 1990 | Jeanne Steed, Mac Synchro Masters | 2003 | Miriam Larson, Southern California Unsyncables |
| 1991 | Nanette Zack, Aquasprite Masters | | |
| 1992 | Sue Bessette, Aqua Masters Synchro | 2004 | Carolyn Madden, Dayton Synchronettes |

## AGE GROUP DEVELOPMENTAL COACHING AWARD

| | | | |
|---|---|---|---|
| 1987 | Cindy Coe, Ken-Ton Kipettes | 1996 | Jeannette Bacigalupo, Los Angeles Synchro |
| 1988 | Patty Olstad, Tucson Sun Rays | 1997 | Carole Mitchell, Dolpholinas of Richmond |
| 1989 | Linda Erholm, Newark Novas | 1998 | Melodie Wallace, Aquanauts of Clear Lake |
| 1990 | Karen Paulk, Largo Waterworks | 1999 | Christie Bober, Brecksville Blue Dolphins |
| 1991 | Kathryn Blevens-Freer, Sacramento Synchro | 2000 | Shellie Boskey, Sioux Falls Cygnets |
| 1993 | Lisa Muiznicks, Puget Sound Athletic Club | 2001 | Kelly Eakin, Kansas City Terrafins |
| 1994 | Carol Valles, New Canaan Aquianas | 2002 | Samantha Derrick, New York |
| 1995 | Lorraine Valerino, Lakeland Family YMCA Flamingos | 2003 | Cheryl Cook, Austin Angelfish |
| | | 2004 | Joanne Kutzler, West Metro Synchronettes |

## AGE GROUP COACHING MERIT AWARD

| | | | |
|---|---|---|---|
| 1998 | Laura LaCursia, Walnut Creek Aquanuts | | Tina Kasid, Leanne Cameron Arielink, |
| 1999 | Janet Wiecking, Santa Clara Aquamaids | | Jung Shin Chun, Laura LaCursia |
| 2000 | Patti Andresan, Santa Clara Aquamaids | 2003 | Jennifer Muzyk, New Canaan Aquiaanas |
| 2001 | Cheryl Abrahams, Riverside Aquettes | 2004 | Debbie Latchford, Buffalo Swimkins |
| 2002 | Coaching Staff, Walnut Creek Aquanuts: | | |

## AGE GROUP DEVELOPMENTAL COACH OF THE YEAR

| | | | |
|---|---|---|---|
| 1986 | Mary Tope, Riverside Aquettes | 1995 | Mary Ellen Wiegand, Buffalo Swimkins |
| | Marilyn Deister, Kansas City Sea Sprites | 1996 | Julie Thaden, Indy Synchro |
| 1987 | Donn Squire, Cypress Swim Club | 1997 | Joanne Wright, Tonawanda Aquettes/Cani- |
| 1988 | Fred Day, Briarwood Synchro | | sius College |
| 1989 | Terry Forman, Fort Lauderdale Terryettes | 1998 | Ginny Jasontek, Cincinnati Synchrogators |
| 1990 | Barbara Kuhl, Cincinnati Sea Lyons | 1999 | Sue Nesbitt, Riverside Aquettes |
| 1991 | Betty Hess, Pennsbury Falconettes | 2000 | Julie Howell, Sweetwater Dolphins |
| 1992 | Candy Kraemerer, Tucson Synchro | 2001 | Patti Barton, Pirouettes of Texas |
| 1993 | Emma Gene Edwards, Dade County Blue | 2002 | Laura LaCursia, Walnut Creek Aquanuts |
| | Sharkettes | 2003 | Shari Darst, Rocky Mountain Splash |
| 1994 | Dee Dent, Canton Tailspinners | 2004 | Lori Eaton, Indy Synchro |

# Appendix B:
# U.S. National Champions,
# 1946–2004

UNITED STATES SYNCHRONIZED SWIMMING
SENIOR NATIONAL SOLO CHAMPIONS
1950–2004

*I. = Indoor, O. = Outdoor*

1950 I. June Taylor, Kia Ora Swim Club
    O. Beulah Gundling, Cedar Rapids
1951 I. June Taylor, Kia Ora Swim Club
    O. Beulah Gundling, Cedar Rapids
1952 I. June Taylor, Kia Ora Swim Club
    O. Beulah Gundling, Cedar Rapids
1953 I. June Taylor, Hollywood Athletic Club
    O. Beulah Gundling, Cedar Rapids
1954 I. Beulah Gundling, Cedar Rapids
    Jo Ann Speer, KRNT Des Moines
    O. Joanne Royer, Riverside Aquettes
1955 I. Joanne Royer, Riverside Aquettes
    O. Joanne Royer, Riverside Aquettes
  Men Donn Squire, Unattached, Oakland
1956 I. Joanne Royer, Unattached, Long Beach
    O. Linda Ridings, Fort Lauderdale
1957 I. Tony Stewart, Unattached, Chicago
    O. Betty Vickers, Hollywood Athletic Club
1958 I. Tony Stewart, Chicago Town Club
    O. Sandy Giltner, Lansing Sea Sprites
1959 I. Sandy Giltner, Lansing Sea Sprites
    O. Betty Vickers, University Club, Hollywood
1960 I. Papsie Georgian, Athens Athletic Club, Oakland
    O. Papsie Georgian, Athens Athletic Club, Oakland

1961 I. Papsie Georgian, Athens Athletic Club, Oakland
    O. Papsie Georgian, Athens Athletic Club, Oakland
1962 I. Barbara Burke, University Club, Hollywood
    O. Barbara Burke, University Club, Hollywood
1963 I. Roberta Armstrong, Paso Robles
    O. Roberta Armstrong, Paso Robles
1964 I. Roberta Armstrong, Paso Robles
    O. Roberta Armstrong, Paso Robles
1965 I. Pam Morris, San Francisco Merionettes
    O. Pam Morris, San Francisco Merionettes
1966 I. Margo McGrath, San Francisco Merionettes
    O. Margo McGrath, San Francisco Merionettes
1967 I. Margo McGrath, San Francisco Merionettes
    O. Margo McGrath, San Francisco Merionettes
1968 I. Margo McGrath, San Francisco Merionettes
    O. Kim Welshons, Santa Clara Aquamaids
1969 I. Kim Welshons, Santa Clara Aquamaids

205

O.   Kim Welshons, Santa Clara Aquamaids
1970   I.   Carol Reynolds, Santa Clara Aquamaids
O.   Barbara Trantina, San Francisco Merionettes
1971   I.   Heidi O'Rourke, San Francisco Merionettes
O.   Heidi O'Rourke, San Francisco Merionettes
1972   I.   Gail Johnson, Santa Clara Aquamaids
O.   Gail Johnson, Santa Clara Aquamaids
1973   I.   Teresa Andersen, Santa Clara Aquamaids
O.   Gail Johnson, Santa Clara Aquamaids
1974   I.   Kathy Kretschmer, San Francisco Merionettes
O.   Gail Johnson, Santa Clara Aquamaids
1975   I.   Gail Johnson, Santa Clara Aquamaids
O.   Gail Johnson, Santa Clara Aquamaids
1976   I.   Robin Curren, Santa Clara Aquamaids
O.   Sue Baross, Santa Clara Aquamaids
1977   I.   Sue Baross, Santa Clara Aquamaids
O.   Sue Baross, Santa Clara Aquamaids
1978   I.   Pam Tryon, Santa Clara Aquamaids
O.   Linda Shelley, Santa Clara Aquamaids
1979   I.   Linda Shelley, Santa Clara Aquamaids
O.   Linda Shelley, Santa Clara Aquamaids

*Indoor/Outdoor discontinued; one championship
per year beginning in 1980.*

1980   Linda Shelley, Santa Clara Aquamaids
1981   Tracie Ruiz, Seattle Aqua Club
1982   Tracie Ruiz, Seattle Aqua Club
1983   Tracie Ruiz, Seattle Aqua Club
1984   Tracie Ruiz, Seattle Aqua Club
1985   Sarah Josephson, Ohio State University
1986   Sarah Josephson, Walnut Creek Aquanuts
1987   Tracie Ruiz-Conforto, Seattle Aqua Club
1988   Tracie Ruiz-Conforto, Seattle Aqua Club
1989   Kristen Babb, Walnut Creek Aquanuts
1990   Kristen Babb, Walnut Creek Aquanuts
1991   Kristen Babb-Sprague, Walnut Creek Aquanuts
1992   Kristen Babb-Sprague, Walnut Creek Aquanuts
1993   Becky Dyroen-Lancer, Santa Clara Aquamaids
1994   Becky Dyroen-Lancer, Santa Clara Aquamaids
1995   Becky Dyroen-Lancer, Santa Clara Aquamaids
1996   Anna Kozlova, Santa Clara Aquamaids
1997   Anna Kozlova, Santa Clara Aquamaids
1998   Anna Kozlova, Santa Clara Aquamaids
1999   Anna Kozlova, Santa Clara Aquamaids
2000   Bill May, Santa Clara Aquamaids
2001   Bill May, Santa Clara Aquamaids
2002   Anna Kozlova, Santa Clara Aquamaids
2003   Bill May, Santa Clara Aquamaids
2004   Bill May, Santa Clara Aquamaids

## SENIOR NATIONAL DUET CHAMPIONS 1946–2004

1946   O.   Ruth Geduldig, Gloria Geduldig, Chi-
cago Town Club
1947   I.   Ruth Geduldig, Gloria Geduldig, Chi-
cago Town Club
O.   Alice Micus, Marilyn Stanley, St. Clair
Synchronettes
1948   I.   Alice Micus, Marilyn Stanley, St. Clair
Synchronettes
O.   Alice Micus, Marilyn Stanley, St. Clair
Synchronettes
1949   I.   Billie Voelker, Rosemarie Voelker, Chi-
cago Town Club
O.   Shirley Simpson, Connie Todoroff, St.
Clair Synchronettes
1950   I.   Marilyn Stanley, Shirley Simpson, St.
Clair Synchronettes
O.   Shirley Simpson, Marilyn Stanley, St.
Clair Synchronettes
1951   I.   Ellen Richard, Connie Todoroff, St. Clair
Synchronettes
O.   Ellen Richard, Connie Todoroff, St. Clair
Synchronettes
1952   I.   Jo Ann Speer, Carla Courter, KRNT Des
Moines
O.   Ellen Richard, Connie Todoroff, St. Clair
Synchronettes

1953   I.   Jo Ann Speer, Carla Courter, KRNT Des
Moines
O.   Joan Pawson, Lynn Pawson, Athens Ath-
letic Club, Oakland
1954   I.   Ellen Richard, Connie Todoroff, St. Clair
Synchronettes
O.   Joan Pawson, Lynn Pawson, Athens Ath-
letic Club, Oakland
1955   I.   Joan Pawson, Lynn Pawson, Athens Ath-
letic Club, Oakland
O.   Joanne Berthelson, Jackie Brown, Athens
Athletic Club, Oakland
1956   I.   Joanne Berthelson, Jackie Brown, Athens
Athletic Club, Oakland
O.   Judy Haga, Sandy Giltner, Lansing Sea
Sprites
1957   I.   Judy Haga, Sandy Giltner, Lansing Sea
Sprites
O.   Judy Haga, Sandy Giltner, Lansing Sea
Sprites
1958   I.   Roz Calcaterra, Mary Jane Gury, Shaw
Park, St. Louis
O.   Roz Calcaterra, Mary Jane Gury, Shaw
Park, St. Louis
1959   I.   Sue Lawrence, Jackie Vargas, Athens Ath-
letic Club, Oakland

O. Sue Lawrence, Jackie Vargas, Athens Athletic Club, Oakland

1960 I. Sue Lawrence, Jackie Vargas, Athens Athletic Club, Oakland

O. Sue Lawrence, Jackie Vargas, Athens Athletic Club, Oakland

1961 I. Phyllis Firman, Louella Sommers, San Francisco Merionettes

O. Barbara Burke, Joanne Schaack, University Club, Hollywood

1962 I. Claire Vida, Louella Sommers, San Francisco Merionettes

O. Claire Vida, Louella Sommers, San Francisco Merionettes

1963 I. Claire Vida, Judy Wejak, San Francisco Merionettes

O. Claire Vida, Judy Wejak, San Francisco Merionettes

1964 I. Margaret Durbrow, Patty Willard, San Francisco Merionettes

O. Margaret Durbrow, Patty Willard, San Francisco Merionettes

1965 I. Pam Morris, Patty Willard, San Francisco Merionettes

O. Pam Morris, Patty Willard, San Francisco Merionettes

1966 I. Margo McGrath, Carol Redmond, San Francisco Merionettes

O. Margo McGrath, Carol Redmond, San Francisco Merionettes

1967 I. Margo McGrath, Carol Redmond, San Francisco Merionettes

O. Margo McGrath, Carol Redmond, San Francisco Merionettes

1968 I. Nancy Hines, Kim Welshons, Santa Clara Aquamaids

O. Nancy Hines, Kim Welshons, Santa Clara Aquamaids

1969 I. Heidi O'Rourke, Barbara Trantina, San Francisco Merionettes

O. Nancy Hines, Kim Welshons, Santa Clara Aquamaids

1970 I. Heidi O'Rourke, Barbara Trantina, San Francisco Merionettes

O. Heidi O'Rourke, Barbara Trantina, San Francisco Merionettes

1971 I. Joan Lang, Heidi O'Rourke, San Francisco Merionettes

O. Joan Lang, Heidi O'Rourke, San Francisco Merionettes

1972 I. Teresa Andersen, Gail Johnson, Santa Clara Aquamaids

O. Teresa Andersen, Gail Johnson, Santa Clara Aquamaids

1973 I. Teresa Andersen, Gail Johnson, Santa Clara Aquamaids

O. Teresa Andersen, Gail Johnson, Santa Clara Aquamaids

1974 I. Kathy Kretschmer, Amy Miner, San Francisco Merionettes

O. Sue Baross, Gail Johnson, Santa Clara Aquamaids

1975 I. Robin Curren, Amanda Norrish, Santa Clara Aquamaids

O. Robin Curren, Amanda Norrish, Santa Clara Aquamaids

1976 I. Robin Curren, Amanda Norrish, Santa Clara Aquamaids

O. Robin Curren, Amanda Norrish, Santa Clara Aquamaids

1977 I. Sue Baross, Linda Shelley, Santa Clara Aquamaids

O. Sue Baross, Linda Shelley, Santa Clara Aquamaids

1978 I. Michele Barone, Pam Tryon, Santa Clara Aquamaids

O. Michele Barone, Pam Tryon, Santa Clara Aquamaids

1979 I. Michele Barone, Linda Shelley, Santa Clara Aquamaids

O. Michele Barone, Linda Shelley, Santa Clara Aquamaids

*Indoor/Outdoor discontinued; one championship per year beginning in 1980.*

1980 Suzanne Cameron, Linda Shelley, Santa Clara Aquamaids

1981 Candy Costie, Tracie Ruiz, Seattle Aqua Club

1982 Candy Costie, Tracie Ruiz, Seattle Aqua Club

1983 Candy Costie, Tracie Ruiz, Seattle Aqua Club

1984 Candy Costie, Tracie Ruiz, Seattle Aqua Club

1985 Karen Josephson, Sarah Josephson, Ohio State University

1986 Karen Josephson, Sarah Josephson, Walnut Creek Aquanuts

1987 Karen Josephson, Sarah Josephson, Walnut Creek Aquanuts

1988 Karen Josephson, Sarah Josephson, Walnut Creek Aquanuts

1989 Kristen Babb, Tracy Long, Walnut Creek Aquanuts

1990 Karen Josephson, Sarah Josephson, Walnut Creek Aquanuts

1991 Karen Josephson, Sarah Josephson, Walnut Creek Aquanuts

1992 Karen Josephson, Sarah Josephson, Walnut Creek Aquanuts

1993 Becky Dyroen-Lancer, Jill Sudduth, Santa Clara Aquamaids

1994 Becky Dyroen-Lancer, Jill Sudduth, Santa Clara Aquamaids

1995 Becky Dyroen-Lancer, Jill Sudduth, Santa Clara Aquamaids

1996 Becky Dyroen-Lancer, Jill Sudduth, Santa Clara Aquamaids

1997 Anna Kozlova, Charlotte Massardier, Santa Clara Aquamaids

1998 Kristina Lum, Bill May, Santa Clara Aquamaids

| | |
|---|---|
| 1999 Anna Kozlova, Tuesday Middaugh, Santa Clara Aquamaids | 2002 Kristina Lum, Bill May, Santa Clara Aquamaids |
| 2000 Kristina Lum, Bill May, Santa Clara Aquamaids | 2003 Kristina Lum, Bill May, Santa Clara Aquamaids |
| 2001 Anna Kozlova, Bill May, Santa Clara Aquamaids | 2004 Bianca VanderVelden, Sonja VanderVelden, Santa Clara Aquamaids |

## SENIOR NATIONAL TRIO CHAMPIONS 1984–1990

| | |
|---|---|
| 1984 Kristen Babb, Michelle Svitenko, Kim Stanley, Walnut Creek Aquanuts | 1988 Karen Josephson, Sarah Josephson, Lisa Riddell, Walnut Creek Aquanuts |
| 1985 Julie Olsen, Lisa Riddell, Mary Visniski, Walnut Creek Aquanuts | 1989 Lori Dickie, Lori Hatch, Robin Roberts, Santa Clara Aquamaids |
| 1986 Tracy Long, Lisa Riddell, Mary Visniski, Walnut Creek Aquanuts | 1990 Karen Josephson, Sarah Josephson, Nadine Bekker, Walnut Creek Aquanuts |
| 1987 Karen Josephson, Sarah Josephson, Lisa Riddell, Walnut Creek Aquanuts | 1991 *event discontinued* |

## SENIOR NATIONAL TEAM CHAMPIONS, 1946–2004

1946 O. Chicago Town Club: Shirley Brown, Phyllis Burrell, Priscilla Hirsch, Audrey Huettenrauch, Marion Mittlacher, Polly Wesner, Nancy Hanna, Doris Dieskow

1947 I. McFadden-Deauville, FL: B. Covington, Jean Fitzsimmons, Joy Fitzsimmons, D. Freeman, P. Freeman, M. Mountcastle, P. Gray, D. Williams

O. Chicago Town Club: Doris Dieskow, Marion Mittlacher, Priscilla Hirsch, Audrey Huettenrauch, Shirley Brown, Phyllis Burrell, Billie Voelker, Rosemarie Voelker

1948 I. St. Clair Synchronettes: Marilyn Stanley, Connie Todoroff, Alice Micus, Shirley Simpson, Ellen Richard

O. St. Clair Synchronettes: Marilyn Stanley, Alice Micus, Shirley Simpson, Doris Mitman, Connie Todoroff

1949 I. St. Clair Synchronettes: Marilyn Stanley, Connie Todoroff, Shirley Simpson, Ellen Richard

O. St. Clair Synchronettes: Marilyn Stanley, Connie Todoroff, Alice Micus, Shirley Simpson, Doris Mitman

1950 I. St. Clair Synchronettes: Marilyn Stanley, Connie Todoroff, Shirley Simpson, Ellen Richard

O. St. Clair Synchronettes: Shirley Simpson, Connie Todoroff, Ellen Richard, Marilyn Stanley

1951 I. KRNT Des Moines: Joanne Speer, Carla Courter, Barbara Springate, Jean Grossman

O. St. Clair Synchronettes: Shirley Simpson, Connie Todoroff, Ellen Richard, Laurine Stocking

1952 I. KRNT Des Moines: Joanne Speer, Carla Courter, Marilyn Adams, Karen Adams

O. Athens Club, Oakland: Dawn Pawson Bean, Joan Pawson, Lynn Pawson, Sally Phillips

1953 I. Athens Club, Oakland: Dawn Pawson Bean, Joan Pawson, Lynn Pawson, Sally Phillips

O. Peterborough, Canada*: J. Craig, N. Nonks, J. Lynch, B. Welch, D. Bristow, N. Douglas, N. Doubt, S. Moldver, I. Reilly, E. Humphries, J. Russele, T. Carey

Athens Club, Oakland: Dawn Pawson Bean, Joan Pawson, Lynn Pawson, Sally Phillips

1954 I. Athens Club, Oakland: Joan Pawson, Lynn Pawson, Loretta Barrious, Sally Phillips

O. Athens Club, Oakland: Lynn Pawson, Joan Pawson, Sally Phillips, Loretta Barrious

1955 I. Athens Club, Oakland: Loretta Barrious, Dawn Pawson Bean, Joan Pawson, Lynn Pawson, Sally Phillips

O. Athens Club, Oakland: Loretta Barrious, Dawn Pawson Bean, Joan Pawson, Lynn Pawson, Sally Phillips

1956 I. Athens Club, Oakland: Janet Anthony, Loretta Barrious, Joanne Berthelsen, Jackie Brown, Joanne Brobst, Evie Oremus, Lynn Pawson, June Schiele

*honorary

O. Athens Club, Oakland: Janet Anthony, Loretta Barrious, Joanne Berthelsen, Jackie Brown, Joanne Brobst, Evie Oremus, Lynn Pawson, June Schiele

1957 I. Athens Club, Oakland: Lynn Pawson, Joan Pawson, Janet Anthony, Loretta Barrious

O. Athens Club, Oakland: Lynn Pawson, Loretta Barrious, Joanne Brobst, Jackie Vargas, Janet Anthony

1958 I. Athens Club, Oakland: Lynn Pawson, Loretta Barrious, Janet Anthony, Sue Lawrence, Jackie Vargas

O. Athens Club, Oakland: Lynn Pawson, Loretta Barrious, Janet Anthony, Jackie Vargas, Sue Lawrence

1959 I. Athens Club, Oakland: Janet Anthony, Joanne Brobst, Sharon Gray, Sue Lawrence, Jackie Vargas

O. Athens Club, Oakland: Janet Anthony, Joanne Brobst, Sharon Gray, Jackie Vargas, Sue Lawrence

1960 I. Athens Club, Oakland: Janet Anthony, Loretta Barrious, Sharon Gray, Sue Lawrence, Jackie Vargas

O. Athens Club, Oakland: Janet Anthony, Loretta Barrious, Sharon Gray, Sue Lawrence, Jackie Vargas

1961 I. San Francisco Merionettes: Margaret Durbrow, Claire Vida, Sharon Hood, Phyllis Firman, Louella Sommers

O. San Francisco Merionettes: Sharon Hood, Phyllis Firman, Margaret Durbrow, Louella Sommers, Claire Vida

1962 I. San Francisco Merionettes: Margaret Durbrow, Phyllis Firman, Claire Vida, Judy Wejak, Pat Kelly, Louella Sommers

O. San Francisco Merionettes: Margaret Durbrow, Phyllis Firman, Claire Vida, Judy Wejak, Pat Kelly, Louella Sommers

1963 I. San Francisco Merionettes: Margaret Durbrow, Pat Kelly, Karen Marwedel, Pam Morris, Claire Vida, Patty Willard, Judy Wejak, Mary Wybrow

O. San Francisco Merionettes: Margaret Durbrow, Pat Kelly, Pam Morris, Karen Marwedel, Mary Wybrow, Claire Vida, Patty Willard, Judy Wejak

1964 I. San Francisco Merionettes: Margaret Durbrow, Rhea Irvine, Margo McGrath, Patsy Mical, Pam Morris, Claire Vida, Patty Willard

O. San Francisco Merionettes: Margaret Durbrow, Rhea Irvine, Margo McGrath, Patsy Mical, Pam Morris, Claire Vida, Patty Willard

1965 I. San Francisco Merionettes: Rhea Irvine, Sharon Lawson, Pam Morris, Kathy McBride, Margo McGrath, Carol Redmond, Patsy Mical, Patty Willard

O. San Francisco Merionettes: Rhea Irvine, Sharon Lawson, Pam Morris, Kathy McBride, Margo McGrath, Patsy Mical, Carol Redmond, Patty Willard

1966 I. San Francisco Merionettes: Kathy Bryant, Sharon Lawson, Kathy McBride, Margo McGrath, Carol Redmond, Andrea Welles

O. San Francisco Merionettes: Kathy Bryant, Sharon Lawson, Kathy McBride, Margo McGrath, Carol Redmond, Andrea Welles

1967 I. San Francisco Merionettes: Kathy Bryant, Norma Fish, Sharon Lawson, Kathy McBride, Margo McGrath, Carol Redmond, Andrea Welles, Bede Trantina

O. San Francisco Merionettes: Kathy Bryant, Andrea Welles, Sharon Lawson, Kathy McBride, Margo McGrath, Carol Redmond, Barbara Trantina, Norma Fish

1968 I. Santa Clara Aquamaids: Pam Albin, Kathy Craig, Nancy Hines, Dianne Howell, Carol Reynolds, Melinda Sellers, Kim Welshons, Kris Welshons

O. Santa Clara Aquamaids: Pam Albin, Cathy Craig, Nancy Hines, Dianne Howell, Carol Reynolds, Melinda Sellers, Kim Welshons, Kris Welshons

1969 I. Santa Clara Aquamaids: Pam Albin, Teresa Andersen, Kathy Bryant, Nancy Hines, Gail Johnson, Carol Reynolds, Kim Welshons, Kris Welshons

O. Santa Clara Aquamaids: Pam Albin, Teresa Andersen, Kathy Bryant, Nancy Hines, Gail Johnson, Carol Reynolds, Kim Welshons, Kris Welshons

1970 I. San Francisco Merionettes: Barbara Cooney, Lona Gallagher, Chris Jeffers, Joan Lang, Barbara Trantina, Amy Miner, Sue Morris, Heidi O'Rourke

O. Santa Clara Aquamaids: Charlotte Jennings, Diane Smith, Teresa Andersen, Nancy Hines, Jackie Douglass, Gail Johnson, Kathy Graham, Carol Reynolds

1971 I. San Francisco Merionettes: Cinny Anderson, Barbara Cooney, Chris Jeffers, Kathy Kretschmer, Joan Lang, Amy Miner, Sue Morris, Heidi O'Rourke

O. San Francisco Merionettes: Cinny Anderson, Chris Jeffers, Barbara Cooney, Kathy Kretschmer, Joan Lang, Amy Miner, Sue Morris, Heidi O'Rourke

1972 I. Santa Clara Aquamaids: Jackie Douglass, Amanda Norrish, Robin Curren, Gail Gardner, Kim Gonterman, Gail Johnson, Teresa Andersen, Kathy Graham

O. Santa Clara Aquamaids: Teresa Andersen, Jackie Douglass, Robin Curren, Gail Gardner, Kim Gonterman, Gail Johnson, Kathy Graham, Amanda Norrish

1973  I.  Santa Clara Aquamaids: Teresa Andersen, Sue Baross, Dana Moore, Robin Curren, Jackie Douglass, Amanda Norrish, Gail Johnson, Suzanne Randell
      O.  Santa Clara Aquamaids: Teresa Andersen, Jackie Douglas, Suzanne Randell, Sue Baross, Robin Curren, Gail Johnson, Amanda Norrish, Dana Moore
1974  I.  Santa Clara Aquamaids: Sue Baross, Robin Curren, Dana Moore, Gail Johnson, Amanda Norrish, Suzanne Randell, Michele Barone, Pam Tryon
      O.  Santa Clara Aquamaids: Sue Baross, Robin Curren, Michele Barone, Gail Johnson, Dana Moore, Pam Tryon, Suzanne Randell, Amanda Norrish
1975  I.  Santa Clara Aquamaids: Sue Baross, Robin Curren, Gail Johnson, Michele Barone, Mary Ellen Longo, Pam Tryon, Amanda Norrish, Linda Shelley
      O.  Santa Clara Aquamaids: Sue Baross, Robin Curren, Gail Johnson, Michele Barone, Mary Ellen Longo, Pam Tryon, Amanda Norrish, Linda Shelley
1976  I.  Santa Clara Aquamaids: Sue Baross, Michele Barone, Tami Allen, Michelle Beaulieu, Gerri Brandley, Linda Shelley, Pam Tryon, Jane Goeppinger
      O.  Santa Clara Aquamaids: Sue Baross, Michele Barone, Robin Curren, Michelle Beaulieu, Amanda Norrish, Pam Tryon, Linda Shelley, Jennifer Rich
1977  I.  Santa Clara Aquamaids: Tami Allen, Michele Barone, Sue Baross, Michelle Beaulieu, Gerri Brandley, Jane Goeppinger, Linda Shelley, Pam Tryon
      O.  Santa Clara Aquamaids: Tami Allen, Michele Barone, Sue Baross, Gerri Brandley, Jane Goeppinger, Michelle Beaulieu, Linda Shelley, Pam Tryon
1978  I.  Santa Clara Aquamaids: Michele Barone, Linda Shelley, Erin Barr, Jane Goeppinger, Gerri Brandley, Michelle Beaulieu, Pam Tryon, Tami Allen
      O.  Santa Clara Aquamaids: Michele Barone, Linda Shelley, Erin Barr, Jane Goeppinger, Gerri Brandley, Michelle Beaulieu, Pam Tryon, Tami Allen
1979  I.  Santa Clara Aquamaids: Tami Allen, Michele Barone, Kathy Kish, Suzanne Cameron, Becky Price, Linda Shelley, Holly Spencer
      O.  Santa Clara Aquamaids: Tami Allen, Michele Barone, Suzanne Cameron, Kathy Kish, Becky Price, Linda Shelley, Holly Spencer

*Indoor/Outdoor discontinued; one championship per year beginning in 1980.*

1980  Walnut Creek Aquanuts: Monica Mendenhall, Julie Olsen, Jill Van Dalen, Becky Roy, Mary Visniski, Marie White, Sara White
1981  Walnut Creek Aquanuts: Lisa Babb, Julie Olsen, Mary Visniski, Monica Mendenhall, Becky Roy, Marie White, Sara White, Kim Stanley
1982  Walnut Creek Aquanuts: Tara Cameron, Mary Visniski, Becky Roy, Lisa Babb, Julie Olsen, Kim Stanley, Marie White, Sara White
1983  Walnut Creek Aquanuts: Lisa Babb, Ginnylee Roderick, Julie Olsen, Kim Stanley, Becky Roy, Mary Visniski, Marie White, Sara White
1984  Walnut Creek Aquanuts: Kristen Babb, Lisa Babb, Julie Olsen, Ginnylee Roderick, Holly Spencer, Kim Stanley, Michelle Svitenko, Mary Visniski
1985  Walnut Creek Aquanuts: Kristen Babb, Lisa Babb, Tracy Long, Julie Olsen, Susan Reed, Lisa Riddell, Michelle Svitenko, Mary Visniski
1986  Walnut Creek Aquanuts: Kristen Babb, Tracy Long, Susan Reed, Karen Josephson, Sarah Josephson, Lisa Riddell, Michelle Svitenko, Mary Visniski
1987  Walnut Creek Aquanuts: Kristen Babb, Karen Josephson, Sarah Josephson, Tracy Long, Susan Reed, Nathalie Schneyder, Lisa Riddell, Michelle Svitenko
1988  Walnut Creek Aquanuts: Kristen Babb, Karen Josephson, Sarah Josephson, Tracy Long, Susan Reed, Nathalie Schneyder, Lisa Riddell, Michelle Svitenko
1989  Walnut Creek Aquanuts: Kristen Babb, Mikako Kotani, Tracy Long, Lori McCoy, Susan Reed, Jill Savery, Nathalie Schneyder, Michelle Svitenko
1990  Santa Clara Aquamaids: Becky Dyroen, Suzannah Dyroen, Natasha Haynes, Patti Lynn, Laurie Martin, Anna Miller, Heather Simmons, Jill Sudduth
1991  Walnut Creek Aquanuts: Kristen Babb-Sprague, Margot Thien, Karen Josephson, Sarah Josephson, Laurie McClelland, Jill Savery, Nathalie Schneyder, Michelle Svitenko
1992  Walnut Creek Aquanuts: Kristen Babb-Sprague, Margot Thien, Karen Josephson, Sarah Josephson, Jenny Ohanesian, Laurie McClelland, Jill Savery, Nathalie Schneyder
1993  Santa Clara Aquamaids: Suzannah Dyroen, Becky Dyroen-Lancer, Kari Kreitzer, Heather Simmons, Jenny Mayer, Jill Sudduth, Janet Wiecking, Mary Wodka
1994  Santa Clara Aquamaids: Suzannah Dyroen, Becky Dyroen-Lancer, Anna Kozlova, Jenny Mayer, Kari Kreitzer, Heather Simmons, Jill Sudduth, Mary Wodka

1995  Santa Clara Aquamaids: Suzannah Dyroen, Becky Dyroen-Lancer, Anna Kozlova, Kari Kreitzer, Jenny Mayer, Heather Simmons, Jill Sudduth, Mary Wodka

1996  Santa Clara Aquamaids: Carrie Barton, Bridget Finn, Anna Kozlova, Kari Kreitzer, Kristina Lum, Elicia Marshall, Alanna O'Leary, Kim Wurzel

1997  Santa Clara Aquamaids: Carrie Barton, Bridget Finn, Anna Kozlova, Kristina Lum, Elicia Marshall, Charlotte Massardier, Tuesday Middaugh, Alanna O'Leary

1998  Santa Clara Aquamaids: Carrie Barton, Kara Duncan, Bridget Finn, Anna Kozlova, Kristina Lum, Elicia Marshall, Bill May, Tuesday Middaugh

1999  Santa Clara Aquamaids: Carrie Barton, Kara Duncan, Bridget Finn, Anna Kozlova, Kristina Lum, Elicia Marshall, Bill May, Kim Wurzel

2000  Santa Clara Aquamaids: Alison Bartosik, Kara Duncan, Sara Lowe, Becky Martin, Bill May, Lauren McFall, Andrea Nott, Stacey Scott, Vanessa Shaw, Kendra Zanotto

2001  Santa Clara Aquamaids: Allison Bartosik, Kara Duncan, Sara Lowe, Becky Martin, Bill May, Lauren McFall, Andrea Nott, Stacey Scott, Vanessa Shaw

2002  Santa Clara Aquamaids: Allison Bartosik, Anna Kozlova, Sara Lowe, Becky Martin, Bill May, Lauren McFall, Andrea Nott, Kendra Zanotto

2003  Santa Clara Aquamaids: Lidia Birukova, Janet Culp, Jennie Culp, Christina Jones, Kim McKinley, Alicia Rice, Bianca VanderVelden, Sonja VanderVelden

2004  Santa Clara Aquamaids: Janet Culp, Jeannie Culp, Christina Jones, Kim McKinley, Andrea Nott, Alicia Rice, Bianca VandeVelden, Sonja VanderVelden

## COLLEGIATE NATIONAL SOLO CHAMPIONS
### 1977–2004

| | | | |
|---|---|---|---|
| 1977 | Sue Flanders, Ohio State University | 1991 | Maria Guisti, Ohio State University |
| 1978 | Linda Shelley, San Jose State University | 1992 | Emily Porter, Arizona State University |
| 1979 | Pam Tryon, University of Arizona | 1993 | Emily Porter, Arizona State University |
| 1980 | Pam Tryon, University of Arizona | 1994 | Jill Savery, University of Ca., Berkeley |
| 1981 | Tara Cameron, Ohio State University | 1995 | Jenny Mayer, San Jose State University |
| 1982 | Tracie Ruiz, University of Arizona | 1996 | Bridget Finn, Stanford University |
| 1983 | Julie Olsen, University of Arizona | 1997 | Heather Pease, Stanford University |
| 1984 | Sarah Josephson, Ohio State University | 1998 | Heather Pease, Stanford University |
| 1985 | Karen Josephson, Ohio State University | 1999 | Vanessa Shaw, Stanford University |
| 1986 | Lori Donn, University of Arizona | 2000 | Shannon Montague, Stanford University |
| 1987 | Ana Amicarella, Ohio State University | 2001 | Carolina Moraes, Ohio State University |
| 1988 | Ginny Cohn, Stanford University | 2002 | Carolina Moraes, Ohio State University |
| 1989 | Maria Guisti, Ohio State University | 2003 | Katie Norris, Stanford University |
| 1990 | Karen Madsen, Stanford University | 2004 | Katie Norris, Stanford University |

## COLLEGIATE NATIONAL DUET CHAMPIONS
### 1977–2004

| | | | |
|---|---|---|---|
| 1977 | Cory Lamb, Cindy Ott, Ohio State University | 1983 | Karen Josephson, Sarah Josephson, Ohio State University |
| 1978 | Cory Lamb, Cindy Ott, Ohio State University | 1984 | Karen Josephson, Sarah Josephson, Ohio State University |
| 1979 | Marie White, Sara White, University of Arizona | 1985 | Karen Josephson, Sarah Josephson, Ohio State University |
| 1980 | Tara Cameron, Karen Callaghan, Ohio State University | 1986 | Karen Brinkman, Lori Donn, University of Arizona |
| 1981 | Julie Olsen, Becky Roy, University of Arizona | 1987 | Dee Cohen, Ruth Weinberg, Stanford University |
| 1982 | Candy Costie, Tracie Ruiz, University of Arizona | 1988 | Cathy Cramer, Jessica Hudacek, Ohio State University |

1989 Dee Cohen, Karen Madsen, Stanford University

1990 Maria Guisti, Cheryl Schemenauer, Ohio State University

1991 Carrie DeGuerre, Maria Guisti, Ohio State University

1992 Carrie DeGuerre, Kim Oschner, Ohio State University

1993 Carrie DeGuerre, Kim Oschner, Ohio State University

1994 Jill Savery, Margot Thien, University of California–Berkeley

1995 Becky Jasontek, Emily Marsh, Ohio State University

1996 Becky Jasontek, Emily Marsh, Ohio State University

1997 Becky Jasontek, Emily Marsh, Ohio State University

1998 Heather Pease, Vanessa Shaw, Stanford University

1999 Carolina Moraes, Isabela Moraes, Ohio State University

2000 Carolina Moraes, Isabela Moraes, Ohio State University

2001 Carolina Moraes, Isabela Moraes, Ohio State University

2002 Carolina Moraes, Isabela Moraes, Ohio State University

2003 Suzanna Hyatt, Chelsea Luker, Ohio State University

2004 Kate Hooven, Becky Kim, Ohio State University

## COLLEGIATE NATIONAL TRIO CHAMPIONS
### 1977–2004

1977 Cory Lamb, Cindy Ott, Jill Vincent, Ohio State University

1978 Cory Lamb, Cindy Ott, Jill Vincent, Ohio State University

1979 Michele Beaulieu, Gerri Brandley, Marie White, University of Arizona

1980 Karen Callaghan, Tara Cameron, Janet Tope, Ohio State University

1981 Julie Olsen, Becky Roy, Pam Tryon, University of Arizona

1982 Karen Callaghan, Karen Josephson, Sarah Josephson, Ohio State University

1983 Manon Cote, Karen Josephson, Sarah Josephson, Ohio State University

1984 Lori Donn, Kathy Kish, Julie Olsen, University of Arizona

1985 Manon Cote, Karen Josephson, Sarah Josephson, Ohio State University

1986 Karen Miele, Adrienne Lehman, Betsy Visniski, Ohio State University

1987 Cathy Cramer, Ann Brown, Jessica Hudacek, Ohio State University

1988 Cathy Cramer, Jessica Hudacek, Tammy Hunt, Ohio State University

1989 Dee Cohen, Melinda Downey, Karen Madsen, Stanford University

1990 Amy Pryor, Maria Guisti, Cheryl Schemenauer, Ohio State University

1991 Carrie DeGuerre, Tia Harding, Diana Ulrich, Ohio State University

1992 Jenny Dunn, Carrie DeGuerre, Kim Oschner, Ohio State University

1993 Jenny Dunn, Carrie DeGuerre, Kim Ochsner, Ohio State University

1994 Jill Savery, Margot Thien, Tina Kasid, University of California–Berkeley

1995 Becky Jasontek, Emily Marsh, Sadie Pietras, Ohio State University

1996 Becky Jasontek, Emily Marsh, Sadie Pietras, Ohio State University

1997 Bridget Finn, Heather Pease, Vanessa Shaw, Stanford University

1998 Heather Pease, Shannon Montague, Vanessa Shaw, Stanford University

1999 Mary Hofer, Isabela Moraes, Carolina Moraes, Ohio State University

2000 Mary Hofer, Isabela Moraes, Carolina Moraes, Ohio State University

2001 Mary Hofer, Isabela Moraes, Carolina Moraes, Ohio State University

2002 Mary Hofer, Isabela Moraes, Carolina Moraes, Ohio State University

2003 Stephanie Joukoff, Jennifer Kibler, Ashley McHugh, Stanford University

2004 Kate Hooven, Becky Kim, Lindsay Newbill, Ohio State University

## COLLEGIATE NATIONAL TEAM CHAMPIONS
### 1977–2004

1977   Ohio State University: Cindy Ott, Joan Marie Barris, Terry Edwards, Heather Bruce, Jane McGorrum, Donna Burrian, Cory Lamb, Jill Vincent

1978   Ohio State University: Heather Bruce, Kerrie Hein, Martha Boss, Laurette Longmire, Myfanwy Borel, Jill Vincent, Cory Lamb, Cindy Ott

1979   Ohio State University: Myfanwy Borel, Karen Callaghan, Tara Cameron, Dawn Nelson, Cindy Ott, Kathy Rankin, Luanne Saas, Jill Vincent

1980   Ohio State University: Myfanwy Borel, Karen Callaghan, Tara Cameron, Dawn Nelson, Kathy Rankin, Carrie Ruehl, Janet Tope, Jill Vincent

1981   Ohio State University: Myfanwy Borel, Karen Callaghan, Tara Cameron, Kathy Rankin, Dawn Nelson, Carrie Ruehl, Janet Tope, Marie White

1982   Ohio State University: Karen Callaghan, Manon Cote, Karen Josephson, Sarah Josephson, Dawn Nelsen, Chare Muth, Luanne Saas, Holly Vargo

1983   University of Arizona: Becky Roy, Julie Olsen, Kathy Kish, Lori Donn, Alice Smith, Margarita Smith, Tammy Kay

1984   University of Arizona: Eileen Daily, Lori Donn, Christy Foster, Missy Ihrig, Kathy Kish, Julie Olsen, Alice Smith, Margarita Smith

1985   University of Arizona: Eileen Daily, Lori Donn, Christy Foster, Laura Fowler, Lori Hatch, Missy Ihrig, Margarita Smith, Alice Smith

1986   Ohio State University: Ana Amicarella, Kathy Augenstein, Cathy Cramer, Adrienne Lehman, Karen Miele, Anne Schulte, Betsy Visniski, Kathy Zittel

1987   Ohio State University: Ana Amicarella, Cathy Cramer, Tammy Hunt, Jessica Hudacek, Tanya Hybl, Denise Sawicki, Anne Schulte, Kathy Zittel

1988   Ohio State University: Cathy Cramer, Jessica Hudacek, Tammy Hunt, Kristin Eakin, Cheryl Schemenauer, Diana Ulrich, Amy Pryor, Denise Sawicki

1989   Ohio State University: Kristin Eakin, Tia Harding, Jessica Hudacek, Tammy Hunt, Amy Pryor, Diana Ulrich, Cheryl Schemenauer, Cheryl Wiegand

1990   Ohio State University: Kristin Eakin, Maria Guisti, Tia Harding, Tammy Hunt, Amy Pryor, Cheryl Schemenauer, Diana Ulrich, Cheryl Wiegand

1991   Ohio State University: Carrie DeGuerre, Sue Ha, Tia Harding, Maria Guisti, Kim Ochsner, Amy Pryor, Jennie Sprague, Diana Ulrich

1992   Ohio State University: Jenny Dunn, Carrie DeGuerre, Julie Jasontek, Shea Tanabe, Heather Roda, Kim Ochsner, Jenny Sprague, Sandra Valles

1993   Ohio State University: Carrie DeGuerre, Jenny Dunn, Kim Ochsner, Sadie Pietras, Kirsten Reno, Heather Roda, Jenny Sprague, Shea Tanabe

1994   Ohio State University: Carrie DeGuerre, Becky Jasontek, Emily Marsh, Pam Ochsner, Gina Pietras, Sadie Pietras, Chris Bober, Heather Roda

1995   Ohio State University: Christie Bober, Ana Cukie, Becky Jasontek, Emily Marsh, Pam Oschner, Erin Olson, Gina Pietras, Sadie Pietras

1996   Ohio State University: Christie Bober, Ana Cukie, Becky Jasontek, Emily Marsh, Pam Oschner, Erin Olson, Gina Pietras, Sadie Pietras

1997   Ohio State University: Christie Bober, Anna Cukie, Becky Jasontek, Emily Marsh, Pam Ochsner, Erin Olson, Gina Pietras

1998   Ohio State University: Anna Cukie, Katie Edwards, Stephanie Johnson, Dennise Martinez, Andrea McGirr, Heather Moore, Lisa Nielsen, Joy Williams

1999   Stanford University: Julie Enos, Paige Freiheit, Emi Kanayama, Shannon Montague, Vanessa Shaw, Lindsey Wiggington, Kristi Wright

2000   Ohio State University: Alia Arbas, Victoria Bowen, Katie Edwards, Tarin Forbes, Mary Hofer, Beth Kreimer, Heather Moore, Carolina Moraes, Isabela Moraes, Kristen Price

2001   Ohio State University: Victoria Bowen, Katie Edwards, Mary Hofer, Suzannah Hyatt, Beth Kreimer, Anna Eng, Isabela Moraes, Kristin Price

2002   Ohio State University: Victoria Bowen, Mary Hofer, Suzannah Hyatt, Beth Kreimer, Kim Lester, Lauren Marsh, Isabela Moraes, Kristen Price

2003   Ohio State University: Victoria Bowen, Heather Burdick, Carly Grimshaw, Suzannah Hyatt, Chelsea Luker, Lauren Marsh, Lindsay Newbill, Emiko Takyu

2004   Ohio State University: Carly Grimshaw, Heather Burdick, Kate Hooven, Becky Kim, Chelsea Luker, Lauren March, Lindsay Newbill, Chisako Ukai

## Junior National Solo Champions
## 1951–2004

1951  I.  Joan Fogerty, Arrowhead Springs
1952  I.  Nancy Wallace, Athens Athletic Club, Oakland
      O.  Marjorie Repass, Corkettes of Houston, TX
1953  I.  Joanne Millin, San Francisco Crystal Pool
      O.  Rosalind Calcaterra, Shaw Park, St. Louis, MO
1954  I.  Joanne Royer, Riverside Aquettes
      O.  Lorraine Muzenski, Unattached, Newark, NJ
      Men  Bert Hubbard, Detroit City Club
1955  I.  Elizabeth Sunbarger, Corkettes of Houston, TX
      O.  Gretchen Lechner, Berea Aquateens, OH
1956  I.  Tony Stewart, Unattached, Chicago, IL
      O.  Mary Anne Teague, Corkettes of Houston, TX
1957  I.  Dolores Lardieri, Newark Aquabelles, NJ
      O.  Gillian Hall, Bristol Girls Club, CT
1958  I.  Sue Ann Hammel, Unattached, Dayton, OH
      O.  Jill Harms, New Providence, NJ
1959  I.  Paula Bonnier, Detroit Park & Recreation
      O.  Rosemary Ueckert, Corkettes of Houston, TX
1960  I.  Barbara Burke, University Club, Hollywood
      O.  Marcia Blixt, Oakland Naiads
1961  I.  Joanne Schaack, University Club, Hollywood
      O.  Linda Jones, Corkettes of Houston, TX
1962  I.  Nancy Stapenhorst, Shaw Park St. Louis, MO
      O.  Louella Sommers, San Francisco Merionettes
1963  I.  Jan Kupferer, Shaw Park St. Louis, MO
      O.  Vicki Barnhouse, Columbus Coralina, OH
1964  I.  Pam Morris, San Francisco Merionettes
      O.  Patty Willard, San Francisco Merionettes
1965  I.  Nancy Hines, Columbus Coralina, OH
      O.  Kim Welshons, Santa Clara Aquamaids
1966  I.  Jackie Lyle, KRNT Des Moines,
      O.  Dianne Howell, Howell Swim Club
1967  I.  Kathy Kretschmer, Dayton Aquanymphs, OH
      O.  Norma Fish, San Francisco Merionettes
1968  I.  Kris Welshons, Santa Clara Aquamaids
      O.  Kathy Bryant, Unattached, San Francisco
1969  I.  Barbara Trantina, San Francisco Merionettes
      O.  Heidi O'Rourke, San Francisco Merionettes

1970  I.  Carol Reynolds, Santa Clara Aquamaids
      O.  Gail Johnson, Santa Clara Aquamaids
1971  I.  Joan Lang, San Francisco Merionettes
      O.  Teresa Andersen, Santa Clara Aquamaids
1972  I.  Gina Childers, Glendale Swim Club
      O.  Jackie Douglass, Santa Clara Aquamaids
1973  I.  Karen Morris, San Francisco Merionettes
      O.  Amy Miner, San Francisco Merionettes
1974  I.  Amanda Norrish, Santa Clara Aquamaids
      O.  Robin Curren, Santa Clara Aquamaids
1975  I.  Sherry Taylor, Cygnets San Antonio, TX
      O.  Sue Baross, Santa Clara Aquamaids
1976  I.  Michele Barone, Santa Clara Aquamaids
      O.  Pam Tryon, Santa Clara Aquamaids
1977  I.  Michelle Beaulieu, Santa Clara Aquamaids
      O.  Linda Shelley, Santa Clara Aquamaids
1978  I.  Cynthia Engle, California Coralettes
      O.  Gerri Brandley, Santa Clara Aquamaids
1979  I.  Brenda Florio, Hamden Heronettes, CT
      O.  Candy Costie, Seattle Aqua Club
1980  I.  Tracie Ruiz, Seattle Aqua Club
      O.  Becky Roy, Walnut Creek Aquanuts
1981  I.  Robin Waller, Meraquas Irvine
      O.  Sarah Josephson, Hamden Heronettes, CT
1982  I.  Mary Visniski, Walnut Creek Aquanuts
      O.  Lea Bean, Meraquas Irvine
1983  I.  Holly Spencer, Seattle Aqua Club
      O.  Lisa Babb, Walnut Creek Aquanuts
1984  I.  Karen Josephson, Ohio State University
      O.  Kim Stanley, Walnut Creek Aquanuts
1985  I.  Kristen Babb, Walnut Creek Aquanuts
      O.  Patti Lynn, Santa Clara Aquamaids
1986  I.  Susan Reed, Walnut Creek Aquanuts
      O.  Tracy Long, Walnut Creek Aquanuts
1987  I.  Lisa Riddell, Walnut Creek Aquanuts
      O.  Betsy Visniski, Ohio State University
1988  I.  Karen Madsen, Santa Clara Aquamaids
      O.  Heather Simmons, Santa Clara Aquamaids
1989  I.  Michelle Svitenko, Walnut Creek Aquanuts
      O.  Janet Wiecking, Briarwood Anemones, VA
1990  I.  Nathalie Schneyder, Walnut Creek Aquanuts
      O.  Amy Pryor, Ohio State University

*Indoor/Outdoor discontinued; one championship per year beginning in 1991.*

1991   Emily Porter, Arizona Aquastars, AZ
1992   Tammy Cleland, Walnut Creek Aquanuts

| 1993 | Becky Jasontek, Cincinnati Synchrogators, OH |
| 1994 | Emily Marsh, Ohio State University |
| 1995 | Alanna O'Leary, Santa Clara Aquamaids |
| 1996 | Alanna O'Leary, Santa Clara Aquamaids |
| 1997 | Lauren McFall, Santa Clara Aquamaids |
| 1998 | Becky Martin, Santa Clara Aquamaids |

| 1999 | Becky Martin, Santa Clara Aquamaids |
| 2000 | Katie Norris, Tallahassee Serinas, FL |
| 2001 | Alison Bartosik, Santa Clara Aquamaids |
| 2002 | Sara Lowe, Santa Clara Aquamaids |
| 2003 | Barbara Nesbitt, Riverside Aquettes |
| 2004 | Christina Jones, Santa Clara Aquamaids |

## JUNIOR NATIONAL DUET CHAMPIONS
### 1947–2004

1947 O. Lou Schleicher, Ruth Burden, Detroit Aqua-Gals

1948 I. Jean Millard, Iris Reilly, Peterborough, Canada

1949 I. Shirley Simpson, Connie Todoroff, St. Clair Synchronettes

Men Lee Embrey, Bert Hubbard, City Club Detroit

1950 I. Lynne Laue, Carol Nedler, Chicago Town Club, IL

1951 *Not held*

1952 I. Joan Pawson, Lynn Pawson, Athens Club, Oakland

O. Marjorie Repass, Barbara Wilder, Corkettes of Houston, TX

1953 I. Judy Elliott, Maureen O'Connell, St. Clair Synchronettes

1953 O. Paula Bonnier, Pat Chapp, Detroit Park & Recreation

1954 I. Maureen Jordan, Carol Jordan, St. Clair Synchronettes

O. Loretta Barrious, Sally Phillips, Athens Club, Oakland

Men Lee Embrey, Bert Hubbard, Detroit City Club

1955 I. Elizabeth Sunbarger, Laura Payne, Corkettes of Houston, TX

O. Jackie Vargas, Marlene Marshall, Oakland Sea Sirens

1956 I. Benelle Scott, Jean King, Michigan State University

O. Kathy Brooks, Gretchen Lechner, Berea Aquateens, OH

1957 I. Peggy Howard, Doris Payne, Corkettes of Houston, TX

O. Pat Green, Sue Lawrence, Athens Club, Oakland

1958 I. Kayda Zavita, Sue Smith, Lansing Sea Sprites

O. Sharon Dean, Lynn Kristic, Oakland Naiads

1959 I. Pat Heitger, Carol Swanson, Columbus Coralina, OH

O. Gillian Hall, Dayle Benson, Bristol Synchronettes, CT

1960 I. Diana Nelson, Jan Waters, KRNT Des Moines

O. Beth Browning, Linda Jones, Corkettes of Houston, TX

1961 I. Sharon Hood, Claire Vida, San Francisco Merionettes

O. Barbara Burke, Joanne Schaack, University Club Hollywood

1962 I. Vicki Barnhouse, Teri Heitger, Columbus Coralina, OH

O. Jan Kupferer, Nancy Stapenhorst, Shaw Park St. Louis, MO

1963 I. Patsy Kelly, Mary Whybrow, San Francisco Merionettes

O. Mary Jo Capps, Liz Wells, Shaw Park St. Louis, MO

1964 I. Kathy Craig, Debbie Howell, Howell Swim Club

O. Margaret Durbrow, Patty Willard, San Francisco Merionettes

1965 I. Pam Albin, Barbara Shervanick, Riverside Aquettes

O. Margo McGrath, Carol Redmond, San Francisco Merionettes

1966 I. Dianne Howell, Melinda Sellers, Danville Howell Swim

O. Nancy Hines, Kim Welshons, Santa Clara Aquamaids

1967 I. Norma Fish, Sharon Lawson, San Francisco Merionettes

O. Kim Gonterman, Sherrill Gonterman, Shaw Park St. Louis, MO

1968 I. Charlotte Jennings, Diann Smith, Washington Athletic Club Seattle, WA

O. Joan Lang, Barbara Trantina, San Francisco Merionettes

1969 I. Kathy Bryant, Kris Welshons, Santa Clara Aquamaids

O. Angie Taylor, Betsy Hart, Cygnets of San Antonio, TX

1970 I. Teresa Andersen, Gail Johnson, Santa Clara Aquamaids

O. Nancy Doyle, Kathy Jansen, Cygnets of San Antonio, TX

1971 I. Cynthia Anderson, Sue Morris, San Francisco Merionettes

O. Kathy Kretschmer, Amy Miner, San Francisco Merionettes

1972  I. Jackie Douglass, Gail Gardner, Santa Clara Aquamaids

O. Robin Curren, Amanda Norrish, Santa Clara Aquamaids

1973  I. Denise Gallagher, Karen Morris, San Francisco Merionettes

O. Debbie Reagan, Linda Reagan, Walnut Creek Aquanuts

1974  I. Dana Moore, Suzanne Randell, Santa Clara Aquamaids

O. Sherry Taylor, Clare Kenward, Cygnets of San Antonio, TX

1975  I. Michele Barone, Pam Tryon, Santa Clara Aquamaids

O. Sue Duffy, Diane Staatsburg, Tonawanda Aquettes, NY

1976  I. Lori Green, Cynthia Engle, California Coralettes

O. Karen Callaghan, Suzanne Cameron, Walnut Creek Aquanuts

1977  I. Michelle Beaulieu, Gerri Brandley, Santa Clara Aquamaids

O. Marie White, Sara White, Walnut Creek Aquanuts

1978  I. Brenda Florio, Laura Florio, Hamden Heronettes, CT

O. Tara Cameron, Cindy Klein, California Coralettes

1979  I. Candy Costie, Tracie Ruiz, Seattle Aqua Club

O. Julie Olsen, Becky Roy, Walnut Creek Aquanuts

1980  I. Karen Josephson, Sarah Josephson, Hamden Heronettes, CT

O. Kathy Kish, Holly Spencer, Santa Clara Aquamaids

1981  I. Darla Dillan, Gloria Dillan, Seattle Aqua Club

O. Lisa Babb, Kim Stanley, Walnut Creek Aquanuts

1982  I. Alice Smith, Margarita Smith, University of Arizona

O. Lea Bean, Betsy Visniski, Meraquas of Irvine

1983  I. Terri Champ, Barbara Miller, Santa Clara Aquamaids

O. Lorri Harrell, Lisa Riddell, Santa Clara Aquamaids

1984  I. Kristen Babb, Michelle Svitenko, Walnut Creek Aquanuts

O. Karen Madsen, Dee Cohen, Meraquas of Irvine

1985  I. Tracy Long, Susan Reed, Walnut Creek Aquanuts

O. Patti Lynn, Heather Simmons, Santa Clara Aquamaids

1986  I. Laura Fowler, Ruth Weinberg, Santa Clara Aquamaids

O. Tracy Fearnow, Christy Foster, Santa Clara Aquamaids

1987  I. Lori Dickie, Robin Roberts, Santa Clara Aquamaids

O. Cheryl Wiegand, Debbie Wiegand, Ohio State University

1988  I. Becky Dyroen, Jill Sudduth, Santa Clara Aquamaids

O. Suzannah Dyroen, Laurie Martin, Santa Clara Aquamaids

1989  I. Lori McCoy, Jill Savery, Walnut Creek Aquanuts

O. Natasha Haynes, Katie Killebrew, Santa Clara Aquamaids

1990  I. Nathalie Schneyder, Margot Thien, Walnut Creek Aquanuts

O. Yasuko Morikawa, Jenny Munoz, Santa Clara Aquamaids

*Indoor/Outdoor discontinued; one championship per year beginning in 1991.*

1991  Laurie McClelland, Jenny Ohanesian, Walnut Creek Aquanuts

1992  Laurie McClelland, Jenny Ohanesian, Walnut Creek Aquanuts

1993  Becky Jasontek, Kim Ochsner, Cincinnati Synchrogators, OH

1994  Kristina Lum, Alanna O'Leary, Santa Clara Aquamaids

1995  Alanna O'Leary, Elicia Marshall, Santa Clara Aquamaids

1996  Alanna O'Leary, Elicia Marshall, Santa Clara Aquamaids

1997  Becky Martin, Lauren McFall, Santa Clara Aquamaids

1998  Becky Martin, Lauren McFall, Santa Clara Aquamaids

1999  Alison Bartosik, Becky Martin, Santa Clara Aquamaids

2000  Alison Bartosik, Andrea Nott, Santa Clara Aquamaids

2001  Alison Bartosik, Sara Lowe, Santa Clara Aquamaids

2002  Stephanie Nesbitt, Courtney Stewart, Riverside Aquettes

2003  Kate Hooven, Becky Kim, Walnut Creek Aquanuts

2004  Christina Jones, Jessica McMahon, Santa Clara Aquamaids

## JUNIOR NATIONAL TRIO CHAMPIONS
## 1983–2004

1983  I.  Candy Costie, Tracie Ruiz, Holly Spencer, Seattle Aqua Club
      O.  Mary Beldin, Carrie Bull, Terri Champ, Santa Clara Aquamaids
1984  I.  Tammy Kay, Alice Smith, Margarita Smith, University of Arizona
      O.  Dee Cohen, Lori Dickie, Karen Madsen, Meraquas of Irvine
1985  I.  Manon Cote, Karen Josephson, Sarah Josephson, Ohio State University
      O.  Karen Miele, Adrienne Lehman, Betsy Visniski, Ohio State University
1986  I.  Stephanie Ammirati, Jennifer Lynn, Robin Roberts, Santa Clara University
      O.  Tracy Fearnow, Christy Foster, Ruth Weinberg, Santa Clara Aquamaids
1987  I.  Melinda Downey, Jill Sudduth, Lisa Poggensee, Santa Clara Aquamaids
      O.  Kristin Eakin, Denise Sawicki, Cheryl Wiegand, Ohio State University
1988  I.  Nadine Bekker, Lori McCoy, Jill Savery, Walnut Creek Aquanuts
      O.  Dana Hunsinger, Margot Thien, Kristina Vorheis, Walnut Creek Aquanuts
1989  I.  Cathy Cramer, Tammy Hunt, Jessica Hudacek, Ohio State University
      O.  Mandy Blake, Khadija Cutcher, Jenny Munoz, Santa Clara Aquamaids
1990  I.  Jenny Dunn, Kim Ochsner, Alison Prout, Cincinnati Synchrogators, OH
      O.  Annmarie Alm, Shala Larsen, Monika Niessner, Santa Clara Aquamaids

*Indoor/Outdoor discontinued; one championship per year beginning in 1991.*

1991  Kristine Fripp, Tammy Cleland, Tina Kasid, Walnut Creek Aquanuts
1992  Sarah Andrews, Tina Kasid, Dawn Wales, Walnut Creek Aquanuts
1993  Shannon Cerveny, Rachel Kozower, Jodi Wiegand, Buffalo Swimkins, NY
1994  Amy McDaniel, Amber McDaniel, Vanessa Shaw, Sweetwater Dolphins
1995  Christina McClelland, Lisa Velez, Lindsey Wiggington, Sweetwater Dolphins
1996  Stacey Park, Ana Shon, Kendra Zanotto, Santa Clara Aquamaids
1997  Alyssa Jones, Andrea Nott, Bora Suh, Santa Clara Aquamaids
1998  Tiffany Bye, Bora Suh, Lauren McFall, Santa Clara Aquamaids
1999  Carrie Arnold, Tiffany Mockler, Kimberly McKinley, Santa Clara Aquamaids
2000  Kim McKinley, Sepeedeh Nikabakht, Ashley Rule, Santa Clara Aquamaids
2001  Becky Kim, Ashley McHugh, Lauren Rettberg, Walnut Creek Aquanuts
2002  Elizabeth-Anne Markman, Courtney Stewart, Cassidy Ramage, Riverside Aquettes
2003  Brooke Abel, Meryl Grandia, Caitlin Stewart, Riverside Aquettes
2004  Poppy Carlig, Layla Smith, Carolyn Watts, Santa Clara Aquamaids

## JUNIOR NATIONAL TEAM CHAMPIONS
## 1946–2004

1946  O.  Chicago Town Club, IL, Doris Dieskow, Priscilla Hirsch, Shirley Brown, Phyllis Burrell, Billie Voelker, Rosemarie Voelker, Audrey Huettenrauch, Marion Mittlacher
1947  O.  Chicago Marlin Club, IL, N. Koe, J. Levinson, M. Levinson, S. Levinson, V. Pauley, L. Prosby, D. Pullman, D. Timmins
1948  I.  St. Clair Synchronettes, P. Boetcher, Laurine Stocking, J. Micus, B. Micus
1949      *Not held*
1950      *Not held*
1951  I.  Pacific Coast Club, Joanne Royer, Joanne Willis, Mary Lou Engle, Stephanie Witt, Pearl Redding, Pat Semanski, Sharon Powell, Diane McKinney

1952  I.  Athens Club, Oakland, Dawn Pawson Bean, Joan Pawson, Lynn Pawson, Sally Phillips, Maura Stone, June Young
      O.  Corkettes of Houston, TX, Margie Repass, Elizabeth Sunbarger, B. Wilder, Joy Cushman
1953  I.  Athens Club, Oakland, Joanne Berthelson, Sandy Kalunki, Jackie Brown, Joanne Brobst
      O.  Houston Crystal Pool, TX, Anne Lewis, Lolly Anderson, Marian Jobst, Stephanie Mosheim
1954  I.  St. Clair Synchronettes, Pat Chapp, Judy Elliott, Paula Bonnier, Maureen O'Donnell
      O.  Corkettes of Houston, Laura Lee Payne,

Beth Browning, Carole Jacobs, Martha Ann Kaufman

1955    I.    San Francisco Synchronettes, Miriam McDonald, Pat Cronin, F. Lett, Barbara Engle

        O.    KRNT Des Moines, M. Moran, E. McDonald, S. Bell, G. Annable, K. Biesenmeyer

1956    I.    Athens Club, Oakland, Jackie DuFosse, Jaclyn Ryan, Pat Green, Carol Reidt, Jan Theoni, Laura Baldwin

        O.    *Kiwettes, Canada, L. Wood, D. Gibson, C. Morton, H. Costers
              Bristol Synchronettes, D. Benson, A. Dimeo, G. Hall, R. Lott, C. Cavaliere

1957    I.    Berea Aquateens, Kathy Brooks, Gretchen Lechner, Karen Luedke, Mary Ann Davis

        O.    Dallas Catalinas, Sue Hammel, Maewin Clem, Alice McRedmond, Carolyn Carroll

1958    I.    Salt Lake Deseret, Irene Humphries, Linda Blackham, Norma Becker, Maryann Olsen

        O.    Coralina Club, Sue Hauck, Gloria Hauck, Carol Swanson, Pat Heitger

1959    I.    Lansing Sea Sprites, Mary Jean Campbell, Betsy Fox, Anne Harrison, Susan Lundberg, Susan Montgomery, Kayda Zavitz

        O.    Corkettes of Houston, Janet Loeffler, Janie Lozo, Carole Stephson, Rosemarie Ueckert

1960    I.    Lansing Sea Sprites, Mary Flewelling, Bonnie Kruger, Meredy Menzies, Paula Stiles, Virginia Wahl

        O.    San Francisco Merionettes, Margaret Durbrow, Sharon Hood, Phyllis Firman, Sydonia Fisher, Louella Sommers, Mary Whybrow

1961    I.    Columbus Coralina Club, Vicki Barnhouse, Nancy Hines, Sally Kinney, Teri Heitger, Kathy Sullivan

        O.    Shaw Park St. Louis. MO, Mary Jo Capps, Jan Kupferer, Nancy Staphenhorst, Liz Wells

1962    I.    Athens Club, Oakland, Margie Lawrence, Pat Brehm, Cathy Hamburg, Marion Whitner, Marcia Blixt, Barbara Newman

        O.    Dayton Aquanymphs, OH, Rosie Clark, Margaret Constable, Linda Davenport, Barbara Henry, Joann Layford

1963    I.    Lansing Sea Sprites, Mary Beuerle, Becky Day, Donna McDonald, Sue Murphy, Sue Shackleton, Cindy Snyder

        O.    San Francisco Merionettes, Roberta Gleason, Rhea Irvine, Sharon Lawson, Kathy McBride, Margo McGrath, Patsy Mical

1964    I.    Columbus Coralina Club, Karen Blackburn, Anne Dueler, Janet Van Atta, Holly Barnhouse, Connie Williams, Linda Williams

        O.    Howell Club, Concord, Kathy Craig, Gail Gardner, Debbie Howell, Dianne Howell, Kathy Knibbe, Melinda Sellers

1965    I.    Shaw Park, St. Louis, MO, Nancy Bock, Kathy Dryden, Laurie Jordan, Sandy Gambaro, Kathy Stephens, Kathy McMullin, Suzanne Leppo, Marsha Steinback

        O.    Riverside Aquettes, Pam Albin, Molly Baross, Kathy Faure, Ginger Norris, Barbara Shervanick, Sally Silva

1966    I.    Dayton Aquanymphs, OH, Sue Henger, Linda King, Sue Nordquist, Kathy Kretschmer, Vickey Weir

        O.    Cygnets of San Antonio, Cindy Banker, Susan Jordan, Jan Buchanan, Betsy Hart, Babs Bazar, Jo Anne Glauberg, Mary Wiedenfeld, Sherry Wiedenmann

1967    I.    San Francisco Merionettes, Norma Fish, Judy Hardiman, Joan Lang, Kathy Nordhausen, Heidi O'Rourke, Barbara Trantina

        O.    Howell Club, Concord, Nancy Lee, Gail Johnson, Pat Torrenga, Nancy Olson

1968    I.    Shaw Park, St. Louis, MO, Jackie Douglass, Sherrill Gonterman, Kim Gonterman, Jan Breckenridge, Sharon Langenbeck, Sandy Langenbeck

        O.    San Francisco Merionettes, Barbara Cooney, Maureen Daly, Amy Miner, Lona Gallagher, Sue Morris, Carrie Turman

1969    I.    Cygnets of San Antonio, Angie Taylor, Nancy Doyle, Jeannie Hayden, Kathy Jansen, Karen Acree, Sherry Taylor

        O.    Seattle Aqua Club, Connie Brewer, Charlotte Jennings, Karen Anderson, Diane Smith, Renee Couchee, Sue Pearson, Colleen Jones, Elaine Zarkades

1970    I.    Berea Aquateens, OH, Joan Barris, Sandy Beran, Nancy Mancini, Jo Anne Ferguson, Pat Leake, Kay Ruenzel, Pat Sandhoff, Becky Storey

        O.    San Francisco Merionettes, Cinny Anderson, Denise Gallagher, Sunny Horstmeyer, Joan Hillsman, Karen Morris, Nancy Hunt, Anne Kraemer, Ann Stevens

1971    I.    Cygnets of San Antonio, Jo Claire Oliverio, Lynn Hooper, Melody Farquahr, Margo Hernandez, Linda Gardner, Kris Berry, Gaye Maxey, Shannon Carmody

        O.    Santa Clara Aquamaids, Amanda Norrish, Robin Curren, Pam Tryon, Suzanne

*honorary

Randell, Susan Martin, Ruthann Cross, Debbie Gartner, Michele Barone

1972 I. Tustin Meraquas, Nanette Arpin, Kevis Bean, Diana Nelson, Lori Nelson, Roberta Morgan, Bunny Stickler, Robin Summerl, Kathi Sunner

O. Walnut Creek Aquanuts, Leslie Ahlf, Shannon Everist, Linda Reagan, Cathy Lagomarsino, Denise Laughrey, Anne McCormick, Debbie Reagan, Mary Irion

1973 I. San Francisco Merionettes, Linda Adams, Laura Cameron, Carol Clark, Kimberly Evart, Linda Gray, Jane Johnson, Diane Lang, Lori Nelson

O. California Coralettes, Cynthia Engle, Lori Green, Mindy Haines, Barbara Koch, Diane Reese, Lee Ann Reese, Marie White, Sara White

1974 I. Santa Clara Aquamaids, Cindy Anderson, Erin Barr, Mary Ellen Longo, Roxanne Herrick, Jill Schroyer, Linda Shelley, Helene Sheptin

O. Tonawanda Aquettes, NY, Kathy Krempholtz, Mary Beth Sowers, Marilyn Marciano, LuAnn Benfanti, Diane Staatsburg, Kathy Rankin, Pam Menth, Sue Duffy

1975 I. Walnut Clara Aquanuts, Karen Callaghan, Suzanne Cameron, Paula Everist, Sue Flanders, Diane Jones, Julie Olsen, Margaret Schremp, Sue Templeton

O. Cygnets of San Antonio, Robyn Stearns, Janet Yates, Becky Price, Rene Ratliff, Betty Longstaff, Melodie Kay, Clare Kenward, Leslie Mason

1976 I. Tustin Meraquas, Avilee Bean, Kerrie Hein, Robin Ikeda, Cory Lamb, Mary Lou Ott, Mary Ann Parker, Sue Toltzman, Janet Tope

O. Hamden Heronettes, CT, Brenda Florio, Laura Florio, Ann Foley, Melissa Irvine, Regina Ketchale, Rita McHugh, Karen Rascale, Janine Sacramone

1977 I. Cygnets of San Antonio, Carla Dunlap, Janet Easton, Linda Lampe, Leslie Ringrose, Pam Rowland, Shellie Swan, Diana Tedder, Kim Watta

O. Walnut Creek Aquanuts, Beth Denison, Ruth Fleming, Becky Roy, Jan Hall, Monica Mendenhall, Dawn Nelson, Sherry Phipps, Leslie Schremp

1978 I. Tonawanda Aquettes, NY, Laurie Beitz, Chris Keleher, Barbara Earsing, Gigi Darlich, Cathy Mineo, Heidi Greiner, Cathleen O'Brien

O. Seattle Aqua Club, Candy Costie, Tracie Ruiz, Gloria Dillan, Darla Dillan, Lezlee Powell, Lisa Mork, Melissa Berg, Amy Campbell

1979 I. Meraquas of Irvine, Pamela Fox, Linda

Lewis, Lori Moore, Ginnylee McGilton, Linda Sliff, Gina Verrecchia, Robin Waller, Sara Woollett

O. Santa Clara Aquamaids, Laura Solomon, Kathy Dent, Jenny Lauck, Michelle Markey, Krista Andreini, Angie Alkire, Ann Motekatis, Debbie Tippett

1980 I. Santa Clara Aquamaids, Mary Beldin, Carrie Bull, Terri Champ, Stacey Dahl, Lorri Harrell, Joy Gilbert, Julie Montgomery, Charlene Stahlke

O. Walnut Creek Aquanuts, Lisa Babb, Kathy Fehely, Becky Dewees, Janice Rubin, Angela Schaub, Jackie Sieh, Kim Stanley, Mary Visniski

1981 I. Tonawanda Aquettes, Karey Buchanan, Lori Donn, Kathy McCall, Kim Rankin, Erin O'Shaughnessy, Krista Greiner, Cindy Stachowicz, Kim Buchanan

O. Hamden Heronettes, Sarah Josephson, Valerie Luedee, Dawn Del Vecchio, Kathy Gillon, Cindy Gillon, Karen Gillon, Heidi Schmidt, Susan Reilly

1982 I. Meraquas of Irvine, Kathy Augenstein, Lea Bean, Arlene Boda, Lori Dickie, Karen Madsen, Candy Murphy, Kim Van Gent, Betsy Visniski

O. Walnut Creek Aquanuts, Kristen Babb, Kristen Burke, Christy Choate, Joan Friedman, Moneka Jhala, Mikako Kotani, Michelle Moon, Michelle Svitenko

1983 I. Seattle Aqua Club, Angie Atkinson, Christy Foster, Katie Dent, Stephanie Ammirati, Susan Galloway, Kip Knappett, Kirsten Wagner, Ruth Weinberg

O. Santa Clara Aquamaids, Barbara Miller, Lisa Riddell, Lori Hatch, Laura Fowler, Robin Roberts, Trish Frese, Katie Dittman, Jennifer Lynn

1984 I. University of Arizona, Connie Cope, Tammie Kay, Alice Smith, Margarita Smith, Eileen Daily, Susan Decker, Missy Ihrig

O. Walnut Creek Aquanuts, Debi Brear, Tiffany Gee, Jessica Hudacek, Susan Hudspeth, Marla McGatlin, Nathalie Schneyder, Kelly Moore, Jackie Rush

1985 I. Ohio State University, Penny Billingham, Cathy Cramer, Adrienne Lehman, Carol Korpi, Karen Miele, Anne Schulte, Holly Vargo, Kathy Zittel

O. Santa Clara Aquamaids, Ginny Cohn, Melinda Downey, Michelle Nance, Dawn Graybill, Shannon Green, Heather Simmons, Carey Shumway, Patti Lynn

1986 I. University of Arizona, Casey O'Shaughnessy, Cheryl Madsen, Debbie Weber, Julie DeEsch, April Brennan, Karen Brinkman, Osena Violette, Kristin Fischer

O. Walnut Creek Aquanuts, Nadine Bekker, Yvonne Bekker, Melissa Matosian, Tabby Camp, Stephanie Moon, Lori McCoy, Sara May, Jill Savery

1987   I.   Santa Clara Aquamaids, Mandy Blake, Kathy Dillon, Becky Dyroen, Laurie Martin, Anna Miller, Jill Sudduth, Lisa Poggensee, Jennifer Sogawa

O. Ohio State University, Kristin Eakin, Maria Guisti, Tanya Hybl, Denise Sawicki, Cheryl Wiegand, Debbie Wiegand

1988   I.   Walnut Creek Aquanuts, Nicole Banks, Kim Cuffe, Debbie Downes, Dana Hunsinger, Tina Kasid, Margot Thien, Michelle Troy, Kristina Vorheis, Rachel Kozower

O. Tonawanda Aquettes, Maureen Wortman, Traci Urbino, Kristy Donn, Kathy Szwejbka, Jennifer Bagley, Sue Springer, Anne Hammer, Kathy Manley

1989   I.   Ohio State University, Julie Jasontek, Tia Harding, Tammy Hunt, Terri Collins, Johanna Monko, Diana Ulrich, Cheryl Schemenauer, Amy Pryor

O. Santa Clara Aquamaids, Khadija Cutcher, Natasha Haynes, Kari Kreitzer, Shala Larsen, Jenny Munoz, Keva Nelson, Monika Niessner, Jill Schlichting

1990   I.   Ohio State University, Jacinta Beckman, Jenny Dunn, Sue Ha, Kim Ochsner, Alison Prout, Jennie Sprague, Shea Tanabe, Sandra Valles.

O. Walnut Creek Aquanuts, Janine Bekker, Kristine Fripp, Stefana Lemings, Kaori Takahashi, Kendra Tomcik, Jennifer Vorheis

*Indoor/Outdoor championships discontinued; one championship a year beginning in 1991.*

1991   Walnut Creek Aquanuts, Tammy Cleland, Kristine Fripp, Tina Kasid, Laurie McClelland, Kristin Smith, Kaori Takahashi, Jennifer Vorheis

1992   Walnut Creek Aquanuts, Sarah Andrews, Tammy Cleland, Laurie McClelland, Tina Kasid, Kristin Smith, Lesley Riddervold, Jennifer Vorheis, Dawn Wales

1993   Arizona Aquastars, Lisa Burton, Heidi Dunham, Julie Gibson, Stephanie Johnson, Sarah Mayfield, Lorette Nichols, Casey Taylor, Shannon Taylor

1994   Santa Clara Aquamaids, Lisa Cunanan, Season Flores, Christine Frankewich, Kristina Lum, Emily Nelson, Alanna O'Leary, Susan Polley, Kim Wurzel

1995   Santa Clara Aquamaids, Kristin Blockie, Kara Butzman, Judy Chiang, Julie Enos, Brianne MacNaughton, Elicia Marshall, Stacey Scott, Ana Shon

1996   Santa Clara Aquamaids, Brynn Butzman, Katie Enos, Karen Green, Brianne MacNaughton, Lauren McFall, Bill May, Becky Martin, Ana Shon

1997   Santa Clara Aquamaids, Alison Bartosik, Erin Blockie, Tiffany Bye, Alyssa Jones, Marlena Marshall, Andrea Nott, Bora Suh, Kendra Zanotto

1998   Santa Clara Aquamaids, Carrie Arnold, Tiffany Bye, Sarah Beddingfield, Cristina Martinez-Canton, Maresea Nelson, Bora Suh, Emiko Takyu, Kerstin Voeller.

1999   Walnut Creek Aquanuts, Erin Dobratz, Julie Drexler, Amanda Graff-Baker, Melissa Iagulli, Stephanie Joukoff, Sharon Mejia, Joanne Taylor, Mary Tschann

2000   Santa Clara Aquamaids, Alison Bartosik, Lidia Birukova, Teresa Liccardo, Sara Lowe, Kim McKinley, Emiko Takyu, Carolyn Steinwedel

2001   Santa Clara Aquamaids, Alison Bartosik, Lidia Birukova, Teresa Liccardo, Sara Lowe, Kim McKinley, Alicia Rice, Ashley Rule, Emiko Takyu

2002   Walnut Creek Aquanuts, Kate Hooven, Becky Kim, Ashley McHugh, Suzanne Alborg, Annabelle Orme, Rachael Rife, Rebekah Rife, Lesley Wallace

2003   Walnut Creek Aquanuts, Kate Hooven, Missy Knight, Becky Kim, Annabelle Orme, Rachel Rife, Rebekah Rife, Lesley Wallace

2004   Santa Clara Aquamaids, Poppy Carlig, Christina Jones, Hae-Rin Lee, Jessica McMahon, Bahereh Nikbakht, Lauren Oyle, Layla Smith, Carolyn Watts

---

## MASTERS OVERALL NATIONAL CHAMPIONS
## 1975–2003

1975   D.C. Masters, District of Columbia
1976   *No championship held*
1977   Dayton Synchronettes, Dayton
1978   D.C. Masters, District of Columbia
1979   D.C. Masters, District of Columbia

1980   D.C. Masters, District of Columbia
1981   Dayton Synchronettes, Dayton
1982   Dayton Synchronettes, Dayton
1983   Santa Clara Aquamaids, Santa Clara
1984   Dayton Synchronettes, Dayton

| | | | |
|---|---|---|---|
| 1985 | D.C. Masters, District of Columbia | 1995 | D.C. Masters, District of Columbia |
| 1986 | D.C. Masters, District of Columbia | 1996 | D.C. Masters, District of Columbia |
| 1987 | Dayton Synchronettes, Dayton | 1997 | Unsyncables, Southern California |
| 1988 | Dayton Synchronettes, Dayton | 1998 | Unsyncables, Southern California |
| 1989 | Dayton Synchronettes, Dayton | 1999 | Unsyncables, Southern California |
| 1990 | Aqua Masters, New York | 2000 | Dayton Synchronettes, Dayton |
| 1991 | Columbus Synch or Swim, Columbus | 2001 | Unsyncables, Southern California |
| 1992 | Dayton Synchronettes, Dayton | 2002 | Dayton Synchronettes, Dayton |
| 1993 | Dayton Synchronettes, Dayton | 2003 | Dayton Synchronettes, Dayton |
| 1994 | Dayton Synchronettes, Dayton | 2004 | Unsyncables, Southern California |

# Appendix C:
# Major International Championships, 1955–2004

### XXVIII Olympic Games, Athens, Greece
### Aug. 13–29, 2004

TEAM (8 ENTRIES)

1. Russia . . . . . . . . . . 99.501
2. Japan . . . . . . . . . . . 98.501
3. United States . . . . . 97.418
4. Spain . . . . . . . . . . . 96.751
5. Canada . . . . . . . . . 95.251
6. China . . . . . . . . . . 94.584
7. Italy . . . . . . . . . . . . 94.084
8. Greece . . . . . . . . . 92.750

**Russia:** Elena Azarova, Olga Brusnikina, Anastasia Davydova, Anastasia Ermakova, Maria Gromova, Maria Kiseleva, Olga Novokshchenova, Anna Shorina, Elvira Khasyanova.
**Team USA:** Alison Bartosik, Tamara Crow, Erin Dobratz, Rebecca Jasontek, Anna Kozlova, Sara Lowe, Lauren McFall, Stephanie Nesbitt, Kendra Zanotto.

DUET FINALS (12)

1. Anastasia Davydova,
   Anastasia Ermakova, RUS . . . . . . . . . . 99.833
2. Miya Tachibana,
   Miho Takeda, JPN . . . . . . . . . . . . . . . 98.833
3. Anna Kozlova,
   Alison Bartosik, USA . . . . . . . . . . . . . 97.167
4. Gemma Mengual,
   Paola Tirados, ESP . . . . . . . . . . . . . . . 96.667
5. Virginie Dedieu,
   Laure Thibaid, FRA . . . . . . . . . . . . . . 95.833
6. Fanny Letourneau,
   Courteney Stewart, CAN . . . . . . . . . . 95.667
7. Beibei Gu,
   Zhang Xiaohuan, CHN . . . . . . . . . . . . 94.167
8. Beatrice Spaziani,
   Lorena Zaffalon, ITA . . . . . . . . . . . . . 93.500
9. Eleftheria Ftouli,
   Christina Thalassinidou, GRE . . . . . . . 93.167
10. Magdalena Brunner,
    Belinda Schmid, SUI . . . . . . . . . . . . . 92.167
11. Iryna Gayvoronska,
    Darya Yuhko, UKR . . . . . . . . . . . . . . 91.667
12. Carolina Moraes,
    Isabela Moraes, BRA . . . . . . . . . . . . . 91.500

**Countries Entered (24):** Australia, Belarus, Brazil, Bulgaria, Canada, China, Czech Republic, Egypt, France, Greece, Holland, Israel, Italy, Japan, Kazakhstan, Korea, Mexico, Puerto Rico, Russia, Slovakia, Spain, Switzerland, Ukraine, United States.

### XXVII Olympic Games, Sydney, Australia
### Sept. 15–Oct. 1, 2000

TEAM (8 ENTRIES)

1. Russia . . . . . . 99.14
2. Japan . . . . . . . 98.86
3. Canada . . . . . . 97.35
4. France . . . . . . 96.46

5. United States . . . . . . 96.10
6. Italy . . . . . . . . . . . . 95.17
7. China . . . . . . . . . . . 94.59
8. Australia . . . . . . . . 89.49

**Russia:** Elena Antonova, Elena Azarova, Olga Brusnikina, Maria Kisseleva, Olga Novokshchenova, Irina Perchina, Elena Soia, Yulia Vasilieva, Olga Vassioukova.

**Team USA:** Carrie Barton, Tammy Cleland McGregor, Bridget Finn, Anna Kozlova, Kristina Lum, Elicia Marshall, Heather Pease-Olson, Kim Wurzel.

DUET FINALS (12)

1. Olga Brusnikina,
   Maria Kisseleva, RUS . . . . . . . . . . . . . . 99.58
2. Miya Tachibana,
   Miho Takeda, JPN . . . . . . . . . . . . . 98.65
3. Virginie Dedieu,
   Myriam Lignot, FRA . . . . . . . . . . . . . . 97.43
4. Anna Kozlova,
   Tuesday Middaugh, USA . . . . . . . . . . . . 96.99
5. Claire Carver-Dias,
   Fanny Letourneau, CAN . . . . . . . . . . . . . 95.98
6. Maurizio Cecconi,
   Alessia Lucchini, ITA . . . . . . . . . . . . . . 95.38
7. Min Li,
   Yuanyuan Li, CHN . . . . . . . . . . . . . . . 94.78
8. Gemma Mengual,
   Paola Tirados, ESP . . . . . . . . . . . . . . 94.52
9. Erica Leal,
   Lillian Leal, MEX . . . . . . . . . . . . . . . 92.76
10. Madeleine Park,
    Belinda Schmid, SUI . . . . . . . . . . . . . . 92.03
11. Yoon-Kyeong Jang,
    Na-Mi Yoo, KOR . . . . . . . . . . . . . . . . 91.82
12. Carolina Moraes,
    Isabela Moraes, BRA . . . . . . . . . . . . . . 90.74

**Countries Entered** (23): Australia, Belarus, Brazil, Canada, China, Cuba, Czech Republic, Egypt, France, Greece, Hungary, Italy, Japan, Kazakhstan, Korea, Mexico, Russia, Slovakia, Spain, Switzerland, Ukraine, United States, Venezuela.

## XXVI Olympic Games, Atlanta, Georgia
### July 30–Aug. 2, 1996

TEAM (8)

1. United States . . . . . 99.72
2. Canada . . . . . . . . . 98.36
3. Japan . . . . . . . . . . . 97.53
4. Russia . . . . . . . . . . 97.26
5. France . . . . . . . . . . 96.07
6. Italy . . . . . . . . . . . 95.25
7. China . . . . . . . . . . 94.12
8. Mexico . . . . . . . . . 93.83

**Team USA:** Suzannah Bianco, Tammy Cleland, Becky Dyroen-Lancer, Emily LeSueur, Heather Pease, Jill Savery, Nathalie Schneyder, Heather Simmons-Carrasco, Jill Sudduth, Margot Thien.

**Countries Entered** (16): Australia, Brazil, Canada, China, Czech Republic, France, Great Britain, Italy, Japan, Korea, Mexico, Netherlands, Russia, Switzerland, Ukraine, United States.

## XXV Olympic Games, Barcelona, Spain
### July 25–Aug. 9, 1992

SOLO (21)

1. Kristen Babb-Sprague, USA . . . . . . . . . . 191.84
2. Sylvie Frechette, CAN . . . . . . . . . . . . 191.71
3. Fumiko Okuno, JPN . . . . . . . . . . . . . . 187.05
4. Olga Sedakova, EUN . . . . . . . . . . . . . 185.10
5. Anne Capron, FRA . . . . . . . . . . . . . . 182.44
6. Kristina Thalissinidou, GRE . . . . . . . . . 180.24
7. Kerry Shacklock, GBR . . . . . . . . . . . . 179.83
8. Marjolijn Both, NED . . . . . . . . . . . . . 179.35

DUET (18)

1. Karen Josephson,
   Sarah Josephson, USA . . . . . . . . . . . . . 192.17
2. Penny Vilagos,
   Vicky Vilagos, CAN . . . . . . . . . . . . . . 189.39
3. Fumiko Okuno,
   Aki Takayama, JPN . . . . . . . . . . . . . . 186.86
4. Anna Kozlova,
   Olga Sedakova, EUN . . . . . . . . . . . . . . 184.08
5. Anne Capron,
   Marianne Aeschbacher, FRA . . . . . . . . . 181.79
6. Kerry Shacklock,
   Laila Vakil, GBR . . . . . . . . . . . . . . . 179.36
7. Marjolijn Both,
   Tamara Zwart, NED . . . . . . . . . . . . . . 179.34
8. Zewen Guan,
   Xiaojie Wang, CHN . . . . . . . . . . . . . . 177.84

**Countries Entered** (22): Australia, Austria, Brazil, Canada, China, Czech Republic, Finland, France, Germany, Great Britain, Greece, Islands of Philippines, Italy, Japan, Mexico, Netherlands, South Africa, Spain, Switzerland, Unified Team, United States, Venezuela.

## XXIV Olympic Games, Seoul, Korea
### Sept. 17–Oct. 2, 1988

SOLO (18)

1. Carolyn Waldo, CA . . . . . . . . . . . . . . 200.15
2. Tracie Ruiz-Conforto, USA . . . . . . . . . . 197.63
3. Mikako Kotani, JPN . . . . . . . . . . . . . . 191.85
4. Muriel Hermine, FRA . . . . . . . . . . . . . 190.10
5. Karin Singer, SUI . . . . . . . . . . . . . . . 185.60
6. Nicola Shearn, GBR . . . . . . . . . . . . . . 181.93
7. Kristina Falasinidi, URS . . . . . . . . . . . 180.65
8. Gerlind Scheller, FRG . . . . . . . . . . . . . 175.98

DUET (15)

1. Carolyn Waldo,
   Michele Cameron, CAN ............ 197.71
2. Karen Josephson,
   Sarah Josephson, USA .............. 197.28
3. Mikako Kotani,
   Miyako Tanaka, JPN .............. 190.15
4. Anne Capron,
   Karine Schuler, FRA .............. 184.79
5. Edith Boss,
   Karin Singer, SUI ................ 183.95
6. Tatiana Titova,
   Maria Tscherniaeva, URS ........... 182.66
7. Lian Goodwin,
   Nicola Shearn, GBR .............. 179.07
8. Lourdes Candini,
   Sonia Cardenas, MEX .............. 175.83

**Countries Entered (19):** Aruba, Australia, Belgium, Brazil, Canada, China, Egypt, France, Great Britain, Japan, Korea, Mexico, Soviet Union, Spain, Sweden, Switzerland, United States, Venezuela, West Germany.

DUET (18)

1. Tracie Ruiz,
   Candy Costie, USA ................ 195.58
2. Sharon Hambrook,
   Kelly Kryczka, CAN ................ 194.23
3. Saeko Kimura,
   Miwako Motoyoshi, JPN ........... 187.99
4. Caroline Holmyard,
   Carolyn Wilson, GBR .............. 184.05
5. Edith Boss,
   Karin Singer, SUI ................ 180.10
6. Catrien Eijken,
   Marijke Engelen, NED ............. 179.05
7. Pascale Besson,
   Muriel Hermine, FRA .............. 176.70
8. Claudia Novelo,
   Pilar Ramirez, MEX ................ 176.40

**Countries Entered (19):** Aruba, Australia, Austria, Belgium, Brazil, Canada, Dominican Republic, Egypt, France, Great Britain, Japan, Mexico, Netherlands, New Zealand, Spain, Switzerland, United States, Venezuela, West Germany.

### *XXIII Olympic Games, Los Angeles, California August 6–9, 1984*

SOLO (17)

1. Tracie Ruiz, USA ................. 198.46
2. Carolyn Waldo, CAN ............. 195.30
3. Miwako Motoyoshi, JPN ........... 187.05
4. Marijke Engelen, NED ............. 182.63
5. Gudrun Hanisch, FRG ............. 182.01
6. Caroline Holmyard, GBR .......... 182.00
7. Muriel Hermine, FRA ............. 180.53
8. Karin Singer, SUI ................ 178.38

### *U.S. Demonstrators at the Olympic Games 1952–68*

1968, Mexico City — Santa Clara Aquamaids, CA
1964, Tokyo, Japan — Lansing Sea Sprites; Shaw Park, St. Louis, MO
1960, Rome, Italy — Tour group: swimmers from clubs throughout U.S.
1956, Melbourne — Athens Club, Oakland; Corkettes of Houston; Riverside Aquettes
1952, Helsinki, Finland — St. Clair Synchronettes, Detroit; Cedar Rapids, IA

## WORLD CHAMPIONSHIPS

### *X World Aquatic Championships, Barcelona, Spain July 12–27, 2003*

SOLO (31)

1. Virginie Dedieu, FRA ............ 99.251
2. Anastasia Ermakova, RUS ........... 97.417
3. Gemma Mengual, ESP ............ 97.334
4. Miya Tachibana, JPN ............. 96.667
5. Anna Kozlova, USA .............. 95.751
6. Jessica Chase, CAN ............... 94.751
7. Lorena Zafflon, ITA .............. 92.583
8. Darya Shemiakin, UKR ........... 92.167
9. Christina Thalassinidou, GRE ....... 92.000
10. Li Zhen, CHN ................... 91.833
11. Belinda Schmid, SUI ............. 90.667
12. Min Jeong Kim, KOR ............. 90.667

DUET (34)

1. Anastasia Davydova,
   Anastassia Ermakova, RUS ........... 99.084
2. Miya Tachibana,
   Miho Takeda, JPN ................ 98.084
3. Gemma Mengual,
   Paola Tirados, ESP ................ 96.667
4. Alison Bartosik,
   Anna Kozlova, USA ................ 96.334
5. Fanny Letourneau,
   Courtney Stewart, CAN ............. 95.417
6. Virginie Dedieu,
   Laure Thibaud, FRA ............... 95.084
7. Xiaohuan Zhang,
   Beibei Gu, CHN ................. 93.084
8. Beatrice Spaziani,
   Lorena Zaffalon, ITA ............... 92.834

9. Belinda Schmid,
   Magdelena Brunner, SUI . . . . . . . . . . 92.250
10. Christina Thalassinidou,
   Eleftheria Ftouli, GRE . . . . . . . . . . . . 92.168
11. Iryna Gayouronska,
   Durya Yusnko, UKR . . . . . . . . . . . . . 91.834
12. Min Jeong Kim,
   Ho Kyung Son, KOR . . . . . . . . . . . . . 90.834

TEAM (21)

1. Russia . . . . . . . . . . 98.750
2. Japan . . . . . . . . . . . 98.334
3. United States . . . . . 96.834
4. Spain . . . . . . . . . . . 96.251
5. Canada . . . . . . . . . 95.917
6. China . . . . . . . . . . 94.334
7. Italy . . . . . . . . . . . . 93.917
8. Ukraine . . . . . . . . . 92.418
9. France . . . . . . . . . . 92.167
10. Greece . . . . . . . . . . 92.084
11. Korea . . . . . . . . . . . 91.750
12. Switzerland . . . . . . . 90.834

FREE ROUTINE COMBINATION (12)

1. Japan . . . . . . . . . . . 98.500
2. Spain . . . . . . . . . . . 97.333
3. United States . . . . . 97.333
4. Canada . . . . . . . . . 96.000
5. China . . . . . . . . . . 93.833
6. Ukraine . . . . . . . . . 93.500
7. Italy . . . . . . . . . . . . 93.333
8. France . . . . . . . . . . 92.667
9. Greece . . . . . . . . . . 92.000
10. Switzerland . . . . . . . 91.333
11. Venezuela . . . . . . . . 83.000
12. Germany . . . . . . . . 82.667

**Russia:** Olga Brusnikina, Anastasia Davydova, Anastassia Ermakova, Maria Gromova, Elena Jouravleva, Elvira Khassianova, Maria Kisseleva, Elena Ovtchinkkikova, Anna Shorina, Irina Tolkacheva.

**Japan (combo):** Michiyo Fujimaru, Saho Harada, Naoko Kawashima, Karanko Kitao, Emiko Suzuki, Juri Tatsumi, Chiaki Watanabe, Yoko Yoneda.

**USA Team:** Alison Bartosik, Erin Dobratz, Mary Hofer, Becky Jasontek, Anna Kozlova, Sara Lowe, Lauren McFall, Stephanie Nesbitt, Katie Norris, Kendra Zanotto.

**Countries Entered (33):** Armenia, Aruba, Belarus, Brazil, Bulgaria, Canada, China, Costa Rica, Cuba, Czech Republic, Dominican Republic, France, Germany, Greece, Hungary, Israel, Italy, Japan, Kazakhstan, Korea, Malaysia, Mexico, Netherlands, New Zealand, Puerto Rico, Russia, Slovakia, Spain, Switzerland, Ukraine, United States, Uzbekistan, Venezuela.

## IX World Aquatic Championships, Fukuoka, Japan
### July 16–29, 2001

SOLO (30)

1. Olga Brusnikina, RUS . . . . . . . . . . . . . 99.434
2. Virginie Dedieu, FRA . . . . . . . . . . . . . 98.287
3. Miya Tachibana, JPN . . . . . . . . . . . . . 97.870
4. Anna Kozlova, USA . . . . . . . . . . . . . . 96.543
5. Claire Carver-Dias, CAN . . . . . . . . . . 95.314
6. Gemma Mengual, ESP . . . . . . . . . . . . 95.142
7. Yuanyuan Li, CHN . . . . . . . . . . . . . . . 93.837
8. Giada Ballan, ITA . . . . . . . . . . . . . . . . 93.044
9. Christina Thalassinidou, GRE . . . . . . . 92.441
10. Yoon Kyeong Jang, KOR . . . . . . . . . . . 91.389
11. Darya Shemyakina, UKR . . . . . . . . . . . 90.017
12. Belinda Schmid, SUI . . . . . . . . . . . . . . 87.964

DUET (27)

1. Miya Tachibana,
   Miho Takeda, JPN . . . . . . . . . . . . . . . 98.910
2. Anastasia Davydova,
   Anastasia Ermakova, RUS . . . . . . . . . . 98.390
3. Claire Carver-Dias,
   Fanny Letourneau, CAN . . . . . . . . . . . 96.704
4. Becky Martin,
   Lauren McFall, USA . . . . . . . . . . . . . . 96.387
5. Gemma Mengual,
   Paola Tirados, ESP . . . . . . . . . . . . . . . 94.977
6. Virginie Dedieu,
   Myriam Glez, FRA . . . . . . . . . . . . . . . 94.547
7. Lorena Zaffalon,
   Clara Porchetto, ITA . . . . . . . . . . . . . . 93.693
8. Ye Xia,
   Xiaohuan Zhang, CHN . . . . . . . . . . . . 93.423
9. Yoon Kyeong Jang,
   Min Jeong Kim, KOR . . . . . . . . . . . . . 91.763
10. Christina Thalassinidou,
   Eleftheria Ftouli, GRE . . . . . . . . . . . . 91.137
11. Carolina de Moraes,
   Isabela de Moraes, BRA . . . . . . . . . . . 90.171
12. Annastasya Pavelyeva,
   Darya Shemyakina, UKR . . . . . . . . . . 89.743

TEAM (12)

1. Russia . . . . . . . . . . 98.917
2. Japan . . . . . . . . . . . 98.088
3. Canada . . . . . . . . . 97.453
4. USA . . . . . . . . . . . 95.941
5. Spain . . . . . . . . . . . 95.081
6. Italy . . . . . . . . . . . . 94.486
7. China . . . . . . . . . . 93.577
8. France . . . . . . . . . . 92.537
9. Greece . . . . . . . . . . 90.806
10. Ukraine . . . . . . . . . 90.287
11. Brazil . . . . . . . . . . 89.557
12. Switzerland . . . . . . . 88.221

**Russia:** Elena Azarova, Olga Brusnikina, Maria Kisseleva, Anna Louriaeva, Olga Medvedeva, Olga

Novokchtchenova, Olga Sedakova, Alexandra Vassina.

**Team USA:** Carrie Barton, Bridget Finn, Rebecca Jasontek, Tina Kasid, Kristina Lum, Emily Marsh, Elicia Marshall, Kim Wurzel.

**Countries Entered (30):** Aruba, Australia, Austria, Belarus, Brazil, Canada, China, Colombia, Cuba, Czech Republic, France, Great Britain, Greece, Hungary, Italy, Japan, Kazakhstan, Malaysia, Mexico, Netherlands, Russia, Slovakia, South Africa, South Korea, Spain, Sweden, Switzerland, Ukraine, United States, Venezuela.

### VIII World Aquatic Championships, Perth, Australia January 8–18, 1998

SOLO (29)

1. Olga Sedakova, RUS . . . . . . . . . . . . . . . 99.304
2. Virginie Dedieu, FRA . . . . . . . . . . . . . . 98.154
3. Miya Tachibana, JPN . . . . . . . . . . . . . . 97.530
4. Kristina Lum, USA . . . . . . . . . . . . . . . . 95.790
5. Giovanna Burlando, ITA . . . . . . . . . . . . 95.697
6. Kasia Kulesza, CAN . . . . . . . . . . . . . . . 95.340
7. Li Min, CHN . . . . . . . . . . . . . . . . . . . . . 94.224
8. Christina Thalassinidou, GRE . . . . . . . . 93.611

DUET (29)

1. Olga Brousnikina,
   Olga Sedakova, RUS . . . . . . . . . . . . . . . 99.073
2. Miya Tachibana,
   Miho Takeda, JPN . . . . . . . . . . . . . . . . 98.060
3. Virginie Didieu,
   Myriam Lignot, FRA . . . . . . . . . . . . . . . 97.323
4. Carrie Barton,
   Elicia Marshall, USA . . . . . . . . . . . . . . . 96.237
5. Kasia Kulesza,
   Jacinthe Taillon, CAN . . . . . . . . . . . . . . 95.899
6. Li Min,
   Long Yan, CHN . . . . . . . . . . . . . . . . . . . 94.667
7. Lillian Leal,
   Erika Leal, MEX . . . . . . . . . . . . . . . . . . 94.224
8. Gaida Ballan,
   Serena Bianchi, ITA . . . . . . . . . . . . . . . 94.039

TEAM (17)

1. Russia . . . . . . . . . . 99.317
2. Japan . . . . . . . . . . . 98.104
3. USA . . . . . . . . . . . . 96.829
4. Canada . . . . . . . . . 96.687
5. France . . . . . . . . . . 96.567
6. Italy . . . . . . . . . . . . 94.754
7. China . . . . . . . . . . . 94.590
8. South Korea . . . . . 93.380

**Russia:** Elena Azarova, Elena Barantseva, Anna Iouriaeva, Olga Brusnikina, Maria Kisseleva, Anna Maslova, Olga Medvedeva, Olga Novokchtchenova, Olga Sedakova, Alexandra Vassina.

**Team USA:** Carrie Barton, Bridget Finn, Rebecca Jasontek, Tina Kasid, Kristina Lum, Emily Marsh, Elicia Marshall, Kim Wurzel.

**Countries Entered (30):** Aruba, Australia, Austria, Belarus, Brazil, Belarus, Canada, Colombia, Cuba, Czech Republic, France, Great Britain, Greece, Hungary, Italy, Japan, Kazakhstan, Malaysia, Mexico, Netherlands, Russia, Slovakia, South Africa, South Korea, Spain, Sweden, Switzerland, Ukraine, United States, Venezuela.

### VII World Aquatic Championships, Rome, Italy September 9–11, 1994

SOLO (30)

1. Becky Dyroen-Lancer, USA . . . . . . . . . . 191.04
2. Fumiko Okuno, JPN . . . . . . . . . . . . . . . 187.30
3. Lisa Alexander, CAN . . . . . . . . . . . . . . . 186.82
4. Olga Sedakova, RUS . . . . . . . . . . . . . . . 186.21
5. Maria Guisti, VEN . . . . . . . . . . . . . . . . . 181.39
6. Marianne Aeschbacher, FRA . . . . . . . . . 179.36
7. Giovanna Burlando, ITA . . . . . . . . . . . . . 179.25
8. Sonia Cardenas, MEX . . . . . . . . . . . . . . . 178.38

DUET (27)

1. Becky Dyroen-Lancer,
   Jill Sudduth, USA . . . . . . . . . . . . . . . . . 187.00
2. (tie)Fumiko Okuno,
   Miya Tachibana, JPN . . . . . . . . . . . . . . . 186.25
2. (tie) Lisa Alexander,
   Erin Woodley, CAN . . . . . . . . . . . . . . . . 186.25
4. Marianne Aeschbacher,
   Myriam Lignot, FRA . . . . . . . . . . . . . . . 180.87
5. Olga Brousnikina,
   Irena Pankratova, RUS . . . . . . . . . . . . . . 179.34
6. Sonia Cardenas,
   Lillian Leal, MEX . . . . . . . . . . . . . . . . . . 178.93
7. Giovanna Burlando
   Paola Celli, ITA . . . . . . . . . . . . . . . . . . . 178.34
8. Kerry Shacklock,
   Laila Vakil, GBR . . . . . . . . . . . . . . . . . . 177.67

TEAM (20)

1. USA . . . . . . . . 185.88
2. Canada . . . . . . 183.26
3. Japan . . . . . . . 183.21
4. Russia . . . . . . 182.95
5. France . . . . . . 180.13
6. Italy . . . . . . . . 178.09
7. China . . . . . . . 176.98
8. Mexico . . . . . . 176.15

**Team USA:** Tammy Cleland, Suzannah Dyroen, Becky Dyroen-Lancer, Jill Savery, Nathalie Schneyder, Heather Simmons, Jill Sudduth, Margot Thien.

**Countries Entered (30):** Argentina, Australia, Austria, Belarus, Brazil, Bulgaria, Canada, China, Colombia, Cuba, Egypt, France, Czech Republic, Germany, Great Britain, Hungary, Italy, Japan, Kazakhstan, Korea, Mexico, Netherlands, New Zealand, Russia, Slovakia, Sweden, Switzerland, Ukraine, United States, Venezuela.

### *VI World Aquatic Championships, Perth, Australia January 3–13, 1991*

SOLO (20)

1. Sylvie Frechette, CAN . . . . . . . . . . . . . . 201.01
2. Kristen Babb, USA . . . . . . . . . . . . . . . . 196.31
3. Mikako Kotani, JPN . . . . . . . . . . . . . . . 195.11
4. Olga Sedakova, URS . . . . . . . . . . . . . . 192.52
5. Karine Schuler, FRA . . . . . . . . . . . . . . 188.24
6. Maria Guisti, VEN . . . . . . . . . . . . . . . . 182.09
7. Marjolijn Both, NED . . . . . . . . . . . . . . 181.44
8. Paola Celli, ITA . . . . . . . . . . . . . . . . . . 179.16

DUET (18)

1. Karen Josephson,
   Sarah Josephson, USA . . . . . . . . . . . . . . 199.76
2. Mikako Kotani,
   Aki Takayama, JPN . . . . . . . . . . . . . . . 194.30
3. Lisa Alexander,
   Kathy Glen, CAN . . . . . . . . . . . . . . . . . 192.56
4. Gana Maximova,
   Olga Sedakova, URS . . . . . . . . . . . . . . 192.26
5. Anne Capron,
   Karine Schuler, FRA . . . . . . . . . . . . . . 188.36
6. Zewen Guan,
   Xiaojie Wang, CHN . . . . . . . . . . . . . . . 179.10
7. Giovanna Burlando,
   Paola Celli, ITA . . . . . . . . . . . . . . . . . . 178.74
8. Sonia Cardenas,
   Lourdes Olivera, MEX . . . . . . . . . . . . . 178.71

TEAM (13)

1. USA . . . . . . . . . . . 196.14
2. Canada . . . . . . . . . 193.25
3. Japan . . . . . . . . . . 189.75
4. Soviet Union . . . . . 188.20
5. France . . . . . . . . . . 182.88
6. China . . . . . . . . . . 179.83
7. Italy . . . . . . . . . . . 178.64
8. Great Britain . . . . . 176.77

**Team USA:** Kristen Babb, Becky Dyroen, Karen Josephson, Sarah Josephson, Jill Savery, Nathalie Schneyder, Heather Simmons, Michelle Svitenko.

**Countries Entered (20):** Australia, Austria, Brazil, Canada, China, France, Great Britain, Germany, Italy, Japan, Korea, Mexico, Netherlands, New Zealand, Spain, Sweden, Switzerland, Soviet Union, United States, Venezuela.

### *V World Aquatic Championships, Madrid, Spain August 14–24, 1986*

SOLO (24)

1. Carolyn Waldo, CAN . . . . . . . . . . . . . . 200.03
2. Sarah Josephson, USA . . . . . . . . . . . . . . 194.96
3. Muriel Hermine, FRA . . . . . . . . . . . . . . 186.25
4. Meiko Tanaka, JPN . . . . . . . . . . . . . . . 183.90
5. Alexandra Worisch, AUT . . . . . . . . . . . 180.13
6. Mariella van de Heijde, NED . . . . . . . . 179.58
7. Karin Singer, SUI . . . . . . . . . . . . . . . . . 178.50
8. Alexandra Dodd, GBR . . . . . . . . . . . . . 176.28

DUET (20)

1. Michelle Cameron,
   Carolyn Waldo, CAN . . . . . . . . . . . . . . 196.26
2. Sarah Josephson,
   Karen Josephson, USA . . . . . . . . . . . . . 193.40
3. Megumi Ito,
   Mikako Kotani, JPN . . . . . . . . . . . . . . . 185.46
4. Edith Boss,
   Karin Singer, SUI . . . . . . . . . . . . . . . . . 180.90
5. Alexandra Dodd,
   Nicola Shearn, GBR . . . . . . . . . . . . . . . 178.37
6. Marjolein Philipsen,
   Mariella von de Heijde, NED . . . . . . . . 177.35
7. Alfia Zhanaletdinova,
   Maria Cherniaeva, URS . . . . . . . . . . . . . 175.20
8. Anne Capron,
   Karine Schuler, FRA . . . . . . . . . . . . . . . 174.16

TEAM (15)

1. Canada . . . . . . . . . 191.20
2. USA . . . . . . . . . . . 190.82
3. Japan . . . . . . . . . . 185.76
4. France . . . . . . . . . . 176.62
5. Soviet Union . . . . . 176.44
6. Netherlands . . . . . . 172.75
7. Switzerland . . . . . . . 171.17
8. Mexico . . . . . . . . . 169.91

**Canada:** Natalie Audet, Michelle Cameron, Sylvie Frechette, Karin Larsen, Chantal Laviolette, Traci Meades, Missy Morlock, Carolyn Waldo.

**Team USA:** Kristen Babb, Lori Hatch, Karen Josephson, Sarah Josephson, Karen Madsen, Lisa Riddell, Michelle Svitenko, Mary Visniski, Susan Reed, Margarita Smith.

**Countries Entered (24):** Aruba, Australia, Austria, Barbados, Brazil, Canada, China, Colombia, Denmark, Dominican Republic, Egypt, France, Great Britain, Italy, Japan, Mexico, Netherlands, New Zealand, Spain, Sweden, Switzerland, Soviet Union, United States, Venezuela.

## IV World Aquatic Championships, Guayaquil, Ecuador
### July 29–Aug. 8, 1982

SOLO (22)

1. Tracie Ruiz, USA . . . . . . . . . . . . . . . . . . 192.30
2. Kelly Kryczka, CAN . . . . . . . . . . . . . . 188.98
3. Miwako Motoyoshi, JPN . . . . . . . . . . . 181.60
4. Carolyn Wilson, GBR . . . . . . . . . . . . . 176.51
5. Marijke Engelen, NED . . . . . . . . . . . . . 171.18
6. Gudrun Haenisch, FRG . . . . . . . . . . . . . 167.65
7. Carol Sturzenegger, SUI . . . . . . . . . . . . 166.58
8. Muriel Hermine, FRA . . . . . . . . . . . . . . 166.04

DUET (21)

1. Sharon Hambrook,
   Kelly Kryczka, CAN . . . . . . . . . . . . . . 190.54
2. Candy Costie,
   Tracie Ruiz, USA . . . . . . . . . . . . . . . . . . 188.65
3. Ikuko Abe,
   Masae Fujiwara, JPN . . . . . . . . . . . . . . 181.90
4. Caroline Holmyard,
   Carolyn Wilson, GBR . . . . . . . . . . . . . 176.73
5. Marijke Engelen,
   Catrien Eijken, NED . . . . . . . . . . . . . . . 174.65
6. Maya Mast,
   Carol Sturzenegger, SUI . . . . . . . . . . . . 167.12
7. Pascale Besson,
   Muriel Hermine, FRA . . . . . . . . . . . . . . 165.34
8. Eva Edinger,
   Alexandra Worisch, AUT . . . . . . . . . . . 162.85

TEAM (12)

1. Canada . . . . . . . . . . . . . . . . . . . . . . . 188.25
2. USA . . . . . . . . . . . . . . . . . . . . . . . . . 186.05
3. Japan . . . . . . . . . . . . . . . . . . . . . . . . 182.05
4. Netherlands . . . . . . . . . . . . . . . . . . . 172.68
5. Great Britain . . . . . . . . . . . . . . . . . . 172.10
6. Switzerland . . . . . . . . . . . . . . . . . . . 166.69
7. Federal Republic of Germany . . . . . 163.69
8. Mexico . . . . . . . . . . . . . . . . . . . . . . . 160.58

**Canada:** Janet Arnold, Wendy Barber, Sharon Hambrook, Kelly Kryczka, Chantal Laviolette, Renee Paradis, Penny Vilagos, Vicky Vilagos, Susan Clarke, Carolyn Waldo.

**Team USA:** Tara Cameron, Candy Costie, Sarah Josephson, Holly Spencer, Tracie Ruiz, Mary Visniski, Robin Waller, Marie White.

**Countries Entered (22):** Australia, Austria, Brazil, Canada, Colombia, Cuba, Dominican Republic, Egypt, France, Great Britain, Italy, Japan, Mexico, Netherlands, Puerto Rico, Sweden, Switzerland, United States, Uruguay, Venezuela, West Germany, Zimbabwe.

## III World Aquatic Championships, Berlin, West Germany
### August 18–28, 1978

SOLO (15)

1. Helen Vanderburg, CAN . . . . . . . . . . . . 187.84

2. Pamela Tryon, USA . . . . . . . . . . . . . . . 181.49
3. Yasuko Unezaki, JPN . . . . . . . . . . . . . . 179.65
4. Jacqueline Cox, GBR . . . . . . . . . . . . . . 177.36
5. Renate Baur, SUI . . . . . . . . . . . . . . . . . 164.33
6. Marijke Engelen, NED . . . . . . . . . . . . . 161.16
7. Donella Burridge, AUS . . . . . . . . . . . . . 157.36
8. Sally Ann Jenkins, NZL . . . . . . . . . . . . 155.23

DUET (15)

1. Michele Calkins,
   Helen Vanderburg, CAN . . . . . . . . . . . . 183.00
2. Masako Fujiwara,
   Yasuko Fujiwara, JPN . . . . . . . . . . . . . . 181.84
3. Pamela Tryon,
   Michele Barone, USA . . . . . . . . . . . . . . 180.75
4. Jacqueline Cox,
   Andrea Holland, GBR . . . . . . . . . . . . . . 170.75
5. Renate Baur,
   Carolyn Sturzenegger, SUI . . . . . . . . . . . 164.12
6. Ines Boermann,
   Gudrun Haenisch, FRG . . . . . . . . . . . . . 160.13
7. Catrien Eijken,
   Marijke Engelen, NED . . . . . . . . . . . . . 158.16
8. Mireya Andrade,
   Gabriela Terroba, MEX . . . . . . . . . . . . . 157.75

TEAM (9)

1. USA . . . . . . . . . . . . . . . . . . . . . . . . . 182.30
2. Japan . . . . . . . . . . . . . . . . . . . . . . . . 181.53
3. Canada . . . . . . . . . . . . . . . . . . . . . . . 177.91
4. Great Britain . . . . . . . . . . . . . . . . . . 165.82
5. Switzerland . . . . . . . . . . . . . . . . . . . 160.34
6. Netherlands . . . . . . . . . . . . . . . . . . . 159.05
7. Federal Republic of Germany . . . . . 158.57
8. Egypt . . . . . . . . . . . . . . . . . . . . . . . . 117.62

**Team USA:** Tami Allen, Michele Barone, Erin Barr, Michele Beaulieu, Gerri Brandley, Jane Goeppinger, Linda Shelley, Pamela Tryon.

**Countries Entered (15):** Australia, Austria, Canada, Denmark, Egypt, Fed. Rep. of Germany, Great Britain, Italy, Japan, Mexico, Netherlands, New Zealand, Sweden, Switzerland, United States.

## II World Aquatic Championships, Cali, Colombia
### July 18–27, 1975

SOLO (6)

1. Gail Johnson Buzonas, USA . . . . . . . . . . 133.00
2. Sylvie Fortier, CAN . . . . . . . . . . . . . . . . 131.30
3. Yasuko Unezaki, JPN . . . . . . . . . . . . . . 126.60
4. (tie) Jane Holland, GBR . . . . . . . . . . . . 114.80
4. (tie) Angelika Honsbeek, NED . . . . . . . . 114.80
6. Donella Burridge, AUS . . . . . . . . . . . . . 111.80

DUET (10)

1. Robin Curren,
   Amanda Norrish, USA . . . . . . . . . . . . . . 129.40

2. Carol Stuart,
   Laura Wilkin, CAN . . . . . . . . . . . . . . . 127.70
3. Masako Fujiwara,
   Yasuko Fujiwara, JPN . . . . . . . . . . . . . 126.00
4. Jane Holland,
   Josephine Mitchell, GBR . . . . . . . . . . . . 115.70
5. Angelika Honsbeek,
   Helma Gluvers, NED . . . . . . . . . . . . . . 110.00
6. Donella Burridge,
   Lisa Steanes, AUS . . . . . . . . . . . . . . . . 108.40
7. Roselyne Jaqueneau,
   Marie Pons, FRA . . . . . . . . . . . . . . . . . 102.30
8. Sylvia Guedel,
   Esther Meyer, SUI . . . . . . . . . . . . . . . . 100.70

TEAM (8)

1. USA . . . . . . . . . . . 128.81
2. Canada . . . . . . . . . 125.12
3. Japan . . . . . . . . . . 123.69
4. Great Britain . . . . . 113.53
5. Netherlands . . . . . . . 110.77
6. Switzerland . . . . . . 99.39
7. Sweden . . . . . . . . . 99.02
8. Colombia . . . . . . . . 84.37

**Team USA:** Michele Barone, Susan Baross, Gail Johnson Buzonas, Robin Curren, Mary Ellen Longo, Amanda Norrish, Linda Shelley, Pamela Tryon.

**Countries Entered (10):** Australia, Canada, Colombia, France, Great Britain, Japan, Netherlands, Sweden, Switzerland, United States.

### *I World Aquatic Championships, Belgrade, Yugoslavia Sept. 2–4, 1973*

SOLO (14)

1. Teresa Andersen, USA . . . . . . . . . . . . . 120.46
2. Jo Jo Carrier, CAN . . . . . . . . . . . . . . . . 112.53

3. Junko Hasumi, JPN . . . . . . . . . . . . . . . 104.18
4. Leisbeth Wouda, NED . . . . . . . . . . . . . . 97.71
5. Francoise Schuler, FRA . . . . . . . . . . . . . 95.85
6. Jennifer Lane, GBR . . . . . . . . . . . . . . . . 94.85
7. Beverly Balkind, AUS . . . . . . . . . . . . . . 93.98
8. Brigette Serwonski, FRG . . . . . . . . . . . . . 93.07

DUET (12)

1. Teresa Andersen,
   Gail Johnson, USA . . . . . . . . . . . . . . . 118.39
2. Jo Jo Carrier,
   Mado Ramsay, CAN . . . . . . . . . . . . . . 112.91
3. Masuko Fujiwara,
   Yasuko Fujiwara, JPN . . . . . . . . . . . . . 109.72
4. Liesbeth Wouda,
   Monique Gerritsen, NED . . . . . . . . . . . . 96.98
5. Pepita Sanchez,
   Eva Govezensky, MEX . . . . . . . . . . . . . 93.52
6. Jennifer Lane,
   Doris Davis, GBR . . . . . . . . . . . . . . . . 94.14
7. Francoise Schuler,
   Elysabeth Gazelles, FRA . . . . . . . . . . . . 91.14
8. Barbro Ansehn,
   Marie Cervin, SWE . . . . . . . . . . . . . . . 88.75

TEAM (11)

1. USA . . . . . . . . . . . 117.61
2. Canada . . . . . . . . . 112.91
3. Japan . . . . . . . . . . 107.31
4. Mexico . . . . . . . . . 98.30
5. Great Britain . . . . . 97.91
6. Netherlands . . . . . . 96.64

**Team USA:** Teresa Andersen, Susan Baross, Robin Curren, Jackie Douglass, Gail Johnson, Dana Moore, Amanda Norrish, Suzanne Randell.

**Countries Entered (15):** Australia, Austria, Canada, Denmark, France, Great Britain, Japan, Mexico, Netherlands, Norway, Spain, Sweden, Switzerland, United States, West Germany.

## FINA SYNCHRONIZED SWIMMING WORLD CUPS

### *X FINA World Cup, Zurich, Switzerland September 12–15, 2002*

SOLO (23)

1. Virginie Dedieu, FRA . . . . . . . . . . . . . . 99.167
2. Miya Tachibana, JPN . . . . . . . . . . . . . . 97.334
3. Anastasia Davydova, RUS . . . . . . . . . . . 97.000
4. Anastasia Ermakova, RUS . . . . . . . . . . . 96.334
5. Anna Kozlova, USA . . . . . . . . . . . . . . . 95.917
6. Gemma Mengual, ESP . . . . . . . . . . . . . 95.833
7. Claire Carver-Dias, CAN . . . . . . . . . . . . 94.750
8. Miho Takeda, JPN . . . . . . . . . . . . . . . . 93.750
9. Darya Shemiakin, UKR . . . . . . . . . . . . . 92.167

10. Lauren McFall, USA . . . . . . . . . . . . . . . 92.833
11. Hu Ni, CHN . . . . . . . . . . . . . . . . . . . . 92.084

DUET (23)

1. Anastasia Davydova,
   Anastasia Ermakova, RUS . . . . . . . . . . . 98.501
2. Miya Tachibana,
   Miho Takeda, JPN . . . . . . . . . . . . . . . . 98.250
3. Fanny Letourneau,
   Claire Carver-Dias, CAN . . . . . . . . . . . . 96.500
4. Alison Bartosik,
   Anna Kozlova, USA . . . . . . . . . . . . . . . 96.001
5. Myriam Glez,
   Virginie Dedieu, FRA . . . . . . . . . . . . . . 95.667

6. Gemma Mengual,
   Andrea Fuentes, ESP .............. 94.834
7. Elvira Khassianova,
   Anna Shorina, RUS .............. 94.167
8. Juri Tatsumi,
   Yoko Yoneda, JPN ................ 94.001
9. Gu Beibei,
   Zhang Xiaohuan, CHN ............ 92.917
10. Sara Lowe,
    Stephanie Nesbitt, USA ............ 92.583

TEAM (12)

1. Russia ........... 98.883
2. Japan ............ 98.000
3. United States ..... 96.501
4. Canada .......... 96.167
5. Spain ............ 95.417
6. China ........... 94.001
7. Italy ............. 93.333
8. Greece .......... 91.667
9. Switzerland ....... 90.918
10. France ........... 90.667

**Russia:** Olga Brusnikina, Yulia Chestakovitch, Anna Chorina, Anastasia Ermakova, Maria Gromova, Elena Jouravleva, Elvira Khassianova, Elena Ovtchinikova, Alexandra Shumkova, Irina Tolkatcheva.

**Team USA:** Alison Bartosik, Tammy Crow, Erin Dobratz, Becky Jasontek, Anna Kozlova, Tracy Long, Sara Lowe, Lauren McFall, Stephanie Nesbitt, Katie Norris, Gina Pietras, Kendra Zanotto.

**Countries Entered (12):** Brazil, Canada, China, Egypt, France, Greece, Italy, Japan, Russia, Spain, Switzerland, United States.

### IX FINA World Cup,
### Seoul, Korea
### September 8–12, 1999

SOLO (24)

1. Olga Brusnikina, RUS .............. 99.406
2. Virginie Dedieu, FRA .............. 97.747
3. Miya Tachibana, JPN ............. 97.583
4. Kristina Lum, USA ................ 96.370
5. Irene Perchina, RUS .............. 96.281
6. Claire Carver-Dias, CAN .......... 96.250
7. Giovanna Burlando, ITA ............ 95.447
8. Miho Takeda, JPN ................ 95.097
9. Valerie Hould-Marchand, CAN ...... 93.826
10. Becky Martin, USA ................ 93.696

DUET (24)

1. Olga Brusnikina,
   Maria Kisseleva, RUS .............. 99.364
2. Miya Tachibana,
   Miho Takeda, JPN ................ 97.773
3. Elena Azorova,
   Olga Novokschenova, RUS .......... 97.643

4. Myriam Lignot,
   Virginie Dedieu, FRA .............. 97.177
5. Carrie Barton,
   Elicia Marshall, USA .............. 96.374
6. Fanny Letourneau,
   Claire Carver-Dias, CAN .......... 95.923
7. Rei Jimbo,
   Raiki Fuji, CHN .................. 95.195
8. Becky Jasontek,
   Emily Marsh, USA ................ 94.853
9. Kristin Normand,
   Reidun Tatham, CAN .............. 94.397
10. Maurizia Cecconi,
    Giovanna Burlando, ITA ............ 94.170

TEAM (12)

1. Russia ............ 99.650
2. Japan ............ 98.527
3. Canada ........... 97.253
4. United States ..... 97.123
5. France ........... 95.233
6. Italy ............. 95.081
7. China ............ 94.120
8. Spain ............ 93.660
9. Korea ............ 92.821
10. Switzerland ....... 92.203

**Russia:** Elena Azarova, Olga Brusnikina, Anna Chorina, Maria Kisseleva, Olga Novokshchenova, Irina Perchina, Elena Soia, Yulia Vasilieva, Olga Vassioukova.

**Team USA:** Carrie Barton, Tammy Crow, Bridget Finn, Becky Jasontek, Kristina Lum, Emily Marsh, Elicia Marshall, Tuesday Middaugh, Lauren McFall, Kim Wurzel.

**Countries Entered (12):** Brazil, Canada, China, France, Italy, Japan, Korea, Mexico, Russia, Spain, Switzerland, United States.

### VIII FINA World Cup,
### Guangzhou, China
### July 16–19, 1997

SOLO

1. Olga Sedakova, RUS .............. 95.792
2. Karen Clark, CAN .............. 94.267
3. Virginie Dedieu, FRA .............. 93.641
4. Miya Tachibana, JPN ............. 93.109
5. Wu Chunlan, CHN ................ 91.907
6. Giovanna Burlando, ITA ............ 91.628
7. Carrie Barton, USA .............. 90.645
8. Choi You-Jin, CHN ................ 90.273

DUET

1. Olga Sedakova,
   Olga Brusnikina, RUS .............. 95.265
2. Miya Tachibana,
   Miho Takeda, JPN ................ 93.544
3. Kasia Kulesza,
   Jacinthe Taillon, CAN .............. 92.853

4. Li Min,
   Long Yan, CHN . . . . . . . . . . . . . . . . . 92.666
5. Virginie Dedieu,
   Myriam Lignot, FRA . . . . . . . . . . . . . 92.663
6. Carrie Barton,
   Elicia Marshall, USA . . . . . . . . . . . . . 91.051
7. Gaida Ballan,
   Serena Bianchi, ITA . . . . . . . . . . . . . . 90.881
8. Choi You-Jin,
   Yoo Na-Mi, KOR . . . . . . . . . . . . . . . 90.426

TEAM

1. Russia . . . . . . . . . . 99.317
2. Japan . . . . . . . . . . . 98.104
3. United States . . . . . 96.829
4. Canada . . . . . . . . . . 96.687
5. France . . . . . . . . . . 96.567
6. Italy . . . . . . . . . . . . 94.754
7. China . . . . . . . . . . . 94.590
8. Korea . . . . . . . . . . . 93.380

**Russia:** Elena Arazova, Olga Brusnikina, Ann Touriaeva, Olga Novokchtchenova, Elana Barantseva, Maria Kisseleva, Olga Medvedeva, Natalia Gruzdeva

**Team USA:** Carrie Barton, Bridget Finn, Becky Jasontek, Tina Kasid, Kristina Lum, Emily Marsh, Elicia Marshall, Kim Wurzel, Tracy Gayeski, Laurie McClelland

**Countries Entered (9):** Canada, China, France, Italy, Japan, Korea, Mexico, Russia, United States.

### VII FINA World Cup, Atlanta, Georgia August 1–5, 1995

SOLO (12)

1. Becky Dyroen-Lancer, USA . . . . . . . . . 97.163
2. Lisa Alexander, CAN . . . . . . . . . . . . . . 96.193
3. Olga Sedakova, RUS . . . . . . . . . . . . . . 95.710
4. Miya Tachibana, JPN . . . . . . . . . . . . . 94.714
5. Lisa Alexander, CAN . . . . . . . . . . . . . . 93.397
6. Chunlan Wu, CHN . . . . . . . . . . . . . . 91.715
7. Laila Vakil, GBR . . . . . . . . . . . . . . . . 91.205
8. Lillian Leal, MEX . . . . . . . . . . . . . . . . 90.274
9. Paola Celli, ITA . . . . . . . . . . . . . . . . . 89.715
10. Naomi Young, AUS . . . . . . . . . . . . . . 87.904

DUET (10)

1. Jill Sudduth,
   Becky Dyroen-Lancer, USA . . . . . . . . . 96.535
2. Lisa Alexander,
   Erin Woodley, CAN . . . . . . . . . . . . . . 95.563
3. Maria Kisseleva,
   Elena Azarova, RUS . . . . . . . . . . . . . . 95.309
4. Miya Tachibana,
   Akiko Kawase, JPN . . . . . . . . . . . . . . . 94.943
5. Marianne Aeschbacher,
   Myriam Lignot, FRA . . . . . . . . . . . . . 92.780

6. Giovanna Burlando,
   M. Carnini, ITA . . . . . . . . . . . . . . . . 92.175
7. Min Li,
   Yan Long, CHN . . . . . . . . . . . . . . . . . 91.466
8. Collette Geir,
   Karen Thomson, GBR . . . . . . . . . . . . 88.702
9. Sylvia Donker,
   Iris Sentrop, NED . . . . . . . . . . . . . . . 87.433
10. M. Ali,
    Rania Kamel, EGY . . . . . . . . . . . . . . . 83.437

TEAM (16)

1. USA . . . . . . . . . . . . 96.615
2. Canada . . . . . . . . . . 95.530
3. Russia . . . . . . . . . . . 94.899
4. Japan . . . . . . . . . . . . 94.702
5. France . . . . . . . . . . . 92.963
6. China . . . . . . . . . . . 92.339
7. Italy . . . . . . . . . . . . 91.664
8. Mexico . . . . . . . . . . 91.254
9. Korea . . . . . . . . . . . 91.113
10. Great Britain . . . . . . 89.395

OLYMPIC TEAM QUALIFYING (12)

1. USA . . . . . . . . 99.790
2. Canada . . . . . . 98.483
3. Japan . . . . . . . 98.216
4. Russia . . . . . . 97.816
5. France . . . . . . 97.057
6. China . . . . . . . 95.616
7. Italy . . . . . . . . 94.940
8. Mexico . . . . . . 94.673

**Team USA:** Suzannah Bianco, Tammy Cleland, Becky Dyroen-Lancer, Emily LeSueur, Heather Pease, Jill Savery, Nathalie Schneyder, Heather Simmons-Carrasco, Jill Sudduth, Margot Thien.

**Countries Entered (18):** Australia, Brazil, Canada, China, Czech Republic, Egypt, France, Great Britain, Italy, Japan, Korea, Mexico, Netherlands, Russia, Switzerland, Ukraine, United States, Venezuela.

### VI FINA World Cup Lausanne, Switzerland July 7–10, 1993

SOLO (9)

1. Becky Dyroen-Lancer, USA . . . . . . . . 193.459
2. Lisa Alexander, CAN . . . . . . . . . . . . . 190.747
3. Olga Sedakova, RUS . . . . . . . . . . . . . 190.434
4. Fumiko Okuno, JPN . . . . . . . . . . . . . 190.149
5. Marianne Aeschbacher, FRA . . . . . . . 186.488
6. Maria Guisti, VEN . . . . . . . . . . . . . . 183.866
7. Marjolein Both, NED . . . . . . . . . . . . 183.674
8. Kerry Shacklock, GBR . . . . . . . . . . . . 183.152
9. Rachel Hobi, SUI . . . . . . . . . . . . . . . 179.396

### DUET (9)

1. Jill Sudduth,
   Becky Dyroen-Lancer, USA ......... 191.987
2. Olga Sedakova,
   Anna Kozlova, RUS ............... 190.394
3. Cari Read,
   Karen Fonteyne, CAN ............. 189.768
4. Akiko Kawase,
   Miya Tachibana, JPN ............. 188.305
5. Celine Leveque,
   Charlotte Massardier, FRA ......... 184.495
6. Laila Vakil,
   Kerry Shacklock, GBR ............. 183.099
7. Marjolijn Both,
   Frouke van Beeck, NED ........... 181.717
8. Jie Jiang,
   Min Tan, CHN ................... 180.285
9. Helen Kaser,
   Caroline Imoberdorf, SUI .......... 177.871

### TEAM (9)

1. USA ............ 191.757
2. Canada .......... 190.456
3. Japan ........... 187.993
4. Russia .......... 187.706
5. France .......... 185.343
6. Italy ........... 182.382
7. China .......... 180.611
8. Great Britain ..... 180.136
9. Switzerland ...... 178.192

**Team USA:** Tammy Cleland, Becky Dyroen-Lancer, Suzannah Dyroen, Heather Pease, Emily Porter, Jill Savery, Nathalie Schneyder, Heather Simmons, Jill Sudduth, Margot Thien.

**Countries Entered (11):** Canada, China, France, Great Britain, Italy, Japan, Netherlands, Russia, Switzerland, United States, Venezuela.

### V FINA World Cup,
### Bonn, Germany
### September 12–15, 1991

#### SOLO (8)

1. Sylvie Frechette, CAN ............... 96.16
2. Kristen Babb-Sprague, USA ......... 95.99
3. Fumiko Okuno, JPN ............... 94.88
4. Olga Sedakova, RUS ............... 93.73
5. Anne Capron, FRA ................ 92.78
6. Maria Guisti, VEN ................ 92.74
7. Marjolijn Both, NED .............. 91.74
8. Monika Muller, GER ............... 90.86

#### DUET (8)

1. Karen Josephson,
   Sarah Josephson, USA ............. 96.86
2. Fumiko Okuno,
   Aki Takayama, JPN ............... 95.25
3. Christine Larson,
   Kathy Glen, CAN ................. 94.92

4. Olga Sedakova,
   Anna Kozlova, RUS ............... 93.89
5. Clarisse Chesnneau,
   Celine Leveque, FRA .............. 91.87
6. Giovanna Burlando,
   Paola Celli, ITA .................. 91.01
7. Zewen Guan,
   Xiaojie Wang, CHN ............... 90.09
8. Monika Muller,
   Ines Haller, GER ................. 88.58

### TEAM (8)

1. USA ............ 96.10
2. Canada .......... 95.21
3. Soviet Union ...... 93.75
4. Japan ........... 93.67
5. China .......... 91.78
6. Italy ........... 91.30
7. France .......... 91.09
8. Germany ........ 85.84

**Team USA:** Kristen Babb-Sprague, Becky Dyroen, Suzannah Dyroen, Karen Josephson, Sarah Josephson, Jill Savery, Nathalie Schneyder, Heather Simmons, Jill Sudduth, Michelle Svitenko.

**Countries Entered (10):** Canada, China, France, Germany, Italy, Japan, Netherlands, Soviet Union, United States, Venezuela.

### IV World Cup
### Paris, France
### September 7–9, 1989

#### SOLO (8)

1. Tracy Long, USA ................. 192.64
2. Sylvie Frechette, CAN ............. 192.40
3. Mikako Kotani, JPN .............. 191.76
4. Karine Schuler, FRA .............. 187.73
5. Christina Falasinidi, URS .......... 184.53
6. Kerry Shacklock, GBR ............ 182.24
7. Claudia Peczinka, SUI ............ 179.69
8. Doris Eisenhofer, FRG ............ 175.33

#### DUET (8)

1. Tracy Long,
   Michele Svitenko, USA ............ 191.03
2. Mikako Kotani,
   Aki Takayama, JPN ............... 190.03
3. Sylvie Frechette,
   Nathalie Guay, CAN .............. 189.45
4. Marianne Aeschbacher,
   Karine Schuler, FRA .............. 186.29
5. Maria Cherniava,
   Elena Foschevaskaia, URS .......... 183.34
6. Sarah Northey,
   Kerry Shacklock, GBR ............ 180.37
7. Claudia Muralt,
   Claudia Peczinka, SUI ............ 176.51
8. Sonia Cardenas,
   Lordes Oliviera, MEX ............. 175.25

TEAM (8)

1. USA ............ 188.94
2. Canada .......... 188.85
3. Japan ........... 186.70
4. Soviet Union ...... 183.66
5. France ........... 182.97
6. Switzerland ....... 176.44
7. Netherlands ....... 175.28
8. Mexico .......... 173.36

**Team USA:** Cathy Cramer, Becky Dyroen, Tracy Long, Patti Lynn, Lori McCoy, Jill Savery, Nathalie Schneyder, Heather Simmons, Jill Sudduth, Michelle Svitenko.

**Countries Entered (10):** Canada, France, Germany, Great Britain, Japan, Mexico, Netherlands, Soviet Union, Switzerland, United States.

### III FINA World Cup, Cairo, Egypt October 1–3, 1987

SOLO (9)

1. Carolyn Waldo, CAN ............... 198.36
2. Tracie Ruiz-Conforto, USA .......... 197.45
3. Muriel Hermine, FRA .............. 188.86
4. Mikako Kotani, JPN ............... 187.63
5. Karin Singer, SUI ................. 183.93
6. Nicola Shearn, GBR .............. 178.50
7. Marjolijn Both, NED .............. 173.58
8. Beatrix Mullner, AUT ............. 171.98
9. Dalia Mokbel, EGY ................ 166.53

DUET (9)

1. Carolyn Waldo,
   Michelle Cameron, CAN ............ 195.54
2. Karen Josephson,
   Sarah Josephson, USA .............. 195.06
3. Mikako Kotani,
   Miyako Tanaka, JPN ............... 187.46
3. Muriel Hermine,
   Karine Schuler, FRA ............... 185.46
5. Karin Singer,
   Edith Boss, SUI ................... 183.42
6. Tatiana Titova,
   Irina Zhukova, URS ............... 180.40
7. Nicola Shearn,
   Nicola Batchelor, GBR ............. 177.34
8. Marjolijn Both,
   Joanni Janssens, NED .............. 175.21
9. Dalia Mokbel,
   Sahar Farouk, EGY ................ 164.34

TEAM (8)

1. USA ............ 193.49
2. Canada .......... 191.63
3. Japan ........... 185.85
4. France ........... 182.11
5. Soviet Union ...... 181.57

6. Switzerland ....... 178.95
7. Netherlands ....... 174.56
8. Egypt ............ 165.83

**Team USA:** Kristen Babb, Lori Hatch, Karen Josephson, Sarah Josephson, Tracy Long, Lisa Riddell, Tracie Ruiz-Conforto, Michelle Svitenko, Karen Madsen, Susan Reed.

**Countries Entered (10):** Austria, Canada, Egypt, France, Great Britain, Japan, Netherlands, Soviet Union, Switzerland, United States.

### II FINA World Cup, Indianapolis, Indiana August 23–27, 1985

SOLO (7)

1. Carolyn Waldo, CAN ............... 195.20
2. Sarah Josephson, USA .............. 191.66
3. Saeko Kimura, JPN ................. 185.38
4. Muriel Hermine, FRA .............. 184.85
5. Gerlind Scheller, FRG .............. 176.48
6. Edith Boss, SUI ................... 174.61
7. Marjolein Philipsen, NED ........... 173.70

DUET (7)

1. Carolyn Waldo,
   Michelle Cameron, CAN ........... 191.66
2. Karen Josephson,
   Sarah Josephson, USA .............. 190.76
3. Saeko Kimura,
   Takiyo Sasao, JPN ................. 185.83
4. Muriel Hermine,
   Pascale Besson, FRA ............... 180.95
5. Edith Boss,
   Karin Singer, SUI ................. 174.77
6. Lourdes Candini,
   Veronica Rodriquez, MEX ........... 170.96
7. Marjolein Van Kolck,
   Marion Jansen, NED ............... 167.55

TEAM (7)

1. Canada .................... 189.90
2. USA ...................... 187.71
3. Japan .................... 184.71
4. Netherlands .............. 170.90
5. Federal Republic Germany ..... 169.57
6. Switzerland ............... 167.99
7. Mexico ................... 166.14

**Canada:** Michelle Cameron, Sylvie Frechette, Karin Larsen, Chantal Laviolette, Traci Meades, Penny Vilagos, Vicky Vilagos, Carolyn Waldo.

**Team USA:** Kristen Babb, Sarah Josephson, Karen Josephson, Susan Reed, Lisa Riddell, Alice Smith, Margarita Smith, Mary Visniski.

**Countries Entered (8):** Canada, France, Germany, Japan, Mexico, Netherlands, Switzerland, United States.

### I FINA World Cup,
### Tokyo, Japan
### August 29–31, 1979

SOLO (7)

1. Helen Vanderburg, CAN . . . . . . . . . . 193.03
2. Michelle Beaulieu, USA . . . . . . . . . . . 188.53
3. Yuki Ishi, JPN . . . . . . . . . . . . . . . . . . . 179.18
4. Marijke Engelen, NED . . . . . . . . . . . . 167.86
5. Andrea Holland, GBR . . . . . . . . . . . . . 167.23
6. Gudrun Haenisch, FRG . . . . . . . . . . . 162.58
7. Caroline Sturzenegger, SUI . . . . . . . . . 160.95

DUET (7)

1. Helen Vanderburg,
   Kelly Kryczka, CAN . . . . . . . . . . . . . 187.41
2. Linda Shelley,
   Michele Barone, USA . . . . . . . . . . . . 186.14
3. Yasuko Unezaki,
   Kinyuyo Okada, JPN . . . . . . . . . . . . . 179.60
4. Andrea Holland,
   Carolyn Wilson, GBR . . . . . . . . . . . . 169.39

5. Marijke Engelen,
   Catrien Eijken, NED . . . . . . . . . . . . . . 169.31
6. Gabriella De Wrova,
   Helen Andrade, MEX . . . . . . . . . . . . . 167.43
7. Gudrun Haenisch,
   Ingrid May, FRG . . . . . . . . . . . . . . . . . 161.90

TEAM (6)

1. USA . . . . . . . . . . . . . 188.49
2. Japan . . . . . . . . . . . . 183.39
3. Canada . . . . . . . . . . 183.07
4. Netherlands . . . . . . . 168.82
5. Great Britain . . . . . . 168.11
6. Switzerland . . . . . . . 163.71

**Team USA:** Michele Barone, Gerri Brandley, Suzanne Cameron, Tracie Ruiz, Michelle Beaulieu, Pam Tryon, Karen Callaghan, Tara Cameron, Linda Shelley, Robin Waller.

**Countries Entered (8):** Canada, Germany, Great Britain, Japan, Mexico, Netherlands, Switzerland, United States.

---

# FINA JUNIOR WORLD SYNCHRONIZED SWIMMING CHAMPIONSHIPS

### IX Junior World Championships
### Moscow, Russia
### July 21–25, 2004

SOLO (29)

1. Natalia Ichtchenko, RUS . . . . . . . . . . . 89.902
2. Christina Jones, USA . . . . . . . . . . . . . 86.346
3. Elsie Marcotte, CAN . . . . . . . . . . . . . 84.599
4. Takako Konishi, JPN . . . . . . . . . . . . . 84.510
5. Beatrice Adelizzi, ITA . . . . . . . . . . . . . 83.991
6. Evanthia Makrygianni, GRE . . . . . . . . 83.809
7. Xin Shi, CHN . . . . . . . . . . . . . . . . . . . 82.419
8. Carmen Moraes, BRA . . . . . . . . . . . . . 80.933
9. Alba Cabello, ESP . . . . . . . . . . . . . . . . 79.985
10. Ganna Gezvesilna, UKR . . . . . . . . . . . 79.911
11. Perrine Penart, FRA . . . . . . . . . . . . . . 79.274
12. Rosanne Klein Geltink, NED . . . . . . . . 78.858

DUET (24)

1. Svetlana Romashina,
   Alexandra Eltchinova, RUS . . . . . . . . . 88.431
2. Annabelle Orme,
   Christina Jones, USA . . . . . . . . . . . . . 85.086
3. Takako Konishi,
   Chisa Ichikawa, JPN . . . . . . . . . . . . . . 84.386
4. Evanthia Marygianni,
   Aglaia Anastasiou, GRE . . . . . . . . . . . 83.848
5. Xi Luo,
   Ou Liu, CHN . . . . . . . . . . . . . . . . . . . 83.805
6. Federica Tommasi,
   Elisa Bozzo, ITA . . . . . . . . . . . . . . . . . 83.102

7. Lila Meesseman-Bakir,
   Anne Lone, FRA . . . . . . . . . . . . . . . . . 81.990
8. Kseniya Sydorenko,
   Oksana Samokhvalova, UKR . . . . . . . . 81.236
9. Anne Claude LeMay,
   Eve Lamoureux, CAN . . . . . . . . . . . . . 81.164
10. Lara Teixeira,
    Carmen Lucia Moraes, BRA . . . . . . . . . 79.667
11. Cristina Violan,
    Lia Abante, ESP . . . . . . . . . . . . . . . . . . 79.332
12. Arna Toktagan,
    Anna Kulinka, KAZ . . . . . . . . . . . . . . 79.261

TEAM (20)

1. Russia . . . . . . . . . . . 87.596
2. Japan . . . . . . . . . . . . 84.760
3. China . . . . . . . . . . . . 84.480
4. United States . . . . . 83.798
5. Italy . . . . . . . . . . . . 83.711
6. Canada . . . . . . . . . . 83.172
7. Greece . . . . . . . . . . . 82.377
8. France . . . . . . . . . . . 81.238

**Russia:** Elizaveta Stephanova, Yulia Shepeleva, Svetlana Romashini, Daria Litvinova, Natalia Ichtchenko, Veronika Fedulova, Alexandra Eltchinova, Ekaterina Efremova.

**Team USA:** Carolyn Watts, Annabelle Orme, Jessica McMahon, Melissa Knight, Meghan Kinney, Christina Jones, Poppy Carlig, Brooke Abel.

FREE ROUTINE COMBINATION (18)

1. Russia ...... 96.600
2. Japan ...... 94.900
3. China ...... 94.000
4. Italy ....... 92.600
5. Canada ..... 91.900
6. Greece ..... 91.300
7. Ykraine ..... 89.100
8. Spain ....... 88.800

**Russia:** Ekaterina Efremova, Alexandra Eltchinova, Veronika Fedulova, Anastasia Gritsenko, Natalia Ichtchenko, Daria Litvinova, Anna Nassekina, Svetlana Romashina, Yulia Stepheleva, Elizaveta Stephanova.

**Countries Entered (31):** Australia, Austria, Belarus, Brazil, Canada, China, Costa Rica, Egypt, France, Germany, Great Britain, Greece, Israel, Italy, Japan, Kazakhstan, Macau China, Malaysia, Mexico, Netherlands, Portugal, Russia, Serbia and Montenegro, Slovakia, Spain, Switzerland, Thailand, Ukraine, United States, Uzbekistan.

### VIII Junior World Championships, Montreal, Canada August 15–18, 2002

SOLO (30)

1. Natalia Ichtchenko, RUS ............. 88.376
2. Nicole Cargill, CAN ................ 86.596
3. Tina Fuentes, ESP .................. 86.110
4. Sara Lowe, USA .................... 85.594
5. Hiromi Kobayashi, JPN ............. 85.285
6. Anastasia Gloushkov, ISR .......... 84.854
7. Beatrice Spaziani, ITA ............. 84.131
8. Zhao Chi Mei, CHN ................ 84.104

Duet (25)

1. Natalia Zlobina,
   Olga Larkina, RUS ................ 87.264
2. Courtney Stewart,
   Nicole Cargill, CAN .............. 86.608
3. Sara Lowe,
   Stephanie Nesbitt, USA ............ 85.724
4. Jiang TingTing,
   Jiang WenWen, CHN .............. 85.293
5. Hiromi Kobayashi,
   Toshiko Lizuka, JPN .............. 85.162
6. Laia Fileia,
   Tina Fuentes, ESP ................ 84.764
7. Sara Savoia,
   Raisa D'Attilia, ITA .............. 83.331
8. Effrosyni Gouda,
   Evgfenia Koutsoudi, GRE ........... 83.032

Team (19)

1. Russia ........... 87.511
2. Japan ............ 85.745
3. Canada .......... 85.601

4. China .......... 85.048
5. Italy ........... 84.214
6. Spain ........... 83.633
7. United States ...... 83.628
8. Greece .......... 82.492

FREE COMBINATION FINAL (9)

1. Japan ............ 94.600
2. Canada .......... 94.000
3. Spain ........... 92.700
4. United States ...... 92.400
5. Italy ............. 92.200
6. Greece .......... 90.700
7. China ........... 90.500
8. Switzerland ...... 85.700
9. Germany ........ 81.800

**Russia:** Svetlana Blokhina, Natalia Ichtchenko, Oleysa Karpova, Olga Koujela, Olga Larkina, Valeria Mozgovaia, Elana Psabtseva, Aleksandra Sergeeva, Natalia Tarassova, Natalia Zlobina.

**Japan (combo):** Ai Aoki, Reiko Fujimori, Chisa Ichikawa, Tomoko Iizuka, Toshiko Iizuka Hiromi Kobayashi, Saki Kobayashi, Takako Konishi, Hinako Kubo, Erina Suzuki.

**Team USA:** Kate Hooven, Christina Jones, Becky Kim, Sara Lowe, Barbara Nesbitt, Stephanie Nesbitt, Cassidy Ramage, Ashley Rule, Elizabeth-Anne Markman, Kim McKinley.

**Countries entered (28):** Australia, Austria, Brazil, Canada, China, Columbia, Costa Rica, Dominican Republic, Egypt, Germany, Great Britain, Greece, Israel, Italy, Japan, Kazakhstan, Korea, Malaysia, Mexico, Netherlands New Zealand, Russia, Slovakia, Spain, Switzerland, Ukraine, United States, Venezuela, Yugoslavia.

### VII Junior World Championships, Federal Way, Washington August 19–25, 2001

SOLO (27)

1. Anastasia Davydova, RUS ............ 91.76
2. Anouk Reniere-Lafreniere, CAN ...... 89.56
3. Tomomi Kago, JPN ................ 89.32
4. Alison Bartosik, USA ............. 86.96
5. Andrea Fuentes, ESP ............. 86.89
6. Beatice Spaziani, ITA ............. 86.46
7. Yajing Pan, CHN .................. 86.33
8. Darya Yushiko, UKR ............. 86.19
9. Anastasia Gloushkov, ISR ............ 85.70
10. Magdalena Brunner, SUI ............ 84.70
11. Maud Egond, FRA ............... 83.53
12. Hyou Mi Kim, KOR .............. 82.73

DUET (12)

1. Anastassia Ermakova,
   Anastasia Davydova, RUS ............ 92.69
2. Tomomi Kago,
   Masako Tachivana, JPN ............. 90.06

3. Trina Fuentes,
Andrea Fuentes, ESP . . . . . . . . . . . . . . . 89.73
4. Jessika Dubuc,
Anouk Reniere-Lafreniere, CAN . . . . . . 89.22
5. Xiaochu He,
Na Wang, CHN . . . . . . . . . . . . . . . . . . . 88.08
6. Alison Bartosik,
Sara Lowe, USA . . . . . . . . . . . . . . . . . . 87.06
7. Darya Yushko,
Iryna Gayvoronska, UKR . . . . . . . . . . . 86.53
8. Fedrica Andolfi,
Beatrice Spanizni, ITA . . . . . . . . . . . . . 85.12
9. Effosyni Gouda,
Eleni Georgiou, GRE . . . . . . . . . . . . . . 83.51
10. Audrey Abodie,
Carole-Anne Berger, FRA . . . . . . . . . . . 83.50
11. Hyun Kyung Chun,
Myong Kyoung Cho, KOR . . . . . . . . . . 82.29
12. Anastasia Gloushkov,
Moran Bar-Lev, ISR . . . . . . . . . . . . . . . 81.93

## Team (17)

1. Russia . . . . . . . . . . . 91.25
2. Japan . . . . . . . . . . . . 89.45
3. China . . . . . . . . . . . 89.28
4. Canada . . . . . . . . . . 88.68
5. United States . . . . . . 86.43
6. Ukraine . . . . . . . . . . 85.71
7. Italy . . . . . . . . . . . . 85.68
8. Greece . . . . . . . . . . . 84.62
9. France . . . . . . . . . . . 82.22
10. Brazil . . . . . . . . . . . . 81.50
11. Switzerland . . . . . . . 79.78
12. Colombia . . . . . . . . 78.71

**Russia:** Joulia Chakhova, Anastasia Davydova, Anastassia Ermakova, Maria Gromova, Elena Jouravleva, Olessia Karpova, Olga Larkina, Valeria Mozgovaia, Alexandra Shumkova, Anastassia Zaitseva.

**Team USA:** Alison Bartosik, Kate Hooven, Becky Kim, Teresa Liccardo, Sara Lowe, Lauren Marsh, Ashley McHugh, Stephanie Nesbitt, Emiko Takyu, Alison Wible.

**Countries Entered** (28): Australia, Brazil, Canada, Chile, China, Colombia, Dominican Republic, Egypt, France, Germany, Great Britain, Greece, Israel, Italy, Japan, Kazakhstan, Korea, Mexico, Netherlands, Puerto Rico, Russia, Slovakia, South Africa, Spain, Switzerland, Ukraine, United States, Yugoslavia.

## VI Junior World Championships, Cali, Colombia July 7–11, 1999

### Solo Finals (12)

1. Anastasia Davydova, RUS . . . . . . . . . . . . . 89.63
2. Charlotte Fabre, FRA . . . . . . . . . . . . . . . 87.64
3. Lorena Zaffalon, ITA . . . . . . . . . . . . . . . . 86.95

4. Mon Jeong Kim, KOR . . . . . . . . . . . . . . . 86.36
5. Darya Shemyakina, UKR . . . . . . . . . . . . 84.96
6. Joana Fiella, ESP . . . . . . . . . . . . . . . . . . 84.83
7. Juan Du, CHN . . . . . . . . . . . . . . . . . . . . 83.63
8. Katerina Kudelkova, CZE . . . . . . . . . . . . 83.36
9. Jaqueline Gomina, COL . . . . . . . . . . . . . 81.23
10. Camille Oliveira, BRA . . . . . . . . . . . . . 79.94

### Duet Finals (12)

1. Anastasia Davydova,
Anastasia Ermakova, RUS . . . . . . . . . . . 89.09
2. Xiaochu He,
Ha Wang, CHN . . . . . . . . . . . . . . . . . . . 86.60
3. Lorena Zaffalon,
Joey Paccagnella, ITA . . . . . . . . . . . . . . 86.10
4. Mon Jeong Kim,
Ha Koh Yun, KOR . . . . . . . . . . . . . . . . 85.60
5. Joana Filella,
Andrea Fuentes, ESP . . . . . . . . . . . . . . . 84.91
6. Darya Shemyakina,
Anastasiya Pavelyena, UKR . . . . . . . . . . 84.50
7. Maeva Morieau,
Geraldi Gibert, FRA . . . . . . . . . . . . . . . 83.98
8. Camile Oliveira,
Rob Fernandos, BRA . . . . . . . . . . . . . . . 81.60
9. Barbora Kudelkova,
Katerina Kudelkova, CZE . . . . . . . . . . . 79.85
10. Alejandra Miranda,
Cla Valdez, COL . . . . . . . . . . . . . . . . . . 78.77

### Team Finals (12)

1. Russia . . . . . . . . 89.04
2. China . . . . . . . . 87.14
3. Italy . . . . . . . . . 86.08
4. France . . . . . . . . 85.36
5. Spain . . . . . . . . 84.63
6. Brazil . . . . . . . . 81.76
7. Columbia . . . . . 80.51
8. Venezuela . . . . . 78.36
9. Mexico . . . . . . . 74.79
10. China . . . . . . . . 73.65

**Russia:** Anastasia Davydova, Anastasia Ermakova, Maria Gromova, Elvira Khassianova, Elisaveta Grouchina, Joulia Chestakovich, Trina Tolkatcheva, Daria Gurban

**Team USA:** Alison Bartosik, Tiffany Bye, Erin Dobratz, Julie Drexler, Stephanie Joukoff, Becky Martin, Katie Norris, Andrea Nott, Kimberly Probst, Kendra Zanotto.

**Countries Entered** (14) Brazil, Chile, China, Colombia, Czech Republic, France, Italy, Korea, Mexico, Russia, Slovakia, Spain, Ukraine, United States, Venezuela.

## V Junior World Championships, Moscow, Russia
### June 29–July 3, 1997

SOLO (20)

1. Alexandra Vassina, RUS .............91.390
2. Yoon Kyeong Jang, KOR .............90.639
3. Valerie Hould Marchand, CAN, .......89.961
4. Ayano Egami, JPN .................89.251
5. Lauren McFall, USA ................89.052
6. Ye Xia, CHN .....................87.610
7. Paola Tirados, ESP .................87.140
8. Myriam Glez, FRA ................86.696

DUET (26)

1. Yoon Kyeong Jang,
   Min-Jeong Kim, KOR ..............91.286
2. Alexandra Vassina,
   Ekaterina Androchina, RUS .........90.608
3. Ayano Egami,
   Ikuyo Kihusawa, JAP .............89.282
4. Becky Martin,
   Lauren McFall, USA ...............87.876
5. Myriam Glez,
   Charlotte Fabre, FRA ..............87.757
6. Ye Xia,
   Xiaohuan Zhang, CHN .............87.218
7. Melissa Dickner,
   Katia Savignac, CAN ..............87.144
8. Paola Tirados,
   Ana Montero, ESP .................86.832

TEAM (19)

1. Russia ......91.194
2. Japan .......89.396
3. USA ........89.357
4. China .......88.097
5. Canada ......88.093
6. France ......86.567
7. Italy .......86.221
8. Spain .......85.740

**Russia:** Alexandra Vassina, Daria Gurban, Ekaterina Androchina, Tatiana Zoueva, Olga Leonova, Anna Shorina, Olga Vassioukova, Elena Soia, Anna Melnikova, Elvira Khassianova.

**Team USA:** Victoria Bowen, Brynn Butzman, Erin Dobratz, Kathryn Enos, Marlene Marshall, Becky Martin, Christina McClelland, Lauren McFall, Kristin Schneider, Lindsey Wiggington.

**Countries Entered:** (27) Australia, Belarus, Belgium, Brazil, Bulgaria, Canada, Chile, China, Egypt, France, Germany, Great Britain, Greece, Hungary, Israel, Italy, Japan, Mexico, Netherlands, New Zealand, Poland, Republic of South Africa, Russia, Spain, Switzerland, Ukraine, United States.

## IV Junior World Championships, Bonn, Germany
### July 20–23, 1995

SOLO (28)

1. Olga Brusnikina, RUS ..............93.089
2. Virginie Dedieu, FRA ..............89.819
3. Estella Warren, CAN ...............89.533
4. Riho Nakajima, JPN ...............88.365
5. Alanna O'Leary, USA .............87.934
6. Clara Porchetto, ITA ..............85.989
7. Hou Yingshu, CHN ...............85.746
8. Paola Tirados, ESP ................83.833

DUET (26)

1. Olga Brusnikina,
   Alexandra Vassina, RUS ...........90.871
2. Riho Nakajima,
   Yoko Isoda, JPN .................88.802
3. Elicia Marshall,
   Alanna O'Leary, USA .............88.183
4. Chantale Sauvageau,
   Tyna Agostinelli, CAN ............88.028
5. Virginie Dedieu,
   Lise Kong, FRA .................86.586
6. Clara Porchetto,
   Laura Vecchietti, ITA .............85.801
7. Xia Ye,
   Zhou Jing, CHN .................84.755
8. Ione Serrano,
   Paola Tirados, ESP ...............83.563

TEAM (18)

1. Canada ......90.747
2. Japan .......89.482
3. Russia ......89.416
4. USA ........87.560
5. Italy .......86.637
6. France ......86.532
7. China .......85.760
8. Spain .......82.778

**Canada:** Tyna Agostinelli, Lyne Beaumont, Melanie Gagne, Catherine Garceau, Valarie Hould-Marchand, Fanny Letourneau, Reidun Tatham, Estella Warren.

**Team USA:** Lori Barbaglia, Amanda Burkett, Julie Enos, Elicia Marshall, Heather Moore, Shannon Montague, Alanna O'Leary, Becky Percy, Lisa Velez, Lindsay Wiggington, Lauren McFall.

**Countries Entered** (28): Belarus, Brazil, Bulgaria, Canada, China, Colombia, Czech Republic, Egypt, France, Great Britain, Germany, Greece, Hungary, Israel, Italy, Japan, Kazakhstan, Korea, Mexico, Netherlands, Russia, Slovakia, South Africa, Spain, Switzerland, United States, Uzbekistan, Yugoslavia.

## III Junior World Championships, Leeds, Great Britain
### August 27–30, 1993

SOLO (30)

1. Olga Brusnikina, RUS . . . . . . . . . . . . . . 174.603
2. Kasia Kulesza, CAN . . . . . . . . . . . . . . 173.667
3. Miho Takeda, JPN . . . . . . . . . . . . . . . 172.456
4. Naomi Young, AUS . . . . . . . . . . . . . . . 171.308
5. Kristina Lum, USA . . . . . . . . . . . . . . . 170.680
6. Mara Brunetti, ITA . . . . . . . . . . . . . . . 166.044
7. Xuan Chen, CHN . . . . . . . . . . . . . . . . 165.120
8. Anna Martyniouk, UKR . . . . . . . . . . . 164.806

DUET

1. Olga Brousnikina,
   Yulia Pankratova, RUS . . . . . . . . . . . . 173.117
2. Kasia Kulesza,
   Marie-Miche Cloutier, CAN . . . . . . . . 173.021
3. Miho Takeda,
   Akiko Miyazaki, JPN . . . . . . . . . . . . . 171.365
4. Kristina Lum,
   Kim Wurzel, USA . . . . . . . . . . . . . . . . 170.031
5. Marie-Pierre Moynot,
   Julie Fabre, FRA . . . . . . . . . . . . . . . . . 166.742
6. Brunella Carrafelli,
   Mara Brunetti, ITA . . . . . . . . . . . . . . . 165.791
7. Bianca Van der Velden,
   Sonja Van der Velden, NED . . . . . . . . . 164.206
8. Karina Volkova,
   Ana Martyniouk, UKR . . . . . . . . . . . . . 162.287

TEAM

1. Canada . . . . . . . . . 172.492
2. Japan . . . . . . . . . . . 171.515
3. Russia . . . . . . . . . . 169.958
4. USA . . . . . . . . . . . 169.653
5. Italy . . . . . . . . . . . . 167.331
6. France . . . . . . . . . . 166.255
7. China . . . . . . . . . . 164.626
8. Netherlands . . . . . 163.903

**Canada:** Stephanie Bissonette, Marie-Miche Cloutier, Ann Cukic, Jennifer De Foy, Kasia Kulesza, Jacinthe Taillon, Estella Warren, Leslie Wright.

**Team USA:** Carrie Barton, Laura Brands, Season Flores, Tracy Gayeski, Deanie Hickox, Kristina Lum, Amber McDaniel, Vanessa Shaw, Tammy Taylor, Kim Wurzel.

**Countries Entered** (30): Australia, Austria, Belarus, Brazil, Bulgaria, Canada, China, Czech Republic, Egypt, France, Germany, Great Britain, Hungary, Italy, Japan, Kazakhstan, Mexico, Netherlands, New Zealand, Poland, Republic of South Africa, Russia, Slovakia, Spain, Sweden, Switzerland, Ukraine, United States.

## II Junior World Championships, Salerno, Italy
### July 25–28, 1991

SOLO

1. Miya Tachibana, JPN . . . . . . . . . . . . . . 161.14
2. Laila Vakil, GBR . . . . . . . . . . . . . . . . . 159.09
3. Janice Bremner, CAN . . . . . . . . . . . . . . 158.59
4. Natalia Gruzdeva, URS . . . . . . . . . . . . . 157.61
5. Heather Pease, USA . . . . . . . . . . . . . . . 157.05
6. Myriam Lignot, FRA . . . . . . . . . . . . . . . 155.03
7. Christine Muellner, AUT . . . . . . . . . . . 154.17
8. Maurizia Cecconi, ITA . . . . . . . . . . . . . 154.12

DUET

1. Miya Tachibana,
   Rei Jimbo, JPN . . . . . . . . . . . . . . . . . . 160.54
2. Natalie Gruzdeva,
   Julie Beloglazova, URS . . . . . . . . . . . . . 158.24
3. Laurie McClelland,
   Jenny Ohanesian, USA . . . . . . . . . . . . . 156.47
4. Magali Rathier,
   Charlotte Massardier, FRA . . . . . . . . . . 155.10
5. Correen Laing,
   Kristin Normand, CAN . . . . . . . . . . . . . 153.92
6. Christina Mullner,
   Francine Zimmer, AUT . . . . . . . . . . . . . 152.13
7. Laila Vakil,
   Rebecca Scales, GBR . . . . . . . . . . . . . . 151.04
8. Sandra Schindler,
   Madeleine Berk, SUI . . . . . . . . . . . . . . . 148.84

TEAM

1. Japan . . . . . . . . . . 160.17
2. USA . . . . . . . . . . . 158.69
3. Soviet Union . . . . . 157.16
4. Canada . . . . . . . . . 157.09
5. France . . . . . . . . . . 155.03
6. Italy . . . . . . . . . . . . 153.45
7. Switzerland . . . . . . . 150.54
8. Egypt . . . . . . . . . . 148.98

**Japan:** Miya Tachibana, Rei Jimbo, Raika Fujii, Mayuko Fujiki, Tomoyo Yoshida, Miho Takeda, Yoko Azuma, Mamiko Imai, Chikako Masuda.

**Team USA:** Annemarie Alm, Tammy Cleland, Heather Pease, Laurie McClelland, Jenny Ohanesian, Kelly Olesen, Sadie Pietras, Jennifer Vorheis, Becky Jasontek, Heidi Dunham.

**Countries Entered** (10): Austria, Canada, Egypt, France, Great Britain, Italy, Japan, Soviet Union, Switzerland, United States.

## I Junior World Championships, Cali, Colombia
### July 17–23, 1989

SOLO (13)

1. Becky Dyroen, USA . . . . . . . . . . . . . . . 174.55
2. Karen Clark, CAN . . . . . . . . . . . . . . . . 171.80

3. Fumiko Okuno, JPN . . . . . . . . . . . . . . 169.65
4. Kerry Shacklock, GBR . . . . . . . . . . . 168.56
5. Gaelie Quelin, FRA . . . . . . . . . . . . . . 166.25
6. Olga Phillipchuk, URS . . . . . . . . . . . 163.71
7. Min Tan, CHN . . . . . . . . . . . . . . . . . . 161.22
8. Marjolijn Both, NED . . . . . . . . . . . . . 160.99

### Duet (12)

1. Becky Dyroen,
   Jill Sudduth, USA . . . . . . . . . . . . . . . . 172.84
2. Karen Clark,
   Keri Closson, CAN . . . . . . . . . . . . . . . 171.60
3. Chiaki Yamamura,
   Nina Enkaku, JPN . . . . . . . . . . . . . . . . 168.34
4. Kerry Shacklock,
   Sara Northey, GBR . . . . . . . . . . . . . . . 167.60
5. Gaelle Quelin,
   Celine Leveque, FRA . . . . . . . . . . . . . . 165.64
6. Elena Azarova,
   Natalia Gruzdeva, URS . . . . . . . . . . . . 164.33

7. Min Tan,
   Jiang Jie, CHN . . . . . . . . . . . . . . . . . . . 163.55
8. Marjolijn Both,
   Sandra Braaksma, NED . . . . . . . . . . . . 160.07

### Team (8)

1. USA . . . . . . . . . . . 169.75
2. Canada . . . . . . . . . 169.43
3. Japan . . . . . . . . . . 167.01
4. Soviet Union . . . . . 164.91
5. China . . . . . . . . . . 160.69
6. Italy . . . . . . . . . . . 156.53
7. Brazil . . . . . . . . . . 153.99
8. Colombia . . . . . . . . 149.39

**Team USA:** Kristy Donn, Becky Dyroen, Suzannah Dyroen, Lori McCoy, Jill Savery, Mary Spencer, Jill Sudduth, Margot Thien.
**Countries Entered** (13): Aruba, Brazil, Canada, China, Colombia, France, Great Britain, Italy, Japan, Netherlands, Russia, Sweden, United States.

---

## Goodwill Games

### IV Goodwill Games, Long Island, New York July 19–20, 1998

### Duet (8)

1. Olga Brousnikina,
   Maria Kisseleva, RUS . . . . . . . . . . . . . . 99.016
2. Kristina Lum,
   Bill May, USA . . . . . . . . . . . . . . . . . . . . 97.979
3. Miya Tachibana,
   Miho Takeda, JPN . . . . . . . . . . . . . . . . 97.286
4. Kasia Kulesza,
   Jacinthe Taillon, CAN . . . . . . . . . . . . . 96.967
5. Virginie Dedieu,
   Cathy Geoffroy, FRA . . . . . . . . . . . . . . 95.706
6. Gaida Ballan,
   Giovanna Burlando, ITA . . . . . . . . . . . . 94.497
7. Li Min,
   Long Yan, CHN . . . . . . . . . . . . . . . . . . 93.663
8. Na-Mi Yoo,
   Yoon-Kyeong Jang, KOR . . . . . . . . . . . . 93.556

### Team (8)

1. Russia . . . . . . 98.774
2. USA . . . . . . . . 97.943
3. Japan . . . . . . . 97.374
4. Canada . . . . . . 96.447
5. France . . . . . . 95.797
6. China . . . . . . . 93.961
7. Italy . . . . . . . . 93.920
8. Korea . . . . . . . 93.621

**Team USA:** Carrie Barton, Bridget Finn, Becky Jasontek, Tina Kasid, Kristina Lum, Emily Marsh, Elicia Marshall, Bill May, Tuesday Middaugh, Kim Wurzel.
**Countries entered** (8): Canada, China, France, Italy, Japan, Korea, Russia, United States.

### III Goodwill Games, St. Petersburg, Russia July 31–August 1, 1994

### Solo (8)

1. Olga Sedakova, RUS . . . . . . . . . . . . . . . 197.20
2. Becky Dyroen-Lancer, USA . . . . . . . . . . 197.02
3. Marianne Aeschbacher, FRA . . . . . . . . . 194.06
4. Akiko Kawase, JPN . . . . . . . . . . . . . . . . 192.54
5. Estella Warren, CAN . . . . . . . . . . . . . . . 190.70
6. Kerry Shacklock, GBR . . . . . . . . . . . . . . 189.68
7. Maria Guisti, VEN . . . . . . . . . . . . . . . . . 189.66
8. Tamara Zwart, NED . . . . . . . . . . . . . . . . 184.76

### Duet (8)

1. Becky Dyroen-Lancer,
   Jill Sudduth, USA . . . . . . . . . . . . . . . . . 197.88
2. Olga Brusnikina,
   Yulia Pankratova, RUS . . . . . . . . . . . . . 195.00
3. Marianne Aeschbacher,
   Myriam Lignot, FRA . . . . . . . . . . . . . . . 193.72
4. Rei Jimbo,
   Kaori Takahashi, JPN . . . . . . . . . . . . . . 193.28
5. Claire Carver,
   Estella Warren, CAN . . . . . . . . . . . . . . . 190.38
6. Kerry Shacklock,
   Laila Vakil, GBR . . . . . . . . . . . . . . . . . . 189.14

7. Iris Sentrop,
   Tamara Zwart, NED ............... 185.44
8. Caroline Imoberdorf,
   Helen Kaeser, SUI ................. 184.70

**Countries entered** (9): Canada, France, Great Britain, Japan, Netherlands, Russia, Switzerland, United States, Venezuela.

### II Goodwill Games, Seattle, Washington July 30, 1990

SOLO (8)

1. Kristen Babb, USA .................. 98.80
2. Mikako Kotani, JPN ................. 97.96
3. Nathalie Guay, CAN ................ 96.60
4. Kristina Falasinidi, URS ............. 96.08
5. Anne Capron, FRA .................. 94.76
6. Kerry Shacklock, GBR .............. 93.16
7. Sonia Cardenas, MEX ............... 93.00
8. Claudia Peczinka, SUI .............. 90.52

DUET (8)

1. Karen Josephson,
   Sarah Josephson, USA ............... 98.88
2. Karen Clark,
   Lisa Alexander, CAN ................ 97.12
3. Hisako Aoishi,
   Aki Takayama, JPN ................. 96.92
4. Kristina Falasinidi,
   Elena Foshchevskaya, USR ........... 95.36
5. Kerry Shacklock,
   Sarah Northey, GBR ................ 92.96
6. Sonia Cardenas,
   Lourdes Olivera, MEX .............. 92.04
7. Maria Carenta,
   Rachel LeBozec, FRA ............... 91.76
8. Claudia Peczinka,
   Daniela Jordi, SUI .................. 91.00

**Countries entered** (8): Canada, Japan, Soviet Union, Great Britain, Mexico, France, Switzerland, United States.

## PAN AMERICAN GAMES

### XIV Pan American Games, Santo Domingo, Dominican Republic August 1–17, 2003

*Solo discontinued, Olympic program only.*

DUET (10)

1. Anna Kozlova,
   Alison Bartosik, USA .............. 95.917
2. Fanny Letourneau,
   Courtney Stewart, CAN ............ 95.584
3. Carolina Moraes,
   Isabela Moraes, BRA ............... 91.833
4. Nara Falcon,
   Olga Vargas, MEX ................. 87.834
5. Luna Aguilu,
   Leilani Torres, PUR ............... 84.000
6. Eglen Martinez,
   Nineth Martinez, VEN ............. 82.833
7. Claudia Cueli,
   Maricarmen Saleta, DOM ........... 80.084
8. Nadezhda Gomez,
   Violeta Mitinian, CRC ............. 73.084
9. Deevah Leenheer,
   Kemberly Vinck, ARU ............. 73.000
10. Florence Corleto,
    Andrea Esquivel, ESA .............. 69.334

TEAM (7)

1. USA ................. 96.500
2. Canada ............... 96.333
3. Brazil ................ 90.833
4. Mexico ............... 88.250
5. Venezuela ............. 84.500
6. Dominican Republic ..... 81.250
7. El Salvador ........... 68.250

**Team USA:** Alison Bartosik, Erin Dobratz, Becky Jasontek, Anna Kozlova, Sara Lowe, Lauren McFall, Stephanie Nesbitt, Kendra Zanotto, Katie Norris.

**Countries Entered** (10): Aruba, Brazil, Canada, Costa Rica, Dominican Republic, El Salvador, Mexico, Puerto Rico, United States, Venezuela.

### XIII Pan American Games, Winnipeg, Canada August 4–7, 1999

*Solo discontinued, Olympic program only.*

DUET (10)

1. Claire Carver-Dias,
   Fanny Letourneau, CAN ............. 97.289
2. Becky Jasontek,
   Emily Marsh, USA ................. 96.047
3. Isabela Moraes,
   Carolina Moraes, BRA .............. 93.874
4. Beatrix Jacobo,
   Erika Leal, MEX ................... 91.933
5. Patricia Gomez,
   Kenya Guerro, CUB ................ 89.587
6. Jacqueline Gonima,
   Erika Piedrahita, COL ............. 88.117

7. M. Saleta Rodriguez,
Hortensia de Trueba, DOM . . . . . . . . 84.134
8. Paola Capucci,
Cecilia Zunzunegui, ARG . . . . . . . . . . 83.010
9. Jessica Hermans,
Amanda Maduro, ARU . . . . . . . . . . . . 75.003
10. Maria Pavlovskaia,
Nadia Sapoyako, CRC . . . . . . . . . . . . . 74.413

TEAM (5)

1. Canada . . . . . . 97.396
2. USA . . . . . . . . 97.317
3. Mexico . . . . . . 93.373
4. Brazil . . . . . . . 92.489
5. Cuba . . . . . . . 91.731

**Canada:** Claire Carver-Dias, Jessica Chase, Valarie Hould-Marchand, Fanny Letourneau, Kristin Normand, Jacinthe Taillon, Reidun Tatham, Lesley Wright, Leslie Beaumont.

**Team USA:** Carrie Barton, Bridget Finn, Becky Jasontek, Kristina Lum, Emily Marsh, Elicia Marshall, Lauren McFall, Tuesday Middaugh, Kim Wurzel.

**Countries Entered** (10): Argentina, Aruba, Brazil, Canada, Colombia, Costa Rica, Cuba, Dominican Republic, Mexico, United States.

### *XII Pan American Games, Mar del Plata, Argentina March 21–25, 1995*

SOLO (7)

1. Becky Dyroen-Lancer, USA . . . . . . . . . 97.090
2. Karen Clark, CAN . . . . . . . . . . . . . . . . 95.595
3. Maria Elena Guisti, VEN . . . . . . . . . . . 95.381
4. I. Ramirez, MEX . . . . . . . . . . . . . . . . . 91.226
5. P. Olivera, BRA . . . . . . . . . . . . . . . . . . 88.750
6. M. Bolvin, URU . . . . . . . . . . . . . . . . . 85.385
7. J. Yelin, ARG . . . . . . . . . . . . . . . . . . . . 85.190

DUET (5)

1. Becky Dyroen-Lancer,
Jill Sudduth, USA . . . . . . . . . . . . . . . 96.451
2. Lisa Alexander,
Erin Woodley, CAN . . . . . . . . . . . . . . 95.471
3. Wendy Aguilar,
Perla Ramirez, MEX . . . . . . . . . . . . . . 92.270
4. R. Periller,
F. Monteiro, BRA . . . . . . . . . . . . . . . . 88.839
5. J. Yelin,
C. Maria, ARG . . . . . . . . . . . . . . . . . . 84.832

TEAM (5)

1. USA . . . . . . . . . . 96.164
2. Canada . . . . . . . . 95.099
3. Mexico . . . . . . . . 92.997
4. Brazil . . . . . . . . . 89.167
5. Argentina . . . . . . 85.003

**Team USA:** Tammy Cleland, Suzannah Dyroen, Becky Dyroen-Lancer, Jill Savery, Nathalie Schneyder, Heather Simmons, Jill Sudduth, Margot Thien.

**Countries entered** (7): Argentina. Brazil, Canada, Mexico, United States, Uruguay, Venezuela.

### *XI Pan American Games, Havana, Cuba August 4–10 1991*

SOLO (8)

1. Becky Dyroen, USA . . . . . . . . . . . . . . . 181.37
2. Maria Guisti, VEN . . . . . . . . . . . . . . . 180.02
3. Sonia Cardenas, MEX . . . . . . . . . . . . . 176.62
4. Teresa Perez, CUB . . . . . . . . . . . . . . . 175.59
5. Julie Bibby, CAN . . . . . . . . . . . . . . . . 173.42
6. Fernanda Bamargo, BRA . . . . . . . . . . 168.24
7. Maria Quintela, CHI . . . . . . . . . . . . . . 160.38
8. Maria Pardinas, URU . . . . . . . . . . . . . 156.45

DUET (6)

1. Diana Ulrich,
Tia Harding, USA . . . . . . . . . . . . . . . 177.99
2. Sonia Cardenas,
Lourdes Olivera, MEX . . . . . . . . . . . . 174.93
3. Julie Bibby,
Corrine Keddie, CAN . . . . . . . . . . . . 174.45
4. Teresa Perez,
Ivette Bacaliao, CUB . . . . . . . . . . . . . 173.23
5. Glaucia Arbon,
Cristina Silveria, BRA . . . . . . . . . . . . 166.39
6. Maria Quintela,
Ana Espinoza, CHI . . . . . . . . . . . . . . 162.65

TEAM (4)

1. USA . . . . . . . . 177.64
2. Canada . . . . . . 176.40
3. Cuba . . . . . . . 171.77
4. Mexico . . . . . . 170.88

**Team USA:** Tia Harding, Laurie Martin, Anna Miller, Kim Ochsner, Emily Porter, Diana Ulrich, Janet Wiecking, Mary Wodka.

**Countries entered** (8): Brazil, Canada, Chile, Cuba, Mexico, United States, Uruguay, Venezuela.

### *X Pan American Games, Indianapolis, Indiana August 7–29, 1987*

SOLO (8)

1. Tracie Ruiz-Conforto, USA . . . . . . . . . 195.48
2. Sylvie Frechette, CAN . . . . . . . . . . . . . 188.18
3. Teresa Perez, CUB . . . . . . . . . . . . . . . 178.15
4. Lourdes Candini, MEX . . . . . . . . . . . . 177.85
5. Maria Guisti, VEN . . . . . . . . . . . . . . . 169.08
6. Monica Berrio, COL . . . . . . . . . . . . . . 161.00
7. Laura Daners, URU . . . . . . . . . . . . . . . 153.31

## Duet (8)

1. Karen Josephson,
   Sarah Josephson, USA . . . . . . . . . . . . . . 192.11
2. Karen Scribney,
   Karen Fonteyne, CAN . . . . . . . . . . . . . . 183.45
3. Lourdes Cardinas,
   Susana Cardinas, MEX . . . . . . . . . . . . . 177.51
4. Teresa Perez,
   Raisa Suarez, CUB . . . . . . . . . . . . . . . . 175.00
5. Ana Amicarella,
   Maria Guisti, VEN . . . . . . . . . . . . . . . . 171.77
6. Chris Albuquerque,
   Eva Riera, BRA . . . . . . . . . . . . . . . . . . . 168.85
7. Nancy Duque,
   Monica Berrio, COL . . . . . . . . . . . . . . . 163.98
8. Laura Daners,
   Raquela Carpin, URU . . . . . . . . . . . . . . 154.74

## Team (5)

1. USA . . . . . . . . . . 190.59
2. Canada . . . . . . . 183.77
3. Mexico . . . . . . . 174.85
4. Brazil . . . . . . . . . 171.19
5. Colombia . . . . . 166.34

**Team USA:** Kristen Babb, Karen Josephson, Sarah Josephson, Lori Hatch, Tracy Long, Tracie Ruiz-Conforto, Lisa Riddell, Michele Svitenko.

**Countries entered** (8): Brazil, Canada, Colombia Cuba, Mexico, United States, Uruguay, Venezuela.

### IX Pan American Games, Caracas. Venezuela August 14–19, 1983

## Solo (10)

1. Tracie Ruiz, USA . . . . . . . . . . . . . . . . . . 190.49
2. Sharon Hambrook, CAN . . . . . . . . . . . 187.06
3. Ana Amicarella, VEN . . . . . . . . . . . . . . 166.68
4. Pilar Ramirez, MEX . . . . . . . . . . . . . . . 165.33
5. Teresa Perez Sole, CUB . . . . . . . . . . . . 164.48
6. Paula Carvalho, BRA . . . . . . . . . . . . . . 161.53
7. Zimena Carias, DOM . . . . . . . . . . . . . . 157.49
8. Azul Martoreli, URU . . . . . . . . . . . . . . . 157.26
9. Nancy Duque, COL . . . . . . . . . . . . . . . 156.15
10. Robin Cody, PUR . . . . . . . . . . . . . . . . 152.95

## Duet (10)

1. Tracie Ruiz,
   Candy Costie, USA . . . . . . . . . . . . . . . . 188.85
2. Penny Vilagos,
   Vicky Vilagos, CAN . . . . . . . . . . . . . . . 187.23
3. Pilar Ramirez,
   Claudia Novelo, MEX . . . . . . . . . . . . . . 165.14
4. Teresa Perez Sole,
   Natalie Daujonovich, CUB . . . . . . . . . . 164.90
5. Paula Carvalho,
   Tessa Carvalho, BRA . . . . . . . . . . . . . . . 162.50

6. Ximena Carias,
   Maribel Solis, DOM . . . . . . . . . . . . . . . 160.05
7. Ana Amicarella,
   Monica Maldonado, VEN . . . . . . . . . . 159.20
8. Nitsa Vivoni,
   Maryrim Ramos, PUR . . . . . . . . . . . . . 155.00
9. Azul Martoreli,
   Martha Sucunza, URU . . . . . . . . . . . . . 154.87
10. Monica Adames,
    Maria Martinez, COL . . . . . . . . . . . . . . 152.83

## Team (8)

1. USA . . . . . . . . . . 188.42
2. Canada . . . . . . . . . 186.44
3. Mexico . . . . . . . . 163.90
4. Cuba . . . . . . . . . . . 163.40
5. Brazil . . . . . . . . . . 161.01
6. Colombia . . . . . . . 156.60
7. Venezuela . . . . . . . 153.89
8. Puerto Rico . . . . . . 152.64

**Team USA:** Karen Callaghan, Candy Costie, Karen Josephson, Sarah Josephson, Becky Roy, Tracie Ruiz, Holly Spencer, Mary Visniski.

**Countries entered** (10): Brazil, Canada, Colombia, Cuba, Dominican Republic, Mexico, Puerto Rico, United States, Uruguay, Venezuela.

### VIII Pan American Games, San Juan, Puerto Rico July 1–8, 1979

## Solo (6)

1. Helen Vanderburg, CAN . . . . . . . . . . . 197.30
2. Michele Beaulieu, USA . . . . . . . . . . . . . 196.90
3. Lourdes de LaGuardia, CUB . . . . . . . . . 172.80
4. Mireya Andrade, MEX . . . . . . . . . . . . . 172.70
5. Martha Aristizabal, COL . . . . . . . . . . . . 162.30
6. Victoria Lasala, PUR . . . . . . . . . . . . . . 150.50

## Duet (6)

1. Helen Vanderburg,
   Kelly Kryczka, CAN . . . . . . . . . . . . . . . 196.30
2. Michele Barone,
   Linda Shelley, USA . . . . . . . . . . . . . . . . 194.80
3. Mireya Andrade,
   Gabriela Terroba, MEX . . . . . . . . . . . . . 179.20
4. Lourdes de la Guardia,
   Silvia Espinosa, CUB . . . . . . . . . . . . . . . 172.70
5. Martha Aristizabel,
   Dinora Arias, COL . . . . . . . . . . . . . . . . 159.50
6. Michele Hernandez,
   Robin Cody, PUR . . . . . . . . . . . . . . . . . 154.10

## Team (6)

1. USA . . . . . . . . . . . 196.50
2. Canada . . . . . . . . . 193.57
3. Mexico . . . . . . . . . 174.50
4. Cuba . . . . . . . . . . . 173.60

5. Colombia ....... 157.80
6. Puerto Rico ...... 154.90

**Team USA:** Michele Barone, Michele Beaulieu, Gerri Brandley, Suzanne Cameron, Laura Florio, Tracie Ruiz, Linda Shelley, Pam Tryon.

**Countries entered** (6): Canada, Colombia, Cuba, Mexico, Puerto Rico, United States.

### VII Pan American Games, Mexico City Oct. 12–26, 1975

Solo (4)

1. Gail Johnson Buzonas, USA .......... 139.70
2. Sylvie Fortier, CAN ................ 138.37
3. Lourdes de la Guardia, CUB .......... 112.66
4. Pepita Sanchez, MEX ............... 107.92

Duet (4)

1. Robin Curren,
   Amanda Norrish, USA .............. 135.46
2. Carol Stewart,
   Laura Wilkin, CAN ................ 131.39
3. Sara Martinez,
   Alicia Foyo, CUB .................. 109.71
4. Pepita Sanchez,
   Constanza Noreiga, MEX ............ 107.43

Team (4)

1. USA ........ 135.31
2. Canada ...... 129.47
3. Mexico ...... 108.63
4. Cuba ....... 107.79

**Team USA:** Sue Baross, Michele Barone, Gail Johnson, Mary Ellen Longo, Amanda Norrish, Linda Shelley, Pam Tryon, Michelle Beaulieu.

**Countries entered** (4): Canada, Cuba, Mexico, United States.

### VI Pan American Games, Cali, Colombia August 2–7, 1971

Solo (4)

1. Heidi O'Rourke, USA ............... 130.58
2. JoJo Carrier, CAN .................. 116.31
3. Eva Govezensky, MEX ............... 105.43
4. Marcela Escobar, COL .............. 89.32

Duet (4)

1. Heidi O'Rourke,
   Joan Lang, USA, .................. 132.50
2. Mado Ramsey,
   JoJo Carrier, CAN ................. 116.62
3. Eva Govezensky,
   Malke Govezensky, MEX ............ 106.66
4. Pascela Escobar,
   Beatriz de Gomez, COL ............. 105.55

Team (4)

1. USA .......... 128.87
2. Canada ........ 107.98
3. Mexico ........ 101.10
4. Colombia ...... 86.44

**Team USA:** Cinny Anderson, Barbara Cooney, Chris Jeffers, Kathy Kretschmer, Joan Lang, Amy Miner, Susan Morris, Heidi O'Rourke.

**Countries entered** (4): USA, Canada, Colombia, Mexico.

### IV Pan American Games, Canada, 1967

*Synchronized swimming events not held.*

### IV Pan American Games, Sao Paulo, Brazil May 1–3, 1963

*Note: Two entries were allowed in solo and duet.*

Solo (7)

1. Roberta Armstrong, USA ............. 89.15
2. Barbara Burke, USA ................ 88.54
3. Sandra Marks, CAN ................ 87.81
4. Marilyn Malefant, CAN ............. 80.09
5. Ofalia Botella, MEX ............... 77.40
6. Eulalia Martinez de Castro, MEX ....... 72.88
7. Idamys Busin, BRA ................. 53.40

Duet (6)

1. Barbara Burke,
   Joanne Schaak, USA ................ 91.51
2. Marian Whitner,
   Marcia Blixt, USA ................. 86.85
3. Marilyn Malefant,
   Sandra Marks, CAN ................ 82.95
4. Maria Villicana,
   Elvia Ramirez, MEX ................ 77.54
5. Ofelia Botella,
   Eulalia de Castro, MEX .............. 77.14
6. Leny Fillellini,
   Maria Nascimiento, BRA ............. 51.36

Team (3)

1. USA ........ 87.39
2. Mexico ...... 76.86
3. Brazil ....... 61.13

**Team USA:** Marcia Blixt, Papsie Georgian, Margaret Lawrence, Judy McFadden, Linda McFadden, Kim Welshons, Marian Whitner.

**Countries entered** (4): Brazil, Canada, Mexico, United States.

### III Pan American Games, Chicago, 1959

*Synchronized swimming events not held; too few countries in 1955.*

### II Pan American Games, Mexico City March 21–25, 1955

*Note: Two entries were allowed in solo and duet.*

SOLO (6)

1. Beulah Gundling, USA . . . . . . . . . . . . . . 94.00
2. Rebecca Garcia, MEX . . . . . . . . . . . . . . . 93.14
3. Joanne Royer, USA . . . . . . . . . . . . . . . . . 90.00
4. Eila Lindell, CAN . . . . . . . . . . . . . . . . . 87.22
5. Giesselie Boulin, CAN . . . . . . . . . . . . . . 80.71
6. Rosa de la Fuente, MEX . . . . . . . . . . . . . 79.14

DUET (6)

1. Ellen Richard,
   Connie Todoroff, USA . . . . . . . . . . . . . . 91.85

2. Rebecca Alverez,
   Gloria Botello, MEX . . . . . . . . . . . . . . . . 91.14
3. Beverly McKnight,
   Diane Baker, CAN . . . . . . . . . . . . . . . . . 88.85
4. Joanne Berthelsen,
   Jackie Brown, USA . . . . . . . . . . . . . . . . . 85.00
5. Christine Villicana,
   Gloria Martinez, MEX . . . . . . . . . . . . . . 84.42
6. Eila Lindell,
   Louise Genereau, CAN . . . . . . . . . . . . . . 83.28

TEAM (3)

1. USA . . . . . . . . 93.92
2. Canada . . . . . . 91.57
3. Mexico . . . . . . 84.42

**Team USA:** Loretta Barrious, Dawn Pawson Bean, Joan Pawson, Lynn Pawson, Sally Phillips.
**Countries entered** (3): Canada, Mexico, United States.

---

## AMERICAN CUP

### VIII American Cup Juniors, Cerritos, California July 27–August 2, 1998

SOLO (21)

1. Naoko Kawashima, JPN . . . . . . . . . . . . . . 86.72
2. Becky Martin, USA . . . . . . . . . . . . . . . . . 86.54
3. Anouk LaFreniere, CAN . . . . . . . . . . . . . 85.58

DUET (17)

1. Satoe Hokoda,
   Kanako Kitao, JPN . . . . . . . . . . . . . . . . . 86.82
2. Becky Martin,
   Andrea Nott, USA . . . . . . . . . . . . . . . . . 85.57
3. Jessika Dubuc,
   Anouk LaFreniere, CAN . . . . . . . . . . . . . 85.34

TEAM (5)

1. USA . . . . . . . . 86.31
2. Canada . . . . . . 85.54
3. Mexico . . . . . . 79.18

**Team USA:** Alison Bartosik, Erin Dobratz, Julie Drexler, Stephanie Joukoff, Christine McClelland, Katie Norris, Andrea Nott, Kimberly Probst.
**Countries entered** (12): Australia, Canada, Chile, Colombia, Germany, Korea, Liechtenstein, Mexico, Puerto Rico, Switzerland, United States, Venezuela.

### VII American Cup Juniors, St. Peters, Missouri August 23–25, 1996

SOLO (22)

1. Alanna O'Leary, USA . . . . . . . . . . . . . . . 90.54
2. Yoon-Kyung Jang, KOR . . . . . . . . . . . . . 90.47
3. Ayano Egami, JPN . . . . . . . . . . . . . . . . . 88.13

DUET (18)

1. Yoon-Kyung Jang,
   Min-Jeong Kim, KOR . . . . . . . . . . . . . . . 90.29
2. Elicia Marshall,
   Alanna O'Leary, USA . . . . . . . . . . . . . . . 90.04
3. Juri Tatsumi,
   Michiyo Fujimaru, JPN . . . . . . . . . . . . . . 89.41

TEAM (4)

1. USA . . . . . . . . 89.67
2. Brazil . . . . . . . 86.12
3. Canada . . . . . . 85.86

**Team USA:** Amanda Burkett, Elicia Marshall, Becky Martin, Bill May, Christina McClelland, Lauren McFall, Shannon Montague, Alanna O'Leary, Stacey Scott, Lindsey Wiggington.
**Countries entered** (12): Aruba, Belgium, Brazil, Canada, Costa Rica, Dominican Republic, Japan, Korea, Mexico, Peru, Puerto Rico, Russia, United States, Venezuela.

## VI American Cup Juniors, Cerritos, California August 19–21, 1994

SOLO (13)

1. Riho Nakajima, JPN ............... 170.74
2. Estella Warren, CAN ............... 170.35
3. Alanna O'Leary, USA .............. 168.27

DUET (11)

1. Yoko Isoda,
   Riho Nakajima, JPN .............. 170.88
2. Claire Carver,
   Estella Warren, CAN ............. 168.65
3. Elicia Marshall,
   Alanna O'Leary, USA ............. 168.01

TEAM (5)

1. Japan ....... 169.19
2. Canada ...... 168.52
3. USA ........ 167.20

**Japan:** Riho Nakajima, Yoko Isoda, Mamiko Imai, Ayano Egami, Emi Fujii, Kayo Higami, Azusa Ishibashi, Kimiko Doi, Aki Sato.

**Team USA:** Lisa Cunanan, Kara Duncan, Julie Enos, Elicia Marshall, Amber McDaniel, Alanna O'Leary, Hilary Seipelt, Vanessa Shaw, Jennifer Stofel, Lisa Velez.

**Countries entered** (7): Australia, Brazil, Canada, Japan, Mexico, Puerto Rico, United States.

## V American Cup Juniors, Fort Lauderdale, Florida August 20–23, 1992

SOLO (22)

1. Tammy Cleland, USA ............... 163.41
2. Katia Seremo, CAN ................ 159.55
3. Mayuko Fujiki, JPN ............... 158.90

DUET (16)

1. Tammy Cleland,
   Heather Pease, USA ............... 162.90
2. Katia Sereno,
   Kasia Kulesza, CAN ............... 159.53
3. Miho Takeda,
   Yuko Yoneda, JPN ................. 157.67

TEAM (7)

1. USA ........ 161.00
2. Canada ...... 157.45
3. Korea ....... 155.24

**Team USA:** Christie Bober, Lisa Burton, Michelle Friend, Becky Jasontek, Kristina Lum, Emily Marsh, Heather Pease, Leslie Riddervold, Kim Wurzel, Gina Pietras.

**Countries entered** (15): Argentina, Aruba, Australia, Brazil, Canada, Czechoslovakia, Germany, Japan, Korea, Mexico, Peru, Switzerland, United States, Uruguay, Venezuela.

## IV American Cup Juniors, Irvine, California August 1–5, 1990

SOLO (26)

1. Jill Savery, USA .................... 177.51
2. Fumiko Okuno, JPN ............... 174.51
3. Tan Min, CHN .................... 169.17

DUET (19)

1. Jill Savery,
   Lori McCoy, USA ................. 177.45
2. Fumiko Okuno,
   Miya Tachibana, JPN ............. 173.73
3. Tan Min,
   Tao Hong, CHN ................. 167.88

TEAM (8)

1. USA ........ 168.49
2. Canada ...... 167.50
3. China ....... 167.41

**Team USA:** Tammy Cleland, Khadija Cutcher, Kari Kreitzer, Jenny Mayer, Laurie McClelland, Jenny Ohanesian, Emily Porter, Jill Schlichting, Stephanie Sogawa, Janet Wiecking.

**Countries entered** (14): Australia, Belgium, Brazil, Canada, China, Egypt, France, Hong Kong, Japan, Mexico, Puerto Rico, Switzerland, United States, West Germany.

## III American Cup, Orlando, Florida July 27–August 2, 1987

SOLO (13)

1. Tracie Ruiz-Conforto, USA .......... 197.25
2. Mikako Kotani, JPN ............... 188.77
3. Alexandra Worisch, AUT ........... 181.17

DUET (10)

1. Karen Josephson,
   Sarah Josephson, USA .............. 192.70
2. Mikako Kotani,
   Miyako Tanaka, JPN ................ 186.27
3. Edith Boss,
   Karin Singer, SUI ................. 181.19

TEAM (7)

1. USA .......... 181.96
2. Canada ......... 178.92
3. Switzerland ..... 175.55

**Team USA:** Tracy Fearnow, Jessica Hudacek, Jennifer Lynn, Patti Lynn, Robin Roberts, Nathalie Schneyder, Anne Schulte, Heather Simmons.

**Countries entered** (9): Austria, Brazil, Canada,

Japan, Korea Mexico, Switzerland, Sweden, United States.

**Countries entered** (14): Australia, Austria, Belgium, Canada, Denmark, Great Britain, Japan, Mexico, Netherlands, Netherlands Antilles, Switzerland, United States, Uruguay, West Germany.

### II American Cup,
### Los Angeles, California
### August 5–7, 1983

*Two entries; highest scoring goes to final event.*

SOLO (25)

1. Tracie Ruiz, USA . . . . . . . . . . . . . . . . . . 190.10
2. Sharon Hambrook, CAN . . . . . . . . . . . . 187.43
3. Miwako Motoyoshi, JPN . . . . . . . . . . . . 179.96

CONSOLATION SOLO

1. Kelly Kryczka, CAN . . . . . . . . . . . . . . . 184.35
2. Candy Costie, USA . . . . . . . . . . . . . . . . 182.03
3. Saeko Kimura, JPN . . . . . . . . . . . . . . . . 177.53

DUET (17)

1. Tracie Ruiz,
   Candy Costie, USA . . . . . . . . . . . . . . . 186.50
2. Sharon Hambrook,
   Kelly Kryczka, CAN . . . . . . . . . . . . . . 185.49
3. Ikuko Abe,
   Miwako Motoyoshi, JPN . . . . . . . . . . . 180.18

CONSOLATION DUET

1. Penny Vilagos,
   Vicky Vilagos, CAN . . . . . . . . . . . . . . . 185.76
2. Karen Josephson,
   Sarah Josephson, USA . . . . . . . . . . . . . 184.15
3. Saeko Kimura,
   Kazuno Fujiwara, JPN . . . . . . . . . . . . . 176.55

TEAM (7)

1. Canada . . . . . . 185.62
2. USA . . . . . . . . 184.29
3. Japan . . . . . . . 179.96

**Canada:** Nathalie Audet, Sharon Hambrook, Kelly Kryczka, Chantal Laviolette, Renee Paradis, Penny Vilagos, Vicky Vilagos, Carolyn Waldo.

**Team USA:** Karen Callaghan, Candy Costie, Karen Josephson, Sarah Josephson, Becky Roy, Tracie Ruiz, Holly Spencer, Mary Visniski.

### I American Cup,
### Concord, California
### June 20–22, 1980

SOLO (14)

1. Linda Shelley, USA . . . . . . . . . . . . . . . . 192.26
2. Lyna Carrier, CAN . . . . . . . . . . . . . . . . 188.06
3. Marijke Engelen, NED . . . . . . . . . . . . . 178.10

CONSOLATION SOLO

1. Tracie Ruiz, USA . . . . . . . . . . . . . . . . . 189.06
2. Kelly Kryczka, CAN . . . . . . . . . . . . . . . 186.03
3. Masae Fujiwara, JPN . . . . . . . . . . . . . . 175.86

DUET (13)

1. Linda Shelley,
   Suzanne Cameron, USA . . . . . . . . . . . . 190.15
2. Lyne Carrier,
   Lyna Carrier, CAN . . . . . . . . . . . . . . . 187.65
3. Kazuno Fujiwara,
   Miwako Motoyoshi, JPN . . . . . . . . . . . 180.91

CONSOLATION DUET

1. Tracie Ruiz,
   Candy Costie, USA . . . . . . . . . . . . . . . 188.55
2. Penny Vilagos,
   Vicky Vilagos, CAN . . . . . . . . . . . . . . . 182.97
3. Ikuko Abe,
   Masae Fujiwara, JPN . . . . . . . . . . . . . . 178.25

TEAM (6)

1. USA . . . . . . . . 191.00
2. Canada . . . . . . 185.56
3. Japan . . . . . . . 181.78

**Team USA:** Linda Shelley, Tracie Ruiz, Robin Waller, Tara Cameron, Candy Costie, Ruth Pickett, Julie Olsen, Suzanne Cameron.

**Countries entered** (7): Canada, Mexico, Japan, Netherlands, Puerto Rico, United States, West Germany.

# Appendix D:
# U.S. Participation in
# International Events, 1951–2004

## 1951

**I Pan American Games**—Buenos Aires, Argentina—USA and Canada demonstrate. Solo: Beulah Gundling (USA), Marjorie Coachland (Canada); duet: Marilyn Stanley and Connie Todoroff (USA), June and Gayle Taylor (Canada). Leaders: Henry Gundling (USA), Lillian MacKellar (Canada).

## 1952

**XV Olympic Games**—Helsinki, Finland—Olympic Gala demonstrations by USA and Canada. USA swimmers: Solo: Beulah Gundling; duet: Connie Todoroff and Ellen Richard; team: St. Clair Synchronettes: Todoroff, Richard, Shirley Simpson, Laurine Stocking. Leaders: Mary Derosier and Peg Sellar (Canada).

**Clinics**—Mary Derosier leads clinics in England, Finland and Denmark, exhibitions by the Synchronettes.

## 1953

**Canadian-American Championships**—Niagara Falls, USA—USA wins solo and duet. Solo: Joanne Royer (Riverside); duet: Judy Haga and Sandy Giltner (Lansing Sea Sprites); team: (Peterborough) Canada.

**Clinics/Exhibitions**—Clinics in England, Paris (International Congress on Physical Education for Women and Girls), and Israel (Maccabiah World Games). Swimmer: Beulah Gundling. Leader: Henry Gundling.

**Exhibition Tours**—U.S. State Department tours begin at U.S. Eastern and Southern military bases.

Swimmers: Oakland Athens Club, Corkettes of Houston and Riverside Aquettes. Leader: Norma Olsen. Joy Cushman gave clinics in Mexico.

## 1954

**Clinics/Exhibitions**—Clinics in Germany, Italy and Canada, Swimmer: Beulah Gundling. Leader: Henry Gundling.

**Exhibition Tours**—First Far East Tour, to Korea, Japan under U.S. State Department auspices. Swimmers: Oakland Athens Club. Leader: Norma Olsen.

## 1955

**II Pan American Games**—Mexico City—USA wins all gold. Results Appendix C.

**Clinics/Exhibitions**—Australia—Swimmer: Beulah Gundling. Leader: Henry Gundling.

**Exhibition Tours**—Far Eastern Tour—Swimmers: Oakland Athens Club, Oakland Naiads, Riverside Aquettes. Leaders: Norma Olsen and Florence Anderson. Joy Cushman leads clinics in Guatemala. Demonstrators: Joanne Royer, Riverside; Joanne Berthelsen, June Schiele, Janet Anthony and Jackie Brown, Athens Club.

## 1956

**XVI Olympic Games**—Melbourne—Olympic Gala demonstrations. Swimmers: Janet Anthony, Loretta Barrious, Joanne Berthelsen, Joanne Brobst, Jackie Brown, Evelyn Oremus, Lynn Pawson, June Scheile, Athens Club; Doris Payne, Peggy Howard, Corkettes; Joanne Royer, Riverside Aquettes.

**Exhibition Tours**—Round-the-World Tour—England, Italy, Denmark, Sweden, Holland, Switzerland, Egypt, Pakistan, India, Malaysia, New Zealand, Australia. Swimmers above, leaders Norma Olsen, Teresa Andersen, Lawrence Johnson, AAU.

### 1957

**Mexican National Championships/Invitational**— Mexico City — Athens Club wins duet and team. Cuba, Mexico, U.S. participate. Solo: Rebecca Garcia (Mexico) 1st; Sue Lawrence 2nd, Jackie Vargas 3rd; duet: Joan and Lynn Pawson 1st, Janet Anthony and Lorretta Barrious 2nd; team: USA 1st: Janet Anthony, Loretta Barrious, Joey Brobst, Jackie Vargas, Lynn Pawson; Mexico 2nd, Cuba 3rd.

**Exhibition Tours**— Far Eastern Tour — Five weeks in Japan. Swimmers: Sharon Dean, Lynn Kristie, Lida Ridings, Frances Stewart, Nancy Millett, Susan Peat and Rosalind Calcaterra, from clubs in Fort Lauderdale, Chicago, St. Louis, and Oakland Naiads. Leader: Joy Cushman.

### 1958

**Paris, Brussels and Barcelona Competitions**— USA wins all competitions. Solo: Linda Ridings (Fort Lauderdale); duet: Rosalind Calcaterra and Sandy Giltner (St. Louis Shaw Park); team: Athens Club: Janet Anthony, Loretta Barrious, Sue Lawrence, Lynn Pawson, Jackie Vargas. Leader: Norma Olsen.

**Exhibition Tours**— Three Tours: European Tour (1) — France, Spain, Belgium [ends at the Brussels Worlds Fair]. Swimmers: Athens Club, Shaw Park. leader Dorothy Donnelley; Far East Tour (2). Swimmers: Oakland Naiads, Hollywood AC. Leaders: Betty Brandelein and Marge Dineen; Brazil Tour (3). Swimmers: Athens Club Water Sprites. Leaders: Helene Harms, Rose Georgian.

### 1959

**III Pan American Games**— Chicago, Illinois — Exhibition only. USA (Athens Club) and Canada demonstrate.

**Exhibition Tours**— Far East Tour — Swimmers: Athens Club, Hollywood AC. Leaders: Bill Royer and Norma Olsen.

### 1960

**XVII Olympic Games**— Rome — Olympic Gala demonstrations. Swimmers from European tours below.

**Exhibition Tours**— Four separate tours. Director Norma Olsen. The American Aquacade. Swimmers by application from clubs throughout the U.S. Tour (1) Denmark, Sweden, Finland, Holland. Leaders: Florence Anderson, Bob Baldwin; Tour (2) West Germany, Czechoslovakia. Leaders: Jay Howell, Chauncey Whitner. Tour (3) France, Belgium, Spain. Leaders: Ella Kovacs, Dot Muhly, Marge Warren (Canada). Tours 1, 2, 3 end at the

Olympic Games. Sixty swimmers participate in the Olympic Gala. Joy Cushman joined the tours in Rome. Tour (4) Far East. Swimmers: St. Louis Shaw Park, Athens Club. Leader: Marge Dineen.

### 1961

**Exhibition Tours**— Last Far East Pacific Command tours — Swimmers: Athens Club, San Francisco Merionettes, Hollywood AC. Leader: Re Calcaterra.

### 1963

**IV Pan American Games**— Sao Paulo — USA wins all events. Results Appendix C.

### 1964

**XVIII Olympic Games**— Tokyo — Olympic Gala demonstrations. Swimmers: St. Louis Shaw Park, Lansing Sea Sprites, New York Community College.

**Exhibition Tours**— Last Round-the-World tour — Exhibitions, clinics in England, France, Germany, Switzerland, Rome, Greece, Istanbul, Egypt, Syria, India, Thailand, Singapore, Hong Kong, Formosa; tour ends at the Olympic Games in Japan. Leaders: Frances Jones, Cora Mae Kintz Judy Haga McDonald, Joyce Lindeman.

### 1965

**Canadian Open**— Montreal, Canada — Pam Morris USA (San Francisco Merionettes) wins solo and figures.

**Clinics/Exhibitions**— Pam Morris in Montreal; Columbus Coralina Club, Edna Hines in Guadalajara, Mexico, and Ontario, Canada.

### 1966

**Canadian Open**— Three gold for USA (San Francisco Merionettes) Solo and figures: Margo McGrath; duet: McGrath and Carol Redmond.

**Tours**— First Japanese Goodwill Exchange — Hamadera Club of Tokyo trains with clubs in 12 U.S. cities.

### 1967

**V Pan American Games**— Winnipeg, Canada — Exhibition only. Canada and U.S. swimmers demonstrate.

**Golden Gate International Solo**— San Francisco — USA wins 1st International meet held in the U.S. Margo McGrath 1st; Cinde Stevens (Canada) 2nd; Carrie Berensen (Holland) 3rd. Seven nations participate.

**Canadian Open**— USA wins all events — San Francisco and Santa Clara participate. Solo: Carol Redmond 1st, Margo McGrath 2nd; duet: Redmond and McGrath; team: Merionettes 1st, Aquamaids 2nd.

**Criterium d' Europe**— Amsterdam, Holland —

Gold for USA (Merionettes). Solo: Carol Redmond; duet: Redmond and Margo McGrath; team: Redmond, McGrath, Kathy Bryant and Barbara Trantina; Netherlands 2nd, France 3rd.

**Clinics and Exhibitions**— Merionettes, Marion Kane, Joy Cushman in Austria, Denmark, England, France, Holland, Spain, West Germany; Corkettes and Joy Cushman in Mexico.

### 1968

**XIX Olympic Games**— Mexico City — Last Olympic Gala exhibition — Santa Clara Aquamaids demonstrate.

**All Japan Competition**— Tokyo— USA (Santa Clara) wins all events. Solo: Kim Welshons; duet: Welshons and Nancy Hines; team: Welshons, Hines, Pam Albin, Kathy Craig, Diane Howell, Melinda Sellers, Carol Reynolds, Kris Welshons.

**Tours**— Japan-USA Goodwill exchange — Santa Clara Aquamaids, Kay Vilen in Japan.

### 1969

**Canadian Open**— USA (Santa Clara) sweeps all events— Solo and figures Kim Welshons; duet: Welshons and Nancy Hines; team: Welsons, Hines, Gail Johnson, Carol Reynolds, Kathy Bryant, Terry Andersen, Kris Welshons, Pam Albin.

**England Open**— London — USA (Merionettes) win all events. Solo: Heidi O'Rourke; duet: O'Rourke and Joan Lang; team: O'Rourke, Lang, Barbara Cooney, Lona Gallagher, Sue Morris, Mary Kay Prejean, Barbara Trantina.

**Tours**— Margo McGrath and Carol Redmond (Merionettes) 10-month clinic-exhibition tour of Europe — England, Holland, Switzerland, France, Austria, West Germany, Denmark, Sweden, Norway, Canada.

**Clinics**— Merionettes, Marion Kane in England and Scotland; San Antonio Cygnets, Margaret Swan in Mexico.

### 1970

**Expo '70 Competition**— Osaka — USA (Santa Clara, San Francisco) wins all events. USA takes top 14 places in figures. Solo: Bede Trantina; duet: Trantina and Heidi O'Rourke; team: San Francisco 1st, Santa Clara 2nd. Merionettes: Barbara Cooney, Lona Gallagher, Chris Jeffers, Joan Lang, Amy Miner, Sue Morris, Heidi O'Rourke, and Bede Trantina. Aquamaids: Terry Andersen, Jackie Douglass, Nancy Hines, Charlotte Jennings, Gail Johnson, Carol Reynolds, Diane Smith.

**Danish International**— Copenhagen — USA (Santa Clara) wins solo, Canada duet and team. Solo: Kim Welshons, Cinde Stevens (Canada) 2nd.

**Clinics**— Kim Welshons in France, Germany, Netherlands, Switzerland; Corkettes, Joy Cushman in Mexico.

**International Coaching**— Claire Vida (Merionettes) in South Africa; Sue Morris (Merionettes) in England and Holland; Vicky Weir (Dayton Aquanymphs) in Resario, Argentina, then with a professional watershow in Buenos Aires.

### 1971

**VI Pan American Games**— Cali, Colombia — USA wins all events. Results Appendix C.

**Clinics**— Kim Welshons clinics in Latin America.

**Coaching**— Nancy Hines (Aquamaids) in Japan; Sue Morris (Merionettes) in England and Holland; Joanna and Elizabeth Wulff (Springfield Aqualinas) in England and Scotland.

### 1972

**Canadian Open**— Canada wins solo, USA (Santa Clara) duet and team. Solo: JoJo Carrier (Canada); duet: Gail Johnson and Terry Andersen 1st; team: USA (Aquamaids) 1st.

**Exhibitions and Clinics**— Demonstrations— Merionettes in Chile at XXI South American Championships; exhibitions in Colombia, Panama; clinics in Argentina, Brazil, Bolivia, Chile, Ecuador, Peru, Paraguay, Uruguay, Venezuela; Kay Vilen and Aquamaids in Germany, England.

**Coaching**— Chris Jeffers (Merionettes) in Switzerland; Diana and Lori Nelson (Tustin Meraquas) in Sweden, Denmark.

### 1973

**I World Aquatic Championships**— Belgrade, Yugoslavia — USA (Santa Clara) wins all events. Results, Appendix C.

**International Junior Invitational**— USA (California Coralettes, Santa Clara Aquamaids) win gold in Dusseldorf, Germany and Holland. Germany — USA solos 1–3: Cynthia Engle (CC), Michele Barone (SC), Lori Green (CC); duet: Michele Barone, Pam Tryon (SC) 1st, Sara and Marie White (CC) 2nd; team: Engle, Green, S. White, M. White, Mindy Haines, Lee Ann and Diane Reese (CC). Holland: Engle wins solo, Green and Barone take 2–3; duet and team results same as above.

**German Open/Holland Open**— USA (Merionettes) win all events. Solo: Amy Miner; duet: Denise Gallagher, Karen Morris; team: Miner, Gallagher, Morris, Cinny Anderson, Pat Leake, Nancy Hunt, Carol Clark, Jane Johnson, Lori Nelson.

**Exhibitions and Clinics**— Merionettes, Marion Kane in West Germany, Denmark, Holland; Walnut Creek Aquanuts, Sue Ahlf, Joan Nelson in Norway, Denmark and Sweden; Tustin Meraquas, Dawn Bean in France; Corkettes, Joy Cushman in Mexico.

**Coaching**— Heidi O'Rourke (Merionettes) in Switzerland; Joan Lang (Merionettes) in Denmark; Kathy Knibbe (Aquanuts) in Vancouver; Kim Welshons (Aquamaids) in Mexico.

## 1974

**I Pan Pacific Invitational**— Honolulu, Hawaii — USA (Santa Clara) wins all events. Solo: Gail Johnson; duet: Johnson and Sue Baross; team: Johnson, Baross, Amanda Norrish, Robin Curren, Dana Moore, Susanne Randell, Pam Tryon and Michele Barone. Competitors from Canada, Japan, Australia, New Zealand and the USA.

**All Japan Invitational**— USA (Santa Clara) wins all events. Solo: Gail Johnson; duet: Johnson, Sue Baross; team: Santa Clara as above for Pan Pac.

**International Solo**— Ottawa — USA wins gold — Kathy Kretschmer (Merionettes) wins solo Sylvie Fortier (Canada) 2nd. Competitors from Japan, Holland, West Germany, New Zealand, France and Mexico.

**Exhibitions and Clinics**— Aquamaids, Kay Vilen in Japan and Taiwan; San Antonio Cygnets and the Women's Army Corps team, Margaret Swan in Germany; Dawn Bean and Sue Ahlf in Vancouver; Marion Kane in Rhodesia and South Africa.

**Coaching**— Nancy Doyle (Cygnets) in Austria; Gina Childers (Glendale) in Holland; Terry Andersen (Aquamaids) in West Germany; Nancy Hines (Aquamaids) in Japan.

**1st International Conference** for Coaches and Judges. Ottawa. US participants Billie MacKellar, Dawn Bean, Don Kane, Marian Kretschmer, Judy McGowan.

## 1975

**II World Aquatic Championships**— Cali, Colombia — USA (Santa Clara) wins all events. Results Appendix C.

**VII Pan American Games**— Mexico City — USA wins all events. Results Appendix C.

**West German/Mid-Atlantic Dual Meet**— Cologne and Karmen, West Germany. USA wins events. Solo: Jill Van Dalen; duet: Van Dalen and Lillian Buckley; team: Pennsbury Falconettes.

## 1976

**II Pan Pacific Championships**— Nagoya — USA (Santa Clara) wins duet and team, Canada wins solo: Sylvie Fortier (Canada) 1st, Robin Curren 2nd; duet: Curren and Amanda Norrish 1st; team: Curren, Norrish, Michele Barone, Sue Baross, Michelle Beaulieu, Jennifer Rich, Pam Tryon, Linda Shelley.

**Scandinavian Open**— Nassajo, Sweden — Canada wins solo and team, USA (Santa Clara) wins duet. Solo: Sylvie Fortier (Canada) 1st, Sue Baross 2nd; duet: Baross and Linda Shelley 1st; team: Canada 1st, USA (Coralettes) 2nd: Cynthia Engle, Lori Green, Lee Ann Reese, Sara and Marie White, Cindy Bull, Tara Cameron.

**Holland Invitational**— USA (Coralettes) win all events. Solo: Lee Ann Reese; duet: Sara and Marie White; team: Coralettes above.

**Clinics and Exhibitions**— Coralettes, Judy Graun in Sweden, Holland; Tustin Meraquas, Dawn Bean in Gien, Marle, Paris, France.

**Coaching**— Kathy Kretschmer (Merionettes) in Holland; Amanda Norrish (Aquamaids) in South Africa; Billie MacKellar in Mexico.

## 1977

**III Pan Pacific Championships**— Mexico City — USA (Santa Clara) wins solo and team, Canada duet. Solo: Sue Baross 1st, Helen Vanderburg (Canada) 2nd; duet: Vanderburg and Michelle Calkins (Canada) 1st, Baross and Linda Shelley 2nd; team: USA 1st: Baross, Shelley, Michelle Beaulieu, Michele Barone, Jane Goeppinger, Gerri Brandley, Pam Tryon, Tami Allen.

**Swiss Open**— Bern — USA wins all events — Santa Clara and Walnut Creek take top 15 places in figures. USA takes top four places in solo and duet. Solo: Sue Baross; duet: Baross and Linda Shelley; team: Aquamaids 1st: Baross, Shelley, Tami Allen, Michele Barone, Michelle Beaulieu, Gerri Brandley, Jane Goeppinger, Pam Tryon; Aquanuts 2nd: Suzanne Cameron, Ruth Fleming, Dawn Nelsen, Julie Olsen, Sherry Phipps, Becky Roy, Leslie Schremp.

**Exhibitions and Clinics**— Aquanuts, Sue Ahlf in Holland; Cygnets, Margaret Swan in Czechoslovakia; University of Arizona in Hermosillo, Mexico.

## 1978

**III World Aquatic Championships**— Berlin, West Germany — USA (Santa Clara) wins team, Canada wins solo and duet. Results Appendix C.

**Swiss Open**— Zurich — USA (Walnut Creek) wins all events. Solo: Suzanne Cameron; duet: Cameron and Karen Callaghan; team: USA (Aquanuts) 1st: Cameron, Callaghan, Becky Roy, Dawn Nelsen, Sherry Phipps, Julie Olsen, Monica Mendenhall, Leslie Schremp.

**West German International Cities Competition**— USA (Hamden) wins all events. Both the Hamden Heronettes and the San Francisco Merionettes compete in Mannheim and Berlin. Solo: Laura Florio; duet: Laura and Brenda Florio; team: Heronettes 1st: L. and B. Florio, Regina Ketchale, Janine Sacramone, Ann and Mary Foley, Melissa Irvine, Rita McHugh; Merionettes 2nd: Shelley Wentker, Brigid Schneider, Ellen Smyth, Diane Donchez, Kathy Marlborough, Cookie Bichard, Diana Nelson, Nadine Nanbu, Cindy Borbeck.

**South American Games**— Guayaquil, Ecuador. Exhibitions by Coralettes: Sara White, Marie White, Tara Cameron, Cindy Bull-Klein, and Sue Baross.

**Masters — Senior Age Aquatic Games**— Etobicoke, Canada — USA participants Diane Tully, Helen Ryker, Jane Katz, Louise Wing. Wing and Katz won gold in their age events.

Clinics— Tustin Meraquas, Dawn Bean in Holland.

Coaching— Sue Flanders (Ohio State) in Puerto Rico; Lori White (Lakewood Synchronettes) in Australia.

### 1979

USA Team I: Michele Barone, Gerri Brandley, Suzanne Cameron, Tracie Ruiz, Michelle Beaulieu, Pam Tryon, Karen Callaghan, Tara Cameron, Linda Shelley, Laura Florio (Pan Am), Robin Waller (FINA Cup).

USA Team II: Julie Olsen, Robin Waller, Candy Costie, Monica Mendenhall, Ruth Pickett, Becky Roy, Mary Visniski, Ginnylee McGilton, Brenda Florio, Janet Tope.

VIII Pan American Games— San Juan, Puerto Rico— USA Team I wins, Canada wins solo and duet. Results Appendix C.

I FINA World Cup— Tokyo, Japan— Canada wins solo and duet, USA team. Results Appendix C.

Swiss Open— Kloten— USA wins gold. Solo: Linda Shelley; duet: Shelley and Michele Barone; team: USA Team II wins.

IV Pan Pacifics— Christchurch, New Zealand— Canada wins solo and team, USA (Santa Clara) duet. Solo: Helen Vanderburg (Canada) 1st, Linda Shelley 2nd; duet: Shelley and Michele Barone 1st; team: Canada 1st, Japan 2nd, USA 3rd: Aquamaids: Michele Barone, Linda Shelley, Becky Price, Suzanne Cameron, Holly Spencer, Kathy Kish, Jenny Lauck, Julie Montgomery, Angie Alkire, Krista Andreini.

Eygptian Open— Alexandria— USA (Santa Clara) wins all gold medals. Solo: Linda Shelley; duet: Shelley and Sue Baross; team: Aquamaids (above) 1st.

I Mallorca Open— USA wins all events— Solo: Michelle Beaulieu; duet: Beaulieu and Pam Tryon 1st, Tracie Ruiz and Candy Costie 2nd; team: USA 1st: Ohio State beats Holland, Sweden. OSU: Karen Callaghan, Dawn Nelsen, Cindy Ott, Jill Vincent, Kathy Rankin, Tara Cameron, Luanne Saas, Myfanwy Borel.

International Duet— Washington, D.C.— USA wins. Linda Shelley and Michele Barone (Santa Clara) win duet held with the World Conference. 10 nations participate.

World Conference— Washington, D.C.— Conference for Judges, 1st FINA Judge Training Manual developed, presented. Judy McGowan, seminar chair.

### 1980

USA Team I: Linda Shelley, Tracie Ruiz, Robin Waller, Tara Cameron, Candy Costie, Ruth Pickett, Julie Olsen, Suzanne Cameron, Marie White, Becky Roy.

USA Team II: Marie White, Sara White, Mary Visniski, Ginnylee McGilton, Kathy Rankin, Holly Spencer, Kathy Kish, Karen Josephson, Sarah Josephson, Monica Mendenhall.

American Cup I— Concord, California— USA wins all events. Results Appendix C.

All Japan Open— Tokyo— USA wins all gold. Solo: Linda Shelley; duet: Shelley and Suzanne Cameron; team: USA Team I 1st.

Swiss Open— Feisch— USA wins solo and team, Canada duet. Solo: Tracie Ruiz; duet: Penny and Vicky Vilagos (Canada) 1st, Ruiz and Candy Costie 2nd; team: USA Team II 1st.

Egyptian International— USA wins all gold. Solo: Linda Shelley; duet: Shelley and Suzanne Cameron; team: Aquanuts: Lisa Babb, Monica Mendenhall, Julie Olsen, Becky Roy, Kim Stanley, Mary Visniski, Marie White, Sara White, Jill Van Dalen.

II Mallorca Open— Spain — USA (Ohio State) wins all events. Solo: Tara Cameron; duet: Cameron and Karen Callaghan; team: USA 1st: Cameron, Callaghan, Ruth Pickett, Janet Tope, Kathy Rankin, Luann Saas, Cathy O'Brien.

Mazda Car Invitational— Coventry, England — Canada wins solo and duet, USA (Santa Clara) silver. Solo: Kelly Kryczka (Canada) 1st, Linda Shelley 2nd; duet: Kryczka and Sharon Hambrook (Canada) 1st, Shelley and Suzanne Cameron 2nd.

Coaching— Nancy Hunt Weiman (Merionettes) in the Soviet Union.

### 1981

USA Team I: Tracie Ruiz, Tara Cameron, Marie White, Candy Costie, Becky Roy, Mary Visniski, Julie Olsen, Robin Waller.

USA Team II: Ginnylee McGilton, Sarah and Karen Josephson, Holly Spencer, Monica Mendenhall, Kathy Kish, Sara White, Kathy Rankin, Jill Van Dalen, Darla Dillan.

V Pan Pacific Championships— Calgary— USA wins solo and duet, Canada team. Solo: Tracie Ruiz; duet: Ruiz and Candy Costie; team: Canada 1st, USA Team I 2nd.

III Mallorca Open— Spain — USA wins all golds. Solo: Ginny McGilton; duet: Kathy Kish and Holly Spencer; team: USA Team II 1st. Largest European competition to date, 105 competitors, 16 countries. Soviets enter for the first time.

ASUA Age Group— Mexico City— USA (Santa Clara) wins all events. *11–12* solo: Patricia Frese; duet: Frese and Robin Roberts; *13–14* solo: Mary Beldin; duet: Beldin and Laura Fowler.

World Conference— Calgary— World Coaching Conference follows Pan Pacific Championships.

Coaching— Amy Miner (Merionettes) in Switzerland; Michelle Beaulieu (Aquamaids) in Egypt.

## 1982

**USA Team I:** Tara Cameron, Candy Costie, Sarah Josephson, Holly Spencer, Tracie Ruiz, Mary Visniski, Robin Waller, Marie White.

**USA Team II:** Lisa Babb, Karen Callaghan, Karen Josephson, Kathy Kish, Ginnylee McGilton, Julie Olsen, Kim Stanley, Sara White.

**IV World Aquatic Championships**— Guayaquil, Ecuador — USA wins solo, Canada wins duet and team. Results Appendix C.

**IV Mallorca Open**— Spain — Canada wins all gold. Solo: Renee Paradis (Canada) 1st, Mary Visniski 2nd, Robin Waller 3rd; duet: Paradis and Nathalie Audet (Canada) 1st, Sara and Marie White 2nd; Karen and Sarah Josephson 3rd; team: USA Team II 2nd.

**1st Soviet Women's Day Competition**— Moscow — USA wins gold — Solo: Tracie Ruiz, Candy Costie 2nd; duet: Ruiz and Costie 1st. No team event.

**Roma Sincro**— Canada wins all gold — Solo: Renee Paradis (Canada) 1st, Holly Spencer 2nd; duet: Paradis and Nathalie Audet (Canada) 1st, Spencer and Kathy Kish 2nd; team: Canada 1st, No USA team entry.

**ASUA Age Group**— Orlando, Florida —1st ASUA Age Group in the US. *12 and under* solo: Patti Lynn 1st; duet: Tracie Rennie and Christine DeMassa 1st; *13–14* solo: Sylvie Frechette (Canada) 1st, Patricia Frese 2nd; duet: Nathalie Guay and Martine LaBelle (Canada) 1st, Trish Frese and Robin Roberts 2nd; *15–17* solo: Karen Josephson 1st; duet: Lisa Babb and Kim Stanley 1st; team: *12–17* Santa Clara 1st: Michelle Svitenko, Kim Stanley, Michelle Moon, Joan Friedman, Christy Choate, Kristine Burke, Lisa Babb, Kristen Babb.

## 1983

**USA Team I:** Karen Callaghan, Candy Costie, Karen Josephson, Sarah Josephson, Becky Roy, Tracie Ruiz, Holly Spencer, Mary Visniski.

**USA Team II:** Lorri Harrell, Lisa Babb, Sara White, Barbara Miller, Lori Donn, Margarita Smith, Kim Stanley, Ginnylee McGilton, Kathy Kish, Julie Olsen.

**American Cup II**— Los Angeles, California — USA wins gold in Pre-Olympic Event. Results Appendix C.

**IX Pan American Games**— Caracas, Venezuela — USA wins solo and duet, Canada wins team. Results Appendix C.

**VI Pan Pacifics**— Melbourne, Australia — Canada wins all gold, USA (Walnut Creek) takes silver in solo and duet. Solo: Sharon Hambrook (Canada) 1st, Mary Visniski 2nd; duet: Hambrook and Kelly Kryczka (Canada) 1st, Marie and Sara White 2nd; team: Canada 1st, Japan 2nd, Australia 3rd. No U.S. team entry.

**Roma Sincro**— Canada wins all gold. Solo: Chantal Laviolette (Canada) 1st, Sarah Josephson 2nd, Karen Josephson 3rd; duet: Vicky and Penny Vilagos (Canada) 1st, Josephson's 2nd; team: Canada wins, No US team entry.

**Hans Christian Andersen Cup**— Odense, Denmark — USA (Meraquas/Aquettes) win duet and team, Austria wins solo. Solo: Alexandra Worisch (Aut) 1st, Kathy Judge 2nd; duet: Judge and Michelle Cooper 1st, Lea Bean and Lori Dickie 3rd; team: USA 1st: Bean, Dickie, Judge, Cooper, Karen Madsen, Candy Murphy, Amanda Wilcox, Erin Caskey.

**Mexico Age Group**— Oaxtepec-Morelos— USA wins 7 of 11 golds. *12 and under* solo: Aki Takayama (Japan) 1st, Patti Lynn and Melinda Downey 2-3; duet: Takayama and Kurimoto (Japan) 1st; Lynn and Downey 2nd; *13–14* solo: Kristen Babb 1st; duet: Trish Frese and Robin Roberts 1st; *15–17* solo: Mikako Kotani (Japan) 1st; Karey Buchanan 2nd; duet: Mary Beldin and Laura Fowler 1st; Sr. solo: Lisa Riddell 1st; Sr. duet: Riddell and Lorri Harrell 1st; *13–17* team: Santa Clara 1st.

**Japan Age Group**— Tokyo— USA wins 3 events. *13–14* solo: Kristen Babb; duet: Trish Frese and Robin Roberts; *15–17* solo: Karey Buchanan, duet: Itoh and Tanaka (Japan) 1st.

**World Conference**— Los Angeles—109 representatives from 22 countries attend the World Conference for Coaches and Judges at UCLA.

## 1984

**Olympic Team:** Candy Costie, Tracie Ruiz, Sarah Josephson.

**USA Team I:** Mary Visniski, Karen Josephson, Holly Spencer, Lisa Babb, Margarita Smith, Julie Olsen, Ginnylee McGilton, Kim Stanley, Alice Smith.

**USA Team II:** Lisa Riddell, Barbara Miller, Lori Donn, Kristen Babb, Lorri Harrell, Lori Hatch, Karey Buchanan, Tammy Kay, Laura Fowler

**XXIII Olympic Games**— Los Angeles — USA Wins Gold in 1st Olympics for Synchro. Results Appendix C.

**VI Mallorca Open**— USA wins solo, Canada duet and team. Solo: Karen Josephson; duet: Penny and Vicky Vilagos (Canada) 1st, Mary Visniski and Lisa Babb 2nd; team: Canada 1st, USA Team I 2nd.

**Swiss Open**— Monthey Valais— USA wins solo and team, Canada duet. Solo: Mary Visniski 1st, Sylvie Frechette (Canada) 2nd; duet: Penny and Vicky Vilagos (Canada) 1st, Visniski and Lisa Babb 2nd; team: USA Team I 1st.

**French Open**— Paris— Gold for Canada. Solo: Renee Paradis (Canada) 1st, Lisa Riddell 3rd; duet: Paradis and Nathalie Audet (Canada) 1st, Riddell and Lorri Harrell 4th; team: Canada 1st, USA Team II 2nd.

**Roma Sincro**— USA wins solo and duet — Solo: Tracie Ruiz 1st, Candy Costie 2nd; duet: Costie and Ruiz score a perfect 100, Karen and Sarah Josephson 2nd. No USA team entry.

**Scandinavian Open**— Linkoping, Sweden — USA wins solo and duet, Great Britain team. Solo: Mary Visniski; duet: Visniski and Lisa Babb. No USA team entry.

**Clinics**— Billie MacKellar, Mary Visniski (Aquanuts) in Australia.

**Coaching**— Heidi O'Rourke (Merionettes) in Switzerland; Karen Callaghan (Ohio State) in Venezuela; Sue Baross (Santa Clara) in Australia; Jane Goeppinger (Santa Clara) in Czechoslovakia, Margo Erickson in Mexico, then Italy after the Olympics.

## 1985

**USA Team I:** Sarah and Karen Josephson, Kristen Babb, Mary Visniski, Susan Reed, Lisa Riddell, Alice Smith, Margarita Smith, Barbara Rudin.

**USA Team II:** Michelle Svitenko, Karen Madsen, Tracy Long, Lorri Harrell, Teri Champ, Holly Vargo, Lori Hatch, Lori Donn, Anne Schulte.

**II FINA World Cup**— Indianapolis— Clean sweep for Canada. Results Appendix C.

**VII Pan Pacifics**— Honolulu, Hawaii — Canada, Japan and USA share golds. Solo: Missy Morlock (Canada) 1st, Karen Madsen 3rd; duet: Mikako Kotani and Megumi Ito (Japan) 1st, Michelle Svitenko and Karen Madsen 3rd; team: USA Team II 1st.

**Swiss Open**— St. Moritz — Great Britain wins all events. Solo: Carolyn Wilson (Great Britain) 1st, Julie Doyle 7th; duet: Wilson and Amanda Dodd (Great Britain) 1st, Doyle and Beth Hines 6th; team: Great Britain 1st, USA (Cincinnati Synchrogators) 4th: Kim Crumrine, Julie Doyle, Beth Hines, Julie Jasontek, Maureen May, Shannon Kelley, Christine Youngpeters, Terri Collins, Marsha Schreiber.

**VII Mallorca Open**— Canada wins all events— Solo: Carolyn Waldo 1st, Patti Lynn 10th; duet: Waldo and Michelle Cameron (Canada) 1st, Lynn and Heather Simmons 9th; team: Canada 1st, USA (Santa Clara) 2nd: Lynn, Simmons, Ginny Cohn, Michelle Nance, Melinda Downey, Carey Shumway, Dawn Graybill, Shannon Green.

**Australia Inaugural Games**— Melbourne — Canada takes gold, USA (Santa Clara) silver. Solo: Sylvie Frechette 1st, Lori Hatch 2nd; duet: Frechette and Nathalie Audet (Canada) 1st, Hatch and Laura Fowler 2nd.

**1st French Grand Prix**— Toulouse, France — USA wins solo and duet. Solo: Sarah Josephson 1st, Karen Josephson, 2nd; duet: Josephsons 1st, Alice and Margarita Smith 2nd.

**I Masters World Games**— Toronto, Canada — Seven golds for USA. Solos: Sue Welch, Peg Hogan, Barbara Browne; duets: Hogan and Rich, Dunn and Jourdian, Eastwood and McMaken; trios: Lenz, Madden, Strawser.

**Coaching**— Cathy O'Brien Romani (Tonawanda Aquettes) in Italy; Kathy Judge (Riverside Aque-ttes) in Switzerland; Kathy Dent in Puerto Rico; and Margo Erickson in Rome.

**International Seminar**— Indianapolis, following World Cup.

## 1986

**USA Team I:** Kristen Babb, Lori Hatch, Karen Josephson, Sarah Josephson, Karen Madsen, Susan Reed, Lisa Riddell, Margarita Smith, Michelle Svitenko, Mary Visniski.

**USA Team II:** Lori Dickie, Lori Donn, Tracy Fearnow, Laura Fowler, Tracy Long, Anne Shulte, Alice Smith, Betsy Visniski, Ruth Weinberg.

**USA Team III:** Karen Brinkman, Jennifer Lynn, Patti Lynn, Michelle Nance, Robin Roberts, Nathalie Schneyder, Heather Simmons, Kathy Zittel.

**V World Aquatic Championships**— Madrid — Canada wins all gold. Results Appendix C.

**French Open**— Issy Les Moulineaux — USA wins duet and team, France solo. Solo: Muriel Hermine (France) 1st, Susan Reed 2nd; duet: Reed and Tracy Long 1st; USA Team II 1st.

**Soviet Women's Day**— Moscow — Canada wins solo, USA duet. Solo: Sylvie Frechette (Canada) 1st, Kristen Babb 2nd; duet: Josephsons 1st, Babb and Michelle Svitenko 2nd.

**Lotte Cup**— Tokyo — USA wins gold. Solo: Sarah Josephson; duet: Josephsons.

**VIII Mallorca Open**— Canada wins solo and duet, Japan team. Solo: Carolyn Waldo (Canada) 1st; Lisa Riddell 2nd; duet: Waldo and Michelle Cameron (Canada) 1st; Kristen Babb and Michelle Svitenko 2nd; team: Canada 1st, No US entry.

**Scandinavian Open**— Odense, Denmark — Great Britain wins duet and team, Sweden solo. Solo: Marie Jacobsson (Sweden) 1st, Leslie Tackett (Tarpons, Colorado) 4th; duet: Joanne Preston and Samantha Allen (Great Britain) 1st, Leslie and Marci Tackett 2nd; team: Great Britain 1st, Tarpons 3rd: Kristen Fischer, Cara Davis, Nancy Strouse, Ingrid Anderson, Shawna Carleton, Melanie Stanton, Leslie Tackett, Marci Tackett.

**Swiss Open Juniors**— Fiesch — Santa Clara wins two golds. Solo: Patti Lynn; duet: Lynn and Heather Simmons.

**Clinics**— Jasana Pacifica, Pat Hixenbaugh, Mission Viejo aquatic exchange to Morocco; Dawn Bean and Lea Bean (Meraquas) in Korea; Diane DeRosier in Beijing, China.

**Coaching**— Linda Edwards (Ohio State) in Peru; Adrienne Lehman (Ohio State) in Switzerland.

**International Seminar**— Madrid — FINA seminar following World Championships.

## 1987

**USA Team I:** Kristen Babb, Karen Josephson, Sarah Josephson, Lori Hatch, Tracy Long, Tracie Ruiz-Conforto, Lisa Riddell, Michelle Svitenko, Karen Madsen, Susan Reed.

**USA Team II**: Tracy Fearnow, Jessica Hudacek, Jennifer Lynn, Patti Lynn, Robin Roberts, Nathalie Schneyder, Anne Schulte, Heather Simmons, Lori Dickie.

**USA Junior Team:** Melinda Downey, Julie Doyle, Becky Dyroen, Jill Sudduth, Lori McCoy, Lisa Poggensee, Jill Savery, Cheryl Schemenauer, Christine Youngpeters.

**III FINA World Cup**— Cairo, Egypt — USA wins solo and team, Canada duet. Results Appendix C.

**X Pan American Games**— Indianapolis— USA reigns supreme. Results Appendix C.

**American Cup III**— Orlando— USA wins all gold. Results Appendix C.

**VIII Pan Pacifics**— Tokyo— Gold to Canada in all events. Solo: Carolyn Waldo 1st, Tracy Fearnow 3rd; duet: Waldo and Michelle Cameron 1st, Heather Simmons and Patti Lynn 3rd; team: Canada 1st, USA Team II 2nd.

**Swiss Open**— St. Moritz — Switzerland wins solo and duet, gold for USA's Junior Team. Solo: Karin Singer 1st, Jill Savery 4th; duet: Singer and Lippuner 1st, Julie Doyle and Christine Youngpeters 4th; team: USA Junior Team 1st.

**Soviet Women's Day**— Moscow Invitational — USA wins solo, Canada duet. Solo: Kristen Babb; duet: Karen Larsen and Tracie Meades (Canada) 1st, Susan Reed and Tracy Long 2nd.

**Roma Sincro**— Italy — USA wins solo and duet, Canada team. Solo: Tracie Ruiz-Conforto; duet: Kristen Babb and Lisa Riddell; team: Canada 1st, no USA team.

**IX Mallorca Open**— Spain — USA wins duet, France solo, Japan team. Solo: Muriel Hermine (France) 1st, Kristen Babb 2nd; duet: Babb and Lisa Riddell 1st; team: Japan 1st, No USA team.

**French Open**— Issy Les Moulinbeaux — France wins solo and duet, USA team. Solo: Muriel Hermine (France) 1st, Becky Dyroen 2nd; duet: Hermine and Sylvie Moisson (France) 1st, Lori McCoy and Jill Savery 2nd; team: USA Junior 1st.

**Vienna Age Group**— Austria — USA wins all golds. Solo: Lori McCoy; duet: McCoy and Jill Savery; USA Juniors top four in figures. No team event.

## *1988*

**Olympic Team:** Tracie Ruiz-Conforto, Karen Josephson, Sarah Josephson.

**USA Team I:** Lori Hatch, Kristen Babb, Lisa Riddell, Becky Dyroen, Lori Dickie, Tracy Long, Michelle Svitenko, Karen Madsen, Susan Reed, Patti Lynn.

**USA Team II:** Heather Simmons, Lori McCoy, Robin Roberts, Jill Savery, Nathalie Schneyder, Jennifer Lynn, Jill Sudduth, Cathy Cramer, Anna Miller, Lisa Poggensee.

**XXIV Olympic Games**— Seoul — Canada wins gold, USA silver. Results Appendix C.

**X Mallorca Open**— USA wins all gold — Solo: Kristen Babb; duet: Babb and Michelle Svitenko; team: USA Team I.

**French Open**— Issy Le Moulineaux — USA wins gold. Solo: Kristen Babb; duet: Svitenko and Babb; team: USA Team I.

**Swiss Open**— Zurich — USA wins gold. Solo: Ruiz-Conforto; duet: Karen and Sarah Josephson; team: USA Team II.

**Petro Cup**— Calgary — Gold for Canada, Silver for USA Team II No solo/duet events.

**Soviet Women's Day**— Moscow — USA wins gold. Solo: Kristen Babb 1st, Tracie Ruiz-Conforto 2nd, Sylvie Frechette (Canada) 3rd; duet: Karen and Sarah Josephson 1st, Babb and Michele Suitenko 2nd, Frechette and Nathalie Guay (Canada), 3rd. No team event.

**Seoul Pre-Olympic**— USA wins solo, Canada duet. Solo: Tracie Ruiz-Conforto 1st, Carolyn Waldo (Canada) 2nd; duet: Waldo and Michele Cameron (Canada) 1st, Karen and Sarah Josephson 2nd. No team event.

**Roma Sincro**— Canada wins all gold, USA (Santa Clara) silver. Solo: Sylvie Frechette (Canada) 1st, Patti Lynn 3rd; duet: Frechette and Nathalie Guay (Canada) 1st, Lynn and Heather Simmons 2nd; team: Canada 1st, USA 2nd, Aquamaids: Lynn, Simmons, Laurie Martin, Mandy Blake, Khadija Cutcher, Jennifer Sogawa, Stephanie Sogawa, Mary Spencer.

**Hans Christian Andersen Cup**— Odense, Denmark — USA (Troy Sculpins) wins all gold. Solo: Alison Prout; duet: Prout and Samantha Derrick; team: USA 1st (Sculpins): Prout, Derrick, Maureen Dewine, Karen Orlet, Adrienne Kerwin, Kim Trumbull, Kerin Banker, Jennifer Darling.

**Loano Cup**— Italy — Canada wins all gold. USA (Sweetwater Dolphins) makes team finals. Solo: Carolyn Waldo (Canada) 1st; duet: Waldo and Michelle Cameron (Canada); team: Canada 1st, USA 8th (Dolphins): Megan Egoscue, Tracy Egoscue, Kindahl Hunter, Brooke Hunter, Candy Aldrich, Laurie McClelland, Jenny Munoz, Tiffany Hernandez.

**Scandinavian Open**— Kuopio, Finland — USA (Cincinnati Synchrogators) wins three events.

**Scotch Centenary**— Greenock, Scotland — Great Britain wins all gold, USA (Jasana Pacifica) silver. Solo: Kerry Shacklock (Great Britain) 1st, Tricia Bisbee 2nd; duet: Shacklock and Sarah Northey (Great Britain) 1st, Bisbee and Kim Glasner 2nd; team: Great Britain 1st, USA 2nd (Jasana Pacifica): Bisbee, Glasner, Summer Velez, Wendy Castillo, Devon Nameth, Jennifer Dodson, Leanna Eaton, Michelle Kroen, Stacie Bantle, Stacey Silva.

**Ontario Masters Invitational**— USA wins six golds— USA solo winners: Sue Bessette, Louise Wing; duet gold: Beth Carey and Carol Motyka-Miller, Helen Ryker and Nancy Schoepperle; trio gold: Bessette, Carey, Miller; team: Suffern Aquatics.

**Clinics**— Cygnets, Nancy Doyle in Monterrey, Mexico.

## 1989

**USA Team I:** Cathy Cramer, Becky Dyroen, Tracy Long, Patti Lynn, Lori McCoy, Jill Savery, Nathalie Schneyder, Heather Simmons, Jill Sudduth, Michelle Svitenko.

**USA Team II:** (Swiss Open) Tracy Long, Nathalie Schneyder, Michelle Svitenko, Patti Lynn, Cathy Cramer, Lisa Poggensee, Jessica Hudacek, Nadine Bekker. (Pan Pacs) Cramer, Poggensee, Hudacek, Bekker, Tia Harding, Anna Miller, Diana Ulrich, Cheryl Schemenauer, Tammy Hunt, Laurie Martin.

**USA Junior Team:** Becky Dyroen, Jill Savery, Jill Sudduth, Lori McCoy, Suzannah Dyroen, Mary Spencer, Margo Thien, Kristy Donn, Stephanie Sogawa, Tina Vorheis.

**IV World Cup**— Paris, France — USA clean sweep. Results Appendix C.

**Swiss Open**— Renens, Switzerland — USA wins duet and team, Japan solo. Solo: Mikako Kotani (Japan) 1st, Tracy Long 2nd; duet: Long and Michelle Svitenko 1st; team: USA Team II 1st.

**IX Pan Pacifics**— Mexico City — USA wins all events. Solo: Lisa Poggensee; duet: Poggensee and Nadine Bekker; team: USA Team II beats Canada Team II by 0.46.

**I Junior World Championships**— Cali, Colombia — First World Championship for Juniors. USA takes all gold. Results Appendix C.

**Soviet Women's Day**— Moscow — USA and Canada split golds. Solo: Kristen Babb 1st, Sylvie Frechette (Canada) 2nd; duet: Frechette and Nathalie Guay (Canada) 1st, Patti Lynn and Heather Simmons 5th.

**Japan Open**— Tokyo — USA wins duet, Japan solo: Solo: Mikako Kotani (Japan) 1st, Tracy Long 2nd; duet: Long and Michelle Svitenko 1st.

**Roma Sincro**— USA (Walnut Creek) wins duet and team, Canada solo. Solo: Kathy Glen (Canada) 1st, Tracy Long 2nd; duet: Long and Svitenko; team: USA 1st (Aquanuts): Nadine Bekker, Tracy Long, Lori McCoy, Susan Reed, Jill Savery, Nathalie Schneyder, Michelle Svitenko, Margot Thien.

**XI Mallorca Open**— Canada wins all gold — USA (Ohio State) against top in world. Solo: Sylvie Frechette (Canada) 1st, Cheryl Schemenauer 14th; duet: Frechette and Nathalie Guay (Canada) 1st, Schemenauer and Jessica Hudacek 7th; team: Canada 1st, Russia 2nd, France 3rd, USA 4th (Ohio State): Amy Pryor, Cheryl Schemenauer, Tammy Hunt, Jessica Hudacek, Diana Ulrich, Kristin Eakin, Tia Harding, Cheryl Wiegand.

**Hans Christian Andersen Cup**— Odense, Denmark — USA (Tonawanda Aquettes) takes all gold. Solo: Kristy Donn; duet: Donn and Maureen Wortman; team: USA team 1st (Aquettes): Donn, Wortman, Nicole Columbus, Ann Hammer, Jean Hilbert, Mimi Laumadue, Tammy Schuman, Traci Urbino.

**4th International Juniors**— Wuppertal, Germany — Golds to USA (solo), Great Britain (duet) and Holland (team). Solo: Janet Wiecking (Briarwood); duet: Collette Geier and Louise Skidmore (Great Britain) 1st, Becky Jasontek and Pam Ochsner (Synchrogators) 2nd; team: Holland, no USA team entry.

**Scandinavian Open**— Oslo, Norway — Sweden wins solo and duet, Canada team. USA (Buffalo Swimkins) take all silver. Solo: Eva Johnsson (Sweden) 1st, Amy Reidel 2nd; duet: Johnsson and Nina Holpers (Sweden) 1st, Riedel and Patti Wiegand 2nd; team: Canada 1st, USA 2nd (Swimkins): Riedel, P. Wiegand, Kristin Yuhnke, Katie McCall, Jodi Wiegand, Shannon Cerveny, Amy Markezich, Rachael Kozower.

**French Open**— La Tour Du Pan — France wins all gold. Solo: Karine Schuler (France) 1st, Laurie Martin 5th; duet: Marianne Aeschbacher and Anne Capron (France) 1st, Martin and Katie Killebrew 4th; team: France 1st, USA 2nd (Santa Clara): Martin, Killebrew, Mandy Blake, Khadija Cutcher, Natasha Haynes, Kari Kreitzer, Shala Larsen, Keva Nelson.

**Pan Pacific Masters**— Indianapolis — USA Masters win all but one gold. 125 masters from the USA attend with a duet from West Germany (wins other gold.)

**World Masters Games**— Arthus, Denmark — 116 competitors from USA, Canada, Denmark. USA takes 10 golds; solos: Jackie Douglass, Nancy Weiman, Eleanor Rissmeyer, Barbara Browne, Louise Wing; duets: Beth Carey and Carol Motyka-Miller, Eva Lenz and Marjorie McClung, Jessie Eastwood and Jean McMaken; trios: Eva Lenz, Carolyn Madden, Martha Strawser; Jesse Eastwood, Marjorie McClung, Jean McMaken.

## 1990

**USA Team I:** Kristen Babb, Becky Dyroen, Karen and Sarah Josephson, Jill Savery, Nathalie Schneyder, Heather Simmons, Michelle Svitenko, Lori McCoy, Jill Sudduth.

**USA Team II:** Kristin Eakin, Jessica Hudacek, Tia Harding, Cheryl Schemenauer, Tammy Hunt, Margot Thien, Suzannah Dyroen, Nadine Bekker, Diana Ulrich, Anna Miller.

**USA Junior Team:** Jill Schlichting, Tammy Cleland, Emily Porter, Kari Kreitzer, Laurie McClelland, Jenny Mayer, Khadija Cutcher, Janet Wiecking, Jenny Ohanesian, Stephanie Sogawa.

**Swiss Open**— Lancy, Switzerland — Canada wins all events. Solo: Sylvie Frechette 1st, Suzannah Dyroen 3rd; duet: Christine Larsen and Kathy Glen (Canada) 1st, Suzannah Dyroen and Nadine Bekker 3rd; team: Canada 1st, Japan 2nd, USA Team II 3rd.

**American Cup IV Junior**— Irvine, California — USA wins all gold. (14 countries from six continents compete). Results Appendix C.

**Soviet Women's Day**— Moscow — USA wins gold. Solo: Tracy Long, Kristina Falasinidi (URS) 2nd; duet: Patti Lynn and Heather Simmons 1st, Jill Sudduth and Becky Dyroen, 2nd.

**II Goodwill Games**— Seattle, Washington — USA takes golds. Results Appendix C.

**Scandinavian Open**— Orebro, Sweden — Russia wins solo and duet, Sweden team. Solo: Kristina Falasinidi (URS) 1st, Kim Ochsner 4th; duet: Anna Kozlova and Ellen Dolzenko (Russia) 1st, Allison Prout and Jenny Dunn 4th; team: Sweden 1st, USA 2nd (Ohio State): Ochsner, Dunn, Prout, Tiffany Williams, Jenny Sprague, Sandra Valles, Valerie Kerscher, Julie Jasontek.

**Vienna Open**— Austria — USA wins solo and duet, Russia team. Solo: Heather Simmons; duet: Becky Dyroen and Jill Sudduth; team: Russia 1st, no USA team entry.

**XII Mallorca Open**— Spain — USA wins duet, Japan solo, Canada team. Solo: Mikako Kotani (Japan) 1st, Becky Dyroen 2nd; duet: Josephsons win by eight points. No USA team entry.

**French Open**— Paris, France — France wins all events, USA (Arizona Aquastars) silver in team. Solo: Anne Capron (France) 1st, Ann Henry, USA, 5th; duet: Capron and Stephane Miermont (France) 1st, Sara Mayfield and Dawn Witkin 4th; team: France 1st, USA 2nd (Aquastars): Henry, Mayfield, Witkin, Molly Dragiewicz, Heidi Dunham, Stephanie Stafford, Amber Vincent, Ali Vincent.

**Moscow Invitational Junior**— Russia wins solo and duet. Solo: Elena Azarova (Russia) 1st, Heather Pease (Cypress Swim Club) 6th; duet: Azarova and Natalia Gruzdeva (Russia) 1st, Pease and Desiree Castro 4th. No team event.

**Hans Christian Andersen Cup**— Odense, Denmark — USA (Troy Sculpins) win all events.

**Finnish Open**— Helsinki — Soviet Juniors win— Solo: Elena Azarova (Russia) 1st, Laurie McClelland 2nd; duet: Azarova and Natalia Gruzdeva (Russia) 1st, Michele Foy and Michele Mahe (Tarpons) 2nd; team: Russia 1st, USA 2nd: Angela and Heather Abbott, Melanie Stanton, Brenda Clabaugh, Michele Mahe, Michele Foy (Tarpons), Amy Santmyer (Air Force Academy), Laurie McClelland (Sweetwater Dolphins).

**III FINA World Masters Championships (1st FINA World Masters for Synchro)**— Rio de Janeiro—12 USA swimmers participate: 11 USA, 1 Brazil: USA wins seven events: Solos: Mary Dorst, Debra Smith, Nancy Weiman, Bernadine Crookshanks, Louise Wing; duets: Weiman and Linda Thomson, Louise and Fred Wing.

**International Coaches and Judges Seminar**— Irvine, California. International Coaches and Judges Seminar following the American Cup, 79 participants from 20 countries.

## 1991

**USA Team I:** Kristen Babb-Sprague, Becky Dyroen, Karen and Sarah Josephson, Jill Savery, Nathalie Schneyder, Heather Simmons, Michelle Svitenko, Jill Sudduth, Suzannah Dyroen.

**USA Team II:** Diana Ulrich, Mary Wodka, Tia Harding, Emily Porter, Laurie Martin, Janet Wiecking, Kim Ochsner, Anna Miller, Kari Kreitzer, Khadija Cutcher.

**USA Junior Team:** Annemarie Alm, Tammy Cleland, Heather Pease, Laurie McClelland, Jenny Ohanesian, Kelly Olsen, Sadie Pietras, Jennifer Vorheis, Becky Jasontek, Heidi Dunham.

**VI World Aquatic Championships**— Perth, Australia — USA wins duet and team, Canada wins solo. Results Appendix C.

**V FINA World Cup**— Bonn, Germany — USA wins duet and team, Canada solo — Solo: Sylvie Frechette (Canada) 1st, Kristen Babb-Sprague 2nd; duet: Karen and Sarah Josephson; team: USA Team I 1st. Canada 2nd, Russia 3rd.

**X Pan Pacifics**— Tokyo— USA Team I wins all gold. Solo: Kristen Babb-Sprague; duet: Karen and Sarah Josephson; team: USA Team I wins by more than four points over Japan.

**XI Pan American Games**— Havana — USA wins all events Eight nations competed. Results Appendix C.

**II Junior World Championships**— Salerno, Italy — Japan wins all events, USA takes silver in team, bronze in duet. Results Appendix C.

**Roma Sincro**— Italy — USA wins duet and team, Canada solo. Solo: Sylvie Frechette (Canada) 1st, Kristen Babb 2nd; duet: Karen and Sarah Josephson 1st; team: USA 1st (Walnut Creek): Kristen Babb, Karen Josephson, Sarah Josephson, Laurie McClelland, Jill Savery, Nathalie Schneyder, Michelle Svitenko, Margot Thien.

**XIII Mallorca Open**— Spain — USA wins all events. Solo: Heather Simmons; duet: Becky Dyroen and Jill Sudduth; team: USA 1st (Aquamaids): Becky and Suzannah Dyroen, Kari Kreitzer, Laurie Martin, Anna Miller, Heather Simmons, Jill Sudduth, Janet Wiecking, Mexico 2nd.

**French Open**— Narbonnne — USA wins all events. Solo: Becky Dyroen; duet: Dyroen and Jill Sudduth; team: USA 1st (Aquamaids) as above.

**Scottish Open**— Glasgow, Scotland — Great Britain wins solo and duet; USA (Sweetwater Dolphins) team. Solo: Kerry Shacklock (Great Britain) 1st, Amy McDaniel 4th; Jr. Solo: Amy McDaniel 1st; duet: Angela Davenport and Melanie Harris (Great Britain) 1st, Emily Marsh and Jolie Taylor 2nd, Amber McDaniel and Tammy Taylor 3rd; team: USA 1st (Sweetwater Dolphins): McDaniel, Marsh, Taylor, Tamara Taylor, Klara Schovanec, Amber McDaniel, Tania Guzman, Ann Marie Kimbell, Shannon-Cremer Martin, Charlotte Gregson.

**Czechoslovakia Cup**— Brno— Canada wins solo

and duet, USA silver. Solo: Sylvie Frechette (Canada) 1st, Becky Jasontek 2nd; duet: Penny and Vicky Vilagos (Canada) 1st, Jasontek and Pam Ochsner 2nd.

**Moscow Invitational Junior**— Moscow — Russia wins solo and duet. Solo: Elizabeta Filakin (Russia) 1st, Heather Pease (Cypress) 3rd; duet: Olga Novokshchenova and Tatiyana Tkachenko (Russia), Pease and Desiree Castro 3rd. No team event.

**Barcelona Pre-Olympic**— Spain — USA and Canada split golds. Solo: Sylvie Frechette (Canada) 1st, USA's Kristen Babb-Sprague 2nd (0.10 behind); duet: Josephsons five-point winners over Japan, Canada 3rd.

### *1992*

**Olympic Team:** Kristen Babb-Sprague, Karen Josephson, Sarah Josephson.

**USA Team I:** Becky Dyroen, Heather Simmons, Jill Sudduth, Jill Savery, Suzannah Dyroen, Nathalie Schneyder, Margot Thien, Emily Porter, Tammy Cleland, Laurie McClelland.

**USA Team II:** Khadija Cutcher, Annemarie Alm, Jill Schlichting, Janet Wiecking, Kim Ochsner, Jenny Ohanesian, Jenny Mayer, Kari Kreitzer, Mary Wodka, Jenny Dunn.

**USA Junior Team:** Emily Marsh, Kim Wurzel, Lisa Burton, Heather Pease, Becky Jasontek, Kristina Lum, Michelle Friend, Gina Pietras, Leslie Riddervold, Christie Bober.

**XXV Olympic Games**— Barcelona — USA wins solo and duet. IOC awards duplicate gold to Canada. Results Appendix C.

**Swiss Open**— Locarno— USA wins all events. Solo: Becky Dyroen; duet: Dyroen and Jill Sudduth; team: USA Team I, Canada 2nd, Japan 3rd. Announcer called this "The Olympic Team Event."

**Loano Open**— Italy — Canada wins all gold. Solo: Cari Read (Canada) 1st, Heather Simmons 2nd; duet: Reed and Karen Fonteyne (Canada) 1st, Becky Dyroen and Jill Sudduth 2nd; team: Canada Team I 1st, USA Team II 2nd.

**V American Cup, Juniors**— Fort Lauderdale, Florida — USA wins all events. Competitors from 14 countries, six continents, had to hurry out to make it to safety before Hurricane Andrew hit the area. Results Appendix C.

**III German Open**— Bonn — Medals split three ways, Canada wins solo, USA duet, Commonwealth of Independent States (Soviet) team. Solo: Sylvie Frechette (Canada) 1st; duet: Sarah and Karen Josephson 1st, team: Commonwealth of Independent States (CIS) wins. No USA solo or team entry.

**XIV Mallorca Open**— Spain — USA wins solo and duet, Great Britain team. Solo: Kristen Babb-Sprague; duet: Karen and Sarah Josephson; team: Great Britain 1st, USA 3rd (Aquanuts): Heather Pease, Jennifer Vorheis, Tina Kasid, Kristin Smith, Lesley Ridervold, Sarah Andrews, Dawn Wales, Kristine Smith.

**XI Roma Sincro**— Italy — Canada wins solo and duet, China team. Solo: Sylvie Frechette (Canada) 1st, Kim Ochsner 7th, Heather Roda 19th; duet: Penny and Vicky Vilagos (Canada), Heather Roda, Jenny Dunn 13th, Jenny Sprague, Kim Oschner 14th; team: China 1st, USA 5th (Ohio State): Jenny Dunn, Kim Ochsner, Heather Roda, Shea Tanabe, Julie Jasontek, Kylan Guenin, Jennie Sprague, Sandra Valles.

**Scandinavian Open**— Kuopio, Finland — USA wins team, Mexico wins solo and duet. Solo: Sonia Cardenas (Mexico) 1st, Becky Jasontek 2nd; duet: Cardenas and Lourdes Olivera (Mexico) 1st, Jasontek, Pam Ochsner 2nd; team: USA 1st (Cincinnati Synchrogators): Jasontek, Liz Collins, Ochsner, Emily Geddes, Lynda Ludwig, Shelley Daniel, Debbie Meister, Jenni Uhl.

**Vienna Open Juniors**— Austria — Greece wins solo, USA duet, Canada team. Solo: Kristina Thalassinidou (Greece) 1st, Kari Kreitzer (Santa Clara), 2nd; duet: Kreitzer and Janet Wiecking 1st. Team: Canada, no U.S. team.

**Scottish Open**—Canada wins solo, USA (Walnut Creek) wins duet. Solo: Lisa Alexander (Canada); duet: Tracey Gayeski and Paige Freiheit.

**IV FINA World Masters**—Indianapolis— USA wins many golds. 128 athletes, 21 USA clubs, three Canadian clubs, plus solo entries from Japan and Switzerland. U.S. winners solos: Violet Royer, Louise Wing, Barbara Eaton, Jeanne Ulrich, Nancy Weiman, Patricia Serneels; duets: Larson and Royer, Greenhill and Zack, Carey and Miller, Bell and Lash, Lamberg and Nichols, Moyer and Serneels; trios: Denlinger, Madden, Strawser; Bessette, Carey, Miller; Kalil, McCormick, Millman; McBride, Ratcliff, Tobler; teams: Dayton Synchronettes, Southern California Unsyncables, Michigan Synchro Masters, Aqua Sprite Masters.

**World Coaches Seminar**— Olympia, Greece —104 participants from 57 nations, the first IOC World Coaches Seminar.

**Coaching Abroad**— Valerie Luedee (Hamden Heronettes) in Switzerland; Robin Roberts (Aquamaids) in France; Anne Schulte (Ohio State) in Switzerland; Tracie Lundsford (Ohio State) in Netherlands; Denise Sawicki (Ohio State) in Germany; Debbie Wiegand (Buffalo Swimkins/Ohio State) in Italy; Carol Dentch in Puerto Rico; Patti Lynn (Aquamaids) in Australia.

*Ed. Note: information incomplete from this point forward due to scarcity of published results in the U.S.*

### *1993*

**USA Team I:** Becky Dyroen-Lancer, Jill Sudduth, Nathalie Schneyder, Tammy Cleland, Heather Simmons, Jill Savery, Suzannah Dyroen, Emily Porter, Heather Pease, Margot Thien.

**USA Team II:** Jenny Ohanesian, Jenny Mayer, Laurie McClelland, Khadija Cutcher, Jennifer Vorheis, Kari Kreitzer, Janet Wiecking, Mary Wodka, Kim Ochsner, Jill Schlichting.

**USA Junior Team:** Carrie Barton, Tracey Gayeski, Laura Brands, Kristina Lum, Season Flores, Tammy Taylor, Amber McDaniel, Deanie Hickox, Kim Wurzel, Vanessa Shaw.

**VI World Cup**—Lausanne, Switzerland—USA wins all gold. Results Appendix C.

**Swiss Open**—Lausanne—USA wins all gold. Solo: Becky Dyroen-Lancer; duet: Dyroen-Lancer and Jill Sudduth; team: USA Team I wins gold.

**Pan Pacifics**—Calgary, Canada—Japan wins all gold. Solo: Fumiko Okuno (Japan) 1st, Heather Simmons 3rd; duet: Okuno and Aki Takayama (Japan) 1st, Kari Kreitzer and Janet Wiecking 3rd; team: Japan 1st, USA Team II 2nd.

**III Junior Worlds**—Leeds, Great Britain—Russia wins solo and duet, Canada team. Results Appendix C.

**VIII German Junior Open**—Dusseldorf—USA and Holland share golds. Solo: Kristina Lum, Kim Wurzel place 1-2; duet: Van der Veldens (Netherlands) 1st, Carrie Barton and Shannon Montague 2nd.

**Finland Open**—Kuopio—USA (Walnut Creek) wins solo and duet. Solo: Tracey Gayeski, Paige Freiheit (USA) place 1-2, duet: Gayeski and Freiheit (USA) 1st.

**Athens Synchro**—Greece—USA (New Canaan) wins solo, Belarus duet and team. Solo: Sandra Valles; duet: Tatiana Medvedeva and Svetlana Vichnevcka (Bel), Valles and Cindy Donofrio 2nd; team: Belarus 1st, no U.S. team entry.

**China Open**—Tianjin—Japan wins solo and duet. Solo: Fumiko Okuno (Japan) 1st, Jill Savery 2nd; duet: Okuno and Miya Tachibana (Japan) 1st, Margot Thien and Nathalie Schneyder 2nd.

**Scottish Open**—Greenock—USA wins senior solo and duet, junior duet and team. Senior solo: Tammy Cleland, Heather Pease place 1-2; senior duet: Cleland and Pease 1st; junior solo: I. Rudenok (Russia) 1st, Becky Percy 2nd; junior duet: Percy and Kristen Moore 1st, Catherine Chen, Trisha Santos 2nd; junior team: USA 1st (Aquanuts): Percy, Moore, Tammy Crow, Catherine Chen, Trisha Santos, Hillary Seipelt, Jennifer Stofiel, Amanda Burkett, Sarah Reidenbach; Russia 2nd, France 3rd.

**Eurosync Masters**—Antwerp, Belgium—Three clubs participate from USA. USA wins nine gold medals. Solos: Patricia Serneels, Jill Clarke, Evelyn Hutchings, Barbara Pedersen, Louise Wing; duets: Clarke and Jakobsen, Hutchings and Pedersen, Wing and Wing; team: Southern California Unsyncables.

## 1994

**USA Team I:** Suzannah Bianco, Tammy Cleland, Becky Dyroen-Lancer, Heather Pease, Emily Porter, Jill Savery, Nathalie Schneyder, Heather Simmons, Jill Sudduth, Margot Thien.

**USA Team II:** Annemarie Alm, Lisa Burton, Becky Jasontek, Tina Kasid, Kari Kreitzer, Jenny Mayer, Emily Marsh, Laurie McClelland, Dawn Wales, Mary Wodka.

**USA Junior Team:** (France) Lori Barbaglia, Julie Enos, Elicia Marshall, Shannon Montague, Heather Moore, Kristin Moore, Alanna O'Leary, Hilary Seipelt, Jennifer Stoifel, Lisa Velez. (American Cup) O'Leary, Marshall, Enos, Stofiel, Velez, Seipelt, Lisa Cunanan, Vanessa Shaw, Kara Duncan, Amber McDaniel.

**VII World Aquatic Championships**—Rome—USA reigns supreme in all events. Dyroen-Lancer gets 5th consecutive grand slam win. Results Appendix C.

**French Open**—Paris—USA wins all events. Solo: Becky Dyroen-Lancer; duet: Dyroen-Lancer and Jill Sudduth; team: USA Team I wins close battle with Canada 183.77–183.64.

**Swiss Open**—Lausanne—Japan, Canada and Russia share golds. Solo: Fumiko Okuno (Japan) 1st, Mary Wodka 5th; duet: Lisa Alexander and Erin Woodley (Canada) 1st, Laurie McClelland and Kari Kreitzer 6th; team: Russia 1st, USA Team II 2nd.

**American Cup VI Juniors**—Cerritos, California—Japan wins all golds, Canada silver, USA bronze. Results Appendix C.

**French Junior International**—Vichy—USA wins all gold. Solo: Alanna O'Leary; duet: O'Leary and Elicia Marshall; team: USA Junior Team beats France, Mexico, and Switzerland.

**Goodwill Games**—St. Petersburg—USA and Russia share golds. Results Appendix C.

**French Winter Nationals**—Paris—USA (Santa Clara) wins solo and duet. Solo: Becky Dyroen-Lancer; duet: Dyroen-Lancer and Jill Sudduth.

**Hans Christian Andersen Cup:**—Odense, Denmark—USA (Troy Sculpins) wins team gold. Solo: Allison Dewine 2nd, Jessie DiFabio 4th; Katie Hogan and Jessie Hall 2nd; team: USA team 1st (Sculpins): Dewine, Hogan, Hall, DiFabio, Jennifer Berg, Meghan Reilly, Rachael Beale, Maria Virgoni, Kristina Schling.

**Dusseldorf International**—Germany—USA (Santa Clara) wins all golds. 13–14 solo: Lisa Cunanan; duet: Cunanan and Sharon Polley; 15–17 solo: Alanna O'Leary; duet: O'Leary and Elicia Marshall; team: Santa Clara 13–17 beats Canada and Spain: Aquamaids: Marshall, O'Leary, Cunanan, Polley, Julie Enos, Deanie Hickox, Season Flores, Judy Chang.

**Loano Cup**—Italy—Solo: Estella Warren (Canada), Paige Freiheit (Walnut Creek) 5th.

**Mallorca Open:** USA (Cincinnati Synchrogators) Team: 4th.

**Trygg Hansa Synchro Open**—Gothenburg, Sweden—Solo: Kristina Moore (Tonawanda Aquettes) 3rd; duet: Moore and Jill Evans 4th.

Flanders Open— Belgium — USA wins duet: A. Ensign and I. Frances (Cypress Swim Club), L. Sherling and S. Tobias 5th.

Slavia Stu Cup— Bratislava, Slovakia — USA (Connecticut Laurels) wins solo and duet, Slovakia team. Solo: Sandra Valles 1st, Julie Jasontek 4th; duet: Valles and Jasontek; team: Slovakia 1st, No USA entry.

V FINA World Masters Championships—Montreal— USA Masters win 9 events— USA solo winners: Nancy Weiman, Jane Katz, Louise Wing; duet winners: Lambert and Nichols, Munchhof and Larson; trio winners: Moore, Thompson, Kaminski; Miller, Carey, Van Alstyne; Hutchings, Huntley, Pedersen; team: Michigan Synchro Masters.

FINA Judges Seminar— Toronto, Canada — 80 participants, emphasis on judging the new Technical routines.

## 1995

USA Team I: Suzannah Bianco, Tammy Cleland, Becky Dyroen-Lancer, Emily Porter-LeSueur, Jill Savery, Nathalie Schneyder, Heather Simmons, Jill Sudduth, Margot Thien, Kari Kreitzer.

USA Team II: Emily Marsh, Lisa Burton, Mandi Keener, Tina Kasid, Annemarie Alm, Becky Jasontek, Kristina Lum, Carrie Barton, Bridget Finn, Kim Wurzel.

USA Junior Team: Lindsey Wiggington, Julie Enos, Shannon Montague, Alanna O'Leary, Amanda Burkett, Elicia Marshall, Heather Moore, Lisa Velez, Lori Barbaglia, Becky Percy.

VII FINA World Cup— Atlanta, Georgia — USA wins all events. USA Team I scores perfect 10s in win. Dyroen-Lancer wins 9th consecutive grand slam. Results Appendix C.

XII Pan American Games— Mar del Plata, Argentina — USA Team I takes all gold. Results Appendix C.

Swiss Open— Geneva, Switzerland — Japan wins duet and team, Russia takes solo. Solo: Olga Sedakova (Russia) 1st, Annemarie Alm 7th; duet: Miho and Mika Kawabe (Japan) 1st, Emily Marsh and Becky Jasontek 3rd; team: Japan 1st, USA Team II 3rd.

IV Junior World Championships— Bonn, Germany — Russia wins solo and duet, Canada team. USA seeks to move up from previous placing and does. Results Appendix C.

French Open— Lille, France — USA wins solo and duet; solo: Anna Kozlova; duet: Kozlova and Mary Wodka.

Mallorca Open— Mallorca, Spain — Japan wins all events. Solo: Miya Tachibana (Japan) 1st, Sandra Valles 4th; duet: Tachibana and Akiko Kawabe (Japan), Julie Jasontek and Sandra Valles 3rd; team: Japan 1st, No U.S. entry.

Scottish Open— Greenock, Scotland — USA wins gold. Sr. solo: Lisa Velez; Jr. Christina McClel-

land; Jr. duet: McClelland and Lindsey Wiggington; team (Sweetwater Dolphins): Velez, McClelland, Wiggington, Sara Bonnell, Jennifer Bullock, Nicole Capatanos, Mary Hofer, Amy McDaniel.

## 1996

Olympic Team: Suzannah Bianco, Tammy Cleland, Becky Dyroen-Lancer, Emily LeSueur, Heather Pease, Jill Savery, Nathalie Schneyder, Heather Simmons-Carrasco, Jill Sudduth, Margot Thien.

USA Team I: Carrie Barton, Lisa Burton, Bridget Finn, Becky Jasontek, Tina Kasid, Kari Kreitzer, Kristina Lum, Emily Marsh, Laurie McClelland, Kim Wurzel.

USA Junior Team: Amanda Burkett, Elicia Marshall, Becky Martin, Bill May, Christina McClelland, Lauren McFall, Shannon Montague, Alanna O'Leary, Stacey Scott, Lindsey Wiggington.

Olympic Games XXVI— Atlanta, Georgia — First team event in the Olympic Games. USA wins gold. Results Appendix C.

Swiss Open— Lausanne — USA wins duet and team, Canada solo. Solo: Jacinthe Taillon (Canada) 1st, Kari Kreitzer 2nd; duet: Kreitzer and Kristina Lum; team: USA Team I 1st, Japan 2nd, Russia 3rd.

American Cup VII Juniors— St. Peters, Missouri — USA wins solo and team, Korea wins duet. Results Appendix C.

French Open— Paris— Team: USA 1st (Santa Clara Aquamaids): Brynn Butzman, Karen Green, Brianne MacNaughton, Becky Martin, Katie Enos, Lauren McFall, Bill May, Anna Shon.

III Athens Synchro— Greece wins solo, Canada duet and team, USA bronze. Solo: Kristina Thalassinidiou (Greece) 1st, Tiffany Mockler 5th; duet: Reidun Tatham and Erin Chan (Canada) 1st, Mockler and Julie Drexler 5th; team: Canada 1st, USA 3rd (New Canaan Aquianas): Mockler, Drexler, Jen Mueyk, Gabriella Nanni, Cindy Elsman, Nicole Querze, Laura Ingraham, Carrie Dougherty.

Junior Open— Budapest, Hungary — Hungary wins solo and duet, Canada wins team. Solo: Hamori Zsuzsanna (Hungary) 1st, Tiffany Mockler 4th, Julie Drexler 5th; duet: Susanna Hamori and Petra Marschalko (Hungary), Drexler and Mockler 2nd; team: Canada 1st, no USA team entry.

FINA World Championship Qualifying— Inverclyde, Scotland, Becky Dyroen-Lancer and Jill Sudduth secured qualifying places for the USA by winning both solo and duet events.

Scottish Open— Inverclyde — USA wins all events. Solo: Anna Kozlova; duet: Kari Kreitzer and Kristina Lum; team: USA 1st (Aquamaids): Carrie Barton, Tuesday Middaugh, Anna Kozlova, Kari Kreitzer, Kristina Lum, Elicia Marshall, Alanna O'Leary, Kim Wurzel.

VI FINA World Masters— Sheffield, England — USA wins 11 gold medal events in largest World

Synchro Masters. USA winners include, Solo: Nancy Weiman, Penny DeMeules; duets: Jamie Buckiewicz and Debbie Anderson, Peggy Beyda and Dot Guenther, Fred and Louise Wing; trio: Clark, DeMeules, MacInness; Buckiewicz, Anderson, Borgmeier; Jakobsen, Larson, Munchhof; teams: Southern California Unsyncables, Ramapo Aqua Masters.

**World Conference**— Albany, New York — World seminar for coaches and judges.

## 1997

**USA Team I:** Carrie Barton, Bridget Finn, Rebecca Jasontek, Tina Kasid, Kristina Lum, Emily Marsh, Elicia Marshall, Kim Wurzel, Tracey Gayeski, Laurie McClelland.

**USA Team II:** Dawn Wales, Paige Freiheit, Stacey Scott, Bill May, Lianne Cameron, Vanessa Shaw, Gina Pietras, Lesley Riddervold, Tammy Crow, Kara Duncan.

**USA Junior Team:** Christina McClelland, Marlene Marshall, Lindsey Wiggington, Lauren McFall, Becky Martin, Erin Dobratz, Brynn Butzman, Victoria Bowen, Katie Enos, Kris Schneider.

**VIII World Cup**— Guangzhou, China — Russia wins all gold. Results Appendix C.

**Swiss Open**— St. Moritz, Switzerland — USA wins solo and duet, Canada team. Solo: Bill May led the USA team to solo and duet wins; duet: May and Stacey Scott; team: Canada 1st, USA Team II 2nd.

**V Junior World Championships**— Moscow, Russia — Russia wins solo and team, Korea duet. Results Appendix C.

**Roma Sincro**— Rome — Russia wins solo and duet. Solo: Olga Sedakova (Russia) 1st, Amanda Burkett 4th; duet: Sedakova and Olga Brusnikina (Russia) 1st, Burkett and Becky Percey 5th; team: Russia 1st, no USA team.

**Slovakia Synchro**— Ukraine wins all events — USA (New Canaan Aquianas) silver in team. Solo: Marina Zdanevich (Ukraine) 1st, Tiffany Mockler 4th; duet: Zdanevich and Irina Ustenko (Ukraine) 1st, Elizabeth McIntyre and Blaire Fraser 5th; team: Ukraine 1st, USA 2nd (Aquianas): Fraser, McIntyre, Mockler, Elizabeth Clerkin, Laura Mase, Kim Probst.

**FINA Coaching and Judging Clinic**— Bangkok — World Seminar, 125 participants.

## 1998

**USA Team I:** Carrie Barton, Bridget Finn, Rebecca Jasontek, Tina Kasid, Kristina Lum, Emily Marsh, Elicia Marshall, Kim Wurzel

**USA Team II:** Tammy Crow, Brynn Butzman, Tracey Gayeski, Heather Moore, Paige Freiheit, Lindsey Wiggington, Gina Pietras, Becky Martin, Vanessa Shaw, Stacey Scott, Lianne Cameron, Kelli Bonzoumet.

**USA Junior Team:** Alison Bartosik, Erin Dobratz, Julie Drexler, Stephanie Joukoff, Christine Mc-

Clelland, Katie Norris, Andrea Nott, Kimberly Probst.

**VIII World Championships**— Perth, Australia — Russia wins gold in all events, USA bronze in team. Results Appendix C.

**Goodwill Games**— Long Island, New York — Russia wins duet and team; USA takes silver in both events. Results Appendix C.

**Swiss Open**— Monthey, Switzerland — Japan wins all events, USA team silver; solo: Juri Tatsumi (Japan) 1st, Becky Martin 2nd; duet: M. Fujimaru and Y. Toneda (Japan) 1st, C. Sauvageau and T. Agostinelli (Canada) 2nd, Tammy Crow and Gina Pietras 3rd; team: Japan 1st, USA Team II 2nd.

**American Cup VIII**— Cerritos, California — Japan wins solo and duet, USA wins team. Results Appendix C.

**VII FINA World Masters**—Casablanca, Morocco— USA wins eight golds. USA winners include solos: Joanne Lyons, Cynthia McKenney; duet: Beyda and Guenther; trio: Bean, Beay, Rudolph; Motyka-Miller, Carey, Pollok; Steiner, Beyda, Guenther; team: two teams from Ramapo.

## 1999

**U.S.A. Team I:** Carrie Barton, Kara Duncan, Bridget Finn, Becky Jasontek, Kristina Lum, Emily Marsh, Elicia Marshall, Tuesday Middaugh, Kim Wurzel, Laurel McFall.

**U.S.A. Team II:** Brynn Butzman, Kelli Bonzoumet, Tammy Crow, Bill May, Lauren McFall, Gina Pietras, Stacey Scott, Vanessa Shaw, Lindsey Wiggington.

**U.S.A. Junior Team:** Alison Bartosik, Tiffany Bye, Erin Dobratz, Julie Drexler, Stephanie Joukoff, Becky Martin, Katie Norris, Andrea Nott, Kimberly Probst, Kendra Zanotto.

**FINA World Cup**— Seoul, Korea — Russia wins all events, Results Appendix C.

**Junior World Championships**— Cali, Colombia — Russia 1st in all events, France, China, Italy took the other medal places. Security advisories by the U.S. State Department kept the USA Junior Team at home. Results Appendix C.

**Pan American Games**— Winnipeg, Canada — Canada wins duet and team, USA takes silver. duet: Claire Carver-Dias and Fanny Letourneau, Becky Jasontek and Emily Marsh (USA) 2nd; team: Canada 1st with 97.39 to USA's 97.31 for 2nd. See Appendix C.

**Japan Open**— Tokyo, Japan — Russia wins solo, duet, Japan wins team. USA (Santa Clara Aquamaids) takes 3rd and 4th. Solo: Olga Brusnikina (Russia) 1st, Anna Kozlova (USA) 3rd; duet: Brusnikina and Kisseleva (Russia) 1st, Kozlova and Tuesday Middaugh (USA) 3rd. Team: Japan 1st, no USA team entry.

**German Open**— Bonn, Germany — USA (Santa Clara Aquamaids) wins all golds, solo, duet and team. Solo: Anna Kozlova (USA) 1st; duet: Carrie Barton and Elicia Marshall (USA) 1st. USA National Team II 1st.

**Rome Open**— Rome, Italy — Gold medals to France, Russia and Canada. USA team wins bronze. Solo: Virginie Dedieu (France) 1st, Lianne Cameron (USA) 8th; duet: Elena Azarova and Olga Novokchtchanova (Russia) 1st, Tammy Cleland-McGregor and Heather Pease (USA) 4th; team: Canada 1st, USA National Junior Team 3rd.

**Swiss Open**— Zurich, Switzerland — USA takes all gold. Solo: Bill May (USA) 1st; duet: Bill May and Kristina Lum (USA) 1st; team: USA Team II 1st.

### 2000

**USA Olympic Team**— Carrie Barton, Tammy Cleland-McGregor, Bridget Finn, Anna Kozlova, Kristin Lum, Elicia Marshall, Tuesday Middaugh, Heather Pease-Olson, Kim Wurzel.

**USA Team I**— Alison Bartosik, Tammy Crow, Becky Jasontek, Becky Martin, Bill May, Lauren McFall, Andrea Nott, Gina Pietras, Vanessa Shaw, Kendra Zanotto.

**USA Junior Team**— Amanda Graff-Baker, Erin Dobratz, Jennifer Kibler, Stacy Leiker, Kim Lester, Sara Lowe, Stephanie Nesbitt, Katie Norris, Lauren Rettberg, Allison Wible.

**XXVII Olympic Games**— Sydney, Australia — Russia wins team and duet. USA 5th in team, 4th in duet (Anna Kozlova and Tuesday Middaugh). Results Appendix C.

**Olympic Qualifying Event**— Sydney, Australia. duet: 28 entries: Olga Brusnikina and Maria Kisseleva (Russia) 1st, Japan 2nd, France 3rd, Tammy Cleland-McGregor, Heather Pease-Olson (USA) 5th; team: (16 entries) Russia 1st, Japan 2nd, Canada 3rd, USA 4th.

**Swiss Open**— Locarno, Switzerland — USA wins gold in solo, silver in duet. Solo: Bill May (USA) 1st, China 2nd and 3rd; duet: Claire Carver-Dias and Fanny Letourneau (Canada) 1st, Anna Kozlova and Tuesday Middaugh (USA) 2nd, China 3rd.

**Rome Open**— Rome — USA National Team I sweeps Gold. Solo: Anna Kozlova 1st, Becky Jasontek 2nd, Italy 3rd; duet: Anna Kozlova and Tuesday Middaugh 1st, Japan 2nd, Becky Martin and Lauren McFall (USA) 3rd; team: USA Team I 1st, Japan 2nd, Canada 3rd.

**American Cup**— Tallahassee, Florida — USA National Junior Team takes silver in solo and team, bronze in duet. Solo: Anouk Lefreniere (Canada) 1st, Katie Norris (USA) 2nd, Japan 3rd; duet: Ayako Matsumura and Eika Kamura (Japan) 1st; Anouk Lefreniere, Jessika Dubuc (Canada) 2nd; Erin Dobratz and Sara Lowe (USA) 3rd; team: Canada 1st, USA Junior Team 2nd, Brazil 3rd.

**VIII World Masters**— Munich — 262 swimmers from 12 countries participated. USA represented by Southern California Unsyncables, Redwood Empire, DC Masters, Ramapo (NY) and the Michigan Synchro Masters. Gold medals to the following USA swimmers: Solos Larson, Jakobsen, Kyle, Weiman, Schroeder; duets Kyle and Schroeder, Hipp and Gaither; trios Gaither, DeMeules, MacInness; Bean, Beay, Hipp; teams Ramapo and two teams from the Unsyncables.

### 2001

**U.S.A. Team I:** Alison Bartosik, Tammy Crow, Becky Jasontek, Anna Kozlova, Becky Martin, Lauren McFall, Katie Norris, Gina Pietras, Lindsey Wiggington, Kendra Zanotto.

**U.S.A. Team II:** Victoria Bowen, Erin Dobratz, Katie Edwards, Anna Eng, Mary Hofer, Suzannah Hyatt, Kim Lester, Elizabeth-Anne Markman, Bill May, Andrea Nott, Kim Probst.

**U.S.A. Junior Team:** Alison Bartosik, Kate Hooven, Becky Kim, Teresa Liccardo, Sara Lowe, Lauren Marsh, Ashley McHugh, Stephanie Nesbitt, Emiko Takyu, Alison Wible.

**IX FINA World Championships**— Fukuoka — Russia wins solo and team. Japan wins duet. Results Appendix C.

**Junior World Championships**—Federal Way, Washington — Russia wins all events. Results Appendix C.

**Swiss Open**— St. Mauritz, Switzerland — Team II earned gold in solo and bronze in duet and team. Solo: Bill May 1st, China 2nd, Canada 3rd and Victoria Bowen (USA) 4th; duet: Anne Davenport and Margie Davenport (Canada) 1st, China 2nd, Mary Hofer and Andrea Nott (USA) 3rd; Erin Dobratz and Suzannah Hyatt (USA) 4th; team: China 1st, Canada 2nd, USA Team II 3rd.

### 2002

**USA Team I:** Alison Bartosik, Tammy Crow, Erin Dobratz, Becky Jasontek, Anna Kozlova, Tracy Long, Sara Lowe, Lauren McFall, Stephanie Nesbitt, Katie Norris, Gina Pietras, Kendra Zanotto.

**USA Team II:** Victoria Bowen, Anna Eng, Mary Hofer, Suzannah Hyatt, Beth Kreimer, Lindsay Newbill, Andrea Nott, Bill May, Kim Probst, Shella Sadovnik, Emiko Takyu.

**USA Junior Team:** Kate Hooven, Christina Jones, Becky Kim, Sara Lowe, Barbara Nesbitt, Stephanie Nesbitt, Cassidy Ramage, Ashley Rule, Elizabeth-Anne Markman, Kim McKinley.

**X FINA World Cup A**— Zurich, Switzerland — France wins solo, Russia wins duet and team. Results Appendix C.

**IX FINA Junior World Championships**— Toronto, Canada — Russia wins all events. Results Appendix C.

**Swiss Open**— Geneva, Switzerland — U.S. wins three events: Solo: Bill May 1st; duet: Alison Bartosik and Anna Kozlova 1st; team: Japan 1st, USA Team I 3rd; Combo team: USA Team I 1st.

**IX FINA World Masters**— Christchurch, New Zealand — Seven countries participated with eight gold medals to USA swimmers, seven to Canada, Japan and Great Britain each won two events and Switzerland won one. USA participants include the Southern California Unsyncables, Redwood Empire Synchro and Sacramento Swim Team. Gold medals to solo: Lea Bean, Carol Mellows, Holly Kyle, Lizzi Jakobsen; duet: Kyle and Chris Schroeder, Penny DeMeules and Jakobsen, trio: Bean, Beay, Melanie Stanton; Kyle, Schroeder, Mellows.

## 2003

**USA Team I:** Alison Bartosik, Erin Dobratz, Mary Hofer, Becky Jasontek, Anna Kozlova, Sara Lowe, Lauren McFall, Stephanie Nesbitt, Katie Norris, Kendra Zanotto.

**USA Team II:** Janet Culp, Jennie Culp, Kate Hooven, Becky Kim, Elizabeth-Anne Markman, Ashley McHugh, Kim McKinley, Lindsay Newbill, Andrea Nott, Kim Probst.

**Pan American Games Team:** Alison Bartosik, Erin Dobratz, Becky Jasontek, Anna Kozlova, Sara Lowe, Lauren McFall, Stephanie Nesbitt, Katie Norris, Kendra Zanotto.

**USA Junior Team:** Brooke Abel, Erin Bell, Poppy Carlig, Christina Jones, Danielle Kramer, Nicole Langley, Barbara Nesbitt, Annabelle Orme, Leah Pinette, Lesley Wallace.

**X FINA World Championships**— Barcelona, Spain — France wins solo, Russia duet and team. Japan wins free combination team. Results Appendix C.

**Pan American Games**— Santo Domingo, Dominican Republic — USA wins both duet and team gold. Results Appendix C.

**Rome Open**— Rome, Italy — USA swept all the gold medals. Solo: Anna Kozlova 1st; duet: Kozlova and Allison Bartosik 1st; Moraes twins (Brazil) 2nd; team: USA Team I wins.

## 2004

**USA Olympic Team:** Alison Bartosik, Tammy Crow, Erin Dobratz, Becky Jasontek, Anna Kozlova, Sara Lowe, Lauren McFall, Stephanie Nesbitt, Kendra Zanotto, Andrea Nott (alternate).

**USA National Team II:** Janet Culp, Jennie Culp, Ellen Hacker, Kate Hooven, Becky Kim, Danielle Kramer, Kimberley McKinley, Leah Pinette, Kimberly Probst, Alicia Rice.

**USA Junior National Team:** Brooke Abel, Poppy Carlig, Debbie Chen, Christina Jones, Meghan Kinney, Melissa Knight, Jessica McMahon, Annabelle Orne, Jillian Penner, Carolyn Watts.

**XXVIII Olympic Games**—Athens Greece — Russia wins team and duet. USA 3rd in team, 3rd in duet (Anna Kozlova and Alison Bartosik). Results Appendix C.

**Olympic Qualifying Event** —Athens, Greece — Russia wins duet and team events. Anna Kozlova and Alison Bartosik 4th in duet of 24 qualifiers; USA Olympic Team takes 3rd of 8 qualifiers.

**U.S. Open International competition** —New Orleans, Louisiana — National Team II wins gold in solo, team and combo events. Kim Probst wins solo for the U.S. Canada takes gold in duet with U.S.'s Kate Hooven and Becky Kim 2nd, and Janet and Jennie Culp 3rd.

**Junior World Championships** —Moscow, Russia — Russia wins all events. USA's Christina Jones and Annabelle Orne take silver in duet, Jones silver in solo. U.S. Junior team is 4th. Results Appendix C.

**German Open Junior Championships** —Germany — Russia wins all events. Christina Jones and Jessica McMahon place 2nd in duet. Jones and McMahon take 2nd and 4th in solo.

# Notes

## Chapter 1

1. Armbrust, "Magical Maidens." *International Swimming & Water Polo*, Winter 1981, p. 54+.
2. Kerper, *Splash*, p. 12.
3. *Ibid.*, p. 14.
4. Armbrust, "Magical Maidens," *International Swimming & Water Polo,* Winter 1981, p. 54+.
5. Dawson, *Weissmuller to Spitz*, p. 18.
6. *Ibid.*, p. 125.
7. Kroll, personal collection.
8. Harvey, "Rippling Rhythm," ISHOF, n.pg.
9. J. Henning, "How It Began," *International Swimming & Water Polo*, Spring 1987, p. 36+.
10. Strubbe, "Origins and Development of," *Synchro-News,* June 1958, p. 83+.
11. Dawson, p. 19.
12. AAU "Women's Sport Committee Report," ISHOF, n.pg.
13. Dawson, p. 19.
14. Zajac, "History of S.S. in England," *Synchro-Info,* June 1969, p. 18+.
15. Harvey, "Rippling Rhythm," ISHOF, n.pg.
16. Zajac, "History of S.S. in England," *Synchro-Info,* June 1969, p. 18+.
17. Strubbe, "Origins and Development of," *Synchro-News,* June 1958, p. 83+.
18. AAU "Women's Sport Committee Report," ISHOF, n.pg.
19. Strubbe, "Origins and Development of…" *Synchro-News,* June 1958, p. 83+.
20. Rackham, *Synchronized Swimming*, p. 22.
21. Dawson, *Weissmuller to Spitz*, p. 18.
22. *Ibid.*, p. 166.
23. *Ibid.*
24. Cordell, "The Original Mermaid."
25. Kellerman, *How to Swim*, p. 30.
26. Dawson, p. 166.
27. Cordell, "The Original Mermaid."
28. Kellerman, *How to Swim*, p. 30.
29. Cordell, "The Original Mermaid."
30. Dawson, p. 166.
31. "Annette Kellerman Dies." *Synchro-Info*, December 1975, p. 14.
32. Cordell, "The Original Mermaid."
33. Dawson, p. 166.
34. Corsan, *At Home in the Water*, p. 113.
35. Stoerker, "The Origin and Development…" masters thesis, p. 12.
36. Stoerker, p. 13.
37. Strubbe, "Origins and Development of…" *Synchro-News*, June 1958, p. 83+.
38. Strubbe, *Synchro-News*, p. 88.
39. Stoerker, p. 17.
40. *Ibid.*, p. 19.
41. Leach, Letters, ISHOF, n.pg.
42. Strubbe, "Origins and Development of…" *Synchro-News*, June 1958, p. 83+.
43. Dawson, p. 19.
44. Strubbe, "Origins and Development of…" *Synchro-News*, June 1958, p. 83+.
45. "In Memorium … Goss" *Synchro-Info*, February 1981, p. 24.
46. Goss, *Water Ballet Charts*.
47. Beshunsky, unpublished, ISHOF, n.pg.
48. "In Memorium … Goss," *Synchro-Info*, February 1981, p. 24.
49. Curtis, *Rhythmic Swimming*, p. 1.
50. Stoerker, p. 16.
51. Trilling, "History of Physical Education…," p. 110.
52. Curtis, *Rhythmic Swimming*, p. 1.
53. Leach, Letters, ISHOF, n.pg.
54. Stoerker, p. 17.
55. Beshunsky, n.pg.
56. Stoerker, p. 14.
57. Hass, *Synchronized Swimmer*, December 1952, p. 3.
58. Bullock, *Synchronized Swimmer*, February 1952, p. 3.
59. Kerth, *Synchronized Swimmer*, June 1952, p. 12.
60. "Swan Club Holds Tryouts," *Ohio State Monthly*, November 1928, ISHOF, n.pg.
61. Stoerker, p. 21.

62. Glass, *Synchronized Swimmer*, February 1955, p. 3.

63. Stoerker, p. 44.

64. Harper, *Synchro Swimming USA*, Spring 2003, p. 9.

65. Stoerker, p. 35.

66. "Terrapins of Mundelein...," *Discus*, January 1939, p. 9.

67. Beshunsky, n.pg.

68. Stoerker, p. 38+.

69. Patterson, *Amateur Athlete*, March 1941, p. 9.

70. D. Bean, personal collection.

71. Synchro Canada, *Highlights of Synchro Swim*, p. 5.

72. Leach, n.pg.

73. Synchro Canada, p. 5.

74. Clark, *60 Years to Celebrate*, p. 6.

75. Curtis, "Competitive SS," *Journal Health & P.E.*, January 1941.

76. Synchro Canada, p. 2.

77. Leach, n.pg.

78. *Ibid.*

79. Thomas, "The Man Who Made the Musical."

80. Albert, "A Century of Progress View Book."

81. Lundholm, "The Story...," *Synchro-Info*, December 1976, p. 16+.

82. "A Century of Progress" Aquacade contract.

83. J. Henning, "How it Began," *Synchro*, August 1985, p. 19+.

84. Curtis.

85. A Century of Progress, Publicity Release, August 24, 1934.

86. Curtis.

87. A Century of Progress, Publicity Release.

88. A Century of Progress Administrative Staff Correspondence.

89. Feinstein, telephone interview, 1997.

90. Curtis, *Rhythmic Swimming*, p. 1.

91. A Century of Progress, Publicity Release.

92. McCormick, *Water Pageants & Games*, 1933.

93. Curtis, *A Source Book of Water Pageantry*, 1936.

94. Curtis, *Rhythmic Swimming*, p. 1.

95. Dawson, p. 110.

96. M. Rose, Interview, April 19, 1997.

97. Brookman, "The Golden Age of Swimming," *Synchro*, December 1979, p. 22+.

98. Beshunsky.

99. B. Rose, *World's Fair Program*, p. 5.

100. Derosier, "History of Water Ballet and...," unpublished, ISHOF, n.pg.

101. B. Rose, *World's Fair Program*, p. 5.

102. Dawson, 152.

103. B. Rose, *World's Fair Program*, p. 5.

104. Crabbe, telephone interview, January 1998.

105. H. Johnson, *Fitness Swimmer*, Summer 1995, p. 32.

106. B. Rose, *World's Fair Program*, p. 7.

107. H. Johnson, *Fitness Swimmer*, Summer 1995, p. 32.

108. B. Rose, *World's Fair Program*, p. 7.

109. H. Johnson, *Fitness Swimmer*, Summer 1995, p. 32.

110. *Ibid.*, p. 34.

111. "Minneapolis Aquatennial," ISHOF, n.pg.

112. "Premier of Aqua Follies...," *Minneapolis Tribune*, August 12, 1950.

113. "Minneapolis Aquatennial," ISHOF, n.pg.

114. L. Michael, "Aqua's Folly," *Freeway News*, p. 8+.

115. S. Martin, "Aqua Follies Spectacle...," *Seattle Post Intelligencer*, p. 3.

116. Detroit Riverama *[16th] Official Program*, "Aqua Follies of 1955, p. 3.

117. Kerper, p. 29+.

118. Crabbe, telephone interview, January 1998.

119. Curtis, "Stars & Stripes," *Synchronized Swimmer*, June 1952, p. 14.

## *Chapter 2*

1. "Steed Twins...," *Chicago Tribune*, February 28, 1938.

2. Stoerker, "The Origin," *master's thesis*, p. 34.

3. *Ibid.*, p. 47.

4. Curtis, *Rhythmic Swimming*, p. 4.

5. *Ibid.*, p. 1.

6. Curtis, "A Plea," *Official Aquatics Guide*, 1928-29.

7. Curtis, *Rhythmic Swimming*, p. 1.

8. "Pool Demonstration [Program]," May 27, 1939, ISHOF, n.pg.

9. Curtis, *Rhythmic Swimming*, p. 2.

10. "Swim Club Wins Trick" *Synchro-Info*, February 1972, p. 9.

11. Leach, "To Set the Record Straight" Unpublished, ISHOF, n.pg.

12. Hayes, *Synchronized Swimmer*, March 1952, p. 6.

13. Leach.

14. Leach, c. 1940, undated personal papers, ISHOF, n.pg.

15. "AAU Women's Sport ... Report," ISHOF, n.pg.

16. Leach, "To Set the Record Straight," Unpublished, ISHOF, n.pg.

17. J. Henning, "A Brief History," ISHOF, n.pg.

18. "1940 Central AAU Women's," Entry, ISHOF, n.pg.

19. "Swimming News. First," *Discus*, May 1940, p. 19.

20. "1940 Central AAU Women's," Entry, ISHOF, n.pg.

21. "Synchronizers Cop Title," *Synchro-Info*, February 1972, p.9.

22. Curtis, *Rhythmic Swimming*, p. 2.

23. "Synchro Swimmers Beat Wright," *Chicago Tempo*, c.1940.

24. Leach, "To Set the Record Straight," Unpublished, ISHOF, n.pg.

25. J. Henning, "How It Began," *International Swim & Water Polo*, p. 36+.

26. "Clark Leach, Father of," ISHOF, n.pg.

27. Paterson, "Memorabilia," *Synchro*, October 1985, p. 13.

28. *AAU Official Swimming Handbook*, 1941-42.

29. Harvey, "Rippling Rhythm," ISHOF, n.pg.

30. Paterson.

31. *AAU Official Swimming Handbook*, 1945-46.

32. Hayes, "Synchronized … at Wright," *Synchronized Swimmer*, March 1952, p. 6.

33. Hayes, Untitled personal records, ISHOF, n.pg.

34. "Wright S.S. … Revived," *Northwest Leader*, July 2, 1997.

35. "Lakeshore Swim Stars Continue," *Discus*, September 1941, p. 8.

36. Hayes, Untitled personal records, ISHOF, n.pg.

37. "CAAU Championships," *Discus*, May 1941, p. 22.

38. "Lakeshore Captures CAAU Duet," *Discus*, June 1941, p. 9.

39. "Lakeshore Girls Capture," *Discus*, August 1941, p. 13.

40. "Lakeshore Swim Stars Continue…" *Discus*. Sept 1941. p. 8.

41. Leach, "Sport Sub-Committee Report," ISHOF, n.pg.

42. *Ibid.*

43. "Lakeshore Shore's Swim Stars," August 10, 1942, ISHOF, n.pg.; "Water Ballet … Aquatennial," *Discus*, August 1943, p. 20.; "Final CAAU Meet … Idylwild," *Discus*, October 1943, p. 22.

44. "Jeanne Wilson … Lakeshore," *Discus*, November 1943, p. 15.

45. "Ballet Champs in H-A Meet," *Chicago Herald American*, August 10, 1945.

46. "Lakeshore Water Ballet Never," *Discus*, February 1942, p. 14.

47. "Capacity Crowd … Swim Meet," *Chicago Herald-American*, August 13, 1945.

48. Kerper, *Splash*, p. 19.

49. Engerrand, telephone interview, October 1997.

50. "Water Ballet Will Go to Neenah," *Discus*, August 1942, p. 13.

51. "Women's National AAU," *Official Program*, ISHOF, n.pg.

52. "1942 National Championships," *Neenah Daily News*, August 12-17, 1942.

53. "Water Ballet Gave … Neenah," *Discus*, September 1942. p. 9.

54. Potter, "Reminiscing," *Synchronized Swimmer*, February 1952. p. 7.

55. "Senior National," *Neenah Daily News*, August 12, 1942.

56. Turner, "Answers … Questions." Unpublished. ISHOF, n.pg.

57. Potter, "Reminiscing." *Synchronized Swimmer*. February 1952. p. 7.

58. "Life … Visits the Lakeshore Club," *Life Magazine*, July 4, 1944.

59. Leach, "Request for Association Activity," Reports, ISHOF, n.pg.

60. Kiphuth, "Connecticut Association," November 11, 1942, ISHOF, n.pg.

61. Sawin, "Indiana Association," November 18, 1942, ISHOF, n.pg.

62. Olsen, "Activity in Iowa," November 1942, ISHOF, n.pg.

63. Meyer, "Activity in New Jersey," November 12, 1942, ISHOF, n.pg.

64. Foster, "Southeastern," November 24, 1942, ISHOF, n.pg.

65. Allen, "Southern Pacific," November 13, 1942, ISHOF, n.pg.

66. Quinn, "S.S. in New Jersey," c. 1954, ISHOF, n.pg.

67. Derosier, "Record … St. Clair," ISHOF, n.pg.

68. Potter, p. 7.

69. J. Henning, "Early SS," Letter, October 28, 1997.

70. J. Henning, "How it Began," *Synchro*, August 1985, p. 19+.

71. Turner, "Early Synchronized Swimming," August 1993, ISHOF, n.pg.

72. "Steed Twins … Rhythm into Crawl," *Chicago Tribune*, February 28, 1938.

73. "Medinah Girls Sparkle," *Chicago Tribune*. January 22, 1939.

74. Paterson, "Memorabilia," *Synchro*, October 1985, p. 13.

75. Paterson, "Early Development … Chicago," Letter, December 13, 1996.

76. "Palm Beach Nights Aquacade," *Discus*, March 1941, p. 13.

77. "Lakeshore Welcomes," *Discus*, April 1940, p. 13.

78. Heath, telephone interview, January 1997.

79. Rosenthal, "Honored," *San Francisco Call-Bulletin*, May 8, 1942.

80. Eaton, "Synchro … DC," Letter, May 1997.

81. "Baltimore Aqualites," *Synchro-Info*, August 1975, p. 23.

82. H. Gundling, "Letters," *Synchro-Info*, August 1972, p. 2.

83. "Canada Adopts Term S.S. 1949," ISHOF, n.pg.

84. Kerper, p. 17.

85. Paterson, "Memorabilia," p. 13.

86. Zink, "SS in Minnesota," Letter, February 21, 1997.

87. Sowers, "Development … in N.Y.," Letter, October 1997.

88. Moore, "Development … in Oregon," Letter, March 1997.

89. Huntley, "Development … So, California." Letter, July 1997.

90. Close, "Dolphins, Bangor," *Synchronized Swimmer*, August 1953, p. 2.

## *Chapter 3*

1. Schleuter, "Mermaids and Music," c. 1946, ISHOF, n.pg.

2. *Ibid.*

3. Derosier, "Report … Forum," c. 1948, ISHOF, n.pg.

4. D. Bean, personal collection.

5. "Record Crowd … H-A Meet," *Chicago Herald American*, August 13, 1946, ISHOF, n.pg.

6. "First National Championships," *Chicago Herald American*, c. August 1946, ISHOF, n.pg.

7. "Town Club Wins Water Ballet," ISHOF, n.pg.

8. Engerrand, telephone interview, October 1997.

9. Rauworth, telephone interview, November 8, 1997.

10. Feinstein, Lena, telephone interview, November 1997.

11. "CAAU Championships, Shawnee," *Discus*, May 1941, p. 66.

12. "Capacity ... Meet," *Chicago Herald-American*, August 13, 1945, ISHOF, n.pg.

13. Rauworth.

14. Schleuter.

15. Derosier.

16. "First National Championships."

17. "Personalities, Ruth Geduldig," *Synchronized Swimmer*, October 1952, p. 9.

18. "Stanley and Micus Win," news clipping, ISHOF, n.pg.

19. Cathy Goodwin, telephone interview, April 1997.

20. Theresa Anderson, personal recollections.

21. Huntley, "Development ... Southern California," Letter, July 1997.

22. J. Henning, "How it Began," *Intnl. Swim & Water Polo*, p. 36+.

23. Dodson. "About the A.A.U.," *Synchronized Swimmer*, November 1952. p. 2+.

24. AAU Official S.S. Handbook, 1956 p. 57.

25. Yates & Andersen, *Synchronized Swimming*.

26. AAU Official S.S. Handbook, 1957. p. 60.

27. "Record Crowd ... H-A Meet," *Chicago Herald American*. August 13, 1946, ISHOF.

28. J. Henning, "Early Synchronized Swimming," Letter, October 28, 1997.

29. Aspinal, "Thoughts ... Mixed SS," news clipping, October 13, 1948, ISHOF, n.pg.

30. Derosier, "Record ... St. Clair," unpublished, c. 1953, ISHOF.

31. Derosier, "Rule Changes for 1950," unpublished, ISHOF, n.pg.

32. Olsen, "SS Goes West," *Beach and Pool*, March 1952, p. 15.

33. *AAU Official Swimming Handbook*. 1945-46, p. 40+.

34. *AAU Official Swimming Handbook*. 1947-48, p. 42.

35. *AAU Official Swimming Handbook*. 1949-50, p. 157.

36. *AAU Official Swimming Handbook*. 1951-52, p. 156.

37. *Ibid*.

38. Derosier, "Report ... Forum," news clipping, ISHOF, n.pg.

39. *AAU Official Swimming Handbook*, 1951-52, p. 156.

40. McFadden, "Synchro's Come," *Synchro Swimming USA*, Fall 1998, p. 12.

41. Harvey, "Rippling Rhythm," news clipping, c. 1946, ISHOF, n.pg.

42. *AAU Official Swimming Handbook*, 1947-48, p. 42.

43. *AAU Official Swimming Handbook*, 1949-50, p. 159.

44. *Ibid*., p. 160.

45. Derosier. -

46. "Canada Adopts Term S.S.," news clipping, ISHOF, n.pg.

47. Derosier.

48. *Ibid*.

49. Seller, "Canadian Tribute ... Derosier," *Synchronized Swimmer*, February 1953, p. 1.

50. "Canada Adopts Term S.S.," news clipping, ISHOF, n.pg.

51. Strubbe, "Origins and Development," *Synchro-News*, June 1958, p. 83+.

52. *Ibid*.

53. "Parade of Champions," *Philippines Herald*, July 26, 1949.

54. Dunbar, "Suspended ... Return," *Oakland Tribune*, August 16, 1949.

55. Schleuter.

56. Derosier.

57. Ostos, "The Past, Present," *International Swim & Water Polo*, Summer 1984. p. 42+.

58. Derosier.

59. Derosier, "History ... in Detroit," unpublished, c. 1946, ISHOF, n.pg.

60. "Exhibitions ... 1951 Pan Am Games," news clipping, ISHOF, n.pg.

61. FINA Rules, "Artistic Swimming," *Synchronized Swimmer*, July 1953, p. 5+.

62. Olsen, "Competition to Music," *Amateur Athlete*, July 1951, p. 19.

63. Huntley, "Development ... Southern California," letter, July 1997.

64. Wing, "Syn ... in New England," letter, October 1997.

65. Quinn, "SS ... New Jersey," news clipping, c. 1954, ISHOF, n.pg.

66. Harvey.

67. Derosier, "Record ... St. Clair," unpublished, c. 1953, ISHOF.

68. Fleming, "SS ... Temple University," *Synchronized Swimmer*, May 1952, p. 3+.

69. "Pennsylvania Member," news clipping, June 15, 1950, ISHOF, n.pg.

70. Chase, "Development ... Texas," letter, August 1997.

71. "Joy Cushman," *Shell Employee News*, news clipping, ISHOF, n.pg.

72. Gregerson, "Regional Development," *Synchro-Info*, February 1972, p. 32+.

73. Calcaterra, "Development ... Ozark," letter, May 1997.

74. Murphy, "Development ... Inland Empire," letter, May 1997.

75. Hinrichs, "Development ... Colorado," letter, March 28, 1997.

## *Chapter 4*

1. Lineer, "SS and ... Olympics," *Beach & Pool*, April 1954.

2. Lineer, "SS ... Add to Olympics," *San Francisco Chronicle*, March 6, 1954.

3. Kahn, "It Says Here," *Daytona Beach Evening News*, August 14, 1953.

4. "The Pool Players," *Sports Illustrated*, June 6, 1955.

5. White, "Following the Ball," *Santa Monica Outlook*, August 18, 1954.

6. Kauffman, "Spectacle, Water Ballet," *Sports Illustrated*, June 6, 1955.

7. Griggs, "Swimming Plus," *Sports Illustrated*, June 6, 1955.

8. Noble, "Prettiest Things Afloat," *Saturday Evening Post*, July 2, 1955.

9. Wilson, "Muscles Aren't Everything," *Parade*, July 17, 1955.

10. Noble.

11. Lineer, "Olympic Funds ... Athens," *San Francisco Chronicle*, December 6, 1954.

12. Ward, "On Second Thought," *Oakland Tribune*, April 23, 1953.

13. "Champions Through the Year," *Synchro-Info*, February 1972, p. 14+.

14. Olsen, "From Aquabelles to Aquachamps," *Amateur Athlete*, November 1952, p. 19+.

15. Elliott, "Frank Elliott Writes," *Synchronized Swimmer*, October 1954, p. 7.

16. R. Bean, "Reply to Mr. Elliott," *Synchronized Swimmer*, January 1955, p. 5+.

17. "The Pool Players."

18. Hubbard, "Mixed S.S. Needs You Now," *Synchronized Swimmer*, November 1953, p. 7.

19. "Exhibitions ... Olympic Games," news clip, ISHOF, n.pg.

20. *AAU Official Synchronized Swimming Handbook*, 1954.

21. Bennett, Coleen and Gordon, *Handbook of Synchronized Swimming*.

22. Helen Cardan, *Synchronized Swimming Stunts*.

23. Ward, "Local Girls ... Movie Short," *Oakland Tribune*, February 13, 1954.

24. Olsen, "SS Goes West," *Beach and Pool*, March 1, 1952, p. 15.

25. Jones, "Synchro ... Michigan," letter, March 23, 1997.

26. *AAU Official Synchronized Swimming Handbook*, 1957.

27. Anderson, "University of Illinois ... Intercollegiate," *Synchronized Swimmer*, March 1952, p. 3+.

28. "Midwest Intercollegiate," *Synchronized Swimmer*, May 1953, p. 7.

29. NSGWS National Section, *Official Aquatics Guide*, 1953-55, p. 66+.

30. "3rd Intercollegiate Conference and..." *Synchronized Swimmer*. January 1954. p. 11+.

31. "Proceedings SS Symposium...," *Synchronized Swimmer*, February 1955, p. 5+.

32. Moran, "Intercollegiate SS Meet, *Synchronized Swimmer*, February 1955, p. 5+.

33. Lloyd, "Swimmers Show Skill," news clip, November 12, 1955, ISHOF, n.pg.

34. "Penguinettes ... in National Conference," *Penn News*, November 16, 1956, ISHOF.n.pg.

35. Beshunsky, news clip, unpublished, ISHOF, n.pg.

36. Hubbard, "Bert Hubbard Writes," *Synchronized Swimmer*, April 1953, p. 21.

37. R. Bean, "On SS Rule Changes," *Synchronized Swimmer*, October 1953, p. 1+.

38. Dodson, "We are ... Bitterly Divided," *Synchronized Swimmer*, August 1954, p. 1+.

39. R. Bean, "The Question, Right," *Synchronized Swimmer*, October 1954, p. 15.

40. H. Gundling, "SS Rules," *Synchronized Swimmer*, November 1953, p. 3.

41. R. Bean, "The Question, Right," *Synchronized Swimmer*, October 1954, p. 15.

42. Elliott, "Frank Elliott Writes," *Synchronized Swimmer*, October 1954, p. 7.

43. International Academy of Aquatic Art, *www.Aquatic-Art.org*.

44. "FINA Rules, Proposals ... (Ornamental) Swimming," *Synchronized Swimmer*, June 1952, p. 8.

45. Seller, "Peg Seller Says," *Synchronized Swimmer*, September 1953, p. 13+.

46. Derosier, "SS in Helsinki," *Synchronized Swimmer*, August 1952, p. 1+.

47. B. Gundling, "SS ... Olympics," *Synchronized Swimmer*, October 1952, p. 2.

48. Cushman, letter, September 29, 2003.

49. "FINA Rules, Artistic Swimming," *Synchronized Swimmer*, July 1953, p. 8+.

50. *FINA Federacion Internationale de Natation Amateur Handbook*, 1953–56, p. 99.

51. T. Anderson, "Show or Sport?" *Synchro-Info*, April 1970, p. 5.

52. Hale, personal interviews.

53. Griggs, p. 19.

54. "U.S. Wins Pan-American S.S.," *AAU Synchronized Swimming Handbook*, 1956, p. 39.

55. Noonan, "Our First SS ... in Sao Paulo," *Synchronized Swimmer*, February 1952, p. 6+.

56. Clark, *S.S. 60 Years to Celebrate*, 1985, p. 6.

57. Seller, "Canadian Tribute ... Derosier," *Synchronized Swimmer*, February 1953, p. 1.

58. Olsen, "Highlights ... Japan, Korea," *Synchronized Swimmer*, August 1954, p. 11+.

59. Strubbe, "Origin and," *Synchro-News*, June 1958, p. 83+.

60. "Beulah Gundling ... Paris," *Daytona Beach Morning Journal*, August 1953.

61. B. Gundling, "International Progress in SS," *Synchronized Swimmer*, May 1954, p. 5.

62. Seller, "SS in England," *Synchronized Swimmer*, October 1953, p. 10.

63. Zajac, ""History of SS in England," *Synchro-Info*, June 1969, p. 18+.

64. "International Activity," news clip, ISHOF, n.pg.

65. Rackham, *Synchronized Swimming*.

66. Olsen, "Swim Tour ... Cinemascope Short," *Synchronized Swimmer*, November 1953, p. 13+.

67. Noble.

68. Olsen, "Report from Egypt," *Amateur Athlete*, December 1956, p. 24.

69. D. Bean, personal collection.

70. "A Brilliant ... SS," [Bombay], *Times of India*, May 15, 1954, ISHOF, n.pg.

71. Strubbe.

72. H. Smith, "The Windham ... Dolphin," *Synchronized Swimmer*, April 1952, p. 5.

73. Oppenheim, "Synchro ... Adirondack Association," letter, January 1997.

74. Olsen, "Joanne Royer Wins," *Amateur Athlete*, August 1953.

75. "West Coast ... Mission Beach," news clip, ISHOF, n.pg.

76. Withers, "Wesleyan College," *Synchronized Swimmer*, November 1952, p. 4.

77. "Water Sprites," news clip, ISHOF, n.pg.

78. Maeys, "Clinic ... Gundling," *Synchronized Swimmer*, February 1953, p. 5.

79. Eytchison, "Synchro ... Potomac Valley," letter, March 5, 1997.

80. Hogan, "Baltimore Aqualites," letter, April 1997.

81. Kennemer, "To Put Montana," *Synchronized Swimmer*, October 1952, p. 4.

82. Hass, "The Ducks Club ... Oklahoma," *Synchronized Swimmer*, December 1952, p. 3+.

83. Quinn, "SS in New Jersey," news clip, ISHOF, n.pg.

84. "Lansing ... Has New Club," *Synchronized Swimmer*, August 1952, p. 9.

85. Jones, "Synchro ... Michigan," letter, January 1997.

86. Eakin, "Synchro ... Berea, Ohio," letter, April 1997.

87. Kretschmer, "Synchro ... Ohio," letter, May 1997.

88. Moore, "Development ... Oregon," letter, March 1997.

89. Forbes, "Synchro ... San Antonio," letter, April 1997.

## *Chapter 5*

1. Georgian, "Success Story ... Oakland," *KGO News Release*, July 1957.

2. King, "East Bay Story," *Berkeley Daily Gazette*, July 3, 1957.

3. "Olsen Gets Olympic Dream," news clip, ISHOF, n.pg.

4. Elston, "History ... Merionettes," telephone interview, May 1997.

5. "Rule Changes Through the Years," *Synchro-Info*, February 1970, p. 10+.

6. "She Grew Up Swimming," *Synchro-Info*, February 1972, p. 31.

7. "Pan American Games Trials," *Synchro-Info*, February 1963, p. 8.

8. Ostos, "The Past, Present," *International Swimming & Water Polo*, Summer 1984, p. 42+.

9. Strubbe, "The Origin," *Synchro-News*, June 1958, p. 83+.

10. "First Competition in Europe," news clip, 1958, ISHOF, n.pg.

11. Krajicek, "Synchro ... Czechoslovakia," *Synchro-Info*, July-August 1965, p. 8+.

12. Rackham, *Synchronized Swimming*, 1968.

13. Kane, "International News," *Synchro-Info*, April 1972, p. 17+.

14. "Olsen Gets Olympic Dream," news clip, ISHOF, n.pg.

15. Olsen, "SS Meet at Oakland," *Amateur Athlete*, September 1957.

16. Donnelly, "AAU Sponsored Tour, Off," *Synchro-News*, June 1958, p. 80+.

17. Van den Broeck, "AAU Sponsored Tour," *Synchro-News*, January-February 1959, p. 24+.

18. Donnelly, "USSS Team Tours Europe," *Amateur Athlete*, July 1958. p. 34.

19. Donnelly, "AAU Sponsored Tour, Off," *Synchro-News*, June 1958. p. 80+.

20. Donnelly, "USSS Team Tours Europe," *Amateur Athlete*, July 1958. p. 34.

21. Dineen, "AAU Sponsored Tour," *Synchro-News*, August 1958, p. 122.

22. Dineen, "AAU Sponsored Tour," *Synchro-News*, September-October 1958, p. 140+.

23. "Poolside ... Tour to Brazil," *Synchro-News*, September-October 1958, p. 133.

24. Olsen, "Rome in 1960," *Synchro-News*, November-December 1958, p. 168+.

25. "Olympic Tour Plans Nearing," *Synchro-News*, January 1960, p. 18.

26. "Additional Exhibitions ... Aquacade," *Synchro-News*, March-April 1960, p. 29.

27. *AAU Official Synchronized Swimming Handbook*, 1961, p. 80.

28. *AAU Official Synchronized Swimming Handbook*, 1962, p. 243.

29. "Poolside ... Olsen FINA Secretary." *Synchro-News*, January 1958, p. 3.

30. "Poolside ... Nationals Televised Live," *Synchro-News*, July 1958, p. 99.

31. "Poolside ... Convention Numbers Grow," *Synchro-News*, November-December 1958, p. 157.

32. "AAU News," *Synchro-News*, June 1958, p. 90+.

33. R.J. Dodson, ed., *The Synchronized Swimmer*, 1951–1955.

34. R.J. Dodson, ed., *The Aquatic Artist*, 1955–1996.

35. Wilbur Luick, publisher, *Synchro-News*, 1958–1960.

36. Cushman, "Chairman's Report, *Synchro-News*, January-February 1960. p. 26.

37. Goss, *Stunts and Synchronized Swimming*, 1957.

38. Yates & Anderson, *Synchronized Swimming*, 1958.

39. Spears, *Beginning Synchronized Swimming*.

40. *AAU Official Synchronized Swimming Handbook*, 1959.

41. Provisor, "The Housewife ... Movie," *Synchro-News*, June 1958, p. 77.

42. Olsen, "SS Meet at Oakland," *Amateur Athlete*, September 1957.

43. "Who's News. Florence Anderson," *Synchro-News*, September-October 1958, p. 137.

44. *AAU Official Synchronized Swimming Handbook*, 1958.

45. *AAU Official Synchronized Swimming Handbook*, 1959.

46. Eakin, "Synchro ... Berea, Ohio," letter, April 1997.

47. "AAU News," *Synchro-News*, September-October 1958, p. 147+.

48. "Poolside ... Host Nationals," *Synchro-News*, March-April 1958, p. 37.

49. "Poolside ... 1st National 12 & under," *Synchro-News*, July 1958, p. 99.

50. "AAU News," *Synchro-News*, May 1958, p. 67+.

51. "AAU News," *Synchro-News*, September-October 1958, p. 147+.

52. "AAU News … Bristol in Yale Carnival," *Synchro-News*, February 1958, p. 12+.

53. "AAU News," *Synchro-News*, May 1958, p. 67+.

54. "AAU News," *Synchro-News*, March-April 1958, p. 47+.

55. "YMCA/ … /CYO News," *Synchro-News*. January-February 1959, p. 10+.

56. "AAU News," *Synchro-News*, May 1958, p. 67+.

57. "AAU News," *Synchro-News*, August 1958, p. 129.

58. Harrell, "Synchro … New Mexico," letter, February 1997.

59. "Championship Team," *Riverside Daily Press*, July 7, 1958.

60. "AAU News," *Synchro-News*, November-December 1958, p. 175+.

61. "Three SS Champions," *Seattle Today*, August 24, 1974.

62. H. Smith, "Synchro … Washington," letter, March 1997.

63. Hester, "Synchro … Nebraska," letter, April 1997.

64. Zamonski, "Water Sports," *Rocky Mountain Sportsman*, September 1959.

65. "Madge Noble Heads … Show," news clip, ISHOF, n.pg.

66. "AAU News," *Synchro-News*, November-December 1958, p. 175+.

67. Forbes [Swan], letter, March 1997.

68. "The Helms Story," *Amateur Athlete*, August 1961; reprint *Synchro-Info*, June 1963, p. 13+.

69. Olsen, "The Helms Hall of Fame," Synchro-News, January 1958, p. 5.

70. "Synchers … Kay Curtis Writes," *Synchro-News*, August 1958, p. 129.

## *Chapter 6*

1. "Miss AAU Synchronized Swimming," *Synchro-Info*, January-February 1964, p. 3.

2. "What's News: A Refreshing," *Synchro-Info*, September-October 1964, p. 6.

3. "Pan American Trials," *Synchro-Info*, February 1963, p. 8.

4. "1963 Indoor … Championships," *Synchro-Info*, May-June 1963, p. 5+.

5. "Merionettes … Shutout," *Amateur Athlete*, May 1965, *Synchro-Info*, May-June 1965, p. 10+.

6. D. Bean, "Impressions of Nationals," *Synchro-Info*, March-April 1967, p. 30+.

7. Treadway, "Final Results: 1968 … Championships," *Synchro-Info*, March-April 1968, p. 4+.

8. "Athlete's Corner," *Synchro-Info*, July-August 1968, p. 21.

9. D. Bean, "Impressions of Nationals," *Synchro-Info*, March-April 1966, p. 6+.

10. D. Bean, "Impressions of Nationals," *Synchro-Info*, March-April 1967, p. 30+.

11. Cushman, "News: ABC Satisfied," *Synchro-Info*, May-June 1963, p. 3.

12. Howell, "One Fabulous Trip," *Synchro-Info*, July-August 1967, p. 20+.

13. Hainsworth, "Letters … Mailbox," *Synchro-Info*, October 1969, p. 4.

14. T. Anderson, "News … Chairman," *Synchro-Info*, May-June 1965, p. 5.

15. Kane, "Association News," *Synchro-Info*, May-June 1966, p. 16.

16. T. Anderson, "Golden Gate … Solo," *Synchro-Info*, November-December 1967, p. 16+.

17. Cushman, "Report … Criterium D' Europe," *Synchro-Info*, May-June 1967, p. 16+.

18. H. Henning, "75 Years … FINA, Part II," *International Swim & Water Polo*, Summer 1983, p. 2+.

19. Rackham, *Synchronized Swimming*.

20. Kitamura, "International News: Japan Growth," *Synchro-Info*, July-August 1967, p. 23.

21. "Poolside … Joy Cushman," *Synchro-News*, July 1958, p. 99.

22. Bauch, "Letters … Mailbox," *Synchro-Info*, January-February 1969, p. 5.

23. Ahlf, "Letters … Mailbox," *Synchro-Info*, September-October 1968, p. 4.

24. "What's News … Sound Equipment," *Synchro-Info*, May-June 1964, p. 11.

25. "AAU News: Advantage … Tapes," *Synchro-News*, June 1958, p. 90+.

26. Swartz, "Letters … Mailbox," *Synchro-Info*, July-August 1965, p. 2+.

27. "Notes … National SS Clinic," *Synchro-Info*, November-December 1965, p. 12+.

28. B. Gundling, *Exploring Aquatic Art*.

29. R. Bean, "Book … Exploring Aquatic Art," *Synchro-Info*, October 1963, p. 8+.

30. Donnelly, *SS Instruction Book*.

31. Vickers, *Teaching Synchronized Swimming*.

32. Spears, *Fundamentals of Synchronized Swimming*.

33. Rackham, *Synchronized Swimming*.

34. Marion Kane, *Judges Training Manual*.

35. Marion Kane, *Meet Manager's Guide*.

36. Donald T. Kane, *Press Relations Guide*. 1966.

37. Donald T. Kane, *Guide to the Administration of S.S.*

38. D. Bean, *Synchro-Info*, 1963–78; *Synchro*, 1979–92.

39. Calcaterra, "Booming Age Group," *Synchro-Info*, May-June 1964, p. 10.

40. Hogan, *USSS … Collegiate … Manual.*

41. D. Bean, "My Impressions," *Synchro-Info*, March-April 1964. p. 6+.

42. D. Bean, "Freight Train Figures," *Synchro-Info*, July-August 1967. p. 3.

43. G. Ahlf, "A Proposal … Judges," *Synchro-Info*, September-October 1968, p. 21.

44. Sellers, "Code … for Judging SS," *Synchro-Info*, September-October 1966, p. 6+.

45. D. Bean, "Improvements in Judging SS," *Synchro-Info*, July-August 1965, p. 4+.

46. McGowan, "Letters … Mailbox," *Synchro-Info*, November-December 1965, p. 2+.

47. Kane, "Canadian … Championships," *Synchro-Info*, March-April 1967, p. 18.

48. "The Lawrence Johnson Trophy," *Synchro-Info*, November-December 1968, p. 2.

49. "Pam Morris ... Swimming Hall of Fame," *Synchro-Info*, November-December 1965, p. 16.

50. Coffin, "Who's News: Peg Seller," *Synchro-Info*, July-August 1966, p. 8.

## *Chapter 7*

1. "Swimmer's View of Nationals," *Synchro-Info*, June 1975, p. 11.

2. "1973 National Convention Report," *Synchro-Info*, December 1973, p. 6+.

3. Ireland, "People ... Fast Paced Retirement; Kane," *Press-Democrat, Synchro-Info*, February 1975, p. 26.

4. Ammirati, "Letters to the Mailbox," *Synchro-Info*, October 1975, p. 2.

5. Forbes, "Synchro Development in San Antonio," letter, March-April 1997.

6. Courtney, "Comment," *Synchro-Info*, June 1971, p. 10.

7. Matthews, "Best of Synchronized Swimming," *Toledo Blade*, September 14, 1969.

8. "News and Notes, Synchro in Magazines," *Synchro-Info*, October 1975, p. 5.

9. Theresa Anderson, "Show or Sport?" *Synchro-Info*, April 1970, p. 5.

10. Hollyburn Synchronettes, "International News," *Synchro-Info*, October 1969, p. 10.

11. "The Editor's Notes, Local Meet Guest," *Synchro-Info*, January-February 1969, p. 6.

12. "1973 National Convention Report," *Synchro-Info*, December 1973, p. 6+.

13. D. Smith, "Letters to the Mailbox," *Synchro-Info*, February 1975, p. 4.

14. "News and Notes: Newsweek Videos," *Synchro-Info*, December 1975, p. 7.

15. D. Smith, "Santa Clara Sweeps ... Honors," *The Journal*, April 9, 1972, p. 9.

16. "1972 Indoor National Championships," *Synchro-Info*, April 1972, p. 5+.

17. Elston, "History of San Francisco Merionettes," telephone interview, May 1997.

18. "1969 Outdoor National Championships," *Synchro-Info*, August 1969, p. 6+.

19. "The 1973 Indoor National Championships." *Synchro-Info*, June 1973, p. 6+.

20. "National Review," *Synchro-Info*, October 1973, p. 22+.

21. "The WAC's 'Merry Mermaids,'" *San Antonio Light*, May 19, 1973; *Synchro-Info*, August 1974, p. 27.

22. Swan Forbes, "WACS, Cygnets Tour Germany," *Synchro-Info*, February 1974, p. 20.

23. "The 1970 Indoor National Championships," *Synchro-Info*, April 1970, p. 8+.

24. "International News: Pan Am Games in Cali.," *Synchro-Info*, August 1969, p. 26.

25. "1971 Pan American Games Trials," *Synchro-Info*, June 1970, p. 6+.

26. "VI Juegos Panamericanos, the Competition," *Synchro-Info*, October 1971, p. 8.

27. "The VII Pan American Games," *Synchro-Info*, December 1975, p. 8.

28. H. Henning, "Seventy Five Years of FINA, Part II," *International Swimming & Water Polo*, Summer 1983, p. 2+.

29. Cushman, "The First World Aquatic Games," *Synchro-Info*, October 1973, p. 6+.

30. Goff, "Synchro at the World Games," *Swimming World*, September 1975; *Synchro-Info*, October 1975, p. 8+.

31. *Ibid.*

32. "International News: First International Conference," *Synchro-Info*, October 1974, p. 28.

33. "The First National Judges Seminar," *Synchro-Info*, April 1969, p. 5.

34. "National Coaches Seminar," *Synchro-Info*, August 1970, p. 11+.

35. "News & Notes: First National Coaches' Camp," *Synchro-Info*, August 1974, p. 5.

36. "Joy Cushman Accepts Interim Chairmanship," *Synchro-Info*, June 1970, p. 6.

37. "1970 National Convention Report." *Synchro-Info*, December 1970. p. 8+.

38. "Joy Cushman Appointed to USOC Board of Directors," *Synchro-Info*, October 1969, p. 13.

39. "1972 National Convention Report," *Synchro-Info*, December 1972, p. 5+.

40. *AAU Official Aquatics Handbooks*, New York, Indianapolis, 1954–1979.

41. "1972 National Convention Report," *Synchro-Info*, December 1972, p. 5+.

42. "Synchro All-Stars of 1969," *Synchro-Info*, February 1970, p. 17+.

43 "1970 National Convention Report," *Synchro-Info*, December 1970, p. 8+.

44. *AAU Official Synchronized Swimming Handbook*, 1974.

45. "News and Notes, Computer Scoring," *Synchro-Info*, June 1972, p. 5.

46. Hasbrouck, *Synchronized Swimming Self Taught*.

47. Jones and Lindeman. *Components of Synchronized Swimming*.

48. "Preview ... Jole Loop Films," *Synchro-Info*, June 1971, p. 10.

49. DeSha, "Letters to the Mailbox," *Synchro-Info*, August 1970, p. 3.

50. Canadian Amateur SS Association, *Synchronized Canada*, 1971–1985.

51. Japan Synchronized Swimming Academy, *Synchronized Japan*, 1975–1990.

52. *AAU Official Synchronized Swimming Handbook*, 1972, pg. 8.

53. "News and Notes, Junior Olympic News," *Synchro-Info*, February 1974, p. 4.

54. Ruggieri, "Intercollegiate SS, 'Do or Die,'" *Synchro-Info*, April 1974, p. 15.

55. Ruggieri, "Intercollegiate Synchro," *Synchro-Info*, February 1975, p. 9.

56. Ruggieri, "Intercollegiate Synchro: Proposed Rules," *Synchro-Info*, June 1975, p. 20.

57. Ruggieri, "Report of the Intercollegiate Fall Meetings," *Synchro-Info*, December 1975, p. 12.

58. Wing, "Letters to the Mailbox," *Synchro-Info*, April 1975, p. 2.

59. MacKellar, "National Committee Reports," *Synchro-Info*, August 1975, p. 6.

60. Murphy, "Letters to the Mailbox," *Synchro-Info*, December 1975, p. 5.

61. "1969 Outdoor National Championships," *Synchro-Info*, August 1969, p. 6+.

62. "1970 Outdoor National Championships." *Synchro-Info*, August 1970. p. 5.

63. "1970 National Convention Report," *Synchro-Info*, December 1970, p. 8+.

64. "1973 Junior National Outdoor Solo Championships," *Synchro-Info*, October 1973, p. 33.

65. "1974 Junior National Championships," *Synchro-Info*, June 1974, p. 22.

66. "1974 National Convention Report," *Synchro-Info*, December 1974, p. 6+.

67. "1969 National Convention Report," *Synchro-Info*, December 1969, p. 5+.

68. Bauch, "Letters to the Mailbox," *Synchro-Info*, January-February 1969. p. 5.

69. Douglass. "The Athlete's Page," *Synchro-Info*, April 1973, p. 26.

70. "1973 Indoor National Championships," *Synchro-Info*, June 1973, p. 6+.

71. "1971 National Convention," *Synchro-Info*, October 1971, p. 4.

72. "Officials Training Committee ... Report," *Synchro-Info*, February 1974, p. 8+.

73. Paulus, *Report ... Major-Minor Sub-Committee on Degrees of Difficulty.*

74. "1972 Outdoor National Championships," *Synchro-Info*, August 1972, p. 5+.

75. D. Bean and R. Bean, "From the Hot Seat," *Synchro-Info*, July-August 1968, p. 17+.

76. "1968 National Convention," *Synchro-Info*, November-December 1968. p. 6+.

77. Gene Ahlf, "Annual Report, Evaluation Study," *Synchro-Info*, December 1971, p. 22.

78. Menish, "Letters to the Mailbox," *Synchro-Info*, February 1974, p. 2.

79. McGinnis, "Letters to the Mailbox," *Synchro-Info*, April 1976, p. 4+.

80. Heeger, "Hall of Fame Museum," *Synchro-Info*, December 1972, p. 10+.

81. "1971 National Convention," *Synchro-Info*, October 1971, p. 4.

82. "Gail Johnson Wins Top Award," *Synchro*, December 1974, p. 5.

83. "News from the National (1968) Convention," *Synchro-Info*, November-December 1968, p. 6+.

# *Chapter 8*

1. "U.S.O.C. Sports Festival," *Olympian*, reprinted in *Synchro-Info*, November 1978, p. 14+.

2. "Report ... 1977 Convention," *Synchro-Info*, December 1977, p. 12+.

3. R. Bean, "Festival Insights," *Synchro-Info*, November 1978, p. 13.

4. "1978 National Convention," *Synchro-Info*, December 1978, p. 10+.

5. "Pan Am ... Trials," *Synchro*, June 1979, p. 6+.

6. Makowsky, "Competitive Image," *Synchro-Info*, April 1976, p. 3.

7. "Olympic Games, Past and Coming," *Los Angeles Times Home Magazine*, July 25, 1982.

8. Motoyoshi, "Water Fairies," *International Swim & Water Polo*, Winter 1982, p. 22+.

9. "Synchro ... Making the News," *Synchro*, August 1982, p. 8.

10. Georges, "A Male's ... View," *Swimming World*, February 1979; *Synchro*, June 1980, p. 34.

11. Ostos, "The Past, Present and Future," *International Swim & Water Polo*, Summer 1984, p. 42+.

12. D. Bean, "Hope for the Olympics," *Synchro-Info*, December 1977, p. 27.

13. H. Henning, "Seventy Five ... FINA," *International Swim & Water Polo*, Summer 1983, p. 2+.

14. "News & Notes: IOC Approves Duet ... '84," *Synchro*, June 1980, p. 7.

15. Kane, "The World Aquatic Games," *Synchro-Info*, November 1978, p. 8+.

16. "Thoughts ... World Aquatic Games," *Synchro-Info*, November 1978, p. 11.

17. "IV World ... Championships," *Synchro*, August 1982, p. 9+.

18. "You Said It!" *Synchro*, February 1983, p. 29.

19. Georges, "Swimming World Views," *Swimming World*, October 1982; *Synchro*, December 1982, p. 8+.

20. "Thoughts ... World Aquatic Games," *Synchro-Info*, November 1978, p. 11.

21. R. Bean, "Swimming ... Nielsens," *Synchro*, August 1982, p. 5.

22. "The VIII Pan Am ... Games," *Synchro*, August 1979, p. 8+.

23. Kane, "U.S. Triumphs in Moscow," *Synchro*, April 1982, p. 8+.

24. "First American Cup," *Synchro*, August 1980, p. 9+.

25. Kane, "International News," *Synchro-Info*, December 1976, p. 24.

26. "Pan Pacific Championships," *Synchro-Info*, October 1977, p. 15+.

27. "Pan Pacific Games," *Synchro*, December 1979, p. 19.

28. D. Bean, "Editor's Notes: Show or Sport?" *Synchro*, June 1982, p. 3.

29. "First FINA World Cup," *Synchro*, December 1979, p. 18.

30. D. Smith, "Central Am ... Caribbean," *Synchro-Info*, August 1977, p. 17.

31. Helmick, "Letters ... Mailbox," *Synchro-Info*, April 1977, p. 8.

32. Cushman, "The First ... ASUA Age," *Synchro*, June 1982, p. 13.

33. "1976 Indoor National," *Synchro-Info*, June 1976, p. 16+.

34. "1979 Indoor National Championships," *Synchro*, April 1979, p. 6+.

35. "1980 National Championships," *Synchro*, August 1980, p. 14+.

36. "1980 National Convention," *Synchro*, October 1980, p. 6+.

37. "Ohio State Wins ... Competition," *Synchro-Info*, June 1977, p. 23.

38. "1977 National Convention," *Synchro-Info*, December 1977, p. 12+.

39. "1976 National Convention," *Synchro-Info*, December 1976, p. 8+.

40. "Editor's Notes: Donations," *Synchro*, June 1980, p. 3.

41. "1981 National Convention," *Synchro*, October 1981, p. 9.

42. "U.S.O.C. Report," *Synchro-Info*, June 1977, p. 9.

43. "News & Notes: USOC Training Camp," *Synchro*, December 1977, p. 9.

44. "USOC ... Camp Successful," *Synchro-Info*, February 1978, p. 10+.

45. Tope, "Letters ... Mailbox," *Synchro-Info*, February 1979, p. 30.

46. "USOC Camps ... International, Elite," *Synchro-Info*, December 1978, p. 24+.

47. "USOC ... Camp Successful," *Synchro*, February 1979, p. 18+.

48. "1979 Elite Camp," *Synchro*, February 1980, p. 8.

49. "USOC Training Camps Set," *Synchro*, April 1978, p. 5.

50. "The First National Coaches Camp," *Synchro-Info*, August 1974, p. 5.

51. "News & Notes: Coaches Camp," *Synchro*, June 1976, p. 7.

52. Kretschmer, "USOC Coaches Camp," *Synchro*, October 1979, p. 18.

53. Ruggieri and Lundholm, *Introduction to Synchronized Swimming*.

54. Wenz, "Sports Medicine Meets SS."

55. Wightman and Chiefari, *Better SS for Girls*.

56. *The 1982 Yearbook*," US Synchronized Swimming, 1982.

57. Harrison, "Letters ... Mailbox," *Synchro*, August 1981, p. 3.

58. "Report ... 1977 Convention," *Synchro-Info*, December 1977, p. 12+.

59. "First National Age Group," *Synchro*, April 1982, p. 13+.

60. "Report ... 1981 Convention," *Synchro*, October 1981, p. 7+.

61. Ruggieri, "News & Notes: Collegiate," *Synchro-Info*, December 1976, p. 7.

62. D. Bean, "Editor's Notes: Club/Club Tension," *Synchro-Info*, April 1978, p. 3.

63. Lamb, personal contact, April 1976.

64. Gorman, "Letters ... Mailbox," *Synchro-Info*, April 1978, p. 2+.

65. "Report ... 1977 Convention," *Synchro-Info*, December 1977, p. 12+.

66. "News & Notes: 2nd ... Masters," *Synchro-Info*, December 1976, p. 7.

67. "Region 4: Masters ... Championships," *Synchro-Info*, February 1978, p. 31.

68. "1982 Masters National," *Synchro*, December 1982, p. 24+.

69. "Masters ... Golden Age Games," *Synchro*, December 1982, p. 27.

70. "Report: 1979 ... Convention," *Synchro-Info*, December 1979, p. 10+.

71. "1978 ... Convention," *Synchro-Info*, December 1978, p. 10+.

72. "Report: 1979 ... Convention," *Synchro-Info*, December 1979, p. 10+.

73. Jones, "Impressions of Nationals," *Synchro-Info*, October 1977, p. 14.

74. Synchro USA, *Official Rules Synchronized Swimming*, 1980, p. 17.

75. Synchro USA, *Official Rules Synchronized Swimming*, 1978, p. 18.

76. "Convention Honors: USAS Award," *Synchro*, October 1982, p. 4.

## *Chapter 9*

1. Dorst, "Letters ... Mailbox," *Synchro*, April 1984, p. 2.

2. "Synchro Demonstrates for the I.O.C.," *Synchro*, February 1983, p. 7.

3. Koch, "Letters ... Mailbox," *Synchro*, October 1984, p. 5+.

4. Rubin, "Eyes are ... Olympics," *San Francisco Chronicle*, September 22, 1983. Reprinted in *Synchro*. December 1983. p. 14.

5. O'Connor, "Letters ... Mailbox," *Synchro*, October 1984, p. 5.

6. Gritten, "XXIIIrd Olympiad," *Synchro*, October 1984, p. 11+.

7. Goodbody. "Synchronized Swimming and the Olympics," *London Times Sports News*, June 18, 1987; Reprinted in *Synchro*, August 1987, p. 4.

8. D. Bean, "Quick Quotes: Tracie Ruiz," *Synchro*, October 1987, p. 8.

9. "Editor's Notes: No TV ... Pan Ams," *Synchro*, October 1987, p. 3.

10. "1988 Olympic Games," *Synchro*, October 1988, p. 10+.

11. "American Cup II," *Synchro*, August 1983, p. 7+.

12. Hester, "Letters ... Mailbox," *Synchro*, February 1984, p. 2.

13. "Olympic Trials 1984 ... National Championships," *Synchro*, June 1984, p. 12+.

14. "News & Notes: Synchro Sold Out," *Synchro*, August 1983, p. 5.

15. "The Sport, Synchronized Swimming," *The Olympian*, October-November 1984.

16. "1984 Olympic Games," *Synchro*, August 1984, p. 10.

17. Gritten, "XXIIIrd Olympiad."

18. Weyler, "Ruiz ... to Go It Alone," *Los Angeles Times*, August 11, 1984.

19. Gritten, "XXIIIrd Olympiad."

20. Weyler, "Ruiz, Costie are No. 1 ... Figures," *Los Angeles Times*, August 9, 1984.

21. Weyler, "Routine Performance," *Los Angeles Times*, August 7, 1984.

22. Mehren, "Unhappy Duo, 'American Hype' Led to Loss," *Los Angeles Times*, August 10, 1984.

23. Weyler, "Ruiz & Costie Make Winning ... Last Duet," *Los Angeles Times*, August 10, 1984.

24. Weyler, "Sport's Olympic ... Double Golden Opportunity," *Los Angeles Times*, July 28, 1984.

25. "1984 Olympic Games," *Synchro*, August 1984, p. 10.

26. Weyler, "For Ruiz, Boycott Added ... Another Gold," *Los Angeles Times*, August 13, 1984.

27. *Ibid.*

28. Gritten, "XXIIIrd Olympiad."

29. D. Bean, "XXIIIrd Olympiad," *Synchro*, October 1984, p. 11+.

30. Ostos, "The Past, Present," *Synchro*, October 1984, p. 19+.

31. Ostos, "Solo, Duet ... Team?" *International Swim & Water Polo*, Winter 1984, p. 30+.

32. D. Bean, "XXIIIrd Olympiad."

33. "News and Notes: McGowan Heads FINA TSSC," *Synchro*, October 1984, p. 9.

34. L. Bean, "World Aquatic," *Synchro*, October 1986, p. 9+.

35. "1987 FINA World Cup," *Synchro*, December 1987, p. 13+.

36. "Victory in Moscow," *Synchro*, April 1988, p. 10+.

37. "Seoul Pre-Olympic ... Meet," *Synchro*, August 1988, p. 20+.

38. "1988 Olympic Games," *Synchro*, October 1988, p. 10+.

39. "Ready to Dazzle Again," *Sports Illustrated*, August 8, 1988; excerpted in *Synchro*, August 1988, p. 45+.

40. "1988 Olympic Games," *Synchro*, October 1988, p. 10+.

41. The Olympian, "1988 Olympic Games," *Synchro*, October 1988, p. 10+.

42. Saito, "Mikako Kotani, Japan's Rising Star," *Synchro*, December 1987, p. 32.

43. "1988 Olympic Trials/National Championships," *Synchro*, June 1988, p. 10+.

44. "1983 Convention Report," *Synchro*, December 1983, p. 9+.

45. "News & Notes: McDonald's New Sponsor," *Synchro*, October 1983, p. 5.

46. Minich, "Synchro's National Coach, Charlotte Davis," *Synchro*, April 1985, p. 11.

47. Atwater and Roby, "Sports Science & SS," *Synchro*, February 1989, p. 32+.

48. "News & Notes: Watanabe New Exec. Director," *Synchro*, October 1985, p. 5.

49. "News & Notes: McDonald's Drops Sponsorship," *Synchro*, February 1986, p. 7.

50. McGowan, "Convention ... From the Chair," *Synchro*, December 1983, p. 9.

51. "Editor's Notes: Litigation Ended," *Synchro*, October 1986, p. 3.

52. "News ... Board of Directors: End of Lawsuit," *Synchro*, April 1988, p. 9.

53. Forbes (Swan), *Coaching SS Effectively.*

54. Van Buskirk, *Coaching Intermediate SS Effectively.*

55. "*Coaching Intermediate SS Effectively Video*," Human Kinetics.

56. D. Bean and C. Davis. *Three Month Curriculum ... Beginning SS Class.*

57. "1986 National Convention," *Synchro*, October 1986, p. 22.

58. Gemma, "Letters ... Mailbox," *Synchro*, August 1985, p. 2+.

59. Bernard, "Letters ... Mailbox," *Synchro*, December 1988, p. 2.

60. Mitchell, "Letters ... Mailbox," *Synchro*, February 1988, p. 2.

61. FINA *Federation Internationale de Natation Amateur* Handbook.

62. "News & Notes: FINA Eligibility Change," *Synchro*, April 1986, p. 8.

63. "Editor's Notes: Creativity is Back," *Synchro*, June 1987, p. 3.

64. L. Bean, "World Aquatic," *Synchro*, October 1986, p. 9+.

65. In the Spotlight. Tracie Wins Olympia," *Synchro*, December 1983, p. 9.

66. "People. Wing Wins Olympia Award, *Synchro*, August 1983, p. 35.

67. "People. Costie Wins Olympia Award," *Synchro*, June 1985, p. 39.

68. "Cover Story. Sarah Josephson Wins Olympia," *Synchro*, December 1986, p. 3.

69. "News & Notes: McDonald's Wins ... WSF," *Synchro*, December 1985, p. 7.

## *Chapter 10*

1. "First World Coaches Seminar," *Synchro*, June 1992, p. 19.

2. "News & Notes: Time Underwater," *Sports Illustrated*, November 28, 1989; reprint *Synchro*, June 1989, p. 9.

3. "News & Notes: Health, SS Almost...," *Health*, June 1990; reprint *Synchro*, June 1990, p. 7.

4. Lewis, "SS Deserve Some Respect," *San Francisco Chronicle*, July 1991; reprint *Synchro*, October 1991, p. 26.

5. L. Bean, "1991 Olympic Festival," *Synchro*, August 1991, p. 12+.

6. Downey, "Olympian or Not: It's a Festival," *Los Angeles Times*, July 10, 1991.

7. O'Heron, "No Sweat Sport Sport ... Olympian?" *Pasadena Weekly*; *Synchro*, April 1992, p. 17.

8. Hudson, "Fans Still Not Getting," *Los Angeles Times*; reprint *Synchro*, April 1992, p. 16.

9. "Thoughts ... from a Couple of Couch Potatoes," *Synchro*, August 1992, p. 15.

10. Wodka, "Boardroom Comments," *Synchro Swimming USA*, April–June, 1994, p. 4.

11. "USA Wins FINA Cup in Bonn," *Synchro*, October 1991, p. 12+.

12. McGowan, "World Beat," *Synchro Swimming USA*, July–September 1993, p. 5.

13. "IV FINA World Cup," *Synchro*, October 1989, p. 8+.

14. "First Junior World..." *Synchro*. August 1989. p. 10+.

15. "II Junior World Championships." *Synchro*, August 1991, p. 22.

16. "Goodwill Games," *Synchro*, August 1990, p. 10.

17. "Miscellany: Flag Bearers," *Synchro*, April 1991, p. 49.

18. Emery, "Barcelona ... Coaches Eyes," *Synchro*, December 1992, p. 20.

19. "USA ... Two Golds at World," *Synchro*, February 1991, p. 7+.

20. "National News: Josephsons'/Team ... World Champions," *Synchro/USA News*, January 1991.

21. "USA ... Two Golds at World," *Synchro*, February 1991, p. 7+.

22. "News & Notes: In the News," *Sports Illustrated*, February 18, 1991; reprint *Synchro*, April 1991, p. 6.

23. McGowan, "Americans Dominate ... Barcelona," *Synchro*, August 1992, p. 10+.

24. Johnson, "Out of Sync," *Sports Illustrated*, August 17, 1992.

25. McGowan, "Americans Dominate ... Barcelona."

26. LaMarca, "IOC ... Second Gold Medal," *Synchro Swimming USA*, January-March 1994, p. 8.

27. LaMarca, "U.S. Sweeps ... World Cup," *Synchro Swimming USA*, July–September 1993, p. 8.

28. LaMarca, "Team USA ... Nation's Best," *Synchro Swimming USA*, October–December 1993, p. 15.

29. "Dyroen-Lancer/Sudduth Strike Gold ... Russia," *Synchro Swimming USA*, July–September 1994, p. 12.

30. LaMarca, "Team USA ... Grand Slam," *Synchro Swimming USA*, July–September 1994, p. 16+.

31. "1989 U.S. National Championships," *Synchro*, June 1989, p. 14+.

32. LaMarca, "Team USA ... Grand Slam," *Synchro Swimming USA*, July–September 1994, p. 16+.

33. "1989 U.S. National Championships," *Synchro*.

34. "News & Notes: Josephsons Return," *Synchro*, October 1989, p. 7.

35. LaMarca, "The Award Stand: National/International Competitions," *Synchro Swimming USA*, April–June 1993, p. 8+.

36. LaMarca, "Santa Clara Sweeps ... Championships," *Synchro Swimming USA*, April–June 1994, p. 16+.

37. Eaton, "College Bound Athletes," *Synchro Swimming USA*, Spring 1999, p. 11.

38. Wightman, "Board Room Comments," *Synchro Swimming USA*, January-March 1993, p. 3.

39. La Marca, "From the Editor," *Synchro Swimming USA*, January-March 1993, p. 2.

40. "News & Notes: Swimmers ... Sea World," *Synchro*, August 1990, p. 6.

41. "Jantzen Signs ... Sponsor," *Synchro Swimming USA*, October–December 1993, p. 10.

42. S. Josephson, "Swimmer's Ear, *Synchro Swimming USA*, July-August-September 1993, p. 4.

43. "New Baby: Zone Clinics," *Synchro*, February 1989, p. 18+.

44. *USSS Figures Book*, 1989.

45. Hammell, *The Adapted Manual*, USSS, 1990.

46. Forbes, *The Safety Manual*, USSS, 1990.

47. Skidmore Tucker, *Sport Training Manual*, USSS, 1992.

48. Hazle, *Meet Management Guide*, USSS, 1994.

49. Gray, "Miscellany," *Synchro World*, Winter 1991-92, *Synchro*, April 1991, p. 49.

50. "National News: Dyroen Award," *Synchro Swimming USA*, October–December 1994, p. 6.

## *Chapter 11*

1. FINA *Federation Internationale de Natation Amateur Handbook*, 1996, p. 271.

2. McGowan, "World Beat: Two Judging Panels," *Synchro Swimming USA*, Fall 1995, p. 6.

3. LaMarca, "U.S. Reigns ... Pan Ams," *Synchro Swimming USA*, April–June 1995, p. 13.

4. "Going for the Goal!" *Synchro Swimming USA*, Fall 1995, p. 18.

5. LaMarca, "Selecting ... Dream Team," *Synchro Swimming USA*, Winter 1995/96, p. 12+.

6. LaMarca, "Perfect Harmony," *Synchro Swimming USA*, Fall 1995, p. 16+.

7. Savery, "Olympic Dreams ... for Gold," *Synchro Swimming USA*, Spring 1996, p. 14+.

8. Barry, "Now a Trained Eggbeater," *Synchro Swimming USA*, Summer/Fall 1996, p. 24+.

9. M. Johnson, "After Winning Gold ... Time to Be a Spectator," *USA Today*, August 3, 1996.

10. LaMarca, "Perfect Olympic Moment," *Synchro Swimming USA*, Summer/Fall 1996, p. 14+.

11. Eaton, "New Team I Makes ... Debut," *Synchro Swimming USA*, Fall 1997, p. 19.

12. Eaton, "May Strikes Alpine Gold," *Synchro Swimming USA*, Fall 1997, p. 20.

13. Eaton, "Juniors Snare Bronze," *Synchro Swimming USA*, Fall 1997, p. 21.

14. Eaton, "Team USA Surpasses Goals," *Synchro Swimming USA*, Winter 1997/98, p. 12+.

15. Eaton, "Team Strikes Silver," *Synchro Swimming USA*, Fall 1998, p. 14+.

16 . Eaton, "Elvis Lives During ... Sweep," *Synchro Swimming USA*, Fall 1999, p. 13.

17. Eaton, "Team USA ... #3 World Ranking," *Synchro Swimming USA*, Winter 1999, p. 16.

18. Eaton, "Going for the Dream," *Synchro Swimming USA*, Fall 1999, p. 16.

19. LaMarca, "Santa Clara 'Three Peats'," *Synchro Swimming USA*, April–June 1995, p. 16+.

20. Saurman, "Dawning of New Era," *Synchro Swimming USA*, Spring 1996, p. 16+.

21. Riemen, "Just ... Aquamaids Sweep," *Synchro Swimming USA*, Summer 1998, p. 14+.

22. Riemen, "Legends in the Making," *Synchro Swimming USA*, Summer 1997, p. 16.

23. Riemen, "David vs Goliath," *Synchro Swimming USA*, Summer 1997, p. 18+.

24. Eaton, "Stanford Tops Ohio State," *Synchro Swimming USA*, Summer 1998, p. 13+.

25. Eaton, "Cardinal Makes the Grade," *Synchro Swimming USA*, Summer 1999, p. 13.

26. Lindeman, "Boardroom: YMCA Program Help," *Synchro Swimming USA*, October–December 1993, p. 5.

27. "Synchronized Swimming & the Komen Foundation," *Synchro Swimming USA*, April–June 1995, p. 12.

28. National Exhibition Team," *Synchro Swimming USA*, Winter 1995/96, p. 9.

29. "President's Message: Promoting the Sport," *Synchro Swimming USA*, Summer 1999, p. 8.

30. Hesse, "Boardroom Comments: Hesse Begins," *Synchro Swimming USA*, July–September 1994, p. 8.

31. Eaton, "Official Program ... National Champi-

onships," 1998.

32. "New Sponsors Team-Up," *Synchro Swimming USA*, Fall 1995, p. 11.

33. "National News: Kodak Posters," *Synchro Swimming USA*, Summer 1999, p. 6.

34. Hesse, "Note from ... USOC Joint Marketing," *Synchro Swimming USA*, Summer 1997, p. 11.

35. Wightman, "Boardroom: USOC Funding Changes," *Synchro Swimming USA*, January-March 1995, p. 4.

36. "Synchro Music Goes Digital," *Synchro Swimming USA*, Winter 1995/96, p. 15.

37. "Boardroom Comments: New Clinic Format Introduced," *Synchro Swimming USA*, Winter 1995/96, p. 5.

38. S. Josephson, "Swimmer's Ear," *Synchro Swimming USA*, July–September 1993, p. 4.

39. LaMarca, "Festival's Final Flame," *Synchro Swimming USA*, Fall 1995, p. 20.

40. Wightman, "Boardroom: College Plans," *Synchro Swimming USA*, January-March 1994, p. 4.

41. Eaton, "Canisius Sweeps ... ECAC Meet," *Synchro Swimming USA*, Summer 1998, p. 12.

42. "Friends for Life," *Synchro Swimming USA*, October–December 1994, p. 15.

43. Eaton, "O, What a Show," *Synchro Swimming USA*, Spring 1999, p. 12.

44. Longmire, "Boardroom: Competitive ... Change," *Synchro Swimming USA*, Winter 1996/97, p. 5.

45. Douglass, "Validation of ... Rating Systems," *Synchro*, June 1988, p. 28+.

46. LaMarca, "U.S. Reigns ... Pan Ams," *Synchro Swimming USA*, April–June 1995, p. 13.

47. "National News: American Wins FINA Prize," *Synchro Swimming USA*, Winter 1995/96, p. 8.

48. Riemen, "Gail Emery Inducted ... WSHOF," *Synchro Swimming USA*, Fall 1997, p. 16+.

49. "National News: Emery Honored, California Legislature," *Synchro Swimming USA*, Summer 1998, p. 7.

50. "National News: Mervyn's Honors Bean, Emery," *Synchro Swimming USA*, Fall 1999, p. 5.

51. "National News: Nesbitt ... Honors Weekend," *Synchro Swimming USA*, Winter 1999, p. 7.

## *Chapter 12*

1. "Olsen Gets Olympic Dream," news clip, 1984, ISHOF, n.pg.

2. Carvalho, "The Mermaid's Club," *Perception Films*.

3. "Traffic Police," *Houston Chronicle*, June 24, 2001.

4. Jon Drummond, "SS ... Inspiring," *Los Angeles Times Sports*, November 15, 2002.

5. "Underrated & Overrated Sports," *Sports Illustrated*, November 4, 2002.

6. "Get Trendy," *Synchro Swimming USA*, Winter 2001, p. 14.

7. "USA Storms Into Olympic Bid," *Synchro Swimming USA*, Summer 2000, p. 14+.

8. "Olympic Duet Tests Mettle," *Synchro Swimming USA*, Fall 2000, p. 12.

9. "Team ... Gold in Rome," *Synchro Swimming USA*, Fall 2000, p. 13+.

10. "Olympic Team Stars ... Sydney," *Synchro Swimming USA*, Winter 2000, p. 13+.

11. Synchro USA Web site, *wwww.usasynchro.org*, Summer 2000.

12. "Olympic Team Stars ... Sydney," *Synchro Swimming USA*, Winter 2000, p. 13+.

13. "Movin' On Up: USA Team 4th," *Synchro Swimming USA*, Summer/Fall, 2001. p. 10+.

14. "Junior World SS Competition," *Seattle Times*, August 26, 2001.

15. "Russia Knocks Out ... Junior Worlds," *Synchro Swimming USA*, Summer/Fall 2001, p. 9.

16. "USA Wins Bronze in World Cup," *Synchro Swimming USA*, Winter 2002, p. 9.

17. FINA Web site, *www.fina.org*, July 13, 2002.

18. "USA Wins Bronze in World Cup," *Synchro Swimming USA*, Winter 2002, p. 9.

19. "From Geveva with Love," *Synchro Swimming USA*, Fall 2002, p. 13.

20. FINA Web site, *www.fina.org*, August 19, 2002.

21. "Duet Gets Chance," *Synchro Swimming USA*, Fall 2002, p. 9.

22. "Results, Rome Open," *USA Newsletter*, *www.usasynchro.org*, June 16, 2003.

23. FINA World Championships ... Barcelona, *www.fina.org*, July 12-27, 2003.

24. "Barcelona World Championships," *www.usasynchro.org*, August 9, 2003.

25. McClintoc, "Team USA Claims Bronze," *Synchro Swimming USA*, Fall 2003, p. 11.

26. "Checkmate, Santa Clara ... #11," *Synchro Swimming USA*, Summer 2002, p. 14.

27. "Santa Clara Sets Record," *Synchro Swimming USA*, Summer 2003, p. 14.

28. "Synchro's Golden Boy," *Synchro Swimming USA*, Summer 2002, p. 16.

29. "2001 National Championships," *Synchro Swimming USA*, Summer 2001, p. 12+.

30. "Checkmate, Santa Clara ... #11," *Synchro Swimming USA*, Summer 2002, p. 14.

31. "Anna in Her Own Words," *Synchro Swimming USA*, Winter 1999, p. 15.

32. "President's: Hazle Begins," *Synchro Swimming USA*, Winter 2000, p. 8.

33. "President's: Convention: 9-11," *Synchro Swimming USA*, Winter 2000, p. 7.

34. "National News: Davis Retires," *Synchro Swimming USA*, Winter 2000, p. 5+.

35. "National News: Pease ... Stanford Coach," *Synchro Swimming USA*, Summer/Fall 2001, p. 5.

36. "National News: DeNegri New," *Synchro Swimming USA*, Winter 2001, p. 6.

37. "President's...," *Ibid*.

38. "Synchro News: Bye Bye Brian," *Synchro Swimming USA*, Spring 2003, p. 5.

39. "National News: USSS Hosts Sponsor Summit," *Synchro Swimming USA*, Spring 2000, p. 5.

40. "Synchro News: Founder's Society," *Synchro Swimming USA*, Winter 2002, p. 5+.

41. "President's: New Format, U.S. Open," *Synchro*

*Swimming USA*, Winter 2002, p. 7.

42. "Collegiate Program Update," *Synchro Swimming USA*, Spring 2000, p. 23.

43. "Education in the New Millenium," *Synchro Swimming USA*, Spring 2000, p. 20.

44. "2003 Coaches College," *Synchro Swimming USA*, Spring 2003, p. 20.

45. "A-May-Zing, Mixed Pairs," *Synchro Swimming USA*, Winter 2000, p. 17.

46. FINA Report, "Guideline," distributed January 1998.

47. "Get Trendy," *Synchro Swimming USA*, Winter 2001, p. 14.

48. Women's Sports Foundation, "25 Years," *Synchro Swimming USA*, Winter 2000, p. 15.

49. "National News: Xerox Top 100 Olympic Athletes of All Time," *Synchro Swimming USA*, Winter 2000, p. 15.

50. "National News: Ruiz ... Swimmer of Century," *Synchro Swimming USA*, Summer 2001, p. 6.

## *Epilogue*

1. Schleuter, "Mermaids and Music," 1946, ISHOF, n.pg.

2. Griggs, "Swimming Plus," *Sports Illustrated*, June 6, 1955, p. 19+

3. Olsen, "AAU ... Tours Face a Challenge," *Synchro-News*, February 1958, p. 23.

4. "Mermaid Who Started a New Olympic Sport," c. 1984, ISHOF, n.pg.

5. "President's: Convention on 9/11," *Synchro Swimming USA*, Winter 2001, p. 7.

6. Marc Salyers, "College Basketball," *Sports Illustrated*, March 8, 1999.

7. R. Bean, "On SS Rule Changes," *Synchronized Swimmer*, October 1953, p. 2+; "Where Do We Go from Here? (I)," *Synchro-News*, January 1960, p. 5+; "Where Do We Go from Here? (II)," *Synchro-News*, March-April 1960, p. 6+; "Where Do We Go from Here? (III)," *Synchro-News*, June 1960, p. 7+; "Where Do We Go from Here?" *Synchro-Info*, August 1973, p. 10+; "Where Do We Go from Here?" *Synchro*, December 1992, p. 10+.

8. D. Bean, "Editor's Notes: Show or Sport," *Synchro*, June 1982, p. 3.

9. "Overview ... Free Routine," *Synchro Swimming USA*, Summer/Fall 1996, p. 18.

10. FINA, *Manual for Judges, Coaches and Referees*. Lausanne, Switzerland, 2003, p. 91.

11. Eaton, "Duet Returns for 2000 Olympics," *Synchro Swimming USA*, Spring 1997, p. 15.

12. Carver, "Clean Up Your Routines," *Synchro Swimming USA*, Winter 2002, p. 13.

13. "Get Trendy," *Synchro Swimming USA*, Winter 2001, p. 14.

14. D. Bean, "Editor's Notes: Show or Sport?"

15. "A-May-Zing, Mixed Pairs," *Synchro Swimming USA*, Winter 2000, p. 17.

16. "Synchro Is Making the News," *Synchro*, August 1982.

17. "Mermaid Who Started a New Olympic Sport," c. 1984, ISHOF, n.pg.

18. Cushman, Joy. Letter. Telephone, September 29, 2003.

19. "Official Press Bulletins: World Aquatic Games," *Synchro-Info*, November 1978, p. 10.

# Bibliography

"Additional Exhibitions Set for American Aquacade." *Synchro-News* (San Jose, CA), March–April 1960.

Ahlf, Gene. "Annual Report, Evaluation Study." *Synchro-Info* (Santa Ana, CA), December 1971.

_____. "Letters to the Mailbox." *Synchro-Info* (Santa Ana, CA), September-October 1968.

_____. "A Proposal for the Selection of Judges." *Synchro-Info* (Santa Ana, CA), September-October 1968.

Albert, Allen D. *Official View Book: A Century of Progress Exposition*. New York: Reuben H. Donnelley, 1933.

Allen, Aileen. "Southern Pacific Association Report." S.S. Scrapbooks [1940s]. Henning Library, International Swimming Hall of Fame, Ft. Lauderdale, Fl. [ISHOF]. November 13, 1942.

"AAU News." *Synchro-News* (San Jose, CA), March-April 1958.

"AAU News." *Synchro-News* (San Jose, CA), May 1958.

"AAU News." *Synchro-News* (San Jose, CA), June 1958.

"AAU News." *Synchro-News* (San Jose, CA), July 1958.

"AAU News." *Synchro-News* (San Jose, CA), August 1958.

"AAU News." *Synchro-News* (San Jose, CA), September 1958.

"AAU News." *Synchro-News* (San Jose, CA), November-December 1958.

"AAU News: Bristol in Yale Carnival." *Synchro-News* (San Jose, CA), February 1958.

*Amateur Athletic Union Official Aquatics Handbook* (New York), 1973.

*Amateur Athletic Union Official Swimming Handbook* (New York), 1941–1953.

*AAU Official Synchronized Swimming Handbooks* (New York), 1954–1979.

"AAU Women's Sport Committee [Report]." AAU 53rd Annual Meeting. Philadelphia, Pa. S.S. Scrapbooks [1940s]. Henning Library, ISHOF. November 17, 1941.

"A-May-Zing, Mixed Pairs to Join FINA Program." *Synchro Swimming USA* (Indianapolis), Winter 2000.

"American Cup II." *Synchro* (Santa Ana, CA), August 1983.

Ammirati, Roberta. "Letters to the Mailbox." *Synchro-Info* (Santa Ana, CA), October 1975.

Anderson, Katherine. "University of Illinois Holds Intercollege Meet." *The Synchronized Swimmer* (Chicago, IL), March 1952.

Anderson, Theresa. "From Your National Chairman." *Synchro-Info* (Santa Ana, CA), January-February 1964.

_____. "Golden Gate International Solo." *Synchro-Info* (Santa Ana, CA), November-December 1967.

_____. "News from Your National Chairman." *Synchro-Info* (Santa Ana, CA), May–June 1965.

_____. "Show or Sport?" *Synchro-Info* (Santa Ana, CA), April 1970.

"Anna in Her Own Words." *Synchro Swimming USA*, Winter 1999.

"Annette Kellerman Dies." [News & Notes]. *Synchro-Info* (Santa Ana, CA), December 1975.

Armbrust, January "Magical Maidens." *International Swimming and Water Polo*, Winter 1981.

Aspinall, J. Edwin. "Thoughts on Mixed Synchronized Swimming." Unpublished. S.S. Scrapbooks [1940s]. Henning Library, ISHOF. October 13, 1948.

"Athlete's Corner." *Synchro-Info* (Santa Ana, CA), July-August 1968.

Atwater, A.E., J.L. Puhl, and F.B. Roby. "Sports Science and Synchronized Swimming." *Synchro* (Santa Ana, CA), February 1989.

"Ballet Champs in H-A Meet." *Chicago Herald-American*. S.S. Scrapbooks [1940s]. Henning Library, ISHOF. August 10, 1945.

"Baltimore Aqualites, 25th Anniversary." *Synchro-Info* (Santa Ana, CA), August 1975.

"Barcelona World Championships," www.usasynchro.org. 2002.

"[Barcelona] World Championships." *USA Synchro Newsletter. www.usasynchro.org.* Santo Domingo. Days 11–14, 2003.

Barry, Dave. "I Am Now a Trained Eggbeater." *Synchro Swimming USA* (Indianapolis, IN), Summer/Fall 1996.

Bauch, Patsy. "Letters to the Mailbox." *Synchro-Info* (Santa Ana, CA), January-February 1969.

_____. "This Is a Sport?" *Ibid.*

Bean, Dawn. News Clippings/Photos/Programs. Personal collection. Santa Ana, CA, 1941–1958.

_____. "College/Club Tension." *Synchro-Info* (Santa Ana, CA), April 1978.

_____. "Creativity Is Back." *Synchro* (Santa Ana, CA), June 1987.

_____. "The Editor's Notes: 'Freight Train' Stunt Proposals." *Synchro-Info* (Santa Ana, CA), July-August 1967.

_____. "The Editor's Notes, Local Meet Guest." *Synchro-Info* (Santa Ana, CA), January-February 1969.

_____. "The Editor's Notes: National Team Funding." *Synchro* (Santa Ana, CA), June 1980.

_____. "The Editor's Notes: Show or Sport?" *Synchro* (Santa Ana, CA), June 1982.

_____. "Hope for the Olympics." *Synchro-Info* (Santa Ana, CA), December 1977.

_____. "Impressions of Nationals [1964]," *Synchro-Info* (Santa Ana, CA), March-April 1964.

_____. "Impressions of Nationals [1966]." *Synchro-Info* (Santa Ana, CA), March-April 1966.

_____. "Impressions of Nationals [1967]." *Synchro-Info* (Santa Ana, CA), March-April 1967.

_____. "Improvements in Judging." *Synchro-Info* (Santa Ana, CA), July-August 1965.

_____. "Litigation Ended." *Synchro* (Santa Ana, CA), October 1986.

_____. "No TV Coverage of Pan Ams." *Synchro* (Santa Ana, CA), October 1987.

_____. "Quick Quotes: Tracie Ruiz." *Synchro* (Santa Ana, CA), October 1987.

_____. "Thoughts on the World Games." *Synchro-Info* (Santa Ana, CA), November 1978.

_____. "XXIII Olympiad: The Solo Competition." *Synchro* (Santa Ana, CA), October 1984.

_____, ed. *Synchro* (Santa Ana, CA), 1979–92.

_____, ed. *Synchro-Info* (Santa Ana, CA), 1963–78.

_____, and Charlotte Davis. *Three Month Curriculum for the Beginning Synchronized Swimming Class* (Indianapolis, IN), 1988.

Bean, Lea. "The 1991 Olympic Festival." *Synchro* (Santa Ana, CA), August 1991.

_____. "The World Aquatic Championships." *Synchro* (Santa Ana, CA), October 1986.

Bean, Ross C. "Exploring Aquatic Art [Book Review]." *Synchro-Info* (Santa Ana, CA), October 1963.

_____. "Festival Insights." *Synchro-Info* (Santa Ana, CA), November 1978.

_____. "Highlights of the National Competition." *Synchro-Info* (Santa Ana, CA), May-June 1965.

_____. "National Review." *Synchro-Info* (Santa Ana, CA), October 1973.

_____. "On Synchronized Swimming Rule Changes." *The Synchronized Swimmer*, October 1953.

_____. "The Question, Right, Left and Center." *The Synchronized Swimmer*, October 1954.

_____. "Reply to Mr. Elliott." *The Synchronized Swimmer*, January 1955.

_____. "Swimming vs the Nielsens." *Synchro* (Santa Ana, CA), August 1982.

_____. "Where Do We Go from Here? [Part I]." *Synchro-News* (San Jose, CA), January 1960.

_____. "Where Do We Go from Here? [Part II]." *Synchro-News* (San Jose, CA), March-April 1960.

_____. "Where Do We Go from Here? [Part III]." *Synchro-News* (San Jose, CA), June 1960.

_____. "Where Do We Go from Here? [1973]." *Synchro-Info* (Santa Ana, CA), August 1973.

_____. "Where Do We Go from Here? [1993]." *Synchro* (Santa Ana, CA), December 1992-January 1993.

_____, and Dawn Bean. "From the Hot Seat." *Synchro-Info* (Santa Ana, CA), July-August 1968.

_____, and _____. "Thoughts on the Olympics from a Couple of Couch Potatoes." *Synchro* (Santa Ana, CA), August-September 1992.

Bennett, Colleen and Gordon, "Handbook of Synchronized Swimming — The Origin of Aquatic Clubs" (Ann Arbor, MI), 1955.

Bernard, Barbara. "Letters to the Mailbox." *Synchro* (Santa Ana, CA), December 1988.

Beshunsky, Doris Dannenhirsch. News clippings/Unpublished Papers/Correspondence. S.S. Scrapbooks [1940s]. Henning Library, ISHOF.

"Beulah Gundling Demonstrates in Paris." *Daytona Beach Morning Herald*, August 1953.

"Bill May Led Santa Clara to its 10th…" *Synchro Swimming USA*, Summer 2001.

"Boardroom Comments: New Clinic Format Introduced." *Synchro Swimming USA*, Winter 1995/96.

"A Brilliant Exhibition of Synchronized Swimming." *Times of India*. May 15, 1954, S.S. Scrapbooks [1950s], Henning Library, ISHOF. 1954.

Brookman, Linda. "The Golden Age of Swimming." *Synchro* (Santa Ana, CA), December 1979.

Bullock, Doris. "The Terrapin Club of the University of Illinois." *The Synchronized Swimmer*, February 1952.

"CAAU [Central Association] Championships. Shawnee Country Club, April 17th." *Discus*. May 1941.

Calcaterra, Re. "The Booming Age Group Program." *Synchro-Info* (Santa Ana, CA), May-June 1964.

_____. "Development of Synchronized Swimming in the Ozark Association." Letter. St. Louis, MO. May 1997.

"Canada Adopts Term 'Synchronized Swimming' and Holds First Championships." S.S. Scrapbooks [1940s]. Henning Library, ISHOF. 1949.

Canadian Amateur Synchronized Swimming Association, Inc. *Synchronized Canada*. 1971–85.

Canham, Don, "Champions on Film, Synchronized Swimming," Demonstrator Beulah Gundling (Ann Arbor, MI), 1958.

"Capacity Crowd at H-A Swim Meet." *Chicago Herald American*. News Clipping. S.S. Scrapbooks [1940s]. Henning Library, ISHOF. August 13, 1945.

Cardan, Helen, "This Is Synchronized Swimming," Demonstrator Betty Vickers, The Jole Co. (San Jose, CA), 1958.

Carvalho, Paul. "The Mermaid's Club." *Perception Films*, Fall 2002.

Carver, Chris. "Clean Up Your Routines." *Synchro Swimming USA*, Winter 2002.

A Century of Progress. "Administrative Staff/U.S. Rubber Co Correspondence." The University of Illinois at Chicago. The University Library, Department of Special Collections. 1934.

_____. "Official [Aquacade] Contract." The University of Illinois at Chicago. The University Library, Department of Special Collections. 1934.

_____. "Publicity Release. August 24, 1934." The University of Illinois at Chicago. The University Library, Department of Special Collections. 1934.

_____. "Publicity Release." Century of Progress World's Fair/Special Collections, The University Library, University of Illinois at Chicago. September 20, 1934.

"Champions Through the Years." *Synchro-Info* (Santa Ana, CA), February 1972.

"Championship Team Will Exhibit Talents." *Riverside Daily Press*, July 7, 1958.

Chase, Jeanette. "Development of Synchronized Swimming in Texas." Letter. Seabrook, TX. August 1997.

"Checkmate, Santa Clara Brings Home #11." *Synchro Swimming USA*, Summer 2002.

Clark, Laurene. *Synchronized Swimming — 60 Years to Celebrate*. Ottawa, Canada: Canadian Amateur Synchronized Swimming Association, 1985.

"Clark Leach, Father of Synchronized Swimming." S.S. Scrapbooks [1950s]. Henning Library, ISHOF. 1941.

Close, Binnie. "The Dolphins of Bangor, Maine." *The Synchronized Swimmer*, August 1953.

"Coach Walter Player." *Chicago Tribune*, October 22, 1939. S.S. Scrapbooks [1940s]. Henning Library, ISHOF. 1939.

*Coaching Intermediate S.S. Effectively Video*. Champaign, IL: Human Kinetics, 1988.

Coffin, Joyce. "Who's News: Margaret 'Peg' Seller." *Synchro-Info* (Santa Ana, CA), July-August 1966.

"Collegiate Program Update." *Synchro Swimming USA*, Spring 2000.

"Convention Honors: United States Aquatic Sports Award." *Synchro* (Santa Ana, CA), 1982.

"Convention News: Address by Senor Ostos." *Synchro-Info* (Santa Ana, CA), December 1978.

Cordell, Michael. "The Original Mermaid [Annette Kellerman]." A Hilton Cordell Film Production. Bondi, NSW, Australia. 2001.

Corsan, George H. *At Home in the Water*. New York: Association, 1914.

_____. *The Swimming and Diving Book*." New York: 1924.

Courtney, Miriam. "Comment." *Synchro-Info* (Santa Ana, CA), June 1971.

"Cover Story: Sarah Josephson Wins Olympia Award." *Synchro* (Santa Ana, CA), December 1986.

Crabbe, Virginia. Telephone interview. Scottsdale, AZ. January 1998.

Curtis, Katharine Whitney. "Competitive Synchronized Swimming." *Journal of Health and Physical Education*, January 1941.

_____. "Kay Curtis." *Stars & Stripes*. European edition. Reprinted in *The Synchronized Swimmer*, June 1952.

_____. "A Plea for More Interest in Stunt and Fancy Swimming." *AAU Official Aquatic Guide*. New York: AAU, 1928-29.

_____. *Rhythmic Swimming*, Minneapolis, MN: Burgess, 1936, 1942.

_____. *A Source Book of Water Pageantry*. Chicago, IL: College Press, 1936.

Cushman, Joy. "Chairman's Report," *Synchro-News* (San Jose, CA), January-February 1960.

_____. "The First ASUA Age Group Championships." *Synchro* (Santa Ana, CA), June 1982.

_____. "The First World Aquatic Games." *Synchro-Info* (Santa Ana, CA), October 1973.

_____. Letter. Houston, TX. September 29, 2003.

_____. "Miss AAU Synchronized Swimming," *Synchro-Info* (Santa Ana, CA), January-February 1964.

_____. "News from Your National Chairman: ABC Satisfied." *Synchro-Info* (Santa Ana, CA), May-June 1963.

_____. "Report of the Criterium D' Europe." *Synchro-Info* (Santa Ana, CA), May-June 1967.

Dawson, Buck. *Weissmuller to Spitz*. Fort Lauderdale, FL: International Swimming Hall of Fame, 1987.

"Demonstrations of Synchronized Swimming at the Maccabiah Games." S.S. Scrapbooks [1950s]. Henning Library, ISHOF. c. 1953.

Derosier, Mary. "History of Water Ballet and Synchronized Swimming in Detroit." Unpublished. S.S. Scrapbooks [1940s]. Henning Library, ISHOF. 1946.

_____. "Record of the St. Clair Synchronettes." Unpublished. S.S. Scrapbooks [1950s]. Henning Library, ISHOF. c. 1953.

_____. "Report of the Women's National Aquatic Forum." S.S. Scrapbooks [1940s]. Henning Library, ISHOF. c. 1948.

_____. "Rule Changes for 1950." Report. S.S. Scrapbooks [1950s]. Henning Library, ISHOF. c. 1950.

_____. "Synchronized Swimming in Helsinki." *The Synchronized Swimmer*, August 1952.

DeSha, Lillian. "Letters to the Mailbox." *Synchro-Info* (Santa Ana, CA), August 1970.

Detroit Riverama. *Official Program. 1955 Detroit Riverama*. S.S. Scrapbooks [1950s]. Henning Library, ISHOF. 1955.

Dineen, Marge. "AAU Sponsored Tour." *Synchro-News* (San Jose, CA), August 1958.

_____. "AAU Sponsored Tour." *Synchro-News* (San Jose, CA), September-October 1958.

"Directories: Club News." *Synchro-News* (San Jose, CA), February 1958.

"Directories: Clubs in Washington." *Synchro-News* (San Jose, CA), September-October 1958.

*Discus*. Magazine of the Lakeshore Athletic Club. Chicago Historical Society.

Dodson, R.J., ed. "About the A.A.U." *The Synchronized Swimmer*, November 1952.

_____. *The Aquatic Artist*. Chicago, 1955–1996.

_____. "Last Issue of *The Synchronized Swimmer*." *The Synchronized Swimmer*, July 1955.

_____. *The Synchronized Swimmer*, November 1951-July 1955.

_____. "We Are Now Sharply, Even Bitterly, Divided..." *The Synchronized Swimmer*, August 1954.

Donnelly, Dorothy. "AAU Sponsored Tour, Off to the World's Fair." *Synchro-News* (San Jose, CA), June 1958.

_____. *Synchronized Swimming Instruction Book* [Swimming Handbook]. New York: Girls Clubs of America, 1963.

_____. "U.S. Synchronized Swim Team Tours Europe." *The Amateur Athlete*, September 1958.

Dorst, Mary. "Letters to the Mailbox." *Synchro* (Santa Ana, CA), April 1984.

Douglass, Jackie. "The Athlete's Page." *Synchro-Info* (Santa Ana, CA), April 1973.

_____. "Validation of Two Subjective Rating Systems for Synchronized Swimming." *Synchro* (Santa Ana, CA), June 1988.

Downey, Mike. "Olympian or Not, It's a Festival." *Los Angeles Times Sports*, July 10, 1991.

Drummond, Jon. "Synchro Athletes Are Inspiring." *Los Angeles Times Sports*, November 15, 2002.

"Duet Event Returns for 2000 Olympics." *Synchro Swimming USA*, Summer 1997.

"Duet Gets Its Chance, Junior World Championships." *Synchro Swimming USA*, Fall 2002.

Dunbar, Bill. "Suspended Aquatic Stars Return Home." *Oakland Tribune*, August 16, 1949.

"Dyroen-Lancer and Sudduth Strike Gold in Russia." *Synchro Swimming USA*, July–September 1994.

Eakin, Karin. "Synchro Development in Berea [Ohio]." Letter. April 1997.

Eaton, Barbara. "Synchro Development in the D.C. Area." Letter. Virginia Beach, Va. May 1997.

Eaton, Brian. "Canisius Sweeps Inaugural ECAC Meet." *Synchro Swimming USA*, Summer 1998.

_____. "Cardinal Makes the Grade." *Synchro Swimming USA*, Summer 1999.

_____. "College Bound Athletes, Beware." *Synchro Swimming USA*, Spring 1999.

_____. "Duet Event Returns for 2000 Olympics." *Synchro Swimming USA*, Summer 1997.

_____. "Elvis Lives During USA's Swiss Open Sweep." *Synchro Swimming USA*, Fall 1999.

_____. "Going for the Dream." *Synchro Swimming USA*, Fall 1999.

_____. "Juniors Snare Bronze in Moscow." *Synchro Swimming USA*, Fall 1997.

_____. "May Strikes Alpine Gold." *Synchro Swimming USA*, Fall 1997.

_____. "New Team I Makes International Debut." *Synchro Swimming USA*, Fall 1997.

_____. "'O', What a Show." *Synchro Swimming USA*, Spring 1999.

_____. "Program, U.S. National Championships." United States Synchronized Swimming, 1998.

_____. "Stanford Tops Ohio State for Overall Title." *Synchro Swimming USA*, Summer 1998.

_____, ed. *Synchro Swimming USA*, Summer 1997–Spring 2003.

_____. "Team Strikes Silver in Team, Duet, '98 Goodwill Games." *Synchro Swimming USA*, Fall 1998.

_____. "Team USA Earns No. 3 World Ranking." *Synchro Swimming USA*, Winter 1999.

_____. "Team USA Surpasses Goals at 8th World Championships." *Synchro Swimming USA*, Winter 1997/98.

"Education in the New Millenium." *Synchro Swimming USA*, Spring 2000.

Edwards, Emma Gene. "Synchro Development in Florida." Letter. Miami, FL. March 28, 1997.

"The VIII Pan American Games." *Synchro-Info* (Santa Ana, CA), August 1979.

Elkington, Helen, and Jane Chamberlain. *Synchronized Swimming*. Newton Abbot, Devon, UK: David & Charles, 1977.

Elliott, Frank L. "Frank L. Elliott Writes." *The Synchronized Swimmer*, October 1954.

Elston, Marion [Kane]. "History of San Francisco Merionettes." Telephone interview. Santa Rosa, CA, May 1997.

Emery, Gail. "Barcelona Seen from the Coaches' Eyes." *Synchro* (Santa Ana, CA), December 1992-January 1993.

Engerrand, Doris Dieskow. Telephone interview. 1997.

"Exhibitions at the 1951 Pan American Games." S.S. Scrapbooks [1950s]. Henning Library, ISHOF. c. 1951.

"Exhibitions at the 1952 Olympic Games." News clippings. S.S. Scrapbooks [1950s], Henning Library, ISHOF. 1952.

Eytchison, Vernon. "Synchro Development in Potomac Valley." Letter. Silver Springs, Md. March 5, 1997.

Feinstein, Lena [Zimmerman]. Telephone interview. Wilmette, IL, November 1997.

FINA *Federation Internationale de Natation Amateur* Handbook. Quadrennial. Lausanne, Switzerland.

FINA "Guideline." Distributed at 8th World Championships. FINA Technical S.S. Committee. Lausanne, Switzerland. January 1998.

*FINA Handbook* (Lausanne, Switzerland), 1953–1956.

*FINA Handbook* (Lausanne, Switzerland), 1994–1996.

"FINA Rules, Artistic Swimming." *The Synchronized Swimmer*, July 1953.

"FINA Rules: Proposals for Ornamental Swimming." *The Synchronized Swimmer*, June 1952.

FINA. *Synchronized Swimming Judges' Training Manual*. Second Edition. Lausanne, Switzerland. 1995.

FINA *Synchronized Swimming Manual for Judges, Coaches and Referees*. Lausanne, Switzerland. 2002, p. 91+.

FINA Website (Lausanne, Switzerland), www.fina.org.

"FINA World Championships." *www.fina.org*. Barcelona, Spain. July 12–27, 2003.

"Final CAAU Meet, Idylwild Park." *Discus*, September 5, 1943.

"The First American Cup." *Synchro* (Santa Ana, CA), August 1980.

"The First Competition in Europe." News Clipping. S.S. Scrapbooks [1950s]. Henning Library, ISHOF. c. 1958.

"The First FINA World Cup." *Synchro* (Santa Ana, CA), December 1979.

"The First Junior World Championships." *Synchro* (Santa Ana, CA), August 1989.

"The First National Age Group Championships." *Synchro* (Santa Ana, CA), April 1982.

"The First National Championships." *Chicago Herald-American*. S.S. Scrapbooks [1940s]. Henning Library, ISHOF. c. August 1946.

"The First National Coaches Camp," *Synchro-Info* (Santa Ana, CA), August 1974.

"The First National Judges Seminar." *Synchro-Info* (Santa Ana, CA), April 1969.

[The First Rules.] "Synchronized Swimming Rules." AAU Convention. S.S. Scrapbooks [1940s], Henning Library, ISHOF. c. 1940.

"The First Synchronized Swim Championship in the World." News Clipping. S.S. Scrapbooks [1940s], Henning Library, ISHOF. March 1, 1940.

"The First World Coaches Seminar at Olympia, Greece." *Synchro* (Santa Ana, CA), June-July 1992.

Fleming, Prudence. "Synchronized Swimming Experiment at Temple University." *The Synchronized Swimmer*, May 1952.

Forbes, Margaret [Swan]. *The Safety Manual*. U.S. Synchronized Swimming. 1990.

_____. "Synchro Development in San Antonio." Letters. San Antonio, TX, March-April 1997.

Foster, John. "Southeastern Association Report." S.S. Scrapbooks [1940s]. Henning Library, ISHOF. November 24, 1942.

"The IV FINA World Cup." *Synchro* (Santa Ana, CA), October 1989.

"IV World Swimming Championships." *Synchro* (Santa Ana, CA), August 1982.

Franklin, Dr. Benjamin. "The Art of Swimming Rendered Easy." Glasgow 1781. Kroll, private collection.

"Friends for Life." *Synchro Swimming USA*, October–December 1994.

"From Geneva with Love." *Synchro Swimming USA*, Fall 2002.

"Gail Johnson Wins Top Aquatic Award." *Synchro-Info* (Santa Ana, CA), December 1974.

Gemma, Kathy. "Letters to the Mailbox." *Synchro* (Santa Ana, CA), August 1985.

Georges, Chris. "A Male's Point of View." *Swimming World*, February 1979. Reprinted in *Synchro* (Santa Ana, CA), June 1980.

_____. "Swimming World Views Synchro at the World Championships." *Swimming World*, October 1982. Reprinted in *Synchro* (Santa Ana, CA), December 1982.

Georgian, Rose. "Success Story Comes to Oakland." *KGO News Release*, July 1957.

"Get Trendy." *Synchro Swimming USA*, Winter 2001.

Glass, Marie. "Marie Glass Writes." *The Synchronized Swimmer*, February 1955.

Glinka, Donna, ed. *The Aquatic Artist*. 1997-1998, Prospect Heights, IL.

Goff, Bob. "Synchro at the World Games." *Swimming World*, September 1975. Reprinted in *Synchro-Info* (Santa Ana, CA), October 1975.

"Going for the Goal!" *Synchro Swimming USA*, Fall 1995.

Goodbody, John. "Synchronized Swimming and the Olympics." *London Times Sports News*, June 18, 1984. Reprinted in *Synchro* (Santa Ana, CA), August 1987.

"The Goodwill Games." *Synchro* (Santa Ana, CA), August-September 1990.

Goodwin, Kathy. Telephone interviews. Chicago April 1997, December 2003.

Gorman, Pat, "Letters to the Mailbox." *Synchro-Info*. (Santa Ana, CA), June 1978.

Goss, Gertrude. *Stunts and Synchronized Swimming*. Boston: Spaulding-Moss Co., 1957.

_____. "Swim to Music." *NSWA Aquatics Guide*. Washington, DC, 1947–49.

_____. *Swimming Analyzed*. Boston: Spaulding-Moss, Co., 1949.

_____. *Water Ballet Charts*. North Hampton, MA: Smith College, 1946.

_____. "The Water Show." *Beach and Pool* 24, 1950.

Gray, Jennifer. *Coaching Synchronized Swimming Figure Transitions*. Maidenhead, Berkshire, U.K.: Standard Studio Publishers, 1993.

_____. "Miscellany." *Synchro World*, Winter 1991-92. Excerpts in *Synchro* (Santa Ana, CA), April 1991.

Gregerson, Lois. "Regional Development: Utah." *Synchro-Info* (Santa Ana, CA), February 1972.

Griggs, Lee. "Swimming Plus." *Sports Illustrated*, Cedar Rapids, IA: June 6, 1955.

Gritten, David, "The XXIII Olympic Games," *Los Angeles Examiner* (Los Angeles, CA), August 10, 1984.

Gundling, Beulah. *Exploring Aquatic Art*. Cedar Rapids, IA: International Academy of Aquatic Art, 1963.

_____. "International Progress in Synchronized Swimming." *The Synchronized Swimmer*, May 1954.

_____. "Synchronized Swimming Experiences During the Olympic Games." [Helsinki]. *The Synchronized Swimmer*, October 1952.

_____, and Jill White. *Creative Synchronized Swimming*. Champaign, IL: Leisure Press, 1988.

Gundling, Henry. "Letter to the Mailbox." *Synchro-Info* (Santa Ana, CA), August 1972.

_____. "Synchronized Swimming Rules." *The Synchronized Swimmer*, November 1953.

Hainsworth, Harry. "Letters to the Mailbox." *Synchro-Info* (Santa Ana, CA), September-October 1969.

Hale, Lynn [Pawson]. Personal conversations. Sonoma, CA. December 1997.

Hammell, Vera. *The Adapted Manual*. U.S. Synchronized Swimming. 1990.

Harper, Jennie. "Clues from the Past, Leads for the Future." *Synchro Swimming USA*, Spring 2003.

Harrell, Barbara. "Synchro Development in New Mexico." Letter. Albuquerque, NM. February 1997.

Harrison, Chris. "Letters to the Mailbox: Magazine for England." *Synchro* (Santa Ana, CA), August 1981.

Harvey, Bud. "Rippling Rhythm — A New Sport, Synchronized Swimming, Puts Bubbles Into the Ballet and the Girls Love It." News Clipping, S.S. Scrapbooks [1940s]. Henning Library. ISHOF. c. 1947.

Hasbrouck, Bernard J., S.J. *Synchronized Swimming Self Taught*. Creighton University, Omaha, NE, 1971.

Hass, Carole. "The Ducks Club at the University of Oklahoma." *The Synchronized Swimmer*, December 1952.

Hayes, Bernice Lorber. "Synchronized Swimming at Wright Junior College." *The Synchronized Swimmer*, March 1952.

_____. Untitled personal records. The University of Illinois at Chicago. The University Library, Department of Special Collections. 1973.

Hazle, Betty. *Meet Management Guide*. U.S. Synchronized Swimming. 1994.

Heath, Frances. *Synchronized Swimming Routine Choreography*. Synchro Swim Alberta, Edmonton, Canada, 1989.

Heath, Millicent. Telephone interview. Cambria, CA. January 1997.

Heeger, Jack J. "Hall of Fame Museum." *Synchro-Info* (Santa Ana, CA), December 1972.

Helmick, Robert. "Letters to the Mailbox." *Synchro-Info* (Santa Ana, CA), April 1977.

"The Helms Story." *Amateur Athlete*. Reprinted in *Synchro-Info* (Santa Ana, CA), June 1963.

Henning, Harold. "Seventy Five Years of FINA, Part II." *International Swimming and Water Polo Magazine*, Summer 1983.

Henning, Jean. "Early Synchronized Swimming." Letter. Marco Island, FL. October 28, 1997.

_____. "How It Began." *International Swimming and Water Polo*, Spring 1987.

_____. "How It Began." *Synchro* (Santa Ana, CA), August 1985.

_____. "Synchronized Swimming, a Brief History." S.S. Scrapbooks [1990s]. Henning Library, ISHOF. June 26, 1996.

Hesse, Debbie. "Boardroom Comments." *Synchro Swimming USA*, July–September 1994.

_____. "A Note from Our Executive Director." *Synchro Swimming USA*, Summer 1997.

Hester, Chelys. "Letters to the Mailbox." *Synchro* (Santa Ana, CA), February 1984.

_____. "Synchro Development in Nebraska." Letter. Lincoln, NE. April 7, 1997.

Hinrichs, Gertrude. "Development of Synchronized Swimming in Colorado." Letter. Denver, CO. March 28, 1997.

Hogan, Peg. "Baltimore Aqualites Development." Letter. Midlothian, VA. April 1997.

_____. *U.S.S.S. Collegiate Synchronized Swimming Manual*. Indianapolis: 1996.

Hollyburn Synchronettes. "International News." *Synchro-Info* (Santa Ana, CA), October 1969.

Howell, Jae. "One Fabulous Trip." *Synchro-Info* (Santa Ana, CA), January-February 1967.

Hubbard, Bert. "Bert Hubbard Writes." *The Synchronized Swimmer*. Chicago, IL. April 1953.

_____. "Men in Synchro." *The Synchronized Swimmer*, February 1953.

_____. "Mixed Synchronized Swimming Needs You Now." *The Synchronized Swimmer*, November 1953.

Hudson, Mary Ann. "Fans Still Not Getting the Picture." *Los Angeles Times Sports*. Reprinted in *Synchro* (Santa Ana, CA), April-May 1992.

Huntley, Pearl Redding. "Development of Synchronized Swimming in Southern California and Oregon." Letter. Huntington Beach, CA. July 1997.

"Impressions of Nationals [Competitor's Views]." *Synchro-Info* (Santa Ana, CA), March-April 1967.

"In Memoriam, Gertrude Goss." *Synchro* (Santa Ana, CA), February 1981.

"In the Spotlight. Tracie Wins Olympia…" *Synchro* (Santa Ana, CA), December 1983.

International Academy of Aquatic Art. *www.AquaticArt.org*.

"International Activity: Demonstrations in Germany and Europe." News Clipping. S.S. Scrapbooks [1950s]. Henning Library, ISHOF. c. 1954.

"International News: The First World Conference." *Synchro-Info* (Santa Ana, CA), October 1974.

"International News: Pan American Games in Cali," *Synchro-Info* (Santa Ana, CA), August 1969.

Ireland, Celia. "Fast Paced Retirement for Marion Kane." *Press Democrat*. Reprinted in *Synchro-Info* (Santa Ana, CA), February 1975.

"Jantzen Signs as U.S.S.S National Sponsor." *Synchro Swimming USA*, October–December 1993.

Japan Synchronized Swimming Academy. *Synchronized Japan*. Tokyo, 1975–1990. Reprinted *Synchro-Info* (Santa Ana, CA), April 1972.

"Jeanne Wilson, Star of the Lakeshore Team." *Discus*, November 1943.

Johnson, Harald. "Esther Williams, America's Swimming Sweetheart." *Fitness Swimmer*, Summer 1995.

Johnson, Michael. "After Winning Gold in 200, 400 Meters, Time to Be Spectator." *USA Today*, August 3, 1996.

Johnson, William Oscar. "Out of Sync." *Sports Illustrated*, August 17, 1992.

Jones, Frances L. "Impressions of Nationals." *Synchro-Info* (Santa Ana, CA), October 1977.

_____. "Synchro Development in Michigan." Letter. Lansing, MI. March 23, 1997.

_____, and Joyce Lindeman. *Components of Synchronized Swimming*. Englewood Cliffs, NJ: Prentice-Hall, Inc., 1975.

Jones, Nancy. "Synchronized Swimming a Hit at Aquatic Forum." News Clipping. *Miami Herald*. S.S. Scrapbooks, Henning Library, ISHOF. c. December 1960.

Jones, Will. "Strip Tease No Aqua Folly." *Minneapolis Morning Tribune*, August 31, 1950, S.S. Scrapbooks [1950s]. Henning Library, ISHOF. 1950.

Josephson, Sarah. "Swimmer's Ear." *Synchro Swimming USA*, July–September 1993.

"Joy Cushman." *Shell Employee News*. News Clipping. S.S. Scrapbooks [1960s]. Henning Library, ISHOF. c. 1960s.

"Joy Cushman Accepts Interim Chairmanship." *Synchro-Info* (Santa Ana, CA), June 1970.

"Joy Cushman Appointed to USOC Board of Directors," *Synchro-Info* (Santa Ana, CA), October 1969.

"The Junior World Synchronized Swimming Competition. *Seattle Times*. News clipping. August 26, 2001.

Kahn, Bernard. "It Says Here, One Way to Learn About Synchronized Swimming." *Daytona Beach Evening News*, August 14, 1953.

Kane, Donald T. "Association News." *Synchro-Info* (Santa Ana, CA), May-June 1966.

_____. "Canadian Dominion Championships." *Synchro-Info* (Santa Ana, CA), March-April 1967.

_____. "Guide to the Administration…." December 1968. p. 4.

_____. "International News." *Synchro-Info* (Santa Ana, CA), April 1972.

_____. "International News." *Synchro-Info* (Santa Ana, CA), December 1976.

_____. "Press Relations Guide." *Synchro-Info*, July-August 1966. p. 10.

_____. "U.S. Triumphs in Moscow." *Synchro* (Santa Ana, CA), April 1982.

_____. "The World Aquatic Games." *Synchro-Info* (Santa Ana, CA), November 1978.

Kane, Marion. "How to Run a S.S. Meet, Part I." *Synchro-Info* (Santa Ana, CA), October 1964. p. 13.

_____. "How to Run a S.S. Meet, Parts II, III." *Synchro-Info* (Santa Ana, CA), December 1964. p. 10.

_____. "How to Run a S.S. Meet, Part IV." *Synchro-Info* (Santa Ana, CA), February 1965. p. 5.

_____. "Meet Managers Guide." AAU Synchronized Swimming. 1964.

_____. "Steps to Be Taken ... Judge." *Synchro-Info* (Santa Ana, CA), August 1964. p. 9.

_____. "The Training and Rating of Judges." *Synchro-Info*, February 1964. p. 5.

Kauffman, Mark. "Spectacle, Water Ballet." *Sports Illustrated*, June 6, 1955.

"Kay Curtis." *Stars & Stripes*, European Edition. Reprinted in *The Synchronized Swimmer*, June 1952.

Kellerman, Annette. *How to Swim*. New York: Duran, 1918.

Kennemer, Dorothy. "To Put Montana on the Map." *The Synchronized Swimmer*, October 1952.

Kerper, Robert E. Jr. *Splash, Aquatic Shows from A to Z*. 1st ed. West Chester, PA. 2002.

Kerth, Dorothy. "The Green Splash of Michigan State." *The Synchronized Swimmer*, June 1952.

King, Glen. "East Bay Story." *Berkeley Daily Gazette*, July 3, 1957.

Kiphuth, Bob. "Report from the Connecticut Association." Unpublished. S.S. Scrapbooks [1940s], Henning Library, ISHOF. November 11, 1942.

Kitamura, Saburo. "International News." *Synchro-Info* (Santa Ana, CA), July-August 1967.

Koch, Barbara. "Letters to the Mailbox." *Synchro* (Santa Ana, CA), October 1984.

Krajicek, Stanislav. "Synchro-Swim in Czechoslovakia." *Synchro-Info* (Santa Ana, CA), July-August 1965.

Kretschmer, Marian. "Synchronized Development in Ohio." Letter. Dayton, OH. May 1997.

_____. "U.S.O.C. Coaches Camp." *Synchro* (Santa Ana, CA), October 1979.

Kroll, Charles R. "A Lifeguard Odyssey." Personal collection. Seattle.

"Lake Shore's Swim Stars Continue Their Winning Ways." News Clipping. S.S. Scrapbooks [1940s]. Henning Library, ISHOF. August 10, 1942.

"Lakeshore Athletic Club Welcomes New Coach." *Discus*, April 1940.

"Lakeshore Captures the CAAU Duet Championship." *Discus*, June 1941.

"Lakeshore Girls Capture CAAU Water Ballet Championship." *Discus*, August 1941.

"Lakeshore Swim Stars Continue Winning Ways." *Discus*, September 1941.

"Lakeshore Water Ballet Never Defeated in Competition." *Discus*, February 1942.

LaMarca, Laura. "The Award Stand: National and International Competitions." *Synchro Swimming USA*, April–June 1993.

_____. "Festival's Final Flame." *Synchro Swimming USA*, Fall 1995.

_____. "From the Editor." *Synchro Swimming USA*, January–March 1993.

_____. "IOC Awards Second Gold Medal." *Synchro Swimming USA*, January–March 1994.

_____. Perfect Harmony." *Synchro Swimming USA*, Fall 1995.

_____. "The Perfect Olympic Moment." *Synchro Swimming USA*, Summer/Fall 1996.

_____. "Santa Clara Sweeps Jantzen Synchronized Swimming Championships." *Synchro Swimming USA*, April–June 1994.

_____. "Santa Clara 'Three Peats' at Jantzen National Championships." *Synchro Swimming USA*, April–June 1995.

_____. "Selecting Synchro's Dream Team." *Synchro Swimming USA*, Winter 1995/96.

_____, ed. *Synchro Swimming USA*, Spring 1993-Spring 1997.

_____. "Team USA Hits Grand Slam at World Championships." *Synchro Swimming USA*, July–September 1994.

_____. "Team USA, Our Nation's Best." *Synchro Swimming USA*, October–December 1993.

_____. "United States Reigns at Pan American Games." *Synchro Swimming USA*, April–June 1995.

_____. "U.S. Sweeps VI World Cup." *Synchro Swimming USA*, July–September 1993.

Lamb, Inez. Interview. Tustin, CA. April 1976.

"Lansing [Michigan] Has a New Club." *The Synchronized Swimmer*, August 1952.

"The Lawrence J. Johnson Trophy 1968." *Synchro-Info* (Santa Ana, CA), November-December 1968.

Leach, Clark. "Request for Association Activity, November 1942." Letters. S.S. Scrapbooks [1940s]. Henning Library, ISHOF. Fort. Lauderdale, FL. 1942.

_____. "Sport Sub-Committee Report, Synchronized Swimming." 1941 AAU Convention. S.S. Scrapbooks. [1940s]. Henning Library, ISHOF. c. 1941.

_____. "To Set the Record Straight." Letter, July 25, 1973, S.S. Scrapbooks [1970s], Henning Library, ISHOF. 1973.

_____. Undated letters/reports. S.S. Scrapbooks [1940s-1950s], Henning Library, ISHOF. Henning Library, ISHOF. c. 1941.

Lewis, Brad. "Synchronized Swimmers Deserve Some Respect." *San Francisco Chronicle*, July 1991. Reprinted in *Synchro* (Santa Ana, CA), October-November 1991.

"Life Magazine Visits Lake Shore Swim Team." *Life [Magazine]*. S.S. Scrapbooks [1940s]. Henning Library, ISHOF. July 4, 1944.

Lindeman, Joyce. "Boardroom Comments." *Synchro Swimming USA*, October–December 1993.

Lineer, George. "Athens Swimmers Escape from Cairo." *San Francisco Chronicle*, November 15, 1956.

_____. "A Bid at Olympics for New Type Event." *San Francisco Chronicle Sporting Green*, January 10, 1956.

_____. "Olympic Funds: Athens Club Mermaids Help Provide Money for U.S. Team." *San Francisco Chronicle*, December 6, 1954.

_____. "Synchronized Swimming and the Olympics." *Beach and Pool*, April 1954.

_____. "Synchronized Swimming Would Add to the Olympics." *San Francisco Chronicle Sporting Green*, Mar. 6, 1954.

Lloyd, Margaret. "Swimmers Show Skill as Dancers at Wheaton." News Clipping. S.S. Scrapbooks [1950s]. Henning Library, ISHOF. November 12, 1955.

Longmire, Laurette. "Boardroom Comments: Competitive Structure Changes." *Synchro Swimming USA*, Winter 1996.

Luick, Wilbur, ed. *Synchro-News* (San Jose, CA), January 1957–April 1962.

Lundholm, Jean. "The Story of Synchronized Swimming." *Synchro-Info* (Santa Ana, CA), December 1976.

MacKellar, Lillian. "National Committee Reports." *Synchro-Info* (Santa Ana, CA), August 1975.

_____. "Synchronized Swimming Stunts," Demonstrator: June Taylor, Classroom Film Distributors (Hollywood, CA), 1955.

"Madge Noble Heads 12th Aquatic Show." S.S. Scrapbooks [1970s], Henning Library, ISHOF. 1975.

Maeys, Jean. "Clinic in Synchronized Swimming Featuring Beulah Gundling." *The Synchronized Swimmer*, February 1953.

Makowsky, Lyle. "Competitive Image." *Synchro-Info* (Santa Ana, CA), April 1976.

Martin, Suzanne. "Aqua Follies Spectacle of Rhythm, Color, Fun." *Seattle Post Intelligencer*. S.S. Scrapbooks. Henning Library, ISHOF. August 12, 1950.

"Masters News: Golden Age Games." *Synchro* (Santa Ana, CA), December 1982.

Matthews, Melissa. "Best of Synchronized Swimming." *Toledo Blade*, September 14, 1969.

McClintoc, Amy, ed. *Synchro Swimming USA*, Summer 2003.

_____. "Team USA Claims Bronze...."*Synchro Swimming USA*, Fall 2003. p. 11.

McCormick, Olive. *Water Pageants, Games and Stunts.* Barnes, 1933.

McFadden, Jeanette and Ogurek, Minnette. "Synchro's Come a Long Way, Baby." *Synchro Swimming USA*, Fall 1998.

McGowan, Judy. "Americans Dominate in Barcelona." *Synchro* (Santa Ana, CA), August-September 1992.

_____. "Convention Report: From the Chair." *Synchro* (Santa Ana, CA), December 1983.

_____. "Letters to the Mailbox." *Synchro-Info* (Santa Ana, CA), November-December 1965.

_____. "World Beat." *Synchro Swimming USA*, July–September 1993.

_____. "World Beat." *Synchro Swimming USA*, Fall 1995.

McInnis, Bette. "Letters to the Mailbox." *Synchro-Info* (Santa Ana, CA), April 1976.

McNally, Joe. "Naked Power, Amazing Grace." *Life Magazine*, July 1996.

"Medinah Girl Stars Sparkle in and Out of the Pool." *Chicago Tribune.* January 22, 1939. S.S. Scrapbooks [1940s]. Henning Library, ISHOF. 1939.

Mehren, Elizabeth. "This Isn't Like Being in Movies." *Los Angeles Times*, August 13, 1984.

_____. "Unhappy Duo, Canadians Say 'American Hype' Led to their Loss in Synchronized Swimming." *Los Angeles Times*, August 10, 1984.

"Members of the Lakeshore Athletic Club Will Compete in Synchronized Swimming Championships at the Shawnee." *Chicago Sun Times.* S.S. Scrapbooks [1940s]. Henning Library, ISHOF. c. 1940.

Menish, Frieda. "Letters to the Mailbox." *Synchro-Info* (Santa Ana, CA), February 1974.

"Merionettes Score Synchronized Shutout." *Amateur Athlete*, May 1965. Reprinted in *Synchro-Info* (Santa Ana, CA), May-June 1965.

"Mermaid Who Started a New Olympic Sport." 1984, S.S. Scrapbooks [1980s]. Henning Library, ISHOF. 1984.

Meyer, Catherine D. "Activity in New Jersey." S.S. Scrapbooks [1940s]. Henning Library, ISHOF. November 12, 1942.

Michael, Laurie. "Aqua's Folly." *Freeway News*. Aquatennial Souvenir Ed. July 15, 1987.

"Midwest Intercollegiate Synchronized Swimming Meet." *The Synchronized Swimmer*, May 1953.

Minich, Michael J. "Synchro's National Coach, Charlotte Davis." *Synchro* (Santa Ana, CA), April 1985.

"Minneapolis Aquatennial." News clippings. S.S. Scrapbooks [1940s], Henning Library, ISHOF. 1941.

Mitchell, Carol. "Letters to the Mailbox." *Synchro* (Santa Ana, CA), February 1988.

Moore, Marna. "Development of Synchronized Swimming in Oregon." Letter. Beaverton, OR. March 1997.

Moran, Jean. "Intercollegiate Synchronized Meet." *The Synchronized Swimmer*, February 1955.

Motoyoshi, Miwako. "Water Fairies." *International Swimming and Water Polo Magazine*, Winter 1982.

"Movin' on Up: USA Team 4th Across the Board." *Synchro Swimming USA*, Summer [Fall] 2001.

Murphy, Ann. "Development of Synchronized Swimming in the Inland Empire." Spokane, WA. May 1997.

Murphy, Marjorie. "Letters to the Mailbox." *Synchro-Info* (Santa Ana, CA), December 1975.

"The National Coaches Seminar." *Synchro-Info* (Santa Ana, CA), August 1970.

"National Exhibition Team Performs at West Point." *Synchro Swimming USA*, Winter 1995/96.

"National News: American Wins FINA Prize." *Synchro Swimming USA*, Winter 1995/96.

"National News: Davis Retires." *Synchro Swimming USA*, Winter 2000.

"National News: DeNegri New National Team Director." *Synchro Swimming USA*, Winter 2001.

"National News: Dyroen-Lancer Named World Synchro Swimmer of the Year." *Synchro Swimming USA*, October–December 1994.

"National News: Emery Honored." *Synchro Swimming USA*, Summer 1998.

"National News: ISHOF Honors Bean, Sowers." *Synchro Swimming USA*, Spring 1996.

"National News: Kodak Posters." *Synchro Swimming USA*, Summer 1999.

"National News: Mervyn's Honors Bean, Emery." *Synchro Swimming USA*, Fall 1999.

"National News: Nesbitt Attends Coaches Recognition Weekend." *Synchro Swimming USA* (Indianapolis, IN), Winter 1999.

"National News: Pease New Stanford Coach." *Synchro Swimming USA*, Summer [Fall] 2001.

"National News: Ruiz ... Swimmer of Century." *Synchro Swimming USA*, Summer 2001.

"National News: USSS Hosts Sponsor Summit." *Synchro Swimming USA* (Indianapolis, IN), Spring 2000.

"National News: Xerox Names Top 100 Athletes of All Time." *Synchro Swimming USA* (Indianapolis, IN), Winter 2000.

National Section for Girls and Women's Sports. *Official Aquatics Guide.* Washington D.C. July 1953–July 1955.

Nelson, Joan Pawson. Personal conversations. Forestville, CA. December 1997.

"The New Baby: Zone Clinics." *Synchro* (Santa Ana, CA), February 1989.

"New Sponsors Team-Up with Synchro Swimming USA." *Synchro Swimming USA*, Fall 1995.

"News: Litigation Ended." *Synchro* (Santa Ana, CA), April 1988.

"News & Notes: Coaches Camp in Dallas." *Synchro-Info* (Santa Ana, CA), June 1976.

"News & Notes: Computer Scoring." *Synchro-Info* (Santa Ana, CA), June 1972.

"News & Notes: FINA Eligibility Change." *Synchro* (Santa Ana, CA), April 1986.

"News & Notes: 1st National Masters." *Synchro-Info* (Santa Ana, CA), December 1975.

"News & Notes: In the News." *Sports Illustrated*, February 18, 1991. Excerpted in *Synchro* (Santa Ana, CA), April 1991.

"News & Notes: I.O.C. Approves Duet for '84 Games." *Synchro* (Santa Ana, CA), June 1980.

"News & Notes: Josephson's Return to Competitive Life." *Synchro* (Santa Ana, CA), October 1989.

"News & Notes: Junior Olympic News." *Synchro-Info* (Santa Ana, CA), February 1974.

"News & Notes: McDonald's Drops Sponsorship." *Synchro* (Santa Ana, CA), February 1986.

"News & Notes: McDonald's New Sponsor." *Synchro* (Santa Ana, CA), October 1983.

"News & Notes: McDonald's Wins Award at WSF Banquet." *Synchro* (Santa Ana, CA), December 1985.

"News & Notes: McGowan Heads FINA TSSC." *Synchro* (Santa Ana, CA), October 1984.

"News & Notes: Michigan State Announces Meet." *Synchro-Info* (Santa Ana, CA), December 1976.

"News & Notes: National Committee Schedules First Coaches Camp." *Synchro-Info* (Santa Ana, CA), August 1974.

"News & Notes: Newsweek Videos," *Synchro-Info* (Santa Ana, CA), December 1975.

"News & Notes: Olympic Venue Sold Out." *Synchro* (Santa Ana, CA), August 1983.

"News & Notes: 2nd National Masters Meet." *Synchro-Info* (Santa Ana, CA), December 1976.

"News & Notes: Synchro in Magazines." *Synchro-Info* (Santa Ana, CA), October 1975.

"News & Notes: Synchro Swimmers Perform at Sea World." *Synchro* (Santa Ana, CA), August 1990.

"News & Notes: Synchronized Swimming Almost Looks Easy." *Health*, June 1990. Excerpted in *Synchro* (Santa Ana, CA), June 1990.

"News & Notes: Synchro's Time Underwater." *Sports Illustrated*, November 28, 1988. Excerpted in *Synchro*, June 1989.

"News & Notes: U.S.O.C. Training Camp for Synchro." *Synchro-Info* (Santa Ana, CA), December 1977.

"News & Notes: Watanabe New Executive Director." *Synchro* (Santa Ana, CA), October 1985.

"1940 Central AAU Women's Swimming and Diving Championships and Central AAU Water Ballet and Synchronized Swimming Championships, Official Entry." S.S. Scrapbooks [1940s]. Henning Library, ISHOF. c.1940.

"1942 National Championships." *Neenah Daily News-Times*. S.S. Scrapbooks [1940s]. Henning Library, ISHOF. August 12–17, 1942.

"The 1946 Minneapolis Aquatennial, Souvenir Program." S.S. Scrapbooks [1940s], Henning Library, ISHOF. 1946.

"The 1963 Indoor National Championships." *Synchro-Info* (Santa Ana, CA), May-June 1963.

"The 1963 Pan American Games Trials." *Synchro-Info* (Santa Ana, CA), February 1963.

"The 1968 National Convention." *Synchro-Info* (Santa Ana, CA), November-December 1968.

"The 1969 National Convention." *Synchro-Info* (Santa Ana, CA), December 1969.

"1969 Outdoor National Championships." *Synchro-Info* (Santa Ana, CA), August 1969.

"The 1970 Indoor National Championships." *Synchro-Info* (Santa Ana, CA), April 1970.

"The 1970 National Convention." *Synchro-Info* (Santa Ana, CA), December 1970.

"1970 Outdoor National Championships." *Synchro-Info* (Santa Ana, CA), August 1970.

"The 1971 National Convention." *Synchro-Info* (Santa Ana, CA), October 1971.

"The 1971 Pan American Games Trials." *Synchro-Info* (Santa Ana, CA), June 1971.

"The 1972 Indoor National Championships." *Synchro-Info* (Santa Ana, CA), April 1972.

"The 1972 National Convention." *Synchro-Info* (Santa Ana, CA), December 1972.

"1972 Outdoor National Championships." *Synchro-Info* (Santa Ana, CA), August 1972.

"The 1973 Indoor National Championships." *Synchro-Info* (Santa Ana, CA), June 1973.

"The 1973 Junior National Outdoor Solo Championships." *Synchro-Info* (Santa Ana, CA), October 1973.

"The 1973 National Convention." *Synchro-Info* (Santa Ana, CA), December 1973.

"The 1974 Junior National Championships." *Synchro-Info* (Santa Ana, CA), June 1974.

"The 1974 National Convention." *Synchro-Info* (Santa Ana, CA), December 1974.

"The 1975 Indoor National Championships." *Synchro-Info* (Santa Ana, CA), June 1975.

"The 1976 Indoor National Championships." *Synchro-Info* (Santa Ana, CA), June 1976.

"The 1976 National Convention." *Synchro-Info* (Santa Ana, CA), December 1976.

"The 1977 National Convention." *Synchro-Info* (Santa Ana, CA), December 1977.

"The 1978 National Convention." *Synchro-Info* (Santa Ana, CA), December 1978.

"1979 Elite Camp." *Synchro* (Santa Ana, CA), February 1980.

"The 1979 Indoor National Championships." *Synchro-Info* (Santa Ana, CA), April 1979.

"The 1979 National Convention." *Synchro* (Santa Ana, CA), December 1979.

"The 1979 Pan American Games." *Synchro* (Santa Ana, CA), August 1979.

"[The 1979] Pan American Games Trials." *Synchro* (Santa Ana, CA), June 1979.

"The 1980 National Championships." *Synchro-Info* (Santa Ana, CA), August 1980.

"The 1980 National Convention." *Synchro* (Santa Ana, CA), October 1980.

"The 1980 Senior National Championships." *Synchro* (Santa Ana, CA), August 1980.

"The 1981 National Convention." *Synchro* (Santa Ana, CA), October 1981.

"The 1982 Masters National Championships." *Synchro* (Santa Ana, CA), December 1982.

*The 1982 Yearbook.* United States Synchronized Swimming. Indianapolis. 1982.

"The 1983 [National] Convention Report." *Synchro* (Santa Ana, CA), December 1983.

"The 1984 Olympic Games." *Synchro* (Santa Ana, CA), August 1984.

"The 1984 Olympic Trials/National Championships." *Synchro* (Santa Ana, CA), June 1984.

"The 1984 XXIIIrd Olympiad." *Synchro* (Santa Ana, CA), October 1984.

"The 1986 [National] U.S.A.S. Convention." *Synchro* (Santa Ana, CA), October 1986.

"The 1987 FINA World Cup." *Synchro* (Santa Ana, CA), December 1987.

"The 1987 [National] U.S.A.S. Convention." *Synchro* (Santa Ana, CA), December 1987.

"The 1987 Pan American Games." *Synchro* (Santa Ana, CA), October 1987.

"The 1988 Olympic Games." *Synchro* (Santa Ana, CA), October 1988.

"The 1988 Olympic Trials/National Championships." *Synchro* (Santa Ana, CA), June 1988.

"The 1989 National Championships." *Synchro* (Santa Ana, CA), June 1989.

Noble, John Wesley. "Prettiest Things Afloat." *Saturday Evening Post*, July 2, 1955.

Noonan, Claudia. "Our First Synchronized Swimming Competition, Sao Paulo." *The Synchronized Swimmer*, February 1952.

"Notes from the National Synchronized Swimming Clinic." *Synchro-Info* (Santa Ana, CA), November-December 1965.

O'Connor, Jennifer. "Letters to the Mailbox." *Synchro* (Santa Ana, CA), October 1984.

"Official Press Bulletins, World Aquatic Games." *Synchro-Info* (Santa Ana, CA), November 1978.

"Officials Training Report." *Synchro-Info* (Santa Ana, CA), February 1974.

O'Heron, Dan. "No Sweat Sport, Is It Olympian Enough?" *Pasadena Weekly Sports*. Reprinted in *Synchro* (Santa Ana, CA), April-May 1992.

"Ohio State Wins First Intercollegiate Synchro Competition." *Synchro-Info* (Santa Ana, CA), June 1977.

Olsen, Norma J. "AAU World Tours Face a Challenge," *Synchro-News* (San Jose, CA), February 1958.

_____. "Activity in Iowa." S.S. Scrapbooks [1940s], Henning Library, ISHOF. November 1942.

_____. "Competition to Music." *The Amateur Athlete*, July 1951.

_____. "From Aquabelles to Aquachamps." *The Amateur Athlete*, November 1952.

_____. "Helms Hall of Fame." *Synchro-News* (Santa Ana, CA), January 1957.

_____. "Highlights of the Swimming Tour of Japan and Korea." *The Synchronized Swimmer*, August 1954.

_____. "Joanne Royer Wins Far Western Title." *The Amateur Athlete*, August 1953.

_____. "Report from Egypt." *The Amateur Athlete*, December 1956.

_____. "Rome in 1960." *Synchro-News* (San Jose, CA), November-December 1958.

_____. "Swimming Tour and Cinemascope Short." *The Synchronized Swimmer*, November 1953.

_____. "Synchronized Swim Meet at Oakland." *The Amateur Athlete*, September 1957.

_____. "Synchronized Swimming Goes West." *Beach and Pool*, March 1, 1952.

"Olsen Gets Olympic Dream." S.S. Scrapbooks [1980s]. Henning Library, ISHOF. 1984.

"The Olympian." U.S.O.C. Daily Newspaper, Olympic Village. Seoul. 1988.

"Olympic Duet Tests Mettle at Swiss Open." *Synchro Swimming USA*, Fall 2000.

"Olympic Games, Past and Coming." *Los Angeles Times Home Magazine*, July 25, 1982.

"Olympic Team Stars, Earns its Stripes…" *Synchro Swimming USA*, Winter 2000.

"Olympic Tour Plans Nearing Completion." *Synchro-News* (San Jose, CA), January 1960.

Oppenheim, Mary. "Synchro Development in Adirondack Association." Letter. Deerfield Beach, FL. January 1997.

Ostos, Lic. Javier. "The Past, Present and Future of Synchronized Swimming." *International Swimming and Water Polo*, Summer 1984.

_____. "The Past, Present, and Future of Synchronized Swimming." *Synchro* (Santa Ana, CA), October 1984.

_____. "Solo, Duet … Team?" *International Swimming and Water Polo Magazine*, Winter 1984.

"Overview of the USA Free Routine." *Synchro Swimming USA*, Summer/Fall 1996.

"Palm Beach Nights Aquacade." *Discus*, January 1941.

"Pam Morris Elected to [International] Swimming Hall of Fame." *Synchro-Info* (Santa Ana, CA), November-December 1965.

"Pan Pacific Championships." *Synchro-Info* (Santa Ana, CA), October 1977.

"Pan Pacific Games." *Synchro* (Santa Ana, CA), December 1979.

"Parade of Champions Gets Underway Tonight." *Philippines Herald*, July 26, 1949. Bean personal collection. (Santa Ana, CA).

Paterson, Pat. "Early Development in the Chicago Area." Letter. Oak Park, IL. December 13, 1996.

_____. "Memorabilia." *Synchro* (Santa Ana, CA), October 1985.

Patterson, Phillip. "Synchronized Swimming." *The Amateur Athlete*, March 1941.

Paulus, Jan. "Report of the Results of the Major-Minor Sub-Committee on Degrees of Difficulty." U.S.S.S Inc. 1975.

"Penguinettes Travel to Massachusetts to Swim in National Conference." *Penn News*, November 16, 1956. S.S. Scrapbooks [1950s]. Henning Library, ISHOF. 1956.

"Pennsylvania Member Doing a Big Job." International Federation of Swimming Coaches and Instructors. S.S. Scrapbooks [1950s]. Henning Library, ISHOF. June 15, 1950.

"People. Costie Wins Olympia Award." *Synchro* (Santa Ana, CA), June 1985.

"People. Wing Wins Olympia Award." *Synchro* (Santa Ana, CA), August 1983.

"Personalities, Ruth Geduldig." *The Synchronized Swimmer*, October 1952.

"Pool Demonstration. Chicago Teachers Day. May 27, 1939." [First Competition Entry, Program]. Chicago Teachers College. S.S. Scrapbooks [1940s], Henning Library, ISHOF. 1939.

"The Pool Players, Synchronized Swimming, Ever Hear of It, Mac?" *Sports Illustrated*, August 30, 1954.

"Poolside with Joy Cushman: Convention Numbers Grow." *Synchro-News* (San Jose, CA), November-December 1958.

"Poolside with Joy Cushman: First National 12 & Under Competition." *Synchro-News* (San Jose, CA), July 1958.

"Poolside with Joy Cushman: Michigan/Iowa Host Nationals." *Synchro-News* (San Jose, CA), March-April 1958.

"Poolside with Joy Cushman: Nationals Televised Live." *Synchro-News* (San Jose, CA), July 1958.

"Poolside with Joy Cushman: Olsen FINA Secretary." *Synchro-News* (San Jose, CA), January 1958.

"Poolside with Joy Cushman: Tour to Brazil." *Synchro-News* (San Jose, CA), September-October 1958.

Potter, Adeline. "Reminiscing." *The Synchronized Swimmer*, February 1952.

"Premiere of Aqua Follies Watershow." *Minneapolis Morning Tribune*. S.S. Scrapbooks [1940s]. Henning Library, ISHOF. c. June 1942.

"President's Message: Convention on 9/11." *Synchro Swimming USA*, Winter 2001.

"President's Message: Hazle Begins Term." *Synchro Swimming USA*, Winter 2000.

"President's Message: New Format for U.S. Open." *Synchro Swimming USA*, Winter 2002.

"President's Message: Promoting the Sport." *Synchro Swimming USA*, Summer 1999.

"Preview of the Jole Loop Films." *Synchro-Info* (Santa Ana, CA), June 1971.

"Proceedings of the Synchronized Swimming Symposium." Michigan State College. *The Synchronized Swimmer*, February 1955.

Provisor, Henry. "The Housewife Who Made a Movie." *Synchro-News* (San Jose, CA), June 1958.

Quinn, Bill. "Synchronized Swimming in New Jersey." News clipping. S.S. Scrapbooks [1950s], Henning Library, ISHOF. c. 1954.

Rackham, George. *Synchronized Swimming*. London: Farber & Farber, 1968.

Rauworth, Nancy [Hanna]. Telephone interview. November 8, 1997.

"Ready to Dazzle Again." *Sports Illustrated*, August 8, 1988. Excerpted in *Synchro* (Santa Ana, CA), August 1988.

"Record Crowd at the Herald American Swim Meet." *Chicago Herald-American*, August 13, 1946.

"Region 4, Masters Synchro Meet." *Synchro-Info* (Santa Ana, CA), February 1978.

"Results, Rome Open." USA Synchro Newsletter. *www. usasynchro.org.* June 16, 2003.

Rieman, Kaylene. "David vs Goliath." *Synchro Swimming USA*, Summer 1997.

_____. "Gail Emery Inducted Into Women's Sports Hall of Fame." *Synchro Swimming USA*, Fall 1997.

_____. "Just Doing It. Aquamaids Sweep Jantzen Nationals for 7th Consecutive Year." *Synchro Swimming USA*, Summer 1998.

_____. "Legends in the Making." *Synchro Swimming USA*, Summer 1997.

Rose, Billy. "Official Program, Billy Rose's Aquacade." Golden Gate International Exposition. San Francisco, CA 1940.

Rose, Mary. Interview. Altamonte Springs, FL. April 19, 1997.

Rosenthal, Ed. "Honored Girls Swim at Y Opening." News clipping. *San Francisco Call-Bulletin*, May 8, 1942.

Rubin, Sylvia. "In the News. Their Eyes Are on the Olympics." *San Francisco Chronicle*, September 22, 1983. Reprinted in *Synchro* (Santa Ana, CA), December 1983.

Ruggieri, Mary Jo. "Intercollegiate Synchronized Swimming. 'Do or Die.'" *Synchro-Info* (Santa Ana, CA), April 1974.

_____. "Intercollegiate Synchronized Swimming." *Synchro-Info* (Santa Ana, CA), June 1975.

_____. "News & Notes: Collegiate Synchronized Swimming," *Synchro-Info* (Santa Ana, CA), December 1976.

_____. "Proposed Intercollegiate Rules." *Synchro-Info* (Santa Ana, CA), February 1975.

_____. "Report of the Intercollegiate Fall Meetings." *Synchro-Info* (Santa Ana, CA), December 1975.

_____, and Lundholm, Jean. *Introduction to Synchronized Swimming*, Minneapolis: Burgess, 1976.

"Rule Changes Through the Years." *Synchro-Info* (Santa Ana, CA), February 1972.

"Russia Knocks Out the Competition at Junior Worlds." *Synchro Swimming USA*, Summer [Fall] 2001.

Saito, Nakako. "Mikako Kotani, Japan's Rising Star." *Synchro* (Santa Ana, CA), December 1987.

Salyers, Marc. College Basketball excerpt. *Sports Illustrated*, March 8, 1999.

"Santa Clara Sets Record." *Synchro Swimming USA*, Summer 2003.

Saurman, Wendy. "The Dawning of New Era." *Synchro Swimming USA*, Spring 1996.

Savery, Jill. "Olympic Dreams, Synchronizing for Gold." *Synchro Swimming USA*, Spring 1996.

Sawin, Bud. "Indiana Association Activity Report." S.S. Scrapbooks [1940s]. Henning Library, ISHOF. November 18, 1942.

Schleuter, Walter J. "Mermaids and Music." News clipping. S.S. Scrapbooks [1940s]. Henning Library, ISHOF. c. 1946.

"The II Junior World Championships." *Synchro* (Santa Ana, CA), August 1991.

Seller, Margaret [Peg]. "Canadian Tribute to Mary Derosier." *The Synchronized Swimmer*, February 1953.

_____. "Peg Seller Says." *The Synchronized Swimmer*, September 1953.

_____. "Synchronized Swimming in England." *The Synchronized Swimmer*, October 1953.

Seller, Peg, and Beulah Gundling. *Aquatic Art*. Cedar Rapids, IA: Pioneer Litho, 1957.

Sellers, G.S. "Code of Performance for Judging Synchronized Swimming." *Synchro-Info* (Santa Ana, CA), September-October 1966.

Senior National Outdoor Competition." *Neenah Daily News*. News clipping. S.S. Scrapbooks [1940s], Henning Library, ISHOF. August 12, 1942.

"Seoul Pre-Olympic Synchro and Diving Meet." *Synchro* (Santa Ana, CA), August 1988.

"The VII Pan American Games." *Synchro-Info* (Santa Ana, CA), December 1975.

"She Can Swim, and Cute Too." *San Francisco Chronicle Sporting Green*, March 15, 1955. News clipping.

"She Grew Up Swimming," *Synchro-Info* (Santa Ana, CA), February 1972.

"VI Juegos Panamericanos, the Competition." *Synchro-Info* (Santa Ana, CA), October 1971.

Skidmore, Rebecca, and Marti Tucker, "Sports Training Manual," U.S. Synchronized Swimming, 1989.

Smith, Donalda. "Central American and Caribbean Age Group Championships." *Synchro-Info* (Santa Ana, CA), August 1977.

_____. "Letters to the Mailbox." *Synchro-Info* (Santa Ana, CA), February 1975.

Smith, Doug. "Santa Clara Sweeps Lorain Swim Honors." *The Journal*, Lorain, Ohio. 1972.

Smith, Helen. "Synchro in Washington." Letter. Seattle. March 1997.

Smith, Hope M. "The Windham High School Dolphin Club." *The Synchronized Swimmer*, April 1952.

Sowers, Dorothy. "Development of Synchronized Swimming in New York." Letter. Tonawanda, NY. October 1997.

Spears, Betty. *Beginning Synchronized Swimming*." Minneapolis: Burgess, 1950.

_____. *Fundamentals of Synchronized Swimming*." Minneapolis: Burgess, 1966.

"The Sport, Synchronized Swimming." *The Olympian*, October-November 1984.

"Stanley and Micus Win Senior Duet." News Clipping. S.S. Scrapbooks [1940s]. Henning Library, ISHOF. c. 1947.

"Steed Twins, Ruth & Minnie, Putting Rhythm Into The Crawl." *Chicago Tribune*, February 28, 1938. S.S. Scrapbooks [1940s]. Henning Library, ISHOF. 1938.

Stoerker, Marian L. "The Origin and Development of Synchronized Swimming in the United States." Master's thesis, University of Wisconsin, 1956.

Strubbe, Albert B.P. "The Origins and Development of Synchronized Swimming." *Synchro-News* (San Jose, CA), June 1958.

Swan, Margaret, Donald Kane, and Dawn Bean. *Coaching Synchronized Swimming Effectively*. Champaign, IL: Human Kinetics, 1984.

"Swan Club Hold Tryouts." *Ohio State University Monthly*. News clipping. S.S. Scrapbooks [1940s], Henning Library, ISHOF. March 1928.

Swan Forbes, Margaret. "WACS, Cygnets Tour Germany." *Synchro-Info* (Santa Ana, CA), February 1974.

Swartz, Roberta. "Letters to the Mailbox." *Synchro-Info* (Santa Ana, CA), July-August 1965.

_____. "Letters to the Mailbox." *Synchro-Info* (Santa Ana, CA), September-October 1965.

"Swim Club Wins Trick Aquatic Tilt." *Wright College News*. Reprinted in *Synchro-Info* (Santa Ana, CA), February 1972.

"Swimmer's View of Nationals." *Synchro-Info* (Santa Ana, CA), June 1975.

"Swimming News: First Synchronized Swimming Championship in the World." *Discus*, May 1940.

"Synchers." *Synchro-News* (San Jose, CA), August 1958.

"Synchro All-Stars of 1969." *Synchro-Info* (Santa Ana, CA), February 1970.

Synchro Canada. *Highlights of Synchro Swim — 1925–1975*. Commemorative Issue. Canadian Amateur Synchronized Swim Association. Ottawa, Ontario, Canada. 1975.

"Synchro Demonstrates for the I.O.C." *Synchro* (Santa Ana, CA), February 1983.

"Synchro Is Making the News." *Sports Illustrated*, August 2, 1982. Excerpted in *Synchro* (Santa Ana, CA), August 1982.

"Synchro Music Goes Digital at Olympic Festival." *Synchro Swimming USA*, Winter 1995/96.

"Synchro News: Bye Bye Brian." *Synchro Swimming USA*, Spring 2003.

"Synchro News: Founder's Society." *Synchro Swimming USA*, Winter 2002.

"Synchro Swimmers Beat Wright in Demonstration." *Chicago Tempo*, Sunday Magazine News clipping, S.S. Scrapbooks [1940s]. Henning Library, ISHOF. c. 1940.

"Synchro Swimming and the Komen Foundation," *Synchro Swimming USA* (Indianapolis, IN), April–June 1995.

"Synchro Swimming USA and Komen Foundation Launch Partnership in Fight Against Breast Cancer." *Synchro Swimming USA*, April–June 1995.

Synchro USA. *Official Rules Synchronized Swimming*. Indianapolis, 1981–2003.

*Synchro USA News*. "Josephson's, Team Crowned World Champions." December 1990-January 1991.

Synchro USA website [*usasynchro.org*]. News, events, teams, results, history.

"Synchronizers Cop AAU Title." *Wright College News*. Reprinted in *Synchro-Info* (Santa Ana, CA), February 1972.

"Synchro's Golden Boy." *Synchro Swimming USA*, Summer 2000.

Tait, Hollis, John Shaw, and Katherine Ley. *A Manual of Physical Education Activities*, 3rd ed. Philadelphia & London: Saunders, 1967.

"Team USA Finds Gold in Rome." *Synchro Swimming USA*, Fall 2000.

"Terrapin Club of Mundelein College." *Discus*, January 1939.

"The 3rd Intercollegiate Conference and Competition Trials." *The Synchronized Swimmer*, January 1954.

Thomas, Tony. "The Man Who Made the Musical." *Compact Disc.* "Lullaby of Broadway, the Best of Busby Berkeley at Warner Bros." Warner Bros. Hollywood, CA.

"Three Synchronized Swimming Champions Pool Talents." *Seattle Today Magazine*, August 28, 1974.

Tope, Mary. "Letters to the Mailbox." *Synchro-Info* (Santa Ana, CA), February 1979.

"Town Club Wins Water Ballet." News clipping. S.S. Scrapbooks [1940s]. Henning Library, ISHOF. August 1946.

"Traffic Police, Like Synchronized Swimming." [Photo Caption]. *Houston Chronicle*, June 24, 2001.

Treadway, Kenneth. "1968 Indoor National Championships." *Synchro-Info* (Santa Ana, CA), March-April 1968.

Trilling, Blanche M. "History of Physical Education for Women at the University of Wisconsin, 1898–1946." The University Library. Madison, WI. 1951.

Tucker, Marti, and Rebecca Skidmore. "Sport Training Manual." U.S. Synchronized Swimming. 1989.

Turner, Marge. "Answers to Your Questions." Unpublished, S.S. Scrapbooks [1990s], Henning Library, ISHOF. 1996.

_____. "Early Synchronized Swimming." Unpublished. S.S. Scrapbooks [1990s]. Henning Library, ISHOF. August 1993.

"The 2001 National Championships." *Synchro Swimming USA* (Indianapolis, IN), Summer 2001.

"2003 Coaches College." *Synchro Swimming USA*, Spring 2003.

"Underrated and Overrated Sports." *Sports Illustrated*, November 4, 2002.

"University of Oklahoma Hosts Scholastic Competition." *Synchro-News* (San Jose, CA), February 1962.

"USA Storms Into Olympic Bid." *Synchro Swimming USA*, Summer 2000.

"USA Takes Two Golds at World Championships." *Synchro* (Santa Ana, CA), February 1991.

"USA Wins Bronze in World Cup Team Final." *Synchro Swimming USA*, Winter 2002.

"U.S.O.C. Camps, Intermediate, Elite." *Synchro-Info* (Santa Ana, CA), December 1978.

"U.S.O.C. Report." *Synchro-Info* (Santa Ana, CA), June 1977.

"U.S.O.C. Sports Festival." *Synchro-Info* (Santa Ana, CA), November 1978.

"U.S.O.C. Training Camp Successful." *Synchro-Info* (Santa Ana, CA), February 1978.

"U.S.O.C. Training Camp Successful." *Synchro-Info* (Santa Ana, CA), February 1979.

"U.S.O.C. Training Camps Set." *Synchro-Info* (Santa Ana, CA), April 1978.

*U.S. Synchronized Swimming Figures Book.* U.S.S.S. 1989.

"U.S. Wins FINA World Cup in Bonn." *Synchro* (Santa Ana, CA), October-November 1991.

"U.S. Wins Pan-American S.S." AAU Synchronized Swimming Handbook. 1956.

Van Buskirk, Kim. *Coaching Intermediate Synchronized Swimming Effectively.* Champaign, IL: Human Kinetics, 1987.

Van den Broeck, Gill. "AAU Sponsored Tour." *Synchro-News* (San Jose, CA), January-February 1959.

Vickers, Betty J. *Teaching Synchronized Swimming.* Englewood Cliffs, N.J.: Prentice-Hall, 1965.

"Victory in Moscow." *Synchro* (Santa Ana, CA), April 1988.

Von Wietersheim, Juliane. "An Approach to the Teaching of Composition in a Synchronized Swimming Course." Master's thesis, Smith College, Northampton, MA, 1955.

"The WAC's 'Merry Mermaids.'" *San Antonio Light*, May 19, 1973. Reprinted in *Synchro-Info* (Santa Ana, CA), August 1974.

Ward, Alan. "Local Girls in Sports Movie Short." *Oakland Tribune*, February 13, 1954.

_____. "On Second Thought." *Oakland Tribune*, April 23, 1953.

"Water Ballet Gave Beautiful Showing in Neenah." *Discus*, September 1942.

"Water Ballet Team Featured in Minneapolis Aquatennial." *Discus*, August 1943.

"Water Ballet Will Go to Neenah, Wisconsin." *Discus*, August 1942.

"Water Sprites of Minden." News clippings. S.S. Scrapbooks [1950s], Henning Library, ISHOF. c. 1952.

Welshons Smith, Kim. "Historical Development of S.S." Master's thesis, San Diego State University, 1982.

Wenz, Betty J. *Sports Medicine Meets Synchronized Swimming.* Reston, VA: National Association for Girls & Women in Sports, 1980.

"West Coast Indoor Swim Meet at Mission Beach." News clipping. S.S. Scrapbooks [1950s]. Henning Library, ISHOF. May 3, 1953.

Weyler, John. "For Ruiz, Boycott Has Added Something to Games, Another Gold." *Los Angeles Times*, August 13, 1984.

_____. "Routine Performance for Ruiz, Costie." *Los Angeles Times*, August 7, 1984.

_____. "Ruiz and Costie Make Winning Performance Out of Their Last Duet." *Los Angeles Times*, August 10, 1984.

_____. "Ruiz, Costie Are No. 1 in Figures Competition." *Los Angeles Times*. August 9, 1984.

_____. "Ruiz Gets Set to Go It Alone." *Los Angeles Times*, August 11, 1984.

_____. "Sport's Olympic Is a Double Golden Opportunity for Tracie Ruiz." *Los Angeles Times*, July 28, 1984.

"What's News: Innovations in Sound Equipment." *Synchro-Info* (Santa Ana, CA), May–June 1964.

"What's News: A 'Refreshing' Golden Gate Swim." *Synchro-Info* (Santa Ana, CA), September–October 1963.

White, Carl. "Following the Ball." *Santa Monica Outlook*, August 18, 1954.

"Who's News: Florence Anderson, Trainer of Judges." *Synchro-News* (San Jose, CA), September-October 1958.

Wightman, Nancy. "Board Room Comments: U.S.S.S. Begins Magazine Publication." *Synchro Swimming USA*, January–March 1993.

_____. "Boardroom Comments: Collegiate Plan." *Synchro Swimming USA*, January–March 1994.

_____. "Boardroom Comments: USOC Funding

Changes." *Synchro Swimming USA*, January–March 1995.

_____, and Nancy Chiefari. *Better Synchronized Swimming for Girls*. New York: Dodd, Meade, 1981.

Wilson, Lonnie. "Muscles Aren't Everything." *Parade*, July 17, 1955.

Wing, Louise. "Letters to the Mailbox." *Synchro-Info* (Santa Ana, CA), April 1975.

_____. "Synchro Development in New England." Letter. Lynn, MA. 1997.

Withers, Julie. "Wesleyan College. Macon, Georgia." *The Synchronized Swimmer*, November 1952.

Wodka, Ed. "Boardroom Comments: Developing Club Marketing." *Synchro Swimming USA*, April–June, 1994.

Women's National AAU Outdoor Swimming & Diving Championships." [*Official Program*]. Neenah, Wisconsin. S.S. Scrapbooks [1940s]. Henning Library, ISHOF. August 14–16, 1942.

Women's Sports Foundation. "25 Years of Making a Difference." *Synchro Swimming USA*, Winter 2000.

"Wright [College] Synchronized Swimming Is Revived." *Northwest Leader*, July 2, 1997. News clipping, S.S. Scrapbooks. Henning Library, ISHOF.

Yates, Fern and Theresa Anderson. *Synchronized Swimming*. New York: Ronald, 1958.

"YMCA … CYO News." *Synchro-News* (San Jose, CA), February 1959.

"You Said It!" *Synchro* (Santa Ana, CA), February 1983.

Zajac, Dawn. "The History of Synchronized Swimming in England." *Synchro-Info* (Santa Ana, CA), June 1969.

Zamonski, Stan. "Water Sports Feature, the Synchronettes." *Rocky Mountain Sportsman*, September 1959.

Zink, Ruth Fife. "Synchronized Swimming in Minnesota." Letter. Stillwater, MN. February 21, 1997.

# Index